Modern American Poets

Their Voices and Visions

Modern American Poets

Their Voices and Visions

Second Edition

Robert DiYanni

Pace University, Pleasantville

Imaginary gardens with real toads in them. — M. Moore

McGraw-Hill, Inc.

New York St. Louis San Francisco Auckland Bogotá Caracas Lisbon London Madrid Mexico City Milan Montreal New Delhi San Juan Singapore Sydney Tokyo Toronto

For Steve, once again with gratitude

This book was developed by STEVEN PENSINGER, Inc.

MODERN AMERICAN POETS
Their Voices and Visions

Copyrights and Acknowledgments appear on pages 793–801, and on this page by reference.

This book is printed on acid-free paper.

1 2 3 4 5 6 7 8 9 0 DOC DOC 9 0 9 8 7 6 5 4 3

ISBN 0-07-016957-8

This book was set in Bembo by ComCom, Inc.
The editors were Steve Pensinger and Scott Amerman;
the production supervisor was Annette Mayeski.
The cover was designed by Carol Couch.
R. R. Donnelley & Sons Company was printer and binder.

Library of Congress Cataloging-in-Publication Data

Modern American poets: their voices and visions / Robert DiYanni;
[developed by Steven Pensinger]. — 2nd ed.
p. cm.
Includes index.
ISBN 0-07-016957-8 (alk. paper)
1. American poetry—20th century. I. DiYanni, Robert.
II. Pensinger, Steven. III. Title.
PS613.M55 1994
811'.508—dc20 93-14414

About the Author

Robert DiYanni is Professor of English and Director of Interdisciplinary Studies at Pace University, Pleasantville, New York, where he teaches courses in literature, writing, and humanities. He has also taught at Queens College of the City University of New York, at New York University in the Graduate Rhetoric Program, and most recently in the Expository Writing Program at Harvard University. He received his B.A. from Rutgers University (1968) and his Ph.D. from the City University of New York (1976).

Professor DiYanni has written articles and reviews on various aspects of literature, composition, and pedagogy. His books include *Literature; The Art of Reading; Women's Voices; Reading Poetry; Like Season'd Timber: New Essays on George Herbert;* and *The McGraw-Hill Book of Poetry*. Current projects include a college handbook, an introduction to the humanities, and with Kraft Rompf, *The McGraw-Hill Book of Fiction,* scheduled for publication in 1994.

Contents

Preface

Modern American Poets: Their Voices and Visions, Second Edition, introduces modern American poetry by means of a rich selection of poems. The book divides into three parts: an introduction to reading poetry, an extensive collection of poems by thirteen major poets, and additional poems representing the voices and visions of more than fifty other modern American poets.

The introduction to reading poetry attends first to the act of reading poems—to what readers do as they read. This discussion considers the subjectivity of readers' responses, along with the intellectual acts they perform in reading. Also included is a demonstration of one form of active involvement with a poem—annotation. By far the largest part of the introduction is the section entitled "Aspects of Poetry," which provides a critical vocabulary that isolates significant poetic elements: voice, diction, imagery, syntax, symbolism, figurative language, rhythm, rhyme, and meter. This section concludes with a discussion of revision, which explores how poets transform their own work, how they play off work by other poets, and how they receive inspiration from other arts.

The heart of *Modern American Poets* is the poetry itself. The thirteen distinctive and important poets chosen for extensive representation are each the subject of a one-hour film produced by the New York Center for Visual History. Their poetry is complemented and extended by the work of the many other fine poets whose poems demonstrate the influence of their predecessors while exhibiting the range and variety of poetry in our time.

Accompanying the work of each poet is a biographical and critical headnote. For the second, larger group of poets, these headnotes are brief biographies. For the thirteen more heavily represented poets, the headnotes are longer and more detailed, establishing a critical and biographical perspective for reading the poems. The headnotes overall attempt to do three things: provide a literary and historical context, identify central features of the work of each poet, and help readers overcome specific stumbling blocks in reading modern American poetry.

Poems are footnoted where necessary. Five poets monopolized most of the notes: T. S. Eliot, Ezra Pound, Hart Crane, Robert Lowell, and Sylvia Plath. Although glosses could have been provided sporadically for the work of the others (and occasional poems are so glossed), for the most part the other poets are left alone. A glossary of poetic terms completes the book's pedagogical apparatus.

For assistance of varying kinds in completing the book I am indebted to Steve Pensinger, who invited my participation in this project and who graciously and generously supported my part in it. His associate at McGraw-Hill, Scott Amerman, offered his expertise with courtesy, enthusiasm, and professionalism. My colleague and friend, Kraft Rompf, contributed heavily to the headnotes for Sylvia Plath and Marianne Moore. I wish to acknowledge his contribution and thank him for allowing me to use here material we prepared jointly for *The McGraw-Hill Book of Poetry* (1993).

Thanks also to the New York Center for Visual History, especially Lawrence Pitkethly, director, and Robert Carnevale, literary researcher. They extended me every courtesy in previewing the films and offered helpful advice as I developed the book. An additional adviser who deserves special thanks is my colleague and friend Donald Ryan, whose knowledge of American poetry and commitment to teaching it well have helped me very much.

I am also happy to acknowledge the assistance of my wife, Mary, whose support has once again proven invaluable. And I gratefully dedicate the book to Steve Pensinger, whose good judgment made it all possible.

Robert DiYanni

Changes in the Second Edition

The major difference between this edition and the first edition of *Modern American Poets* is the increased number of poems in Part Two: Major Voices and Visions. *Modern American Poets* now includes nearly every poem quoted in the series of films (with the exception of juvenilia). The vast majority appear complete, including such long works as *Song of Myself* and *The Wasteland.* Some poems, however, have been excerpted, including four of Pound's "Cantos" (though two appear intact). In the excerpts we have been careful to include the lines quoted in the Pound film.

Part Three, "Other Voices and Visions," has been freshened with the addition of new voices, which have been added to those from the first edition. Every poet included in this section in the first edition has been retained, though to make room for the new voices, some poets with multiple selections have been cut back. A dozen women's voices have been added to this edition, including those of Alice Fulton, Marilyn Hacker, Mary Oliver, and Jorie Graham. Minority representation has been increased for both sexes with the inclusion of Lucille Clifton, Audre Lorde, Rita Dove, and Jerry Ward, Jr. Hispanic and Native American contributions appear by Julia Alvarez, Alberto Rios, Jimmy Santiago Baca, and Cathy Song. Still other poets have been included either because they had been previously overlooked (Robert

Duncan, Robert Pinsky, and David Wagoner) or because they have recently come to my attention (Christopher Corkery, Barbara Holder, Sheryl Noethe, Sandra Schor, and Baron Wormser). The inclusion of these and the other newly added poets coupled with the increase in the number of poems by the film-affiliated poets should make *Modern American Poets* an even more valuable resource for all readers of American poetry.

Robert DiYanni

PART ONE

Introduction

Reading Poetry

We read poems for pleasure; they entertain us. And we read them for instruction; they enlighten us. Poems draw us into their imaginative worlds, charming us with their voices and engaging us with their visions. They may echo our sentiments, expressing our perceptions and thoughts in memorable language. They may also make us aware of things we didn't know or of things we knew only dimly. Good poems help us to see more clearly, to feel more acutely, and to understand more deeply what we see and feel and think.

These qualities of poetry in general are particularly apparent in the poetry of our country and century. American poets have made available images of ourselves in their poems. They have shown us who we are and from whence we came. And they have envisioned, in their singular ways, where they believe we are going. Taking their cue from Ralph Waldo Emerson, the spiritual father of modern American literature, our modern poets, beginning with Walt Whitman and Emily Dickinson, have created a distinctive body of original American poetry that speaks in a variety of specifically American voices as it presents diverse visions of America.

Emerson proclaimed repeatedly—but perhaps most notably in his lecture-essay "The American Scholar"—that American literature had too long been subservient to British literature. He urged and challenged the young country to produce poets who would do for America what continental European poets had done for their respective countries. Whitman was the first poet of stature to answer Emerson's call. And he did it in his customary grandiloquent way by setting himself up as an American bard, a national poet whose verse and poetic personality would be at one with the land, culture, and people his poems celebrated. Following Whitman came Dickinson with her markedly different voice and vision, bearing vestiges of her New England Puritan heritage.

These three writers—Emerson, Whitman, and Dickinson—have been the primary and seminal influences on the American poets of the twentieth century: Emerson for his philosophical perspective; Whitman for his public celebration of the American themes of democracy, idealism, solidarity, equality, and love of nature; Dickinson for her finely discriminating probings of the soul in a spare poetic style, original in its elliptical syntax, its metaphorical daring, and its unconventional rhythm and rhyme. The twentieth-century poets have had to come to terms with what these nineteenth-century precursors represented. And they did this in splendidly various ways. Whether their poems look toward historical moments in the past or project visions of the future, and whether their visions are hopefully optimistic or desperately pessimistic, our poets have consistently responded to the natural landscape of the American continent, to its history both recent and remote, and to its brief but ongoing literary tradition. Their poems testify to what Helen Vendler has described as "the range and play of the American imagination, a sense of the complication, depth, and grandeur of American poetry."* Before introducing you, however, to the distinctive accomplishments of America's modern poets and a rich sampling of their major work, we offer an overview of the process of reading poetry and a set of critical terms that one needs to discuss it.

THE EXPERIENCE OF READING POETRY

When we read poetry, we invoke our entire range of experience with life and language. We read a poem, that is, in light of what we know about its subject, what we notice about its language, and what we recognize from our previous encounters with liter-

* See Helen Vendler's introductory essay in *Voices and Visions: The Poet in America* (New York: Random House, 1987).

ary works, especially other poems. In addition, because of the characteristic density and compression of poetry, we read it with particular attention to the connotations of its words and to the expressive qualities of its sound and rhythm. We attend painstakingly to the linguistic and structural features of poems, since it is these elements that distill meaning, embody feeling, and convey experience.

To see how our experience influences our response to a poem and how our attention to language directs us toward what it expresses, let us consider the following brief poem.

ROBERT HAYDEN

[1913–1980]

Those Winter Sundays

Sundays too my father got up early
and put his clothes on in the blueblack cold,
then with cracked hands that ached
from labor in the weekday weather made
banked fires blaze. No one ever thanked him.

I'd wake and hear the cold splintering, breaking.
When the rooms were warm, he'd call,
and slowly I would rise and dress,
fearing the chronic angers of that house,

Speaking indifferently to him,
who had driven out the cold
and polished my good shoes as well.
What did I know, what did I know
of love's austere and lonely offices?

Even from a single reading we see that the speaker of "Those Winter Sundays," now an adult, is remembering how his father used to get up on cold Sunday mornings and light the fires that would warm the house for his sleeping family. We sense his regret at how unappreciative of his father he was as a child. We may wonder what prompts these memories and feelings. Our initial reading may also call up a memory much like the one described in Hayden's poem. But even if our experience does not echo the speaker's or if our feelings differ from his, we may respond nonetheless to the description of waking up on a cold day in a warm house. Such personal responses, whatever their precise nature, are important to our reading of poetry, for in arriving at a sense of a poem's meaning and value, we often begin with them.

Let us consider what Hayden's poem implies by returning for a second, more deliberate reading. In this reading we might notice, for example, that the first words, "Sundays too," indicate that the speaker's father performed his house-warming chores every day, including Sundays. We might notice also that the poem contrasts cold and warmth, with the cold dissipated as the warmth of the fires the father has started suffuses the house. And we might note further that the poem shifts from father to son, from "him" to "I." The first stanza, for example, describes the father's act, the second the boy's awakening to a warm house, while the third records a different kind of awakening—the speaker's understanding of his earlier indifference and of his father's love. It is in this third and final stanza that we feel most strongly the contrast between the speaker's past and present, between the then and the now of the poem, between the love that the speaker neither noticed nor acknowledged and now acknowledges and understands.

So far we have centered on the poem's speaker and its subject. (The *speaker* refers to the voice of the character we hear in the poem; the *subject* indicates what the poem is literally about.) Our first readings of a poem will usually focus on who is speaking about what, and why. In considering speaker and subject, we solidify our sense of what the poem implies, whether its implications concern, primarily, ideas or feelings. When the speaker notes that he feared "the chronic angers of that house," we may sense that he points toward something important. Presumably he feared his father's anger, which on occasion must have been directed at him. But by using the plural form of the word rather than the singular ("angers" rather than "anger") the speaker may be suggesting that there was discord between the father and other members of the family as well. Whatever the specific nature of his fear, the speaker intimates that this fear was the source of his own wariness and indifference toward his father.

The lines that convey the speaker's feeling most intensely, however, are those that end the poem:

What did I know, what did I know
of love's austere and lonely offices?

In these lines we sense the speaker's remorse and regret for not being aware of all his father did for him; we sense further that even though he didn't understand and feel the extent of his father's devotion, he certainly does later. Moreover, we sense the intensity of his feelings both in his repetition of the phrase "what did I know," and in the words that describe his father's actions: "love's austere and lonely offices." "Austere" suggests both the rigor and self-discipline of the father's acts and perhaps the stern severity with which he may have performed them. "Lonely" indicates that the father performed his early morning labors alone, without help from the other members of the family. It also suggests that the father was emotionally isolated from the speaker and perhaps from other members of the family.

But the word "offices" conveys other ideas as well. It implies both the duties the father fulfills and the corresponding authority he possesses. In addition, it suggests something done for another, as in the good offices of a friend. Beyond these related meanings, "offices" also refers to the daily prayers recited by clerics. Thus, the words "austere" and "offices" convey the speaker's understanding of his father's sacrifices for him. Moreover, the highly abstract language of the conclusion—so different from the concrete details of the preceding stanzas—may also indicate the speaker's inability to express affection directly (an inadequacy he intimates his father suffered from as well).

THE PROCESS OF READING POETRY

To read poetry well we need to slow down enough to observe details of language, form, and sound. By reading slowly and deliberately we give ourselves a chance to form connections among the individual elements of the poem. Read the following poem through without stopping and then again with the accompanying commentary.

ROBERT FROST

[1874–1963]

Mending Wall

Something there is that doesn't love a wall,
That sends the frozen-ground-swell under it,
And spills the upper boulders in the sun;

And makes gaps even two can pass abreast.
The work of hunters is another thing:
I have come after them and made repair
Where they have left not one stone on a stone,
But they would have the rabbit out of hiding,
To please the yelping dogs. The gaps I mean,
No one has seen them made or heard them made,
But at spring mending-time we find them there.
I let my neighbor know beyond the hill;
And on a day we meet to walk the line
And set the wall between us once again.
We keep the wall between us as we go.
To each the boulders that have fallen to each.
And some are loaves and some so nearly balls
We have to use a spell to make them balance:
"Stay where you are until our backs are turned!"
We wear our fingers rough with handling them.
Oh, just another kind of outdoor game,
One on a side. It comes to little more:
There where it is we do not need the wall:
He is all pine and I am apple orchard.
My apple trees will never get across
And eat the cones under his pines, I tell him.
He only says, "Good fences make good neighbors."
Spring is the mischief in me, and I wonder
If I could put a notion in his head:
"*Why* do they make good neighbors? Isn't it
Where there are cows? But here there are no cows.
Before I built a wall I'd ask to know
What I was walling in or walling out,
And to whom I was like to give offense.
Something there is that doesn't love a wall,
That wants it down." I could say "Elves" to him,
But it's not elves exactly, and I'd rather
He said it for himself. I see him there
Bringing a stone grasped firmly by the top
In each hand, like an old-stone savage armed.
He moves in darkness as it seems to me,
Not of woods only and the shade of trees.
He will not go behind his father's saying,
And he likes having thought of it so well
He says again, "Good fences make good neighbors."

During your second excursion through the poem, read more slowly and deliberately. Try to discover things that you didn't pick up on the first reading. Also reflect on the observations made and the questions raised in the commentary.

Mending Wall

Something there is that doesn't love a wall,
That sends the frozen-ground-swell under it
And spills the upper boulders in the sun,
And makes gaps even two can pass abreast.
The work of hunters is another thing:
I have come after them and made repair
Where they have left not one stone on a stone,
But they would have the rabbit out of hiding,
To please the yelping dogs. The gaps I mean,
No one has seen them made or heard them made,
But at spring mending-time we find them there.

Comment

"Mending Wall" opens with a speaker suggesting that not everybody likes walls. The opening line, cast in an impersonal form, exhibits an unusual sentence pattern. Its deviation from the normal word order of the English sentence draws attention to it, elevating it above a flat statement in ordinary language. The opening lines invite us to consider the wall symbolically, since they suggest that even nature objects to it. The speaker seems to attribute to nature human intentionality, an intentionality that, of course, reflects his own attitude toward walls. That is, in offering an explanation of how stone walls fall into disrepair—seasonal variations in temperature cause the ground to swell and the stones to fall from the wall—he enlists nature's support for his dislike of walls.

In addition to nature's groundswell, the speaker offers another reason for the wall's disarray: hunters tear down parts of it when hunting rabbits. He implies that he has seen the disrepair being caused by the hunters, but has only discovered nature's antiwall activities after the fact. His last observation—"at spring mending-time we find them there"—suggests two more things: (1) that the walls are broken and repaired annually; (2) that he participates in repairing the wall with others.

I let my neighbor know beyond the hill;
And on a day we meet to walk the line
And set the wall between us once again.
We keep the wall between us as we go.
To each the boulders that have fallen to each.
And some are loaves and some so nearly balls
We have to use a spell to make them balance:
"Stay where you are until our backs are turned!"
We wear out fingers rough with handling them.
Oh, just another kind of outdoor game,
One on a side. It comes to little more:

Comment

Perhaps the first thing that strikes us about the way the poem continues is that the speaker initiates the ritualistic spring wall repair. Perhaps he dislikes broken walls even more than unbroken ones. A second detail worth noting is the manner in which the speaker and his neighbor go about their work. Instead of working together on one side of the wall, they "keep the wall between" them as they work. This image neatly illustrates one symbolic dimension of walls: their disposition to keep people apart.

Frost, however, merely hints at this idea. He describes a scene that shows two men working together yet divided, the wall they are repairing, simultaneously uniting and separating them. The image is provocative because it is paradoxical: the men come together in order to separate themselves; they join in rebuilding the wall that will continue to sunder them. This double-edged image, moreover, is sustained through additional details: in the repeated use of language suggesting the solidarity of the men: *"we* have to use a spell"; "till *our* backs are turned"; *"we* wear *our* fingers rough." This unifying language is counterpointed, however, by contrasting images indicative of separation: "To *each* the boulders that have fallen to *each"; "One* on a *side."*

One additional point is made in these lines: that the work is also play, a "game." This second paradox indicates more generally that their action is simultaneously both serious and humorous, a matter of importance for each, yet "just another kind of outdoor game."

There where it is we do not need the wall:
He is all pine and I am apple orchard.

My apple trees will never get across
And eat the cones under his pines, I tell him.
He only says, "Good fences make good neighbors."
Spring is the mischief in me, and I wonder
If I could put a notion in his head:
"*Why* do they make good neighbors? Isn't it
Where there are cows? But here there are no cows.
Before I built a wall I'd ask to know
What I was walling in or walling out,
And to whom I was like to give offense.

Comment

This next section continues the emphasis of the previous ones. The speaker heightens the separateness of the two men by referring to the different species of tree that inhabit the adjoining properties. (The trees themselves differ in appearance and with respect to the climate and soil in which they grow. The narrator's apple trees bear leaves and fruit; the neighbor's pine trees bear needles and pine cones.) And the speaker further accentuates their differences when he playfully teases the neighbor by remarking that his apple trees won't intrude on the neighbor's pines. Impervious to wit and lacking the speaker's sense of humor, the neighbor retorts, "Good fences make good neighbors," counter-balancing the speaker's view expressed in the opening line. The speaker can't resist undermining the neighbor's viewpoint by asking why he maintains it. What we see taking shape here is not merely a set of contrasting opinions about the value and usefulness of walls, but something more fundamental: contrasting approaches to thought and action. The speaker questions things; he wants to know why walls exist, what purposes they serve, and whether this particular wall is necessary. In contrast, the neighbor seems to lack the speaker's impulse to wonder why things are the way they are, walls included. He seems neither to need nor want a logical explanation.

Something there is that doesn't love a wall,
That wants it down." I could say "Elves" to him,
But it's not elves exactly, and I'd rather
He said it for himself. I see him there,
Bringing a stone grasped firmly by the top
In each hand, like an old-stone savage armed.

He moves in darkness as it seems to me,
Not of woods only and the shade of trees.
He will not go behind his father's saying,
And he likes having thought of it so well
He says again, "Good fences make good neighbors."

Comment

The final section begins with a repetition of the opening line. This time it is spoken to the neighbor, whereas earlier it was directed at the reader. These last ten lines of the poem seem to emphasize the primitive quality of the neighbor as seen from the speaker's perspective. As the neighbor carries two stones to place on the wall, one in each hand, the speaker envisions him as a savage, a primitive being, precivilized and perhaps prerational as well. The stones he carries as part of a cooperative effort to repair the wall are momentarily seen by the speaker as weapons. Once again a double perspective is implied: the men as neighborly workers, the neighbors as deadly enemies.

Perhaps even more damning to the neighbor is the speaker's comment that he "moves in darkness," a darkness both literal (since the neighbor moves in the shade of his trees) and figurative (since it is not a darkness of woods alone). At this point the poet invites us to consider the symbolic implications of what he is describing. The neighbor's darkness, the speaker suggests, is a darkness of ignorance, superstition, and fear. The neighbor operates without the logic of rational explanation. And there is more than a touch of satire in the speaker's remark that the neighbor "likes having thought of it so well" that he repeats, "Good fences make good neighbors." This is ironic, of course, since the neighbor didn't *think* of this saying so much as *remember* it. He merely repeats what he's heard, presumably without thinking about what it means or why he should accept it.

A few final observations. Both characters present their views twice. Neither changes his view; neither crosses the wall. And the wall is repaired after all, regardless of the speaker's objections.

And some lingering questions. Does Frost share the speaker's point of view? The neighbor's? Does Frost seem to be criticizing or at least questioning the value of traditional explanations? Is he suggesting that a stubborn persistence, however blind and unthinking, is more powerful than the logic of rational explanation? What, finally, are we left with as the poem's meaning?

THE PRACTICE OF ACTIVE READING

Thus far we have read two poems, each followed by comments and questions emphasizing the experience and process of reading. Next we illustrate active reading—what we actually do when we read and reread a poem. Some of the marginal annotations record observations, others raise questions; all are abbreviated notes that reflect a reading that embodies both thought and feeling. In making notes about a poem in this manner, we become actively engaged in seeing and thinking. Our observations and questions lead us to notice details of language and to think about the poem's implications. As we formulate provisional answers to our questions, we find ourselves exploring both its meaning and its value.

The annotations for Theodore Roethke's "My Papa's Waltz" are unconcerned with technical matters such as the poem's form, rhyme scheme, and meter, or with what such technical elements contribute to its meaning and feeling. Another set of annotations, of course, could be made specifically highlighting these features. In fact, some technical consideration of Roethke's poem appears later in the discussion "Words," on pages 26–28. For now, however, we focus on the poem's situation and subject. Here it is without annotation:

THEODORE ROETHKE

[1908–1963]

My Papa's Waltz

The whiskey on your breath
Could make a small boy dizzy;
But I hung on like death:
Such waltzing was not easy.

We romped until the pans
Slid from the kitchen shelf;
My mother's countenance
Could not unfrown itself.

The hand that held my wrist
Was battered on one knuckle;

At every step you missed
My right ear scraped a buckle.

You beat time on my head
With a palm caked hard by dirt,
Then waltzed me off to bed
Still clinging to your shirt.

And here is it again with annotations:

An affectionate term for his father—papa.

My Papa's Waltz

What kind of waltzing and who instigated it?

The whiskey on your breath
Could make a small boy dizzy;
But I hung on like death:
Such waltzing was not easy.

"Waltzed" or "danced" for "romped"?

"Face" or "expression" for "countenance"?

The mother—angry? disapproving? mother as audience—as nonparticipant—

We romped until the pans
Slid from the kitchen shelf;
My mother's countenance
Could not unfrown itself.

The father misses steps but he can dance—not drunk.

The hand that held my wrist
Was battered on one knuckle;
At every step you missed
My right ear scraped a buckle.

Clinging—how? Fearfully? Joyfully? Both?

You beat time on my head
With a palm caked hard by dirt,
Then waltzed me off to bed
Still clinging to your shirt.

The boy's father, a manual laborer, is "waltzing" with his son. But his "dance" is more a romp through the house with a stop in the kitchen and another at the boy's bedroom, where presumably he is unceremoniously dumped into bed. The mother watches, her frown indicating disapproval, perhaps even anger.

The dance is somewhat rough because the boy's father has been drinking. It is also rough because he scrapes the child's ear on his belt buckle as he keeps a steady rhythm by beating time on the boy's head. The boy is described as "clinging" to his father's shirt, but the language doesn't clarify whether that clinging is purely out of terror—or whether it is part of the game father and son enjoy together. Possibly this bedtime romp is a regular ritual rather than a one-time occurrence.

The tone of the poem seems nostalgic, though not sentimentally so. The boy, now a man, remembers his father as "papa," clearly an affectionate term. The high-spirited bouncing rhythm of the poem seems to counter any indication that the father's drinking or the son's fear are its central concerns.

CENTERING ON SUBJECT AND THEME

A poem's subject is, simply, what the poem is about. Roethke's and Hayden's poems are about memories of the poets' fathers and, more specifically, about the poets' responses to those memories. Frost's poem is about two men repairing a stone wall. And it's also about the significance of walls and the values associated with them. But we sense that all three poems are about more than these things, and it is this sense that renders our preliminary descriptions inadequate.

Hayden's "Those Winter Sundays" is also about love and sacrifice, indifference and regret. It is about how understanding sometimes comes too late. This more amplified and generalized statement comes closer to what seems central to the poem. But it also moves beyond description of the poem's subject into interpretation of *theme,* an idea about the subject. But let us be more precise about what we mean by theme.

Theme is an abstraction or generalization drawn from the details of a literary work. In other words, theme refers to an idea or intellectually comprehensible meaning inherent and implicit in a work. In determining a poem's theme we should be careful neither to oversimplify nor to distort the poem's meaning. And although there is no sure-fire way to determine whether we are doing either of these things, at the very least we should be alert to the possibility that we may be. To suggest, for example, that the theme of "Those Winter Sundays" is a father's loving concern for his family is to highlight only part of the poem's meaning, since it omits the speaker's regret about his indifference to his father. Or to see Roethke's "My Papa's Waltz" as a statement about a child's fear of his father's behavior is to misrepresent the complexity of the speaker's responses to his memories of his father.

We should also recognize that a poem can have several themes:

a poem can be interpreted from more than one perspective, can yield more than one meaning. We have indicated multiple possibilities of meaning in our running commentary on Frost's "Mending Wall." And we have also seen something of the complexity of meaning in "Those Winter Sundays" and "My Papa's Waltz." We now consider briefly another poem, this time focusing on its theme.

ELIZABETH BISHOP

[1911–1979]

One Art

The art of losing isn't hard to master;
so many things seem filled with the intent
to be lost that their loss is no disaster.

Lose something every day. Accept the fluster
of lost door keys, the hour badly spent.
The art of losing isn't hard to master.

Then practice losing farther, losing faster:
places, and names, and where it was you meant
to travel. None of these will bring disaster.

I lost my mother's watch. And look! my last, or
next-to-last, of three loved houses went.
The art of losing isn't hard to master.

I lost two cities, lovely ones. And, vaster,
some realms I owned, two rivers, a continent.
I miss them, but it wasn't a disaster.

—Even losing you (the joking voice, a gesture
I love) I shan't have lied. It's evident
the art of losing's not too hard to master
though it may look like *(Write it!)* like disaster.

The central idea of "One Art" is expressed in its opening line: that "the art of losing isn't hard to master." In other words, losing isn't merely something that happens, but is instead an "art" that one can learn. The line is repeated three times, once with a slight variation. An additional line, line 3, also repeated with slightly greater variations, strengthens the point of the first, that loss is no disaster. Taken together, these two lines and ideas sum up the poem's theme, which we can paraphrase as follows: human loss is inescapable; we all experience it frequently. Because of our repeated practice at losing, we can learn to accept our losses, however great; no loss is too overwhelming for us.

Although this is what the poem says, it's not what it means, or at least it's not the poem's only meaning. We can offer a fuller explanation of its meaning based on a closer look at its details and a consideration of its *tone* (the writer's implied attitude toward the subject).

Besides making the central points outlined in our initial interpretation, the opening stanza implies that things get lost of their own inclination. The implication of this hyperbolic suggestion is that we can't do much, if anything, to prevent their loss. From this we move to the advice of stanzas 2 and 3: practice losing things; learn to accept the inconvenience and frustration of doing without them.

In stanza 4 we are given a glimpse of lost things that seem to undercut the flat statement that loss is easy to take. The loss of one's mother's watch, while not necessarily a disaster, could be gravely disappointing if one attached sentimental value to it. The lost houses, too, could represent not merely the loss of a residence, easily enough replaced, but possibly of a spouse or of a segment of one's life. The same can be said for the losses described in stanza 5: cities, a river, a continent. Though the speaker claims that these losses weren't significant, she does miss them, rather more, we expect, than she misses a lost hour or set of keys. Finally, in the last stanza, we are shown a much greater loss—the loss of someone the speaker loves. Here, too, we read that the loss can be accommodated, that the speaker can come to terms with it, presumably without too much trouble.

As we make our way through the poem, perhaps near the end, perhaps upon a second reading, we may begin to wonder whether the speaker's repeated claims that losing is neither difficult nor consequential are not a bit too heavily pressed. That is, the speaker's insistently repeated claim may suggest the opposite of what she explicitly says. We wonder whether she may be trying to talk herself into accepting what her words literally say. We may suspect that the opposite case more nearly approximates reality: that losing is indeed difficult to master—if it can ever be mastered—and that it may cause, at times, very real disasters.

The poem can thus be read two ways: literally or ironically. In a literal reading, we accept the speaker's words for what they actually state. In an ironic reading, we reverse the literal meaning of her claim and realize that the speaker has not mastered the art of losing.

Centering on a poem's theme then, we work toward understanding a poem's significance—what it says, what it implies, what it means. As we have suggested previously, our sense of a poem's significance may change as we reread it. Moreover, our understanding of any poem's theme depends on our experience—both our literary experience and our experience in living, and as these develop so will our understanding of poetry.

Aspects of Poetry

We can interpret and appreciate poems by attending to their basic elements. The elements of a poem include a *speaker* whose voice we hear in it; its *diction* or selection of words; its *syntax* or the order of those words in phrase and sentence; its *imagery* or details of sight, sound, taste, smell, and touch; its *figures of speech* or nonliteral ways of expressing one thing in terms of another, such as symbol and metaphor; its *sound effects,* especially rhyme, assonance, and alliteration; its *rhythm and meter* or the pattern of accents we hear in the poem's words, phrases, lines, and stanzas; and its *structure* or formal pattern of organization. All the elements of a poem work together harmoniously to convey feeling and embody meaning. We will consider them individually, however, to sharpen our perception of what each element contributes.

VOICES

When we read or hear a poem, we hear a speaker's voice. It is this voice that conveys the poem's *tone.* Tone is an abstraction we make from the details of a poem's language; the inclusion of certain kinds of details and the exclusion of other kinds; the use of meter and rhyme (or lack of them); particular choices of words and sentence pattern, of imagery and figurative language. In listening to a poem's language, in hearing the voice of its speaker, we catch its tone and feeling and ultimately its meaning.

In listening to the speaker's voice, for example, in Roethke's "My Papa's Waltz" (p. 13), we hear a tone different from that of the speaker in Hayden's "Those Winter Sundays" (p. 5). Roethke's speaker remembers his father fondly and addresses him ("your breath," "you missed"). He remembers and celebrates their spirited cavorting as a "romp" and a "waltz," and he includes such comic details as the mother frowning while pans slide off the kitchen shelves and the father keeping time by patting the boy's head. The complex tone of the poem comes from its varied details: the boy's hanging on "like death," his ear scraping his father's belt buckle, and his "clinging" to his father's shirt.

The speaker of Hayden's "Those Winter Sundays," in contrast, admires his father and perhaps feared him as a child. His attitude is suggested by the details he remembers and by the way he meticulously describes his father's attentive labors. But his tone conveys more than admiration; it conveys also a sense of regret, disappointment, and perhaps anguish at having been indifferent toward him as a child. The tone of Hayden's poem has none of the ease and playfulness of Roethke's; it is serious in its portrayal of the speaker's father and solemn in its account of the speaker's subsequent feelings.

The range of tones we find in poems is as diverse and complex as the range of voices and attitudes we discern in everyday experience. One of the more important and persistent is the *ironic tone* of voice. Irony is a way of speaking that implies a discrepancy or opposition between what is said and what is meant. You may have heard irony in Elizabeth Bishop's "One Art" (p. 16). The poem below is more insistently and clearly ironic.

STEPHEN CRANE

[1871–1900]

War Is Kind

Do not weep, maiden, for war is kind.
Because your lover threw wild hands toward the sky
And the affrighted steed ran on alone,

Do not weep.
War is kind.

Hoarse, booming drums of the regiment,
Little souls who thirst for fight,
These men were born to drill and die.
The unexplained glory flies above them,
Great is the battle god, great, and his kingdom
A field where a thousand corpses lie.

Do not weep, babe, for war is kind.
Because your father tumbled in the yellow trenches,
Raged at his breast, gulped and died,
Do not weep.
War is kind.

Swift blazing flag of the regiment,
Eagle with crest of red and gold,
These men were born to drill and die.
Point for them the virtue of slaughter,
Make plain to them the excellence of killing
And a field where a thousand corpses lie.

Mother whose heart hung humble as a button
On the bright splendid shroud of your son,
Do not weep.
War is kind.

How do we know that the speaker's attitude toward war is not what his words indicate, that his words are ironic? We know because the details of death in battle are antithetical to the consoling refrain of stanzas 1, 3, and 5: "Do not weep. War is kind." Moreover the details of stanzas 2 and 4 also work toward the same ironic end, but in a different way. Instead of the ironic consoling voice of stanzas 1, 3, and 5 (which of course offers no real consolation given the brutality described), stanzas 2 and 4 sound more supportive of military glory. Crane uses a marchlike rhythm along with words connoting military glory in a context that makes them sound hollow and false.

We hear a rather different voice in the following poem.

WILLIAM CARLOS WILLIAMS

[1883–1963]

The Widow's Lament in Springtime

Sorrow is my own yard
where the new grass
flames as it has flamed
often before but not
with the cold fire
that closes round me this year.
Thirtyfive years
I lived with my husband.
The plumtree is white today
with masses of flowers.
Masses of flowers
load the cherry branches
and color some bushes
yellow and some red
but the grief in my heart
is stronger than they
for though they were my joy
formerly, today I notice them
and turn away forgetting.
Today my son told me
that in the meadows,
at the edge of the heavy woods
in the distance, he saw
trees of white flowers.
I feel that I would like
to go there
and fall into those flowers
and sink into the marsh near them.

Williams's speaker is a widow whose voice is heavy with grief. Her first word, in fact, is "sorrow." And her last statement indicates how desperate her hopelessness is. By entitling the poem "The Widow's Lament in Springtime," Williams directs our attention to its sorrowful tone. Part of the power of the poem comes from the steady lament of its voice. The widow, relentless in her expression of grief, appropriates everything to her sorrow.

She sees as contributing to her grief things we normally associate with feelings of joy and elation, especially the spring blossoms and the new growth of grass, traditional symbols of life and renewal. Her heaviness of heart is conveyed by the repetition of details, the heavy reliance on accented syllables, the use of short lines, and a steady, insistent contrast between former joy and present unassuageable grief.

For some additional practice in listening to the voices of poems, read the following and consider the questions that accompany them.

T. S. ELIOT

[1888–1965]

Journey of the Magi

'A cold coming we had of it,
Just the worst time of the year
For a journey, and such a long journey:
The ways deep and the weather sharp,
The very dead of winter.'
And the camels galled, sore-footed, refractory,
Lying down in the melting snow.
There were times we regretted
The summer palaces on slopes, the terraces,
And the silken girls bringing sherbet.
Then the camel men cursing and grumbling
And running away, and wanting their liquor and women,
And the night-fires going out, and the lack of shelters,
And the cities hostile and the towns unfriendly
And the villages dirty and charging high prices:
A hard time we had of it.
At the end we preferred to travel all night,
Sleeping in snatches,
With the voices singing in our ears, saying
That this was all folly.

Then at dawn we came down to a temperate valley,
Wet, below the snow line, smelling of vegetation,

With a running stream and a water-mill beating the
  darkness,
And three trees on the low sky.
And an old white horse galloped away in the meadow.
Then we came to a tavern with vine-leaves over the lintel,
Six hands at an open door dicing for pieces of silver,
And feet kicking the empty wine-skins.
But there was no information, and so we continued
And arrived at evening, not a moment too soon
Finding the place; it was (you may say) satisfactory.

All this was a long time ago, I remember,
And I would do it again, but set down
This set down
This: were we led all that way for
Birth or Death? There was a Birth, certainly,
We had evidence and no doubt. I had seen birth and death,
But had thought they were different; this Birth was
Hard and bitter agony for us, like Death, our death.
We returned to our places, these Kingdoms,
But no longer at ease here, in the old dispensation,
With an alien people clutching their gods.
I should be glad of another death.

QUESTIONS

1. The first five lines are adapted from a Christmas sermon by Lancelot Andrewes (1555–1626). The speaker is one of the three Wise Men, or Magi, who came to Bethlehem, guided by a star, to witness the birth of Christ. Why is he speaking? And what is the tone of his voice?
2. Notice how many lines begin with "And." How does this repetition contribute to the poem's tone? Notice also how, near the poem's conclusion, the "Ands" disappear and "But" emerges. Characterize the change of tone you hear at this transition.
3. Consider the effect of the repetition of "set down/This set down/This." What other repetitions occur in the poem? How do they contribute to its tone?

GWENDOLYN BROOKS

[*b.* 1917]

The Mother

Abortions will not let you forget.
You remember the children you got that you did not get,
The damp small pulps with a little or with no hair,
The singers and workers that never handled the air.
You will never neglect or beat
Them, or silence or buy with a sweet.
You will never wind up the sucking-thumb
Or scuttle off ghosts that come.
You will never leave them, controlling your luscious sigh,
Return for a snack of them, with gobbling mother-eye.
I have heard in the voices of the wind the voices of my dim killed children.
I have contracted. I have eased
My dim dears at the breasts they could never suck.
I have said, Sweets, if I sinned, if I seized
Your luck
And your lives from your unfinished reach,
If I stole your births and your names,
Your straight baby tears and your games,
Your stilted or lovely loves, your tumults, your marriages, aches, and your deaths,
If I poisoned the beginnings of your breaths,
Believe that even in my deliberateness I was not deliberate.
Though why should I whine,
Whine that the crime was other than mine?—
Since anyhow you are dead.
Or rather, or instead,
You were never made.
But that too, I am afraid,
Is faulty: oh, what shall I say, how is the truth to be said?
You were born, you had body, you died.
It is just that you never giggled or planned or cried.

Believe me, I loved you all.
Believe me, I knew you, though faintly, and I loved, I loved you
All.

QUESTIONS

1. Whom is the speaker addressing? Why?
2. What words and phrases express the speaker's state of mind most powerfully?
3. Characterize the poem's voices.

WORDS

In reading any poem it is necessary to know what the words mean, but it is equally important to understand what those words imply or suggest. The *denotation,* or dictionary meaning, of *dictator,* for example, is "a person exercising absolute power, especially one who assumes absolute control without the free consent of the people." But *dictator* also carries additional *connotations* or associations both personal and public. Beyond its dictionary meaning, *dictator* may suggest repressive force and tyrannical oppression; it may call up images of bloodbaths, purges, executions; it may trigger associations that prompt us to think of Hitler, for example, or Mussolini. The same kind of associative resonance occurs with a word like *vacation,* the connotations of which far outstrip its dictionary definition: "a period of suspension of work, study, or other activity."

Because poets often hint indirectly at more than their words directly state, it is necessary to develop the habit of considering the connotations of words as well as their denotations. Often for both poets and readers the "best words" are those that do the most work; they convey feelings and indirectly imply ideas rather than state them outright. Poets choose a particular word because it suggests what they want to suggest. Its appropriateness is a function of both its denotation and its connotation. Consider, for example, the second stanza of "My Papa's Waltz":

We romped until the pans
Slid from the kitchen shelf;
My mother's countenance
Could not unfrown itself.

"Romped" could be replaced by *danced* since the poet is describing a dance, specifically a waltz. Why "romped" then? For one thing, it means something different from *danced.* That is, its denotation provides a different meaning, indicating play or frolic of a boisterous nature. Although "romped" is not really a dance word at all, here it suggests a kind of rough, crude dancing, far less elegant and systematic than waltzing. But it also connotes the kind of vigorous roughhousing that fathers and sons occasionally engage in and from which many mothers are excluded—though here, of course, the romp is occasioned by the father's having had too much to drink. "Romped" then both describes more precisely the kind of dance and suggests the speaker's attitude toward the experience.

Perhaps the most unusual words in the stanza, however, are "countenance" and "unfrown." "Countenance" is less familiar and more surprising than face. This is also true of "unfrown," a word you won't find in the dictionary. What makes these words noticeable is not just their uncommonness but their strangeness in the context of the stanza. "Countenance," a formal word, contrasts with the informal language of the two lines before it, lines that describe the informal romp of a dance; it suggests the mother's formality as she watches the informal play of her husband and son. Although her frown indicates disapproval, perhaps annoyance that her pans are falling, the disapproval and annoyance may be put on, part of an act. It is possible that she is responding as she is expected to respond.

If we look up *countenance* in the *Random House College Dictionary,* here is what we find:

noun 1. appearance, esp. the expression of the face . . .
2. the face; visage
3. calm facial expression; composure
4. (obsolete) bearing; behavior . . .
trans. verb 6. to permit or tolerate
7. to approve, support, or encourage. . . .

Let's consider briefly the implications of these multiple denotations. The second meaning is more general than the first. It is this first meaning to which we gave priority in the discussion above. We determined our sense of the kind of expression on the mother's face from the line, "Could not unfrown itself." But in looking at definitions 3 and 4, we encounter a problem, or at least a complication. Isn't the mother's "frown" a sign of *dis*composure rather than one of the "composure" suggested by a "calm facial expression"? Or is it possible that Roethke has used *countenance* with two meanings in mind: the meaning of "facial expression" on one hand; the meaning of "tolerate and permit, approve and encourage" on the other? Or is the poet using the word ironically? This double sense of *countenance* thus parallels the double sense of the experience for the child as both pleasurable and frightening.

To gain practice in discerning and appreciating diction in poetry, read the following poems with special attention to their words.

EDWIN ARLINGTON ROBINSON

[1869–1935]

Miniver Cheevy

Miniver Cheevy, child of scorn,
  Grew lean while he assailed the seasons;
He wept that he was ever born,
  And he had reasons.

Miniver loved the days of old
  When swords were bright and steeds were prancing;
The vision of a warrior bold
  Would set him dancing.

Miniver sighed for what was not,
  And dreamed, and rested from his labors;
He dreamed of Thebes and Camelot,
  And Priam's neighbors.

Miniver mourned the ripe renown
  That made so many a name so fragrant;
He mourned Romance, now on the town,
  And Art, a vagrant.

Miniver loved the Medici,
  Albeit he had never seen one;
He would have sinned incessantly
  Could he have been one.

11**Thebes:** Greek city famous in history and legend 11**Camelot:** the seat of King Arthur's court 12**Priam:** king of Troy during the Trojan War. 17**the Medici:** family of powerful merchants and bankers, rulers of Florence in the fourteenth, fifteenth, and sixteenth centuries, who were known for their patronage of the arts.

Miniver cursed the commonplace
  And eyed a khaki suit with loathing;
He missed the mediæval grace
  Of iron clothing.

Miniver scorned the gold he sought,
  But sore annoyed was he without it;
Miniver thought, and thought, and thought,
  And thought about it.

Miniver Cheevy, born too late,
  Scratched his head and kept on thinking;
Miniver coughed, and called it fate,
  And kept on drinking.

QUESTIONS

1. List the words in the poem that illustrate what is said in line 5: that "Miniver loved the days of old." List all the verbs that describe Miniver's action or inaction. What do they reveal about him?
2. What are the connotations of "ripe"? (line 13) and "fragrant" (line 14)? What does the combination of each respectively with ideas of fame and nobility suggest about these ideas? And how do the connotations of "on the town" (to describe Romance) and "a vagrant" (to characterize Art) suggest what has happened to Art and Romance?

ADRIENNE RICH

[*b.* 1929]

Rape

There is a cop who is both prowler and father:
he comes from your block, grew up with your brothers,
had certain ideals.
You hardly know him in his boots and silver badge,
on horseback, one hand touching his gun.

You hardly know him but you have to get to know him:
he has access to machinery that could kill you.

He and his stallion clop like warlords among the trash,
his ideals stand in the air, a frozen cloud
from between his unsmiling lips.

And so, when the time comes, you have to turn to him,
the maniac's sperm still greasing your thighs,
your mind whirling like crazy. You have to confess
to him, you are guilty of the crime
of having been forced.

And you see his blue eyes, the blue eyes of all the family
whom you used to know, grow narrow and glisten,
his hand types out the details
and he wants them all
but the hysteria in your voice pleases him best.

You hardly know him but now he thinks he knows you:
he has taken down your worst moment
on a machine and filed it in a file.
He knows, or thinks he knows, how much you imagined;
he knows, or thinks he knows, what you secretly wanted.

He has access to machinery that could get you put away;
and if, in the sickening light of the precinct,
and if, in the sickening light of the precinct,
your details sound like a portrait of your confessor,
will you swallow, will you deny them, will you lie your way
   home?

QUESTION

The man referred to in the poem is described as a "cop," "prowler," "father," and "confessor." What are the implications of each? Also, explain the different implications of line 8 and the alternative listed below:

Rich: He and his stallion clop like warlords among the trash.

Alternate: He and his horse walk with authority through the neighborhood.

ELIZABETH BISHOP

[1911–1979]

Filling Station

Oh, but it is dirty!
—this little filling station,
oil-soaked, oil-permeated
to a disturbing, over-all
black translucency.
Be careful with that match!

Father wears a dirty,
oil-soaked monkey suit
that cuts him under the arms,
and several quick and saucy
and greasy sons assist him
(it's a family filling station),
all quite thoroughly dirty.

Do they live in the station?
It has a cement porch
behind the pumps, and on it
a set of crushed and grease-
impregnated wickerwork;
on the wicker sofa
a dirty dog, quite comfy.

Some comic books provide
the only note of color—
of certain color. They lie
upon a big dim doily
draping a taboret
(part of the set), beside
a big hirsute begonia.

Why the extraneous plant?
Why the taboret?
Why, or why, the doily?

(Embroidered in daisy stitch
with marguerites, I think,
and heavy with gray crochet.)

Somebody embroidered the doily.
Somebody waters the plant,
or oils it, maybe. Somebody
arranges the rows of cans
so that they softly say:
ESSO—SO—SO—SO
to high-strung automobiles.
Somebody loves us all.

QUESTIONS

1. List the words suggesting dirt or oil. What is their cumulative effect?
2. Single out two words that surprised you, and comment on their appropriateness.

IMAGES

Poems are grounded in the concrete and the specific—in details that stimulate our senses—for it is through our senses that we perceive the world. We see daylight break and fade; we hear dogs bark and children laugh; we feel the sting of a bitterly cold wind; we smell the heavy aroma of perfume; we taste the tartness of lemon and the sweetness of chocolate. Poems include such particularities, thereby triggering our memories, stimulating our feelings, and commanding our response.

Such specific details when they appear in poems are called images. An *image* is a concrete representation of a sense impression, feeling, or idea. Images appeal to one or more of our senses—or, more precisely, they trigger our imaginative reenactment of sensory experience by rendering feeling and thought in concrete details related directly to our physical perception of the world. Images may be visual (something seen), aural (something heard), tactile (something felt), olfactory (something smelled), or gustatory (something tasted).

Tactile images of heat and cold inform Hayden's "Those Winter Sundays" (p. 5), with the speaker's father waking up early "in the blueblack cold" to make "banked fires blaze." Visual and tactile images appear in Frost's "Mending Wall" (pp. 7–8), whose speaker describes the boulders used to build the wall as "loaves" and "balls" that "wear" the fingers "rough with handling them."

For an indication of how images work together to convey feelings and ideas, consider the images in the following poem.

ELIZABETH BISHOP

[1911–1979]

First Death in Nova Scotia

In the cold, cold parlor
my mother laid our Arthur
beneath the chromographs:
Edward, Prince of Wales,
with Princess Alexandra,
and King George with Queen Mary.
Below them on the table
stood a stuffed loon
shot and stuffed by Uncle
Arthur, Arthur's father.

Since Uncle Arthur fired
a bullet into him,
he hadn't said a word.
He kept his own counsel
on his white, frozen lake,
the marble-topped table.
His breast was deep and white,
cold and caressable;
his eyes were red glass,
much to be desired.

"Come," said my mother,
"Come and say good-bye
to your little cousin Arthur."
I was lifted up and given
one lily of the valley
to put in Arthur's hand.

Arthur's coffin was
a little frosted cake,
and the red-eyed loon eyed it
from his white, frozen lake.

Arthur was very small.
He was all white, like a doll
that hadn't been painted yet.
Jack Frost had started to paint him
the way he always painted
the Maple Leaf (Forever).
He has just begun on his hair,
a few red strokes, and then
Jack Frost had dropped the brush
and left him white, forever.

The gracious royal couples
were warm in red and ermine;
their feet were well wrapped up
in the ladies' ermine trains.
They invited Arthur to be
the smallest page at court.
But how could Arthur go,
clutching his tiny lily,
with his eyes shut up so tight
and the roads deep in snow?

The poem describes a child's view of death. Through images, specifically through what the little girl sees and hears, it renders her incomprehension and confused feelings about her cousin Arthur's death. It accomplishes this by filtering the child's perceptions through an adult sensibility. In a similar way, Bishop presents a voice childlike in its syntactic constructions and adult in its vocabulary. By means of the double perspective of adult/child we gain a complex inner view of the speaker's impressions and understanding of her experience, vividly rendered in the poem's images.

Our first sense impression is tactile: we imagine "the cold, cold parlor." Immediately after, we see two things: a picture of the British royal family and a stuffed loon, which had been shot by the dead boy's father, also named Arthur. The second stanza describes the loon in more detail. It sits on a marble-topped table, a detail that conveys two tactile impressions, hardness and coldness. This imagery is emphasized in the description of the marble table top as the loon's "white, frozen lake."

These visual images are continued in the third stanza, in which the speaker sees her dead cousin in his coffin. She holds a long-stemmed white flower which she puts in the dead boy's hand. The images of whiteness and cold (the frozen lake, marble table top, and the dead, stuffed white loon of the previous stanzas) are continued: the speaker describes Arthur's coffin as a "frosted cake." The birthday cake image also indicates the limited extent of the speaker's comprehension of the reality and finality of death.

With the repeated details about the loon's red eyes and its frozen posture and base, the child unconsciously (and the poet consciously) associate the dead boy and the dead loon. Moreover, this connection is further established by the imagery of the fourth stanza, in which Arthur is described as "all white," with "a few red strokes" for his hair. Unlike the maple leaf with its complete and thorough redness, little Arthur is left "unpainted" by Jack Frost (another image of the cold) and is thus left white "forever." On the one hand, such a description clearly indicates the child's fantastic incomprehension of Arthur's death; on the other, it suggests that she intuitively senses that Arthur has been drained of color and of life. A similar combination of intuitive understanding and conscious ignorance is echoed in the speaker's comparison of Arthur with a doll. She sees how similar they look on the surface, but she does not consciously register their similar lifelessness.

The images of the final stanzas recall those of stanza 1. The royal couples of the chromograph are described as dressed in red clothes with white fur trim, details that connect directly with the dead loon. Moreover, the lily of the third stanza (white and short-lived like the boy) reappears clutched in Arthur's hand. The final image is one of whiteness and coldness: deep snow covers the cold ground where Arthur will soon lie.

The poem's concrete details, mostly visual and tactile images, strongly evoke the coldness and lifelessness of the dead child. But they suggest other things as well. The portrait of the royal family and the stuffed loon suggest something of the family's social identity—its conservatism and propriety in particular. More importantly, however, these details, along with the others noted above, reveal the limitation of the speaker's understanding. She sees the loon, for example, as quiet: "he hadn't said a word," and "he kept his own counsel." In addition, she fantasizes that the royal family (which she sees as very much alive in their warm furs) have invited little Arthur to serve as "the smallest page at court." Even though this may be the speaker's way of coping with death, the final two images of white lily and cold snow, and the tone in which she asks her final question all point toward her near acknowledgment of the truth.

It should prove useful to return at this point to a few of the poems considered in earlier sections of this introduction and examine their imagery. For further practice in responding to poetic images, read the following poems.

HD

[1886–1961]

Heat

O wind, rend open the heat,
cut apart the heat,
rend it to tatters.

Fruit cannot drop
through this thick air—
that presses up and blunts
the points of pears
and rounds the grapes.

Cut the heat—
plow through it,
turning it on either side
of your path.

QUESTION

By asking the wind to "rend open," "cut apart," and "plow through" the heat, the poet creates an image of it. Identify this image and explain what stanza 2 contributes to it.

ROBERT LOWELL

[1917–1977]

The Drinker

The man is killing time—there's nothing else.
No help now from the fifth of Bourbon
chucked helter-skelter into the river,
even its cork sucked under.

Stubbed before-breakfast cigarettes
burn bull's-eyes on the bedside table;
a plastic tumbler of alka seltzer
champagnes in the bathroom.

No help from his body, the whale's
warm-hearted blubber, foundering down
leagues of ocean, gasping whiteness.
The barbed hooks fester. The lines snap tight.

When he looks for neighbors, their names blur in the window,
his distracted eye sees only glass sky.
His despair has the galvanized color
of the mop and water in the galvanized bucket.

Once she was close to him
as water to the dead metal.

He looks at her engagements inked on her calendar.
A list of indictments.
At the numbers in her thumbed black telephone book.
A quiver full of arrows.

Her absence hisses like steam,
the pipes sing . . .
even corroded metal somehow functions.
He snores in his iron lung,

and hears the voice of Eve,
beseeching freedom from the Garden's

perfect and ponderous bubble. No voice
outsings the serpent's flawed, euphoric hiss.

The cheese wilts in the rat-trap,
the milk turns to junket in the cornflakes bowl,
car keys and razor blades
shine in an ashtray.

Is he killing time? Out on the street,
two cops on horseback clop through the April rain
to check the parking meter violations—
their oilskins yellow as forsythia.

QUESTIONS

1. Identify the images in each stanza, and explain their implications. What does the poem's imagery suggest about the drinker?
2. Make a list (or a series of lists) of related images, and explain what they have in common.

EZRA POUND

[1885–1972]

The River-Merchant's Wife: A Letter

While my hair was still cut straight across my forehead
I played about the front gate, pulling flowers.
You came by on bamboo stilts, playing horse,
You walked about my seat, playing with blue plums.
And we went on living in the village of Chokan:
Two small people, without dislike or suspicion.

At fourteen I married My Lord you.
I never laughed, being bashful.
Lowering my head, I looked at the wall.
Called to, a thousand times, I never looked back.

At fifteen I stopped scowling,
I desired my dust to be mingled with yours
Forever and forever and forever.
Why should I climb the look out?

At sixteen you departed,
You went into far Ku-to-yen by the river of swirling eddies,
And you have been gone five months.
The monkeys make sorrowful noise overhead.

You dragged your feet when you went out.
By the gate now, the moss is grown, the different mosses
Too deep to clear them away!

The leaves fall early this autumn, in wind.
The paired butterflies are already yellow with August,
Over the grass in the West garden;
They hurt me. I grow older.
If you are coming down through the narrows of the river
  Kiang,
Please let me know beforehand,
And I will come out to meet you
          As far as Cho-fu-Sa.

By Rihaku

QUESTIONS

1. Identify the images in the first three stanzas and comment on their implications.
2. Explain the significance of the following details in stanza 4: (a) the monkeys; (b) the mosses; (c) the fallen leaves; (d) the butterflies.

COMPARISONS

Language can be conveniently classified as either literal or figurative. When we speak literally, we mean exactly what each word conveys; when we use *figurative language* we mean something other than the actual meaning of the words. "Go jump in the lake," for example, if meant literally would be intended as a command to leave (go) and jump (not dive or wade) into a lake

By Rihaku: Pound's poem translates the Chinese of Li Po, whose Japanese name was Rihaku.

(not a pond or stream). Usually, however, such an expression is not literally meant. In telling someone to go jump in the lake we are telling them something, to be sure, but what we mean is different from the literal meaning of the words. To get lost, perhaps, which is itself a figurative expression.

Rhetoricians have catalogued more than 250 different *figures of speech,* expressions or ways of using words in a nonliteral sense. They include *hyperbole* or exaggeration (I'll die if I miss that game"); *litotes* or understatement ("Being flayed alive is somewhat painful"); *synecdoche* or using a part to signify the whole ("Lend me a hand"); *metonymy* or substituting an attribute of a thing for the thing itself ("step on the gas"); *personification,* endowing inanimate objects or abstract concepts with animate characteristics or qualities ("the lettuce was lonely without tomatoes and cucumbers for company"). We will not go on to name and illustrate the others but instead will concentrate on two specially important for poetry: simile and metaphor.

The heart of both these figures is comparison—the making of connections between normally unrelated things, seeing one thing in terms of another. More than 2,300 years ago Aristotle defined *metaphor* as "an intuitive perception of the similarity in dissimilars." And he suggested further that to be a "master of metaphor" is the greatest of a poet's achievements. In our century, Robert Frost has echoed Aristotle by suggesting that metaphor is central to poetry, and that, essentially, poetry is a way of "saying one thing and meaning another, saying one thing in terms of another."

Although both figures involve comparisons between unlike things, *simile* establishes the comparison explicitly with the words *like* or *as*. *Metaphor,* on the other hand, employs no such explicit verbal clue. The comparison is *implied* in such a way that the figurative term is substituted for or identified with the literal one. "My daughter dances like an angel" is a simile; "my daughter is an angel" is a metaphor. In this example the difference involves more than the word *like:* the simile is more restricted in its comparative suggestion than is the metaphor. That is, the daughter's angelic attributes are more extensive in the unspecified and unrestricted metaphor. In the simile, however, she only dances like an angel. (There's no suggestion that she possesses other angelic qualities.)

Consider as an example of comparison the following lines from Bishop's "First Death in Nova Scotia":

Arthur was very small.
He was all white, like a doll
That hadn't been painted yet.

Here the poet conveys a sense of the child's world through a simile ("like a doll"). The young speaker sees the lifelessness of her cousin Arthur and compares his appearance with something familiar—a doll. In this case, however, Arthur is "unpainted," left "white, forever," as she notes later. The comparison suggests that the speaker recognizes, with one part of her mind, that her cousin is dead. But rather than register that brute fact with full force, her mind tempers its harshness. By means of the simile, the poet conveys both the child's subconscious acknowledgment of Arthur's death and the psychic strategy that enables her to cope with the fact.

As an additional example, consider the uses of comparison in Lowell's "The Drinker." Lowell compares the drinker's physical state to a fish in trouble: "the barbed hooks fester. The lines snap tight." Since the poet is not describing a fish, the fishy language must be seen as metaphorically describing the situation of the drinker. Lowell renders the drinker's state of mind in an additional comparison: "His despair has the galvanized color / of the mop and water in the galvanized bucket." And he further indicates by means of simile how impoverished the drinker's relationship with his wife has been: "Once she was close to him / as water to the dead metal." Taken together, these comparisons and additional images vividly render the drinker's hopeless desperation.

As a final example of the way comparison can animate a poem, consider the following selection.

LANGSTON HUGHES

[1902–1967]

Dream Deferred

What happens to a dream deferred?

Does it dry up
like a raisin in the sun?
Or fester like a sore—
And then run?

Does it stink like rotten meat?
Or crust and sugar over—
like a syrupy sweet?

Maybe it just sags
like a heavy load.

Or does it explode?

Once we realize that by "dream," the poet means a hope, desire, or ambition, we can return to the series of similes that answer the question with which the poem begins. Each simile appears as an image that stimulates a different sense: a dried-up raisin; a festering, running sore; "rotten meat"; "a syrupy sweet." Cumulatively, the similes suggest decay or deterioration over time: something dries up, festers, rots, crusts over. With the fifth simile, "Maybe it just sags / like a heavy load," the speaker illustrates how an unfulfilled dream can become a burden, a weight on one's mind and heart. And the final comparison—a metaphor—reveals yet another way the dream can result in destruction: through an explosion of both the dream itself and the spirit of the dreamer, who, by being denied its fulfillment, is led to abandon all hope of its realization. Enraged, he explodes into violence.

As an exercise in interpreting comparative figures, read the two poems that follow and consider the questions that accompany them.

ROBERT WALLACE

[*b.* 1932]

The Double-Play

In his sea lit
distance, the pitcher winding
like a clock about to chime comes down with

the ball, hit
sharply, under the artificial
banks of arc-lights, bounds like a vanishing string

over the green
to the shortstop magically
scoops to his right whirling above his invisible

shadows
in the dust redirects
its flight to the running poised second baseman

pirouettes
leaping, above the slide, to throw
from mid-air, across the colored tightened interval,

to the leaning-
out first baseman ends the dance
drawing it disappearing into his long brown glove

stretches. What
is too swift for deception
is final, lost, among the loosened figures

jogging off the field
(the pitcher walks), casual
in the space where the poem has happened.

QUESTIONS

1. As its title suggests, the poem describes a double play in baseball—getting two offensive players out on a single play. Throughout the poem the double play is compared to a dance. Pinpoint the words and phrases that establish this metaphorical connection, and explain what precisely about the double play makes it like a dance.
2. Besides the central metaphor that controls the poem, the poet has introduced other comparisons to illuminate and describe aspects or details of the double play. Identify and explain these comparisons.
3. In what way has the double play occurred "in the space where the poem has happened" (line 24)? How has a double play occurred both on the page and in the poem?

SYLVIA PLATH

[1932–1963]

Metaphors

I'm a riddle in nine syllables,
An elephant, a ponderous house,
A melon strolling on two tendrils.

O red fruit, ivory, fine timbers!
This loaf's big with its yeasty rising.
Money's new-minted in this fat purse.
I'm a means, a stage, a cow in calf.
I've eaten a bag of green apples,
Boarded the train there's no getting off.

QUESTION

To understand this riddling poem, you have to make sense of its metaphors. Identify the metaphors, and explain what they have in common.

MARIANNE MOORE

[1887–1972]

The Mind Is an Enchanting Thing

is an enchanted thing
    like the glaze on a
katydid-wing
        subdivided by sun
        till the nettings are legion.
Like Gieseking playing Scarlatti;

like the apteryx-awl
    as a beak, or the
kiwi's rain-shawl
        of haired feathers, the mind
        feeling its way as though blind,
walks along with its eyes on the ground.

It has memory's ear
    that can hear without
having to hear.
        Like the gyroscope's fall,
        truly unequivocal
because trued by regnant certainty,

it is a power of
    strong enchantment. It

is like the dove-
neck animated by
sun; it is memory's eye;
it's conscientious inconsistency.

It tears off the veil; tears
the temptation, the
mist the heart wears,
from its eyes—if the heart
has a face; it takes apart
dejection. It's fire in the dove-neck's

iridescence; in the
inconsistencies
of Scarlatti.
Unconfusion submits
its confusion to proof; it's
not a Herod's oath that cannot change.

QUESTION

Moore's poem is organized as a series of comparisons, which taken together reveal some of the powers and enchantments of the mind. Identify at least three of Moore's comparisons, indicate whether they are similes or metaphors, and explain what each suggests about the mind.

SYMBOLS

A *symbol* is any object or action that means more than itself, any object or action that represents something beyond itself. A rose, for example, can represent beauty or love or transience. A tree may represent a family's roots and branches. A soaring bird might stand for freedom. Light might symbolize hope or knowledge or life. These and other familiar symbols may represent different, even opposite things, depending on how they are deployed in a particular poem. Natural symbols like light and darkness, fire and water can stand for contradictory things. Water, for example, which typically symbolizes life (rain, fertility, food, life) can also stand for death (tempests, hurricanes, floods). And fire, which often indicates destruction, can represent purgation or purification. The meaning of any symbol, whether an object, an action, or a gesture, is controlled by its context.

How then do we know if a poetic detail is symbolic? How do we decide whether to leap beyond the poem's factual detail into a symbolic interpretation? There are no simple answers to these questions. Like any interpretive connections we make in reading, the decision to view something as symbolic depends partly on our skill in reading and partly on whether the poetic context invites and rewards a symbolic reading. The following questions can guide our thinking about interpreting symbols:

1. Is the object, action, gesture, or event important to the poem? Is it described in detail? Does it occur repeatedly? Does it appear at a climactic moment in the poem?
2. Does the poem seem to warrant our granting its details more significance than their immediate literal meaning?
3. Does our symbolic reading make sense? Does it account for the literal details without either ignoring or distorting them?

Even in following such guidelines, there will be occasions when we are not certain that a poem is symbolic. And there will be times when, though we are fairly confident *that* certain details are symbolic, we are not confident about *what* they symbolize. Such uncertainty is due largely to the nature of interpretation, which is an art rather than a science. But these interpretive complications are also due to the differences in complexity and variability with which poets use symbols. The most complex symbols resist definitive and final explanation. We can circle around them, but we neither exhaust their significance nor define their meaning.

As an example of how literal details assume symbolic significance, observe their use in the following poem.

PETER MEINKE

[*b.* 1932]

Advice to My Son

The trick is, to live your days,
as if each one may be your last
(for they go fast, and young men lose their lives

in strange and unimaginable ways)
but at the same time, plan long range
(for they go slow: if you survive
the shattered windshield and the bursting shell
you will arrive
at our approximation here below
of heaven or hell).

To be specific, between the peony and the rose
plant squash and spinach, turnips and tomatoes;
beauty is nectar
and nectar, in a desert, saves—
but the stomach craves stronger sustenance
than the honied vine.

Therefore, marry a pretty girl
after seeing her mother;
show your soul to one man,
work with another,
and always serve bread with your wine.

But, son,
always serve wine.

The concrete details that invite symbolic reading are these: peony and rose; squash, spinach, turnips, and tomatoes; bread and wine. If we read the poem literally and assume the advice is meant that way, we learn something about the need to plant and enjoy these flowers and foods. But if we suspect that the speaker is advising his son about more than food and flowers, we will look toward their symbolic implications.

What then do the various plants and the bread and wine symbolize? How is the speaker's advice about them related to the more general advice about living? In the first stanza the general advice implies two contradictory courses of action: (1) live each day to the fullest as if it will be the last; (2) look to the future and plan wisely so your future will not be marred by unwise decisions. In advising his son to plant peonies and roses, the speaker urges him to see the need for beauty and luxury, implying that he needs food for the spirit as well as sustenance for the body.

The symbols of bread and wine suggest a related point. The speaker urges his son to serve both bread and wine as bread is a dietary staple, something basic and common, but wine enhances the bread, making it seem more than mere common fare. Wine symbolizes something festive; it provides a touch of celebration. Thus the speaker's advice about bread and wine parallels his earlier suggestions. In each case, he urges his son to balance and blend, to fulfill both his basic and his spiritual needs. By making his advice concrete the speaker does indeed advocate literally what he says: plant roses and peonies with your vegetables; drink wine with your bread. But by including such specific instructions in a poem that contains other more serious advice about living (live for today, live for the future) the poet invites us to see bread and wine, vegetables and flowers more than literally. If our interpretation of their symbolic dimension is congruent with other parts of the poem, and if it makes sense, then we should feel confident that we are not imposing a symbolic reading where it is not warranted.

Consider the symbolic implications of the three poems that follow.

ROBERT FROST

[1874–1963]

The Road Not Taken

Two roads diverged in a yellow wood,
And sorry I could not travel both
And be one traveler, long I stood
And looked down one as far as I could
To where it bent in the undergrowth;

Then took the other, as just as fair,
And having perhaps the better claim,
Because it was grassy and wanted wear;
Though as for that the passing there
Had worn them really about the same,

And both that morning equally lay
In leaves no step had trodden black.
Oh, I kept the first for another day!
Yet knowing how way leads on to way,
I doubted if I should ever come back.

I shall be telling this with a sigh
Somewhere ages and ages hence:
Two roads diverged in a wood, and I—
I took the one less traveled by,
And that has made all the difference.

QUESTIONS

1. On one level, this is a poem about walking in the woods and choosing one of two paths to follow. What invites us to see the poem as something more? What is this something more?
2. Frost is careful not to specify what the two roads represent: he does not limit their possible symbolic meanings. And yet the nature of the experience he describes does pivot the poem on a central human problem: the inescapable necessity to make choices. Specify some of the kinds of choices we all must make that could be represented by the two roads of the poem.

EMILY DICKINSON

[1830–1886]

Because I could not stop for Death

Because I could not stop for Death—
He kindly stopped for me—
The Carriage held but just Ourselves—
And Immortality.

We slowly drove—He knew no haste
And I had put away
My labor and my leisure too,
For His Civility—

We passed the School, where Children strove
At Recess—in the Ring—
We passed the Fields of Gazing Grain—
We passed the Setting Sun—

Or rather—He passed Us—
The Dews drew quivering and chill—

For only Gossamer, my Gown—
My Tippet—only Tulle—

We paused before a House that seemed
A Swelling of the Ground—
The Roof was scarcely visible—
The Cornice—in the Ground—

Since then—'tis Centuries—and yet
Feels shorter than the Day
I first surmised the Horses' Heads
Were toward Eternity—

QUESTION

Explain the symbolic significance of the details in lines 9–12 and 17–20.

HART CRANE

[1899–1932]

Royal Palm

FOR GRACE HART CRANE

Green rustlings, more-than-regal charities
Drift coolly from that tower of whispered light.
Amid the noontide's blazed asperities
I watched the sun's most gracious anchorite

Climb up as by communings, year on year
Uneaten of the earth or aught earth holds,
And the grey trunk, that's elephantine, rear
Its frondings sighing in æthereal folds.

Forever fruitless, and beyond that yield
Of sweat the jungle presses with hot love
And tendril till our deathward breath is sealed—
It grazes the horizons, launched above

BECAUSE I COULD NOT STOP FOR DEATH 16 **Tippet:** scarf or stole.

Mortality—ascending emerald-bright,
A fountain at salute, a crown in view—
Unshackled, casual of its azured height
As though it soared suchwise through heaven too.

QUESTION

What aspects of the palm tree does Crane single out? What words suggest his attitude toward the tree? And what, finally, does the tree come to represent? (Consider especially the last two stanzas.)

SENTENCES

Poets use sentences as they do imagery, diction, structure, sound, and rhythm—to express meaning and convey feeling. Part of a poem's effect derives from the poet's choices in the length and form and shape of its sentences. Consider, for example, how sentences contribute to some of the poems discussed earlier. In "Those Winter Sundays" (p. 5), Robert Hayden uses normal word order for each of the poem's four sentences, but he varies their lengths dramatically. In the first stanza, for example, Hayden follows a long sentence with a short one. The effect is to heighten the emphasis of the short sentence: "No one ever thanked him." In the last stanza, Hayden uses a question rather than a statement to express the speaker's remembrance of his father's acts of love. Both the question and the repetition of the phrase "What did I know" reveal the intensity of the speaker's regret at his belated understanding.

In "Stopping by Woods on a Snowy Evening" (p. 57), Robert Frost achieves emphasis differently—through *inversion,* or the reversal of the standard order of words in a line or sentence. The word order of the first line of the poem is inverted:

Whose woods these are I think I know.

Normal word order would be:

I think I know whose woods these are.

In the more conversational alternative, emphasis falls on what the speaker knows or thinks he knows. In Frost's line emphasis falls on "whose woods," which becomes more important than what the speaker thinks he knows. Perhaps more important still is the difference in tone between the two versions. Frost's inverted *syntax,* or order of words in a sentence, lifts the line, giving it a more even rhythm and slowing it down slightly. The more everyday version lacks the rhythmic regularity of Frost's line and reads much more like a casual statement.

The seven sentences in Langston Hughes's "Dream Deferred" (pp. 41–42) are notable for another reason: all but one of them are questions. The lone declarative sentence, however, with its tentative introductory "Maybe," is very much like a question, too. We should also note that even though questions dominate the poem, these questions vary in purpose and force. The first interrogative sentence, "What happens to a dream deferred," states the question to which the rest of the poem is an answer—an answer in the form of additional questions. The final question/answer is set apart from the others visually by the space preceding it and by being italicized. Its importance is thus doubly highlighted, triply if we consider its placement at the end of the poem.

In Adrienne Rich's "Prospective Immigrants Please Note," variations in sentence form and length embody shifts in the poem's tone.

ADRIENNE RICH

[*b.* 1929]

Prospective Immigrants Please Note

Either you will
go through this door
or you will not go through.

If you go through
there is always the risk
of remembering your name.

Things look at you doubly
and you must look back
and let them happen.

If you do not go through
it is possible
to live worthily

to maintain your attitudes
to hold your position
to die bravely

but much will blind you,
much will evade you,
at what cost who knows?

The door itself
makes no promises.
It is only a door.

Unlike the sentences in Hughes's poem, which were predominantly questions, Rich's sentences are largely declarative. Five of the poem's six sentences are statements; one is a question. Moreover, the declarative sentences show a consistency in length: the first three sentences are each three lines; the last two share the final three-line stanza. But the question is different not only in form but in length also: it stretches across three stanzas, filling nine lines. Moreover, its tone shifts from the straightforward either-or of stanza 1 and the if-then of stanza 2 to a greater range of possibilities as the interrogative sentence unfolds ("to live" . . . "to maintain" . . . "to hold" . . . "to die"). Immediately following this list of possibilities comes a pair of counter-probabilities introduced by "but": "much will blind you, / much will evade you." The possibilities inaugurated with this "but" make the alternatives previously announced less attractive. Further accenting the reconsideration of possibilities is the question that comes at the very end of the sentence: "at what cost who knows?" This long interrogative sentence serves, finally, to prepare for the return of the short, crisp declaratives with which the poem began and to suggest that the first alternative proposed—to go through the door—is the one to follow. We are left, however, with the reminder that "The door itself / makes no promises," for "It is only a door."

You can gain additional practice in assessing the contribution of a poem's sentences to its tone and meaning by considering the way they work in the following poems.

ROBERT FROST

[1874–1963]

The Silken Tent

She is as in a field a silken tent
At midday when a sunny summer breeze
Has dried the dew and all its ropes relent,
So that in guys it gently sways at ease,
And its supporting central cedar pole,
That is its pinnacle to heavenward
And signifies the sureness of the soul,
Seems to owe naught to any single cord,
But strictly held by none, is loosely bound
By countless silken ties of love and thought
To everything on earth the compass round,
And only by one's going slightly taut
In the capriciousness of summer air
Is of the slightest bondage made aware.

QUESTION

Perhaps the most astonishing thing about this poem is that it is only a single sentence. Go through the poem again, attending to the way the sentence develops. Account for all the conjunctions: *so* (line 4), *and* (line 5), *And* (line 7), *But* (line 9), *And* (line 12). How do these conjunctions help us follow the sentence?

E. E. CUMMINGS

[1894–1962]

Me up at does

Me up at does

out of the floor
quietly Stare

a poisoned mouse

still who alive

is asking What
have i done that

You wouldn't have

QUESTIONS

1. Rearrange the syntax of this poem to approximate the normal word order of an English sentence. Where do you have to make the heaviest adjustment?
2. How is cummings's word order related to the situation the poem describes? What does cummings gain by ordering his words as he does?

WALLACE STEVENS

[1879–1955]

No Possum, No Sop, No Taters

He is not here, the old sun,
As absent as if we were asleep.

The field is frozen. The leaves are dry.
Bad is final in this light.

In this bleak air the broken stalks
Have arms without hands. They have trunks

Without legs or, for that, without heads.
They have heads in which a captive cry

Is merely the moving of a tongue.
Snow sparkles like eyesight falling to earth,

Like seeing fallen brightly away.
The leaves hop, scraping on the ground.

It is deep January. The sky is hard.
The stalks are firmly rooted in ice.

It is in this solitude, a syllable,
Out of these gawky flitterings,

Intones its single emptiness,
The savagest hollow of winter-sound.

It is here, in this bad, that we reach
The last purity of the knowledge of good.

The crow looks rusty as he rises up
Bright is the malice in his eye . . .

One joins him there for company.
But at a distance, in another tree.

QUESTIONS

1. Notice how frequently Stevens uses the short sentence. What is the effect of accumulating short sentences in stanzas 2 and 7?
2. Consider the effect of the inverted sentence in the next-to-last stanza:

   Bright is the malice in his eye.

   What is different about the following alternative?

   The malice in his eye is bright.

3. Why is the last line a separate sentence, rather than a continuation of the sentence begun on the previous line?

SOUNDS

The most familiar element of poetry is *rhyme,* which can be defined as the matching of final vowel and consonant sounds in two or more words. When the corresponding sounds occur at the ends of lines we have *end rhyme;* when they occur within lines we have *internal rhyme.* The opening stanza of Edgar Allan Poe's "The Raven" illustrates both:

Once upon a midnight dreary, while I pondered weak and weary,
Over many a quaint and curious volume of forgotten lore—

While I nodded nearly napping, suddenly there came a tapping,
As of some one gently rapping, rapping at my chamber door.
"Tis some visitor," I muttered, "tapping at my chamber door—
Only this and nothing more."

For the reader rhyme is a pleasure, for the poet a challenge. Part of its pleasure for the reader is in anticipating and hearing a poem's echoing song. Part of its challenge for the poet is in rhyming naturally, without forcing the rhythm, the syntax, or the sense. When the challenge is met successfully, the poem is a pleasure to listen to; it sounds natural to the ear.

ROBERT FROST

[1874–1963]

Stopping by Woods on a Snowy Evening

Whose woods these are I think I know.
His house is in the village, though;
He will not see me stopping here
To watch his woods fill up with snow.

My little horse must think it queer
To stop without a farmhouse near
Between the woods and frozen lake
The darkest evening of the year.

He gives his harness bells a shake
To ask if there is some mistake.
The only other sound's the sweep
Of easy wind and downy flake.

The woods are lovely, dark and deep,
But I have promises to keep,
And miles to go before I sleep,
And miles to go before I sleep.

Notice how in each of the first three stanzas, three of the four lines rhyme (lines 1, 2, and 4). And note also how Frost picks up the nonrhymed sound of each stanza (the third line) and links it with the rhyming sound of the stanza that follows it, until the fourth stanza when he closes with four matching rhymes. Part of our pleasure in Frost's rhyming may derive from the pattern of departure and return it voices. Part may stem also from the way the rhyme pattern supports the poem's meaning. The speaker is caught between his desire to remain still, peacefully held by the serene beauty of the woods, and his contrasting need to leave, to return to his responsibilities. In a similar way, the poem's rhyme is caught between a surge forward toward a new sound and a return to a sound repeated earlier. The pull and counterpull of the rhyme reflect the speaker's ambivalence.

The rhymes in Frost's poem are *exact* or *perfect rhymes:* that is, the rhyming words share corresponding sounds and stresses and a similar number of syllables. While Frost's poem contains perfect rhymes ("know," "though," and "snow," for example), we sometimes hear in poems a less exact, *imperfect, approximate,* or *slant rhyme.* Emily Dickinson's "Because I could not stop for Death" (p. 49) includes such slant rhymes ("away,"—"Civility," "chill"—"Tulle"). Theodore Roethke's "My Papa's Waltz" (p. 13) contains a slant rhyme on ("dizzy"—"easy"), which also exemplifies *feminine rhyme.* In feminine rhyme the final syllable of a rhymed word is unstressed; in *masculine rhyme* the final syllable is stressed—or the words rhymed are each only one syllable.

Besides rhyme, two other forms of sound play prevail in poetry: *alliteration* or the repetition of consonant sounds, especially at the beginning of words, and *assonance* or the repetition of vowel sounds. In his witty guide to poetic technique, *Rhyme's Reason,* John Hollander describes alliteration and assonance like this:

> Assonance is the spirit of a rhyme,
> A common vowel, hovering like a sigh
> After its consonantal body dies . . .
>
> . . . .
>
> Alliteration lightly links
> Stressed syllables with common consonants.

Walt Whitman's "When I Heard the Learn'd Astronomer," though lacking in end rhyme, possesses a high degree of assonance. The long *i*'s in lines 1, 3, and 4 accumulate and gather force as the poem glides into its last four lines: *"I,"* "t*i*red," "r*i*sing," "gl*i*ding," "I," "m*y*self," "n*i*ght," "t*i*me," and "s*i*lence." This assonance sweetens the sound of the second part of the poem, highlighting its radical shift of action and feeling.

WALT WHITMAN

[1819–1892]

When I Heard the Learn'd Astronomer

When I heard the learn'd astronomer,
When the proofs, the figures, were ranged in columns before me,
When I was shown the charts and diagrams, to add, divide, and
  measure them,
When I sitting heard the astronomer where he lectured with much
  applause in the lecture-room,
How soon unaccountable I became tired and sick,
Till rising and gliding out I wander'd off by myself,
In the mystical moist night-air, and from time to time,
Look'd up in perfect silence at the stars.

Both alliteration and assonance are clearly audible in "Stopping by Woods," particularly in the third stanza:

He gives his harness bells a shake
To ask if there is some mistake.
The only other sound's the sweep
Of easy wind and downy flake.

Notice that the long *e* of "sweep" is echoed in "*ea*-sy" and "down-*y*," and that the *ow* of "d*ow*ny" echoes the same sound in "s*ou*nd's." These repetitions of sound accentuate the images the words embody, aural images (wind-blow and snow-fall), tactile images (the soft fluff of down and the feel of thc gently blowing wind), and the visual images (the white flakes of snow).

The alliterative *s*'s in "*s*ome," and "*s*weep" are supported by the internal and terminal *s*'s: "Give*s*," "hi*s*," "harne*ss* bell*s*," and "i*s*," and also by mid-word *s*'s: "a*s*k," "mi*s*take," and "ea*s*y." There is a difference in the weight of these sounds; some are heavier than others—the two similar heavy *s*'s of "easy" and "his" contrast the lighter softer "*s*" in "harness" and "mistake."

Listen to the sound effects of rhyme, alliteration, and assonance in the following poem. Try to determine what sound contributes to its meaning.

WALLACE STEVENS

[1879–1955]

Peter Quince at the Clavier

I

Just as my fingers on these keys
Make music, so the self same sounds
On my spirit make a music, too.

Music is feeling, then, not sound;
And thus it is that what I feel,
Here in this room, desiring you,

Thinking of your blue-shadowed silk,
Is music. It is like the strain
Waked in the elders by Susanna.

Of a green evening, clear and warm,
She bathed in her still garden, while
The red-eyed elders watching, felt

The basses of their beings throb
In witching chords, and their thin blood
Pulse pizzicati of Hosanna.

II

In the green water, clear and warm,
Susanna lay.
She searched
The touch of springs,
And found
Concealed imaginings.
She sighed,
For so much melody.

Upon the bank, she stood
In the cool
Of spent emotions.
She felt, among the leaves,

The dew
Of old devotions.

She walked upon the grass,
Still quavering.
The winds were like her maids,
On timid feet,
Fetching her woven scarves,
Yet wavering.

A breath upon her hand
Muted the night.
She turned—
A cymbal crashed,
And roaring horns.

III

Soon, with a noise like tambourines.
Came her attendant Byzantines.

They wondered why Susanna cried
Against the elders by her side;

And as they whispered, the refrain
Was like a willow swept by rain.

Anon, their lamps' uplifted flame
Revealed Susanna and her shame.

And then, the simpering Byzantines
Fled, with a noise like tambourines.

IV

Beauty is momentary in the mind—
The fitful tracing of a portal;
But in the flesh it is immortal.

The body dies; the body's beauty lives.
So evenings die, in their green going,
A wave, interminably flowing.

So gardens die, their meek breath scenting
The cowl of winter, done repenting.
So maidens die, to the auroral
Celebration of a maiden's choral.

Susanna's music touched the bawdy strings
Of those white elders; but, escaping,
Left only Death's ironic scraping.
Now, in its immortality, it plays
On the clear viol of her memory,
And makes a constant sacrament of praise.

Before listening to the sound play of the poem, we should perhaps say a few words about its speaker and situation. Peter Quince, the title character, is the speaker. As he plays on a clavier (a keyboard instrument similar to a harpsichord), he is thinking about his sexual desire for a woman, whom he imagines, or perhaps remembers, in a blue silk dress. His feelings are connected in his mind with the Biblical story of Susanna, who was falsely accused of adultery by two lustful elders who themselves wanted to have sexual intercourse with her. Their immoral proposition occurs offstage, so to speak, in the second section. Its aftermath is described in section III. The fourth and final section offers a set of speculations, in part on the incident, especially on Susanna's chastity, and more generally on the nature of beauty and its relation to thought.

Our interest, however, for the moment, is in the poem's music. One of its more notable sound effects is the way it becomes more musical as it progresses. Throughout the first section, for example, end rhyme is minimal. So too is the use of sound play in the first four stanzas of the section. Only at the end of section I do we hear Stevens employing sound effects to describe the old men's lust for Susanna. Stevens's musical effects here are achieved largely through alliteration of b's and p's, which imitate the sound of plucking a stringed instrument such as a violin. Contributing to the pinched music of these last lines of section I is the repetition of short i's:

Ĭn wĭtching chords, and their thĭn blood

Pulse pĭzzĭcati of Hosanna.

The sound play increases in section II, which begins with the melodious rhymes of repeated long vowels and with soft consonantal alliteration. We hear a pleasant music throughout three stanzas of section II until it is interrupted by the jarring cymbal crash of hard consonants. This change in sound from a pleasing harmony to a dissonant cacophony imitates the intrusion of the lustful elders and indicates abrupt changes of direction in the action and feelings the poem describes.

Without pursuing the poem's sound effects in detail, we should note that each section corresponds to the movement of a symphonic work. Each section is written in a different tempo. The first is like an allegro (a fast tempo); the second, an andante (a moderate, walking tempo); the third, a scherzo (a rapid tempo in vigorous rhythm); and the fourth, a return to the rhythms of the opening. The rhymes and repetitions of section IV emphasize the poem's themes, resolve its disharmonies, and effectively integrate sound and sense, music and meaning. Listen to the language of the following examples.

HELEN CHASIN

[*b.* 1938]

The Word Plum

The word *plum* is delicious

pout and push, luxury of
self-love, and savoring murmur

full in the mouth and falling
like fruit

taut skin
pierced, bitten, provoked into
juice, and tart flesh

question
and reply, lip and tongue
of pleasure.

QUESTIONS

1. How is the word *p-l-u-m* sounded and resounded in the poem? Look at and listen to lines 2–3 in particular.
2. Map out the poem's patterns of alliteration and vowel repetition.

MAY SWENSON

[*b.* 1919]

The Universe

What
is it about,
the universe,
the universe about us stretching out?
We, within our brains,
within it,
think
we must unspin
the laws that spin it.
We think *why*
because we think
because.
Because we think,
we think
the universe about us.

But does it think,
the universe?
Then what about?
About us?
If not,
must there be cause
in the universe?
Must it have laws?
And what
if the universe
is not about us?
Then what?
What
is it about?
And what
about *us?*

QUESTION

Is this poem merely a witty game of repeating words, or does it employ sound effects to sound effect? Note lines 10–15 and 24–31.

RHYTHMS

Rhythm is the pulse or beat we feel in a phrase of music or a line of poetry. Rhythm refers to the regular recurrence of the accent or stress in poem or song. We derive our sense of rhythm from everyday life and from our experience with language and music. We experience the rhythm of day and night, the seasonal rhythms of the year, the beat of our hearts, and the rise and fall of our chests as we breathe in and out.

Perhaps our earliest memories of rhythm in language are associated with nursery rhymes like

JACK and JILL went UP the HILL*
to FETCH a PAIL of WAter.

Later we probably learned songs like "America," whose rhythm we might indicate like this:

MY COUN-TRY 'tis of THEE
SWEET LAND of LIberTY
Of THEE i SING.

Since then we have developed an ear for the rhythm of language in everyday speech:

I THINK I'll HIT the HAY

Did you SEE that?
Or: Did you see THAT?
Or: GO and DON'T come BACK.

Poets rely heavily on rhythm to express meaning and convey feeling. The following brief poem uses rhythm expressively in a way you can readily hear.

* Capitalization indicates stressed syllables, lower case letters unstressed ones.

ROBERT FROST

[1874–1963]

The Span of Life

The OLD DOG BARKS BACKward withOUT GETting UP.
I can reMEMber when HE was a PUP.

The first line is slower than the second. It is harder to pronounce and takes longer to say because Frost clusters the hard consonants (*d, k,* and *g* sounds) in the first line, and because the first line contains seven stresses to the four accents of the second. Three of the seven stresses fall at the beginning of the line, which gets it off to a slow start, whereas the accents of the second line are evenly spaced. The contrasting rhythms of the lines reinforce their contrasting images and sound effects. More importantly, however, the difference in the sound and rhythm in the two lines echoes their contrast of youth and age.

But we cannot proceed any further in this discussion without introducing more precise terms to refer to the patterns of accents we hear in a poem. If rhythm is the pulse or beat we hear in the line, then we can define *meter* as the measure or patterned count of a poetic line. Meter is a count of the stresses we feel in the poem's rhythm. By convention the unit of poetic meter in English is the *foot,* a unit of measure consisting of stressed and unstressed syllables. A poetic foot may be either *iambic* or *trochaic, anapestic* or *dactylic.* An iambic line is composed primarily of *iambs,* an *iamb* being defined as an unaccented syllable followed by an accented one as in the word "preVENT" or "conTAIN." Reversing the order of accented and unaccented syllables we get a *trochee,* which is an accented syllable followed by an unaccented one, as in "FOOTball" or LIquor." We can represent an accented syllable by a ´ and an unaccented syllable by a ˘: thus, prĕveńt (˘´), an iamb, and líquŏr (´˘), a trochee. Because both iambic and trochaic feet contain two syllables per foot, they are called *duple* (or double) meters. These duple meters can be distinguished from *triple* meters (three-syllable meters) like anapestic and dactylic meters. An *anapest* (˘˘´) consists of two unaccented syllables followed by an accented one as in cŏmprĕHEŃD or ĭntĕrVEŃE. A *dactyl* reverses the anapest, beginning with an ac-

cented syllable followed by two unaccented ones. DÁNgĕroŭs and CHÉERfŭlly̆ are examples. So is the word ÁNăpĕst.

Three additional points must be noted about poetic meter. First, anapestic (˘˘´) and iambic (˘´) meters move from an unstressed syllable to a stressed one. For this reason they are called *rising* meters. (They "rise" to the stressed syllable.) Lines in anapestic or iambic meter frequently end with a stressed syllable. Trochaic (´˘) and dactylic (´˘˘) meters, on the other hand, are said to be *falling* meters because they begin with a stressed syllable and decline in pitch and emphasis. (Syllables at the ends of trochaic and dactylic lines are generally unstressed.)

Second, the regularity of a poem's meter is not inflexible. In a predominantly iambic poem every line will not usually conform exactly to the strict metrical pattern. In "Stopping by Woods," for example, Robert Frost avoids metrical monotony by subtly altering the poem's rhythm and, in one important instance, departing from the iambic pattern. We can divide the poem's final stanza into metrical feet and mark the accents in this manner:

> Thĕ woóds / ăre lóve / ly̆, dárk, / ănd deép. /
> Bŭt Í / hăve pró / mĭsĕs / tŏ keép,
> Ănd míles / tŏ gó / bĕfóre / Ĭ sleép,
> Ănd míles / tŏ gó / bĕfóre / Ĭ sleép.

If we regard the pattern of this stanza and the pattern of the poem as a whole as regularly, even insistently, iambic, then the second line of this final stanza marks a slight deviation from that norm. The second and third feet of the line can be read as two accented syllables followed by two unaccented syllables, a spondaic foot followed by a pyrrhic. Two accented syllables together are called a *spondee* (KNÍCK-KNÁCK); two unaccented ones, a *pyrrhic* (ŏf thĕ). Both spondaic and pyrrhic feet serve as substitute feet for iambic and trochaic feet. Neither can serve as the metrical norm of an English poem.

Third, we give names to lines of poetry based on the number of feet they contain. You may have noticed that "Stopping by Woods on a Snowy Evening" consists of eight-syllable, or *octosyllabic,* lines. Since the meter is iambic (˘´) with two syllables per foot, the line contains four iambic feet and is hence called a *tetrameter* line (from the Greek word for "four"). Thus Frost's poem is written in *iambic tetrameter,* unlike Millay's sonnet "Love Is Not All" (p. 78), for example, which contains ten-syllable lines, also predominantly iambic. Such five-foot lines are named *pentameters* (from the Greek *penta,* for "five"), making the sonnet a poem in *iambic pentameter.*

Here is a chart of the various meters and poetic feet.

	Foot	**Meter**	**Example**
Rising or Ascending Feet	iamb	iambic	prevent
	anapest	anapestic	comprehend
Falling or Descending Feet	trochee	trochaic	football
	dactyl	dactylic	cheerfully
Substitute Feet	spondee	spondaic	knick-knack
	pyrrhic	pyrrhic	hit of the year

Duple Meters: two syllables per foot: iambic and trochaic

Triple Meters: three syllables per foot: anapestic and dactylic

Number of feet per line

one foot	monometer
two feet	dimeter
three feet	trimeter
four feet	tetrameter
five feet	pentameter
six feet	hexameter
seven feet	heptameter
eight feet	octameter

You should now be better able to discern the meter and rhythm of a poem. You can make an instructive comparison by taking the measure of two poems written in iambic pentameter, John Crowe Ransom's "Piazza Piece" (p. 80) and Edna St. Vincent Millay's "Love Is Not All" (p. 78). In Ransom's sonnet, see if you can account for the changes in pacing between the poem's opening eight lines and its last six. Consider changes in the basic iambic pattern; listen for caesuras, or pauses, and watch for *enjambed,* or run-on, lines whose sense and grammar run over into the next line. You should also be alert for the way in which parallel sentence structure and sound play collaborate with rhythm and meter to support each poem's feeling and meaning.

Metrical Variation

We noted earlier that Frost's "Stopping by Woods" is written in strict iambic pentameter with only one slight variation in line 14.

How then does Frost manage to avoid the monotony of fifteen lines of ta TUM / ta TUM / ta TUM / ta TUM / ? One way is by varying the reader's focus on different details: woods, snow, and speaker (stanza 1); horse and darkness (stanza 2); horse and snow (stanza 3); woods and darkness and speaker (stanza 4). Another is to vary the syntax, as he does with the inversion of the opening line. A third is simply to use a familiar diction in a normal speaking voice. Fourth and perhaps most important is Frost's masterful control of tempo. Of the four stanzas none carry the same pattern of end stopping. Stanza 1 is end-stopped at the first, second, and fourth lines, with line 3 enjambed. Stanza 3 is the closest to the second stanza, with two end-stopped lines and two enjambed lines. Stanza 4 is heavily stopped with two caesuras in its initial line and with end stops at every line. (It is here that we are slowed down to feel the seductive beauty of the woods; it is here that the symbolic weight of the poem is heaviest.) But we should not overlook the contrasting second stanza, which is cast as a single flowing sentence. The iambic pattern inhabits this stanza as it beats in the others. But as a result of the variety of technical resources Frost displays in the poem, we hear the iambic beat but are not overwhelmed by it.

Frost's rhythmical variations can be compared with Whitman's expressive use of metrical variation in "When I Heard the Learn'd Astronomer," a poem in *free verse,* verse without a fixed metrical pattern (p. 59). Whitman's poem is characteristic of much free verse in its varying line lengths and accents per line and in its imitation of the cadences of speech. The poem's final line ("Look'd up in perfect silence at the stars"), however, differs from the others, as Paul Fussell has pointed out in *Poetic Meter and Poetic Form.** It is written in strict iambic pentameter, a variation that carries considerable expressive power, coming after the seemingly casual metrical organization of the previous lines. Because Whitman's line must be read in the context of the whole poem for its expressive impact to be felt, you should turn to it, preferably to read it aloud. In rereading you might like to consider whether, as some readers have suggested, the poem is not really in free verse at all, but rather in *blank verse,* unrhymed iambic pentameter.

Besides this expressive use of metrical variation, Whitman's

* Paul Fussell, *Poetic Meter and Poetic Form* (New York: Random House, 1979), p. 85.

poem exhibits additional elements of rhythmic control: in its consistency of end-stopped lines; in its flexible use of caesura (lines 2, 3, and 7); in its absence of caesura from the shorter lines (1 and 4–8). We can perhaps gain a greater appreciation of Whitman's rhythmical accomplishment by recasting his lines like this:

When I heard the learn'd astronomer,
When the proofs, the figures
Were ranged in columns before me,
When I was shown the charts and diagrams
To add, divide, and measure them,
When I sitting heard the astronomer
Where he lectured to much applause
In the lecture-room. . . .

Or like this:

When I heard
The learn'd astronomer,
When the proofs,
The figures were ranged
In columns
Before me,
When I was shown
The charts and diagrams
To add, divide and
Measure them. . . .

Both versions destroy the poem: they eliminate the sweep of its long lines, destroying its cadences and rhythm, and ultimately inhibiting its expressiveness.

Before leaving the poem, we should note that Whitman's rhythmic effects work together with other devices of sound, structure, and diction. In the same way, for example, that the strict iambic pentameter of the last line varies the prevailing meter expressively, so too does its assonance (the long *i*'s) deviate expressively from the poem's previously established avoidance of vowel music. In addition, the meter of the final line stresses *sílenče* and *stárs,* both of which the speaker values. Finally, the iambic rhythm of the line has us looking UP and AT the stars, an unusual metrical effect since prepositions are almost always unstressed.

Throughout these comments on the rhythm and meter of the poems by Whitman and Frost, we have been engaged in the act of *scansion,* measuring verse, identifying its prevailing meter and

rhythm, and accounting for deviations from the metrical pattern. In scanning a poem, we try to determine its dominant rhythm and meter, and to account for variations from the norm. The pattern we hear as dominant will influence how we read lines that do not conform metrically, and also how we interpret and respond to those lines.

One last note about rhythm and meter. Without the turn of the poetic line, without the division of words into lines, we have no poem. It is the poetic line that distinguishes poetry from prose, since poets decide where one line ends and another begins. And as the poet Wendell Berry has pointed out, it is the line of verse that "checks the merely impulsive flow of speech, subjects it to another pulse, to measure."* Without the measure of meter, without the turn of the line, there is no music and no poem. Meter and rhythm are not merely technical elements, no more than diction and imagery, syntax and structure and sound. All of these interrelated elements of poetry have effects on readers, do things to readers. We sense them and feel them and thereby understand a poem, not just with our minds, but also with our eyes and ears.

Here are a few additional poems for rhythmic and metrical consideration.

LANGSTON HUGHES

[1902–1967]

Ballad of the Landlord

Landlord, landlord,
My roof has sprung a leak.
Don't you 'member I told you about it
Way last week?

Landlord, landlord,
These steps is broken down.
When you come up yourself
It's a wonder you don't fall down.

* Wendell Berry, *Standing By Words* (San Francisco: North Point Press, 1983), p. 28.

Ten Bucks you say I owe you?
Ten Bucks you say is due?
Well, that's Ten Bucks more'n I'll pay you
Till you fix this house up new.

What? You gonna get eviction orders?
You gonna cut off my heat?
You gonna take my furniture and
Throw it in the street?

Um-huh! You talking high and mighty.
Talk on—till you get through.
You ain't gonna be able to say a word
If I land my fist on you.

Police! Police!
Come and get this man!
He's trying to ruin the government
And overturn the land!

Copper's whistle!
Patrol bell!
Arrest.

Precinct Station.
Iron cell.
Headlines in press:

MAN THREATENS LANDLORD
TENANT HELD NO BAIL
JUDGE GIVES NEGRO 90 DAYS IN COUNTY JAIL

QUESTIONS

1. What is the prevailing meter of the poem? How would you characterize its rhythm?
2. Where do rhythm and meter change? How, why, and to what effect?

THEODORE ROETHKE

[1908–1963]

Elegy for Jane

MY STUDENT, THROWN BY A HORSE

I remember the neckcurls, limp and damp as tendrils;
And her quick look, a sidelong pickerel smile;
And how, once startled into talk, the light syllables leaped for her,
And she balanced in the delight of her thought,
A wren, happy, tail into the wind,
Her song trembling the twigs and small branches.
The shade sang with her;
The leaves, their whispers turned to kissing;
And the mold sang in the bleached valleys under the rose.

Oh, when she was sad, she cast herself down into such a pure depth,
Even a father could not find her:
Scraping her cheek against straw;
Stirring the clearest water.

My sparrow, you are not here,
Waiting like a fern, making a spiny shadow.
The sides of wet stones cannot console me,
Nor the moss, wound with the last light.

If only I could nudge you from this sleep,
My maimed darling, my skittery pigeon,
Over this damp grave I speak the words of my love:
I, with no rights in this matter,
Neither father nor lover.

QUESTIONS

1. Mark the accented syllables in each line, taking note of caesuras and end-stopped lines. Does Roethke's elegy have a prevailing meter, or is it variable?

2. Comment on the poem's changes of rhythm. Where does it slow down, and with what effect?

RICHARD WILBUR

[*b.* 1921]

Junk

Huru Welandes
wore ne geswiceð
monna ænigum
ðaru ðe Mimming can
heardne gehealdan.

WALDERE

An axe angles
from my neighbor's ashcan;
It is hell's handiwork,
the wood not hickory,
The flow of the grain
not faithfully followed.
The shivered shaft
rises from a shellheap
Of plastic playthings,
paper plates,
And the sheer shards
of shattered tumblers
That were not annealed
for the time needful.
At the same curbside,
a cast-off cabinet
Of wavily-warped
unseasoned wood
Waits to be trundled

Huru Welandes . . . heardne gehealdan: The epigraph, from *Waldere,* I, 2–4, can be translated: "Indeed Weland's handiwork does not fail any man who hard Mimming can hold." *Waldere,* a long Anglo-Saxon epic poem, survives only as a fragment. Weland is a lengendary Germanic smith, and Mimming is the name of a sword he made. The letter ð is called "eth" and is roughly equivalent to the modern "th."

in the trash-man's truck.
Haul them off! Hide them!
The heart winces
For junk and gimcrack,
for jerrybuilt things
And the men who make them
for a little money,
Bartering pride
like the bought boxer
Who pulls his punches,
or the paid-off jockey
Who in the home stretch
holds in his horse.
Yet the things themselves
in thoughtless honor
Have kept composure,
like captives who would not
Talk under torture.
Tossed from a tailgate
Where the dump displays
its random dolmens,
Its black barrows
and blazing valleys,
They shall waste in the weather
and toward what they were.
The sun shall glory
in the glitter of glass-chips,
Foreseeing the salvage
of the prisoned sand,
And the blistering paint
peel off in patches,
That the good grain
be discovered again.
Then burnt, bulldozed,
they shall all be buried
To the depth of diamonds,
in the making dark
Where halt Hephaestus
keeps his hammer
And Wayland's work
is worn away.

QUESTION

How does the rhythm and meter of "Junk" differ from the meters and rhythms of the other poems in this section?

STRUCTURES

When we analyze a poem's structure, we focus on its patterns of organization. *Form* exists in poems on many levels from patterns of sound and image to structures of syntax and of thought; it is as much a matter of phrase and line as of stanza and whole poem.

Among the most popular forms of poetry has been the *sonnet,* a fourteen-line poem usually written in iambic pentameter. Because the form of the sonnet is strictly constrained, it is considered a *closed* or *fixed form.* We can recognize poems in fixed forms such as the sonnet, sestina, and villanelle by their patterns of rhyme, meter, and repetition. Poems written in fixed form reveal their structural patterns both aurally and visually. We see the shapes of their stanzas and the patterns of their line lengths; we feel their metrical beat, and we hear their play of sound.

The *Shakespearean,* or *English, sonnet* falls into three *quatrains,* or four-line sections, with the rhyme pattern *abab cdcd efef* followed by a *couplet* or pair of rhymed lines with the pattern *gg.* The following poem is an example.

EDNA ST. VINCENT MILLAY

[1892–1950]

I Dreamed I Moved among the Elysian Fields

I dreamed I moved among the Elysian fields,
In converse with sweet women long since dead;
And out of blossoms which that meadow yields
I wove a garland for your living head.
Danae, that was the vessel for a day
Of golden Jove, I saw, and at her side,
Whom Jove the Bull desired and bore away,
Europa stood, and the Swan's featherless bride.

Elysian Fields: in Greek mythology, the land of the virtuous dead.

All these were mortal women, yet all these
Above the ground had had a god for guest;
Freely I walked beside them and at ease,
Addressing them, by them again addressed,
And marvelled nothing, for remembering you,
Wherefore I was among them well I knew.

We can chart the rhyme pattern of the sonnet by designating each rhyming sound with a letter this way:

fields, *a*
dead; *b*
yields *a*
head. *b*
day *c*
side, *d*
away, *c*
bride. *d*
these *e*
guest; *f*
ease, *e*
addressed, *f*
you, *g*
knew. *g*

We have also marked the poem's punctuation, which is congruent with the structure of its rhyme. The organization of the sonnet's sentences approximates its rhyme structure of three quatrains and a couplet.

In the first quatrain, the speaker, wandering in the Elysian Fields, talks with women who died long before. As she talks, she weaves a garland for her lover's head. The second and third quatrains name three women who were seduced by Jove (Zeus), the chief god in Greek and Roman mythology. Jove descended upon Danae as a shower of gold; he carried away Europa after disguising himself as a bull; and, in the form of a swan, he raped Leda. The final couplet contains a surprising twist: the speaker feels comfortable talking with these women whom Jove singled out. She feels similarly honored; she considers her lover a living god.

Although this sonnet follows the Shakespearean pattern carefully, most sonnets deviate from it in some way. Another of Millay's sonnets illustrates one such variation.

Love Is Not All: It Is Not Meat Nor Drink

Love is not all: it is not meat nor drink
Nor slumber nor a roof against the rain;
Nor yet a floating spar to men that sink
And rise and sink and rise and sink again;
Love cannot fill the thickened lung with breath,
Nor clean the blood, nor set the fractured bone;
Yet many a man is making friends with death
Even as I speak, for lack of love alone.
It well may be that in a difficult hour,
Pinned down by pain and moaning for release,
Or nagged by want past resolution's power,
I might be driven to sell your love for peace,
Or trade the memory of this night for food.
It well may be. I do not think I would.

The rhymes of this sonnet also clearly follow the Shakespearean pattern. Moreover, they approximate the logical structure of the poem. Lines 1–4 offer a statement about the limitations of love. Lines 5–6 continue to define love's limits, largely by referring to physical needs that love cannot satisfy and to adverse circumstances that it cannot improve. Midway through the poem's second structural unit (lines 7–8), however, there is a suggestion that even though the power of love is restricted (lines 1–6), its presence is necessary. There is, then, something of a countermovement that suggests the power and prominence of love. Instead of repeating the idea of the first quatrain throughout the second, Millay introduces a qualification and complication. The consequence is a tension between the poem's structure of rhyme and its organization of thought.

In the third quatrain the poem turns from generalized statements about love to the speaker's personal application of them. Here, too, the poem's rhyme pattern is slightly at odds with its organization of idea and feeling. The idea of the third quatrain—that the speaker might trade or abandon love for other things (peace or food, for example)—is continued into the first line of the final couplet. The last line of the poem serves to counterpoint this idea. Its change of tone and rhythm signals a shift in the direction of the speaker's thought and feeling.

An alternative to the Shakespearean sonnet is the *Petrarchan,* or *Italian, sonnet,* which typically falls into two parts: an octave of eight lines and a sestet of six. The octave rhyme pattern is *abba abba;* the rhymes of the sestet are more variable. Some common variations include *cde cde;* or *cde ced;* or *cd cd cd;* or *cde dce.* The following sonnet, again by Millay, exemplifies the form.

What Lips My Lips Have Kissed, and Where, and Why

What lips my lips have kissed, and where, and why,
I have forgotten, and what arms have lain
Under my head till morning; but the rain
Is full of ghosts tonight, that tap and sigh
Upon the glass and listen for reply,
And in my heart there stirs a quiet pain
For unremembered lads that not again
Will turn to me at midnight with a cry.
Thus in the winter stands the lonely tree,
Nor knows what birds have vanished one by one,
Yet knows its boughs more silent than before:
I cannot say what loves have come and gone,
I only know that summer sang in me
A little while, that in me sings no more.

Composed as two sentences of eight and six lines respectively, this poem breaks neatly into syntactic units that parallel the two-part structure of the Petrarchan sonnet. It also adheres to the form's rhyme scheme: *abba abba; cde dce* (with a slight variation in the rhymes of the sestet).

The octave describes the speaker's feelings as she remembers her former lovers. And although she doesn't recall specific details, she feels their loss, as she is presumably now alone. In line 9 the poem turns to an image of a tree in which birds once sang but is now abandoned. The shift to this image after the personal exposition in lines 1–8 is characteristic of the Petrarchan sonnet, which frequently changes direction in the first line of the sestet. In the second half of the sestet (lines 12–14), the poet explicitly compares her lonely predicament with that of the birdless tree.

Although this sonnet follows the Petrarchan schema closely, many Petrarchan sonnets deviate from the pattern. The following example uses the central logical division of octave and sestet, but diverges from the standard rhyme scheme.

JOHN CROWE RANSOM

[1888–1974]

Piazza Piece

—I am a gentleman in a dust coat trying
To make you hear. Your ears are soft and small
And listen to an old man not at all,
They want the young men's whispering and sighing.
But see the roses on your trellis dying
And hear the spectral singing of the moon;
For I must have my lovely lady soon,
I am a gentleman in a dust coat trying.

—I am a lady young in beauty waiting
Until my truelove comes, and then we kiss.
But what gray man among the vines is this
Whose words are dry and faint as in a dream?
Back from my trellis, sir, before I scream!
I am a lady young in beauty waiting.

The structure of Ransom's sonnet is both audible and visible, its two-part form clearly discernible to eye and ear. The rhyme pattern *(abba/acca, dee/ffd)* enforces its visual impression, highlighted by the separation of idea and action into two self-contained units of eight and six lines respectively. This form seems particularly well suited to Ransom's subject, since the poem presents two contrasting attitudes and two different speakers.

In the octave we see and hear an old man in a dust coat (death?) who insists that the beautiful young woman to whom he speaks will soon belong to him. And although Ransom's rhymes do not exactly conform to the standard Petrarchan pattern, the eight lines comprise a unit to be distinguished from the next six. In the sestet we see and hear the beautiful young woman in a set of changing rhymes, again varying slightly from the standard pattern. The different rhymes in the sestet, the space separating it from the octave, and the change of speaker all indicate an important shift. Ransom exploits this shift by making the young lady both unreceptive to the advances of the old man and unaware of who he is and what he represents.

The two sonnet forms discussed here offer different possibilities for poets. The English sonnet is particularly suitable for a theme and variations on it—for example, to the expression of an idea in the first quatrain, followed by a pair of varied restatements with different examples or images, and concluding with a couplet that serves as a summary or ironic commentary on the thrice-imaged idea. The Petrarchan form is especially well suited to the movement from the statement of a problem to its solution. It functions well also to enforce radical shifts of direction, especially contrasts in tone, idea, and feeling. Both Ransom and Millay have capitalized on the structural possibilities of their respective sonnet forms.

But not all poems are written in fixed forms. Many poets have resisted the limitations inherent in using a consistent and specific metrical pattern or in rhyming lines in a prescribed manner. As an alternative to the strictness of fixed form, they developed and discovered looser, more *open* and *free forms*. *Open* or *free form* does not imply formlessness. It suggests, instead, that poets capitalize on the freedom either to create their own forms or to use the traditional fixed forms in more flexible ways. An example of a poem in open form by Walt Whitman is reprinted here.

WALT WHITMAN

[1819–1892]

When I Heard the Learn'd Astronomer

When I heard the learn'd astronomer,
When the proofs, the figures, were ranged in columns before
  me,
When I was shown the charts and diagrams, to add, divide, and
  measure them,
When I sitting heard the astronomer where he lectured with
  much applause in the lecture-room,
How soon unaccountable I became tired and sick,
Till rising and gliding out I wander'd off by myself,
In the mystical moist night-air, and from time to time,
Look'd up in perfect silence at the stars.

Although Whitman's poem is arranged as a single sentence, it can be divided into two parts, each of four lines. The two-part division accumulates a set of contrasts: the speaker with other people and the speaker alone; the speaker sitting inside and the speaker standing outside looking at the stars; the noise inside and the silence outside; the lecturer's activity and the speaker's passivity; the clutter of details in lines 1–4 and the spareness of details in lines 5–8.

These contrasts reflect the poem's movement from one kind of learning about nature to another: from passive listening to active observation; from indirect factual knowledge to direct mystical apprehension. Whether the poet rejects the first form of knowledge for the second or whether he suggests that both are needed is not directly stated. The emphasis, nevertheless, is on the speaker's need to be alone and to experience nature directly.

More elaborate departures from fixed form include poems such as this unusual configuration of e. e. cummings:

E. E. CUMMINGS

[1894–1962]

l(a

l(a

le
af
fa

ll

s)
one
l

iness

Perhaps the first things to notice are the lack of capital letters and the absence of punctuation (except for the parentheses). What we don't see is as important as what we do. We don't see any recognizable words or sentences, to say nothing of traditional stanzas or lines of poetry. The poem strikes the eye as a series of letters that stream down the page, for the most part two to a line. Rearranging the letters horizontally we find these words: *(a leaf falls) loneliness.* (The first *l* of *loneliness* appears before the parenthesis, like this: *l (a leaf falls) oneliness;* to get *loneliness* you have to move the *l* in front of *oneliness.*

A single falling leaf is a traditional symbol of loneliness; this image is not new. What is new, however, is the way cummings has coupled the concept with the image, the way he has formed and shaped them into a nontraditional poem. But what has the poet gained by arranging his poem this way? By breaking the horizontal line of verse into a series of fragments (from the horizontal viewpoint), cummings illustrates visually the separation that is the primary cause of loneliness. Both the word *loneliness* and the image described in *a leaf falls* are broken apart, separated in this way. In addition, by splitting the initial letter from *loneliness,* the poet has revealed the hidden *one* in the word. It's as if he is saying: loneliness is *one*-liness. This idea is further corroborated in the visual ambiguity of "l." Initially we are not sure whether this symbol "l" is a number—*one*—or the letter *l.* By shaping and arranging his poem this way, cummings unites form and content, structure and idea. In addition, he invites us to play the poetry game with him by remaking the poem as we put its pieces together. In doing so we step back and see in the design of the poem a leaf falling

d
o
w
n

the page. By positioning the letters as he does; cummings pictures a leaf fall:

le
af
fa
ll
s.

If "l(a" is a poem for the eye, the following poem, also by cummings, is arranged for voice. From the standpoint of traditional poetic form, it too exhibits peculiarities of sound and structure, line and stanza.

E. E. CUMMINGS

[1894–1962]

[Buffalo Bill's]

Buffalo Bill's
defunct
          who used to
          ride a watersmooth-silver
                                        stallion
and break onetwothreefourfive   pigeons justlikethat
                                                              Jesus
he was a handsome man
                              and what i want to know is
how do you like your blueeyed boy
Mister Death

Before we listen closely to the voice of the poem, let's glance at how it hits the eye. "Buffalo Bill's," "stallion," "defunct," "Jesus," and "Mister Death" are all set on separate lines *as* complete lines. "Buffalo Bill's," "Mister Death," and "Jesus" are the only words capitalized. "Buffalo Bill's" and "Mister Death" frame the poem; "Jesus" is set off on its own as far to the right as the line will go. Other words also receive a visual stress. At two points in line 6, cummings buncheswordstogetherlikethis. Both of these visual effects are translated from eye to voice to ear so that we read the poem acknowledging the stress in each case. Cummings has used typography as a formal way of laying out language on the page to direct our reading. To see and hear what he has accomplished in this respect, read aloud the following rearranged version, which deliberately flattens the special effects cummings highlights.

Buffalo Bill's defunct,
Who used to ride
a water-smooth silver stallion
and break one, two, three, four, five
pigeons just like that
Jesus he was a handsome man
And what I would like to know is

how do you like your
blueeyed boy, Mister Death?

Let us, finally, summarize our remarks about structure and form. In discerning a poem's structure, we gain a clue to its meaning. Moreover, we can increase our ability to apprehend a poem's organization by doing the following:

1. Looking and listening for changes of diction and imagery, tone and mood, rhythm and rhyme, time and place and circumstance.
2. Watching for repeated elements: words, images, patterns of syntax, rhythm and rhyme.
3. Remembering that structure is an aspect of meaning. It is not something independent of meaning, but works with other poetic elements to embody meaning, to formulate it. A poem's structure, its form, is part of what the poem says, part of how it means what it does.

Test out these ideas by analyzing the form of the following poems.

WILLIAM CARLOS WILLIAMS

[1883–1963]

The Dance

In Breughel's great picture, The Kermess,
the dancers go round, they go round and
around, the squeal and the blare and the
tweedle of bagpipes, a bugle and fiddles
tipping their bellies (round as the thick-
sided glasses whose wash they impound)
their hips and their bellies off balance
to turn them. Kicking and rolling about
the Fair Grounds, swinging their butts, those
shanks must be sound to bear up under such
rollicking measures, prance as they dance
in Breughel's great picture, The Kermess.

QUESTION

What is the relationship of the poem's structure to its subject? How, specifically, do the structure and language of Williams's poem accomplish what the title suggests?

THEODORE ROETHKE

[1908–1963]

The Waking

I wake to sleep, and take my waking slow.
I feel my fate in which I cannot fear.
I learn by going where I have to go.

We think by feeling. What is there to know?
I hear my being dance from ear to ear.
I wake to sleep, and take my waking slow.

Of those so close beside me, which are you?
God bless the Ground! I shall walk softly there,
And learn by going where I have to go.

Light takes the Tree; but who can tell us how?
The lowly worm climbs up a winding stair;
I wake to sleep, and take my waking slow.

Great Nature has another thing to do
To you and me; so take the lively air,
And, lovely, learn by going where to go.

This shaking keeps me steady. I should know.
What falls away is always. And is near.
I wake to sleep, and take my waking slow.
I learn by going where I have to go.

QUESTION

Describe the patterns of repetition that prevail in the poem. Consider repeated rhyme and repeated lines. What is their effect on the poem's tone and feeling?

A. R. AMMONS

[*b.* 1926]

Poetics

I look for the way
things will turn
out spiraling from a center,
the shape
things will take to come forth in

so that the birch tree white
touched black at branches
will stand out
wind-glittering
totally its apparent self:

I look for the forms
things want to come as

from what black wells of possibility,
how a thing will
unfold:

not the shape on paper—though
that, too—but the
uninterfering means on paper:

not so much looking for the shape
as being available
to any shape that may be
summoning itself
through me
from the self not mine but ours.

QUESTIONS

1. How does the structure of "Poetics" reflect its central idea?
2. What is the poem saying about form in nature and in poems?

REVISIONS

Unlike the goddess Athena, who sprang full-grown from the head of Zeus, poems rarely emerge fully formed from poets' heads. When they do, however, it is often because the poet worked on them both consciously and subconsciously before putting a word on paper. The product of labor as well as inspiration, good poems are the result of considerable care, of repeated efforts to find the right words and put them in the right order.

And yet for all the effort involved, the words and lines of a poem should seem natural, even inevitable. The great modern Irish poet William Butler Yeats put it this way:

> . . . A line will take us hours maybe;
> Yet if it does not seem a moment's thought,
> Our stitching and unstitching has been nought.

We suspect that these lines and the complete poem from which they are taken, "Adam's Curse," took more than a few moments to compose. So too did the following lines, in which Walt Whitman describes a spider spinning its web.

WALT WHITMAN

[1819–1892]

A Noiseless Patient Spider

A noiseless patient spider,
I mark'd where on a little promontory it stood isolated,
Mark'd how to explore the vacant vast surrounding,
It launch'd forth filament, filament, filament, out of itself,
Ever unreeling them, ever tirelessly speeding them.
And you O my soul where you stand,
Surrounded, detached, in measureless oceans of space,
Ceaselessly musing, venturing, throwing, seeking the spheres
  to connect them,
Till the bridge you will need be form'd, till the ductile anchor
  hold,
Till the gossamer thread you fling catch somewhere,
  O my soul.

QUESTIONS

1. Divide the poem into two parts. Relate the parts, and explain the metaphors that connect them.
2. Identify specific words and phrases in the second part that parallel details in the first. Explain their relationship.

"A Noiseless Patient Spider" appeared in Whitman's book *Leaves of Grass*. The version that follows is an earlier draft. Comment on differences in the language, structure, and idea between the two versions. Explain which version you prefer and why.

The Soul, Reaching, Throwing Out for Love

The Soul, reaching, throwing out for love,
As the spider, from some little promontory, throwing out filament after filament, tirelessly out of itself, that one at least may catch and form a link, a bridge, a connection
O I saw one passing along, saying hardly a word—yet full of love I detected him, by certain signs
O eyes wishfully turning! O silent eyes!
For then I thought of you o'er the world,
O latent oceans, fathomless oceans of love!
O waiting oceans of love! yearning and fervid! and of you sweet souls perhaps in the future, delicious and long:
But Death, unknown on the earth—ungiven, dark here, unspoken, never born:
You fathomless latent souls of love—you pent and unknown oceans of love!

Here is another pair of spider poems by Robert Frost. Consider the differences in the words, sentences, images, comparisons, sound, structure, and meaning between the two versions.

ROBERT FROST

[1874–1963]

Design

I found a dimpled spider, fat and white,
On a white heal-all, holding up a moth
Like a white piece of rigid satin cloth—

Assorted characters of death and blight
Mixed ready to begin the morning right,
Like the ingredients of a witches' broth—
A snow-drop spider, a flower like a froth,
And dead wings carried like a paper kite.

What had that flower to do with being white,
The wayside blue and innocent heal-all?
What brought the kindred spider to that height,
Then steered the white moth thither in the night?
What but design of darkness to appall?—
If design govern in a thing so small.

In White

A dented spider like a snow drop white
On a white Heal-all, holding up a moth
Like a white piece of lifeless satin cloth—
Saw ever curious eye so strange a sight?—
Portent in little, assorted death and blight
Like ingredients of a witches' broth?—
The beady spider, the flower like a froth,
And the moth carried like a paper kite.

What had that flower to do with being white,
The blue prunella every child's delight.
What brought the kindred spider to that height?
(Make we no thesis of the miller's plight.)
What but design of darkness and of night?
Design, design! Do I use the word aright?

The following poem by Emily Dickinson is the result of a series of revisions. The poet tried it a number of ways in an attempt to refine and articulate her poetic idea, but—according to her modern editor and biographer, Thomas H. Johnson—presumably without satisfaction. She sent an early version to her sister-in-law and neighbor, Sue Dickinson, for advice. Complicating matters was Thomas Wentworth Higginson, who brought out an edition of Dickinson's poems in 1890, four years after her death. Dickinson had corresponded with Higginson and once sent him an alternative version of the poem. When Higginson published the work, he concocted his own version of the poem by combining the two that Dickinson had written, forming from them a three-stanza poem that was considered the true version for more than fifty years. Examine the versions below carefully, identifying differences in language, structure, and tone. Decide which version you prefer, and why.

EMILY DICKINSON

[1830–1886]

Safe in their Alabaster Chambers

(1859 VERSION)

Safe in their Alabaster Chambers—
Untouched by Morning
And untouched by Noon—
Sleep the meek members of the Resurrection—
Rafter of satin,
And Roof of stone.

Light laughs the breeze
In her Castle above them—
Babbles the Bee in a stolid Ear,
Pipe the Sweet Birds in ignorant cadence—
Ah, what sagacity perished here!

Safe in their Alabaster Chambers

(1861 VERSION)

Safe in their Alabaster Chambers—
Untouched by Morning—
And untouched by Noon—
Lie the meek members of the Resurrection—
Rafter of Satin—and Roof of Stone!

Grand go the Years—in the Crescent—above them—
Worlds scoop their Arcs—
And Firmaments—row—
Diadems—drop—and Doges—surrender—
Soundless as dots—on a Disc of Snow—

Here are three versions of Marianne Moore's poem about poetry, each shorter than the one before. Notice what each version strips away from its predecessors. Comment on each, and explain which you prefer, and why.

MARIANNE MOORE

[1887–1972]

Poetry

(1921 VERSION)

I, too, dislike it: there are things that are important beyond all this
fiddle.
Reading it, however, with a perfect contempt for it, one
discovers in it after all, a place for the genuine.
Hands that can grasp, eyes
that can dilate, hair that can rise
if it must, these things are important not because a

high-sounding interpretation can be put upon them but because
they are
useful. When they become so derivative as to become
unintelligible,
the same thing may be said for all of us, that we
do not admire what
we cannot understand: the bat
holding on upside down or in quest of something to

eat, elephants pushing, a wide horse taking a roll, a tireless wolf
under
a tree, the immovable critic twitching his skin like a horse that
feels a flea, the base-
ball fan, the statistician—

nor is it valid
to discriminate against "business documents and

school-books"; all these phenomena are important. One must
make a distinction
however: when dragged into prominence by half poets, the result
is not poetry,
nor till the poets among us can be
"literalists of
the imagination"—above
insolence and triviality and can present

for inspection, "imaginary gardens with real toads in them," shall
we have
it. In the meantime, if you demand on the one hand,
the raw material of poetry in
all its rawness and
that which is on the other hand
genuine, you are interested in poetry.

Poetry

(1924 VERSION)

I, too, dislike it:
there are things that are important beyond all this fiddle.
The bat, upside down; the elephant pushing,
the tireless wolf under a tree,
the base-ball fan, the statistician—
"business documents and schoolbooks"—
these phenomena are pleasing,
but when they have been fashioned
into that which is unknowable,
we are not entertained.
It may be said of all of us
that we do not admire what we cannot understand;
enigmas are not poetry.

Poetry

(1967 VERSION)

I, too, dislike it.
    Reading it, however, with a perfect contempt for it, one
    discovers
in it after all, a place for the genuine.

Parodies

A rather different type of poetic revision is the effort of a poet to rewrite the poetry of a precursor, particularly in the form of a *parody,* a humorous and mocking imitation of a work. A parodic poem ridicules by distorting and exaggerating aspects of the poem or the body of poems it imitates. There may be distortions of the tone and purpose of the original poem or exaggerations of its stylistic mannerisms. The best parodists respect the works they parody, for to write parody well writers must understand and appreciate what they poke fun at. Good parodies catch the special manner and flavor of the originals. In them we hear echoes of the voice of the earlier poem. By extending the original beyond its limits, a parodist can point to the virtues of the poem he or she parodies. The following parody of William Carlos Williams's "This Is Just to Say" seems to do this. First, Williams's poem.

WILLIAM CARLOS WILLIAMS

[1883–1963]

This Is Just to Say

I have eaten
the plums
that were in
the icebox

and which
you were probably
saving
for breakfast

Forgive me
they were delicious
so sweet
and so cold

Now Kenneth Koch's parody:

KENNETH KOCH

[*b.* 1925]

Variations on a Theme by William Carlos Williams

1

I chopped down the house that you had been saving to live in
next summer.
I am sorry, but it was morning, and I had nothing to do
and its wooden beams were so inviting.

2

We laughed at the hollyhocks together
And then sprayed them with lye.
Forgive me. I simply do not know what I am doing.

3

I gave away the money that you had been saving to live on for
the next ten years.
The man who asked for it was shabby
and the firm March wind on the porch was so juicy and cold.

4

Last evening we went dancing and I broke your leg.
Forgive me. I was clumsy, and
I wanted you here in the wards, where I am the doctor!

QUESTIONS

1. Explain Koch's title.
2. Would his parody be as effective if he cut it down to one or two stanzas? If the four stanzas were rearranged? How long, in compari-

son, is Williams's poem, and why do you think Koch made his parody four times as long?

3. What do the four variations have in common?
4. Does the parody seem fair to Williams? Is it a coherent and engaging poem in its own right?

Unlike Koch's parody of a single poem by Williams, the next poem parodies not one poem but many. What specific features of the style of T. S. Eliot are parodied in "Chard Whitlow"? How, specifically, does the parodist ridicule Eliot's poetry? (Eliot's poems are reprinted on pp. 447–488.)

HENRY REED

[*b*. 1914]

Chard Whitlow

As we get older we do not get any younger.
Seasons return, and today I am fifty-five,
And this time last year I was fifty-four,
And this time next year I shall be sixty-two.
And I cannot say I should care (to speak for myself)
Fidgeting uneasily under a drafty stair,
Or counting sleepless nights in the crowded Tube.

There are certain precautions—though none of them very
reliable—
Against the blast from bombs, or the flying splinter,
But not against the blast from Heaven, *vento dei venti,*
The wind with a wind, unable to speak for wind;
And the frigid burnings of purgatory will not be touched
By any emollient.
I think you will find this put,
Far better than I could ever hope to express it,
In the words of Kharma: "It is, we believe,
Idle to hope that the simple stirrup-pump
Can extinguish hell."
Oh, listeners,
And you especially who have switched off the wireless,
And sit in Stoke or Basingstoke, listening appreciatively to the
silence

(Which is also the silence of hell), pray not for yourselves but for your souls.

And pray for me also under the drafty stair.
As we get older we do not get any younger.

And pray for Kharma under the holy mountain.

Poems and Paintings

Another type of revision is the re-envisioning that some poets engage in when they are inspired or influenced by a work in another medium, such as painting, and "translate" it into poetry. Inspired by the art of the Flemish Renaissance painter Pieter Breughel the Elder (1525–1569), William Carlos Williams wrote a series of poems entitled *Pictures from Breughel.* In transforming Breughel's paintings from a visual language into a verbal one, Williams also interpreted them. Consider your own interpretation both of Williams's poems and Breughel's paintings *Landscape with the Fall of Icarus* and *Hunters in the Snow.* Also pay attention to the additional considerations raised in the questions that follow the paired poems and paintings.

Landscape with the Fall of Icarus (c. 1558), Pieter Breughel the Elder.

(Musées Royaux Des Beaux-Arts, Brussels)

WILLIAM CARLOS WILLIAMS

[1883–1963]

Landscape with the Fall of Icarus

According to Breughel
when Icarus fell
it was spring

a farmer was ploughing
his field
the whole pageantry

of the year was
awake tingling
near

the edge of the sea
concerned
with itself

sweating in the sun
that melted
the wings' wax

unsignificantly
off the coast
there was

a splash quite unnoticed
this was
Icarus drowning

QUESTIONS

1. Both painting and poem are based on the Greek story of Daedalus, a skilled craftsman who built a labyrinth for the king of Crete to keep the Minotaur, a creature half-bull and half-man. When Daedalus and his son were later imprisoned in the labyrinth, Daedalus made wings of wax and feathers, which they used to fly away. Ignoring his

father's warning, Icarus flew too close to the sun, his wax wings melted, and he fell into the sea. How much of this story is relevant to poem and painting? What details has Breughel invented? What does Williams mean when he begins his poem, "According to Breughel"?

2. What is Williams's purpose in the poem? To memorialize the painter? To imitate his work? Something else?
3. Consider the technical aspects of the poem—its stanzas and short lines, for example. Would it matter if the first stanza were omitted and the "was" of stanzas 2, 5, and 6 were changed to "is"?
4. What is the effect of mentioning Icarus at the end of the poem rather than earlier. What is suggested by the poem's title?

Here is an additional poem inspired by Breughel's painting. Comment on its relation to the painting and to Williams's poem.

W. H. AUDEN

[1907–1973]

Musée des Beaux Arts

About suffering they were never wrong,
The Old Masters: how well they understood
Its human position; how it takes place
While someone else is eating or opening a window or just
 walking dully along;
How, when the aged are reverently, passionately waiting
For the miraculous birth, there always must be
Children who did not specially want it to happen, skating
On a pond at the edge of the wood:
They never forgot
That even the dreadful martyrdom must run its course
Anyhow in a corner, some untidy spot
Where the dogs go on with their doggy life and the torturer's
 horse
Scratches its innocent behind on a tree.

In Breughel's *Icarus,* for instance: how everything turns away
Quite leisurely from the disaster; the ploughman may
Have heard the splash, the forsaken cry.
But for him it was not an important failure; the sun shone

As it had to on the white legs disappearing into the green
Water; and the expensive delicate ship that must have seen
Something amazing, a boy falling out of the sky,
Had somewhere to get to and sailed calmly on.

QUESTIONS

1. "Musée des Beaux Arts" can be divided into two parts, as the text indicates. Explain the relationship between them. What would be the effect of reversing them?
2. What is the meaning of Breughel's painting, according to Auden? What is the relationship of poem to painting?
3. Where is Icarus mentioned? Why? How does Auden end the poem, and what does this ending suggest?
4. Compare the form and language of Auden's poem with Williams's "Landscape with the Fall of Icarus."

Here is the second of Breughel's paintings, *Hunters in the Snow*. Describe what you see after looking closely at each section of the picture. Offer an interpretation of what the painting seems to suggest. Then consider Williams's poem of the same title in relation to the painting.

Hunters in the Snow (1565), Pieter Breughel the Elder.

(Kunsthistorisches Museum, Vienna/Marburg/Art Resource)

WILLIAM CARLOS WILLIAMS

[1883–1963]

The Hunters in the Snow

The over-all picture is winter
icy mountains
in the background the return

from the hunt it is toward evening
from the left
sturdy hunters lead in

their pack the inn-sign
hanging from a
broken hinge is a stag a crucifix

between his antlers the cold
inn yard is
deserted but for a huge bonfire

that flares wind-driven tended by
women who cluster
about it to the right beyond

the hill is a pattern of skaters
Brueghel the painter
concerned with it all has chosen

a winter-struck bush for his
foreground to
complete the picture.

QUESTIONS

1. What details of the painting has Williams included in his poem? Which has he omitted?
2. What is the purpose of Williams's poem? Is there any indication that he is interpreting the painting?

3. What features does this poem share with Williams's poem on Breughel's *Landscape with the Fall of Icarus?*

Here, finally, is another poem inspired by *Hunters in the Snow.* Account for its use of the painting and its relation to it.

JOHN BERRYMAN

[1914–1972]

Winter Landscape

The three men coming down the winter hill
In brown, with tall poles and a pack of hounds
At heel, through the arrangement of the trees,
Past the five figures at the burning straw,
Returning cold and silent to their town,

Returning to the drifted snow, the rink
Lively with children, to the older men,
The long companions they can never reach,
The blue light, men with ladders, by the church
The sledge and shadow in the twilit street,

Are not aware that in the sandy time
To come, the evil waste of history
Outstretched, they will be seen upon the brow
Of that same hill: when all their company
Will have been irrecoverably lost,

These men, this particular three in brown
Witnessed by birds will keep the scene and say
By their configuration with the trees,
The small bridge, the red houses and the fire,
What place, what time, what morning occasion

Sent them into the wood, a pack of hounds
At heel and the tall poles upon their shoulders,
Thence to return as now we see them and
Ankle-deep in snow down the winter hill
Descend, while three birds watch and the fourth flies.

QUESTIONS

1. Which poem better helps you to see the details of the painting? Which helps you to better understand its symbolic implications?
2. Where does each poem depart from the details of the painting? In what ways and for what purposes?
3. Compare the way each poem begins. What is emphasized? How would you describe the tone of each opening stanza? Compare the endings. Which seems least like its beginning? What is implied in each ending?
4. Compare the way each poet organizes his details. Consider especially the use of the birds.
5. Neither poem rhymes, and neither uses a consistent metrical pattern, yet both poems exhibit formal organization. What devices of form, sound, and rhythm exist in each poem? What do they contribute to the meaning and feeling of the work?

PART TWO

Major Voices and Visions

Walt Whitman

[1819–1892]

Walt Whitman is important to American poetry for two reasons: he was a great poet, and he was a seminal influence. As a poet, Whitman revolutionized American verse, inaugurating a poetic tradition remarkable for its energy, diversity, and resilience. Whitman broke new ground in subject matter, form, and style. After Whitman, American poets could take as subjects of their poems any aspect of life. Whitman excluded nothing from his poems. One of his important achievements was to extend the range of poetic subjects to encompass the common, the ordinary, the seemingly unimportant and inconsequential. One result of this change was a renewed interest in the familiar, in things often overlooked or taken for granted such as insects, individual blades of grass, even our own hearing and breathing.

Whitman took as his self-appointed task "to write up America." He did this by making the American land and people his essential subject, celebrating both in a style and set of poetic forms notable for their departure from the prevailing tendencies in British and American poetry of the time. For example, instead of using iambic pentameter, the reigning poetic meter, Whitman wrote verse free of metrical regularity. Instead of closed couplets and tightly symmetrical stanzas, he developed more open, fluid forms. Rather than employing an archaic poetic diction, both formalized and conventional, he used a more familiar and informal language. He also experimented by mixing exalted language with common speech. The result was, as he remarked, a "new style . . . necessitated by new theories, new themes," theories and themes far removed from European models. Whitman's stylistic innovation in *Leaves of Grass,* which he once described as "a language experiment," formed part of his ambition "to give something to our literature which will be our own . . . strengthening and intensifying the national."

Social values and political ideals animate nearly all of Whitman's work. Whitman envisioned a democratic brotherhood of people that cuts across barriers of class, race, and creed. His poetry emphasizes the fundamental equality of human beings, an equality rooted in the intrinsic worth of all living things. Coupled with his concerns for social solidarity and the value of life is an emphasis on self-reliance and individualism, ideas heralded by Emerson, who made reliance on the self a philosophic ideal.

Whitman saw America itself as a great poem. He considered his poetry as analogous to that of the epic bard who mythologizes the distinctive social and cultural characteristics of a country and its people. Epic, too, are the grandeur and sweep of Whitman's subject and tone. Whitman chanted the praises of an expanding country, singing of progress, democracy, freedom, individualism, and brotherhood. His characteristic tone was one of celebration. His characteristic manner of celebration was to name. By naming things American, Whitman called them to the attention of his readers, acknowledging them as worthy of notice and appreciation.

Whitman was something of a prophet—a seer whose vision transcended that of ordinary people, but whose sympathy and imagination united him in spirit with everyone. Allied with Whitman's visionary capacity and his sympathetic imagination is his tendency to embrace and absorb all he comes in contact with. He is the most inclusive of poets, accepting into his embrace all aspects of experience, good and bad, common and unusual. His poetry, moreover, attempts to transcend time and place. It strives to break down boundaries, to abolish differences, eliminate separateness. In "Crossing Brooklyn Ferry," for example, Whitman speaks directly to us across the century that separates him from us. He collapses temporal distinctions and breaks down spatial barriers, making all places a central everywhere and all times a continuous eternal present. Furthermore, his poetry relates people to the natural world and connects them with one another. Its prevailing impulse is to unite, making Whitman one of the most receptive, affirmative, and democratic of poets.

We can illustrate some of these attitudes and values so fundamental to Whitman's poetic vision by quoting a short poem from the "Inscriptions" section of *Leaves of Grass.*

One's Self I Sing

One's Self I sing, a simple separate person,
Yet utter the word Democratic, the word En-Masse.

Of physiology from top to toe I sing,
Not physiognomy alone nor brain alone is worthy for the Muse,
I say the form complete is worthier far,
The Female equally with the Male I sing.

Of Life immense in passion, pulse, and power,
Cheerful, for freest action form'd under the laws divine,
The Modern Man I sing.

These optimistic, affirmative lines celebrate life, especially its vitality, energy, and physicality. Whitman's lines embrace male and female, body and soul, separateness and togetherness. They announce the arrival of a new man, the nineteenth-century American whom Whitman celebrates throughout *Leaves of Grass,* which he saw through no less than nine editions beginning in 1855 and concluding in the famous deathbed edition of 1892. This book of poems was, as Whitman himself said, an attempt "to put a *Person,* a human being (myself in the latter half of the Nineteenth Century, in America) freely, fully, and truly on record."

Whitman has had both a wide influence and a strong impact. Many modern American poets have benefited from his revolutionary poetics. William Carlos Williams, for example, was influenced by Whitman's attention to the commonplace and by his experiments with the poetic line. Wallace Stevens displays the meditative and philosophical cast found in poems such as Whitman's "Crossing Brooklyn Ferry." e. e. cummings echoes Whitman's affirmation and celebration of life as well as his frank avowal of the erotic. These and many other poets have made and continue to make Whitman's legacy a living poetic reality.

The facts of Whitman's life can only hint at the range of his experience and the impulses that animate his poetry. He was born in 1819 on Long Island—in Huntington, New York—and was educated in the Brooklyn public schools. In his youth he worked successively as an office boy and clerk for a doctor, lawyer, and printer. He taught school from 1836 to 1841. His journalistic career involved, at various stages, writing, typesetting, and editing, and included the editorship of the Brooklyn *Daily Eagle,* the New Orleans *Crescent,* the Brooklyn *Freeman,* and the Brooklyn *Daily Times.* Whitman also worked as a carpenter, building a house for himself and his family. During the Civil War he served as a nurse and worked briefly as a clerk in the Bureau of Indian Affairs. He also worked in the attorney general's office in Washington, until he suffered a paralytic stroke. He spent the last two decades of his life in Camden, New Jersey, where he died quietly in 1892, shortly after he prepared the deathbed edition of his life's work.

In reading Whitman's poems it helps to know not only the salient facts of his life but also something about both his reading and his poetic intentions. One of the chief stumbling blocks for readers unfamiliar with Whitman is the largeness of his claims. He seems to boast, to brag about his status, his vision, his amplitude. He seems to claim for himself exemption from the limitations of time and space. Once we realize, however, that the "I" of poems such as *Song of Myself* is not the autobiographical I, that it is not the historical Walt Whitman, we minimize this potential difficulty. The "I" we hear throughout *Leaves of Grass* is the American self—the larger-than-life embodiment of the American spirit that Whitman employs to establish and sustain his vision of America. The "I" who speaks in Whitman's poems is confident, assertive, and authoritative. It possesses knowledge acquired partly from living, partly through observing, but largely through intuition. Whitman's "I" sees and knows all—or nearly all. His "I" shares in the participatory divinity he believed was common to all people. Whitman sees human beings as immortal and eternal, with the potential of transcending the finite boundaries of their physical beings.

As an American poet living in an age of progress and expansionism, Whitman valued material reality as much as its spiritual counterpart. Whitman's spiritualizing of man and nature did not require a corresponding rejection of physical experience. His attitude toward sex, for example, runs counter to the celibate ascetic ideal of Oriental mysticism. But Whitman, like Emerson before him, sees the value of looking beyond appearances, beyond the physical and material differences that separate human beings from one another to the ties of spiritual essence that bind them. Whitman's unifying view extends to the natural world as well as the social one. Nature figures prominently in Whitman's poetry not only as inspiration and symbol but as an important dimension of the way spirit is manifested in the external world.

An additional aspect of Whitman's poetry is his tendency to contradict himself. On one hand, he celebrates the single and simple separate person, praising the virtues of originality and self-reliance. At the same time, however, he urges the claims of community, fraternity, and solidarity. These emphases for Whitman, however, are less contradictory than complementary. "Do I contradict myself?" he asks in *Song of Myself.* "Very well then," he answers, "I contradict myself, (I am large. I contain multitudes.)" Whitman's solution to contradiction was an all-encompassing embrace and a spiritual perspective on the unity of life. He accepted both his own diversity and that of the world.

One additional item of interest is the way Whitman's poetry mirrors the cultural situation of his time. In an important book on Whitman's life and art, *Walt Whitman: The Making of the Poet,* Paul Zweig describes the influence of Whitman's milieu on his work. Zweig recounts Whitman's transformation from an undistinguished journalist into a profoundly original poet, whose journalistic experience and ambitions became part of his poems. Zweig also describes Whitman's love for the theater, suggesting that the relationship between actor and audience provided a model for the relationship Whitman tried to establish with his readers. Whitman's insistent presence in his poems and his effort to assume many roles and speak in other voices, along with his repeated use of direct address, exemplify this attempt.

Besides theater, music also influenced Whitman's poetry. He passionately loved opera, which he describes as "a new world—a liquid world—[that] rushes like a torrent through you." He spoke of dating a new era in his development from his introduction to opera. One aspect of that development affected the structure of his poems. Longer poems like *Song of Myself* and "When Lilacs Last in the Dooryard Bloom'd," exhibit a symphonic rather than a logical structure. They use repetition and refrain, and they blend speech and song in the manner of operatic aria and recitative.

One additional social reality had a decisive impact on Whitman's life and art: the Civil War. It was not as a soldier that Whitman served but as a nurse. On hearing that his brother George had been wounded in battle, Whitman hurried to the military hospital in Washington. Although his brother had not been seriously injured, Whitman, deeply moved by the suffering of the soldiers, remained for twelve years. He nursed the wounded and wrote letters and ran errands for them, giving of his immense reserves of sympathy and compassion. Out of his experience came the series of poems entitled *Drum-Taps,* which contains some of his most affecting poetry.

Finally, we should mention how the cultural conventions and moral attitudes of Whitman's time prevented his poetry from receiving the recognition it deserved. Many contemporary readers were shocked by the frankly erotic quality of some of his poems. Condemned as obscene, vulgar, and depraved, Whitman's poems were considered by many as violations of the morals of the day. Such readers were unprepared for his frank celebration of physical love. They were also unprepared for his inclusion of physical details such as sweating and belching. Not until the twentieth century did the cultural and moral climate change sufficiently for readers to see Whitman's celebration of the body as liberating.

Whitman was a poet who drew sustenance from his culture while rebelling against its stultifying conventions. His poems serve both as journalistic reports of his time and as an imaginative transformation of its raw data into art. His greatest poems transcend their time and place to become universal statements about intensely felt experiences. He remains the greatest and most representative of American poets.

*Song of Myself**

[1]

I celebrate myself,
And what I assume you shall assume,
For every atom belonging to me as good belongs to you.

*Based on the 1855 text. Section numbers have been added to parallel Whitman's later deathbed edition in fifty-two numbered sections.

I loafe and invite my soul,
I lean and loafe at my ease . . . . observing a spear of summer grass.

[2]

Houses and rooms are full of perfumes . . . . the shelves are crowded with perfumes,
I breathe the fragrance myself, and know it and like it,
The distillation would intoxicate me also, but I shall not let it.

The atmosphere is not a perfume . . . . it has no taste of the distillation . . . . it is odorless,
It is for my mouth forever . . . . I am in love with it,
I will go to the bank by the wood and become undisguised and naked,
I am mad for it to be in contact with me.

The smoke of my own breath,
Echoes, ripples, and buzzed whispers . . . . loveroot, silkthread, crotch and vine,
My respiration and inspiration . . . . the beating of my heart . . . . the passing of blood and air through my lungs,
The sniff of green leaves and dry leaves, and of the shore and darkcolored sea-rocks, and of hay in the barn,
The sound of the belched words of my voice . . . . words loosed to the eddies of the wind,
A few light kisses . . . . a few embraces . . . . a reaching around of arms,
The play of shine and shade on the trees as the supple boughs wag,
The delight alone or in the rush of the streets, or along the fields and hillsides,
The feeling of health . . . . the full-moon trill . . . . the song of me rising from bed and meeting the sun.
Have you reckoned a thousand acres much? Have you reckoned the earth much?
Have you practiced so long to learn to read?
Have you felt so proud to get at the meaning of poems?

Stop this day and night with me and you shall possess the origin of all poems,

You shall possess the good of the earth and sun . . . . there are millions of suns left,
You shall no longer take things at second or third hand . . . . nor look through the eyes of the dead . . . . nor feed on the spectres in books,
You shall not look through my eyes either, nor take things from me,
You shall listen to all sides and filter them from yourself.

[3]

I have heard what the talkers were talking . . . . the talk of the beginning and the end,
But I do not talk of the beginning or the end.

There was never any more inception than there is now,
Nor any more youth or age than there is now;
And will never be any more perfection than there is now,
Nor any more heaven or hell than there is now.

Urge and urge and urge,
Always the procreant urge of the world.

Out of the dimness opposite equals advance . . . . Always substance and increase,
Always a knit of identity . . . . always distinction . . . . always a breed of life.

To elaborate is no avail . . . . Learned and unlearned feel that it is so.

Sure as the most certain sure . . . . plumb in the uprights, well entretied, braced in the beams,
Stout as a horse, affectionate, haughty, electrical,
I and this mystery here we stand.

Clear and sweet is my soul . . . . and clear and sweet is all that is not my soul.

Lack one lacks both . . . . and the unseen is proved by the seen,
Till that becomes unseen and receives proof in its turn.

Showing the best and dividing it from the worst, age vexes age,
Knowing the perfect fitness and equanimity of things, while they discuss I am silent, and go bathe and admire myself.

Welcome is every organ and attribute of me, and of any man hearty and clean,
Not an inch nor a particle of an inch is vile, and none shall be less familiar than the rest.

I am satisfied . . . . I see, dance, laugh, sing;
As God comes a loving bedfellow and sleeps at my side all night and close on the peep of the day,
And leaves for me baskets covered with white towels bulging the house with their plenty,
Shall I postpone my acceptation and realization and scream at my eyes,
That they turn from gazing after and down the road,
And forthwith cipher and show me to a cent,
Exactly the contents of one, and exactly the contents of two, and which is ahead?

[4]

Trippers and askers surround me,
People I meet . . . . the effect upon me of my early life . . . . of the ward and city I live in . . . . of the nation,
The latest news . . . . discoveries, inventions, societies . . . . authors old and new,
My dinner, dress, associates, looks, business, compliments, dues,
The real or fancied indifference of some man or woman I love,
The sickness of one of my folks—or of myself . . . . or ill-doing . . . . or loss or lack of money . . . . or depressions or exaltations,
They come to me days and nights and go from me again,
But they are not the Me myself.

Apart from the pulling and hauling stands what I am,
Stands amused, complacent, compassionating, idle, unitary,
Looks down, is erect, bends an arm on an impalpable certain rest,

Looks with its sidecurved head curious what will come next,
Both in and out of the game, and watching and wondering at it.

Backward I see in my own days where I sweated through fog with linguists and contenders,
I have no mockings or arguments . . . . I witness and wait.

[5]

I believe in you my soul . . . . the other I am must not abase itself to you,
And you must not be abased to the other.

Loafe with me on the grass . . . . loose the stop from your throat,
Not words, not music or rhyme I want . . . . not custom or lecture, not even the best,
Only the lull I like, the hum of your valued voice.

I mind how we lay in June, such a transparent summer morning;
You settled your head athwart my hips and gently turned over upon me.
And parted the shirt from my bosom-bone, and plunged your tongue to my barestript heart,
And reached till you felt my beard, and reached till you held my feet.

Swiftly arose and spread around me the peace and joy and knowledge that pass all the art and argument of the earth;
And I know that the hand of God is the elderhand of my own,
And I know that the spirit of God is the eldest brother of my own,
And that all the men ever born are also my brothers . . . . and the women my sisters and lovers,
And that a kelson of the creation is love;
And limitless are leaves stiff or drooping in the fields,
And brown ants in the little wells beneath them,
And mossy scabs of the wormfence, and heaped stones, and elder and mullen and pokeweed.

[6]

A child said, What is the grass? fetching it to me with full hands;
How could I answer the child? . . . . I do not know what it is any more than he.

I guess it must be the flag of my disposition, out of hopeful green stuff woven.

Or I guess it is the handkerchief of the Lord,
A scented gift and remembrancer designedly dropped,
Bearing the owner's name someway in the corners, that we may see and remark, and say Whose?

Or I guess the grass is itself a child . . . . the produced babe of the vegetation.
Or I guess it is a uniform hieroglyphic,
And it means, Sprouting alike in broad zones and narrow zones,
Growing among black folks as among white,
Kanuck, Tuckahoe, Congressman, Cuff, I give them the same, I receive them the same.
And now it seems to me the beautiful uncut hair of graves.

Tenderly will I use you curling grass,
It may be you transpire from the breasts of young men,
It may be if I had known them I would have loved them;
It may be you are from old people and from women, and from offspring taken soon out of their mothers' laps,
And here you are the mothers' laps.

This grass is very dark to be from the white heads of old mothers,
Darker than the colorless beards of old men,
Dark to come from under the faint red roofs of mouths.

O I perceive after all so many uttering tongues!
And I perceive they do not come from the roofs of mouths for nothing.

I wish I could translate the hints about the dead young men and women,

And the hints about old men and mothers, and the offspring
taken soon out of their laps.

What do you think has become of the young and old men?
And what do you think has become of the women and
children?

They are alive and well somewhere;
The smallest sprout shows there is really no death,
And if ever there was it led forward life, and does not wait at
the end to arrest it,
And ceased the moment life appeared.

All goes onward and outward . . . . and nothing collapses,
And to die is different from what any one supposed, and
luckier.

[7]

Has any one supposed it lucky to be born?
I hasten to inform him or her it is just as lucky to die, and I
know it.

I pass death with the dying, and birth with the new-washed
babe . . . . and am not contained between my hat and
boots,
And peruse manifold objects, no two alike, and every one
good,
The earth good, and the stars good, and their adjuncts all good.
I am not an earth nor an adjunct of an earth,
I am the mate and companion of people, all just as immortal
and fathomless as myself;
They do not know how immortal, but I know.

Every kind for itself and its own . . . . for me mine male and
female.
For me all that have been boys and that love women,
For me the man that is proud and feels how it stings to be
slighted,
For me the sweetheart and the old maid . . . . for me mothers
and the mothers of mothers,

For me lips that have smiled, eyes that have shed tears,
For me children and the begetters of children.

Who need be afraid of the merge?
Undrape . . . . you are not guilty to me, nor stale nor discarded,
I see through the broadcloth and gingham whether or no,
And am around, tenacious, acquisitive, tireless . . . . and can never be shaken away.

[8]

The little one sleeps in its cradle,
I lift the gauze and look a long time, and silently brush away flies with my hand.

The youngster and the redfaced girl turn aside up the bushy hill,
I peeringly view them from the top.

The suicide sprawls on the bloody floor of the bedroom,
It is so . . . . I witnessed the corpse . . . . there the pistol had fallen.

The blab of the pave . . . . the tires of carts and sluff of bootsoles and talk of the promenaders,
The heavy omnibus, the driver with his interrogating thumb, the clank of the shod horses on the granite floor,
The carnival of sleighs, the clinking and shouted jokes and pelts of snowballs;
The hurrahs for popular favorites . . . . the fury of roused mobs,
The flap of the curtained litter—the sick man inside, borne to the hospital,
The meeting of enemies, the sudden oath, the blows and fall,
The excited crowd—the policeman with his star quickly working his passage to the centre of the crowd;
The impassive stones that receive and return so many echoes,
The souls moving along . . . . are they visible while the least atom of the stones is visible?
What groans of overfed or half-starved who fall on the flags sunstruck or in fits,

What exclamations of women taken suddenly, who hurry
home and give birth to babes,
What living and buried speech is always vibrating here . . . .
what howls restrained by decorum,
Arrests of criminals, slights, adulterous offers made,
acceptances, rejections with convex lips,
I mind them or the resonance of them . . . . I come again and
again.

[9]

The big doors of the country-barn stand open and ready,
The dried grass of the harvest-time loads the slow-drawn
wagon,
The clear light plays on the brown gray and green intertinged,
The armfuls are packed to the sagging mow:
I am there . . . . I help . . . . I came stretched atop of the load,
I felt its soft jolts . . . . one leg reclined on the other,
I jump from the crossbeams, and seize the clover and timothy,
And roll head over heels, and tangle my hair full of wisps.

[10]

Alone far in the wilds and mountains I hunt,
Wandering amazed at my own lightness and glee,
In the late afternoon choosing a safe spot to pass the night,
Kindling a fire and broiling the freshkilled game,
Soundly falling asleep on the gathered leaves, my dog and gun
by my side.
The Yankee clipper is under her three skysails . . . . she cuts
the sparkle and scud,
My eyes settle the land . . . . I bend at her prow or shout
joyously from the deck.

The boatmen and clamdiggers arose early and stopped for me,
I tucked my trowser-ends in my boots and went and had a
good time,
You should have been with us that day round the
chowder-kettle.

I saw the marriage of the trapper in the open air in the
far-west . . . . the bride was a red girl,

Her father and his friends sat near by crosslegged and dumbly smoking . . . . they had moccasins to their feet and large thick blankets hanging from their shoulders;
On a bank lounged the trapper . . . . he was dressed mostly in skins . . . . his luxuriant beard and curls protected his neck,
One hand rested on his rifle . . . . the other hand held firmly the wrist of the red girl,
She had long eyelashes . . . . her head was bare . . . . her coarse straight locks descended upon her voluptuous limbs and reached to her feet.

The runaway slave came to my house and stopped outside,
I heard his motions crackling the twigs of the woodpile,
Through the swung half-door of the kitchen I saw him limpsey and weak,
And went where he sat on a log, and led him in and assured him,
And brought water and filled a tub for his sweated body and bruised feet,
And gave him a room that entered from my own, and gave him some coarse clean clothes,
And remember perfectly well his revolving eyes and his awkwardness,
And remember putting plasters on the galls of his neck and ankles;
He staid with me a week before he was recuperated and passed north,
I had him sit next me at table . . . . my firelock leaned in the corner.

[11]

Twenty-eight young men bathe by the shore,
Twenty-eight young men, and all so friendly,
Twenty-eight years of womanly life, and all so lonesome.

She owns the fine house by the rise of the bank.
She hides handsome and richly drest aft the blinds of the window.

Which of the young men does she like the best?
Ah the homeliest of them is beautiful to her.

Where are you off to, lady? for I see you,
You splash in the water there, yet stay stock still in your room.

Dancing and laughing along the beach came the twenty-ninth bather,
The rest did not see her, but she saw them and loved them.

The beards of the young men glistened with wet, it ran from their long hair,
Little streams passed all over their bodies.

An unseen hand also passed over their bodies,
It descended tremblingly from their temples and ribs.

The young men float on their backs, their white bellies swell to the sun . . . . they do not ask who seizes fast to them,
They do not know who puffs and declines with pendant and bending arch,
They do not think whom they souse with spray.

[12]

The butcher-boy puts off his killing clothes, or sharpens his knife at the stall in the market,
I loiter enjoying his repartee and his shuffle and breakdown.

Blacksmiths with grimed and hairy chests environ the anvil,
Each has his main-sledge . . . . they are all out . . . . there is a great heat in the fire.

From the cinder-strewed threshold I follow their movements,
The lithe sheer of their waists plays even with their massive arms,
Overhand the hammers roll—overhand so slow—overhand so sure,
They do not hasten, each man hits in his place.

[13]

The negro holds firmly the reins of his four horses . . . . the block swags underneath on its tied-over chain,
The negro that drives the huge dray of the stoneyard . . . .

steady and tall he stands poised on one leg on the stringpiece,
His blue shirt exposes his ample neck and breast and loosens over his hipband,
His glance is calm and commanding . . . . he tosses the slouch of his hat away from his forehead,
The sun falls on his crispy hair and moustache . . . . falls on the black of his polish'd and perfect limbs.

I behold the picturesque giant and love him . . . . and I do not stop there,
I go with the team also.

In me the caresser of life wherever moving . . . . backward as well as forward slueing,
To niches aside and junior bending.

Oxen that rattle the yoke or halt in the shade, what is that you express in your eyes?
It seems to me more than all the print I have read in my life.

My tread scares the wood-drake and wood-duck on my distant and daylong ramble,
They rise together, they slowly circle around.
. . . . I believe in those winged purposes,
And acknowledge the red yellow and white playing within me,
And consider the green and violet and the tufted crown intentional;
And do not call the tortoise unworthy because she is not something else,
And the mockingbird in the swamp never studied the gamut, yet trills pretty well to me,
And the look of the bay mare shames silliness out of me.

[14]

The wild gander leads his flock through the cool night,
Ya-honk! he says, and sounds it down to me like an invitation;
The pert may suppose it meaningless, but I listen closer,
I find its purpose and place up there toward the November sky.

The sharphoofed moose of the north, the cat on the housesill, the chickadee, the prairie-dog,
The litter of the grunting sow as they tug at her teats,
The brood of the turkeyhen, and she with her halfspread wings,
I see in them and myself the same old law.

The press of my foot to the earth springs a hundred affections,
They scorn the best I can do to relate them.

I am enamoured of growing outdoors,
Of men that live among cattle or taste of the ocean or woods,
Of the builders and steerers of ships, of the wielders of axes and mauls, of the drivers of horses,
I can eat and sleep with them week in and week out.

What is commonest and cheapest and nearest and easiest is Me,
Me going in for my chances, spending for vast returns,
Adorning myself to bestow myself on the first that will take me,
Not asking the sky to come down to my goodwill,
Scattering it freely forever.

[15]

The pure contralto sings in the organloft,
The carpenter dresses his plank . . . . the tongue of his foreplane whistles its wild ascending lisp,
The married and unmarried children ride home to their thanksgiving dinner,
The pilot seizes the king-pin, he heaves down with a strong arm,
The mate stands braced in the whaleboat, lance and harpoon are ready,
The duck-shooter walks by silent and cautious stretches,
The deacons are ordained with crossed hands at the altar,
The spinning-girl retreats and advances to the hum of the big wheel,
The farmer stops by the bars of a Sunday and looks at the oats and rye,
The lunatic is carried at last to the asylum a confirmed case,

He will never sleep any more as he did in the cot in his mother's bedroom;
The jour printer with gray head and gaunt jaws works at his case,
He turns his quid of tobacco, his eyes get blurred with the manuscript;
The malformed limbs are tied to the anatomist's table,
What is removed drops horribly in a pail;
The quadroon girl is sold at the stand . . . . the drunkard nods by the barroom stove,
The machinist rolls up his sleeves . . . . the policeman travels his beat . . . . the gatekeeper marks who pass,
The young fellow drives the express-wagon . . . . I love him though I do not know him;
The half-breed straps on his light boots to compete in the race,
The western turkey-shooting draws old and young . . . . some lean on their rifles, some sit on logs,
Out from the crowd steps the marksman and takes his position and levels his piece;
The groups of newly-come immigrants cover the wharf or levee,
The woollypates hoe in the sugarfield, the overseer views them from his saddle;
The bugle calls in the ballroom, the gentlemen run for their partners, the dancers bow to each other;
The youth lies awake in the cedar-roofed garret and harks to the musical rain,
The Wolverine sets traps on the creek that helps fill the Huron,
The reformer ascends the platform, he spouts with his mouth and nose,
The company returns from its excursion, the darkey brings up the rear and bears the well-riddled target,
The squaw wrapt in her yellow-hemmed cloth is offering moccasins and beadbags for sale,
The connoisseur peers along the exhibition-gallery with halfshut eyes bent sideways,
The deckhands make fast the steamboat, the plank is thrown for the shoregoing passengers,
The young sister holds out the skein, the elder sister winds it off in a ball and stops now and then for the knots,

The one-year wife is recovering and happy, a week ago she bore her first child,
The cleanhaired Yankee girl works with her sewing-machine or in the factory or mill,
The nine months' gone is in the parturition chamber, her faintness and pains are advancing;
The pavingman leans on his twohanded rammer—the reporter's lead flies swiftly over the notebook—the signpainter is lettering with red and gold,
The canal-boy trots on the towpath—the bookkeeper counts at his desk—the shoemaker waxes his thread,
The conductor beats time for the band and all the performers follow him,
The child is baptised—the convert is making the first professions,
The regatta is spread on the bay . . . . how the white sails sparkle!
The drover watches his drove, he sings out to them that would stray,
The pedlar sweats with his pack on his back—the purchaser higgles about the odd cent,
The camera and plate are prepared, the lady must sit for her daguerreotype,
The bride unrumples her white dress, the minutehand of the clock moves slowly,
The opium eater reclines with rigid head and just-opened lips,
The prostitute draggles her shawl, her bonnet bobs on her tipsy and pimpled neck,
The crowd laugh at her blackguard oaths, the men jeer and wink to each other,
(Miserable! I do not laugh at your oaths nor jeer you,)
The President holds a cabinet council, he is surrounded by the great secretaries,
On the piazza walk five friendly matrons with twined arms;
The crew of the fish-smack pack repeated layers of halibut in the hold,
The Missourian crosses the plains toting his wares and his cattle,
The fare-collector goes through the train—he gives notice by the jingling of loose change,
The floormen are laying the floor—the tinners are tinning the roof—the masons are calling for mortar,

In single file each shouldering his hod pass onward the laborers;
Seasons pursuing each other the indescribable crowd is gathered . . . . it is the Fourth of July . . . . what salutes of cannon and small arms!
Seasons pursuing each other the plougher ploughs and the mower mows and the winter grain falls in the ground;
Off on the lakes the pikefisher watches and waits by the hole in the frozen surface,
The stumps stand thick round the clearing, the squatter strikes deep with his axe,
The flatboatmen make fast toward dusk near the cottonwood or pekantrees,
The coon-seekers go now through the regions of the Red river, or through those drained by the Tennessee, or through those of the Arkansas,
The torches shine in the dark that hangs on the Chattahoochee or Altamahaw;
Patriarchs sit at supper with sons and grandsons and great grandsons around them,
In walls of adobie, in canvas tents, rest hunters and trappers after their day's sport.
The city sleeps and the country sleeps,
The living sleep for their time . . . . the dead sleep for their time,
The old husband sleeps by his wife and the young husband sleeps by his wife;
And these one and all tend inward to me, and I tend outward to them,
And such as it is to be of these more or less I am.

[16]

I am of old and young, of the foolish as much as the wise,
Regardless of others, ever regardful of others,
Maternal as well as paternal, a child as well as a man,
Stuffed with the stuff that is coarse, and stuffed with the stuff that is fine,
One of the great nations, the nation of many nations—the smallest the same and the largest the same,
A southerner soon as a northerner, a planter nonchalant and hospitable,

A Yankee bound my own way . . . . ready for trade . . . . my
joints the limberest joints on earth and the sternest joints on
earth,
A Kentuckian walking the vale of the Elkhorn in my deerskin
leggings,
A boatman over the lakes or bays or along coasts . . . . a
Hoosier, a Badger, a Buckeye,
A Louisianian or Georgian, a poke-easy from sandhills and
pines,
At home on Canadian snowshoes or up in the bush, or with
fishermen off Newfoundland,
At home in the fleet of iceboats, sailing with the rest and
tacking,
At home on the hills of Vermont or in the woods of Maine or
the Texan ranch,
Comrade of Californians . . . . comrade of free
northwesterners, loving their big proportions,
Comrade of raftsmen and coalmen—comrade of all who
shake hands and welcome to drink and meat;
A learner with the simplest, a teacher of the thoughtfulest,
A novice beginning experient of myriads of seasons,
Of every hue and trade and rank, of every caste and religion,
Not merely of the New World but of Africa Europe or Asia
. . . . a wandering savage,
A farmer, mechanic, or artist . . . . a gentleman, sailor, lover
or quaker,
A prisoner, fancy-man, rowdy, lawyer, physician or priest.
I resist anything better than my own diversity,
And breathe the air and leave plenty after me,
And am not stuck up, and am in my place.

The moth and the fisheggs are in their place,
The suns I see and the suns I cannot see are in their place.
The palpable is in its place and the impalpable is in its place.

[17]

These are the thoughts of all men in all ages and lands, they
are not original with me,
If they are not yours as much as mine they are nothing or
next to nothing,

If they do not enclose everything they are next to nothing,
If they are not the riddle and the untying of the riddle they are nothing,
If they are not just as close as they are distant they are nothing.

This is the grass that grows wherever the land is and the water is,
This is the common air that bathes the globe,

This is the breath of laws and songs and behaviour,
This is the tasteless water of souls . . . . this is the true sustenance,
It is for the illiterate . . . . it is for the judges of the supreme court . . . . it is for the federal capitol and the state capitols,
It is for the admirable communes of literary men and composers and singers and lecturers and engineers and savans,
It is for the endless races of working people and farmers and seamen.

[18]

This is the trill of a thousand clear cornets and scream of the octave flute and strike of triangles.

I play not a march for victors only . . . . I play great marches for conquered and slain persons.

Have you heard that it was good to gain the day?
I also say it is good to fall . . . . battles are lost in the same spirit in which they are won.

I sound triumphal drums for the dead . . . . I fling through my embouchures the loudest and gayest music to them,
Vivas to those who have failed, and to those whose war-vessels sank in the sea, and those themselves who sank in the sea,
And to all generals that lost engagements, and all overcome heroes, and the numberless unknown heroes equal to the greatest heroes known.

[19]

This is the meal pleasantly set . . . . this is the meat and drink
for natural hunger,
It is for the wicked just the same as the righteous . . . . I make
appointments with all,
I will not have a single person slighted or left away,
The keptwoman and sponger and thief are hereby invited
. . . . the heavy-lipped slave is invited . . . . the venerealee
is invited,
There shall be no difference between them and the rest.

This is the press of a bashful hand . . . . this is the float and
odor of hair,
This is the touch of my lips to yours . . . . this is the murmur
of yearning,
This is the far-off depth and height reflecting my own face,
This is the thoughtful merge of myself and the outlet again.

Do you guess I have some intricate purpose?
Well I have . . . . for the April rain has, and the mica on the
side of a rock has.

Do you take it I would astonish?
Does the daylight astonish? or the early redstart twittering
through the woods?
Do I astonish more than they?

This hour I tell things in confidence,
I might not tell everybody but I will tell you.

[20]

Who goes there! hankering, gross, mystical, nude?
How is it I extract strength from the beef I eat?

What is a man anyhow? What am I? and what are you?
All I mark as my own you shall offset it with your own,
Else it were time lost listening to me.

I do not snivel that snivel the world over,
That months are vacuums and the ground but wallow and
filth,

That life is a suck and a sell, and nothing remains at the end but threadbare crape and tears.
Whimpering and truckling fold with powders for invalids . . . . conformity goes to the fourth-removed,
I cock my hat as I please indoors or out.

Shall I pray? Shall I venerate and be ceremonious?

I have pried through the strata and analyzed to a hair,
And counselled with doctors and calculated close and found no sweeter fat than sticks to my own bones.

In all people I see myself, none more and not one a barleycorn less,
And the good or bad I say of myself I say of them.

And I know I am solid and sound,
To me the converging objects of the universe perpetually flow,
All are written to me, and I must get what the writing means.

And I know I am deathless,
I know this orbit of mine cannot be swept by a carpenter's compass,
I know I shall not pass like a child's carlacue cut with a burnt stick at night.

I know I am august,
I do not trouble my spirit to vindicate itself or be understood,
I see that the elementary laws never apologize,
I reckon I behave no prouder than the level I plant my house by after all.

I exist as I am, that is enough,
If no other in the world be aware I sit content,
And if each and all be aware I sit content.

One world is aware, and by far the largest to me, and that is myself,
And whether I come to my own today or in ten thousand or ten million years,

I can cheerfully take it now, or with equal cheerfulness I can
wait.

My foothold is tenoned and mortised in granite,
I laugh at what you call dissolution,
And I know the amplitude of time.

[21]

I am the poet of the body,
And I am the poet of the soul.
The pleasures of heaven are with me, and the pains of hell are
with me,
The first I graft and increase upon myself . . . . the latter I
translate into a new tongue.

I am the poet of the woman the same as the man,
And I say it is as great to be a woman as to be a man,
And I say there is nothing greater than the mother of men.

I chant a new chant of dilation or pride,
We have had ducking and deprecating about enough,
I show that size is only development.

Have you outstript the rest? Are you the President?
It is a trifle . . . . they will more than arrive there every one,
and still pass on.

I am he that walks with the tender and growing night;
I call to the earth and sea half-held by the night.

Press close barebosomed night! Press close magnetic
nourishing night!
Night of south winds! Night of the large few stars!
Still nodding night! Mad naked summer night!

Smile O voluptuous coolbreathed earth!
Earth of the slumbering and liquid trees!
Earth of departed sunset! Earth of the mountains misty-top!
Earth of the vitreous pour of the full moon just tinged with
blue!
Earth of shine and dark mottling the tide of the river!

Earth of the limpid gray of clouds brighter and clearer for my sake!
Far-swooping elbowed earth! Rich apple-blossomed earth!
Smile, for your lover comes!

Prodigal! you have given me love! . . . . therefore I to you give love!
O unspeakable passionate love!

Thruster holding me tight and that I hold tight!
We hurt each other as the bridegroom and the bride hurt each other.

[22]

You sea! I resign myself to you also . . . . I guess what you mean,
I behold from the beach your crooked inviting fingers,
I believe you refuse to go back without feeling of me;
We must have a turn together . . . . I undress . . . . hurry me out of sight of the land,
Cushion me soft . . . . rock me in billowy drowse,
Dash me with amorous wet . . . . I can repay you.

Sea of stretched ground-swells!
Sea breathing broad and convulsive breaths!
Sea of the brine of life! Sea of unshovelled and always-ready graves!
Howler and scooper of storms! Capricious and dainty sea!
I am integral with you . . . . I too am of one phase and of all phases.

Partaker of influx and efflux . . . . extoller of hate and conciliation,
Extoller of armies and those that sleep in each others' arms.
I am he attesting sympathy;
Shall I make my list of things in the house and skip the house that supports them?

I am the poet of commonsense and of the demonstrable and of immortality;

And am not the poet of goodness only . . . . I do not decline
to be the poet of wickedness also.

Washes and razors for foofoos . . . . for me freckles and a
bristling beard.

What blurt is it about virtue and about vice?
Evil propels me, and reform of evil propels me . . . . I stand
indifferent,
My gait is no faultfinder's or rejecter's gait,
I moisten the roots of all that has grown.

Did you fear some scrofula out of the unflagging pregnancy?
Did you guess the celestial laws are yet to be worked over and
rectified?

I step up to say that what we do is right and what we affirm is
right . . . . and some is only the ore of right,
Witnesses of us . . . . one side a balance and the antipodal side
a balance,
Soft doctrine as steady help as stable doctrine,
Thoughts and deeds of the present our rouse and early start.

This minute that comes to me over the past decillions,
There is no better than it and now.

What behaved well in the past or behaves well today is not
such a wonder,
The wonder is always and always how there can be a mean
man or an infidel.

[23]

Endless unfolding of words of ages!
And mine a word of the modern . . . . a word en masse.

A word of the faith that never balks,
One time as good as another time . . . . here or henceforward
it is all the same to me.

A word of reality . . . . materialism first and last imbueing.

Hurrah for positive science! Long live exact demonstration!
Fetch stonecrop and mix it with cedar and branches of lilac;
This is the lexicographer or chemist . . . . this made a grammar of the old cartouches,
These mariners put the ship through dangerous unknown seas,
This is the geologist, and this works with the scalpel, and this is a mathematician.

Gentlemen I receive you, and attach and clasp hands with you,
The facts are useful and real . . . . they are not my dwelling . . . . I enter by them to an area of the dwelling.

I am less the reminder of property or qualities, and more the reminder of life,
And go on the square for my own sake and for others' sakes,
And make short account of neuters and geldings, and favor men and women fully equipped,
And beat the gong of revolt, and stop with fugitives and them that plot and conspire.

[24]

Walt Whitman, an American, one of the roughs, a kosmos,
Disorderly fleshy and sensual . . . . eating drinking and breeding,
No sentimentalist . . . . no stander above men and women or apart from them . . . . no more modest than immodest.
Unscrew the locks from the doors!
Unscrew the doors themselves from their jambs!

Whoever degrades another degrades me . . . . and whatever is done or said returns at last to me.
And whatever I do or say I also return.

Through me the afflatus surging and surging . . . . through me the current and index.

I speak the password primeval . . . . I give the sign of democracy;

By God! I will accept nothing which all cannot have their
counterpart of on the same terms.

Through me many long dumb voices,
Voices of the interminable generations of slaves,
Voices of prostitutes and of deformed persons,
Voices of the diseased and despairing, and of thieves and
dwarfs,
Voices of cycles of preparation and accretion,
And of the threads that connect the stars—and of wombs, and
of the fatherstuff,
And of the rights of them the others are down upon,
Of the trivial and flat and foolish and despised,
Of fog in the air and beetles rolling balls of dung.

Through me forbidden voices,
Voices of sexes and lusts . . . . voices veiled, and I remove the
veil,
Voices indecent by me clarified and transfigured.

I do not press my finger across my mouth,
I keep as delicate around the bowels as around the head and
heart,
Copulation is no more rank to me than death is.

I believe in the flesh and the appetites,
Seeing hearing and feeling are miracles, and each part and tag
of me is a miracle.

Divine am I inside and out, and I make holy whatever I touch
or am touched from;
The scent of these arm-pits is aroma finer than prayer,
This head is more than churches or bibles or creeds.

If I worship any particular thing it shall be some of the spread
of my body;
Translucent mould of me it shall be you,
Shaded ledges and rests, firm masculine coulter, it shall be
you.
Whatever goes to the tilth of me it shall be you,
You my rich blood, your milky stream pale strippings of my
life;

Breast that presses against other breasts it shall be you.
My brain it shall be your occult convolutions,
Root of washed sweet-flag, timorous pond-snipe, nest of guarded duplicate eggs, it shall be you,
Mixed tussled hay of head and beard and brawn it shall be you,
Trickling sap of maple, fibre of manly wheat, it shall be you;
Sun so generous it shall be you,
Vapors lighting and shading my face it shall be you,
You sweaty brooks and dews it shall be you.
Winds whose soft-tickling genitals rub against me it shall be you,
Broad muscular fields, branches of liveoak, loving lounger in my winding paths, it shall be you,
Hands I have taken, face I have kissed, mortal I have ever touched, it shall be you.

I dote on myself . . . . there is that lot of me, and all so luscious,
Each moment and whatever happens thrills me with joy.

I cannot tell how my ankles bend . . . . nor whence the cause of my faintest wish,
Nor the cause of the friendship I emit . . . . nor the cause of the friendship I take again.

To walk up my stoop is unaccountable . . . . I pause to consider if it really be,
That I eat and drink is spectacle enough for the great authors and schools,
A morning-glory at my window satisfies me more than the metaphysics of books.

To behold the daybreak!
The little light fades the immense and diaphanous shadows,
The air tastes good to my palate.

Hefts of the moving world at innocent gambols, silently rising, freshly exuding,
Scooting obliquely high and low.

Something I cannot see puts upward libidinous prongs,
Seas of bright juice suffuse heaven.

The earth by the sky staid with . . . . the daily close of their junction,
The heaved challenge from the east that moment over my head,
The mocking taunt, See then whether you shall be master!

[25]

Dazzling and tremendous how quick the sunrise would kill me,
If I could not now and always send sunrise out of me.

We also ascend dazzling and tremendous as the sun,
We found our own my soul in the calm and cool of the daybreak.

My voice goes after what my eyes cannot reach,
With the twirl of my tongue I encompass worlds and volumes of worlds.

Speech is the twin of my vision . . . . it is unequal to measure itself.

It provokes me forever,
It says sarcastically, Walt, you understand enough . . . . why don't you let it out then?

Come now I will not be tantalized . . . . you conceive too much of articulation.

Do you not know how the buds beneath are folded?
Waiting in gloom protected by frost,
The dirt receding before my prophetical screams,
I underlying causes to balance them at last,
My knowledge my live parts . . . . it keeping tally with the meaning of things,
Happiness . . . . which whoever hears me let him or her set out in search of this day.

My final merit I refuse you . . . . I refuse putting from me the best I am.

Encompass worlds but never try to encompass me,
I crowd your noisiest talk by looking toward you.

Writing and talk do not prove me,
I carry the plenum of proof and every thing else in my face,
With the hush of my lips I confound the topmost skeptic.

[26]

I think I will do nothing for a long time but listen,
And accrue what I hear into myself . . . . and let sounds contribute toward me.
I hear the bravuras of birds . . . . the bustle of growing wheat . . . . gossip of flames . . . . clack of sticks cooking my meals.

I hear the sound of the human voice . . . . a sound I love,
I hear all sounds as they are tuned to their uses . . . . sounds of the city and sounds out of the city . . . . sounds of the day and night;
Talkative young ones to those that like them . . . . the recitative of fish-pedlars and fruit-pedlars . . . . the loud laugh of workpeople at their meals,
The angry base of disjointed friendship . . . . the faint tones of the sick,
The judge with hands tight to the desk, his shaky lips pronouncing a death-sentence,
The heave'e'yo of stevedores unlading ships by the wharves . . . . the refrain of the anchor-lifters;
The ring of alarm-bells . . . . the cry of fire . . . . the whirr of swift-streaking engines and hose-carts with premonitory tinkles and colored lights,
The steam-whistle . . . . the solid roll of the train of approaching cars;
The slow-march played at night at the head of the association,
They go to guard some corpse . . . . the flag-tops are draped with black muslin.

I hear the violincello or man's heart complaint,
And hear the keyed cornet or else the echo of sunset.

I hear the chorus . . . . it is a grand-opera . . . . this indeed is music!

A tenor large and fresh as the creation fills me,
The orbic flex of his mouth is pouring and filling me full.

I hear the trained soprano . . . . she convulses me like the
climax of my love-grip;
The orchestra whirls me wider than Uranus flies,
It wrenches unnamable ardors from my breast,
It throbs me to gulps of the farthest down horror,
It sails me . . . . I dab with bare feet . . . . they are licked by
the indolent waves,
I am exposed . . . . cut by bitter and poisoned hail,
Steeped amid honeyed morphine . . . . my windpipe squeezed
in the fakes of death,
Let up again to feel the puzzle of puzzles,
And that we call Being.

[27]

To be in any form, what is that?
If nothing lay more developed the quahaug and its callous
shell were enough.

Mine is no callous shell,
I have instant conductors all over me whether I pass or stop,
They seize every object and lead it harmlessly through me.

I merely stir, press, feel with my fingers, and am happy,
To touch my person to some one else's is about as much as I
can stand.

[28]

Is this then a touch? . . . . quivering me to a new identity,
Flames and ether making a rush for my veins,
Treacherous tip of me reaching and crowding to help them,
My flesh and blood playing out lightning, to strike what is
hardly different from myself,
On all sides prurient provokers stiffening my limbs,
Straining the udder of my heart for its withheld drip,
Behaving licentious toward me, taking no denial,
Depriving me of my best as for a purpose,
Unbuttoning my clothes and holding me by the bare waist,

Deluding my confusion with the calm of the sunlight and pasture fields,
Immodestly sliding the fellow-senses away,
They bribed to swap off with touch, and go and graze at the edges of me,
No consideration, no regard for my draining strength or my anger,
Fetching the rest of the herd around to enjoy them awhile,
Then all uniting to stand on a headland and worry me.

The sentries desert every other part of me,
They have left me helpless to a red marauder,
They all come to the headland to witness and assist against me.
I am given up by traitors;
I talk wildly . . . . I have lost my wits . . . . I and nobody else am the greatest traitor,
I went myself first to the headland . . . . my own hands carried me there.

You villain touch! what are you doing? . . . . my breath is tight in its throat;
Unclench your floodgates! you are too much for me.

[29]

Blind loving wrestling touch! Sheathed hooded sharptoothed touch!
Did it make you ache so leaving me?
Parting tracked by arriving . . . . perpetual payment of the perpetual loan,
Rich showering rain, and recompense richer afterward.

Sprouts take and accumulate . . . . stand by the curb prolific and vital,
Landscapes projected masculine full-sized and golden.

[30]

All truths wait in all things,
They neither hasten their own delivery nor resist it,
They do not need the obstetric forceps of the surgeon,

The insignificant is as big to me as any,
What is less or more than a touch?

Logic and sermons never convince,
The damp of the night drives deeper into my soul.

Only what proves itself to every man and woman is so,
Only what nobody denies is so.

A minute and a drop of me settle my brain;
I believe the soggy clods shall become lovers and lamps,
And a compend of compends is the meat of a man or woman,
And a summit and flower there is the feeling they have for each other,
And they are to branch boundlessly out of that lesson until it becomes omnific,
And until every one shall delight us, and we them.

[31]

I believe a leaf of grass is no less than the journeywork of the stars,
And the pismire is equally perfect, and a grain of sand, and the egg of the wren,
And the tree-toad is a chef-d'œuvre for the highest,
And the running blackberry would adorn the parlors of heaven,
And the narrowest hinge in my hand puts to scorn all machinery,
And the cow crunching with depressed head surpasses any statue,
And a mouse is miracle enough to stagger sextillions of infidels,
And I could come every afternoon of my life to look at the farmer's girl boiling her iron tea-kettle and baking shortcake.

I find I incorporate gneiss and coal and long-threaded moss and fruits and grains and esculent roots,
And am stucco'd with quadrupeds and birds all over,
And have distanced what is behind me for good reasons,
And call any thing close again when I desire it.

In vain the speeding or shyness,
In vain the plutonic rocks send their old heat against my approach,
In vain the mastodon retreats beneath its own powdered bones,
In vain objects stand leagues off and assume manifold shapes,
In vain the ocean settling in hollows and the great monsters lying low,
In vain the buzzard houses herself with the sky,
In vain the snake slides through the creepers and logs,
In vain the elk takes to the inner passes of the woods,
In vain the razorbilled auk sails far north to Labrador,
I follow quickly . . . . I ascend to the nest in the fissure of the cliff.

[32]

I think I could turn and live awhile with the animals . . . . they are so placid and self-contained,
I stand and look at them sometimes half the day long,
Thcy do not sweat and whine about their condition,
They do not lie awake in the dark and weep for their sins,
They do not make me sick discussing their duty to God,
Not one is dissatisfied . . . . not one is demented with the mania of owning things,
Not one kneels to another nor to his kind that lived thousands of years ago,
Not one is respectable or industrious over the whole earth.

So they show their relations to me and I accept them;
They bring me tokens of myself . . . . they evince them plainly in their possession.

I do not know where they got those tokens,
I must have passed that way untold times ago and negligently dropt them,
Myself moving forward then and now and forever,
Gathering and showing more always and with velocity,
Infinite and omnigenous and the like of these among them;
Not too exclusive toward the reachers of my remembrancers,
Picking out here one that shall be my amie,
Choosing to go with him on brotherly terms.

A gigantic beauty of a stallion, fresh and responsive to my caresses,
Head high in the forehead and wide between the ears,
Limbs glossy and supple, tail dusting the ground,
Eyes well apart and full of sparkling wickedness . . . . ears finely cut and flexibly moving.

His nostrils dilate . . . . my heels embrace him . . . . his well built limbs tremble with pleasure . . . . we speed around and return.

I but use you a moment and then I resign you stallion . . . . and do not need your paces, and outgallop them,
And myself as I stand or sit pass faster than you.

[33]

. . . I visit the orchards of God and look at the spheric product,
And look at quintillions ripened, and look at quintillions green.

I fly the flight of the fluid and swallowing soul,
My course runs below the soundings of plummets.

I help myself to material and immaterial,
No guard can shut me off, no law can prevent me.

I anchor my ship for a little while only,
My messengers continually cruise away or bring their returns to me.

I go hunting polar furs and the seal . . . . leaping chasms with a pike-pointed staff . . . . clinging to topples of brittle and blue.
I ascend to the foretruck . . . . I take my place late at night in the crow's nest . . . . we sail through the arctic sea . . . . it is plenty light enough,
Through the clear atmosphere I stretch around on the wonderful beauty,
The enormous masses of ice pass me and I pass them . . . . the scenery is plain in all directions,

The white-topped mountains point up in the distance . . . .
I fling out my fancies toward them;
We are about approaching some great battlefield in which we are soon to be engaged,
We pass the colossal outposts of the encampment . . . . we pass with still feet and caution;
Or we are entering by the suburbs some vast and ruined city . . . . the blocks and fallen architecture more than all the living cities of the globe.

I am a free companion . . . . I bivouac by invading watchfires.

I turn the bridegroom out of bed and stay with the bride myself,
And tighten her all night to my thighs and lips.

My voice is the wife's voice, the screech by the rail of the stairs,
They fetch my man's body up dripping and drowned.

I understand the large hearts of heroes,
The courage of present times and all times;
How the skipper saw the crowded and rudderless wreck of the steamship, and death chasing it up and down the storm,
How he knuckled tight and gave not back one inch, and was faithful of days and faithful of nights,
And chalked in large letters on a board, Be of good cheer, We will not desert you;
How he saved the drifting company at last,
How the lank loose-gowned women looked when boated from the side of their prepared graves,
How the silent old-faced infants, and the lifted sick, and the sharplipped unshaved men;
All this I swallow and it tastes good . . . . I like it well, and it becomes mine,
I am the man . . . . I suffered . . . . I was there.

The disdain and calmness of martyrs,
The mother condemned for a witch and burnt with dry wood, and her children gazing on;
The hounded slave that flags in the race and leans by the fence, blowing and covered with sweat,

The twinges that sting like needles his legs and neck,
The murderous buckshot and the bullets,
All these I feel or am.

I am the hounded slave . . . . I wince at the bite of the dogs,
Hell and despair are upon me . . . . crack and again crack the marksmen,
I clutch the rails of the fence . . . . my gore dribs thinned with the ooze of my skin,
I fall on the weeds and stones,
The riders spur their unwilling horses and haul close,
They taunt my dizzy ears . . . . they beat me violently over the head with their whip-stocks.

Agonies are one of my changes of garments;
I do not ask the wounded person how he feels . . . . I myself become the wounded person,
My hurt turns livid upon me as I lean on a cane and observe.

I am the mashed fireman with breastbone broken . . . . tumbling walls buried me in their debris,
Heat and smoke I inspired . . . . I heard the yelling shouts of my comrades,
I heard the distant click of their picks and shovels;
They have cleared the beams away . . . . they tenderly lift me forth.

I lie in the night air in my red shirt . . . . the pervading hush is for my sake,
Painless after all I lie, exhausted but not so unhappy,
White and beautiful are the faces around me . . . . the heads are bared of their fire-caps,
The kneeling crowd fades with the light of the torches.
Distant and dead resuscitate,
They show as the dial or move as the hands of me . . . . and I am the clock myself.

I am an old artillerist, and tell of some fort's bombardment . . . . and am there again.

Again the reveille of drummers . . . . again the attacking cannon and mortars and howitzers,

Again the attacked send their cannon responsive.
I take part . . . . I see and hear the whole,
The cries and curses and roar . . . . the plaudits for well aimed shots,
The ambulanza slowly passing and trailing its red drip,
Workmen searching after damages and to make indispensable repairs,
The fall of grenades through the rent roof . . . . the fan-shaped explosion,
The whizz of limbs heads stone wood and iron high in the air.

Again gurgles the mouth of my dying general . . . . he furiously waves with his hand,
He gasps through the clot . . . . Mind not me . . . . mind . . . . the entrenchments.

[34]

I tell not the fall of Alamo . . . . not one escaped to tell the fall of Alamo,
The hundred and fifty are dumb yet at Alamo.

Hear now the tale of a jetblack sunrise,
Hear of the murder in cold blood of four hundred and twelve young men.

Retreating they had formed in a hollow square with their baggage for breastworks,
Nine hundred lives out of the surrounding enemy's nine times their number was the price they took in advance,
Their colonel was wounded and their ammunition gone,
They treated for an honorable capitulation, received writing and seal, gave up their arms, and marched back prisoners of war.
They were the glory of the race of rangers,
Matchless with a horse, a rifle, a song, a supper or a courtship,
Large, turbulent, brave, handsome, generous, proud and affectionate,
Bearded, sunburnt, dressed in the free costume of hunters,
Not a single one over thirty years of age.

The second Sunday morning they were brought out in squads and massacred . . . . it was beautiful early summer,
The work commenced about five o'clock and was over by eight.

None obeyed the command to kneel,
Some made a mad and helpless rush . . . . some stood stark and straight,
A few fell at once, shot in the temple or heart . . . . the living and dead lay together,
The maimed and mangled dug in the dirt . . . . the newcomers saw them there;
Some half-killed attempted to crawl away,
These were dispatched with bayonets or battered with the blunts of muskets;
A youth not seventeen years old seized his assassin till two more came to release him,
The three were all torn, and covered with the boy's blood.

At eleven o'clock began the burning of the bodies;
And that is the tale of the murder of the four hundred and twelve young men,
And that was a jetblack sunrise.

[35]

Did you read in the seabooks of the oldfashioned frigate-fight?
Did you learn who won by the light of the moon and stars?

Our foe was no skulk in his ship, I tell you,
His was the English pluck, and there is no tougher or truer, and never was, and never will be;
Along the lowered eve he came, horribly raking us.
We closed with him . . . . the yards entangled . . . . the cannon touched,
My captain lashed fast with his own hands.

We had received some eighteen-pound shots under the water,
On our lower-gun-deck two large pieces had burst at the first fire, killing all around and blowing up overhead.

Ten o'clock at night, and the full moon shining and the leaks on the gain, and five feet of water reported,
The master-at-arms loosing the prisoners confined in the after-hold to give them a chance for themselves.

The transit to and from the magazine was now stopped by the sentinels,
They saw so many strange faces they did not know whom to trust.

Our frigate was afire . . . . the other asked if we demanded quarters? if our colors were struck and the fighting done?

I laughed content when I heard the voice of my little captain,
We have not struck, he composedly cried, We have just begun our part of the fighting.

Only three guns were in use,
One was directed by the captain himself against the enemy's mainmast,
Two well-served with grape and canister silenced his musketry and cleared his decks.

The tops alone seconded the fire of this little battery, especially the maintop,
They all held out bravely during the whole of the action.

Not a moment's cease,
The leaks gained fast on the pumps . . . . the fire eat toward the powder-magazine,
One of the pumps was shot away . . . . it was generally thought we were sinking.
Serene stood the little captain,
He was not hurried . . . . his voice was neither high nor low,
His eyes gave more light to us than our battle-lanterns.

Toward twelve at night, there in the beams of the moon they surrendered to us.

[36]

Stretched and still lay the midnight,
Two great hulls motionless on the breast of the darkness,

Our vessel riddled and slowly sinking . . . . preparations to pass to the one we had conquered,
The captain on the quarter deck coldly giving his orders through a countenance white as a sheet,
Near by the corpse of the child that served in the cabin,
The dead face of an old salt with long white hair and carefully curled whiskers,
The flames spite of all that could be done flickering aloft and below,
The husky voices of the two or three officers yet fit for duty,
Formless stacks of bodies and bodies by themselves . . . . dabs of flesh upon the masts and spars,
The cut of cordage and dangle of rigging . . . . the slight shock of the soothe of waves,
Black and impassive guns, and litter of powder-parcels, and the strong scent,
Delicate sniffs of the seabreeze . . . . smells of sedgy grass and fields by the shore . . . . death-messages given in charge to survivors,
The hiss of the surgeon's knife and the gnawing teeth of his saw,
The wheeze, the cluck, the swash of falling blood . . . . the short wild scream, the long dull tapering groan,
These so . . . . these irretrievable.

[37]

O Christ! My fit is mastering me!
What the rebel said gaily adjusting his throat to the rope-noose,
What the savage at the stump, his eye-sockets empty, his mouth spirting whoops and defiance,
What stills the traveler come to the vault at Mount Vernon,
What sobers the Brooklyn boy as he looks down the shores of the Wallabout and remembers the prison ships,
What burnt the gums of the redcoat at Saratoga when he surrendered his brigades,
These become mine and me every one, and they are but little,
I become as much more as I like.

I become any presence or truth of humanity here,
And see myself in prison shaped like another man,
And feel the dull unintermitted pain.

For me the keepers of convicts shoulder their carbines and
keep watch,
It is I let out in the morning and barred at night.

Not a mutineer walks handcuffed to the jail, but I am
handcuffed to him and walk by his side,
I am less the jolly one there, and more the silent one with
sweat on my twitching lips.

Not a youngster is taken for larceny, but I go up too and am
tried and sentenced.

Not a cholera patient lies at the last gasp, but I also lie at the
last gasp,
My face is ash-colored, my sinews gnarl . . . . away from me
people retreat.

Askers embody themselves in me, and I am embodied in
them,
I project my hat and sit shamefaced and beg.

[38]

I rise extatic through all, and sweep with the true gravitation,
The whirling and whirling is elemental within me.

Somehow I have been stunned. Stand back!
Give me a little time beyond my cuffed head and slumbers
and dreams and gaping,
I discover myself on a verge of the usual mistake.

That I could forget the mockers and insults!
That I could forget the trickling tears and the blows of the
bludgeons and hammers!
That I could look with a separate look on my own crucifixion
and bloody crowning!

I remember . . . . I resume the overstaid fraction,
The grave of rock multiplies what has been confided to it
. . . . or to any graves,
The corpses rise . . . . the gashes heal . . . . the fastenings roll away.

I troop forth replenished with supreme power, one of an average unending procession,
We walk the roads of Ohio and Massachusetts and Virginia and Wisconsin and New York and New Orleans and Texas and Montreal and San Francisco and Charleston and Savannah and Mexico,
Inland and by the seacoast and boundary lines . . . . and we pass the boundary lines.

Our swift ordinances are on their way over the whole earth,
The blossoms we wear in our hats are the growth of two thousand years.

Eleves I salute you,
I see the approach of your numberless gangs . . . . I see you understand yourselves and me,
And know that they who have eyes are divine, and the blind and lame are equally divine,
And that my steps drag behind yours yet go before them,
And are aware how I am with you no more than I am with everybody.

[39]

The friendly and flowing savage . . . . Who is he?
Is he waiting for civilization or past it and mastering it?

Is he some southwesterner raised outdoors? Is he Canadian?
Is he from the Mississippi country? or from Iowa, Oregon or California? or from the mountains? or prairie life or bush-life? or from the sea?
Wherever he goes men and women accept and desire him,
They desire he should like them and touch them and speak to them and stay with them.

881**Eleves:** pupils or disciples (from French *élève:* "student").

Behaviour lawless as snow-flakes . . . . words simple as grass . . . . uncombed head and laughter and naivete;
Slowstepping feet and the common features, and the common modes and emanations,
They descend in new forms from the tips of his fingers,
They are wafted with the odor of his body or breath . . . . they fly out of the glance of his eyes.

[40]

Flaunt of the sunshine I need not your bask . . . . lie over,
You light surfaces only . . . . I force the surfaces and the depths also.

Earth! you seem to look for something at my hands,
Say old topknot! what do you want?

Man or woman! I might tell how I like you, but cannot,
And might tell what it is in me and what it is in you, but cannot,
And might tell the pinings I have . . . . the pulse of my nights and days.

Behold I do not give lectures or a little charity,
What I give I give out of myself.

You there, impotent, loose in the knees, open your scarfed chops till I blow grit within you,
Spread your palms and lift the flaps of your pockets,
I am not to be denied . . . . I compel . . . . I have stores plenty and to spare,
And any thing I have I bestow.

I do not ask who you are . . . . that is not important to me,
You can do nothing and be nothing but what I will infold you.

To a drudge of the cottonfields or emptier of privies I lean . . . . on his right cheek I put the family kiss,
And in my soul I swear I never will deny him.

899**topknot:** an Indian.

On women fit for conception I start bigger and nimbler
babes,
This day I am jetting the stuff of far more arrogant republics.

To any one dying . . . . thither I speed and twist the knob of
the door,
Turn the bedclothes toward the foot of the bed,
Let the physician and the priest go home.

I seize the descending man . . . . I raise him with resistless
will.

O despairer, here is my neck,
By God! you shall not go down! Hang your whole weight
upon me.

I dilate you with tremendous breath . . . . I buoy you up;
Every room of the house do I fill with an armed force . . . .
lovers of me, bafflers of graves:
Sleep! I and they keep guard all night;
Not doubt, not decease shall dare to lay finger upon you,
I have embraced you, and henceforth possess you to myself,
And when you rise in the morning you will find what I tell
you is so.

[41]

I am he bringing help for the sick as they pant on their backs,
And for strong upright men I bring yet more needed help.

I heard what was said of the universe,
Heard it and heard of several thousand years;
It is middling well as far as it goes . . . . but is that all?

Magnifying and applying come I,
Outbidding at the start the old cautious hucksters,
The most they offer for mankind and eternity less than a spirt
of my own seminal wet,
Taking myself the exact dimensions of Jehovah and laying
them away,
Lithographing Kronos and Zeus his son, and Hercules his
grandson,

936**Kronos, Zeus, Hercules:** divinities in Greek mythology.

Buying drafts of Osiris and Isis and Belus and Brahma and
  Adonai,
In my portfolio placing Manito loose, and Allah on a leaf, and
  the crucifix engraved,
With Odin, and the hideous-faced Mexitli, and all idols and
  images,
Honestly taking them all for what they are worth, and not a
  cent more,
Admitting they were alive and did the work of their day,
Admitting they bore mites as for unfledged birds who have
  now to rise and fly and sing for themselves,
Accepting the rough deific sketches to fill out better in myself
  . . . . bestowing them freely on each man and woman I see,
Discovering as much or more in a framer framing a house,
Putting higher claims for him there with his rolled-up sleeves,
  driving the mallet and chisel;
Not objecting to special revelations . . . . considering a curl of
  smoke or a hair on the back of my hand as curious as any
  revelation;
Those ahold of fire-engines and hook-and-ladder ropes more
  to me than the gods of the antique wars,
Minding their voices peal through the crash of destruction,
Their brawny limbs passing safe over charred laths . . . . their
  white foreheads whole and unhurt out of the flames;
By the mechanic's wife with her babe at her nipple
  interceding for every person born;
Three scythes at harvest whizzing in a row from three lusty
  angels with shirts bagged out at their waists;
The snag-toothed hostler with red hair redeeming sins past
  and to come,
Selling all he possesses and traveling on foot to fee lawyers for
  his brother and sit by him while he is tried for forgery:
What was strewn in the amplest strewing the square rod about
  me, and not filling the square rod then;
The bull and the bug never worshipped half enough,
Dung and dirt more admirable than was dreamed,
The supernatural of no account . . . . myself waiting my time
  to be one of the supremes,

937**Osiris and Isis, Belus and Brahma:** Egyptian and Hindu deities, respectively. 937**Adonai:** in Hebrew, another name for God. 938**Manito:** Algonquin Indian nature spirit. 938**Allah:** Moslem supreme being. 939**Odin:** Norse god of war. 939**Mexitli:** Aztec god of war.

The day getting ready for me when I shall do as much good
as the best, and be as prodigious,
Guessing when I am it will not tickle me much to receive
puffs out of pulpit or print;
By my life-lumps! becoming already a creator!
Putting myself here and now to the ambushed womb of the
shadows!

[42]

.... A call in the midst of the crowd,
My own voice, orotund sweeping and final.

Come my children,
Come my boys and girls, and my women and household and
intimates,
Now the performer launches his nerve .... he has passed his
prelude on the reeds within.

Easily written loosefingered chords! I feel the thrum of their
climax and close.

My head evolves on my neck,
Music rolls, but not from the organ .... folks are around me,
but they are no household of mine.

Ever the hard and unsunk ground,
Ever the eaters and drinkers .... ever the upward and
downward sun .... ever the air and the ceaseless tides,
Ever myself and my neighbors, refreshing and wicked and
real,
Ever the old inexplicable query .... ever that thorned
thumb—that breath of itches and thirsts,
Ever the vexer's hoot! hoot! till we find where the sly one
hides and bring him forth;
Ever love .... ever the sobbing liquid of life,
Ever the bandage under the chin .... ever the tressels of
death.

Here and there with dimes on the eyes walking,
To feed the greed of the belly the brains liberally spooning,

Tickets buying or taking or selling, but in to the feast never once going;
Many sweating and ploughing and thrashing, and then the chaff for payment receiving,
A few idly owning, and they the wheat continually claiming.

This is the city . . . . and I am one of the citizens;
Whatever interests the rest interests me . . . . politics, churches, newspapers, schools,
Benevolent societies, improvements, banks, tariffs, steamships, factories, markets,
Stocks and stores and real estate and personal estate.

They who piddle and patter here in collars and tailed coats . . . . I am aware who they are . . . . and that they are not worms or fleas,
I acknowledge the duplicates of myself under all the scrape-lipped and pipe-legged concealments.

The weakest and shallowest is deathless with me,
What I do and say the same waits for them,
Every thought that flounders in me the same flounders in them.

I know perfectly well my own egotism,
And know my omnivorous words, and cannot say any less,
And would fetch you whoever you are flush with myself.

My words are words of a questioning, and to indicate reality;
This printed and bound book . . . . but the printer and the printing-office boy?
The marriage estate and settlement . . . . but the body and mind of the bridegroom? also those of the bride?
The panorama of the sea . . . . but the sea itself?
The well-taken photographs . . . . but your wife or friend close and solid in your arms?
The fleet of ships of the line and all the modern improvements . . . . but the craft and pluck of the admiral?
The dishes and fare and furniture . . . . but the host and hostess, and the look out of their eyes?
The sky up there . . . . yet here or next door or across the way?
The saints and sages in history . . . . but you yourself?

Sermons and creeds and theology . . . . but the human brain,
and what is called reason, and what is called love, and what is called life?

[43]

I do not despise you priests;
My faith is the greatest of faiths and the least of faiths,
Enclosing all worship ancient and modern, and all between ancient and modern,
Believing I shall come again upon the earth after five thousand years,
Waiting responses from oracles . . . . honoring the gods . . . . saluting the sun,
Making a fetish of the first rock or stump . . . . powowing with sticks in the circle of obis,
Helping the lama or brahmin as he trims the lamps of the idols,
Dancing yet through the streets in a phallic procession . . . . rapt and austere in the woods, a gymnosophist,
Drinking mead from the skull-cup . . . . to shasta and vedas admirant . . . . minding the koran,
Walking the teokallis, spotted with gore from the stone and knife—beating the serpent-skin drum;
Accepting the gospels, accepting him that was crucified, knowing assuredly that he is divine,
To the mass kneeling—to the puritan's prayer rising—sitting patiently in a pew,
Ranting and frothing in my insane crisis—waiting dead-like till my spirit arouses me;
Looking forth on pavement and land, and outside of pavement and land,
Belonging to the winders of the circuit of circuits.

One of that centripetal and centrifugal gang,
I turn and talk like a man leaving charges before a journey.
Down-hearted doubters, dull and excluded,
Frivolous sullen moping angry affected disheartened atheistical,

1009**obis:** i.e., obeah, referring to West African witchcraft and sorcery.
1011**gymnosophist:** Hindu ascetic. 1012**shasta:** i.e., Shastra, a Hindu sacred writing (cf. the Vedas). 1013**teokallis:** Aztec temples.

I know every one of you, and know the unspoken interrogatories,
By experience I know them.

How the flukes splash!
How they contort rapid as lightning, with spasms and spouts of blood!

Be at peace bloody flukes of doubters and sullen mopers,
I take my place among you as much as among any;
The past is the push of you and me and all precisely the same,
And the night is for you and me and all,
And what is yet untried and afterward is for you and me and all.

I do not know what is untried and afterward,
But I know it is sure and alive, and sufficient.

Each who passes is considered, and each who stops is considered, and not a single one can it fail.

It cannot fail the young man who died and was buried,
Nor the young woman who died and was put by his side,
Nor the little child that peeped in at the door and then drew back and was never seen again,
Nor the old man who has lived without purpose, and feels it with bitterness worse than gall,
Nor him in the poorhouse tubercled by rum and the bad disorder,
Nor the numberless slaughtered and wrecked . . . . nor the brutish koboo, called the ordure of humanity,
Nor the sacs merely floating with open mouths for food to slip in,
Nor any thing in the earth, or down in the oldest graves of the earth,
Nor any thing in the myriads of spheres, nor one of the myriads of myriads that inhabit them,
Nor the present, nor the least wisp that is known.

1040**koboo:** Sumatran savage.

[44]

It is time to explain myself. . . . let us stand up.

What is known I strip away . . . . I launch all men and women forward with me into the unknown.

The clock indicates the moment . . . . but what does eternity indicate?

Eternity lies in bottomless reservoirs . . . . its buckets are rising forever and ever,
They pour and they pour and they exhale away.

We have thus far exhausted trillions of winters and summers;
There are trillions ahead, and trillions ahead of them.

Births have brought us richness and variety,
And other births will bring us richness and variety.

I do not call one greater and one smaller,
That which fills its period and place is equal to any.

Were mankind murderous or jealous upon you my brother or my sister?
I am sorry for you . . . . they are not murderous or jealous upon me;
All has been gentle with me . . . . . . I keep no account with lamentation;
What have I to do with lamentation?

I am an acme of things accomplished, and I an encloser of things to be.

My feet strike an apex of the apices of the stairs,
On every step bunches of ages, and larger bunches between the steps,
All below duly traveled—and still I mount and mount.

Rise after rise bow the phantoms behind me,
Afar down I see the huge first Nothing, the vapor from the nostrils of death,
I know I was even there . . . . I waited unseen and always,

And slept while God carried me through the lethargic mist,
And took my time . . . . and took no hurt from the fœtid carbon.

Long I was hugged close . . . . long and long.

Immense have been the preparations for me,
Faithful and friendly the arms that have helped me.

Cycles ferried my cradle, rowing and rowing like cheerful boatmen;
For room to me stars kept aside in their own rings,
They sent influences to look after what was to hold me.

Before I was born out of my mother generations guided me,
My embryo has never been torpid . . . . nothing could overlay it;
For it the nebula cohered to an orb . . . . the long slow strata piled to rest it on . . . . vast vegetables gave it sustenance,
Monstrous sauroids transported it in their mouths and deposited it with care.

All forces have been steadily employed to complete and delight me,
Now I stand on this spot with my soul.

[45]

Span of youth! Ever-pushed elasticity! Manhood balanced and florid and full!

My lovers suffocate me!
Crowding my lips, and thick in the pores of my skin,
Jostling me through streets and public halls . . . . coming naked to me at night,
Crying by day Ahoy from the rocks of the river . . . . swinging and chirping over my head,
Calling my name from flowerbeds or vines or tangled underbrush,
Or while I swim in the bath . . . . or drink from the pump at the corner . . . . or the curtain is down at the opera . . . . or I glimpse at a woman's face in the railroad car;

[1078]**sauroids:** prehistoric reptiles.

Lighting on every moment of my life,
Bussing my body with soft and balsamic busses,
Noiselessly passing handfuls out of their hearts and giving
them to be mine.

Old age superbly rising! Ineffable grace of dying days!

Every condition promulges not only itself . . . . it promulges
what grows after and out of itself,
And the dark hush promulges as much as any.

I open my scuttle at night and see the far-sprinkled systems,
And all I see, multiplied as high as I can cipher, edge but the
rim of the farther systems.

Wider and wider they spread, expanding and always
expanding,
Outward and outward and forever outward.
My sun has his sun, and round him obediently wheels,
He joins with his partners a group of superior circuit,
And greater sets follow, making specks of the greatest inside
them.

There is no stoppage, and never can be stoppage;
If I and you and the worlds and all beneath or upon their
surfaces, and all the palpable life, were this moment
reduced back to a pallid float, it would not avail in the
long run,
We should surely bring up again where we now stand,
And as surely go as much farther, and then farther and
farther.

A few quadrillions of eras, a few octillions of cubic leagues,
do not hazard the span, or make it impatient,
They are but parts . . . . any thing is but a part.

See ever so far . . . . there is limitless space outside of that,
Count ever so much . . . . there is limitless time around that.

Our rendezvous is fitly appointed . . . . God will be there
and wait till we come.

[46]

I know I have the best of time and space—and that I was never measured, and never will be measured.

I tramp a perpetual journey,
My signs are a rain-proof coat and good shoes and a staff cut from the woods;
No friend of mine takes his ease in my chair,
I have no chair, nor church nor philosophy;
I lead no man to a dinner-table or library or exchange,
But each man and each woman of you I lead upon a knoll,
My left hand hooks you round the waist,
My right hand points to landscapes of continents, and a plain public road.

Not I, not any one else can travel that road for you,
You must travel it for yourself.

It is not far . . . . it is within reach,
Perhaps you have been on it since you were born, and did not know,
Perhaps it is every where on water and on land.

Shoulder your duds, and I will mine, and let us hasten forth;
Wonderful cities and free nations we shall fetch as we go.
If you tire, give me both burdens, and rest the chuff of your hand on my hip,
And in due time you shall repay the same service to me;
For after we start we never lie by again.

This day before dawn I ascended a hill and looked at the crowded heaven,
And I said to my spirit, When we become the enfolders of those orbs and the pleasure and knowledge of every thing in them, shall we be filled and satisfied then?
And my spirit said No, we level that lift to pass and continue beyond.

You are also asking me questions, and I hear you;
I answer that I cannot answer . . . . you must find out for yourself.

Sit awhile wayfarer,
Here are biscuits to eat and here is milk to drink,
But as soon as you sleep and renew yourself in sweet clothes I will certainly kiss you with my goodbye kiss and open the gate for your egress hence.

Long enough have you dreamed contemptible dreams,
Now I wash the gum from your eyes,
You must habit yourself to the dazzle of the light and of every moment of your life.

Long have you timidly waded, holding a plank by the shore,
Now I will you to be a bold swimmer,
To jump off in the midst of the sea, and rise again and nod to me and shout, and laughingly dash with your hair.

[47]

I am the teacher of athletes,
He that by me spreads a wider breast than my own proves the width of my own,
He most honors my style who learns under it to destroy the teacher.

The boy I love, the same becomes a man not through derived power but in his own right,
Wicked, rather than virtuous out of conformity or fear,
Fond of his sweetheart, relishing well his steak,
Unrequited love or a slight cutting him worse than a wound cuts,
First rate to ride, to fight, to hit the bull's eye, to sail a skiff, to sing a song or play on the banjo,
Preferring scars and faces pitted with smallpox over all latherers and those that keep out of the sun.

I teach straying from me, yet who can stray from me?
I follow you whoever you are from the present hour;
My words itch at your ears till you understand them.

I do not say these things for a dollar, or to fill up the time while I wait for a boat;
It is you talking just as much as myself . . . . I act as the tongue of you,

It was tied in your mouth . . . . in mine it begins to be
loosened.

I swear I will never mention love or death inside a house,
And I swear I never will translate myself at all, only to him
or her who privately stays with me in the open air.

If you would understand me go to the heights or
water-shore,
The nearest gnat is an explanation and a drop or the motion
of waves a key,
The maul the oar and the handsaw second my words.

No shuttered room or school can commune with me,
But roughs and little children better than they.

The young mechanic is closest to me . . . . he knows me
pretty well,
The woodman that takes his axe and jug with him shall take
me with him all day,
The farmboy ploughing in the field feels good at the sound
of my voice,
In vessels that sail my words must sail . . . . I go with
fishermen and seamen, and love them,
My face rubs to the hunter's face when he lies down alone in
his blanket,
The driver thinking of me does not mind the jolt of his
wagon,
The young mother and old mother shall comprehend me,
The girl and the wife rest the needle a moment and forget
where they are,
They and all would resume what I have told them.

[48]

I have said that the soul is not more than the body,
And I have said that the body is not more than the soul,
And nothing, not God, is greater to one than one's-self is,
And whoever walks a furlong without sympathy walks to his
own funeral, dressed in his shroud,
And I or you pocketless of a dime may purchase the pick of
the earth,

And to glance with an eye or show a bean in its pod confounds the learning of all times,
And there is no trade or employment but the young man following it may become a hero,
And there is no object so soft but it makes a hub for the wheeled universe,
And any man or woman shall stand cool and supercilious before a million universes.

And I call to mankind, Be not curious about God,
For I who am curious about each am not curious about God,
No array of terms can say how much I am at peace about God and about death.

I hear and behold God in every object, yet I understand God not in the least,
Nor do I understand who there can be more wonderful than myself.

Why should I wish to see God better than this day?
I see something of God each hour of the twenty-four, and each moment then,
In the faces of men and women I see God, and in my own face in the glass;
I find letters from God dropped in the street, and every one is signed by God's name,
And I leave them where they are, for I know that others will punctually come forever and ever.

[49]

And as to you death, and you bitter hug of mortality . . . . it is idle to try to alarm me.

To his work without flinching the accoucheur comes,
I see the elderhand pressing receiving supporting,
I recline by the sills of the exquisite flexible doors . . . . and mark the outlet, and mark the relief and escape.

And as to you corpse I think you are good manure, but that does not offend me,
I smell the white roses sweetscented and growing,

I reach to the leafy lips . . . . I reach to the polished breasts of melons.

And as to you life, I reckon you are the leavings of many deaths,
No doubt I have died myself ten thousand times before.
I hear you whispering there O stars of heaven,
O suns . . . . O grass of graves . . . . O perpetual transfers and promotions . . . . if you do not say anything how can I say anything?

Of the turbid pool that lies in the autumn forest,
Of the moon that descends the steeps of the soughing twilight,
Toss, sparkles of day and dusk . . . . toss on the black stems that decay in the muck,
Toss to the moaning gibberish of the dry limbs.

I ascend from the moon . . . . I ascend from the night,
And perceive of the ghastly glitter the sunbeams reflected,
And debouch to the steady and central from the offspring great or small.

[50]

There is that in me . . . . I do not know what it is . . . . but I know it is in me.

Wrenched and sweaty . . . . calm and cool then my body becomes;
I sleep . . . . I sleep long.

I do not know it . . . . it is without name . . . . it is a word unsaid,
It is not in any dictionary or utterance or symbol.

Something it swings on more than the earth I swing on,
To it the creation is the friend whose embracing awakes me.

Perhaps I might tell more . . . . Outlines! I plead for my brothers and sisters.

Do you see O my brothers and sisters?
It is not chaos or death . . . . it is form and union and plan
. . . . it is eternal life . . . . it is happiness.

[51]

The past and present wilt . . . . I have filled them and emptied them,
And proceed to fill my next fold of the future.
Listener up there! Here you . . . . what have you to confide to me?
Look in my face while I snuff the sidle of evening,
Talk honestly, for no one else hears you, and I stay only a minute longer.
Do I contradict myself?
Very well then . . . . I contradict myself;
I am large . . . . I contain multitudes.

I concentrate toward them that are nigh . . . . I wait on the door-slab.

Who has done his day's work and will soonest be through with his supper?
Who wishes to talk with me?

Will you speak before I am gone? Will you prove already too late?

[52]

The spotted hawk swoops by and accuses me . . . . he complains of my gab and my loitering.

I too am not a bit tamed . . . . I too am untranslatable,
I sound my barbaric yawp over the roofs of the world.

The last scud of day holds back for me,
It flings my likeness after the rest and true as any on the shadowed wilds,
It coaxes me to the vapor and the dusk.

I depart as air . . . . I shake my white locks at the runaway sun,

I effuse my flesh in eddies and drift it in lacy jags.

I bequeath myself to the dirt to grow from the grass I love,
If you want me again look for me under your bootsoles.

You will hardly know who I am or what I mean,
But I shall be good health to you nevertheless,
And filter and fibre your blood.

Failing to fetch me at first keep encouraged,
Missing me one place search another,
I stop some where waiting for you.

There Was a Child Went Forth

There was a child went forth every day,
And the first object he looked upon and received with wonder or pity or love or dread, that object he became,
And that object became part of him for the day or a certain part of the day . . . . or for many years or stretching cycles of years.

The early lilacs became part of this child,
And grass, and white and red morningglories, and white and red clover, and the song of the phœbe-bird,
And the March-born lambs, and the sow's pink-faint litter, and the mare's foal, and the cow's calf, and the noisy brood of the barnyard or by the mire of the pondside . . and the fish suspending themselves so curiously below there . . and the beautiful curious liquid . . and the water-plants with their graceful flat heads . . all became part of him.

And the field-sprouts of April and May became part of him . . . wintergrain sprouts, and those of the light-yellow corn, and of the esculent roots of the garden,
And the appletrees covered with blossoms, and the fruit afterward . . . . and woodberries . . and the commonest weeds by the road;
And the old drunkard staggering home from the outhouse of the tavern whence he had lately risen,
And the schoolmistress that passed on her way to the school . . and the friendly boys that passed . . and the quarrelsome

boys . . and the tidy and freshcheeked girls . . and the barefoot negro boy and girl,
And all the changes of city and country wherever he went.

His own parents . . he that had propelled the fatherstuff at night, and fathered him . . and she that conceived him in her womb and birthed him . . . . they gave this child more of themselves than that,
They gave him afterward every day . . . . they and of them became part of him.

The mother at home quietly placing the dishes on the suppertable,
The mother with mild words . . . . clean her cap and gown . . . . a wholesome odor falling off her person and clothes as she walks by:
The father, strong, selfsufficient, manly, mean, angered, unjust,
The blow, the quick loud word, the tight bargain, the crafty lure,
The family usages, the language, the company, the furniture . . . . the yearning and swelling heart,
Affection that will not be gainsayed . . . . The sense of what is real . . . . the thought if after all it should prove unreal,
The doubts of daytime and the doubts of nighttime . . . . the curious whether and how,
Whether that which appears so is so . . . . Or is it all flashes and specks?
Men and women crowding fast in the streets . . if they are not flashes and specks what are they?
The streets themselves, and the facades of houses . . . . the goods in the windows,
Vehicles . . teams . . the tiered wharves, and the huge crossing at the ferries;
The village on the highland seen from afar at sunset . . . . the river between,
Shadows . . aureola and mist . . light falling on roofs and gables of white or brown, three miles off,
The schooner near by sleepily dropping down the tide . . the little boat slacktowed astern,
The hurrying tumbling waves and quickbroken crests and slapping;

The strata of colored clouds . . . . the long bar of maroontint
  away solitary by itself . . . . the spread of purity it lies
  motionless in,
The horizon's edge, the flying seacrow, the fragrance of
  saltmarsh and shoremud;
These became part of that child who went forth every day,
  and who now goes and will always go forth every day,
And these become of him or her that peruses them now.

Crossing Brooklyn Ferry

1

Flood-tide below me! I see you face to face!
Clouds of the west—sun there half an hour high— I see you
  also face to face.

Crowds of men and women attired in the usual costumes,
  how curious you are to me!
On the ferry-boats the hundreds and hundreds that cross,
  returning home, are more curious to me than you suppose,
And you that shall cross from shore to shore years hence are
  more to me, and more in my meditations, than you might
  suppose.

2

The impalpable sustenance of me from all things at all hours
  of the day,
The simple, compact, well-join'd scheme, myself
  disintegrated, every one disintegrated yet part of the
  scheme,
The similitudes of the past and those of the future,
The glories strung like beads on my smallest sights and
  hearings, on the walk in the street and the passage over the
  river,
The current rushing so swiftly and swimming with me far
  away,
The others that are to follow me, the ties between me and
  them,
The certainty of others, the life, love, sight, hearing of others.

Others will enter the gates of the ferry and cross from shore to shore,
Others will watch the run of the flood-tide,
Others will see the shipping of Manhattan north and west, and the heights of Brooklyn to the south and east,
Others will see the islands large and small;
Fifty years hence, others will see them as they cross, the sun half an hour high,
A hundred years hence, or ever so many hundred years hence, others will see them,
Will enjoy the sunset, the pouring-in of the flood-tide, the falling-back to the sea of the ebb-tide.

3

It avails not, time nor place—distance avails not,
I am with you, you men and women of a generation, or ever so many generations hence,
Just as you feel when you look on the river and sky, so I felt,
Just as any of you is one of a living crowd, I was one of a crowd,
Just as you are refresh'd by the gladness of the river and the bright flow, I was refresh'd,
Just as you stand and lean on the rail, yet hurry with the swift current, I stood yet was hurried,
Just as you look on the numberless masts of ships and the thick-stemm'd pipes of steamboats, I look'd.

I too many and many a time cross'd the river of old,
Watched the Twelfth-month sea-gulls, saw them high in the air floating with motionless wings, oscillating their bodies,
Saw how the glistening yellow lit up parts of their bodies and left the rest in strong shadow,
Saw the slow-wheeling circles and the gradual edging toward the south,
Saw the reflection of the summer sky in the water,
Had my eyes dazzled by the shimmering tracks of beams,
Look'd at the fine centrifugal spokes of light round the shape of my head in the sunlit water,
Look'd on the haze on the hills southward and south-westward,
Look'd on the vapor as it flew in fleeces tinged with violet,

Look'd toward the lower bay to notice the vessels arriving,
Saw their approach, saw aboard those that were near me,
Saw the white sails of schooners and sloops, saw the ships at anchor,
The sailors at work in the rigging or out astride the spars,
The round masts, the swinging motion of the hulls, the slender serpentine pennants,
The large and small steamers in motion, the pilots in their pilothouses,
The white wake left by the passage, the quick tremulous whirl of the wheels,
The flags of all nations, the falling of them at sunset,
The scallop-edged waves in the twilight, the ladled cups, the frolicsome crests and glistening,
The stretch afar growing dimmer and dimmer, the gray walls of the granite storehouses by the docks,
On the river the shadowy group, the big steam-tug closely flank'd on each side by the barges, the hay-boat, the belated lighter,
On the neighboring shore the fires from the foundry chimneys burning high and glaringly into the night,
Casting their flicker of black contrasted with wild red and yellow light over the tops of houses, and down into the clefts of streets.

4

These and all else were to me the same as they are to you,
I loved well those cities, loved well the stately and rapid river,
The men and women I saw were all near to me,
Others the same—others who look back on me because I look'd forward to them,
(The time will come, though I stop here to-day and to-night.)

5

What is it then between us?
What is the count of the scores or hundreds of years between us?

Whatever it is, it avails not—distance avails not, and place avails not,

I too lived, Brooklyn of ample hills was mine,
I too walk'd the streets of Manhattan island, and bathed in the waters around it,
I too felt the curious abrupt questionings stir within me,
In the day among crowds of people sometimes they came upon me,
In my walks home late at night or as I lay in my bed they came upon me,
I too had been struck from the float forever held in solution,
I too had receiv'd identity by my body,
That I was I knew was of my body, and what I should be I knew I should be of my body.

6

It is not upon you alone the dark patches fall,
The dark threw its patches down upon me also,
The best I had done seem'd to me blank and suspicious,
My great thoughts as I supposed them, were they not in reality meagre?
Nor is it you alone who know what it is to be evil,
I am he who knew what it was to be evil,
I too knitted the old knot of contrariety,
Blabb'd, blush'd, resented, lied, stole, grudg'd,
Had guile, anger, lust, hot wishes I dared not speak,
Was wayward, vain, greedy, shallow, sly, cowardly, malignant,
The wolf, the snake, the hog, not wanting in me,
The cheating look, the frivolous word, the adulterous wish, not wanting,
Refusals, hates, postponements, meanness, laziness, none of these wanting,
Was one with the rest, the days and haps of the rest,
Was call'd by my nighest name by clear loud voices of young men as they saw me approaching or passing,
Felt their arms on my neck as I stood, or the negligent leaning of their flesh against me as I sat,
Saw many I loved in the street or ferry-boat or public assembly, yet never told them a word,
Lived the same life with the rest, the same old laughing, gnawing, sleeping,
Play'd the part that still looks back on the actor or actress,

The same old role, the role that is what we make it, as great as we like,
Or as small as we like, or both great and small.

7

Closer yet I approach you,
What thought you have of me now, I had as much of you—I laid in my stores in advance,
I consider'd long and seriously of you before you were born.

Who was to know what should come home to me?
Who knows but I am enjoying this?
Who knows, for all the distance, but I am as good as looking at you now, for all you cannot see me?

8

Ah, what can ever be more stately and admirable to me than mast-hemm'd Manhattan?
River and sunset and scallop-edg'd waves of flood-tide?
The sea-gulls oscillating their bodies, the hay-boat in the twilight, and the belated lighter?
What gods can exceed these that clasp me by the hand, and with voices I love call me promptly and loudly by my nighest name as I approach?
What is more subtle than this which ties me to the woman or man that looks in my face?
Which fuses me into you now, and pours my meaning into you?

We understand then do we not?
What I promis'd without mentioning it, have you not accepted?
What the study could not teach—what the preaching could not accomplish is accomplish'd, is it not?

9

Flow on, river! flow with the flood-tide, and ebb with the ebb-tide!
Frolic on, crested and scallop-edg'd waves!

Gorgeous clouds of the sunset! drench with your splendor
me, or the men and women generations after me!
Cross from shore to shore, countless crowds of passengers!
Stand up, tall masts of Mannahatta! stand up, beautiful hills of
Brooklyn!
Throb, baffled and curious brain! throw out questions and
answers!
Suspend here and everywhere, eternal float of solution!
Gaze, loving and thirsting eyes, in the house or street or
public assembly!
Sound out, voices of young men! loudly and musically call me
by my nighest name!
Live, old life! play the part that looks back on the actor or
actress!
Play the old role, the role that is great or small according as
one makes it!
Consider, you who peruse me, whether I may not in
unknown ways be looking upon you;
Be firm, rail over the river, to support those who lean idly,
yet haste with the hasting current;
Fly on, sea-birds! fly sideways, or wheel in large circles high
in the air;
Receive the summer sky, you water, and faithfully hold it till
all downcast eyes have time to take it from you!
Diverge, fine spokes of light, from the shape of my head, or
any one's head, in the sunlit water!
Come on, ships from the lower bay! pass up or down,
white-sail'd schooners, sloops, lighters!
Flaunt away, flags of all nations! be duly lower'd at sunset!
Burn high your fires, foundry chimneys! cast black shadows at
nightfall! cast red and yellow light over the tops of the
houses!
Appearances, now or henceforth, indicate what you are,
You necessary film, continue to envelop the soul,
About my body for me, and your body for you, be hung our
divinest aromas,
Thrive, cities—bring your freight, bring your shows, ample
and sufficient rivers,
Expand, being than which none else is perhaps more spiritual,
Keep your places, objects than which none else is more
lasting.

You have waited, you always wait, you dumb, beautiful ministers,
We receive you with free sense at last, and are insatiate henceforward,
Not you any more shall be able to foil us, or withhold yourselves from us,
We use you, and do not cast you aside—we plant you permanently within us,
We fathom you not—we love you—there is perfection in you also,
You furnish your parts toward eternity,
Great or small, you furnish your parts toward the soul.

Out of the Cradle Endlessly Rocking

Out of the cradle endlessly rocking,
Out of the mocking-bird's throat, the musical shuttle,
Out of the Ninth-month midnight,
Over the sterile sands and the fields beyond, where the child leaving his bed wander'd alone, bareheaded, barefoot,
Down from the shower'd halo,
Up from the mystic play of shadows twining and twisting as if they were alive,
Out from the patches of briers and blackberries,
From the memories of the bird that chanted to me,
From your memories sad brother, from the fitful risings and fallings I heard,
From under that yellow half-moon late-risen and swollen as if with tears,
From those beginning notes of yearning and love there in the mist,
From the thousand responses of my heart never to cease,
From the myriad thence-arous'd words,
From the word stronger and more delicious than any,
From such as now they start the scene revisiting,
As a flock, twittering, rising, or overhead passing,
Borne hither, ere all eludes me, hurriedly,
A man, yet by these tears a little boy again,
Throwing myself on the sand, confronting the waves,
I, chanter of pains and joys, uniter of here and hereafter,

Taking all hints to use them, but swiftly leaping beyond them,
A reminiscence sing.

Once Paumanok,
When the lilac-scent was in the air and Fifth-month grass was growing,
Up this seashore in some briers,
Two feather'd guests from Alabama, two together,
And their nest, and four light-green eggs spotted with brown,
And every day the he-bird to and fro near at hand,
And every day the she-bird crouch'd on her nest, silent, with bright eyes,
And every day I, a curious boy, never too close, never disturbing them,
Cautiously peering, absorbing, translating.

Shine! shine! shine!
Pour down your warmth, great sun!
While we bask, we two together.

Two together!
Winds blow south, or winds blow north,
Day come white, or night come black,
Home, or rivers and mountains from home,
Singing all time, minding no time,
While we two keep together.

Till of a sudden,
May-be kill'd, unknown to her mate,
One forenoon the she-bird crouch'd not on the nest,
Nor return'd that afternoon, nor the next,
Nor ever appear'd again.

And thenceforward all summer in the sound of the sea,
And at night under the full of the moon in calmer weather,
Over the hoarse surging of the sea,
Or flitting from brier to brier by day,
I saw, I heard at intervals the remaining one, the he-bird,
The solitary guest from Alabama.

Blow! blow! blow!
Blow up sea-winds along Paumanok's shore;
I wait and I wait till you blow my mate to me.

Yes, when the stars glisten'd
All night long on the prong of a moss-scallop'd stake,
Down almost amid the slapping waves,
Sat the long singer wonderful causing tears.

He call'd on his mate,
He pour'd forth the meanings which I of all men know.

Yes my brother I know,
The rest might not, but I have treasur'd every note,
For more than once dimly down to the beach gliding,
Silent, avoiding the moonbeams, blending myself with the shadows,
Recalling now the obscure shapes, the echoes, the sounds and sights after their sorts,
The white arms out in the breakers tirelessly tossing,
I, with bare feet, a child, the wind wafting my hair,
Listen'd long and long.

Listen'd to keep, to sing, now translating the notes,
Following you my brother.

Soothe! soothe! soothe!
Close on its wave soothes the wave behind,
And again another behind embracing and lapping, every one close,
But my love soothes not me, not me.

Low hangs the moon, it rose late,
It is lagging—O I think it is heavy with love, with love.

O madly the sea pushes upon the land,
With love, with love.

O night! do I not see my love fluttering out among the breakers?
What is that little black thing I see there in the white?

Loud! loud! loud!
Loud I call to you, my love!

High and clear I shoot my voice over the waves,
Surely you must know who is here, is here,
You must know who I am, my love.

Low-hanging moon!
What is that dusky spot in your brown yellow?
O it is the shape, the shape of my mate!
O moon do not keep her from me any longer.

Land! land! O land!
Whichever way I turn, O I think you could give me my mate back again if you only would,
For I am almost sure I see her dimly whichever way I look.

O rising stars!
Perhaps the one I want so much will rise, will rise with some of you.

O throat! O trembling throat!
Sound clearer through the atmosphere!
Pierce the woods, the earth,
Somewhere listening to catch you must be the one I want.

Shake out carols!
Solitary here, the night's carols!
Carols of lonesome love! death's carols!
Carols under that lagging, yellow, waning moon!
O under that moon where she droops almost down into the sea!
O reckless despairing carols.

But soft! sink low!
Soft! let me just murmur,
And do you wait a moment you husky-nois'd sea,
For somewhere I believe I heard my mate responding to me,
So faint, I must be still, be still to listen,
But not altogether still, for then she might not come immediately to me.

Hither my love!
Here I am! here!
With this just-sustain'd note I announce myself to you,
This gentle call is for you my love, for you.

Do not be decoy'd elsewhere,
That is the whistle of the wind, it is not my voice,

That is the fluttering, the fluttering of the spray,
Those are the shadows of leaves.

O darkness! O in vain!
O I am very sick and sorrowful.
O brown halo in the sky near the moon, drooping upon the sea!
O troubled reflection in the sea!
O throat! O throbbing heart!
And I singing uselessly, uselessly all the night.

O past! O happy life! O songs of joy!
In the air, in the woods, over fields,
Loved! loved! loved! loved! loved!
But my mate no more, no more with me!
We two together no more.

The aria sinking.
All else continuing, the stars shining,
The winds blowing, the notes of the bird continuous echoing,
With angry moans the fierce old mother incessantly moaning,
On the sands of Paumanok's shore gray and rustling,
The yellow half-moon enlarged, sagging down, drooping, the face of the sea almost touching,
The boy ecstatic, with his bare feet the waves, with his hair the atmosphere dallying,
The love in the heart long pent, now loose, now at last tumultuously bursting,
The aria's meaning, the ears, the soul, swiftly depositing,
The strange tears down the cheeks coursing,
The colloquy there, the trio, each uttering,
The undertone, the savage old mother incessantly crying,
To the boy's soul's questions sullenly timing, some drown'd secret hissing,
To the outsetting bard.

Demon or bird! (said the boy's soul,)
Is it indeed toward your mate you sing? or is it really to me?
For I, that was a child, my tongue's use sleeping, now I have heard you,
Now in a moment I know what I am for, I awake,

And already a thousand singers, a thousand songs, clearer, louder and more sorrowful than yours,
A thousand warbling echoes have started to life within me, never to die.

O you singer solitary, singing by yourself, projecting me,
O solitary me listening, never more shall I cease perpetuating you,
Never more shall I escape, never more the reverberations,
Never more the cries of unsatisfied love be absent from me,
Never again leave me to be the peaceful child I was before what there in the night,
By the sea under the yellow and sagging moon,
The messenger there arous'd, the fire, the sweet hell within,
The unknown want, the destiny of me.

O give me the clew! (it lurks in the night here somewhere,)
O if I am to have so much, let me have more!

A word then, (for I will conquer it,)
The word final, superior to all,
Subtle, sent up—what is it? I listen;
Are you whispering it, and have been all the time, you sea-waves?
Is that it from your liquid and wet sands?

Whereto answering, the sea,
Delaying not, hurrying not,
Whisper'd me through the night, and very plainly before daybreak,
Lisp'd to me the low and delicious word death,
And again death, death, death, death,
Hissing melodious, neither like the bird nor like my arous'd child's heart,
But edging near as privately for me rustling at my feet,
Creeping thence steadily up to my ears and laving me softly all over,
Death, death, death, death, death.

Which I do not forget,
But fuse the song of my dusky demon and brother,

That he sang to me in the moonlight on Paumanok's gray beach,
With the thousand responsive songs at random,
My own songs awaked from that hour,
And with them the key, the word up from the waves,
The word of the sweetest song and all songs,
That strong and delicious word which, creeping to my feet,
(Or like some old crone rocking the cradle, swathed in sweet garments, bending aside,)
The sea whisper'd me.

The Dalliance of the Eagles

Skirting the river road, (my forenoon walk, my rest,)
Skyward in air a sudden muffled sound, the dalliance of the eagles,
The rushing amorous contact high in space together,
The clinching interlocking claws, a living, fierce, gyrating wheel,
Four beating wings, two beaks, a swirling mass tight grappling,
In tumbling turning clustering loops, straight downward falling,
Till o'er the river pois'd, the twain yet one, a moment's lull,
A motionless still balance in the air, then parting, talons loosing,
Upward again on slow-firm pinions slanting, their separate diverse flight,
She hers, he his, pursuing.

Cavalry Crossing a Ford

A line in long array where they wind betwixt green islands,
They take a serpentine course, their arms flash in the sun—hark to the musical clank,
Behold the silvery river, in it the splashing horses loitering stop to drink,
Behold the brown-faced men, each group, each person a picture, the negligent rest on the saddles,
Some emerge on the opposite bank, others are just entering the ford—while,
Scarlet and blue and snowy white,
The guidon flags flutter gayly in the wind.

Bivouac on a Mountain Side

I see before me now a traveling army halting,
Below a fertile valley spread, with barns and the orchards of summer,
Behind, the terraced sides of a mountain, abrupt, in places rising high,
Broken, with rocks, with clinging cedars, with tall shapes dingily seen,
The numerous camp-fires scatter'd near and far, some away up on the mountain,
The shadowy forms of men and horses, looming, large-sized, flickering,
And over all the sky—the sky! far, far out of reach, studded, breaking out, the eternal stars.

By the Bivouac's Fitful Flame

By the bivouac's fitful flame,
A procession winding around me, solemn and sweet and slow—but first I note,
The tents of the sleeping army, the fields' and woods' dim outline,
The darkness lit by spots of kindled fire, the silence,
Like a phantom far or near an occasional figure moving,
The shrubs and trees, (as I lift my eyes they seem to be stealthily watching me,)
While wind in procession thoughts, O tender and wondrous thoughts,
Of life and death, of home and the past and loved, and of those that are far away;
A solemn and slow procession there as I sit on the ground,
By the bivouac's fitful flame.

Vigil Strange I Kept on the Field One Night

Vigil strange I kept on the field one night;
When you my son and my comrade dropt at my side that day,
One look I but gave which your dear eyes return'd with a look I shall never forget,

One touch of your hand to mine O boy, reach'd up as you lay on the ground,
Then onward I sped in the battle, the even-contested battle,
Till late in the night reliev'd to the place at last again I made my way,
Found you in death so cold dear comrade, found your body son of responding kisses, (never again on earth responding,)
Bared your face in the starlight, curious the scene, cool blew the moderate night-wind,
Long there and then in vigil I stood, dimly around me the battlefield spreading,
Vigil wondrous and vigil sweet there in the fragrant silent night,
But not a tear fell, not even a long-drawn sigh, long, long I gazed,
Then on the earth partially reclining sat by your side leaning my chin in my hands,
Passing sweet hours, immortal and mystic hours with you dearest comrade—not a tear, not a word,
Vigil of silence, love and death, vigil for you my son and my soldier,
As onward silently stars aloft, eastward new ones upward stole,
Vigil final for you brave boy, (I could not save you, swift was your death,
I faithfully loved you and cared for you living, I think we shall surely meet again,)
Till at latest lingering of the night, indeed just as the dawn appear'd,
My comrade I wrapt in his blanket, envelop'd well his form,
Folded the blanket well, tucking it carefully over head and carefully under feet,
And there and then and bathed by the rising sun, my son in his grave, in his rude-dug grave I deposited,
Ending my vigil strange with that, vigil of night and battle-field dim,
Vigil for boy of responding kisses, (never again on earth responding,)
Vigil for comrade swiftly slain, vigil I never forget, how as day brighten'd,
I rose from the chill ground and folded my soldier well in his blanket,
And buried him where he fell.

A Sight in Camp in the Daybreak Gray and Dim

A sight in camp in the daybreak gray and dim,
As from my tent I emerge so early sleepless,
As slow I walk in the cool fresh air the path near by the hospital tent,
Three forms I see on stretchers lying, brought out there untended lying,
Over each the blanket spread, ample brownish woolen blanket,
Gray and heavy blanket, folding, covering all.

Curious I halt and silent stand,
Then with light fingers I from the face of the nearest the first just lift the blanket;
Who are you elderly man so gaunt and grim, with well-gray'd hair, and flesh all sunken about the eyes?
Who are you my dear comrade?

Then to the second I step—and who are you my child and darling?
Who are you sweet boy with cheeks yet blooming?

Then to the third—a face nor child nor old, very calm, as of beautiful yellow-white ivory;
Young man I think I know you—I think this face is the face of the Christ himself,
Dead and divine and brother of all, and here again he lies.

The Wound-Dresser

1

An old man bending I come among new faces,
Years looking backward resuming in answer to children,
Come tell us old man, as from young men and maidens that love me,
(Arous'd and angry, I'd thought to beat the alarum, and urge relentless war,
But soon my fingers fail'd me, my face droop'd and I resign'd myself,
To sit by the wounded and soothe them, or silently watch the dead;)

Years hence of these scenes, of these furious passions, these chances,
Of unsurpass'd heroes, (was one side so brave? the other was equally brave;)
Now be witness again, paint the mightiest armies of earth,
Of those armies so rapid so wondrous what saw you to tell us?
What stays with you latest and deepest? of curious panics,
Of hard-fought engagements or sieges tremendous what deepest remains?

2

O maidens and young men I love and that love me,
What you ask of my days those the strangest and sudden your talking recalls,
Soldier alert I arrive after a long march cover'd with sweat and dust,
In the nick of time I come, plunge in the fight, loudly shout in the rush of successful charge,
Enter the captur'd works—yet lo, like a swift-running river they fade,
Pass and are gone they fade—I dwell not on soldiers' perils or soldiers' joys,
(Both I remember well—many the hardships, few the joys, yet I was content.)

But in silence, in dreams' projections,
While the world of gain and appearance and mirth goes on,
So soon what is over forgotten, and waves wash the imprints off the sand,
With hinged knees returning I enter the doors, (while for you up there,
Whoever you are, follow without noise and be of strong heart.)

Bearing the bandages, water and sponge,
Straight and swift to my wounded I go,
Where they lie on the ground after the battle brought in,
Where their priceless blood reddens the grass the ground,
Or to the rows of the hospital tent, or under the roof'd hospital,
To the long rows of cots up and down each side I return,

To each and all one after another I draw near, not one do I
miss,

An attendant follows holding a tray, he carries a refuse pail,
Soon to be fill'd with clotted rags and blood, emptied, and
fill'd again.

I onward go, I stop,
With hinged knees and steady hand to dress wounds,
I am firm with each, the pangs are sharp yet unavoidable,
One turns to me his appealing eyes—poor boy! I never knew
you,
Yet I think I could not refuse this moment to die for you, if
that would save you.

3

On, on I go, (open doors of time! open hospital doors!)
The crush'd head I dress, (poor crazed hand tear not the
bandage away,)
The neck of the cavalry-man with the bullet through and
through I examine,
Hard the breathing rattles, quite glazed already the eye, yet life
struggles hard,
(Come sweet death! be persuaded O beautiful death!
In mercy come quickly.)

From the stump of the arm, the amputated hand,
I undo the clotted lint, remove the slough, wash off the matter
and blood,
Back on his pillow the soldier bends with curv'd neck and
side-falling head,
His eyes are closed, his face is pale, he dares not look on the
bloody stump,
And has not yet look'd on it.

I dress a wound in the side, deep, deep,
But for a day or two more, for see the frame all wasted and
sinking,
And the yellow-blue countenance see.

I dress the perforated shoulder, the foot with the
bullet-wound,

Cleanse the one with a gnawing and putrid gangrene, so
sickening, so offensive,
While the attendant stands behind aside me holding the tray
and pail.

I am faithful, I do not give out,
The fractur'd thigh, the knee, the wound in the abdomen,
These and more I dress with impassive hand, (yet deep in my
breast a fire, a burning flame.)

4

Thus in silence in dreams' projections,
Returning, resuming, I thread my way through the hospitals,
The hurt and wounded I pacify with soothing hand,
I sit by the restless all the dark night, some are so young,
Some suffer so much, I recall the experience sweet and sad,
(Many a soldier's loving arms about this neck have cross'd and
rested,
Many a soldier's kiss dwells on these bearded lips.)

Reconciliation

Word over all, beautiful as the sky,
Beautiful that war and all its deeds of carnage must in time be
utterly lost,
That the hands of the sisters Death and Night incessantly softly
wash again, and ever again, this soil'd world;
For my enemy is dead, a man divine as myself is dead,
I look where he lies white-faced and still in the coffin—I draw
near,
Bend down and touch lightly with my lips the white face in
the coffin.

When Lilacs Last in the Dooryard Bloom'd

1

When lilacs last in the dooryard bloom'd,
And the great star early droop'd in the western sky in the
night,
I mourn'd, and yet shall mourn with ever-returning spring.

Ever-returning spring, trinity sure to me you bring,
Lilac blooming perennial and drooping star in the west,
And thought of him I love.

2

O powerful western fallen star!
O shades of night—O moody, tearful night!
O great star disappear'd—O the black murk that hides the star!
O cruel hands that hold me powerless—O helpless soul of me!
O harsh surrounding cloud that will not free my soul.

3

In the dooryard fronting an old farm-house near the
  white-wash'd palings,
Stands the lilac-bush tall-growing with heart-shaped leaves of
  rich green,
With many a pointed blossom rising delicate, with the
  perfume strong I love,
With every leaf a miracle—and from this bush in the
  dooryard,
With delicate-color'd blossoms and heart-shaped leaves of rich
  green.
A sprig with its flower I break.

4

In the swamp in secluded recesses,
A shy and hidden bird is warbling a song.

Solitary the thrush,
The hermit withdrawn to himself, avoiding the settlements,
Sings by himself a song.
Song of the bleeding throat,
Death's outlet song of life, (for well dear brother I know,
If thou wast not granted to sing thou would'st surely die.)

5

Over the breast of the spring, the land, amid cities,
Amid lanes and through old woods, where lately the violets
  peep'd from the ground, spotting the gray debris,

Amid the grass in the fields each side of the lanes, passing the endless grass,
Passing the yellow-spear'd wheat, every grain from its shroud in the dark-brown fields uprisen,
Passing the apple-tree blows of white and pink in the orchards,
Carrying a corpse to where it shall rest in the grave,
Night and day journeys a coffin.

6

Coffin that passes through lanes and streets,
Through day and night with the great cloud darkening the land,
With the pomp of the inloop'd flags with the cities draped in black,
With the show of the States themselves as of crape-veil'd women standing,
With processions long and winding and the flambeaus of the night,
With the countless torches lit, with the silent sea of faces and the unbared heads,
With the waiting depot, the arriving coffin, and the sombre faces,
With dirges through the night, with the thousand voices rising strong and solemn,
With all the mournful voices of the dirges pour'd around the coffin,
The dim-lit churches and the shuddering organs—where amid these you journey,
With the tolling tolling bells' perpetual clang,
Here, coffin that slowly passes,
I give you my sprig of lilac.

7

(Nor for you, for one alone,
Blossoms and branches green to coffins all I bring,
For fresh as the morning, thus would I chant a song for you O sane and sacred death.

All over bouquets of roses,
O death, I cover you over with roses and early lilies,
But mostly and now the lilac that blooms the first,

Copious I break, I break the sprigs from the bushes,
With loaded arms I come, pouring for you,
For you and the coffins all of you O death.)

8

O western orb sailing the heaven,
Now I know what you must have meant as a month since I walk'd,
As I walk'd in silence the transparent shadowy night,
As I saw you had something to tell as you bent to me night after night,
As you droop'd from the sky low down as if to my side, (while the other stars all look'd on,)
As we wander'd together the solemn night, (for something I know not what kept me from sleep,)
As the night advanced, and I saw on the rim of the west how full you were of woe,
As I stood on the rising ground in the breeze in the cool transparent night,
As I watch'd where you pass'd and was lost in the netherward black of the night,
As my soul in its trouble dissatisfied sank, as where you sad orb,
Concluded, dropt in the night, and was gone.

9

Sing on there in the swamp,
O singer bashful and tender, I hear your notes, I hear your call,
I hear, I come presently, I understand you,
But a moment I linger, for the lustrous star has detain'd me,
The star my departing comrade holds and detains me.

10

O how shall I warble myself for the dead one there I loved?
And how shall I deck my song for the large sweet soul that has gone?
And what shall my perfume be for the grave of him I love?

Sea-winds blown from east and west,
Blown from the Eastern sea and blown from the Western sea, till there on the prairies meeting,
These and with these and the breath of my chant,
I'll perfume the grave of him I love.

11

O what shall I hang on the chamber walls?
And what shall the pictures be that I hang on the walls,
To adorn the burial-house of him I love?

Pictures of growing spring and farms and homes,
With the Fourth-month eve at sundown, and the gray smoke lucid and bright,
With floods of the yellow gold of the gorgeous, indolent, sinking sun, burning, expanding the air,
With the fresh sweet herbage under foot, and the pale green leaves of the trees prolific,
In the distance the flowing glaze, the breast of the river, with a wind-dapple here and there,
With ranging hills on the banks, with many a line against the sky, and shadows,
And the city at hand with dwellings so dense, and stacks of chimneys,
And all the scenes of life and the workshops, and the workmen homeward returning.

12

Lo, body and soul—this land,
My own Manhattan with spires, and the sparkling and hurrying tides, and the ships,
The varied and ample land, the South and the North in the light, Ohio's shores and flashing Missouri,
And ever the far-spreading prairies cover'd with grass and corn.

Lo, the most excellent sun so calm and haughty,
The violet and purple morn with just-felt-breezes,
The gentle soft-born measureless light,
The miracle spreading bathing all, the fulfill'd noon,

The coming eve delicious, the welcome night and the stars,
Over my cities shining all, enveloping man and land.

13

Sing on, sing on you gray-brown bird,
Sing from the swamps, the recesses, pour your chant from the bushes,
Limitless out of the dusk, out of the cedars and pines.
Sing on dearest brother, warble your reedy song,
Loud human song, with voice of uttermost woe.

O liquid and free and tender!
O wild and loose to my soul!—O wondrous singer!
You only I hear—yet the star holds me, (but will soon depart,)
Yet the lilac with mastering odor holds me.

14

Now while I sat in the day and look'd forth,
In the close of the day with its light and the fields of spring, and the farmers preparing their crops,
In the large unconscious scenery of my land with its lakes and forests,
In the heavenly aerial beauty, (after the perturb'd winds and the storms,)
Under the arching heavens of the afternoon swift passing, and the voices of children and women,
The many-moving sea-tides, and I saw the ships how they sail'd,
And the summer approaching with richness, and the fields all busy with labor,
And the infinite separate houses, how they all went on, each with its meals and minutia of daily usages,
And the streets how their throbbings throbb'd, and the cities pent—lo, then and there,
Falling upon them all and among them all, enveloping me with the rest,
Appear'd the cloud, appear'd the long black trail,
And I knew death, its thought, and the sacred knowledge of death.

Then with the knowledge of death as walking one side of me,
And the thought of death close-walking the other side of me,
And I in the middle as with companions, and as holding the
hands of companions,
I fled forth to the hiding receiving night that talks not,
Down to the shores of the water, the path by the swamp in
the dimness,
To the solemn shadowy cedars and ghostly pines so still.

And the singer so shy to the rest receiv'd me,
The gray-brown bird I know receiv'd us comrades three,
And he sang the carol of death, and a verse for him I love.
From deep secluded recesses,
From the fragrant cedars and the ghostly pines so still,
Came the carol of the bird.

And the charm of the carol rapt me,
As I held as if by their hands my comrades in the night,
And the voice of my spirit tallied the song of the bird.

Come lovely and soothing death,
Undulate round the world, serenely arriving, arriving,
In the day, in the night, to all, to each,
Sooner or later delicate death.

Prais'd be the fathomless universe,
For life and joy, and for objects and knowledge curious,
And for love, sweet love—but praise! praise! praise!
For the sure-enwinding arms of cool-enfolding death.

Dark mother always gliding near with soft feet,
Have none chanted for thee a chant of fullest welcome?
Then I chant it for thee, I glorify thee above all,
I bring thee a song that when thou must indeed come, come
unfalteringly.

Approach strong deliveress,
When it is so, when thou hast taken them I joyously sing the dead,
Lost in the loving floating ocean of thee,
Laved in the flood of thy bliss O death.

From me to thee glad serenades,
Dances for thee I propose saluting thee, adornments and feastings for thee,
And the sights of the open landscape and the high-spread sky are fitting,
And life and the fields, and the huge and thoughtful night.

The night in silence under many a star,
The ocean shore and the husky whispering wave whose voice I know,
And the soul turning to thee O vast and well-veil'd death,
And the body gratefully nestling close to thee.
Over the tree-tops I float thee a song,
Over the rising and sinking waves, over the myriad fields and the prairies wide,
Over the dense-pack'd cities all and the teeming wharves and ways,
I float this carol with joy, with joy to thee O death.

15

To the tally of my soul,
Loud and strong kept up the gray-brown bird,
With pure deliberate notes spreading filling the night.

Loud in the pines and cedars dim,
Clear in the freshness moist and the swamp-perfume,
And I with my comrades there in the night.

While my sight that was bound in my eyes unclosed,
As to long panoramas of visions.

And I saw askant the armies,
I saw as in noiseless dreams hundreds of battle-flags,
Borne through the smoke of the battles and pierc'd with missiles I saw them,
And carried hither and yon through the smoke, and torn and bloody,
And at last but a few shreds left on the staffs, (and all in silence)
And the staffs all splinter'd and broken.

I saw battle-corpses, myriads of them,
And the white skeletons of young men, I saw them,

I saw the debris and debris of all the slain soldiers of the war,
But I saw they were not as was thought,
They themselves were fully at rest, they suffer'd not,
The living remain'd and suffer'd, the mother suffer'd,
And the wife and the child and the musing comrade suffer'd,
And the armies that remain'd suffer'd.

16

Passing the visions, passing the night,
Passing, unloosing the hold of my comrades' hands,
Passing the song of the hermit bird and the tallying song of my soul,
Victorious song, death's outlet song, yet varying ever-altering song,
As low and wailing, yet clear the notes, rising and falling, flooding the night,
Sadly sinking and fainting, as warning and warning, and yet again bursting with joy,
Covering the earth and filling the spread of the heaven,
As that powerful psalm in the night I heard from recesses,
Passing, I leave thee lilac with heart-shaped leaves,
I leave thee there in the door-yard, blooming, returning with spring.
I cease from my song for thee,
From my gaze on thee in the west, fronting the west, communing with thee,
O comrade lustrous with silver face in the night.

Yet each to keep and all, retrievements out of the night,
The song, the wondrous chant of the gray-brown bird,
And the tallying chant, the echo arous'd in my soul,
With the lustrous and drooping star with the countenance full of woe,
With the holders holding my hand nearing the call of the bird,
Comrades mine and I in the midst, and their memory ever to keep, for the dead I loved so well,
For the sweetest, wisest soul of all my days and lands—and this for his dear sake,
Lilac and star and bird twined with the chant of my soul,
There in the fragrant pines and the cedars dusk and dim.

When I Heard at the Close of the Day

When I heard at the close of the day how my name had been
receiv'd with plaudits in the capitol, still it was not a happy
night for me that follow'd,
And else when I carous'd, or when my plans were
accomplish'd, still I was not happy,
But the day when I rose at dawn from the bed of perfect
health, refresh'd, singing, inhaling the ripe breath of autumn,
When I saw the full moon in the west grow pale and disappear
in the morning light,
When I wander'd alone over the beach, and undressing
bathed, laughing with the cool waters, and saw the sun rise,
And when I thought how my dear friend my lover was on his
way coming, O then I was happy,
O then each breath tasted sweeter, and all that day my food
nourish'd me more, and the beautiful day pass'd well,
And the next came with equal joy, and with the next at
evening came my friend,
And that night while all was still I heard the waters roll slowly
continually up the shores,
I heard the hissing rustle of the liquid and sands as directed to
me whispering to congratulate me,
For the one I love most lay sleeping by me under the same
cover in the cool night,
In the stillness in the autumn moonbeams his face was inclined
toward me,
And his arm lay lightly around my breast—and that night I
was happy.

A Glimpse

A glimpse through an interstice caught,
Of a crowd of workmen and drivers in a bar-room around the
stove late of a winter night, and I unremark'd seated in a
corner,
Of a youth who loves me and whom I love, silently
approaching and seating himself near, that he may hold me
by the hand,
A long while amid the noises of coming and going, of
drinking and oath and smutty jest,

There we two, content, happy in being together, speaking little, perhaps not a word.

Earth, My Likeness

Earth, my likeness,
Though you look so impassive, ample and spheric there,
I now suspect that is not all;
I now suspect there is something fierce in you eligible to burst forth,
For an athlete is enamour'd of me, and I of him,
But toward him there is something fierce and terrible in me eligible to burst forth,
I dare not tell it in words, not even in these songs.

As I Sit Writing Here

As I sit writing here, sick and grown old,
Not my least burden is that dulness of the years, querilities,
Ungracious glooms, aches, lethargy, constipation, whimpering *ennui,*
May filter in my daily songs.

Twilight

The soft voluptuous opiate shades,
The sun just gone, the eager light dispell'd—(I too will soon be gone dispell'd,)
A haze—nirwana—rest and night—oblivion.

Good-Bye My Fancy!

Good-bye my Fancy!
Farewell dear mate, dear love!
I'm going away, I know not where,
Or to what fortune, or whether I may ever see you again,
So Good-bye my Fancy.

Now for my last—let me look back a moment;
The slower fainter ticking of the clock is in me,
Exit, nightfall, and soon the heart-thud stopping.

Long have we lived, joy'd, caress'd together;
Delightful!—now separation—Good-bye my Fancy.

Yet let me not be too hasty,
Long indeed have we lived, slept, filter'd, become really blended into one;
Then if we die we die together, (yes, we'll remain one,)
If we go anywhere we'll go together to meet what happens,
May-be we'll be better off and blither, and learn something,
May-be it is yourself now really ushering me to the true songs, (who knows?)
May-be it is you the mortal knob really undoing, turning—so now finally,
Good-bye—and hail! my Fancy.

Emily Dickinson

[1830–1886]

Emily Dickinson's external life was remarkably circumscribed. Born in 1830 in Amherst, Massachusetts, and educated at Amherst Academy, she lived there her entire life, except for a brief stay at what was later to become Mount Holyoke College. She lived a life of seclusion, leaving Massachusetts only once and rarely leaving her father's house during the last fifteen years of her life. She died in the house where she was born.

If Dickinson's external life was unadventurous, her interior life was not. Her mind was anything but provincial. She read widely in English literature and thought deeply about what she read. She expressed a particular fondness for the poetry of John Keats and Robert Browning, the prose of John Ruskin and Sir Thomas Browne, and the novels of George Eliot and Charlotte and Emily Brontë. And although she disclaimed knowledge of Whitman's work, she treasured a book that significantly influenced both Whitman's poetry and her own: the King James translation of the Bible. She especially liked the Book of Revelation.

Dickinson is often bracketed with Whitman as a cofounder of modern American poetry. Each brought to poetry something new, fresh, and strikingly original. But their poems, however prototypically modern, could not be more different. A mere glance at the page reveals a significant visual difference. Whitman's poems are large and expansive. The lines are long and the poems are typically ample and open. Dickinson's poems, by contrast, are highly compressed. They squeeze moments of intensely felt life and thought into tight four-line stanzas that compress feeling and condense thought.

The openness of Whitman's form is paralleled by the openness of his stance, his public outgoing manner. Dickinson's poetry is much more private, tending toward inwardness. Hers is a more meditative poetry than Whitman's, a poetry rooted partly in the metaphysical poetry of such seventeenth-century writers as John Donne and George Herbert. More directly influential on Dickinson's poetry than the metaphysical poets, however, was the tradition of Protestant hymnology. Her poems frequently employ the meter of hymns and follow their typical stanzaic pattern. Here, for example, is the opening verse of "Our God, Our Help in Ages Past," its accented syllables marked with ′.

> Our God, our help in ages past,
> Our hope for years to come,
> Our shelter from the stormy blast,
> And our eternal home.

The hymn's meter and formal structure are highly regular. The first and third lines are in iambic tetrameter, the second and fourth in iambic trimeter. The lack of metrical variation results in a steady, predictable rhythm, essential for singing. Dickinson varies this standard pattern to suit her poetic purpose. Her numerous variations amply testify to the ingenious and stunning uses to which she put this familiar meter. Consider, for example, "I felt a Funeral, in my Brain," "I like a look of Agony," "I died for Beauty—but was scarce," and "I heard a Fly buzz—when I died."

Dickinson's adaptation of hymn meter accords with her adaptation of the traditional religious doctrines of orthodox Christianity. For although her poems reflect a Calvinist heritage—particularly in their probing self-analysis, in which an intensely religious disposition intersects with profound psychological experience—she was not an orthodox Christian. Her religious ideas, like her life and poetry, were distinctive and individual. And even when her views tend toward orthodox teaching, as in her attitude toward immortality, her literary expression of such a belief is strikingly original. In addition, Dickinson's mischievous wit contrasts sharply with the brooding solemnity characteristic of much Calvinist-inspired religious writing. Finally, her love for nature separates her from her Puritan precursors, allying her instead with such transcendentalist contemporaries as Emerson, Whitman, and Thoreau, though her vision of life is starker than theirs.

Dickinson's poetry requires repeated and careful readings. Her diction is frequently surprising. Her elliptical syntax occasionally departs from the normal pattern. Readers must consequently fill in the gaps her language creates. Her taut lines need to be loosened; her tight poems need to be opened up. Words, phrases, lines cry out for the expansion of interpretive paraphrase.

Though a dictionary is necessary to identify the meanings of many of the words in Dickinson's poems, we need to attend to their richness of connotation as well. In "A narrow Fellow in the Grass," for example, we can explore the connotations of "Fellow," "transport," "cordiality," and "Zero at the Bone," considering how they fuse thought and feeling. In "The Bustle in a House," we can be alert for the fresh treatment of metaphor in the second stanza and attentive to the connotations of "industries," "Morning," and "Enacted" from the opening lines. And in "Tell all the Truth but tell it slant," we can discover the general idea implied by the poem and then apply it to specific areas of our experience. In doing so we will discover how Dickinson treats both nature and human experience obliquely and indirectly. To read her poems requires, in addition, a willingness to wait for the poem's possibilities of meaning to reveal themselves. Since many of her poems are cast as riddles, we must be willing to accept uncertainty, ambiguity, and partial understanding in interpreting them.

We also have to extend our notion of what constitutes acceptable poetic technique—something her contemporaries found nearly impossible. Dickinson was criticized for using inexact rhymes, rough rhythms, and colloquial diction, and for taking liberties with grammar. Her odd punctuation—heavy on dashes—and her peculiar use of capitalization were also unappreciated. But Dickinson exploited these and other poetic resources to convey complex states of mind and feeling. She employed these and other poetic idiosyncrasies not for their own sake, but for emotional and psychological impact.

In his extensive biography of Dickinson, Richard B. Sewall describes her resolve to portray the state of her mind and being in all their unorthodox complexity. He also describes Dickinson's early and futile hopes for publication and appreciation as well as her resignation to what she termed her "barefoot rank: of anonymity." Sewall also reveals her determination to pursue truth and to make poems her way. When Thomas Wentworth Higginson, an influential contemporary critic, advised her to write a more polite poetry, less indirect and metaphoric, smoother in rhythm and rhyme, simpler in thought, and less colloquial in idiom, she replied with a poem. Her answer is that although she could have written otherwise, she chose to write as she did.

326

I cannot dance upon my Toes—
No Man instructed me—
But oftentimes, among my mind,
A Glee possesseth me,

That had I Ballet knowledge—
Would put itself abroad
In Pirouette to blanch a Troupe—
Or lay a Prima, mad,

And though I had no Gown of Gauze—
No ringlet, to my Hair,
Nor hopped to Audiences—like Birds,
One claw upon the Air,

Nor tossed my shape in Eider Balls,
Nor rolled on wheels of snow
Till I was out of sight, in sound,
The House encore me so—

Nor any know I know the Art
I mention—easy—Here—
Nor any Placard boast me—
It's full as Opera

Sewall describes how Dickinson's poems reflect her poetic vocation. He demonstrates how basic religious texts such as the Bible and Thomas à Kempis's *The Imitation of Christ* sustained her both spiritually and poetically. Though allowing that Dickinson's decision to cloister herself in her chamber could have had its roots in neurosis, he argues that her firm resolve was motivated by a commitment to the art of poetry akin to the ascetic discipline of religious devotion. In fact, he cites one of her more famous poems—one usually interpreted as a love poem—to suggest that it be read as a dedication to the spiritual or poetic life. It can also be read as a celebration of individual choice.

303

The Soul selects her own Society—
Then—shuts the Door—
To her divine Majority—
Present no more—

Unmoved—she notes the Chariots—pausing—
At her low Gate—
Unmoved—an Emperor be kneeling
Upon her Mat—

I've known her—from an ample nation—
Choose One—
Then—close the Valves of her attention—
Like Stone—

Sewall's central point about the relationship between Dickinson's life and art is that although we may not be certain which interpretation to favor when considering this and many other poems, we can remain satisfied with our uncertainty because such ambiguity is central to her art. She writes metaphorically, concealing as much as she reveals. As readers we share in apprehending the nature of the experience she describes—in the poem above, the experience of making a decisive choice involving commitment and renunciation. In doing so, however, we also supply specific details from our own lives to render the decision specific and significant. Dickinson's poetry, in other words, conveys the essence of an experience, its heart and core. Her poems, as Sewall aptly notes, do not tell us so much how to live as what it feels like to be alive.

Emily Dickinson's poems do not encompass a wide range of experience; instead they probe deeply into a few of life's major experiences—love, death, doubt, and faith. In examining her experience, Dickinson makes a scrupulous effort to tell the truth, but she tells it "slant." Part of her originality and artistry includes the way she invites us to share in her search for truth. The qualified assertions we frequently find in her poems, their riddles and uncertainties, and their questioning stance demand our participation and response. In considering her representation of intensely felt moments of consciousness, we experience for ourselves her explosive power. And in learning to share Dickinson's acute perceptions and feelings, we also come to understand our own.

67

Success is counted sweetest
By those who ne'er succeed.
To comprehend a nectar
Requires sorest need.

Not one of all the purple Host
Who took the Flag today
Can tell the definition
So clear of Victory

As he defeated—dying—
On whose forbidden ear
The distant strains of triumph
Burst agonized and clear!

108

Surgeons must be very careful
When they take the knife!
Underneath their fine incisions
Stirs the Culprit—*Life!*

185

"Faith" is a fine invention
When Gentlemen can *see*—
But *Microscopes* are prudent
In an Emergency.

199

I'm "wife"—I've finished that—
That other state—
I'm Czar—I'm "Woman" now—
It's safer so—

How odd the Girl's life looks
Behind this soft Eclipse—
I think that Earth feels so
To folks in Heaven—now—

This being comfort—then
That other kind—was pain—
But why compare?
I'm "Wife"! Stop there!

241

I like a look of Agony,
Because I know it's true—
Men do not sham Convulsion,
Nor simulate, a Throe—

The Eyes glaze once—and that is Death—
Impossible to feign
The Beads upon the Forehead
By homely Anguish strung.

249

Wild Nights—Wild Nights!
Were I with thee
Wild Nights should be
Our luxury!

Futile—the Winds—
To a Heart in port—
Done with the Compass—
Done with the Chart!

Rowing in Eden—
Ah, the Sea!
Might I but moor—Tonight—
In Thee!

252

I can wade Grief—
Whole Pools of it—
I'm used to that—
But the least push of Joy
Breaks up my feet—
And I tip—drunken—
Let no Pebble—smile—
'Twas the New Liquor—
That was all!

Power is only Pain—
Stranded, thro' Discipline,
Till Weights—will hang—
Give Balm—to Giants—
And they'll wilt, like Men—
Give Himmaleh—
They'll Carry—Him!

258

There's a certain Slant of light,
Winter Afternoons—
That oppresses, like the Heft
Of Cathedral Tunes—

Heavenly Hurt, it gives us—
We can find no scar,
But internal difference,
Where the Meanings, are—

None may teach it—Any—
'Tis the Seal Despair—
An imperial affliction
Sent us of the Air—

When it comes, the Landscape listens—
Shadows—hold their breath—
When it goes, 'tis like the Distance
On the look of Death—

280

I felt a Funeral, in my Brain,
And Mourners to and fro
Kept treading—treading—till it seemed
That Sense was breaking through—

And when they all were seated,
A Service, like a Drum—
Kept beating—beating—till I thought
My Mind was going numb—

And I heard them lift a Box
And creak across my Soul
With those same Boots of Lead, again,
The Space—began to toll,

As all the Heavens were a Bell,
And Being, but an Ear,
And I, and Silence, some strange Race
Wrecked, solitary, here—

And then a Plank in Reason, broke,
And I dropped down, and down—
And hit a World, at every plunge,
And Finished knowing—then—

306

The Soul's Superior instants
Occur to Her—alone—
When friend—and Earth's occasion
Have infinite withdrawn—

Or She—Herself—ascended
To too remote a Height

For lower Recognition
Than Her Omnipotent—

This Mortal Abolition
Is seldom—but as fair
As Apparition—subject
To Autocratic Air—

Eternity's disclosure
To favorites—a few—
Of the Colossal substance
Of Immortality

321

Of all the Sounds despatched abroad,
There's not a Charge to me
Like that old measure in the Boughs—
That phraseless Melody—
The Wind does—working like a Hand,
Whose fingers Comb the Sky—
Then quiver down—with tufts of Tune—
Permitted Gods, and me—

Inheritance, it is, to us—
Beyond the Art to Earn—
Beyond the trait to take away
By Robber, since the Gain
Is gotten not of fingers—
And inner than the Bone—
Hid golden, for the whole of Days,
And even in the Urn,
I cannot vouch the merry Dust
Do not arise and play
In some odd fashion of its own,
Some quainter Holiday,
When Winds go round and round in Bands—
And thrum upon the door,
And Birds take places, overhead,
To bear them Orchestra.

I crave Him grace of Summer Boughs,
If such an Outcast be—
Who never heard that fleshless Chant—
Rise—solemn—on the Tree,
As if some Caravan of Sound
Off Deserts, in the Sky,
Had parted Rank,
Then knit, and swept—
In Seamless Company—

324

Some keep the Sabbath going to Church—
I keep it, staying at Home—
With a Bobolink for a Chorister—
And an Orchard, for a Dome—

Some keep the Sabbath in Surplice—
I just wear my Wings—
And instead of tolling the Bell, for Church,
Our little Sexton—sings.

God preaches, a noted Clergyman—
And the sermon is never long,
So instead of getting to Heaven, at last—
I'm going, all along.

328

A Bird came down the Walk—
He did not know I saw—
He bit an Angleworm in halves
And ate the fellow, raw,

And then he drank a Dew
From a convenient Grass—
And then hopped sidewise to the Wall
To let a Beetle pass—

He glanced with rapid eyes
That hurried all around—

They looked like frightened Beads, I thought—
He stirred his Velvet Head

Like one in danger, Cautious,
I offered him a Crumb
And he unrolled his feathers
And rowed him softer home—

Than Oars divide the Ocean,
Too silver for a seam—
Or Butterflies, off Banks of Noon
Leap, plashless as they swim.

341

After great pain, a formal feeling comes—
The Nerves sit ceremonious, like Tombs—
The stiff Heart questions was it He, that bore,
And Yesterday, or Centuries before?

The Feet, mechanical, go round—
Of Ground, or Air, or Ought—
A Wooden way
Regardless grown,
A Quartz contentment, like a stone—

This is the Hour of Lead—
Remembered, if outlived,
As Freezing persons, recollect the Snow—
First—Chill—then Stupor—then the letting go—

365

Dare you see a Soul *at the White Heat?*
Then crouch within the door—
Red—is the Fire's common tint—
But when the vivid Ore
Has vanquished Flame's conditions,
It quivers from the Forge
Without a color, but the light
Of unanointed Blaze.

Least Village has its Blacksmith
Whose Anvil's even ring
Stands symbol for the finer Forge
That soundless tugs—within—
Refining these impatient Ores
With Hammer, and with Blaze
Until the Designated Light
Repudiate the Forge—

435

Much Madness is divinest Sense—
To a discerning Eye—
Much Sense—the starkest Madness—
'Tis the Majority
In this, as All, prevail—
Assent—and you are sane—
Demur—you're straightway dangerous—
And handled with a Chain—

448

This was a Poet—It is That
Distills amazing sense
From ordinary Meanings—
And Attar so immense

From the familiar species
That perished by the Door—
We wonder it was not Ourselves
Arrested it—before—

Of Pictures, the Discloser—
The Poet—it is He—
Entitles Us—by Contrast—
To ceaseless Poverty—

Of Portion—so unconscious—
The Robbing—could not harm—
Himself—to Him—a Fortune—
Exterior—to Time—

449

I died for Beauty—but was scarce
Adjusted in the Tomb
When One who died for Truth, was lain
In an adjoining Room—

He questioned softly "Why I failed"?
"For Beauty", I replied—
"And I—for Truth—Themself are One—
We Brethren, are", He said—

And so, as Kinsmen, met a Night—
We talked between the Rooms—
Until the Moss had reached our lips—
And covered up—our names—

465

I heard a Fly buzz—when I died—
The Stillness in the Room
Was like the Stillness in the Air—
Between the Heaves of Storm—

The Eyes around—had wrung them dry—
And Breaths were gathering firm
For the last Onset—when the King
Be witnessed—in the Room—

I will my Keepsakes—Signed away
What portion of me be
Assignable—and then it was
There interposed a Fly—

With Blue—uncertain stumbling Buzz—
Between the light—and me—
And then the Windows failed—and then
I could not see to see—

480

"Why do I love" You, Sir?
Because—
The Wind does not require the Grass
To answer—Wherefore when He pass
She cannot keep Her place.

Because He knows—and
Do not You—
And We know not—
Enough for Us
The Wisdom it be so—

The Lightning—never asked an Eye
Wherefore it shut—when He was by—
Because He knows it cannot speak—
And reasons not contained—
—Of Talk—

There be—preferred by Daintier Folk—
The Sunrise—Sir—compelleth Me—
Because He's Sunrise—and I see—
Therefore—Then—
I love Thee—

501

This World is not Conclusion.
A Species stands beyond—
Invisible, as Music—
But positive, as Sound—
It beckons, and it baffles—
Philosophy—don't know—
And through a Riddle, at the last—
Sagacity, must go—
To guess it, puzzles scholars—
To gain it, Men have borne
Contempt of Generations
And Crucifixion, shown—
Faith slips—and laughs, and rallies—

Blushes, if any see—
Plucks at a twig of Evidence—
And asks a Vane, the way—
Much Gesture, from the Pulpit—
Strong Hallelujahs roll—
Narcotics cannot still the Tooth
That nibbles at the soul—

508

I'm ceded—I've stopped being Theirs—
The name They dropped upon my face
With water, in the country church
Is finished using, now,
And They can put it with my Dolls,
My childhood, and the string of spools,
I've finished threading—too—

Baptized, before, without the choice,
But this time, consciously, of Grace—
Unto supremest name—
Called to my Full—The Crescent dropped—
Existence's whole Arc, filled up,
With one small Diadem.

My second Rank—too small the first—
Crowned—Crowing—on my Father's breast—
A half unconscious Queen—
But this time—Adequate—Erect,
With Will to choose, or to reject,
And I choose, just a Crown—

512

The Soul has Bandaged moments—
When too appalled to stir—
She feels some ghastly Fright come up
And stop to look at her—

Salute her—with long fingers—
Caress her freezing hair—

Sip, Goblin, from the very lips
The Lover—hovered—o'er—
Unworthy, that a thought so mean
Accost a Theme—so—fair—

The soul has moments of Escape—
When bursting all the doors—
She dances like a Bomb, abroad,
And swings upon the Hours,

As do the Bee—delirious borne—
Long Dungeoned from his Rose—
Touch Liberty—then know no more,
But Noon, and Paradise—

The Soul's retaken moments—
When, Felon led along,
With shackles on the plumed feet,
And staples, in the Song,

The Horror welcomes her, again,
These, are not brayed of Tongue—

536

The Heart asks Pleasure—first—
And then—Excuse from Pain—
And then—those little Anodynes
That deaden suffering—

And then—to go to sleep—
And then—if it should be
The will of its Inquisitor
The privilege to die—

547

I've seen a Dying Eye
Run round and round a Room—
In search of Something—as it seemed—

Then Cloudier become—
And then—obscure with Fog—
And then—be soldered down
Without disclosing what it be
'Twere blessed to have seen—

569

I reckon—when I count at all—
First—Poets—Then the Sun—
Then Summer—Then the Heaven of God—
And then—the List is done—

But, looking back—the First so seems
To Comprehend the Whole—
The Others look a needless Show—
So I write—Poets—All—

Their Summer—lasts a Solid Year—
They can afford a Sun
The East—would deem extravagant—
And if the Further Heaven—

Be Beautiful as they prepare
For Those who worship Them—
It is too difficult a Grace—
To justify the Dream—

599

There is a pain—so utter—
It swallows substance up—
Then covers the Abyss with Trance—
So Memory can step
Around—across—upon it—
As one within a Swoon—
Goes safely—where an open eye—
Would drop Him—Bone by Bone.

632

The Brain—is wider than the Sky—
For—put them side by side—
The one the other will contain
With ease—and You—beside—

The Brain is deeper than the sea—
For—hold them—Blue to Blue—
The one the other will absorb—
As Sponges—Buckets—do—

The Brain is just the weight of God—
For—Heft them—Pound for Pound—
And they will differ—if they do—
As Syllable from Sound—

640

I cannot live with You—
It would be Life—
And Life is over there—
Behind the Shelf

The Sexton keeps the Key to—
Putting up
Our Life—His Porcelain—
Like a Cup—

Discarded of the Housewife—
Quaint—or Broke—
A newer Sevres pleases—
Old Ones crack—

I could not die—with You—
For One must wait
To shut the Other's Gaze down—
You—could not—

And I—Could I stand by
And see You—freeze—
Without my Right of Frost—
Death's privilege?

Nor could I rise—with You—
Because Your Face
Would put out Jesus'—
That New Grace

Glow plain—and foreign
On my homesick Eye—
Except that You than He
Shone closer by—

They'd judge Us—How—
For You—served Heaven—You know,
Or sought to—
I could not—

Because You saturated Sight—
And I had no more Eyes
For sordid excellence
As Paradise

And were You lost, I would be—
Though My Name
Rang loudest
On the Heavenly fame—

And were You—saved—
And I—condemned to be
Where You were not—
That self—were Hell to Me—

So We must meet apart—
You there—I—here—
With just the Door ajar
That Oceans are—and Prayer—
And that White Sustenance—
Despair—

650

Pain—has an Element of Blank—
It cannot recollect
When it begun—or if there were
A time when it was not—

It has no Future—but itself—
Its Infinite contain
Its Past—enlightened to perceive
New Periods—of Pain.

657

I dwell in Possibility—
A fairer House than Prose—
More numerous of Windows—
Superior—for Doors—

Of Chambers as the Cedars—
Impregnable of Eye—
And for an Everlasting Roof
The Gambrels of the Sky—

Of Visitors—the fairest—
For Occupation—This—
The spreading wide my narrow Hands
To gather Paradise—

668

"Nature" is what we see—
The Hill—the Afternoon—
Squirrel—Eclipse—the Bumble bee—
Nay—Nature is Heaven—
Nature is what we hear—
The Bobolink—the Sea—
Thunder—the Cricket—
Nay—Nature is Harmony—
Nature is what we know—
Yet have no art to say—

So impotent Our Wisdom is
To her Simplicity.

709

Publication—is the Auction
Of the Mind of Man—
Poverty—be justifying
For so foul a thing

Possibly—but We—would rather
From Our Garret go
White—Unto the White Creator—
Than invest—Our Snow—

Thought belong to Him who gave it—
Then—to Him Who bear
Its Corporal illustration—Sell
The Royal Air—

In the Parcel—Be the Merchant
Of the Heavenly Grace—
But reduce no Human Spirit
To Disgrace of Price—

744

Remorse—is Memory—awake—
Her Parties all astir—
A Presence of Departed Acts—
At window—and at Door—

Its Past—set down before the Soul
And lighted with a Match—
Perusal—to facilitate—
And help Belief to stretch—

Remorse is cureless—the Disease
Not even God—can heal—
For 'tis His institution—and
The Adequate of Hell—

754

My Life had stood—a Loaded Gun—
In Corners—till a Day
The Owner passed—identified—
And carried Me away—

And now We roam in Sovereign Woods—
And now We hunt the Doe—
And every time I speak for Him—
The Mountains straight reply—

And do I smile, such cordial light
Upon the Valley glow—
It is as a Vesuvian face
Had let its pleasure through—

And when at Night—Our good Day done—
I guard My Master's Head—
'Tis better than the Eider-Duck's
Deep Pillow—to have shared—

To foe of His—I'm deadly foe—
None stir the second time—
On whom I lay a Yellow Eye—
Or an emphatic Thumb—

Though I than He—may longer live
He longer must—than I—
For I have but the power to kill,
Without—the power to die—

959

A loss of something ever felt I—
The first that I could recollect
Bereft I was—of what I knew not
Too young that any should suspect

A Mourner walked among the children
I notwithstanding went about

As one bemoaning a Dominion
Itself the only Prince cast out—

Elder, Today, a session wiser
And fainter, too, as Wiseness is—
I find myself still softly searching
For my Delinquent Palaces—

And a Suspicion, like a Finger
Touches my Forehead now and then
That I am looking oppositely
For the site of the Kingdom of Heaven—

986

A narrow Fellow in the Grass
Occasionally rides—
You may have met Him—did you not
His notice sudden is—

The Grass divides as with a Comb—
A spotted shaft is seen—
And then it closes at your feet
And opens further on—

He likes a Boggy Acre
A floor too cool for Corn—
Yet when a Boy, and Barefoot—
I more than once at Noon
Have passed, I thought, a Whip lash
Unbraiding in the Sun
When stooping to secure it
It wrinkled, and was gone—

Several of Nature's People
I know, and they know me—
I feel for them a transport
Of cordiality—

But never met this Fellow
Attended, or alone

Without a tighter breathing
And Zero at the Bone—

1072

Title divine—is mine!
The Wife—without the Sign!
Acute Degree—conferred on me—
Empress of Calvary!
Royal—all but the Crown!
Betrothed—without the swoon
God sends us Women—
When you—hold—Garnet to Garnet—
Gold—to Gold—
Born—Bridalled—Shrouded—
In a Day—
Tri Victory
"My Husband"—women say—
Stroking the Melody—
Is *this*—the way?

1078

The Bustle in a House
The Morning after Death
Is solemnest of industries
Enacted upon Earth—

The Sweeping up the Heart
And putting Love away
We shall not want to use again
Until Eternity.

1100

The last Night that She lived
It was a Common Night
Except the Dying—this to Us
Made Nature different

We noticed smallest things—
Things overlooked before
By this great light upon our Minds
Italicized—as 'twere.

As We went out and in
Between Her final Room
And Rooms where Those to be alive
Tomorrow were, a Blame

That Others could exist
While She must finish quite
A Jealousy for Her arose
So nearly infinite—

We waited while She passed—
It was a narrow time—
Too jostled were Our Souls to speak
At length the notice came.

She mentioned, and forgot—
Then lightly as a Reed
Bent to the Water, struggled scarce—
Consented, and was dead—

And We—We placed the Hair—
And drew the Head erect—
And then an awful leisure was
Belief to regulate—

1129

Tell all the Truth but tell it slant—
Success in Circuit lies
Too bright for our infirm Delight
The Truth's superb surprise

As Lightning to the Children eased
With explanation kind
The Truth must dazzle gradually
Or every man be blind—

1138

A Spider sewed at Night
Without a Light
Upon an Arc of White.

If Ruff it was of Dame
Or Shroud of Gnome
Himself himself inform.

Of Immortality
His Strategy
Was Physiognomy.

1142

The Props assist the House
Until the House is built
And then the Props withdraw
And adequate, erect,
The House support itself
And cease to recollect
The Auger and the Carpenter—
Just such a retrospect
Hath the perfected Life—
A past of Plank and Nail
And slowness—then the Scaffolds drop
Affirming it a Soul.

1705

Volcanoes be in Sicily
And South America
I judge from my Geography—
Volcanoes nearer here
A Lava step at any time
Am I inclined to climb—
A Crater I may contemplate
Vesuvius at Home.

1770

Experiment escorts us last—
His pungent company
Will not allow an Axiom
An Opportunity

1732

My life closed twice before its close—
It yet remains to see
If Immortality unveil
A third event to me

So huge, so hopeless to conceive
As these that twice befell.
Parting is all we know of heaven,
And all we need of hell.

Robert Frost

[1874–1963]

Like Walt Whitman before him, Robert Frost yearned to become America's foremost poet. Aiming for both critical and popular acclaim, Frost hoped to achieve recognition as a major poet and to reach the widest possible audience. And although he did succeed in becoming a popular poet (perhaps the most popular in America's history), in the minds of some readers his very popularity diminished his critical stature. Frost himself, however, was partly responsible for this. The image he projected—folksy, lovable, homespun—undercut his reputation as a major poet. Even today, with Frost's poetic stature amply acknowledged, he is occasionally seen as a less serious, less impressive, less demanding, and hence less important poet than his contemporaries Ezra Pound, T. S. Eliot, and Wallace Stevens.

There is a measure of truth in this assessment, perhaps, but only a small measure. Frost's poems are easier to read than those of Pound, Eliot, or Stevens: his familiar vocabulary and traditional forms enhance their accessibility. But his poems are neither simple nor easy to understand. Their diction is more richly allusive and connotative than at first may appear. Their paraphrasable thought is subtler and more profound than an initial reading might suggest. Moreover, their form, though traditional, is more intricately wrought and more decisively experimental than is generally recognized. Before turning to consider these claims, we should be aware of the course of Frost's poetic career, particularly of his popularity as an honored national poet, who, ironically, was first recognized abroad rather than at home.

Although Robert Frost is considered a New England farmer–poet who captures in his verse the tang of Yankee speech, he was born in San Francisco and lived there until the age of eleven, when his family moved to Lawrence, Massachusetts. He attended high school in Lawrence and was covaledictorian of his graduating class with Elinor White, whom he later married. Frost continued his education at Dartmouth College, where he remained for only one term, and later at Harvard University, where he studied for two years without taking a degree. After working at a succession of odd jobs including farming and factory work, Frost taught at Pinkerton Academy, where from 1906 to 1910 he reformed the English syllabus, directed theatrical productions, and wrote many of the poems later included in his first book, *A Boy's Will.*

In 1911, in an attempt to attract the attention of prominent and influential members in the literary world, he sold his farm in Derry, New Hampshire, and moved with his family to England. There he met and received the support of Ezra Pound, who helped secure publication of his first two volumes of poems, and of Edward Thomas, who reviewed them perceptively. Having launched his career, Frost returned to America in 1915 and quickly secured an American publisher—Henry Holt and Co.—for the two books published in England, *A Boy's Will* (1913) and *North of Boston* (1914), and for subsequent volumes as well. With the publication in 1916 of *Mountain Interval,* Frost's fame grew. In 1917, and periodically thereafter, he was poet in residence at Amherst College and served in a similar capacity at various other colleges and universities including Dartmouth, Wesleyan, Michigan, Harvard, and Yale. Frost received awards and prizes, among them the Bollingen Poetry Prize (1963) and four Pulitzer Prizes (1924, 1931, 1937, and 1943). In addition many honorary degrees, including ones from Oxford and Cambridge universities, were conferred on him. Although Frost was fond of joking that he could make a blanket of the many academic hoods he had acquired, he valued them, particularly those from the British institutions. Later in his life Frost was appointed goodwill emissary to South America and the Soviet Union. At the time he was also the only American poet honored with an invitation to read his work at a presidential inauguration. In January 1961, at the inauguration of John F. Kennedy, Frost read "The Gift Outright" and another poem he had composed for the occasion.

This brief summary of Frost's career, however, oversimplifies what was in reality a more complex and arduous process. Initially an obscure writer, Frost experienced difficulty in breaking into print in a significant way. He later struggled with the decline of his poetic powers, most of his best work being produced when he was younger. And more tragically, he suffered the deaths of his wife and three of his children, one of whom committed suicide. He also saw his sister and one of his daughters succumb to mental illness. And finally, despite his many prizes and awards, Frost was bitter that he never won a Nobel Prize. He died in 1963, two weeks short of his eighty-ninth birthday.

What accounts for Frost's fame and popularity? Three things, at least: his shrewd management of his career, including the cultivation of his poetic image; his use of familiar subjects, especially the natural world and people engaged in recognizable activities; his accessible language and apparent simplicity of thought. From the beginning, Frost skillfully managed his poetic career, going abroad to England to win the approval of the prominent poets and critics of his day. Frost, of course, did not plan every step of his rise to fame; rather he trusted to his highly developed instinct for sizing up opportunities and capitalizing on them. As William Pritchard explains in *Robert Frost: A Literary Life Reconsidered,* Frost retrospectively structured his literary life as one of adversity overcome. The most important aspect of this biographical semifictionalizing was Frost's portrayal of himself as a literary exile unappreciated in his home country. Allied with this biographical myth-making was Frost's control over his public image. He refused, for example, to read his darker, more skeptical poems in public, preferring instead to reveal his more congenial, folksy side. And he carefully masked from public exposure his hunger for fame and an occasional nasty denigration of those poets he considered his strongest rivals.

More important to his popularity than his masterly manipulation of his public persona, however, is the readability of his poetry. Frost avoids obscure language, preferring the familiar word and the idiomatic phrase. He also shuns foreign words and shies away from all but the scantiest of references to economic, literary, and political history. And instead of the structural openness, fragmentation, and discontinuity favored by some of his contemporaries, Frost used traditional poetic forms characterized by coherence and continuity.

That Frost's poems are relatively easy to read does not mean that they are necessarily easy to understand. Frost is a master of concealment, of saying one thing in terms of another, especially of saying two or more things simultaneously. Even his most accessible poems such as "Birches," "Mending Wall," and "The Road Not Taken" contain clear invitations to consider their symbolic ramifications. The symbolic nature of these poems doesn't manifest itself immediately. To appreciate the fullness of Frost's achievement, we need to read with attention to their symbolic detail, whether we are reading the meditative blank verse of "Birches" or "Mending Wall" or the lyrical descriptions of "Desert Places" or "Stopping by Woods on a Snowy Evening."

It is also a mistake to assume, on the basis of a familiarity with a few of Frost's more famous lyrics, that his poetry lacks either drama or humor. "Departmental" reveals Frost's humorous side, while "Home Burial" shows him at work in a longer, more dramatic form. Though his poems are certainly serious, they are not solemn. This is as true of "Stopping by Woods" and "The Road Not Taken" as it is for "The Silken Tent," a witty extended comparison between a woman and a pitched tent; "Provide, Provide," a pragmatic set of admonitions about how to get on in the world; and "A Considerable Speck," a satirical jab at human limitations, particularly the performances of writers. Moreover, Frost himself warned us against taking him too seriously. Although we cannot completely trust him in such matters since he enjoyed teasing his audiences, we can at least regard his work as a mixture of playfulness and seriousness. "If it is with outer seriousness," he once remarked, "it must with inner humor; if with inner seriousness, then with outer humor."

Complicating matters further is Frost's view of nature. More often than not, nature appears as a powerful, dangerous, and cruel force, its purpose and design not immediately apparent. Frost avoids a simple representation of the relationship between the natural and human worlds. He does not share Emerson's belief in nature as a moral teacher. He does not believe, for example, that in reading nature we discover moral and spiritual truths. That romantic view is questioned in poems like "Desert Places" and "The Most of It," where nature seems to express "nothing" to the human observer. Frost's response to nature, essentially, is to question its meaning for human beings, to wonder skeptically just how much it does express. A poem like "Tree at My Window" explores this issue in a way that may at first appear familiar but that changes as the poem progresses. This poem seems to suggest that there are definite connections between trees and people—that the human and the natural worlds intersect. But it also points to radical differences between the two worlds, differences that separate them more than their similarities bind them. At stake in this and many of Frost's other nature poems are the Emersonian and Whitmanesque transcendentalist ideas, in which nature and man form part of a harmonious whole, a unity exemplified by poems such as "The Tuft of Flowers" and "Two Look at Two."

The complexity and richness of Frost's vision of nature are paralleled by the subtlety of his technical achievement. Though he worked in traditional forms—sonnet, heroic couplet, blank verse, four-line stanza—the effects he wrought in them are remarkable for their range and versatility. To take just one example, consider his sonnets, which include poems in both of the traditional forms, Shakespearean and Petrarchan. "Putting in the Seed" is constructed according to the Shakespearean, or English, pattern with three quatrains and a concluding couplet (though Frost alters the rhyme pattern slightly). "Design" follows the Petrarchan model: an octave of eight lines followed by a sestet of six. The octave of "Design" describes a natural scene (a white spider finding on a white flower a white moth that it kills and devours). The sestet explores the significance of the event. Though conventional in logical organization, "Design" exhibits a variation from the Petrarchan rhyme scheme: *abba abba cde cde* (or *cd cd cd*). Frost's poem uses only three rhymes throughout both octave and sestet: *abba abba acc caa.*

Frost's sonnets often diverge in some way from the traditional sonnet and thus make something new and fresh of the form. "Mowing," for example, while composed according to the Petrarchan structure, contains a strong concluding couplet more characteristic of the Shakespearean sonnet. It also varies from the rhyme scheme of both traditional patterns, though using the same number of different sounds as the Shakespearean form: *abca bdec dfeg fg.* The poem displays a curious use of overlapping sound effects that Frost worked out more elaborately and systematically in other lyrics. Other sonnet variations appear in "The Silken Tent," which is constructed as a single sentence spun out over the fourteen lines in a Shakespearean pattern. Working against that rhyme scheme, however, is a logical structure more characteristic of the Petrarchan division into two major sections, with a turn at the ninth line. Such hybrid sonnets are accompanied by other sonnet experiments such as "Once by the Pacific," in seven couplets rhyming *aa bb cc dd ee ff gg,* and "Acquainted with the Night," composed in the interlocking rhymes of *terza rima: aba bcb cdc ded ee.*

Frost was a skilled wordsmith who cared about the sounds of his sentences. He noted more than once how "the sentence sound says more than the words"; how "tones of voice" can "mean more than words." In such voice tones Frost heard the sounds of sense and captured them in his verse, heightening their expressiveness by combining the inflections of ordinary speech with the measured regularity of meter. Because Frost's achievement in this regard surpasses that of most other modern American poets, we should be particularly attentive to the way he makes poetry out of the spoken word. His poems often mask the most elegant and subtle of his technical accomplishments. Perhaps the best way to read Frost's poems is to approach them as performances, as poetic acts of skillful daring, of risks taken, of technical dangers overcome. In doing so we may share the pleasure Frost took in poetic performance. In addition, we can see how Frost's poetry often "begins in delight and ends in wisdom," offering along the way what he called "a momentary stay against confusion."

Mowing

There was never a sound beside the wood but one,
And that was my long scythe whispering to the ground.
What was it it whispered? I knew not well myself;
Perhaps it was something about the heat of the sun,
Something, perhaps, about the lack of sound—
And that was why it whispered and did not speak.
It was no dream of the gift of idle hours,
Or easy gold at the hand of fay or elf:
Anything more than the truth would have seemed too weak
To the earnest love that laid the swale in rows,
Not without feeble-pointed spikes of flowers
(Pale orchises), and scared a bright green snake.
The fact is the sweetest dream that labor knows.
My long scythe whispered and left the hay to make.

Storm Fear

When the wind works against us in the dark,
And pelts with snow
The lower chamber window on the east,
And whispers with a sort of stifled bark,
The beast,
"Come out! Come out"—
It costs no inward struggle not to go,
Ah, no!
I count our strength,
Two and a child,
Those of us not asleep subdued to mark
How the cold creeps as the fire dies at length,—
How drifts are piled,
Dooryard and road ungraded,
Till even the comforting barn grows far away,
And my heart owns a doubt
Whether 'tis in us to arise with day
And save ourselves unaided.

The Tuft of Flowers

I went to turn the grass once after one
Who mowed it in the dew before the sun.

The dew was gone that made his blade so keen
Before I came to view the leveled scene.

I looked for him behind an isle of trees;
I listened for his whetstone on the breeze.

But he had gone his way, the grass all mown,
And I must be, as he had been,—alone,

"As all must be," I said within my heart,
"Whether they work together or apart."

But as I said it, swift there passed me by
On noiseless wing a bewildered butterfly,

Seeking with memories grown dim o'er night
Some resting flower of yesterday's delight.

And once I marked his flight go round and round,
As where some flower lay withering on the ground.

And then he flew as far as eye could see,
And then on tremulous wing came back to me.

I thought of questions that have no reply,
And would have turned to toss the grass to dry;

But he turned first, and led my eye to look
At a tall tuft of flowers beside a brook,

A leaping tongue of bloom the scythe had spared
Beside a reedy brook the scythe had bared.

The mower in the dew had loved them thus,
By leaving them to flourish, not for us,

Nor yet to draw one thought of ours to him,
But from sheer morning gladness at the brim.

The butterfly and I had lit upon,
Nevertheless, a message from the dawn,

That made me hear the wakening birds around,
And hear his long scythe whispering to the ground,

And feel a spirit kindred to my own;
So that henceforth I worked no more alone;

But glad with him, I worked as with his aid,
And weary, sought at noon with him the shade;

And dreaming, as it were, held brotherly speech
With one whose thought I had not hoped to reach.

"Men work together," I told him from the heart,
"Whether they work together or apart."

Home Burial

He saw her from the bottom of the stairs
Before she saw him. She was starting down,
Looking back over her shoulder at some fear.
She took a doubtful step and then undid it
To raise herself and look again. He spoke
Advancing toward her: "What is it you see
From up there always—for I want to know."
She turned and sank upon her skirts at that,
And her face changed from terrified to dull.
He said to gain time: "What is it you see"
Mounting until she cowered under him.
"I will find out now—you must tell me, dear."
She, in her place, refused him any help
With the least stiffening of her neck and silence.
She let him look, sure that he wouldn't see,
Blind creature; and awhile he didn't see.
But at last he murmured, "Oh," and again, "Oh."

"What is it—what?" she said.
"Just that I see."

"You don't," she challenged. "Tell me what it is."

"The wonder is I didn't see at once.
I never noticed it from here before.
I must be wonted to it—that's the reason.
The little graveyard where my people are!
So small the window frames the whole of it.
Not so much larger than a bedroom, is it?
There are three stones of slate and one of marble,
Broad-shouldered little slabs there in the sunlight
On the sidehill. We haven't to mind *those.*
But I understand: it is not the stones,
But the child's mound—"
"Don't, don't, don't,
don't," she cried.

She withdrew shrinking from beneath his arm
That rested on the banister, and slid downstairs;
And turned on him with such a daunting look,

He said twice over before he knew himself:
"Can't a man speak of his own child he's lost?"

"Not you! Oh, where's my hat? Oh, I don't need it!
I must get out of here. I must get air.
I don't know rightly whether any man can."

"Amy! Don't go to someone else this time.
Listen to me. I won't come down the stairs."
He sat and fixed his chin between his fists.
"There's something I should like to ask you, dear."

"You don't know how to ask it."
                                        "Help me, then."

Her fingers moved the latch for all reply.

"My words are nearly always an offense.
I don't know how to speak of anything
So as to please you. But I might be taught
I should suppose. I can't say I see how.
A man must partly give up being a man
With women-folk. We could have some arrangement
By which I'd bind myself to keep hands off
Anything special you're a-mind to name.
Though I don't like such things 'twixt those that love.
Two that don't love can't live together without them.
But two that do can't live together with them."
She moved the latch a little. "Don't—don't go.
Don't carry it to someone else this time.
Tell me about it if it's something human.
Let me into your grief. I'm not so much
Unlike other folks as your standing there
Apart would make me out. Give me my chance.
I do think, though, you overdo it a little.
What was it brought you up to think it the thing
To take your mother-loss of a first child
So inconsolably—in the face of love.
You'd think his memory might be satisfied—"

"There you go sneering now!"
                                        "I'm not, I'm not!

You make me angry. I'll come down to you.
God, what a woman! And it's come to this,
A man can't speak of his own child that's dead."

"You can't because you don't know how to speak.
If you had any feelings, you that dug
With your own hand—how could you?—his little grave;
I saw you from that very window there,
Making the gravel leap and leap in air,
Leap up, like that, like that, and land so lightly
And roll back down the mound beside the hole.
I thought, Who is that man? I didn't know you.
And I crept down the stairs and up the stairs
To look again, and still your spade kept lifting.
Then you came in. I heard your rumbling voice
Out in the kitchen, and I don't know why,
But I went near to see with my own eyes.
You could sit there with the stains on your shoes
Of the fresh earth from your own baby's grave
And talk about your everyday concerns.
You had stood the spade up against the wall
Outside there in the entry, for I saw it."

"I shall laugh the worst laugh I ever laughed.
I'm cursed. God, if I don't believe I'm cursed."

"I can repeat the very words you were saying.
'Three foggy mornings and one rainy day
Will rot the best birch fence a man can build.'
Think of it, talk like that at such a time!
What had how long it takes a birch to rot
To do with what was in the darkened parlor?
You *couldn't* care! The nearest friends can go
With anyone to death, comes so far short
They might as well not try to go at all.
No, from the time when one is sick to death,
One is alone, and he dies more alone.
Friends make pretense of following to the grave,
But before one is in it, their minds are turned
And making the best of their way back to life
And living people, and things they understand.

But the world's evil. I won't have grief so
If I can change it. Oh, I won't, I won't!"

"There, you have said it all and you feel better.
You won't go now. You're crying. Close the door.
The heart's gone out of it: why keep it up.
Amy! There's someone coming down the road!"

"*You*—oh, you think the talk is all. I must go—
Somewhere out of this house. How can I make you—"

"If—you—do!" She was opening the door wider.
"Where do you mean to go? First tell me that.
I'll follow and bring you back by force. I *will!*—"

The Hill Wife

LONELINESS

HER WORD

One ought not to have to care
    So much as you and I
Care when the birds come round the house
    To seem to say good-by;

Or care so much when they come back
    With whatever it is they sing;
The truth being we are as much
    Too glad for the one thing

As we are too sad for the other here—
    With birds that fill their breasts
But with each other and themselves
    And their built or driven nests.

HOUSE FEAR

Always—I tell you this they learned—
Always at night when they returned
To the lonely house from far away
To lamps unlighted and fire gone gray,
They learned to rattle the lock and key
To give whatever might chance to be

Warning and time to be off in flight:
And preferring the out- to the in-door night,
They learned to leave the house-door wide
Until they had lit the lamp inside.

THE SMILE

HER WORD

I didn't like the way he went away.
That smile! It never came of being gay.
Still he smiled—did you see him?—I was sure!
Perhaps because we gave him only bread
And the wretch knew from that that we were poor.
Perhaps because he let us give instead
Of seizing from us as he might have seized.
Perhaps he mocked at us for being wed,
Or being very young (and he was pleased
To have a vision of us old and dead).
I wonder how far down the road he's got.
He's watching from the woods as like as not.

THE OFT-REPEATED DREAM

She had no saying dark enough
    For the dark pine that kept
Forever trying the window-latch
    Of the room where they slept.

The tireless but ineffectual hands
    That with every futile pass
Made the great tree seem as a little bird
    Before the mystery of glass!

It never had been inside the room,
    And only one of the two
Was afraid in an oft-repeated dream
    Of what the tree might do.

THE IMPULSE

It was too lonely for her there,
    And too wild,
And since there were but two of them,
    And no child,

And work was little in the house,
    She was free,
And followed where he furrowed field,
    Or felled tree.

She rested on a log and tossed
    The fresh chips,
With a song only to herself
    On her lips.

And once she went to break a bough
    Of black alder.
She strayed so far she scarcely heard
    When he called her—

And didn't answer—didn't speak—
    Or return.
She stood, and then she ran and hid
    In the fern.

He never found her, though he looked
    Everywhere,
And he asked at her mother's house
    Was she there.

Sudden and swift and light as that
    The ties gave,
And he learned of finalities
    Besides the grave.

After Apple-Picking

My long two-pointed ladder's sticking through a tree
Toward heaven still,
And there's a barrel that I didn't fill
Beside it, and there may be two or three
Apples I didn't pick upon some bough.
But I am done with apple-picking now.
Essence of winter sleep is on the night,
The scent of apples: I am drowsing off.
I cannot rub the strangeness from my sight

I got from looking through a pane of glass
I skimmed this morning from the drinking trough
And held against the world of hoary grass.
It melted, and I let it fall and break.
But I was well
Upon my way to sleep before it fell,
And I could tell
What form my dreaming was about to take.
Magnified apples appear and disappear,
Stem end and blossom end,
And every fleck of russet showing clear.
My instep arch not only keeps the ache,
It keeps the pressure of a ladder-round.
I feel the ladder sway as the boughs bend.
And I keep hearing from the cellar bin
The rumbling sound
Of load on load of apples coming in.
For I have had too much
Of apple-picking: I am overtired
Of the great harvest I myself desired.
There were ten thousand thousand fruit to touch,
Cherish in hand, lift down, and not let fall.
For all
That struck the earth,
No matter if not bruised or spiked with stubble,
Went surely to the cider-apple heap
As of no worth.
One can see what will trouble
This sleep of mine, whatever sleep it is.
Were he not gone,
The woodchuck could say whether it's like his
Long sleep, as I describe its coming on,
Or just some human sleep.

The Wood-Pile

Out walking in the frozen swamp one gray day,
I paused and said, "I will turn back from here.
No, I will go on farther—and we shall see."
The hard snow held me, save where now and then
One foot went through. The view was all in lines

Straight up and down of tall slim trees
Too much alike to mark or name a place by
So as to say for certain I was here
Or somewhere else: I was just far from home.
A small bird flew before me. He was careful
To put a tree between us when he lighted,
And say no word to tell me who he was
Who was so foolish as to think what *he* thought.
He thought that I was after him for a feather—
The white one in his tail; like one who takes
Everything said as personal to himself.
One flight out sideways would have undeceived him.
And then there was a pile of wood for which
I forgot him and let his little fear
Carry him off the way I might have gone,
Without so much as wishing him good-night.
He went behind it to make his last stand.
It was a cord of maple, cut and split
And piled—and measured, four by four by eight.
And not another like it could I see.
No runner tracks in this year's snow looped near it.
And it was older sure than this year's cutting,
Or even last year's or the year's before.
The wood was gray and the bark warping off it
And the pile somewhat sunken. Clematis
Had wound strings round and round it like a bundle.
What held it though on one side was a tree
Still growing, and on one a stake and prop,
These latter about to fall. I thought that only
Someone who lived in turning to fresh tasks
Could so forget his handiwork on which
He spent himself, the labor of his ax,
And leave it there far from a useful fireplace
To warm the frozen swamp as best it could
With the slow smokeless burning of decay.

An Old Man's Winter Night

All out-of-doors looked darkly in at him
Through the thin frost, almost in separate stars,
That gathers on the pane in empty rooms.

What kept his eyes from giving back the gaze
Was the lamp tilted near them in his hand.
What kept him from remembering what it was
That brought him to that creaking room was age.
He stood with barrels round him—at a loss.
And having scared the cellar under him
In clomping here, he scared it once again
In clomping off;—and scared the outer night,
Which has its sounds, familiar, like the roar
Of trees and crack of branches, common things,
But nothing so like beating on a box.
A light he was to no one but himself
Where now he sat, concerned with he knew what,
A quiet light, and then not even that.
He consigned to the moon, such as she was,
So late-arising, to the broken moon
As better than the sun in any case
For such a charge, his snow upon the roof,
His icicles along the wall to keep;
And slept. The log that shifted with a jolt
Once in the stove, disturbed him and he shifted,
And eased his heavy breathing, but still slept.
One aged man—one man—can't keep a house,
A farm, a countryside, or if he can,
It's thus he does it of a winter night.

Birches

When I see birches bend to left and right
Across the lines of straighter darker trees,
I like to think some boy's been swinging them.
But swinging doesn't bend them down to stay
As ice-storms do. Often you must have seen them
Loaded with ice a sunny winter morning
After a rain. They click upon themselves
As the breeze rises, and turn many-colored
As the stir cracks and crazes their enamel.
Soon the sun's warmth makes them shed crystal shells
Shattering and avalanching on the snow-crust—
Such heaps of broken glass to sweep away
You'd think the inner dome of heaven had fallen.

They are dragged to the withered bracken by the load,
And they seem not to break; though once they are bowed
So low for long, they never right themselves:
You may see their trunks arching in the woods
Years afterwards, trailing their leaves on the ground
Like girls on hands and knees that throw their hair
Before them over their heads to dry in the sun.
But I was going to say when Truth broke in
With all her matter-of-fact about the ice-storm,
I should prefer to have some boy bend them
As he went out and in to fetch the cows—
Some boy too far from town to learn baseball,
Whose only play was what he found himself,
Summer or winter, and could play alone.
One by one he subdued his father's trees
By riding them down over and over again
Until he took the stiffness out of them,
And not one but hung limp, not one was left
For him to conquer. He learned all there was
To learn about not launching out too soon
And so not carrying the tree away
Clear to the ground. He always kept his poise
To the top branches, climbing carefully
With the same pains you use to fill a cup
Up to the brim, and even above the brim.
Then he flung outward, feet first, with a swish,
Kicking his way down through the air to the ground.
So was I once myself a swinger of birches.
And so I dream of going back to be.
It's when I'm weary of considerations,
And life is too much like a pathless wood
Where your face burns and tickles with the cobwebs
Broken across it, and one eye is weeping
From a twig's having lashed across it open.
I'd like to get away from earth awhile
And then come back to it and begin over.
May no fate willfully misunderstand me
And half grant what I wish and snatch me away
Not to return. Earth's the right place for love:
I don't know where it's likely to go better.
I'd like to go by climbing a birch tree,
And climb black branches up a snow-white trunk

Toward heaven, till the tree could bear no more,
But dipped its top and set me down again.
That would be good both going and coming back.
One could do worse than be a swinger of birches.

"Out, Out—"

The buzz saw snarled and rattled in the yard
And made dust and dropped stove-length sticks of wood,
Sweet-scented stuff when the breeze drew across it.
And from there those that lifted eyes could count
Five mountain ranges one behind the other
Under the sunset far into Vermont.
And the saw snarled and rattled, snarled and rattled,
As it ran light, or had to bear a load.
And nothing happened: day was all but done.
Call it a day, I wish they might have said
To please the boy by giving him the half hour
That a boy counts so much when saved from work.
His sister stood beside them in her apron
To tell them "Supper." At the word, the saw,
As if to prove saws knew what supper meant,
Leaped out at the boy's hand, or seemed to leap—
He must have given the hand. However it was,
Neither refused the meeting. But the hand!
The boy's first outcry was a rueful laugh,
As he swung toward them holding up the hand,
Half in appeal, but half as if to keep
The life from spilling. Then the boy saw all—
Since he was old enough to know, big boy
Doing a man's work, though a child at heart—
He saw all spoiled. "Don't let him cut my hand off—
The doctor, when he comes. Don't let him, sister!"
So. But the hand was gone already.
The doctor put him in the dark of ether.
He lay and puffed his lips out with his breath.
And then—the watcher at his pulse took fright.
No one believed. They listened at his heart.
Little—less—nothing!—and that ended it.
No more to build on there. And they, since they
Were not the one dead, turned to their affairs.

The Ax-Helve

I've known ere now an interfering branch
Of alder catch my lifted ax behind me.
But that was in the woods, to hold my hand
From striking at another alder's roots,
And that was, as I say, an alder branch.
This was a man, Baptiste, who stole one day
Behind me on the snow in my own yard
Where I was working at the chopping-block,
And cutting nothing not cut down already.
He caught my ax expertly on the rise,
When all my strength put forth was in his favor,
Held it a moment where it was, to calm me,
Then took it from me—and I let him take it.
I didn't know him well enough to know
What it was all about. There might be something
He had in mind to say to a bad neighbor
He might prefer to say to him disarmed.
But all he had to tell me in French-English
Was what he thought of—not me, but my ax,
Me only as I took my ax to heart.
It was the bad ax-helve someone had sold me—
'Made on machine,' he said, plowing the grain
With a thick thumbnail to show how it ran
Across the handle's long drawn serpentine,
Like the two strokes across a dollar sign.
'You give her one good crack, she's snap raght off.
Den where's your hax-ead flying t'rough de hair?'
Admitted; and yet, what was that to him?

'Come on my house and I put you one in
What's las' awhile—good hick'ry what's grow crooked.
De second growt' I cut myself—tough, tough!'

Something to sell? That wasn't how it sounded.

'Den when you say you come? It's cost you nothing.
Tonaght?'

As well tonight as any night.

Beyond an over-warmth of kitchen stove
My welcome differed from no other welcome.

Baptiste knew best why I was where I was.
So long as he would leave enough unsaid,
I shouldn't mind his being overjoyed
(If overjoyed he was) at having got me
Where I must judge if what he knew about an ax
That not everybody else knew was to count
For nothing in the measure of a neighbor.
Hard if, though cast away for life with Yankees,
A Frenchman couldn't get his human rating!

Mrs. Baptiste came in and rocked a chair
That had as many motions as the world:
One back and forward, in and out of shadow,
That got her nowhere; one more gradual,
Sideways, that would have run her on the stove
In time, had she not realized her danger
And caught herself up bodily, chair and all,
And set herself back where she started from.
'She ain't spick too much Henglish—dat's too bad.'

I was afraid, in brightening first on me,
Then on Baptiste, as if she understood
What passed between us, she was only feigning.
Baptiste was anxious for her; but no more
Than for himself, so placed he couldn't hope
To keep his bargain of the morning with me
In time to keep me from suspecting him
Of really never having meant to keep it.

Needlessly soon he had his ax-helves out,
A quiverful to choose from, since he wished me
To have the best he had, or had to spare—
Not for me to ask which, when what he took
Had beauties he had to point me out at length
To insure their not being wasted on me.
He liked to have it slender as a whipstock,
Free from the least knot, equal to the strain
Of bending like a sword across the knee.
He showed me that the lines of a good helve
Were native to the grain before the knife
Expressed them, and its curves were no false curves
Put on it from without. And there its strength lay
For the hard work. He chafed its long white body

From end to end with his rough hand shut round it.
He tried it at the eye-hole in the ax-head.
'Hahn, hahn,' he mused, 'don't need much taking down.'
Baptiste knew how to make a short job long
For love of it, and yet not waste time either.

Do you know, what we talked about was knowledge?
Baptiste on his defense about the children
He kept from school, or did his best to keep—
Whatever school and children and our doubts
Of laid-on education had to do
With the curves of his ax-helves and his having
Used these unscrupulously to bring me
To see for once the inside of his house.
Was I desired in friendship, partly as someone
To leave it to, whether the right to hold
Such doubts of education should depend
Upon the education of those who held them?

But now he brushed the shavings from his knee
And stood the ax there on its horse's hoof,
Erect, but not without its waves, as when
The snake stood up for evil in the Garden,—
Top-heavy with a heaviness his short,
Thick hand made light of, steel-blue chin drawn down
And in a little—a French touch in that.
Baptiste drew back and squinted at it, pleased;
'See how she's cock her head!'

Putting in the Seed

You come to fetch me from my work tonight
When supper's on the table, and we'll see
If I can leave off burying the white
Soft petals fallen from the apple tree
(Soft petals, yes, but not so barren quite,
Mingled with these, smooth bean and wrinkled pea;)
And go along with you ere you lose sight
Of what you came for and become like me,
Slave to a springtime passion for the earth.
How Love burns through the Putting in the Seed

On through the watching for that early birth
When, just as the soil tarnishes with weed,
The sturdy seedling with arched body comes
Shouldering its way and shedding the earth crumbs.

The Oven Bird

There is a singer everyone has heard,
Loud, a mid-summer and a mid-wood bird,
Who makes the solid tree trunks sound again.
He says that leaves are old and that for flowers
Mid-summer is to spring as one to ten.
He says the early petal-fall is past,
When pear and cherry bloom went down in showers
On sunny days a moment overcast;
And comes that other fall we name the fall.
He says the highway dust is over all.
The bird would cease and be as other birds
But that he knows in singing not to sing.
The question that he frames in all but words
Is what to make of a diminished thing.

Fire and Ice

Some say the world will end in fire,
Some say in ice.
From what I've tasted of desire
I hold with those who favor fire.
But if it had to perish twice,
I think I know enough of hate
To say that for destruction ice
Is also great
And would suffice.

Nothing Gold Can Stay

Nature's first green is gold,
Her hardest hue to hold.
Her early leaf's a flower;
But only so an hour.

Then leaf subsides to leaf.
So Eden sank to grief,
So dawn goes down to day.
Nothing gold can stay.

The Need of Being Versed in Country Things

The house had gone to bring again
To the midnight sky a sunset glow.
Now the chimney was all of the house that stood,
Like a pistil after the petals go.

The barn opposed across the way,
That would have joined the house in flame
Had it been the will of the wind, was left
To bear forsaken the place's name.

No more it opened with all one end
For teams that came by the stony road
To drum on the floor with scurrying hoofs
And brush the mow with the summer load.

The birds that came to it through the air
At broken windows flew out and in,
Their murmur more like the sigh we sigh
From too much dwelling on what has been.

Yet for them the lilac renewed its leaf,
And the aged elm, though touched with fire;
And the dry pump flung up an awkward arm;
And the fence post carried a strand of wire.

For them there was really nothing sad.
But though they rejoiced in the nest they kept,
One had to be versed in country things
Not to believe the phoebes wept.

Tree at My Window

Tree at my window, window tree,
My sash is lowered when night comes on;
But let there never be curtain drawn
Between you and me.

Vague dream-head lifted out of the ground,
And thing next most diffuse to cloud,
Not all your light tongues talking aloud
Could be profound.

But, tree, I have seen you taken and tossed,
And if you have seen me when I slept,
You have seen me when I was taken and swept
And all but lost.

That day she put our heads together,
Fate had her imagination about her,
Your head so much concerned with outer,
Mine with inner, weather.

On Looking up by Chance at the Constellations

You'll wait a long, long time for anything much
To happen in heaven beyond the floats of cloud
And the Northern Lights that run like tingling nerves.
The sun and moon get crossed, but they never touch,
Nor strike out fire from each other, nor crash out loud.
The planets seem to interfere in their curves,
But nothing ever happens, no harm is done.
We may as well go patiently on with our life,
And look elsewhere than to stars and moon and sun
For the shocks and changes we need to keep us sane.
It is true the longest drouth will end in rain,
The longest peace in China will end in strife.
Still it wouldn't reward the watcher to stay awake
In hopes of seeing the calm of heaven break
On his particular time and personal sight.
That calm seems certainly safe to last tonight.

West-running Brook

"Fred, where is north?"
"North? North is there, my love.
The brook runs west."
"West-running Brook then call it."

(West-running Brook men call it to this day.)
"What does it think it's doing running west
When all the other country brooks flow east
To reach the ocean? It must be the brook
Can trust itself to go by contraries
The way I can with you—and you with me—
Because we're—we're—I don't know what we are.
What are we?"
"Young or new?"
"We must be something.
We've said we two. Let's change that to we three.
As you and I are married to each other,
We'll both be married to the brook. We'll build
Our bridge across it, and the bridge shall be
Our arm thrown over it asleep beside it.
Look, look, it's waving to us with a wave
To let us know it hears me."
"Why, my dear,
That wave's been standing off this jut of shore—"
(The black stream, catching on a sunken rock,
Flung backward on itself in one white wave,
And the white water rode the black forever,
Not gaining but not losing, like a bird
White feathers from the struggle of whose breast
Flecked the dark stream and flecked the darker pool
Below the point, and were at last driven wrinkled
In a white scarf against the far-shore alders.)
"That wave's been standing off this jut of shore
Ever since rivers, I was going to say,
Were made in heaven. It wasn't waved to us."

"It wasn't, yet it was. If not to you,
It was to me—in an annunciation."

"Oh, if you take it off to lady-land,
As't were the country of the Amazons
We men must see you to the confines of
And leave you there, ourselves forbid to enter,—
It is your brook! I have no more to say."

"Yes, you have, too. Go on. You thought of something."

"Speaking of contraries, see how the brook
In that white wave runs counter to itself.
It is from that in water we were from
Long, long before we were from any creature.
Here we, in our impatience of the steps,
Get back to the beginning of beginnings,
The stream of everything that runs away.
Some say existence like a Pirouot
And Pirouette, forever in one place,
Stands still and dances, but it runs away,
It seriously, sadly, runs away
To fill the abyss's void with emptiness.
It flows beside us in this water brook,
But it flows over us. It flows between us
To separate us for a panic moment.
It flows between us, over us, and *with* us.
And it is time, strength, tone, light, life, and love—
And even substance lapsing unsubstantial;
The universal cataract of death
That spends to nothingness—and unresisted,
Save by some strange resistance in itself,
Not just a swerving, but a throwing back,
As if regret were in it and were sacred.
It has this throwing backward on itself
So that the fall of most of it is always
Raising a little, sending up a little.
Our life runs down in sending up the clock.
The brook runs down in sending up our life.
The sun runs down in sending up the brook.
And there is something sending up the sun.
It is this backward motion toward the source,
Against the stream, that most we see ourselves in,
The tribute of the current to the source.
It is from this in nature we are from.
It is most us."

"Today will be the day
You said so."

"No, today will be the day
You said the brook was called West-running Brook."

"Today will be the day of what we both said."

Once by the Pacific

The shattered water made a misty din.
Great waves looked over others coming in,
And thought of doing something to the shore
That water never did to land before.
The clouds were low and hairy in the skies,
Like locks blown forward in the gleam of eyes.
You could not tell, and yet it looked as if
The shore was lucky in being backed by cliff,
The cliff in being backed by continent;
It looked as if a night of dark intent
Was coming, and not only a night, an age.
Someone had better be prepared for rage.
There would be more than ocean-water broken
Before God's last *Put out the Light* was spoken.

Acquainted with the Night

I have been one acquainted with the night.
I have walked out in rain—and back in rain.
I have outwalked the furthest city light.

I have looked down the saddest city lane.
I have passed by the watchman on his beat
And dropped my eyes, unwilling to explain.

I have stood still and stopped the sound of feet
When far away an interrupted cry
Came over houses from another street,

But not to call me back or say good-by;
And further still at an unearthly height,
One luminary clock against the sky

Proclaimed the time was neither wrong nor right.
I have been one acquainted with the night.

Desert Places

Snow falling and night falling fast, oh, fast
In a field I looked into going past,
And the ground almost covered smooth in snow,
But a few weeds and stubble showing last.

The woods around it have it—it is theirs.
All animals are smothered in their lairs.
I am too absent-spirited to count;
The loneliness includes me unawares.

And lonely as it is, that loneliness
Will be more lonely ere it will be less—
A blanker whiteness of benighted snow
With no expression, nothing to express.

They cannot scare me with their empty spaces
Between stars—on stars where no human race is.
I have it in me so much nearer home
To scare myself with my own desert places.

Departmental

An ant on the tablecloth
Ran into a dormant moth
Of many times his size.
He showed not the least surprise.
His business wasn't with such.
He gave it scarcely a touch,
And was off on his duty run.
Yet if he encountered one
Of the hive's enquiry squad
Whose work is to find out God
And the nature of time and space,
He would put him onto the case.
Ants are a curious race;
One crossing with hurried tread
The body of one of their dead
Isn't given a moment's arrest—

Seems not even impressed.
But he no doubt reports to any
With whom he crosses antennae,
And they no doubt report
To the higher-up at court.
Then word goes forth in Formic:
"Death's come to Jerry McCormic,
Our selfless forager Jerry.
Will the special Janizary
Whose office it is to bury
The dead of the commissary
Go bring him home to his people.
Lay him in state on a sepal.
Wrap him for shroud in a petal.
Embalm him with ichor of nettle.
This is the word of your Queen."
And presently on the scene
Appears a solemn mortician;
And taking formal position,
With feelers calmly atwiddle,
Seizes the dead by the middle,
And heaving him high in air,
Carries him out of there.
No one stands round to stare.
It is nobody else's affair.

It couldn't be called ungentle.
But how thoroughly departmental.

Provide, Provide

The witch that came (the withered hag)
To wash the steps with pail and rag,
Was once the beauty Abishag,

The picture pride of Hollywood.
Too many fall from great and good
For you to doubt the likelihood.

Die early and avoid the fate.
Or if predestined to die late,
Make up your mind to die in state.

Make the whole stock exchange your own!
If need be occupy a throne,
Where nobody can call *you* crone.

Some have relied on what they knew;
Others on being simply true.
What worked for them might work for you.

No memory of having starred
Atones for later disregard
Or keeps the end from being hard.

Better to go down dignified
With boughten friendship at your side
Than none at all. Provide, provide!

Never Again Would Birds' Song Be the Same

He would declare and could himself believe
That the birds there in all the garden round
From having heard the daylong voice of Eve
Had added to their own an oversound,
Her tone of meaning but without the words.
Admittedly an eloquence so soft
Could only have had an influence on birds
When call or laughter carried it aloft.
Be that as may be, she was in their song.
Moreover her voice upon their voices crossed
Had now persisted in the woods so long
That probably it never would be lost.
Never again would birds' song be the same.
And to do that to birds was why she came.

The Gift Outright

The land was ours before we were the land's.
She was our land more than a hundred years
Before we were her people. She was ours
In Massachusetts, in Virginia,
But we were England's, still colonials,
Possessing what we still were unpossessed by,

Possessed by what we now no more possessed.
Something we were withholding made us weak
Until we found out that it was ourselves
We were withholding from our land of living,
And forthwith found salvation in surrender.
Such as we were we gave ourselves outright
(The deed of gift was many deeds of war)
To the land vaguely realizing westward,
But still unstoried, artless, unenhanced,
Such as she was, such as she would become.

The Most of It

He thought he kept the universe alone;
For all the voice in answer he could wake
Was but the mocking echo of his own
From some tree-hidden cliff across the lake.
Some morning from the boulder-broken beach
He would cry out on life, that what it wants
Is not its own love back in copy speech,
But counter-love, original response.
And nothing ever came of what he cried
Unless it was the embodiment that crashed
In the cliff's talus on the other side,
And then in the far distant water splashed,
But after a time allowed for it to swim,
Instead of proving human when it neared
And someone else additional to him,
As a great buck it powerfully appeared,
Pushing the crumpled water up ahead,
And landed pouring like a waterfall,
And stumbled through the rocks with horny tread,
And forced the underbrush—and that was all.

Two Look at Two

Love and forgetting might have carried them
A little further up the mountainside
With night so near, but not much further up.
They must have halted soon in any case
With thoughts of the path back, how rough it was

With rock and washout, and unsafe in darkness;
When they were halted by a tumbled wall
With barbed-wire binding. They stood facing this,
Spending what onward impulse they still had
In one last look the way they must not go,
On up the failing path, where, if a stone
On earthside moved at night, it moved itself;
No footstep moved it. "This is all," they sighed,
"Good-night to woods." But not so; there was more.
A doe from round a spruce stood looking at them
Across the wall, as near the wall as they.
She saw them in their field, they her in hers.
The difficulty of seeing what stood still,
Like some up-ended boulder split in two,
Was in her clouded eyes: they saw no fear there.
She seemed to think that two thus they were safe.
Then, as if they were something that, though strange,
She could not trouble her mind with too long,
She sighed and passed unscared along the wall.
"*This,* then, is all. What more is there to ask?"
But no, not yet. A snort to bid them wait.
A buck from round the spruce stood looking at them
Across the wall, as near the wall as they.
This was an antlered buck of lusty nostril,
Not the same doe come back into her place.
He viewed them quizzically with jerks of head,
As if to ask, "Why don't you make some motion?
Or give some sign of life? Because you can't.
I doubt if you're as living as you look."
Thus till he had them almost feeling dared
To stretch a proffering hand—and a spell-breaking.
Then he too passed unscared along the wall.
Two had seen two, whichever side you spoke from.
"This *must* be all." It was all. Still they stood,
A great wave from it going over them,
As if the earth in one unlooked-for favor
Had made them certain earth returned their love.

Wallace Stevens

[1879–1955]

The poetry of Wallace Stevens is animated by the mind's quest for meaning. As his poem "Of Modern Poetry" suggests, Stevens's work reveals the mind "in the act of finding / What will suffice." Primarily reflective, his poems voice two fundamental questions: (1) What is the relationship between the external world and the human mind, between reality and the imagination? (2) What can human beings substitute for the consolations of traditional religion as a way of giving meaning to their experience? The answer to the first question, briefly put, is that imagination transforms reality; human beings perceive and create the reality they contemplate. Perception, for Stevens, is an imaginative act, not a mere registering or transcribing of what's "out there." The answer to the second question is related to that of the first. For Stevens, the creation of art and the perception of beauty in the natural world order experience and endow it with meaning and value. For Stevens, art in general and poetry in particular thus become necessary fictions. Poetry is a "fiction" because it is an imaginative construct; it is a "necessary" fiction because human beings need order, value, and meaning in their lives, and art provides them best. Thus, poetry, painting, and the arts, in general, compensate for the values formerly offered by religious faith.

These ideas appear in many of Stevens's poems, including

"The Idea of Order at Key West" and his deservedly famous "Sunday Morning." In both poems the speaker discovers and creates meaning through the agency of the imagination. Stevens's speakers note the beauty of the natural world, especially its nuances of shape, sound, and color. This is not surprising for a poet who once noted that "the greatest poverty is not to live in a physical world." We can see this tendency in the final stanza of "Sunday Morning," in which we also notice the symbolic reverberations of its closing details:

Deer walk upon our mountains, and the quail
Whistle about us their spontaneous cries;
Sweet berries ripen in the wilderness;
And, in the isolation of the sky,
At evening, casual flocks of pigeons make
Ambiguous undulations as they sink,
Downward to darkness, on extended wings.

In "The Idea of Order at Key West," Stevens's speaker serves as the model of the artist-poet, the maker who endows the natural world with form and hence with significance. The speaker's singing gives order and meaning to "the dark voice of the sea," to "the outer voice of sky / And cloud," and especially to "The meaningless plungings of water and the wind." For as Stevens notes, the speaker's song is an image of the artist's "Blessed rage for order . . . The maker's rage to order words." As the poem indicates, the artist is

. . . the single artificer of the world
In which she sang. And when she sang, the sea,
Whatever self it had, became the self
That was her song, for she was the maker
. . . there never was a world for her
Except the one she sang and, singing, made.

As Helen Vendler has pointed out, the singer gives voice to the nonarticulated voice of the sea, shaping the sounds of the sea into meaningful language. This imaginative art, for Stevens, exemplifies the poet's task to make the natural world intelligible to human understanding. Stevens's poetry can be compared with that of William Carlos Williams in its attention to pictorial detail. The opening of Stevens's "The Poems of Our Climate" sounds something like Williams, though with more repetition than Williams customarily employed.

The Poems of Our Climate

I

Clear water in a brilliant bowl,
Pink and white carnations. The light
In the room more like a snowy air,
Reflecting snow. A newly-fallen snow
At the end of winter when afternoons return.
Pink and white carnations.

From this descriptive scene painting, however, the rest of Stevens's first stanza moves into his more characteristic meditative mode:

. . . one desires
So much more than that. The day itself
Is simplified: a bowl of white,
Cold, a cold porcelain, low and round,
With nothing more than the carnations there.

Such lines indicate the characteristic restlessness of mind common in Stevens's work, their explanatory touch being alien to Williams. So, too, is the invitation to speculate on the significance of flowers, bowl, and water. In the poem's two remaining stanzas we see Stevens's tendency to accept an imperfect world while reshaping it in the language of art:

II

Say even that this complete simplicity
Stripped one of all one's torments, concealed
The evilly compounded, vital I
And made it fresh in a world of white,
A world of clear water, brilliant edged,
Still one would want more, one would need more,
More than a world of white and snowy scents.

III

There would still remain the never-resting mind,
So that one would want to escape, come back
To what had been so long composed.

The imperfect is our paradise.
Note that, in this bitterness, delight,
Since the imperfect is so hot in us,
Lies in flawed words and stubborn sounds.

Throughout "The Poems of Our Climate," Stevens explores the relationship between the external world and the human mind, especially as the poet's artistic intelligence finds meaning and solace in the eternity of art.

Like Stevens's poems, his life was contemplative, meditative, quiet. Relatively uneventful, both his life and his poems lack the external drama and emotional intensity of the lives and work of Frost, Whitman, or Pound. Born in Reading, Pennsylvania, in 1879, Stevens studied at Harvard (without obtaining a degree), graduated from the New York University School of Law, and practiced law privately before joining the Hartford Accident and Indemnity Company, where he later became a vice president. In college Stevens wrote poetry and served as president of the literary magazine and the literary society. During his years of practicing law and working as an insurance company executive, Stevens wrote many poems. Although his first volume, *Harmonium,* was not published until 1923, he had been publishing poems in literary magazines for ten years. His *Collected Poems,* published in 1955, the year of his death, won both the Pulitzer Prize and the National Book Award.

Perhaps the most difficult thing about Stevens's poetry is its privacy. In reading Stevens we are invited to share the perceptions and reflections of a finely nuanced imagination. We are shown the poet's imaginative life, and we observe him creating meanings out of the recalcitrant details of external reality. We are, however, only witnesses to Stevens's meaning-making, not participants in it. His finely modulated discriminations of thought and feeling may prevent us from sharing broadly in his experience. But if we familiarize ourselves with Stevens's characteristic manner and central concerns, we can share his delicate perceptions.

Another aspect of Stevens's poetry that requires some attention is his wide-ranging vocabulary. By turns familiar and exotic, Stevens's diction is continuously surprising, whether in the nonsense words that appear in much of his early works or the eloquent sound play he often indulges in. For an initial sampling of Stevens's diction, look at "Bantams in Pine-Woods" and "Peter Quince at the Clavier." In these poems, as in some others, Stevens is something of a showman; he seems to enjoy displaying his linguistic virtuosity. This virtuosity with language and sound is further allied with Stevens's imaginative playfulness. Enjoying puns, riddles, and enigmas, Stevens was fond of artists such as Paul Klee, whose paintings exhibit a high degree of whimsy. It is thus important to realize that Stevens, though a serious poet, was also a playful one.

A final consideration in reading Stevens is to be aware that his poems center around a single idea or feeling that is frequently illustrated in multiple ways. Stevens's characteristic form is a theme and variations or a theme and accompanying set of meditative qualifications. A delightful example is "Thirteen Ways of Looking at a Blackbird," in which we are presented with multiple images of a single subject. More important than the blackbird in and of itself is what the poet makes of it. Stevens's imaginative transformations of the blackbird and the ways we perceive it are central to the poem's action and meaning. "Blackbird" also illustrates Stevens's penchant for innuendo, suggestion, and implication; the various images of the blackbird occasionally hint at their varied implications, but the thirteen images remain unexplained. The poem illustrates Stevens's belief in the power of the imagination to create meaning and to delight in that creation.

Although Stevens's poems lack the more democratic virtues of such other modern American poets as Whitman, Williams, and Frost, his poetry emerges just as powerfully from the same Emersonian tradition. Like his Romantic forebears Wordsworth and Keats in England and Whitman and Emerson in America, Stevens wrestles with questions about the individual's relationship to external reality. And like the responses of his modern poetic counterparts, especially Robert Frost, Stevens's answers diverge from those of his Romanticist predecessors. Among modern American poets, his imaginative force and sheer rhetorical brilliance are unequaled. Perhaps more than any other American poet, he reveals and explores how poetry can be a speculative instrument that transforms reality, orders the world, and composes the self.

Sunday Morning

I

Complacencies of the peignoir, and late
Coffee and oranges in a sunny chair,
And the green freedom of a cockatoo

Upon a rug mingle to dissipate
The holy hush of ancient sacrifice.
She dreams a little, and she feels the dark
Encroachment of that old catastrophe,
As a calm darkens among water-lights.
The pungent oranges and bright, green wings
Seem things in some procession of the dead,
Winding across wide water, without sound.
The day is like wide water, without sound,
Stilled for the passing of her dreaming feet
Over the seas, to silent Palestine,
Dominion of the blood and sepulchre.

II

Why should she give her bounty to the dead?
What is divinity if it can come
Only in silent shadows and in dreams?
Shall she not find in comforts of the sun,
In pungent fruit and bright, green wings, or else
In any balm or beauty of the earth,
Things to be cherished like the thought of heaven?
Divinity must live within herself:
Passions of rain, or moods in falling snow;
Grievings in loneliness, or unsubdued
Elations when the forest blooms; gusty
Emotions on wet roads on autumn nights;
All pleasures and all pains, remembering
The bough of summer and the winter branch.
These are the measures destined for her soul.

III

Jove in the clouds had his inhuman birth.
No mother suckled him, no sweet land gave
Large-mannered motions to his mythy mind
He moved among us, as a muttering king,
Magnificent, would move among his hinds,
Until our blood, commingling, virginal,
With heaven, brought such requital to desire
The very hinds discerned it, in a star.

[31]**Jove:** Roman name for Zeus, king of the gods in Greek mythology. Also known as Jupiter.

Shall our blood fail? Or shall it come to be
The blood of paradise? And shall the earth
Seem all of paradise that we shall know?
The sky will be much friendlier then than now,
A part of labor and a part of pain,
And next in glory to enduring love,
Not this dividing and indifferent blue.

IV

She says, "I am content when wakened birds,
Before they fly, test the reality
Of misty fields, by their sweet questionings;
But when the birds are gone, and their warm fields
Return no more, where, then, is paradise?"
There is not any haunt of prophecy,
Nor any old chimera of the grave,
Neither the golden underground, nor isle
Melodious, where spirits gat them home,
Nor visionary south, nor cloudy palm
Remote on heaven's hill, that has endured
As April's green endures; or will endure
Like her remembrance of awakened birds,
Or her desire for June and evening, tipped
By the consummation of the swallow's wings.

V

She says, "But in contentment I still feel
The need of some imperishable bliss."
Death is the mother of beauty; hence from her,
Alone, shall come fulfilment to our dreams
And our desires. Although she strews the leaves
Of sure obliteration on our paths,
The path sick sorrow took, the many paths
Where triumph rang its brassy phrase, or love
Whispered a little out of tenderness,
She makes the willow shiver in the sun
For maidens who were wont to sit and gaze

[52]**Chimera:** in Greek mythology, a monster with a lion's head; more generally, a fanciful image.

Upon the grass, relinquished to their feet.
She causes boys to pile new plums and pears
On disregarded plate. The maidens taste
And stray impassioned in the littering leaves.

VI

Is there no change of death in paradise?
Does ripe fruit never fall? Or do the boughs
Hang always heavy in that perfect sky,
Unchanging, yet so like our perishing earth,
With rivers like our own that seek for seas
They never find, the same receding shores
That never touch with inarticulate pang?
Why set the pear upon those river-banks
Or spice the shores with odors of the plum?
Alas, that they should wear our colors there,
The silken weavings of our afternoons,
And pick the strings of our insipid lutes!
Death is the mother of beauty, mystical,
Within whose burning bosom we devise
Our earthly mothers waiting, sleeplessly.

VII

Supple and turbulent, a ring of men
Shall chant in orgy on a summer morn
Their boisterous devotion to the sun,
Not as a god, but as a god might be,
Naked among them, like a savage source.
Their chant shall be a chant of paradise,
Out of their blood, returning to the sky;
And in their chant shall enter, voice by voice,
The windy lake wherein their lord delights,
The trees, like serafin, and echoing hills,
That choir among themselves long afterward.
They shall know well the heavenly fellowship
Of men that perish and of summer morn.
And whence they came and whither they shall go
The dew upon their feet shall manifest.

[100]**Serafin:** seraphim, an order of high-ranking angels close to God.

VIII

She hears, upon that water without sound,
A voice that cries, "The Tomb in Palestine
Is not the porch of spirits lingering.
It is the grave of Jesus, where he lay."
We live in an old chaos of the sun,
Or old dependency of day and night,
Or island solitude, unsponsored, free,
Of that wide water, inescapable.
Deer walk upon our mountains, and the quail
Whistle about us their spontaneous cries;
Sweet berries ripen in the wilderness;
And, in the isolation of the sky,
At evening, casual flocks of pigeons make
Ambiguous undulations as they sink,
Downward to darkness, on extended wings.

Anecdote of the Jar

I placed a jar in Tennessee,
And round it was, upon a hill.
It made the slovenly wilderness
Surround that hill.

The wilderness rose up to it,
And sprawled around, no longer wild.
The jar was round upon the ground
And tall and of a port in air.

It took dominion everywhere.
The jar was gray and bare.
It did not give of bird or bush,
Like nothing else in Tennessee.

The Emperor of Ice-Cream

Call the roller of big cigars,
The muscular one, and bid him whip
In kitchen cups concupiscent curds.
Let the wenches dawdle in such dress

As they are used to wear, and let the boys
Bring flowers in last month's newspapers.
Let be be finale of seem.
The only emperor is the emperor of ice-cream.

Take from the dresser of deal,
Lacking the three glass knobs, that sheet
On which she embroidered fantails once
And spread it so as to cover her face.
If her horny feet protrude, they come
To show how cold she is, and dumb.
Let the lamp affix its beam.
The only emperor is the emperor of ice-cream.

Bantams in Pine-Woods

Chieftain Iffucan of Azcan in caftan
Of tan with henna hackles, halt!

Damned universal cock, as if the sun
Was blackamoor to bear your blazing tail.

Fat! Fat! Fat! Fat! I am the personal.
Your world is you. I am my world.

You ten-foot poet among inchlings. Fat!
Begone! An inchling bristles in these pines,

Bristles, and points their Appalachian tangs,
And fears not portly Azcan nor his hoos.

Disillusionment of Ten O'Clock

The houses are haunted
By white night-gowns.
None are green,
Or purple with green rings,
Or green with yellow rings,
Or yellow with blue rings.
None of them are strange,
With socks of lace

And beaded ceintures.
People are not going
To dream of baboons and periwinkles.
Only, here and there, an old sailor,
Drunk and asleep in his boots,
Catches tigers
In red weather.

The Snow Man

One must have a mind of winter
To regard the frost and the boughs
Of the pine-trees crusted with snow;

And have been cold a long time
To behold the junipers shagged with ice,
The spruces rough in the distant glitter

Of the January sun; and not to think
Of any misery in the sound of the wind,
In the sound of a few leaves,

Which is the sound of the land
Full of the same wind
That is blowing in the same bare place

For the listener, who listens in the snow,
And, nothing himself, beholds
Nothing that is not there and the nothing that is.

A High-Toned Old Christian Woman

Poetry is the supreme fiction, madame.
Take the moral law and make a nave of it
And from the nave build haunted heaven. Thus,
The conscience is converted into palms,
Like windy citherns hankering for hymns.
We agree in principle. That's clear. But take
The opposing law and make a peristyle,
And from the peristyle project a masque
Beyond the planets. Thus, our bawdiness,

Unpurged by epitaph, indulged at last,
Is equally converted into palms,
Squiggling like saxophones. And palm for palm,
Madame, we are where we began. Allow,
Therefore, that in the planetary scene
Your disaffected flagellants, well-stuffed,
Smacking their muzzy bellies in parade,
Proud of such novelties of the sublime,
Such tink and tank and tunk-a-tunk-tunk,
May, merely may, madame, whip from themselves
A jovial hullabaloo among the spheres.
This will make widows wince. But fictive things
Wink as they will. Wink most when widows wince.

O Florida, Venereal Soil

A few things for themselves,
Convolvulus and coral,
Buzzards and live-moss,
Tiestas from the keys,
A few things for themselves,
Florida, venereal soil,
Disclose to the lover.

The dreadful sundry of this world,
The Cuban, Polodowsky,
The Mexican women,
The negro undertaker
Killing the time between corpses
Fishing for crayfish . . .
Virgin of boorish births,

Swiftly in the nights,
In the porches of Key West,
Behind the bougainvilleas,
After the guitar is asleep,
Lasciviously as the wind,
You come tormenting,
Insatiable,

When you might sit,
A scholar of darkness,
Sequestered over the sea,
Wearing a clear tiara
Of red and blue and red,
Sparkling, solitary, still,
In the high sea-shadow.

Donna, donna, dark,
Stooping in indigo gown
And cloudy constellations,
Conceal yourself or disclose
Fewest things to the lover—
A hand that bears a thick-leaved fruit,
A pungent bloom against your shade.

To the One of Fictive Music

Sister and mother and diviner love,
And of the sisterhood of the living dead
Most near, most clear, and of the clearest bloom,
And of the fragrant mothers the most dear
And queen, and of diviner love the day
And flame and summer and sweet fire, no thread
Of cloudy silver sprinkles in your gown
Its venom of renown, and on your head
No crown is simpler than the simple hair.

Now, of the music summoned by the birth
That separates us from the wind and sea,
Yet leaves us in them, until earth becomes,
By being so much of the things we are,
Gross effigy and simulacrum, none
Gives motion to perfection more serene
Than yours, out of our imperfections wrought,
Most rare, or ever of more kindred air
In the laborious weaving that you wear.

For so retentive of themselves are men
That music is intensest which proclaims
The near, the clear, and vaunts the clearest bloom,
And of all vigils musing the obscure,

That apprehends the most which sees and names,
As in your name, an image that is sure,
Among the arrant spices of the sun,
O bough and bush and scented vine, in whom
We give ourselves our likest issuance.

Yet not too like, yet not so like to be
Too near, too clear, saving a little to endow
Our feigning with the strange unlike, whence springs
The difference that heavenly pity brings.
For this, musician, in your girdle fixed
Bear other perfumes. On your pale head wear
A band entwining, set with fatal stones.
Unreal, give back to us what once you gave:
The imagination that we spurned and crave.

From *The Comedian as the Letter C*

IV

The Idea of a Colony

Nota: his soil is man's intelligence.
That's better. That's worth crossing seas to find.
Crispin in one laconic phrase laid bare
His cloudy drift and planned a colony.
Exit the mental moonlight, exit lex,
Rex and principium, exit the whole
Shebang. Exeunt omnes. Here was prose
More exquisite than any tumbling verse:
A still new continent in which to dwell.
What was the purpose of his pilgrimage,
Whatever shape it took in Crispin's mind,
If not, when all is said, to drive away
The shadow of his fellows from the skies,
And, from their stale intelligence released,
To make a new intelligence prevail?
Hence the reverberations in the words
Of his first central hymns, the celebrants
Of rankest trivia, tests of the strength
Of his æsthetic, his philosophy,
The more invidious, the more desired.

The florist asking aid from cabbages,
The rich man going bare, the paladin
Afraid, the blind man as astronomer,
The appointed power unwielded from disdain.
His western voyage ended and began.
The torment of fastidious thought grew slack,
Another, still more bellicose, came on.
He, therefore, wrote his prolegomena,
And, being full of the caprice, inscribed
Commingled souvenirs and prophecies.
He made a singular collation. Thus:
The natives of the rain are rainy men.
Although they paint effulgent, azure lakes,
And April hillsides wooded white and pink,
Their azure has a cloudy edge, their white
And pink, the water bright that dogwood bears.
And in their music showering sounds intone.
On what strange froth does the gross Indian dote,
What Eden sapling gum, what honeyed gore,
What pulpy dram distilled of innocence,
That streaking gold should speak in him
Or bask within his images and words?
If these rude instances impeach themselves
By force of rudeness, let the principle
Be plain. For application Crispin strove,
Abhorring Turk as Esquimau, the lute
As the marimba, the magnolia as rose.
Upon these premises propounding, he
Projected a colony that should extend
To the dusk of a whistling south below the south,
A comprehensive island hemisphere.
The man in Georgia waking among pines
Should be pine-spokesman. The responsive man,
Planting his pristine cores in Florida,
Should prick thereof, not on the psaltery,
But on the banjo's categorical gut,
Tuck, tuck, while the flamingos flapped his bays.
Sepulchral señors, bibbling pale mescal,
Oblivious to the Aztec almanacs,
Should make the intricate Sierra scan.
And dark Brazilians in their cafés,
Musing immaculate, pampean dits,

Should scrawl a vigilant anthology,
To be their latest, lucent paramour.
These are the broadest instances. Crispin,
Progenitor of such extensive scope,
Was not indifferent to smart detail.
The melon should have apposite ritual,
Performed in verd apparel, and the peach,
When its black branches came to bud, belle day,
Should have an incantation. And again,
When piled on salvers its aroma steeped
The summer, it should have a sacrament
And celebration. Shrewd novitiates
Should be the clerks of our experience.

These bland excursions into time to come,
Related in romance to backward flights,
However prodigal, however proud,
Contained in their afflatus the reproach
That first drove Crispin to his wandering.
He could not be content with counterfeit,
With masquerade of thought, with hapless words
That must belie the racking masquerade,
With fictive flourishes that preordained
His passion's permit, hang of coat, degree
Of buttons, measure of his salt. Such trash
Might help the blind, not him, serenely sly.
It irked beyond his patience. Hence it was,
Preferring text to gloss, he humbly served
Grotesque apprenticeship to chance event,
A clown, perhaps, but an aspiring clown.
There is a monotonous babbling in our dreams
That makes them our dependent heirs, the heirs
Of dreamers buried in our sleep, and not
The oncoming fantasies of better birth.
The apprentice knew these dreamers. If he dreamed
Their dreams, he did it in a gingerly way.
All dreams are vexing. Let them be expunged.
But let the rabbit run, the cock declaim.

Trinket pasticcio, flaunting skyey sheets,
With Crispin as the tiptoe cozener?
No, no: veracious page on page, exact.

Thirteen Ways of Looking at a Blackbird

I

Among twenty snowy mountains,
The only moving thing
Was the eye of the blackbird.

II

I was of three minds,
Like a tree
In which there are three blackbirds.

III

The blackbird whirled in the autumn winds.
It was a small part of the pantomime.

IV

A man and a woman
Are one.
A man and a woman and a blackbird
Are one.

V

I do not know which to prefer,
The beauty of inflections
Or the beauty of innuendoes,
The blackbird whistling
Or just after.

VI

Icicles filled the long window
With barbaric glass.
The shadow of the blackbird
Crossed it, to and fro.
The mood
Traced in the shadow
An indecipherable cause.

VII

O thin men of Haddam
Why do you imagine golden birds?
Do you not see how the blackbird
Walks around the feet
Of the women about you?

VIII

I know noble accents
And lucid, inescapable rhythms;
But I know, too,
That the blackbird is involved
In what I know.

IX

When the blackbird flew out of sight,
It marked the edge
Of one of many circles.

X

At the sight of blackbirds
Flying in a green light,
Even the bawds of euphony
Would cry out sharply.

XI

He rode over Connecticut
In a glass coach.
Once, a fear pierced him,
In that he mistook
The shadow of his equipage
For blackbirds.

XII

The river is moving.
The blackbird must be flying.

XIII

It was evening all afternoon.
It was snowing
And it was going to snow.
The blackbird sat
In the cedar-limbs.

The Idea of Order at Key West

She sang beyond the genius of the sea.
The water never formed to mind or voice,
Like a body wholly body, fluttering
Its empty sleeves; and yet its mimic motion
Made constant cry, caused constantly a cry,
That was not ours although we understood,
Inhuman, of the veritable ocean.

The sea was not a mask. No more was she.
The song and water were not medleyed sound
Even if what she sang was what she heard,
Since what she sang was uttered word by word.
It may be that in all her phrases stirred
The grinding water and the gasping wind;
But it was she and not the sea we heard.

For she was the maker of the song she sang.
The ever-hooded, tragic-gestured sea
Was merely a place by which she walked to sing.
Whose spirit is this? we said, because we knew
It was the spirit that we sought and knew
That we should ask this often as she sang.

If it was only the dark voice of the sea
That rose, or even colored by many waves;
If it was only the outer voice of sky
And cloud, of the sunken coral water-walled,
However clear, it would have been deep air,
The heaving speech of air, a summer sound
Repeated in a summer without end
And sound alone. But it was more than that,

More even than her voice, and ours, among
The meaningless plungings of water and the wind,
Theatrical distances, bronze shadows heaped
On the high horizons, mountainous atmospheres
Of sky and sea.

It was her voice that made
The sky acutest at its vanishing.
She measured to the hour its solitude.
She was the single artificer of the world
In which she sang. And when she sang, the sea,
Whatever self it had, became the self
That was her song, for she was the maker. Then we,
As we beheld her striding there alone,
Knew that there never was a world for her
Except the one she sang and, singing, made.

Ramon Fernandez, tell me, if you know,
Why, when the singing ended and we turned
Toward the town, tell why the glassy lights,
The lights in the fishing boats at anchor there,
As the night descended, tilting in the air,
Mastered the night and portioned out the sea,
Fixing emblazoned zones and fiery poles,
Arranging, deepening, enchanting night.

Oh! Blessed rage for order, pale Ramon,
The maker's rage to order words of the sea,
Words of the fragrant portals, dimly-starred,
And of ourselves and of our origins,
In ghostlier demarcations, keener sounds.

From *The Man with the Blue Guitar*

I

The man bent over his guitar,
A shearsman of sorts. The day was green.

They said, "You have a blue guitar,
You do not play things as they are."

The man replied, "Things as they are
Are changed upon the blue guitar."

And they said then, "But play, you must,
A tune beyond us, yet ourselves,

A tune upon the blue guitar
Of things exactly as they are."

II

I cannot bring a world quite round,
Although I patch it as I can.

I sing a hero's head, large eye
And bearded bronze, but not a man,

Although I patch him as I can
And reach through him almost to man.

If to serenade almost to man
Is to miss, by that, things as they are,

Say that it is the serenade
Of a man that plays a blue guitar.

III

Ah, but to play man number one,
To drive the dagger in his heart,

To lay his brain upon the board
And pick the acrid colors out,

To nail his thought across the door,
Its wings spread wide to rain and snow,

To strike his living hi and ho,
To tick it, tock it, turn it true,

To bang it from a savage blue,
Jangling the metal of the strings . . .

IV

So that's life, then: things as they are?
It picks its way on the blue guitar.

A million people on one string?
And all their manner in the thing,

And all their manner, right and wrong,
And all their manner, weak and strong?

The feelings crazily, craftily call,
Like a buzzing of flies in autumn air,

And that's life, then: things as they are,
This buzzing of the blue guitar.

V

Do not speak to us of the greatness of poetry,
Of the torches wisping in the underground,

Of the structure of vaults upon a point of light.
There are no shadows in our sun,

Day is desire and night is sleep.
There are no shadows anywhere.

The earth, for us, is flat and bare.
There are no shadows. Poetry

Exceeding music must take the place
Of empty heaven and its hymns,

Ourselves in poetry must take their place,
Even in the chattering of your guitar.

VI

A tune beyond us as we are,
Yet nothing changed by the blue guitar;

Ourselves in the tune as if in space,
Yet nothing changed, except the place

Of things as they are and only the place
As you play them, on the blue guitar,

Placed, so, beyond the compass of change,
Perceived in a final atmosphere;

For a moment final, in the way
The thinking of art seems final when

The thinking of god is smoky dew.
The tune is space. The blue guitar

Becomes the place of things as they are,
A composing of senses of the guitar.

Men Made out of Words

What should we be without the sexual myth,
The human revery or poem of death?

Castratos of moon-mash—Life consists
Of propositions about life. The human

Revery is a solitude in which
We compose these propositions, torn by dreams,

By the terrible incantations of defeats
And by the fear that defeats and dreams are one.

The whole race is a poet that writes down
The eccentric propositions of its fate.

The Sense of the Sleight-of-Hand Man

One's grand flights, one's Sunday baths,
One's tootings at the weddings of the soul
Occur as they occur. So bluish clouds
Occurred above the empty house and the leaves
Of the rhododendrons rattled their gold,
As if someone lived there. Such floods of white

Came bursting from the clouds. So the wind
Threw its contorted strength around the sky.

Could you have said the bluejay suddenly
Would swoop to earth? It is a wheel, the rays
Around the sun. The wheel survives the myths.
The fire eye in the clouds survives the gods.
To think of a dove with an eye of grenadine
And pines that are cornets, so it occurs,
And a little island full of geese and stars:
It may be that the ignorant man, alone,
Has any chance to mate his life with life
That is the sensual, pearly spouse, the life
That is fluent in even the wintriest bronze.

Study of Two Pears

I

Opusculum paedagogum.
The pears are not viols,
Nudes or bottles.
They resemble nothing else.

II

They are yellow forms
Composed of curves
Bulging toward the base.
They are touched red.

III

They are not flat surfaces
Having curved outlines.
They are round
Tapering toward the top.

IV

In the way they are modelled
There are bits of blue.

A hard dry leaf hangs
From the stem.

V

The yellow glistens.
It glistens with various yellows,
Citrons, oranges and greens
Flowering over the skin.

VI

The shadows of the pears
Are blobs on the green cloth.
The pears are not seen
As the observer wills.

The Glass of Water

That the glass would melt in heat,
That the water would freeze in cold,
Shows that this object is merely a state,
One of many, between two poles. So,
In the metaphysical, there are these poles.

Here in the centre stands the glass. Light
Is the lion that comes down to drink. There
And in that state, the glass is a pool.
Ruddy are his eyes and ruddy are his claws
When light comes down to wet his frothy jaws

And in the water winding weeds move round.
And there and in another state—the refractions,
The *metaphysica,* the plastic parts of poems
Crash in the mind—But, fat Jocundus, worrying
About what stands here in the centre, not the glass,

But in the centre of our lives, this time, this day,
It is a state, this spring among the politicians
Playing cards. In a village of the indigenes,
One would have still to discover. Among the dogs and dung,
One would continue to contend with one's ideas.

To the Roaring Wind

What syllable are you seeking,
Vocalissimus,
In the distances of sleep?
Speak it.

From *The Auroras of Autumn*

II

Farewell to an idea . . . A cabin stands,
Deserted, on a beach. It is white,
As by a custom or according to

An ancestral theme or as a consequence
Of an infinite course. The flowers against the wall
Are white, a little dried, a kind of mark

Reminding, trying to remind, of a white
That was different, something else, last year
Or before, not the white of an aging afternoon,

Whether fresher or duller, whether of winter cloud
Or of winter sky, from horizon to horizon.
The wind is blowing the sand across the floor.

Here, being visible is being white,
Is being of the solid of white, the accomplishment
Of an extremist in an exercise . . .

The season changes. A cold wind chills the beach.
The long lines of it grow longer, emptier,
A darkness gathers though it does not fall

And the whiteness grows less vivid on the wall.
The man who is walking turns blankly on the sand.
He observes how the north is always enlarging the change,

With its frigid brilliances, its blue-red sweeps
And gusts of great enkindlings, its polar green,
The color of ice and fire and solitude.

A Postcard from the Volcano

Children picking up our bones
Will never know that these were once
As quick as foxes on the hill;

And that in autumn, when the grapes
Made sharp air sharper by their smell
These had a being, breathing frost;

And least will guess that with our bones
We left much more, left what still is
The look of things, left what we felt

At what we saw. The spring clouds blow
Above the shuttered mansion-house,
Beyond our gate and the windy sky

Cries out a literate despair.
We knew for long the mansion's look
And what we said of it became

A part of what it is . . . Children,
Still weaving budded aureoles,
Will speak our speech and never know,

Will say of the mansion that it seems
As if he that lived there left behind
A spirit storming in blank walls,

A dirty house in a gutted world,
A tatter of shadows peaked to white,
Smeared with the gold of the opulent sun.

Angel Surrounded by Paysans

One of the countrymen:

There is
A welcome at the door to which no one comes?

The angel:

I am the angel of reality,
Seen for a moment standing in the door.

I have neither ashen wing nor wear of ore
And live without a tepid aureole,

Or stars that follow me, not to attend,
But, of my being and its knowing, part.

I am one of you and being one of you
Is being and knowing what I am and know.

Yet I am the necessary angel of earth,
Since, in my sight, you see the earth again,

Cleared of its stiff and stubborn, man-locked set,
And, in my hearing, you hear its tragic drone

Rise liquidly in liquid lingerings,
Like watery words awash; like meanings said

By repetitions of half-meanings. Am I not,
Myself, only half of a figure of a sort,

A figure half seen, or seen for a moment, or man
Of the mind, an apparition apparelled in

Apparels of such lightest look that a turn
Of my shoulder and quickly, too quickly, I am gone?

The Plain Sense of Things

After the leaves have fallen, we return
To a plain sense of things. It is as if
We had come to an end of the imagination,
Inanimate in an inert savoir.

It is difficult even to choose the adjective
For this blank cold, this sadness without cause.
The great structure has become a minor house.
No turban walks across the lessened floors.

The greenhouse never so badly needed paint.
The chimney is fifty years old and slants to one side.
A fantastic effort has failed, a repetition
In a repetitiousness of men and flies.

Yet the absence of the imagination had
Itself to be imagined. The great pond,
The plain sense of it, without reflections, leaves,
Mud, water like dirty glass, expressing silence

Of a sort, silence of a rat come out to see,
The great pond and its waste of the lilies, all this
Had to be imagined as an inevitable knowledge,
Required, as a necessity requires.

The Planet on the Table

Ariel was glad he had written his poems.
They were of a remembered time
Or of something seen that he liked.

Other makings of the sun
Were waste and welter
And the ripe shrub writhed.

His self and the sun were one
And his poems, although makings of his self,
Were no less makings of the sun.

It was not important that they survive.
What mattered was that they should bear
Some lineament or character,

Some affluence, if only half-perceived,
In the poverty of their words,
Of the planet of which they were part.

The River of Rivers in Connecticut

There is a great river this side of Stygia,
Before one comes to the first black cataracts
And trees that lack the intelligence of trees.

In that river, far this side of Stygia,
The mere flowing of the water is a gayety,
Flashing and flashing in the sun. On its banks,

No shadow walks. The river is fateful,
Like the last one. But there is no ferryman.
He could not bend against its propelling force.

It is not to be seen beneath the appearances
That tell of it. The steeple at Farmington
Stands glistening and Haddam shines and sways.

It is the third commonness with light and air,
A curriculum, a vigor, a local abstraction . . .
Call it, once more, a river, an unnamed flowing,

Space-filled, reflecting the seasons, the folk-lore
Of each of the senses; call it, again and again,
The river that flows nowhere, like a sea.

Not Ideas about the Thing but the Thing Itself

At the earliest ending of winter,
In March, a scrawny cry from outside
Seemed like a sound in his mind.

He knew that he heard it,
A bird's cry, at daylight or before,
In the early March wind.

The sun was rising at six,
No longer a battered panache above snow . . .
It would have been outside.

It was not from the vast ventriloquism
Of sleep's faded papier-mâché . . .
The sun was coming from outside.

That scrawny cry—It was
A chorister whose c preceded the choir.
It was part of the colossal sun,

Surrounded by its choral rings,
Still far away. It was like
A new knowledge of reality.

The Course of a Particular

Today the leaves cry, hanging on branches swept by wind,
Yet the nothingness of winter becomes a little less.
It is still full of icy shades and shapen snow.

The leaves cry . . . One holds off and merely hears the cry.
It is a busy cry, concerning someone else.
And though one says that one is part of everything,

There is a conflict, there is a resistance involved;
And being part is an exertion that declines:
One feels the life of that which gives life as it is.

The leaves cry. It is not a cry of divine attention,
Nor the smoke-drift of puffed-out heroes, nor human cry.
It is the cry of leaves that do not transcend themselves,

In the absence of fantasia, without meaning more
Than they are in the final finding of the ear, in the thing
Itself, until, at last, the cry concerns no one at all.

Of Modern Poetry

The poem of the mind in the act of finding
What will suffice. It has not always had
To find: the scene was set; it repeated what
Was in the script.
Then the theatre was changed
To something else. Its past was a souvenir.

It has to be living, to learn the speech of the place.
It has to face the men of the time and to meet
The women of the time. It has to think about war
And it has to find what will suffice. It has
To construct a new stage. It has to be on that stage
And, like an insatiable actor, slowly and
With meditation, speak words that in the ear,
In the delicatest ear of the mind, repeat,
Exactly, that which it wants to hear, at the sound

Of which, an invisible audience listens,
Not to the play, but to itself, expressed
In an emotion as of two people, as of two
Emotions becoming one. The actor is
A metaphysician in the dark, twanging
An instrument, twanging a wiry string that gives
Sounds passing through sudden rightnesses, wholly
Containing the mind, below which it cannot descend,
Beyond which it has no will to rise.
                                        It must
Be the finding of a satisfaction, and may
Be of a man skating, a woman dancing, a woman
Combing. The poem of the act of the mind.

Final Soliloquy of the Interior Paramour

Light the first light of evening, as in a room
In which we rest and, for small reason, think
The world imagined is the ultimate good.

This is, therefore, the intensest rendezvous.
It is in that thought that we collect ourselves,
Out of all the indifferences, into one thing:

Within a single thing, a single shawl
Wrapped tightly round us, since we are poor, a warmth,
A light, a power, the miraculous influence.

Here, now, we forget each other and ourselves.
We feel the obscurity of an order, a whole,
A knowledge, that which arranged the rendezvous,

Within its vital boundary, in the mind.
We say God and the imagination are one . . .
How high that highest candle lights the dark.

Out of this same light, out of the central mind,
We make a dwelling in the evening air,
In which being there together is enough.

From *Notes Toward a Supreme Fiction*

TO HENRY CHURCH

And for what, except for you, do I feel love?
Do I press the extremest book of the wisest man
Close to me, hidden in me day and night?
In the uncertain light of single, certain truth,
Equal in living changingness to the light
In which I meet you, in which we sit at rest,
For a moment in the central of our being,
The vivid transparence that you bring is peace.

It Must Be Abstract

I

Begin, ephebe, by perceiving the idea
Of this invention, this invented world,
The inconceivable idea of the sun.

You must become an ignorant man again
And see the sun again with an ignorant eye
And see it clearly in the idea of it.

Never suppose an inventing mind as source
Of this idea nor for that mind compose
A voluminous master folded in his fire.

How clean the sun when seen in its idea,
Washed in the remotest cleanliness of a heaven
That has expelled us and our images . . .

The death of one god is the death of all.
Let purple Phoebus lie in umber harvest,
Let Phoebus slumber and die in autumn umber,

Phoebus is dead, ephebe. But Phoebus was
A name for something that never could be named.
There was a project for the sun and is.

There is a project for the sun. The sun
Must bear no name, gold flourisher, but be
In the difficulty of what it is to be.

II

It is the celestial ennui of apartments
That sends us back to the first idea, the quick
Of this invention; and yet so poisonous

Are the ravishments of truth, so fatal to
The truth itself, the first idea becomes
The hermit in a poet's metaphors,

Who comes and goes and comes and goes all day.
May there be an ennui of the first idea?
What else, prodigious scholar, should there be?

The monastic man is an artist. The philosopher
Appoints man's place in music, say, today.
But the priest desires. The philosopher desires.

And not to have is the beginning of desire.
To have what is not is its ancient cycle.
It is desire at the end of winter, when

It observes the effortless weather turning blue
And sees the myosotis on its bush.
Being virile, it hears the calendar hymn.

It knows that what it has is what is not
And throws it away like a thing of another time,
As morning throws off stale moonlight and shabby sleep.

III

The poem refreshes life so that we share,
For a moment, the first idea . . . It satisfies
Belief in an immaculate beginning

And sends us, winged by an unconscious will,
To an immaculate end. We move between these points:
From that ever-early candor to its late plural

And the candor of them is the strong exhilaration
Of what we feel from what we think, of thought
Beating in the heart, as if blood newly came,

An elixir, an excitation, a pure power.
The poem, through candor, brings back a power again
That gives a candid kind to everything.

We say: At night an Arabian in my room,
With his damned hoobla-hoobla-hoobla-how,
Inscribes a primitive astronomy

Across the unscrawled fores the future casts
And throws his stars around the floor. By day
The wood-dove used to chant his hoobla-hoo

And still the grossest iridescence of ocean
Howls hoo and rises and howls hoo and falls.
Life's nonsense pierces us with strange relation.

IV

The first idea was not our own. Adam
In Eden was the father of Descartes
And Eve made air the mirror of herself,

Of her sons and of her daughters. They found themselves
In heaven as in a glass; a second earth;
And in the earth itself they found a green—

The inhabitants of a very varnished green.
But the first idea was not to shape the clouds
In imitation. The clouds preceded us

There was a muddy centre before we breathed.
There was a myth before the myth began,
Venerable and articulate and complete.

From this the poem springs: that we live in a place
That is not our own and, much more, not ourselves
And hard it is in spite of blazoned days.

We are the mimics. Clouds are pedagogues.
The air is not a mirror but bare board,
Coulisse bright-dark, tragic chiaroscuro

And comic color of the rose, in which
Abysmal instruments make sounds like pips
Of the sweeping meanings that we add to them.

Chaos in Motion and Not in Motion

Oh, that this lashing wind was something more
Than the spirit of Ludwig Richter . . .

The rain is pouring down. It is July.
There is lightning and the thickest thunder.

It is a spectacle. Scene 10 becomes 11,
In Series X, Act IV, et cetera.

People fall out of windows, trees tumble down,
Summer is changed to winter, the young grow old,

The air is full of children, statues, roofs
And snow. The theatre is spinning round,

Colliding with deaf-mute churches and optical trains.
The most massive sopranos are singing songs of scales.

And Ludwig Richter, turbulent Schlemihl,
Has lost the whole in which he was contained,

Knows desire without an object of desire,
All mind and violence and nothing felt.

He knows he has nothing more to think about,
Like the wind that lashes everything at once.

The House Was Quiet and the World Was Calm

The house was quiet and the world was calm.
The reader became the book; and summer night

Was like the conscious being of the book.
The house was quiet and the world was calm.

The words were spoken as if there was no book,
Except that the reader leaned above the page,

Wanted to lean, wanted much most to be
The scholar to whom his book is true, to whom

The summer night is like a perfection of thought.
The house was quiet because it had to be.

The quiet was part of the meaning, part of the mind:
The access of perfection to the page.

And the world was calm. The truth in a calm world,
In which there is no other meaning, itself

Is calm, itself is summer and night, itself
Is the reader leaning late and reading there.

The Rock

I

Seventy Years Later

It is an illusion that we were ever alive,
Lived in the houses of mothers, arranged ourselves
By our own motions in a freedom of air.

Regard the freedom of seventy years ago.
It is no longer air. The houses still stand,
Though they are rigid in rigid emptiness.

Even our shadows, their shadows, no longer remain.
The lives these lived in the mind are at an end.
They never were . . . The sounds of the guitar

Were not and are not. Absurd. The words spoken
Were not and are not. It is not to be believed.
The meeting at noon at the edge of the field seems like

An invention, an embrace between one desperate clod
And another in a fantastic consciousness,
In a queer assertion of humanity:

A theorem proposed between the two—
Two figures in a nature of the sun,
In the sun's design of its own happiness,

As if nothingness contained a métier,
A vital assumption, an impermanence
In its permanent cold, an illusion so desired

That the green leaves came and covered the high rock,
That the lilacs came and bloomed, like a blindness cleaned,
Exclaiming bright sight, as it was satisfied,

In a birth of sight. The blooming and the musk
Were being alive, an incessant being alive,
A particular of being, that gross universe.

II

The Poem as Icon

It is not enough to cover the rock with leaves.
We must be cured of it by a cure of the ground
Or a cure of ourselves, that is equal to a cure

Of the ground, a cure beyond forgetfulness.
And yet the leaves, if they broke into bud,
If they broke into bloom, if they bore fruit,

And if we ate the incipient colorings
Of their fresh culls might be a cure of the ground.
The fiction of the leaves is the icon

Of the poem, the figuration of blessedness,
And the icon is the man. The pearled chaplet of spring,
The magnum wreath of summer, time's autumn snood,

Its copy of the sun, these cover the rock.
These leaves are the poem, the icon and the man.
These are a cure of the ground and of ourselves,

In the predicate that there is nothing else.
They bud and bloom and bear their fruit without change.
They are more than leaves that cover the barren rock

They bud the whitest eye, the pallidest sprout,
New senses in the engenderings of sense,
The desire to be at the end of distances,

The body quickened and the mind in root.
They bloom as a man loves, as he lives in love.
They bear their fruit so that the year is known,

As if its understanding was brown skin,
The honey in its pulp, the final found,
The plenty of the year and of the world.

In this plenty, the poem makes meanings of the rock,
Of such mixed motion and such imagery
That its barrenness becomes a thousand things

And so exists no more. This is the cure
Of leaves and of the ground and of ourselves.
His words are both the icon and the man.

III

Forms of the Rock in a Night-Hymn

The rock is the gray particular of man's life,
The stone from which he rises, up—and—ho,
The step to the bleaker depths of his descents . . .

The rock is the stern particular of the air,
The mirror of the planets, one by one,
But through man's eye, their silent rhapsodist,

Turquoise the rock, at odious evening bright
With redness that sticks fast to evil dreams;
The difficult rightness of half-risen day.

The rock is the habitation of the whole,
Its strength and measure, that which is near, point A
In a perspective that begins again

At B: the origin of the mango's rind.
It is the rock where tranquil must adduce
Its tranquil self, the main of things, the mind,

The starting point of the human and the end,
That in which space itself is contained, the gate
To the enclosure, day, the things illumined

By day, night and that which night illumines,
Night and its midnight-minting fragrances,
Night's hymn of the rock, as in a vivid sleep.

William Carlos Williams

[1883–1963]

Although William Carlos Williams pursued a full-time career as a physician (he was a general practitioner with a specialty in pediatrics), he was equally devoted to literature. Born in Rutherford, New Jersey, in 1883, Williams attended preparatory schools in New York and Switzerland before studying medicine at the University of Pennsylvania, where he met Ezra Pound, who encouraged him to continue writing. Although Williams took Pound's advice and began publishing his poetry, he did not abandon his medical education. He interned in a New York City hospital, did his pediatric training in Leipzig, Germany, then returned to New Jersey to start his own medical practice. He worked there as both a poet and a doctor until his death in 1963.

Like his major contemporaries, Williams received a number of awards for his work, including a National Book Award (1950), a Bollingen Prize (1953), and a Pulitzer Prize (1962). His poetry is infused with the qualities that characterized him as a man: warmth, kindness, gaiety, candor, and a healthy affirmation of life. His poems are noteworthy for their openness of form, imagistic concreteness, and a lack of discursive explanation. They exhibit qualities, moreover, that put them at odds with the poems of his most famous contemporary, T. S. Eliot. Although Williams sought to write innovative poems to make American poetry new,

Williams's way was not Eliot's way. Where Eliot had raided history for allusion and illustration, and where he had used a variety of foreign languages in his poems, Williams avoided allusion and eschewed foreign linguistic borrowings. In fact, in his *Autobiography* Williams wrote that Eliot's highly allusive and erudite poems "returned us to the classroom at a time when American poetry was developing a different aesthetic rooted in the local, the present, and the familiar."

Like the poetry of his most illustrious American poetic forebear, Walt Whitman, Williams's poetry celebrates the common and the ordinary. According to Williams, any object or subject can be regarded poetically. Nothing is too odd or trivial not to be granted the appreciative and illuminating gaze of the poet. A woman standing on a street corner munching plums, a cat tipping over a flowerpot, a red wheelbarrow beside some white chickens—Williams made these and other seemingly inconsequential actions and objects fitting subjects for poems.

More important than the ordinariness of his subjects, however, is the way Williams defamiliarizes and reenvisions them. His poems invite observation, not abstract thinking. Williams is remembered for a credo that came to be associated with the poetic movement of Imagism, which favored concrete detail over discursive explanation. "No ideas but in things," he once wrote. Williams valued an idea as much as Eliot, Frost, or Stevens did. His motto, however, summarizes an aesthetic that does not so much rule out thought as insist that it be embodied in images. By omitting discursive explanation, Williams wrote poems that do not insist on a "meaning." Instead, his poems shape and organize language aesthetically. Such poems present imagistic pictures; more important, they also become objects made of words, aesthetic forms to be contemplated. One example is the following brief poem:

The Red Wheelbarrow

so much depends
upon

a red wheel
barrow

glazed with rain
water

beside the white
chickens.

To focus on the poem's paraphrasable meaning is to severely limit our enjoyment of it. We could ask, of course, just what does depend upon the red wheelbarrow. Although our answers will assuredly vary, to stop with that question is to avoid looking *at* the poem in an attempt to look *through* it.

Looking at Williams's "The Red Wheelbarrow" we see a miniature painting in the primary colors of red and white. Like its colors, its objects are basic, common, familiar. In inspecting the poem this way, we view it as a representation of something. But even this painterly way of seeing the work ignores the fact that it is "a machine made out of words," which is one way Williams once defined a poem. Perhaps we can see just what kind of machine Williams has made by altering it as follows: "So much depends upon a red wheelbarrow glazed with rainwater beside the white chickens."

Without considering the meaning of the statement, we can clearly see that this altered version lacks the formal qualities of Williams's poem. This alternative version does not invite consideration as a poem because its words are not arranged to form a poetic image. By arranging the words as he does, however, Williams challenges us to treat this text *as* a poem, to read it the way we read other, more traditional poems. In doing so, we notice a series of patterns: four two-line stanzas; a single two-syllable word as the second line of each stanza; a highly regularized syllable count in the lines of the poem—4/2, 3/2, 3/2, 4/2. We also see that each of the short lines contains one accented syllable and each of the long ones, two. In addition to this metrical regularity, we hear the poem's sound play in line 5—"gl*a*zed with r*a*in"—and in line 7: "bes*i*de the wh*i*te."

Williams calls our attention to a familiar subject by organizing language and shaping it aesthetically. As a result, we look more closely at the objects depicted in the poem and at the poem itself as an aesthetic object. Beyond this, Williams invites us to listen to his language as well. Perhaps the most remarkable thing about this work is the way Williams splits the two compound words:

wheel/barrow and rain/water; he not only splits them into their constituent parts, he does so by breaking them across the poetic line. In doing this, he makes the words new and thereby makes a poem that sees commonplace words in a fresh way.

The simplicity of Williams's verse forms, the matter-of-factness of his subjects, and the ordinariness of much of his language should not blind us to his poetic resourcefulness. His most successful poems, whether "seeing" poems like "Queen Anne's Lace" or "talking" poems like "Danse Russe," possess the power to surprise, to reveal things we hadn't seen quite that way before. Like Wallace Stevens, Williams had great respect for the power of the imagination. And like English Romantic writers such as William Wordsworth and Samuel Taylor Coleridge, for whom the imagination was a primary epistemological instrument, Williams never tired of celebrating its importance.

Williams reveals an intensely imaginative vision in his most memorable poems: the poetic suite *Pictures from Breughel,* inspired by Pieter Breughel the Elder, his complex epic poem *Paterson,* and his shorter lyrics. This vision also appears in prose works such as *In the Money* and *In the American Grain,* in which Williams scathingly criticizes habitual failures of the American imagination, especially its brutishness, violence, and Puritanical suspicion of pleasure.

Like Whitman before him, Williams performs, through his poetry, acts of reconciliation. He wanted, as he put it in "A Sort of a Song,"

> —through metaphor to reconcile
> the people and the stones.

Spring and All

By the road to the contagious hospital
under the surge of the blue
mottled clouds driven from the
northeast—a cold wind. Beyond, the
waste of broad, muddy fields
brown with dried weeds, standing and fallen

patches of standing water
the scattering of tall trees

All along the road the reddish
purplish, forked, upstanding, twiggy
stuff of bushes and small trees
with dead, brown leaves under them
leafless vines—

Lifeless in appearance, sluggish
dazed spring approaches—

They enter the new world naked,
cold, uncertain of all
save that they enter. All about them
the cold, familiar wind—

Now the grass, tomorrow
the stiff curl of wildcarrot leaf
One by one objects are defined—
It quickens: clarity, outline of leaf

But now the stark dignity of
entrance—Still, the profound change
has come upon them: rooted, they
grip down and begin to awaken

Danse Russe

If when my wife is sleeping
and the baby and Kathleen
are sleeping
and the sun is a flame-white disc
in silken mists
above shining trees,—
if I in my north room
dance naked, grotesquely
before my mirror
waving my shirt round my head
and singing softly to myself:
"I am lonely, lonely.
I was born to be lonely,
I am best so!"

If I admire my arms, my face,
my shoulders, flanks, buttocks
against the yellow drawn shades,—

Who shall say I am not
the happy genius of my household?

The Young Housewife

At ten A.M. the young housewife
moves about in negligee behind
the wooden walls of her husband's house.
I pass solitary in my car.

Then again she comes to the curb
to call the ice-man, fish-man, and stands
shy, uncorseted, tucking in
stray ends of hair, and I compare her
to a fallen leaf.

The noiseless wheels of my car
rush with a crackling sound over
dried leaves as I bow and pass smiling.

Queen Anne's Lace

Her body is not so white as
anemone petals nor so smooth—nor
so remote a thing. It is a field
of the wild carrot taking
the field by force; the grass
does not raise above it.
Here is no question of whiteness,
white as can be, with a purple mole
at the center of each flower.
Each flower is a hand's span
of her whiteness. Wherever
his hand has lain there is
a tiny purple blemish. Each part
is a blossom under his touch

to which the fibres of her being
stem one by one, each to its end,
until the whole field is a
white desire, empty, a single stem,
a cluster, flower by flower,
a pious wish to whiteness gone over—
or nothing.

January Morning

I

I have discovered that most of
the beauties of travel are due to
the strange hours we keep to see them:

the domes of the Church of
the Paulist Fathers in Weehawken
against a smoky dawn—the heart stirred—
are beautiful as Saint Peters
approached after years of anticipation.

II

Though the operation was postponed
I saw the tall probationers
in their tan uniforms
                    hurrying to breakfast!

III

—and from basement entries
neatly coiffed, middle aged gentlemen
with orderly moustaches and
well-brushed coats

IV

—and the sun, dipping into the avenues
streaking the tops of
the irregular red houselets,
                              and
the gay shadows dropping and dropping.

V

—and a young horse with a green bed-quilt
on his withers shaking his head:
bared teeth and nozzle high in the air!

VI

—and a semicircle of dirt-colored men
about a fire bursting from an old
ash can,

VII

—and the worn,
blue car rails (like the sky!)
gleaming among the cobbles!

VIII

—and the rickety ferry-boat "Arden"!
What an object to be called "Arden"
among the great piers,—on the
ever new river!
"Put me a Touchstone
at the wheel, white gulls, and we'll
follow the ghost of the *Half Moon*
to the North West Passage—and through!
(at Albany!) for all that!"

IX

Exquisite brown waves—long
circlets of silver moving over you!
enough with crumbling ice crusts among you!
The sky has come down to you,
lighter than tiny bubbles, face to
face with you!
His spirit is
a white gull with delicate pink feet
and a snowy breast for you to
hold to your lips delicately!

X

The young doctor is dancing with happiness
in the sparkling wind, alone
at the prow of the ferry! He notices
the curdy barnacles and broken ice crusts
left at the slip's base by the low tide
and thinks of summer and green
shell-crusted ledges among
                    the emerald eel-grass!

XI

Who knows the Palisades as I do
knows the river breaks east from them
above the city—but they continue south
—under the sky—to bear a crest of
little peering houses that brighten
with dawn behind the moody
water-loving giants of Manhattan.

XII

Long yellow rushes bending
above the white snow patches;
purple and gold ribbon
of the distant wood:
                what an angle
you make with each other as
you lie there in contemplation.

XIII

Work hard all your young days
and they'll find you too, some morning
staring up under
your chiffonier at its warped
bass-wood bottom and your soul—
out!
—among the little sparrows
behind the shutter.

XIV

—and the flapping flags are at
half mast for the dead admiral.

XV

All this—
            was for you, old woman.
I wanted to write a poem
that you would understand.
For what good is it to me
if you can't understand it?
                  But you got to try hard—
But—
       Well, you know how
the young girls run giggling
on Park Avenue after dark
when they ought to be home in bed?
Well,
that's the way it is with me somehow.

To Elsie

The pure products of America
go crazy—
mountain folk from Kentucky

or the ribbed north end of
Jersey
with its isolate lakes and

valleys, its deaf-mutes, thieves
old names
and promiscuity between

devil-may-care men who have taken
to railroading
out of sheer lust of adventure—

and young slatterns, bathed
in filth
from Monday to Saturday

to be tricked out that night
with gauds
from imaginations which have no

peasant traditions to give them
character
but flutter and flaunt

sheer rags—succumbing without
emotion
save numbed terror

under some hedge of choke-cherry
or viburnum—
which they cannot express—

Unless it be that marriage
perhaps
with a dash of Indian blood

will throw up a girl so desolate
so hemmed round
with disease or murder

that she'll be rescued by an
agent—
reared by the state and

sent out at fifteen to work in
some hard-pressed
house in the suburbs—

some doctor's family, some Elsie—
voluptuous water
expressing with broken

brain the truth about us—
her great
ungainly hips and flopping breasts

addressed to cheap
jewelry
and rich young men with fine eyes

as if the earth under our feet
were
an excrement of some sky

and we degraded prisoners
destined
to hunger until we eat filth

while the imagination strains
after deer
going by fields of goldenrod in

the stifling heat of September
Somehow
it seems to destroy us

It is only in isolate flecks that
something
is given off

No one
to witness
and adjust, no one to drive the car

A Sort of a Song

Let the snake wait under
his weed
and the writing
be of words, slow and quick, sharp
to strike, quiet to wait,
sleepless.

—through metaphor to reconcile
the people and the stones.
Compose. (No ideas
but in things) Invent!
Saxifrage is my flower that splits
the rocks.

The Wind Increases

The harried
earth is swept
The trees
the tulip's bright
tips
sidle and
toss—
Loose your love
to flow

Blow!

Good Christ what is
a poet—if any
exists?
a man
whose words will
bite
their way
home—being actual

having the form
of motion

At each twigtip

new

upon the tortured
body of thought

gripping
the ground

a way
to the last leaftip

At the Ball Game

The crowd at the ball game
is moved uniformly

by a spirit of uselessness
which delights them—

all the exciting detail
of the chase

and the escape, the error
the flash of genius—

all to no end save beauty
the eternal—

So in detail they, the crowd,
are beautiful

for this
to be warned against

saluted and defied—
It is alive, venomous

it smiles grimly
its words cut—

The flashy female with her
mother, gets it—

The Jew gets it straight—it
is deadly, terrifying—

It is the Inquisition, the
Revolution

It is beauty itself
that lives

day by day in them
idly—

This is
the power of their faces

It is summer, it is the solstice
the crowd is

cheering, the crowd is laughing
in detail

permanently, seriously
without thought

Between Walls

the back wings
of the

hospital where
nothing

will grow lie
cinders

in which shine
the broken

pieces of a green
bottle

Nantucket

Flowers through the window
lavender and yellow

changed by white curtains—
Smell of cleanliness—

Sunshine of late afternoon—
On the glass tray

a glass pitcher, the tumbler
turned down, by which

a key is lying— And the
immaculate white bed

To a Poor Old Woman

munching a plum on
the street a paper bag
of them in her hand

They taste good to her
They taste good
to her. They taste
good to her

You can see it by
the way she gives herself
to the one half
sucked out in her hand

Comforted
a solace of ripe plums
seeming to fill the air
They taste good to her

The Last Words of My English Grandmother

There were some dirty plates
and a glass of milk
beside her on a small table
near the rank, disheveled bed—

Wrinkled and nearly blind
she lay and snored
rousing with anger in her tones
to cry for food,

Gimme something to eat—
They're starving me—
I'm all right I won't go
to the hospital. No, no, no

Give me something to eat
Let me take you
to the hospital, I said
and after you are well

you can do as you please.
She smiled, Yes
you do what you please first
then I can do what I please—

Oh, oh, oh! she cried
as the ambulance men lifted
her to the stretcher—
Is this what you call

making me comfortable?
By now her mind was clear—
Oh you think you're smart
you young people,

she said, but I'll tell you
you don't know anything.
Then we started.
On the way

we passed a long row
of elms. She looked at them
awhile out of
the ambulance window and said,

What are all those
fuzzy-looking things out there?
Trees? Well, I'm tired
of them and rolled her head away.

Shadows

I

Shadows cast by the street light
under the stars,
the head is tilted back,
the long shadow of the legs
presumes a world
taken for granted
on which the cricket trills.
The hollows of the eyes
are unpeopled.
Right and left
climb the ladders of night
as dawn races
to put out the stars.
That
is the poetic figure
but we know
better: what is not now
will never
be. Sleep secure,
the little dog in the snapshot
keeps his shrewd eyes
pared. Memory
is liver than sight.
A man
looking out,
seeing the shadows—
it is himself
that can be painlessly amputated
by a mere shifting
of the stars.
A comfort so easily not to be
and to be at once one
with every man.
The night blossoms
with a thousand shadows
so long
as there are stars,
street lights
or a moon and

who shall say
by their shadows
which is different
from the other
fat or lean.

II

Ripped from the concept of our lives
and from all concept
somehow, and plainly,
the sun will come up
each morning
and sink again.
So that we experience
violently
every day
two worlds
one of which we share with the
rose in bloom
and one,
by far the greater,
with the past,
the world of memory,
the silly world of history,
the world
of the imagination.
Which leaves only the beasts and trees,
crystals
with their refractive
surfaces
and rotting things
to stir our wonder.
Save for the little
central hole
of the eye itself
into which
we dare not stare too hard
or we are lost.
The instant

trivial as it is
is all we have
unless—unless
things the imagination feeds upon,
the scent of the rose,
startle us anew.

The Sparrow

(TO MY FATHER)

This sparrow
who comes to sit at my window
is a poetic truth
more than a natural one.
His voice,
his movements,
his habits—
how he loves to
flutter his wings
in the dust—
all attest it;
granted, he does it
to rid himself of lice
but the relief he feels
makes him
cry out lustily—
which is a trait
more related to music
than otherwise.
Wherever he finds himself
in early spring,
on back streets
or beside palaces,
he carries on
unaffectedly
his amours.
It begins in the egg,
his sex genders it:
What is more pretentiously
useless

or about which
we more pride ourselves?
It leads as often as not
to our undoing.
The cockerel, the crow
with their challenging voices
cannot surpass
the insistence
of his cheep!
Once
at El Paso
toward evening,
I saw—and heard!—
ten thousand sparrows
who had come in from
the desert
to roost. They filled the trees
of a small park. Men fled
(with ears ringing!)
from their droppings,
leaving the premises
to the alligators
who inhabit
the fountain. His image
is familiar
as that of the aristocratic
unicorn, a pity
there are not more oats eaten
nowadays
to make living easier
for him.
At that,
his small size,
keen eyes,
serviceable beak
and general truculence
assure his survival—
to say nothing
of his innumerable
brood.
Even the Japanese
know him

and have painted him
sympathetically,
with profound insight
into his minor
characteristics.
Nothing even remotely
subtle
about his lovemaking.
He crouches
before the female,
drags his wings,
waltzing,
throws back his head
and simply—
yells! The din
is terrific.
The way he swipes his bill
across a plank
to clean it,
is decisive.
So with everything
he does. His coppery
eyebrows
give him the air
of being always
a winner—and yet
I saw once,
the female of his species
clinging determinedly
to the edge of
a water pipe,
catch him
by his crown-feathers
to hold him
silent,
subdued,
hanging above the city streets
until
she was through with him.
What was the use
of that?
She hung there

herself,
puzzled at her success.
I laughed heartily.
Practical to the end,
it is the poem
of his existence
that triumphed
finally;
a wisp of feathers
flattened to the pavement,
wings spread symmetrically
as if in flight,
the head gone,
the black escutcheon of the breast
undecipherable,
an effigy of a sparrow,
a dried wafer only,
left to say
and it says it
without offense,
beautifully;
This was I,
a sparrow.
I did my best;
farewell.

Winter Trees

All the complicated details
of the attiring and
the disattiring are completed!
A liquid moon
moves gently among
the long branches.
Thus having prepared their buds
against a sure winter
the wise trees
stand sleeping in the cold.

Complaint

They call me and I go.
It is a frozen road
past midnight, a dust
of snow caught
in the rigid wheeltracks.
The door opens.
I smile, enter and
shake off the cold.
Here is a great woman
on her side in the bed.
She is sick,
perhaps vomiting,
perhaps laboring
to give birth to
a tenth child. Joy! Joy!
Night is a room
darkened for lovers,
through the jalousies the sun
has sent one gold needle!
I pick the hair from her eyes
and watch her misery
with compassion.

Waiting

When I am alone I am happy.
The air is cool. The sky is
flecked and splashed and wound
with color. The crimson phalloi
of the sassafras leaves
hang crowded before me
in shoals on the heavy branches.
When I reach my doorstep
I am greeted by
the happy shrieks of my children
and my heart sinks.
I am crushed.

Are not my children as dear to me
as falling leaves or
must one become stupid
to grow older?
It seems much as if Sorrow
had tripped up my heels.
Let us see, let us see!
What did I plan to say to her
when it should happen to me
as it has happened now?

The Great Figure

Among the rain
and lights
I saw the figure 5
in gold
on a red
firetruck
moving
tense
unheeded
to gong clangs
siren howls
and wheels rumbling
through the dark city.

The Locust Tree in Flower

Among
of
green

stiff
old
bright

broken
branch
come

white
sweet
May

again

Young Love

What about all this writing?

O "Kiki"
O Miss Margaret Jarvis
The backhandspring
I: clean
   clean
   clean: yes . . New York

Wrigley's, appendicitis, John Marin:
skyscraper soup—

Either that or a bullet!

Once
anything might have happened
You lay relaxed on my knees—
the starry night
spread out warm and blind
above the hospital—

Pah!

It is unclean
which is not straight to the mark—

In my life the furniture eats me

the chairs, the floor
the walls
which heard your sobs
drank up my emotion—
they which alone know everything

and snitched on us in the morning—

What to want?

Drunk we go forward surely
Not I

beds, beds, beds
elevators, fruit, night-tables
breasts to see, white and blue—
to hold in the hand, to nozzle

It is not onion soup
Your sobs soaked through the walls
breaking the hospital to pieces
Everything
—windows, chairs
obscenely drunk, spinning—
white, blue, orange
—hot with our passion
wild tears, desperate rejoinders
my legs, turning slowly
end over end in the air!

But what would you have?

All I said was:
there, you see, it is broken
stockings, shoes, hairpins
your bed, I wrapped myself round you—

I watched.

You sobbed, you beat your pillow
you tore your hair
you dug your nails into your sides

I was your nightgown
                                        I watched!

Clean is he alone
after whom stream

the broken pieces of the city—
flying apart at his approaches

but I merely
caressed you curiously
fifteen years ago and you still
go about the city, they say
patching up sick school children

Asphodel, That Greeny Flower

Of asphodel, that greeny flower,
    I come, my sweet,
        to sing to you.

My heart rouses
    thinking to bring you news
        of something

that concerns you
    and concerns many men

        Look at
    what passes for the new.

You will not find it there but in
    despised poems.

    It is difficult

to get the news from poems
    yet men die miserably every day
        for lack

of what is found there.

Here me out
    for I too am concerned

and every man
    who wants to die at peace in his bed
        besides.

From *Paterson*

Paterson lies in the valley under the Passaic Falls
its spent waters forming the outline of his back. He
lies on his right side, head near the thunder
of the waters filling his dreams! Eternally asleep,
his dreams walk about the city where he persists
incognito. Butterflies settle on his stone ear.
Immortal he neither moves nor rouses and is seldom
seen, though he breathes and the subtleties of his machinations
drawing their substance from the noise of the pouring river
animate a thousand automatons. Who because they
neither know their sources nor the sills of their
disappointments walk outside their bodies aimlessly for the
most part,
locked and forgot in their desires—unroused. . . .

Say it! No ideas but in things. Mr.
Paterson has gone away
to rest and write. Inside the bus one sees
his thoughts sitting and standing. His
thoughts alight and scatter—

Who are these people (how complex
the mathematic) among whom I see myself
in the regularly ordered plateglass of
his thoughts, glimmering before shoes and bicycles?
They walk incommunicado, the
equation is beyond solution, yet
its sense is clear—that they may live
his thought is listed in the Telephone
Directory—

A wonder! A wonder!

Around the falling waters the Furies hurl!
Violence gathers, spins in their heads summoning
them:

They begin!
The perfections are sharpened

The flower spreads its colored petals
            wide in the sun
But the tongue of the bee
            misses them
They sink back into the loam
            crying out
—you may call it a cry
that creeps over them, a shiver
            as they wilt and disappear:
Marriage comes to have a shuddering
            implication

            Crying out
or take a lesser satisfaction:
            a few go
to the Coast without gain—
The language is missing them
            they die also
            incommunicado.

The language, the language
            fails them
They do not know the words
            or have not
The courage to use them
            —girls from
families that have decayed and
taken to the hills: no words.
They may look at the torrent in
            their minds
and it is foreign to them.

They turn their backs
and grow faint—but recover!
            Life is sweet
they say: the language!
            —the language
is divorced from their minds,
the language . . . the language!

From *Paterson* (Book Three)

II. THE LIBRARY FIRE

Fire burns; that is the first law.
When a wind fans it the flames

are carried abroad. Talk
fans the flames. They have

manoeuvred it so that to write
is a fire and not only of the blood.

The writing is nothing, the being
in a position to write (that's

where they get you) is nine tenths
of the difficulty: seduction

or strong arm stuff. The writing
should be a relief,

relief from the conditions
which as we advance become—a fire,

a destroying fire. For the writing
is also an attack and means must be

found to scotch it—at the root
if possible. So that

to write, nine tenths of the problem
is to live. They see

to it, not by intellection but
by sub-intellection (to want to be

blind as a pretext for
saying, We're so proud of you!

A wonderful gift! How *do*
you find the time for it in

your busy life? It must be a great
thing to have such a pastime.

But you were always a strange
boy. How's your mother?)

—the cyclonic fury, the fire,
the leaden flood and finally
the cost—

Your father was *such* a nice man.
I remember him well

Or, Geeze, Doc, I guess it's all right
but what the hell does it mean?

With due ceremony a hut would be constructed consisting of twelve poles, each of a different species of wood. These they run into the ground, tie them together at the top, cover them entirely with bark, skins or blankets joined close together. . Now here is where one sits who will address the Spirit of Fire, He-Who-Lies-With-His-Eyes-Bulging-In-The-Smoke-Hole . Twelve *manittos* attend him as subordinate deities, half representing animals and the others vegetables. A large oven is built in the house of sacrifice . heated with twelve large red-hot stones.

Meanwhile an old man throws twelve pipefuls of tobacco upon the hot stones, and directly another follows and pours water on them, which occasions a smoke or vapor almost powerful enough to suffocate the persons in the tent —

Ex qua re, quia sicubi fumus adscendit in altum; ita sacrificulus, duplicata altiori voce, *Kännakä, kännakä!* vel aliquando *Hoo Hoo!* faciem versus orientem convertit.

Whereupon as the smoke ascends on high, the sacrificer crying with a loud voice, *Kännakä, Kännakä!* or sometimes, *Hoo, Hoo!* turns his face towards the east.

While some are silent during the sacrifice, certain make a ridiculous speech, while others imitate the cock, the squirrel and other animals, and make all kinds of noises. During the shouting two roast deer are distributed.

(breathing the books in)
the acrid fumes,
for what they could decipher .
warping the sense to detect the norm, to break

through the skull of custom
                    to a place hidden from
affection, women and offspring—an affection
for the burning   .

It started in the car barns of the street railway company, in the paint shop. The men had been working all day refinishing old cars with the doors and windows kept closed because of the weather which was very cold. There was paint and especially varnish being used freely on all sides. Heaps of paint soaked rags had been thrown into the corners. One of the cars took fire in the night.

Breathless and in haste
the various night (of books) awakes! awakes
and begins (a second time) its song, pending the
obloquy of dawn   .
                    It will not last forever
against the long sea, the long, long
sea, swept by winds, the "wine-dark sea"   .

A cyclotron, a sifting   .

        And there,
in the tobacco hush   :   in a tepee they lie
huddled (a huddle of books)
            antagonistic,
                    and dream of
gentleness—under the malignity of the hush
they cannot penetrate and cannot waken, to be again
active but remain—books
            that is, men in hell,
their reign over the living ended
Clearly, they say. Oh clearly! Clearly?
What more clear than that of all things
nothing is so unclear, between man and
his writing, as to which is the man and
which the thing and of them both which
is the more to be valued

When discovered it was a small blaze, though it was hot but it looked as tho' the firemen could handle it. But at dawn a wind came up and the flames (which they thought were subsiding) got suddenly out of control—sweeping the block and heading toward the business district. Before noon the whole city was doomed —

Beautiful thing
—the whole city doomed! And
the flames towering .

like a mouse, like
a red slipper, like
a star, a geranium,
a cat's tongue or—

thought, thought
that is a leaf, a
pebble, an old man
out of a story by

Pushkin .

Ah!
rotten beams tum-
bling,

. an old bottle

mauled
The night was made day by the flames, flames
on which he fed—grubbing the page
(the burning page)
like a worm—for enlightenment

Of which we drink and are drunk and in the end
are destroyed (as we feed). But the flames
are flames with a requirement, a belly of their
own that destroys—as there are fires that
smolder
smolder a lifetime and never burst
into flame

Papers
(consumed) scattered to the winds. Black.
The ink burned white, metal white. So be it.

Come overall beauty. Come soon. So be it.
A dust between the fingers. So be it.
Come tatterdemalion futility. Win through.
So be it.— So be it.

An iron dog, eyes
aflame in a flame-filled corridor. A drunkenness
of flames. So be it. A bottle, mauled
by the flames, belly-bent with laughter:
yellow, green. So be it—of drunkenness
survived, in guffaws of flame. All fire afire!
So be it. Swallowing the fire. So be
it. Torqued to laughter by the fire,
the very fire. So be it. Chortling at flames
sucked in, a multiformity of laughter, a
flaming gravity surpassing the sobriety of
flames, a chastity of annihilation. Recreant,
calling it good. Calling the fire good.
So be it. The beauty of fire-blasted sand
that was glass, that was a bottle: unbottled.
Unabashed. So be it.
An old bottle, mauled by the fire
gets a new glaze, the glass warped
to a new distinction, reclaiming the
undefined. A hot stone, reached
by the tide, crackled over by fine
lines, the glaze unspoiled .
Annihilation ameliorated: Hottest
lips lifted till no shape but a vast
molt of the news flows. Drink
of the news, fluid to the breath.
Shouts its laughter, crying out—by
an investment of grace in the sand
—or stone: oasis water. The glass
splotched with concentric rainbows
of cold fire that the fire has bequeathed
there as it cools, its flame
defied—the flame that wrapped the glass
deflowered, reflowered there by
the flame: a second flame, surpassing
heat

Hell's fire. Fire. Sit your horny ass
down. What's your game? Beat you
at your own game, Fire. Outlast you:
Poet Beats Fire at Its Own Game! The bottle!
the bottle! the bottle! the bottle! I
give you the bottle! What's burning
now, Fire?

The Library?

Whirling flames, leaping
from house to house, building to building

carried by the wind
the Library is in their path

Beautiful thing! aflame .

a defiance of authority
—burnt Sappho's poems, burned
by intention (or are they still hid
in the Vatican crypts?) :
beauty is
a defiance of authority :

for they were
unwrapped, fragment by fragment, from
outer mummy cases of papier mâché inside
Egyptian sarcophagi .

flying papers
from old conflagrations, picked up
haphazard by the undertakers to make
moulds, layer after layer
for the dead

Beautiful thing

The anthology suppressed, revived even by
the dead, you who understand nothing
of this:

Dürer's *Melancholy,* the gears
lying disrelated to the mathematics of the
machine
Useless.

Beautiful thing, your
vulgarity of beauty surpasses all their
perfections!

Vulgarity surpasses all perfections
—it leaps from a varnish pot and we see
it pass—in flames!

Beautiful thing

—intertwined with the fire. An identity
surmounting the world, its core—from which
we shrink squirting little hoses of
objection—and
I along with the rest, squirting
at the fire

Poet.
Are you there?

How shall I find examples? Some boy
who drove a bull-dozer through
the barrage at Iwo Jima and turned it
and drove back making a path for the others—

Voiceless, his
action gracing a flame
—but lost, lost
because there is no way to link
the syllables anew to imprison him

No twist of the flame
in his own image : he goes nameless
until a Niké shall live in his honor—

And for that, invention is lacking,
the words are lacking:

the waterfall of the
flames, a cataract reversed, shooting
upward (what difference does it make?)

The language,

Beautiful thing—that I
make a fool of myself, mourning the lack
of dedication
mourning its losses,
for you

Scarred, fire swept
(by a nameless fire, that is unknown even
to yourself) nameless,

drunk.

Rising, with a whirling motion, the person
passed into the flame, becomes the flame—
the flame taking over the person

—with a roar, an outcry
which none can afford (we die in silence, we
enjoy shamefacedly—in silence, hiding
our joy even from each other
keeping
a secret joy in the flame which we dare
not acknowledge)

a shriek of fire with
the upwind, whirling the room away—to reveal
the awesome sight of a tin roof (1880)
entire, half a block long, lifted like a
skirt, held by the fire—to rise at last,
almost with a sigh, rise and float, float
upon the flames as upon a sweet breeze,
and majestically drift off, riding the air,
sliding
upon the air, easily and away over
the frizzled elms that seem to bend under
it, clearing the railroad tracks to fall
upon the roofs beyond, red hot

darkening the rooms
                    (but not our minds)

While we stand with our mouths open,
shaking our heads and saying, My God, did
you ever see anything like that? As though
it were wholly out of our dreams, as
indeed it is, unparalleled in our most sanguine
dreams .

                    The person submerged
in wonder, the fire become the person .

But the pathetic library (that contained,
perhaps, not one volume of distinction)
must go down also—

                    BECAUSE IT IS SILENT. IT
IS SILENT BY DEFECT OF VIRTUE IN THAT IT
CONTAINS NOTHING OF YOU

                    That which should be
rare is trash; because it contains
nothing of you. They spit on you,
literally, but without you, nothing. The
library is muffled and dead

                    But you are the dream
of dead men

                    Beautiful Thing!
Let them explain you and you will be
the heart of the explanation. Nameless,
you will appear
                    Beautiful Thing
the flame's lover—

                    The pitiful dead
cry back to us from the fire, cold in
the fire, crying out—wanting to be chaffed
and cherished
          those who have written books

We read: not the flames
but the ruin left
by the conflagration

Not the enormous burning
but the dead (the books
remaining). Let us read .

and digest: the surface
glistens, only the surface.
Dig in—and you have

a nothing, surrounded by
a surface, an inverted
bell resounding, a

white-hot man become
a book, the emptiness of
a cavern resounding

Hi Kid

I know you just about to shot me. But honest Hon. I have really been to busy to write. Here there, and everywhere.

Bab I haven't wrote since October so I will go back to Oct. 31, (Oh by the way are friend Madam B. Harris had a party the 31, but only high browns and *yellow* so I wasn't invited)

But I pay that no mind, cause I really (pitched myself a ball) Went to the show early in the day, and then to the dance at the club. had me a (some kinded fine time) I was feeling good believe me you. child.

But, child, Nov 1, I did crack you know yourself I been going full force on the (jug) will we went out (going to Newark) was raining, car slapped on brakes, car turned around a few times, rocked a bit and stopped facing the other way, from which we was going. Pal, believe me for the next few days. Honey, I couldn't even pick up a half filled bucket of hot water for fear of scalding myself.

Now I don't know which did it the jug or the car skidding but all I know is I was nowhere on nerves. But as they say alls well that ends well So Nov 15, I mean Kid I was so teaed that I didn't know a from z I really mean I was teaed Since Nov 15 I Have been at it again ever since.

But now for the (Boys) How Raymond James People going with Sis but is in jail for giving Joseble Miller a baby.

Robert Blocker has taken his ring from Sally Mitchell

Little Sonny Jones is supposed to be the father of a girl's baby on Liberty St.

Sally Mund Barbara H Jean C and Mary M are all supposed to be going to have kids Nelson W. a boy on 3rd St is father to 3 kids on their way.

. . . .

P.S. Kid do you think in your next letter of your you could tell me how to get over there.

Tell Raymond I said I bubetut hatche isus cashutute
Just a new way of talking kid. It is called (Tut) maybe you heard of it.
Well here hoping you can read it

D
J
B

So long.

Later
Beautiful thing
I saw you:

Yes, said
the Lady of the House to my questioning.
Downstairs
(by the laundry tubs)
and she pointed,
smiling, to the basement, still smiling, and
went out and left me with you (alone in the house)
lying there, ill
(I don't at all think that you
were ill)
by the wall on your damp bed, your long
body stretched out negligently on the dirty sheet .

Where is the pain?
(You put on a simper designed
not to reveal)

—the small window with two panes,
my eye level of the ground, the furnace odor .

Persephone
gone to hell, that hell could not keep with
the advancing season of pity.

—for I was overcome
by amazement and could do nothing but admire
and lean to care for you in your quietness—

who looked at me, smiling, and we remained
thus looking, each at the other . in silence .

You lethargic, waiting upon me, waiting for
the fire and I
attendant upon you, shaken by your beauty

Shaken by your beauty .
Shaken.

—flat on your back, in a low bed (waiting)
under the mud plashed windows among the scabrous
dirt of the holy sheets .
You showed me your legs, scarred (as a child)
by the whip .

Read. Bring the mind back (attendant upon
the page) to the day's heat. The page also is
the same beauty : a dry beauty of the page—
beaten by whips

A tapestry hound
with his thread teeth drawing crimson from
the throat of the unicorn

. . . a yelping of white hounds
—under a ceiling like that of San Lorenzo, the long
painted beams, straight across, that preceded
the domes and arches
more primitive, square edged

. a docile queen, not bothered
to stick her tongue out at the moon, indifferent,
through loss, but .
queenly,
in bad luck, the luck of the stars, the black stars

. the night of a mine

Dear heart
It's all for you, my dove, my
changeling
But you!
—in your white lace dress
"the dying swan"
and high-heeled slippers—tall
as you already were—
till your head
through fruitful exaggeration
was reaching the sky and the
prickles of its ecstasy
Beautiful Thing!
And the guys from Paterson
beat up
the guys from Newark and told
them to stay the hell out
of their territory and then
socked you one
across the nose
Beautiful Thing
for good luck and emphasis
cracking it
till I must believe that all
desired women have had each
in the end
a busted nose
and live afterward marked up
Beautiful Thing
for memory's sake
to be credible in their deeds

Then back to the party!
and they maled
and femaled you jealously
Beautiful Thing
as if to discover whence and
by what miracle
there should escape, what?
still to be possessed, out of
what part
Beautiful Thing

should it look?
        or be extinguished—
Three days in the same dress
        up and down   .

                I can't be half gentle enough,
half tender enough
                toward you, toward you,
inarticulate, not half loving enough

BRIGHTen

                        the cor
                                        ner
where   you   are!

                                —a flame,
        black plush, a dark flame.

Ezra Pound

[1885–1972]

It has been said of Ezra Pound that modern poetry would be substantially poorer without him, that he is the single most important influence on the history of poetry in our century. And although some might disagree with the largeness of this claim, few would deny Pound an important place in modern literary history. Why? Partly because of his own poetry, which consistently sought to find ways to revitalize the past, to make it relevant to the modern world. Partly also because of his prolific output of nearly one hundred volumes, including critical manifestos, anthologies of poems, translations, and literary criticism. In part, finally, because of his generous intervention on behalf of young writers whose works he championed (and sometimes influenced) in an effort to secure their initial publication; among the more famous writers he assisted were T. S. Eliot, Robert Frost, Marianne Moore, William Carlos Williams, Ernest Hemingway, and James Joyce.

Pound's poetry is animated by a desire to retain and renew the great literature of the past. As an editor, critic, and translator, he restored an appreciation of the achievements not only of individual poets such as Homer and Propertius, but also of specific literary genres such as the troubadour poetry of twelfth-century Provence. Pound's cultural impetus was evident in his support of and friendship with artists such as the French sculptor Henri Gaudier-Brzeska and the violinist Olga Rudge, with whom he later lived.

For Pound, art was a way of both preserving history and making it. He considered works of art to be embodiments of their historical moment, bearing signs of their cultural identity and their creator's individuality. Pound also believed that true artists passionately devote themselves to their own specific craft but also exhibit a love of other arts as well. Pound himself exemplified this ideal. Besides his friendship with artists, he contributed art and music reviews to *The New Age,* wrote a book on the American composer George Antheil, and composed an opera, *Villon.* At one point he defined poetry as a composition of words set to music; at another he condemned poets uninterested in art and music as bad poets.

The literary movements with which Pound has most often been associated are Imagism and Vorticism. Imagism, the more important, was less a revolutionary than a purificatory movement in poetry. Reacting against tendencies in late nineteenth-century and early twentieth-century Victorian and Edwardian verse—such as verbosity, didacticism, excessive ornamentation, and metrical regularity—the Imagists advocated precision and concreteness of detail, concentration of language, and a freshness of rhythmic cadence. Pound saw the image as the poet's pigment, the artist's way of making an impression visually, intellectually, and emotionally.

Pound's imagistic tendencies were strongly manifested in his works. Counseling poets to fear abstraction, Pound summed up his principles of Imagism as a set of guidelines in "A Few Don'ts for an Imagist":

1. To present a direct treatment of the thing described.
2. To use absolutely no word that does not contribute to the presentation of the image.
3. To compose on the order of musical cadence and phrasing, not according to strict, unvarying rhythms.

But even though the Imagism of early Pound and H.D., Amy Lowell, William Carlos Williams, and others contributed to a revitalized American poetry, the movement had its limits. Its central limitation was one of its outstanding strengths—its pictorial precision. Imagistic poems tend to be static; they lack movement and tension. Pound's images, however, generally avoid this static pictorialism. Consider, for example, his most famous Imagist poem:

In a Station of the Metro

The apparition of these faces in the crowd;
Petals on a wet, black bough.

In *The Pound Era,* Hugh Kenner has described in illuminating detail the genesis of this poem. He argues that Pound's poem is not merely a static image or pictorial representation, however sharp, of something seen, preserved through memory, and later recorded in verse. Kenner quotes Pound's description of the stimulus for the poem: on a visit to Paris, he emerged from the Metro (Parisian subway) and "saw suddenly a beautiful face, and then another and another, and then a beautiful child's face, and then another beautiful woman, and I tried all that day to find words for what they had meant to me, and I could not find any words that seemed to me worthy, or as lovely as that sudden emotion."

Pound's final words ("that sudden emotion") provide the key to his initial experience and to his poetic intention and achievement. For Pound desired to translate his experience into an imagistic poem that would be the equivalent of an abstract painting—not a verbal portrait of what he had seen, but rather, as Kenner notes, "an abstract equivalent for it, reduced, intensified." Pound wrote a thirty-line poem, which he destroyed; six months later he produced another, shorter poem, which he also destroyed. Then, a year later, he completed the twenty words (title included) of "In a Station of the Metro."

The poem nicely illustrates Pound's definition of an image as "that which presents an intellectual and emotional complex in an instant of time." In calling it a "cluster" and a "VORTEX, from which and through which, and into which, ideas are constantly rushing," Pound went beyond the static Imagism of his contemporaries, moving toward a dynamic Imagism, which he soon termed Vorticism, a short-lived movement he inaugurated with the painter and writer Wyndham Lewis. Its central feature was the vortex or whirlpool of energy that the artist drew on to invent new forms and measures, rather than imitate old ones. But as we have seen, Pound's Imagism also actively sets things into relation with and against one another. "In a Station of the Metro," as Kenner has suggested, exhibits an act of mind by discovering a connection and devising a form of compressed metaphor to express this resemblance and its emotional significance.

There are additional problems, however, with the work of some Imagist poems: a lack of discursiveness, an avoidance of transitions, and an emphasis on particular poetic moments, all of which made it difficult for Imagist poets to sustain a long poem. T. S. Eliot partly solved this problem in *The Waste Land* by using a musical structure that includes repetition, thematic variation, and ironic juxtaposition of images. Pound employed similar techniques in "Hugh Selwyn Mauberley." "Mauberley" has been seen as a collection of fragments comparable to those in Eliot's *The Waste Land.* But whereas the images in Eliot's poem seem to offer a hopeful restoration of meaning to life, Pound's images hold out no such possibility. Instead, the speaker of "Mauberley" ironically depicts the loss of coherence in society, the futility of poetic ambition, the destructive consequences of materialism, and the general cultural decay of modern civilization, especially the British empire. (Some have seen these, however, as basic themes in *The Waste Land,* as well.) Like Eliot's "Gerontion," "Mauberley" anticipates some of the technical devices of *The Waste Land,* especially its shifts of perspective, its amalgam of unidentified quotations in different languages, and its discontinuous structure. It differs from *The Waste Land,* however, and more closely approximates "Gerontion" and "The Love Song of J. Alfred Prufrock" in its focus on a single consciousness, though its scope and ambition have more in common with Eliot's longer poem.

Before "Mauberley," Pound was occupied with translations of poems from Chinese and Provençal, especially the troubadour poetry of Bertrans de Born. In both *Cathay* and *Personae* Pound employed the technique of speaking from behind a mask, speaking in the voice of another. From Provençal, Pound adapted de Born's "Sestina: Altaforte," capturing its vigorous energy and feverish lust for battle. The poem's repetitive structure creates a crescendo of emotional power, well suited to the intensity of the speaker's martial obsession. From the Chinese of Li Po, Pound created versions of poems that were less strictly translations than adaptations. Pound based his versions on the notes of the American Sinologist Ernest Fenollosa, who, like Pound, could not read Chinese, but who had had the poems translated by Japanese scholars. This fact accounts in large measure for Pound's use of Japanese spellings of place names in poems like "The River-Merchant's Wife: A Letter" and for its attribution to Rihaku, the Japanese name of Li Po. What perhaps fascinated Pound most about Chinese was the imagistic quality not only of the poems he adapted, but of the Chinese characters, which embody words and images simultaneously. Later, Pound explored the problems of life and love in the modern world by adapting the persona of the classical Roman poet Sextus Propertius.

Though Pound's poetic activity took him well beyond the land and culture of his birth, his background was distinctively American. He was born in Idaho in 1885 and was educated at Hamilton College and the University of Pennsylvania, from which he earned a B.A. and an M.A., respectively. He taught briefly at Wabash College in Indiana but soon left to travel and live abroad, settling in London (1908–1920), Paris (1920–1924), and Rapallo, Italy (1924–1945). Pound was exceptionally active in literary pursuits of all sorts, particularly in founding and editing literary journals. He was the London editor of *Poetry* (1912–1919) and of *The Little Review* (1917–1919), the cofounder and editor of *The Exile* (1927–1928), and the Paris correspondent for *The Dial.* In 1914, he married Dorothy Shakespear, with whom he lived at Rapallo in alternation with Olga Rudge, by whom he had a child and with whom he lived in Venice.

Pound was more conservative in politics than in literature. For him the measure of a society's political integrity was the degree to which it allowed art to flourish. Pound saw capitalism as evil, and he viewed banking as a curse, associating it with usury, which he believed was contrary to nature. Ideas like these led Pound toward anti-Semitism, which was apparent in a series of broadcasts he made over Italian radio during the Second World War. The broadcasts were savagely critical of American policy and of Jews and were later deemed traitorous by a postwar tribunal. Arrested and imprisoned near Pisa in 1945, Pound was found unfit for trial by reason of insanity and was committed to St. Elizabeths Hospital in Washington, D.C. He was released in 1958, due largely to the persistent efforts of other American poets, including Robert Frost and Archibald MacLeish. Pound returned to Italy, where he lived until his death in 1972.

When Pound was awarded the prestigious Bollingen Poetry Prize in 1948, a heated debate arose about his worthiness to receive it. Those who considered a poet's life and work as inextricably united were angered by the award. Others, separating the writer's politics from his poetry, felt that Pound's poetic achievement had been justly acknowledged. Still others were understandably ambivalent about the tribute. Disputes about this issue are still aired occasionally, though Pound's reputation as a preeminent Modernist poet–critic has been secured.

Pound's most ambitious and complex work of poetry is *The Cantos,* his attempt to write a modern epic. *The Cantos* make sustained and complex use of literary allusion to call up the context of literary works and historical events. Like Eliot, with whom he shared a propensity for learned reference, Pound expected his readers to be conversant with a broad range of humanistic knowledge, including a variety of languages and literatures both classical and modern, along with Italian art, Chinese philosophy, and modern American economic theory. These are among the subjects that appear in *The Cantos,* which together form a body of 117 separate poems and several fragments that combine description, reminiscence, meditation, quotation, and speculation in a complex amalgamation of forms, meters, and voices.

The Cantos occupied Pound for more than fifty years, from 1917 to 1968. Animating the poems is a set of beliefs about the importance and dignity of honest labor, whether that labor is channeled into making poems or furniture, and a corollary notion that what destroys societies is greed. These impulses are most clearly discernible in two of the more accessible *Cantos,* XLV and LXXXI. Although there is widespread disagreement about how effectively Pound has achieved his aims in *The Cantos,* and although his repugnant acts during World War II stained his reputation, there is no doubt that he has been a considerable force in modern poetry. In giving us the fragments of his poems, he assembled, as Donald Hall has suggested, "the best of himself and of the cultures he loved."

Portrait d'une Femme

Your mind and you are our Sargasso Sea,
London has swept about you this score years
And bright ships left you this or that in fee:
Ideas, old gossip, oddments of all things,
Strange spars of knowledge and dimmed wares of price.
Great minds have sought you—lacking someone else.
You have been second always. Tragical?
No. You preferred it to the usual thing:
One dull man, dulling and uxorious,
One average mind—with one thought less, each year.
Oh, you are patient, I have seen you sit
Hours, where something might have floated up.
And now you pay one. Yes, you richly pay.
You are a person of some interest, one comes to you
And takes strange gain away:
Trophies fished up; some curious suggestion;
Fact that leads nowhere; and a tale or two,
Pregnant with mandrakes, or with something else
That might prove useful and yet never proves,
That never fits a corner or shows use,
Or finds its hour upon the loom of days:
The tarnished, gaudy, wonderful old work;
Idols and ambergris and rare inlays,
These are your riches, your great store; and yet
For all this sea-hoard of deciduous things,
Strange woods half sodden, and new brighter stuff:
In the slow float of differing light and deep,
No! there is nothing! In the whole and all,
Nothing that's quite your own.
Yet this is you.

A Pact

I make a pact with you, Walt Whitman—
I have detested you long enough.
I come to you as a grown child
Who has had a pig-headed father;

Portrait d'une Femme French for "portrait of a lady." [1]**Sargasso Sea** a sea in the North Atlantic, named and noted for its large masses of seaweed.

I am old enough now to make friends.
It was you that broke the new wood,
Now is a time for carving.
We have one sap and one root—
Let there be commerce between us.

The Rest

O helpless few in my country,
O remnant enslaved!

Artists broken against her,
A-stray, lost in the villages,
Mistrusted, spoken-against,

Lovers of beauty, starved,
Thwarted with systems,
Helpless against control;

You who can not wear yourselves out
By persisting to successes,
You who can only speak,
Who can not steel yourselves into reiteration;

You of the finer sense,
Broken against false knowledge,
You who can know at first hand,
Hated, shut in, mistrusted:

Take thought:
I have weathered the storm,
I have beaten out my exile.

A Virginal

No, no! Go from me. I have left her lately.
I will not spoil my sheath with lesser brightness,
For my surrounding air hath a new lightness;
Slight are her arms, yet they have bound me straitly
And left me cloaked as with a gauze of aether;

A VIRGINAL **Virginal** A small keyboard instrument, a rectangular harpsichord.

As with sweet leaves; as with subtle clearness.
Oh, I have picked up magic in her nearness
To sheathe me half in half the things that sheathe her.
No, no! Go from me. I have still the flavour,
Soft as spring wind that's come from birchen bowers.
Green come the shoots, aye April in the branches,
As winter's wound with her sleight hand she staunches,
Hath of the trees a likeness of the savour:
As white their bark, so white this lady's hours.

The Seafarer

FROM THE ANGLO-SAXON

May I, for my own self, song's truth reckon,
Journey's jargon, how I in harsh days
Hardship endured oft.
Bitter breast-cares have I abided,
Known on my keel many a care's hold,
And dire sea-surge, and there I oft spent
Narrow nightwatch nigh the ship's head
While she tossed close to cliffs. Coldly afflicted.
My feet were by frost benumbed.
Chill its chains are; chafing sighs
Hew my heart round and hunger begot
Mere-weary mood. Lest man know not
That he on dry land loveliest liveth,
List how I, care-wretched, on ice-cold sea,
Weathered the winter, wretched outcast
Deprived of my kinsmen;
Hung with hard ice-flakes, where hail-scur flew,
There I heard naught save the harsh sea
And ice-cold wave, at whiles the swan cries,
Did for my games the gannet's clamour,
Sea-fowls' loudness was for me laughter,
The mews' singing all my mead-drink.
Storms, on the stone-cliffs beaten, fell on the stern
In icy feathers; full oft the eagle screamed
With spray on his pinion.
Not any protector
May make merry man faring needy.
This he little believes, who aye in winsome life

Abides 'mid burghers some heavy business,
Wealthy and wine-flushed, how I weary oft
Must bide above brine.
Neareth nightshade, snoweth from north,
Frost froze the land, hail fell on earth then,
Corn of the coldest. Nathless there knocketh now
The heart's thought that I on high streams
The salt-wavy tumult traverse alone.
Moaneth alway my mind's lust
That I fare forth, that I afar hence
Seek out a foreign fastness.
For this there's no mood-lofty man over earth's midst,
Not though he be given his good, but will have in his youth
greed;
Nor his deed to the daring, nor his king to the faithful
But shall have his sorrow for sea-fare
Whatever his lord will.
He hath not heart for harping, nor in ring-having
Nor winsomeness to wife, nor world's delight
Nor any whit else save the wave's slash,
Yet longing comes upon him to fare forth on the water.
Bosque taketh blossom, cometh beauty of berries,
Fields to fairness, lands fares brisker,
All this admonisheth man eager of mood,
The heart turns to travel so that he then thinks
On flood-ways to be far departing.
Cuckoo calleth with gloomy crying,
He singeth summerward, bodeth sorrow,
The bitter heart's blood. Burgher knows not—
He the prosperous man—what some perform
Where wandering them widest draweth.
So that but now my heart burst from my breastlock,
My mood 'mid the mere-flood,
Over the whale's acre, would wander wide.
On earth's shelter cometh oft to me,
Eager and ready, the crying lone-flyer,
Whets for the whale-path the heart irresistibly,
O'er tracks of ocean; seeing that anyhow
My lord deems to me this dead life
On loan and on land, I believe not
That any earth-weal eternal standeth
Save there be somewhat calamitous

That, ere a man's tide go, turn it to twain.
Disease or oldness or sword-hate
Beats out the breath from doom-gripped body.
And for this, every earl whatever, for those speaking after—
Laud of the living, boasteth some last word,
That he will work ere he pass onward,
Frame on the fair earth 'gainst foes his malice,
Daring ado, . . .
So that all men shall honour him after
And his laud beyond them remain 'mid the English,
Aye, for ever, a lasting life's-blast,
Delight 'mid the doughty.
                                        Days little durable,
And all arrogance of earthen riches,
There come now no kings nor Cæsars
Nor gold-giving lords like those gone.
Howe'er in mirth most magnified,
Whoe'er lived in life most lordliest,
Drear all this excellence, delights undurable!
Waneth the watch, but the world holdeth.
Tomb hideth trouble. The blade is layed low.
Earthly glory ageth and seareth.
No man at all going the earth's gait,
But age fares against him, his face paleth,
Grey-haired he groaneth, knows gone companions,
Lordly men, are to earth o'ergiven,
Nor may he then the flesh-cover, whose life ceaseth,
Nor eat the sweet nor feel the sorry,
Nor stir hand nor think in mid heart,
And though he strew the grave with gold,
His born brothers, their buried bodies
Be an unlikely treasure hoard.

Ballad of the Goodly Fere

Simon Zelotes speaking after the Crucifixion.
Fere = Mate, Companion.

Ha' we lost the goodliest fere o' all
For the priests and the gallows tree?
Aye lover he was of brawny men,
O' ships and the open sea.

When they came wi' a host to take Our Man
His smile was good to see,
"First let these go!" quo' our Goodly Fere,
"Or I'll see ye damned," says he.

Aye he sent us out through the crossed high spears
And the scorn of his laugh rang free,
"Why took ye not me when I walked about
Alone in the town?" says he.

Oh we drank his "Hale" in the good red wine
When we last made company,
No capon priest was the Goodly Fere
But a man o' men was he.

I ha' seen him drive a hundred men
Wi' a bundle o' cords swung free,
That they took the high and holy house
For their pawn and treasury.

They'll no' get him a' in a book I think
Though they write it cunningly;
No mouse of the scrolls was the Goodly Fere
But aye loved the open sea.

If they think they ha' snared our Goodly Fere
They are fools to the last degree.
"I'll go to the feast," quo' our Goodly Fere,
"Though I go to the gallows tree."

"Ye ha' seen me heal the lame and blind,
And wake the dead," says he,
"Ye shall see one thing to master all:
'Tis how a brave man dies on the tree."

A son of God was the Goodly Fere
That bade us his brothers be.
I ha' seen him cow a thousand men.
I have seen him upon the tree.

He cried no cry when they drave the nails
And the blood gushed hot and free,

The hounds of the crimson sky gave tongue
But never a cry cried he.

I ha' seen him cow a thousand men
On the hills o' Galilee,
They whined as he walked out calm between,
Wi' his eyes like the grey o' the sea,

Like the sea that brooks no voyaging
With the winds unleashed and free,
Like the sea that he cowed at Genseret
Wi' twey words spoke' suddently.

A master of men was the Goodly Fere,
A mate of the wind and sea,
If they think they ha' slain our Goodly Fere
They are fools eternally.

I ha' seen him eat o' the honey-comb
Sin' they nailed him to the tree.

Sestina: Altaforte

LOQUITUR: *En* Bertrans de Born. Dante Alighieri put this man in hell for that he was a stirrer up of strife. Eccovi! Judge ye! Have I dug him up again? The scene is at his castle, Altaforte. "Papiols" is his jongleur. "The Leopard," the *device* of Richard Cœur de Lion.

I

Damn it all! all this our South stinks peace.
You whoreson dog, Papiols, come! Let's to music!
I have no life save when the swords clash.
But ah! when I see the standards gold, vair, purple, opposing
And the broad fields beneath them turn crimson,
Then howl I my heart nigh mad with rejoicing.

II

In hot summer have I great rejoicing
When the tempests kill the earth's foul peace,

And the lightnings from black heav'n flash crimson,
And the fierce thunders roar me their music
And the winds shriek through the clouds mad, opposing,
And through all the riven skies God's swords clash.

III

Hell grant soon we hear again the swords clash!
And the shrill neighs of destriers in battle rejoicing,
Spiked breast to spiked breast opposing!
Better one hour's stour than a year's peace
With fat boards, bawds, wine and frail music!
Bah! there's no wine like the blood's crimson!

IV

And I love to see the sun rise blood-crimson.
And I watch his spears through the dark clash
And it fills all my heart with rejoicing
And pries wide my mouth with fast music
When I see him so scorn and defy peace,
His lone might 'gainst all darkness opposing.

V

The man who fears war and squats opposing
My words for stour, hath no blood of crimson
But is fit only to rot in womanish peace
Far from where worth's won and the swords clash
For the death of such sluts I go rejoicing;
Yea, I fill all the air with my music.

VI

Papiols, Papiols, to the music!
There's no sound like to swords swords opposing,
No cry like the battle's rejoicing
When our elbows and swords drip the crimson

And our charges 'gainst "The Leopard's" rush clash.
May God damn for ever all who cry "Peace!"

VII

And let the music of the swords make them crimson!
Hell grant soon we hear again the swords clash!
Hell blot black for alway the thought "Peace!"

Planh for the Young English King[1]

That is, Prince Henry Plantagenet, elder brother to Richard Cœur de Lion.

If all the grief and woe and bitterness,
All dolour, ill and every evil chance
That ever came upon this grieving world
Were set together they would seem but light
Against the death of the young English King.
Worth lieth riven and Youth dolorous,
The world o'ershadowed, soiled and overcast,
Void of all joy and full of ire and sadness.

Grieving and sad and full of bitterness
Are left in teen the liegemen courteous,
The joglars supple and the troubadours.
O'er much hath ta'en Sir Death that deadly warrior
In taking from them the young English King,
Who made the freest hand seem covetous.
'Las! Never was nor will be in this world
The balance for this loss in ire and sadness!

O skillful Death and full of bitterness,
Well mayst thou boast that thou the best chevalier
That any folk e'er had, hast from us taken;
Sith nothing is that unto worth pertaineth
But had its life in the young English King
And better were it, should God grant his pleasure,

[1]*From the Provençal of Bertrans de Born "Si tuit li dolh elh plor elh marrimen."*

That he should live than many a living dastard
That doth but wound the good to ire and sadness.

From this faint world, how full of bitterness
Love takes his way and holds his joy deceitful,
Sith no thing is but turneth unto anguish
And each to-day 'vails less than yestere'en,
Let each man visage this young English King
That was most valiant 'mid all worthiest men!
Gone is his body fine and amorous,
Whence have we grief, discord and deepest sadness.

Him, whom it pleased for our great bitterness
To come to earth to draw us from misventure,
Who drank of death for our salvacioun,
Him do we pray as to a Lord most righteous
And humble eke, that the young English King
He please to pardon, as true pardon is,
And bid go in with honourèd companions,
There where there is no grief, nor shall be sadness.

Salutation

O generation of the thoroughly smug
        and thoroughly uncomfortable,
I have seen fishermen picnicking in the sun,
I have seen them with untidy families,
I have seen their smiles full of teeth
        and heard ungainly laughter.
And I am happier than you are,
And they were happier than I am;
And the fish swim in the lake
        and do not even own clothing.

The Return

See, they return; ah, see the tentative
Movements, and the slow feet,
The trouble in the pace and the uncertain
Wavering!

See, they return, one, and by one,
With fear, as half-awakened;
As if the snow should hesitate
And murmur in the wind,
                    and half turn back;
These were the "Wing'd-with-Awe,"
                    Inviolable,
Gods of the wingèd shoe!
With them the silver hounds,
                    sniffing the trace of air!

Haie! Haie!
          These were the swift to harry;
These the keen-scented;
These were the souls of blood.

Slow on the leash,
                    pallid the leash-men!

The Garden

En robe de parade.
SAMAIN

Like a skein of loose silk blown against a wall
She walks by the railing of a path in Kensington Gardens,
And she is dying piece-meal
          of a sort of emotional anæmia.

And round about there is a rabble
Of the filthy, sturdy, unkillable infants of the very poor.
They shall inherit the earth.

In her is the end of breeding.
Her boredom is exquisite and excessive.

THE GARDEN **En robe de parade.** French for "dressed for a state occasion." The phrase is from a poem by the French poet Albert Samain (1858–1900).
[7]**They shall inherit the earth** See Matthew 5:5, "Blessed are the meek, for they shall inherit the earth."

She would like some one to speak to her,
And is almost afraid that I
will commit that indiscretion.

Exile's Letter

Tō So-kiu of Rakuyō, ancient friend, Chancellor Gen.
Now I remember that you built me a special tavern
By the south side of the bridge at Ten-shin.
With yellow gold and white jewels, we paid for songs and laughter
And we were drunk for month on month, forgetting the kings and princes.
Intelligent men came drifting in from the sea and from the west border,
And with them, and with you especially
There was nothing at cross purpose,
And they made nothing of sea-crossing or of mountain-crossing,
If only they could be of that fellowship,
And we all spoke out our hearts and minds, and without regret.
And then I was sent off to South Wai,
smothered in laurel groves,
And you to the north of Raku-hoku,
Till we had nothing but thoughts and memories in common.
And then, when separation had come to its worst,
We met, and travelled into Sen-jō,
Through all the thirty-six folds of the turning and twisting waters,
Into a valley of the thousand bright flowers,
That was the first valley;
And into ten thousand valleys full of voices and pine winds.
And with silver harness and reins of gold,
Out came the East of Kan foreman and his company.
And there came also the "True man" of Shi-yō to meet me,
Playing on a jewelled mouth-organ.
In the storied houses of San-ka they gave us more Sennin music,
Many instruments, like the sound of young phœnix broods.

The foreman of Kan-chū, drunk, danced
          because his long sleeves wouldn't keep still
With that music playing,
And I, wrapped in brocade, went to sleep with my head on his lap,
And my spirit so high it was all over the heavens,
And before the end of the day we were scattered like stars, or rain.
I had to be off to So, far away over the waters,
You back to your river-bridge.

And your father, who was brave as a leopard,
Was governor in Hei Shu, and put down the barbarian rabble.
And one May he had you send for me,
          despite the long distance.
And what with broken wheels and so on, I won't say it wasn't hard going,
Over roads twisted like sheep's guts.
And I was still going, late in the year,
          in the cutting wind from the North,
And thinking how little you cared for the cost,
          and you caring enough to pay it.
And what a reception:
Red jade cups, food well set on a blue jewelled table,
And I was drunk, and had no thought of returning.
And you would walk out with me to the western corner of the castle,
To the dynastic temple, with water about it clear as blue jade,
With boats floating, and the sound of mouth-organs and drums,
With ripples like dragon-scales, going grass green on the water,
Pleasure lasting, with courtezans, going and coming without hindrance,
With the willow flakes falling like snow,
And the vermilioned girls getting drunk about sunset,
And the water, a hundred feet deep, reflecting green eyebrows
—Eyebrows painted green are a fine sight in young moonlight,
Gracefully painted—
And the girls singing back at each other,
Dancing in transparent brocade,

And the wind lifting the song, and interrupting it,
Tossing it up under the clouds.
          And all this comes to an end.
          And is not again to be met with.
I went up to the court for examination,
Tried Yō Yū's luck, offered the Chōyō song,
And got no promotion,
          and went back to the East Mountains
          White-headed.
And once again, later, we met at the South bridge-head.
And then the crowd broke up, you went north to San palace,
And if you ask how I regret that parting:
It is like the flowers falling at Spring's end
          Confused, whirled in a tangle.
What is the use of talking, and there is no end of talking,
There is no end of things in the heart.
I call in the boy,
Have him sit on his knees here
          To seal this,
And send it a thousand miles, thinking.

By Rihaku (Li T'ai Po)

From *Homage to Sextus Propertius*

V

Yet you ask on what account I write so many love-lyrics
And whence this soft book comes into my mouth.
Neither Calliope nor Apollo sung these things into my ear,
     My genius is no more than a girl.

If she with ivory fingers drive a tune through the lyre,
     We look at the process.
How easy the moving fingers; if hair is mussed on her forehead,
If she goes in a gleam of Cos, in a slither of dyed stuff,
There is a volume in the matter; if her eyelids sink into sleep,
There are new jobs for the author;

HOMAGE [3]**Calliope** one of the Muses, or goddesses of poetry. [3]**Apollo** Greek god of the sun. [8]**Cos** a Greek island famous for its light transparent dresses.

And if she plays with me with her shirt off,
We shall construct many Iliads.
And whatever she does or says
We shall spin long yarns out of nothing.
Thus much the fates have allotted me, and if, Maecenas,
I were able to lead heroes into armour, I would not,
Neither would I warble of Titans, nor of Ossa
spiked onto Olympus,
Nor of causeways over Pelion,
Nor of Thebes in its ancient respectability,
nor of Homer's reputation in Pergamus,
Nor of Xerxes' two-barreled kingdom, nor of
Remus and his royal family,
Nor of dignified Carthaginian characters,
Nor of Welsh mines and the profit Marus had out of them.

I should remember Caesar's affairs . . .
for a background,
Although Callimachus did without them,
and without Theseus,
Without an inferno, without Achilles attended of gods,
Without Ixion, and without the sons of Menoetius and the
Argo and without Jove's grave and the Titans.

And my ventricles do not palpitate to Caesarial *ore rotundos,*
Nor to the tune of the Phrygian fathers,

[12]**Iliad** Homeric epic poem about the Trojan War. [15]**Maecenas** friend of Roman emperor Augustus; patron of Roman poets Horace and Vergil. [17]**Titans** Legendary giants. [17]**Ossa** mountain locale of the war of the giants in Greek myth. [18]**Olympus** mountain home of the Greek pantheon of gods. [19]**Pelion** mountain with a temple to Zeus and cave of the centaur Chiron. [20]**Thebes** Ancient Greek city, center of military and political power until its decline in the fourth century B.C. [21]**Pergamus** Troy. [22]**Xerxes** Persian king who conquered Greece in the fifth century B.C. [23]**Remus** twin brother of Romulus, who founded the city of Rome. [24]**Carthaginian characters** Carthage was an ancient North African state that rivaled Rome in ecclesiastical and civil importance. [28]**Callimachus** Alexandrian poet. [29]**Theseus** legendary Greek hero who slew the Minotaur. [30]**Achilles** Greek hero of the *Iliad,* a warrior favored by the gods. [31]**Ixion** famous in Greek mythology for being punished by Zeus for an attempted seduction of Hera, Zeus's wife. Ixion was chained to a wheel and rolled through the heavens. [31]**Menoetius** father of Patroclus, Greek warrior and friend of Achilles. [32]**Argo** in Greek mythology, ship in which the Argonauts sailed to search for the Golden Fleece. [34]**Phrygian fathers** influenced the development of early Greek music.

Sailor, of winds; a plowman, concerning his oxen;
Soldier, the enumeration of wounds; the sheep-feeder, of ewes;
We, in our narrow bed, turning aside from battles:
Each man where he can, wearing out the day in his manner.

It is noble to die of love, and honourable to remain
                    uncuckolded for a season.
And she speaks ill of light women,
                    and will not praise Homer
Because Helen's conduct is "unsuitable."

VI

When, when, and whenever death closes our eyelids,
Moving naked over Acheron
Upon the one raft, victor and conquered together,
Marius and Jugurtha together,
                    one tangle of shadows.

Caesar plots against India,
Tigris and Euphrates shall, from now on, flow at his bidding,
Tibet shall be full of Roman policemen,
The Parthians shall get used to our statuary
                    and acquire a Roman religion;

One raft on the veiled flood of Acheron,
          Marius and Jugurtha together.

Nor at my funeral either will there be any long trail
                    bearing ancestral lares and images;
No trumpets filled with my emptiness,

[43]**Helen** Greek woman of great beauty who was seduced by the Trojan soldier Paris and abducted to Troy, an event that precipitated the Trojan War. [45]**Acheron** in Greek mythology, one of the rivers of the Underworld that the dead must cross. [47]**Marius and Jugurtha** Gaius Marius defeated and imprisoned Jugurtha, king of Numidia. [50]**Tigris and Euphrates** the two main rivers in ancient Mesopotamia (present-day Iraq). [52]**The Parthians . . . Roman religion** Caesar had planned to attack the Parthians, who inhabited the lands near Persia. [57]**lares** Roman household spirits, thought to bring good fortune to the living members of the family.

Nor shall it be on an Atalic bed;
The perfumed cloths will be absent.
A small plebeian procession.
Enough, enough and in plenty
There will be three books at my obsequies
Which I take, my not unworthy gift, to Persephone.

You will follow the bare scarified breast
Nor will you be weary of calling my name, nor too weary
To place the last kiss on my lips
When the Syrian onyx is broken.

"He who is now vacant dust
Was once the slave of one passion:"
Give that much inscription
"Death why tardily come?"

You, sometimes, will lament a lost friend,
For it is a custom:
This care for past men,

Since Adonis was gored in Idalia, and the Cytharean
Ran crying with out-spread hair,
In vain, you call back the shade,
In vain, Cynthia. Vain call to unanswering shadow,
Small talk comes from small bones.

VII

Me happy, night, night full of brightness;
Oh couch made happy by my long delectations;
How many words talked out with abundant candles;
Struggles when the lights were taken away;
Now with bared breasts she wrestled against me,
Tunic spread in delay;
And she then opening my eyelids fallen in sleep,

59 **Atalic bed** a reference to Attalus III of Pergamum, famous for his extravagance. 64 **Persephone** queen of the Underworld. 68 **Syrian onyx** the Syrians kept in a casket of onyx the ointments they used to embalm the dead. 77 **Since Adonis . . . out-spread hair** Adonis, the lover of Venus, the goddess from Cythera, was killed by a wild boar in the town of Idalium, on Cyprus. 79 **Cynthia** the name Propertius used for his mistress.

Her lips upon them; and it was her mouth saying:
Sluggard!

In how many varied embraces, our changing arms,
Her kisses, how many, lingering on my lips.
"Turn not Venus into a blinded motion,
Eyes are the guides of love,
Paris took Helen naked coming from the bed of Menelaus,
Endymion's naked body, bright bait for Diana,"
—such at least is the story.

While our fates twine together, sate we our eyes with love;
For long night comes upon you
and a day when no day returns.
Let the gods lay chains upon us
so that no day shall unbind them.

Fool who would set a term to love's madness,
For the sun shall drive with black horses,
earth shall bring wheat from barley,
The flood shall move toward the fountain
Ere love know moderations,
The fish shall swim in dry streams.
No, now while it may be, let not the fruit of life cease.

Dry wreaths drop their petals,
their stalks are woven in baskets,
To-day we take the great breath of lovers,
to-morrow fate shuts us in.

Though you give all your kisses
you give but few.

Nor can I shift my pains to other,
Hers will I be dead,
If she confer such nights upon me,
long is my life, long in years,
If she give me many,
God am I for the time.

[94]**Paris took Helen . . . Menelaus** the abduction of Helen, wife of Menelaus, by Paris, a Trojan, sparked the hostilities that led to the Trojan War.

Hugh Selwyn Mauberley (Life and Contacts)

"VOCAT AESTUS IN UMBRAM"
—NEMESIANUS, *Ec. IV*

E. P. ODE POUR L'ELECTION DE SON SEPULCHRE

For three years, out of key with his time,
He strove to resuscitate the dead art
Of poetry; to maintain "the sublime"
In the old sense. Wrong from the start—

No, hardly, but seeing he had been born
In a half savage country, out of date;
Bent resolutely on wringing lilies from the acorn;
Capaneus, trout for factitious bait;

"Ἴδμεν γάϱ τοι πάνθ', ὅσ' ἐνὶ Τϱοίῃ
Caught in the unstopped ear;
Giving the rocks small lee-way
The chopped seas held him, therefore, that year.

His true Penelope was Flaubert,
He fished by obstinate isles;
Observed the elegance of Circe's hair
Rather than the mottoes on sun-dials.

Unaffected by "the march of events,"
He passed from men's memory in *l'an trentuniesme*

HUGH SELWYN MAUBERLEY Pound described this poem as "a farewell to London . . . a study in form, an attempt to condense the James novel." He also remarked about the poem's speaker: "I'm no more Mauberley than Eliot is Prufrock." **Vocat aestus in umbram** Latin for "Heat summons us into the shade." Nemesianus was a third-century Roman poet. **Ode pour . . . Son Sepulchre** French for "Ode on the choice of his tomb." An adaptation of the title of a poem by Pierre de Ronsard (1524–1585). [8]**Capaneus** one of the seven warriors who attacked Thebes, who after swearing an oath against Zeus, was struck dead with a thunderbolt. [9]This Greek is from Homer's *Odyssey*. It means: "For we know all the things that are in Troy." Part of the song of the Sirens, which was so powerfully seductive that Odysseus plugged the ears of his sailors with wax and lashed himself to the mast of his ship to prevent them all from jumping into the sea. [13]**Penelope** wife of Odysseus, who faithfully awaited his return for twenty years. [13]**Flaubert** French novelist (1821–1880). [15]**Circe** sorceress from Homer's *Odyssey* with whom Odysseus spent a year.

De son eage, the case presents
No adjunct to the Muses' diadem.

II

The age demanded an image
Of its accelerated grimace,
Something for the modern stage,
Not, at any rate, an Attic grace;

Not, not certainly, the obscure reveries
Of the inward gaze;
Better mendacities
Than the classics in paraphrase!

The "age demanded" chiefly a mould in plaster,
Made with no loss of time,
A prose kinema, not, not assuredly, alabaster
Or the "sculpture" of rhyme.

III

The tea-rose tea-grown, etc.
Supplants the mousseline of Cos,
The pianola "replaces"
Sappho's barbitos.

Christ follows Dionysus,
Phallic and ambrosial
Made way for macerations:
Caliban casts out Ariel.

All things are a flowing,
Sage Heracleitus says;

18–19**l'an trentuniesme de son eage** medieval French for "the thirtieth year of his age," an adaptation of the opening line of the *Grand Testament* of François Villon (1431–?): "In the thirtieth year of my life." 31**kinema** Greek for "movement" or "motion." 34**Cos** a Greek island famous for its fabric, especially muslin. 36**barbitos** a lyrelike instrument played by the Greek poet Sappho (c. 600 B.C.). 37**Dionysus** Greek god of fertility and revelry. 39**macerations** fasting. 40**Caliban, Ariel** contrasting characters from Shakespeare's *The Tempest.* Caliban is associated with the earthly and the ugly; Ariel, with the ethereal and the beautiful. 42**Heracleitus** Greek philosopher (c. 550 B.C.) who taught that life is in a constant state of flux or change.

But a tawdry cheapness
Shall outlast our days.

Even the Christian beauty
Defects—after Samothrace;
We see τὸ χαλόν
Decreed in the market place.

Faun's flesh is not to us,
Nor the saint's vision.
We have the press for wafer;
Franchise for circumcision.

All men, in law, are equals.
Free of Pisistratus,
We choose a knave or an eunuch
To rule over us.

O bright Apollo,
τίν' ἄνδρα, τίν' ἥρωα, τίνα θεόν,
What god, man, or hero
Shall I place a tin wreath upon!

IV

These fought in any case,
and some believing,
pro domo, in any case . . .

Some quick to arm,
some for adventure,
some from fear of weakness,
some from fear of censure,
some for love of slaughter, in imagination,
learning later . . .
some in fear, learning love of slaughter;

[46]**Samothrace** a Greek island. [47]The Greek characters mean "the beautiful." [54]**Pisistratus** Athenian tyrant (d. 527 B.C.). [58]The Greek is from Pindar (522–443 B.C.) and means: "What man, what hero, what god." [63]**pro domo** Latin for "for the home."

Died some, pro patria,
non "dulce" non "et decor" . . .
walked eye-deep in hell
believing in old men's lies, then unbelieving
came home, home to a lie,
home to many deceits,
home to old lies and new infamy;
usury age-old and age-thick
and liars in public places.

Daring as never before, wastage as never before.
Young blood and high blood,
fair cheeks, and fine bodies;

fortitude as never before

frankness as never before,
disillusions as never told in the old days,
hysterias, trench confessions,
laughter out of dead bellies.

V

There died a myriad,
And of the best, among them,
For an old bitch gone in the teeth,
For a botched civilization,

Charm, smiling at the good mouth,
Quick eyes gone under earth's lid,

For two gross of broken statues,
For a few thousand battered books.

Yeux Glauques

Gladstone was still respected,
When John Ruskin produced

[71–72]**pro patria . . . non "et decor"** Latin, adapted from Horace *Odes* III, ii, 138. Horace's line translates: "it is sweet and glorious to die for one's country"; Pound's: "For one's native land, not sweetly, not gloriously." **Yeux Glauques** French for "glaucous eyes," referring to a blue-green or sea green eye color, a symptom of glaucoma, which often leads to blindness. [96]**Gladstone** three-time British prime minister (1809–1898).

"King's Treasuries"; Swinburne
And Rossetti still abused.

Foetid Buchanan lifted up his voice
When that faun's head of hers
Became a pastime for
Painters and adulterers.

The Burne-Jones cartoons
Have preserved her eyes;
Still, at the Tate, they teach
Cophetua to rhapsodize;

Thin like brook-water,
With a vacant gaze.
The English Rubaiyat was still-born
In those days.

The thin, clear gaze, the same
Still darts out faun-like from the half-ruin'd face,
Questing and passive. . . .
"Ah, poor Jenny's case" . . .

Bewildered that a world
Shows no surprise
At her last maquero's
Adulteries.

"Siena mi fe'; Disfecemi Maremma"

Among the pickled foetuses and bottled bones,
Engaged in perfecting the catalogue,

97–100**John Ruskin . . . Foetid Buchanan** Ruskin (1819–1900), an art critic, defended the Pre-Raphaelite painters and poets, among them Dante Gabriel Rossetti (1828–1882) and Algernon Swinburne (1837–1909). Robert W. Buchanan (1841–1901) attacked their work. 104**Burne-Jones** Sir Edward Burne-Jones (1833–1898), a Pre-Raphaelite painter whose work hangs in London's Tate Gallery. 110**Rubaiyat** *The Rubaiyat* of Omar Khayyam, translated into English by Edward Fitzgerald and published in 1859. 115**Jenny** a prostitute in a poem by Rossetti. 118**maquero** pimp. **"Siena mi fe'; Disfecemi Maremma"** Italian, from Dante's *Purgatorio* V, 133, meaning, "Siena made me, Maremma undid me." Spoken by a woman condemned to death by her husband, for infidelity.

I found the last scion of the
Senatorial families of Strasbourg, Monsieur Verog.

For two hours he talked of Galliffet;
Of Dowson; of the Rhymers' Club;
Told me how Johnson (Lionel) died
By falling from a high stool in a pub . . .

But showed no trace of alcohol
At the autopsy, privately performed—
Tissue preserved—the pure mind
Arose toward Newman as the whiskey warmed.

Dowson found harlots cheaper than hotels;
Headlam for uplift; Image impartially imbued
With raptures for Bacchus, Terpsichore and the Church
So spoke the author of "The Dorian Mood,"

M. Verog, out of step with the decade,
Detached from his contemporaries,
Neglected by the young,
Because of these reveries.

Brennbaum

The skylike limpid eyes,
The circular infant's face,
The stiffness from spats to collar
Never relaxing into grace;

The heavy memories of Horeb, Sinai and the forty years,
Showed only when the daylight fell
Level across the face
Of Brennbaum "The Impeccable."

[123]**Monsieur Verog** Victor Plarr (1863–1929), poet and member of an association of poets, The Rhymers' Club. [124]**Galliffet** Gaston de Galliffet, a French general (1830–1909). [126]**Johnson (Lionel)** Lionel Johnson (1867–1902), a poet. [131]**Newman** John Henry Newman (1801–1890), an English convert to Catholicism, was ordained a priest and later elevated to cardinal. [134]**Terpsichore** Greek muse of the dance. [144]**Horeb, Sinai and the forty years** Biblical allusions to the wandering of the Israelites for forty years in the desert, to Moses's vision of the burning bush on Mount Horeb, and to his reception of the Ten Commandments on Mount Sinai.

Mr. Nixon

In the cream gilded cabin of his steam yacht
Mr. Nixon advised me kindly, to advance with fewer
Dangers of delay. "Consider
"Carefully the reviewer.

"I was as poor as you are;
"When I began I got, of course,
"Advance on royalties, fifty at first," said Mr. Nixon,
"Follow me, and take a column,
"Even if you have to work free.

"Butter reviewers. From fifty to three hundred
"I rose in eighteen months;
"The hardest nut I had to crack
"Was Dr. Dundas.

"I never mentioned a man but with the view
"Of selling my own works.
"The tip's a good one, as for literature
"It gives no man a sinecure.

"And no one knows, at sight, a masterpiece.
"And give up verse, my boy,
"There's nothing in it."

. . . .

Likewise a friend of Bloughram's once advised me:
Don't kick against the pricks,
Accept opinion. The "Nineties" tried your game
And died, there's nothing in it.

X

Beneath the sagging roof
The stylist has taken shelter,
Unpaid, uncelebrated,
At last from the world's welter

168**a friend of Bloughram's** a reference to "Bishop Bloughram's Apology," a poem by Robert Browning.

Nature receives him;
With a placid and uneducated mistress
He exercises his talents
And the soil meets his distress.

The haven from sophistications and contentions
Leaks through its thatch;
He offers succulent cooking;
The door has a creaking latch.

XI

"Conservatrix of Milésien"
Habits of mind and feeling,
Possibly. But in Ealing
With the most bank-clerkly of Englishmen?

No, "Milésian" is an exaggeration.
No instinct has survived in her
Older than those her grandmother
Told her would fit her station.

XII

"Daphne with her thighs in bark
Stretches toward me her leafy hands,"
Subjectively. In the stuffed-satin drawing-room
I await The Lady Valentine's commands,

Knowing my coat has never been
Of precisely the fashion
To stimulate, in her,
A durable passion;

Doubtful, somewhat, of the value
Of well-gowned approbation

184**"Conservatrix of Milésien"** a reference to the second-century B.C. Greek writer Aristides, whose *Milesian Tales* were considered by some to be licentious. 186**Ealing** an outlying borough of London. 192–193**Daphne . . . leafy hands"** a reference to the Greek myth in which the nymph Daphne was transformed into a laurel tree to escape Apollo, who was pursuing her. Pound translates the version of the French poet Théophile Gautier.

Of literary effort,
But never of The Lady Valentine's vocation:

Poetry, her border of ideas,
The edge, uncertain, but a means of blending
With other strata
Where the lower and higher have ending;

A hook to catch the Lady Jane's attention,
A modulation toward the theatre,
Also, in the case of revolution,
A possible friend and comforter.

. . . .

Conduct, on the other hand, the soul
"Which the highest cultures have nourished"
To Fleet St. where
Dr. Johnson flourished;

Beside this thoroughfare
The sale of half-hose has
Long since superseded the cultivation
Of Pierian roses.

Envoi (1919)

Go, dumb-born book,
Tell her that sang me once that song of Lawes:
Hadst thou but song
As thou has subjects known,
Then were there cause in thee that should condone
Even my faults that heavy upon me lie,
And build her glories their longevity.

Tell her that sheds
Such treasure in the air,
Recking naught else but that her graces give
Life to the moment,

[215]**Dr. Johnson** Samuel Johnson (1709–1764), English writer of didactic fiction and moral essays. [219]**Pieria** in Greek mythology, the birthplace of the Muses, famous for their inspiration of art, especially poetry.

I would bid them live
As roses might, in magic amber laid,
Red overwrought with orange and all made
One substance and one colour
Braving time.

Tell her that goes
With song upon her lips
But sings not out the song, nor knows
The maker of it, some other mouth,
May be as fair as hers,
Might, in new ages, gain her worshippers,
When our two dusts with Waller's shall be laid,
Siftings on siftings in oblivion,
Till change hath broken down
All things save Beauty alone.

Mauberley (1920)

"Vacuos exercet aera morsus."

I

Turned from the "eau-forte
Par Jaquemart"
To the strait head
Of Messalina:

"His true Penelope
Was Flaubert,"
And his tool
The engraver's.

Firmness,
Not the full smile,
His art, but an art
In profile;

242**Waller's** Edmund Waller (1606–1687), English poet whose "Go Lovely Rose" Pound adapts in the *Envoi.* **"Vacuos exercet aera morsus."** Latin from Ovid's *Metamorphoses* VII, 786, meaning: "He snaps vacuously at the empty air." 246–247**"eau-forte / Par Jaquemart** French for "etching by Jacquemart" (Jules), French artist (1837–1880). 249**Messalina** wife of the Roman emperor Claudius.

Colourless
Pier Francesca,
Pisanello lacking the skill
To forge Achaia.

II

"Qu'est ce qu'ils savent de l'amour, et qu'est ce qu'ils peuvent comprendre? S'ils ne comprennent pas la poésie, s'ils ne sentent pas la musique, qu'est ce qu'ils peuvent comprendre de cette passion en comparaison avec laquelle la rose est grossière et le parfum des violettes un tonnerre?"

—CAID ALI

For three years, diabolus in the scale,
He drank ambrosia,
All passes, ANANGKE prevails,
Came end, at last, to that Arcadia.

He had moved amid her phantasmagoria,
Amid her galaxies,
NUKTIS 'AGALMA

. . . .

Drifted . . . drifted precipitate,
Asking time to be rid of . . .
Of his bewilderment; to designate
His new found orchid. . . .

To be certain . . . certain . . .
(Amid aerial flowers) . . . time for arrangements—
Drifted on
To the final estrangement;

[259]**Pier Francesca** Piero della Francesca, Italian painter (1420?–1492). [260]**Pisanello** Italian artist (1397?–1455?) known for his medallions. [261]**Achaia** ancient Greece. **Caid Ali** Caid Ali, the alleged source of the epigraph to Part II, doesn't exist. The epigraph is Pound's. Its French translates: "What do they know of love, and what can they understand? If they do not understand poetry, if they do not respond to music, what can they understand of this passion in comparison to which the rose is gross and the perfume of violets a clap of thunder?" [262]**diabolus** Latin for "devil." In music it denotes the interval of an augmented fourth. [264]**ANANGKE** Greek for "necessity." [265]**Arcadia** in Greek mythology, an idyllic place. [268]**NUKTIS 'AGALMA** Greek for "night's jewel." From the Greek poet Bion (c. 100 B.C.).

Unable in the supervening blankness
To sift TO AGATHON from the chaff

Until he found his sieve . . .
Ultimately, his seismograph:

—Given that is his "fundamental passion,"
This urge to convey the relation
Of eye-lid and cheek-bone
By verbal manifestation;

To present the series
Of curious heads in medallion—

He had passed, inconscient, full gaze,
The wide-banded irides
And botticellian sprays implied
In their diastasis;

Which anaethesis, noted a year late,
And weighed, revealed his great affect,
(Orchid), mandate
Of Eros, a retrospect.

Mouths biting empty air,
The still stone dogs,
Caught in metamorphosis, were
Left him as epilogues.

"The Age Demanded"

For this agility chance found
Him of all men, unfit
As the red-beaked steeds of
The Cytheraean for a chain bit.

The glow of porcelain
Brought no reforming sense

[278]**TO AGATHON** Greek for "the good." [288]**irides** irises, both eyes and flowers. [290]**diastasis** separation. [294]**Eros** Greek god of love. [301–302]**red-beaked steeds of / The Cytheraean** a reference to the doves harnessed to the chariot of Aphrodite.

To his perception
Of the social inconsequence.

Thus, if her colour
Came against his gaze,
Tempered as if
It were through a perfect glaze

He made no immediate application
Of this to relation of the state
To the individual, the month was more temperate
Because this beauty had been.

The coral isle, the lion-coloured sand
Burst in upon the porcelain revery:
Impetuous troubling
Of his imagery.

Mildness, amid the neo-Nietzschean clatter
His sense of graduations,
Quite out of place amid
Resistance to current exacerbations,

Invitation, mere invitation to perceptivity
Gradually led him to the isolation
Which these presents place
Under a more tolerant, perhaps, examination.

By constant elimination
The manifest universe
Yielded an armour
Against utter consternation

A Minoan undulation,
Seen, we admit, amid ambrosial circumstances
Strengthened him against
The discouraging doctrine of chances,

And his desire for survival,
Faint in the most strenuous moods,

[319] **neo-Nietzschean** a reference to Friedrich Nietzsche, German philosopher (1844–1900).

Became an Olympian *apathein*
In the presence of selected perceptions.

A pale gold, in the aforesaid pattern,
The unexpected palms
Destroying, certainly, the artist's urge,
Left him delighted with the imaginary
Audition of the phantasmal sea-surge,

Incapable of the least utterance or composition,
Emendation, conservation of the "better tradition,"
Refinement of medium, elimination of superfluities,
August attraction or concentration.

Nothing, in brief, but maudlin confession,
Irresponse to human aggression
Amid the precipitation, down-float
Of insubstantial manna,
Lifting the faint susurrus
Of his subjective hosannah.

Ultimate affronts to
Human redundancies;

Non-esteem of self-styled "his betters"
Leading, as he well knew,
To his final
Exclusion from the world of letters.

IV

Scattered Moluccas
Not knowing, day to day,
The first day's end, in the next noon;
The placid water
Unbroken by the Simoon;

Thick foliage
Placid beneath warm suns,

[337]**apathein** Greek for "absence of feeling." [360]**Moluccas** islands in the Malay Archipelago. [364]**Simoon** dry, hot wind.

Tawn fore-shores
Washed in the cobalt of oblivions;

Or through dawn-mist
The grey and rose
Of the juridical
Flamingoes;

A consciousness disjunct
Being but this overblotted
Series
Of intermittences;

Coracle of Pacific voyages,
The unforecasted beach;
Then on an oar
Read this:

"I was
And I no more exist;
Here drifted
An hedonist."

Medallion

Luini in porcelain!
The grand piano
Utters a profane
Protest with her clear soprano.

The sleek head emerges
From the gold-yellow frock
As Anadyomene in the opening
Pages of Reinach.

Honey-red, closing the face-oval,
A basket-work of braids which seem as if they were
Spun in King Minos' hall
From metal, or intractable amber;

377**coracle** a small boat. 385**Luini in porcelain** a reference to the Italian painter Bernardino Luini (1475–1532?) 391**Anadyomene** a reference to Aphrodite, meaning "born from foam." Pound alludes to the Apollo of Salomon Reinach (1858–1932). 395**Minos** mythical king of Crete.

The face-oval beneath the glaze,
Bright in its suave bounding-line, as,
Beneath half-watt rays,
The eyes turn topaz.

Canto I

And then went down to the ship,
Set keel to breakers, forth on the godly sea, and
We set up mast and sail on that swart ship,
Bore sheep aboard her, and our bodies also
Heavy with weeping, and winds from sternward
Bore us out onward with bellying canvas,
Circe's this craft, the trim-coifed goddess.
Then sat we amidships, wind jamming the tiller,
Thus with stretched sail, we went over sea till day's end.
Sun to his slumber, shadows o'er all the ocean,
Came we then to the bounds of deepest water,
To the Kimmerian lands, and peopled cities
Covered with close-webbed mist, unpierced ever
With glitter of sun-rays
Nor with stars stretched, nor looking back from heaven
Swartest night stretched over wretched men there.
The ocean flowing backward, came we then to the place
Aforesaid by Circe.
Here did they rites, Perimedes and Eurylochus,
And drawing sword from my hip
I dug the ell-square pitkin;
Poured we libations unto each the dead,
First mead and then sweet wine, water mixed with white flour.
Then prayed I many a prayer to the sickly death's-heads;
As set in Ithaca, sterile bulls of the best
For sacrifice, heaping the pyre with goods,
A sheep to Tiresias only, black and a bell-sheep.
Dark blood flowed in the fosse,

CANTO I Lines 1–68 adapt Book XI of the *Odyssey,* in which Homer describes Odysseus's voyage to the Underworld. [12]**Kimmerians** a mythical people who lived at the edge of the world. [19]**Perimedes and Eurylochus** companions of Odysseus. [21]**pitkin** a small pit.

Souls out of Erebus, cadaverous dead, of brides
Of youths and of the old who had borne much;
Souls stained with recent tears, girls tender,
Men many, mauled with bronze lance heads,
Battle spoil, bearing yet dreory arms,
These many crowded about me; with shouting,
Pallor upon me, cried to my men for more beasts;
Slaughtered the herds, sheep slain of bronze;
Poured ointment, cried to the gods,
To Pluto the strong, and praised Proserpine;
Unsheathed the narrow sword,
I sat to keep off the impetuous impotent dead,
Till I should hear Tiresias.
But first Elpenor came, our friend Elpenor,
Unburied, cast on the wide earth,
Limbs that we left in the house of Circe,
Unwept, unwrapped in sepulchre, since toils urged other.
Pitiful spirit. And I cried in hurried speech:
"Elpenor, how art thou come to this dark coast?
Cam'st thou afoot, outstripping seamen?"

And he in heavy speech:
"Ill fate and abundant wine. I slept in Circe's ingle.
Going down the long ladder unguarded,
I fell against the buttress,
Shattered the nape-nerve, the soul sought Avernus.
But thou, O King, I bid remember me, unwept, unburied,
Heap up mine arms, be tomb by sea-bord, and inscribed:
A man of no fortune, and with a name to come.
And set my oar up, that I swung mid fellows."

And Anticlea came, whom I beat off, and then Tiresias Theban,
Holding his golden wand, knew me, and spoke first:
"A second time? why? man of ill star,
Facing the sunless dead and this joyless region?

[29]**Erebus** the land of the dead. [33]**dreory** bloody. [38]**Proserpine** wife of Pluto, the god of the Underworld. [42]**Elpenor** Odysseus's companion who was left unburied after dying in a fall from the roof of Circe's house. [50]**ingle** corner. [53]**Avernus** entrance to the Underworld. [58]**Anticlea** mother of Odysseus.

Stand from the fosse, leave me my bloody bever
For soothsay."
        And I stepped back.
And he strong with the blood, said then: "Odysseus
Shalt return through spiteful Neptune, over dark seas,
Lose all companions." And then Anticlea came.
Lie quiet Divus. I mean, that is Andreas Divus,
In officina Wecheli, 1538, out of Homer.
And he sailed, by Sirens and thence outward and away
And unto Circe.
        Venerandam,
In the Cretan's phrase, with the golden crown, Aphrodite,
Cypri munimenta sortita est, mirthful, orichalchi, with golden
Girdles and breast bands, thou with dark eyelids
Bearing the golden bough of Argicida. So that:

Canto XIII

Kung walked
        by the dynastic temple
And into the cedar grove,
        and then out by the lower river,
And with him Khieu, Tchi
        and Tian the low speaking
And "we are unknown," said Kung,
"You will take up charioteering?
        Then you will become known,
Or perhaps I should take up charioteering, or archery?
Or the practice of public speaking?"
And Tseu-lou said, "I would put the defences in order,"
And Khieu said, "If I were lord of a province

CANTO I [62]**bever** a libation or offering to the gods. [66]**Neptune** god of the sea. [68]**Andreas Divus** Pound used a Latin translation of Homer by Andrus Divus made in 1538. [72]**Venerandam** Latin for "commanding reverence," a phrase describing Aphrodite, the Greek goddess of love. [74]**Cypri munimenta sortita est** Latin for "The fortresses of Cyprus were her appointed realm." [74]**orichalchi** Latin for "of copper." [76]**Argicida** the Greek god Hermes, who slew the many-eyed Argus. *CANTO XIII* [1]**Kung** Confucius, Kung Fu-Tze (551–479 B.C.), the great Chinese wise man who founded Confucianism. [5–6]**Khieu, Tchi / and Tian** three disciples of Confucius.

I would put it in better order than this is."
And Tchi said, "I would prefer a small mountain temple,
With order in the observances,
with a suitable performance of the ritual,"
And Tian said, with his hand on the strings of his lute
The low sounds continuing
after his hand left the strings,
And the sound went up like smoke, under the leaves,
And he looked after the sound:
"The old swimming hole,
And the boys flopping off the planks,
Or sitting in the underbrush playing mandolins."
And Kung smiled upon all of them equally.
And Thseng-sie desired to know:
"Which had answered correctly?"
And Kung said, "They have all answered correctly,
That is to say, each in his nature."
And Kung raised his cane against Yuan Jang,
Yuan Jang being his elder,
For Yuan Jang sat by the roadside pretending
to be receiving wisdom.
And Kung said
"You old fool, come out of it,
Get up and do something useful."
And Kung said
"Respect a child's faculties
From the moment it inhales the clear air,
But a man of fifty who knows nothing
Is worthy of no respect."
And "When the prince has gathered about him
All the savants and artists, his riches will be fully employed."
And Kung said, and wrote on the bo leaves:
If a man have not order within him
He can not spread order about him;
And if a man have not order within him
His family will not act with due order;
And if the prince have not order within him
He can not put order in his dominions.
And Kung gave the words "order"
And "brotherly deference"
And said nothing of the "life after death."
And he said

"Anyone can run to excesses,
It is easy to shoot past the mark,
It is hard to stand firm in the middle."

And they said: If a man commit murder
Should his father protect him, and hide him?
And Kung said:
He should hide him.

And Kung gave his daughter to Kong-Tch'ang
although Kong-Tch'ang was in prison.
And he gave his niece to Nan-Young
although Nan-Young was out of office.
And Kung said "Wan ruled with moderation,
In his day the State was well kept,
And even I can remember
A day when the historians left blanks in their writings,
I mean for things they didn't know,
But that time seems to be passing."
And Kung said, "Without character you will
be unable to play on that instrument
Or to execute the music fit for the Odes.
The blossoms of the apricot
blow from the east to the west,
And I have tried to keep them from falling."

Canto XLV

WITH *Usura*

With usura hath no man a house of good stone
each block cut smooth and well fitting
that design might cover their face,
with usura
hath no man a painted paradise on his church wall
harpes et luz
or where virgin receiveth message
and halo projects from incision,

CANTO XLV **Usury:** A charge for the use of purchasing power, levied without regard to production; often without regard to the possibilities of production. (Hence the failure of the Medici bank.) [Pound's note] [6]**harpes et luz** Latin for "harps and lutes."

with usura
seeth no man Gonzaga his heirs and his concubines
no picture is made to endure nor to live with
but it is made to sell and sell quickly
with usura, sin against nature,
is thy bread ever more of stale rags
is thy bread dry as paper,
with no mountain wheat, no strong flour
with usura the line grows thick
with usura is no clear demarcation
and no man can find site for his dwelling.
Stone-cutter is kept from his stone
weaver is kept from his loom
WITH USURA
wool comes not to market
sheep bringeth no gain with usura
Usura is a murrain, usura
blunteth the needle in the maid's hand
and stoppeth the spinner's cunning. Pietro Lombardo
came not by usura
Duccio came not by usura
nor Pier della Francesca; Zuan Bellin' not by usura
nor was "La Calunnia" painted.
Came not by usura Angelico; came not Ambrogio Praedis,
Came no church of cut stone signed: *Adamo me fecit.*
Not by usura St Trophime
Not by usura Saint Hilaire,
Usura rusteth the chisel
It rusteth the craft and the craftsman
It gnaweth the thread in the loom
None learneth to weave gold in her pattern;
Azure hath a canker by usura; cramoisi is unbroidered
Emerald findeth no Memling

[10]**Gonzaga** Luigi Gonzaga (1267–1360), a ruler of Mantua. [25]**murrain** a plague. [27–31]**Pietro Lombardo . . . "La Calunnia" painted** Pietro Lombardo, Italian sculptor (1435–1515); Duccio de Buoninsegna (1260?–1318?); Piero della Francesca (1420?–1492?), Giovanni Bellini (1430?–1516)—all Italian painters; *La Calumnia (Rumor),* a painting by Sandro Botticelli (1445–1510). [32]**Angelico . . . Ambrogio Praedis** Fra Angelico (1387–1445), Ambrogio Praedis (1445–1506), Italian painters. [33]**Adamo me fecit** Latin for "Adam made me." These words were carved into the church of San Zeno Maggiore in Verona. [34–35]**St. Trophime . . . Saint Hilaire** medieval French churches. [40]**cramoisi** in French, a heavy crimson cloth. [41]**Memling** Hans Memling (1430–1495), Flemish painter.

Usura slayeth the child in the womb
It stayeth the young man's courting
It hath brought palsey to bed, lyeth
between the young bride and her bridegroom
CONTRA NATURAM
They have brought whores for Eleusis
Corpses are set to banquet
at behest of usura.

From *Canto LXXX*

Tudor indeed is gone and every rose,
Blood-red, blanch-white that in the sunset glows
Cries: "Blood, Blood, Blood!" against the gothic stone
Of England, as the Howard or Boleyn knows.

Nor seeks the carmine petal to infer;
Nor is the white bud Time's inquisitor
Probing to know if its new-gnarled root
Twists from York's head or belly of Lancaster;

Or if a rational soul should stir, perchance,
Within the stem or summer shoot to advance
Contrition's utmost throw, seeking in thee
But oblivion, not thy forgiveness, FRANCE.

as the young lizard extends his leopard spots
along the grass-blade seeking the green midge half an
ant-size
and the Serpentine will look just the same
and the gulls be as neat on the pond
and the sunken garden unchanged
and God knows what else is left of our London
my London, your London
and if her green elegance
remains on this side of my rain ditch
puss lizard will lunch on some other T-bone

sunset grand couturier.

CANTO XLV [46]**CONTRA NATURAM** Latin for "against nature." [47]**Eleusis** ancient Greek city, the home of secret fertility rites honoring Demeter and Persephone.

From *Canto LXXXI*

Yet
Ere the season died a-cold
Borne upon a zephyr's shoulder
I rose through the aureate sky
Lawes and Jenkins guard thy rest
Dolmetsch ever be thy guest,
Has he tempered the viol's wood
To enforce both the grave and the acute?
Has he curved us the bowl of the lute?
Lawes and Jenkins guard thy rest
Dolmetsch ever be thy guest
Hast 'ou fashioned so airy a mood
To draw up leaf from the root?
Hast 'ou found a cloud so light
As seemed neither mist nor shade?

Then resolve me, tell me aright
If Waller sang or Dowland played.

Your eyen two wol sleye me sodenly
I may the beauté of hem nat susteyne

And for 180 years almost nothing.

Ed ascoltando al leggier mormorio
there came new subtlety of eyes into my tent,
whether of spirit or hypostasis,
but what the blindfold hides

CANTO LXXXI This poem is one of the *Pisan Cantos,* written during Pound's imprisonment as he awaited trial for allegedly treasonous wartime broadcasts. [3]**zephyr** the west wind. [5]**Lawes and Jenkins . . . be thy guest** Henry Lawes (1596–1662) and John Jenkins (1592–1678), English composers; Arnold Dolmetsch (1858–1940), musicologist with a special interest in rebuilding old instruments. [17]**Waller** Edmund Waller (1606–1687), English poet, whose "Go Lovely Rose" Lawes set to music and Pound adapted poetically in the *Envoi* to "Mauberley." (see pp. 378–379) [17]**Dowland** John Dowland (1563–1626), composer and lutenist. [18–19]**Your eyen . . . nat susteyne** the lines come from the poem "Merciles Beaute" by Geoffrey Chaucer (1340–1400): "Your two eyes will slay me quickly; I may not withstand their beauty." [21]**Ed ascoltando al leggier mormorio** Italian for "and listening to the light murmur." [23]**hypostasis** Greek for "the essential part of something."

or at carneval
                        nor any pair showed anger
    Saw but the eyes and stance between the eyes,
colour, diastasis,
    careless or unaware it had not the
  whole tent's room
nor was place for the full Ειδως
interpass, penetrate
    casting but shade beyond the other lights
        sky's clear
        night's sea
        green of the mountain pool
        shone from the unmasked eyes in half-mask's space.
What thou lovest well remains,
                        the rest is dross
What thou lov'st well shall not be reft from thee
What thou lov'st well is thy true heritage
Whose world, or mine or theirs
                        or is it of none?
First came the seen, then thus the palpable
    Elysium, though it were in the halls of hell,
What thou lovest well is thy true heritage

The ant's a centaur in his dragon world.
Pull down thy vanity, it is not man
Made courage, or made order, or made grace,
    Pull down thy vanity, I say pull down.
Learn of the green world what can be thy place
In scaled invention or true artistry,
Pull down thy vanity,
                            Paquin pull down!
The green casque has outdone your elegance.

"Master thyself, then others shall thee beare"
    Pull down thy vanity
Thou art a beaten dog beneath the hail,
A swollen magpie in a fitful sun,

28**diastasis** Greek for "separation." 31Ειδως Greek for "image." 45**Elysium** Greek mythological heaven for the good. 54**Paquin** Parisian dress designer. 56**Master thyself . . . thee beare"** adapted from Geoffrey Chaucer's poem "Truth." Chaucer's line reads "Control thyself, who controls the deeds of others."

Half black half white
Nor knowst'ou wing from tail
Pull down thy vanity
        How mean thy hates
Fostered in falsity,
        Pull down thy vanity,
Rathe to destroy, niggard in charity,
Pull down thy vanity,
        I say pull down.

But to have done instead of not doing
        this is not vanity
To have, with decency, knocked
That a Blunt should open
        To have gathered from the air a live tradition
or from a fine old eye the unconquered flame
This is not vanity.
    Here error is all in the not done,
all in the diffidence that faltered,

From *Canto LXXXIV*

    Under white clouds, cielo di Pisa
out of all this beauty something must come,

O moon my pin-up,
                chronometer
Wei, Chi and Pi-kan
Yin had these three men full of humanitas (manhood)
                or jên
Xaire Alessandro
                Xaire Fernando, e il Capo,

CANTO LXXXI [66]**Rathe** Middle English for "quick." [72]**Blunt** Wilfred Blunt (1840–1922), poet and political writer. *CANTO LXXXIV* [5]**Wei, Chi and Pi-kan** Wei Tzu was a twelfth-century B.C. viscount of a Chinese principality. When he became disgusted with the cruelty of the last sovereign of the Yin dynasty, he retired from the court. Chi Tzu, twelfth-century viscount of Chi, protested against the practices of the emperor and was put in prison. Pi-kan, uncle of the same emperor, objected to the emperor's excesses and was executed. [7]**jên** humaneness. [8]**Allesandro** Allesandro Pavolini, secretary of the Italian Fascist Republican party. [9]**Fernando** Fernando Mezzasoma, minister of popular culture of the Republic. Pavolini and Mezzasoma were executed following the Allied victory in the Second World War. [9]**il Capo** the head, or leader of the Fascists, Benvenuto Mussolini.

Pierre, Vidkun,
Henriot
and as to gradations
who went out of industrials into Government
when the slump was in the offing
as against whom, prepense, got OUT of Imperial Chemicals
in 1938
so as not to be nourished by blood-bath?

quand vos venetz al som de l'escalina
ἦθος° gradations ethos
These are distinctions in clarity

ming  these are distinctions

From *Canto LXXXVI*

As a lone ant from a broken ant-hill
from the wreckage of Europe, ego scriptor.

The rain has fallen, the wind coming down
out of the mountain
Lucca, Forti dei Marmi, Berchthold after the other one . . .
parts reassembled.
. . . and within the crystal, went up swift as Thetis
in colour rose-blue before sunset
and carmine and amber,

spiriti questi? personae?
tangibility by no means *atasal*
but the crystal can be weighed in the hand
formal and passing within the sphere: Thetis,
Maya, 'Αφροδίτη,° Aphrodite

CANTO LXXXIV 10–11**Pierre, Vidkun, Henriot** Pierre Laval, premier of Vichy France (1942–1945); Vidkun Quisling, Norwegian who collaborated with the Germans and became head of the Norwegian government under the German occupation; Philippe Henriot, French Fascist journalist who held a ministerial post in the Vichy government during the German occupation. 15**Imperial Chemicals** British chemical combine. 18**quand . . . escalina** "when you come to the top of the stair" (Dante's *Purgatorio,* XXVI, 146) 19**ethos** place or character. 21**ming** light or intelligence.

From *Canto XCI*

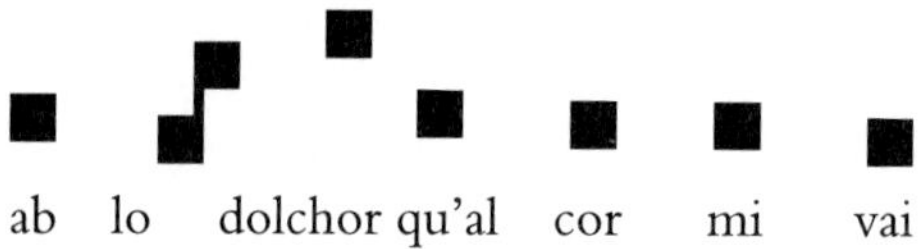

AB LO DOLCHOR QU'AL COR MI VAI

that the body of light come forth
from the body of fire
And that your eyes come to the surface
from the deep wherein they were sunken,
Reina—for 300 years,
and now sunken
That your eyes come forth from their caves
& light then
as the holly-leaf
qui laborat, orat
Thus Undine came to the rock,
by Circeo
and the stone eyes again looking seaward
Thus Apollonius
(if it was Apollonius)
& Helen of Tyre
by Pithagoras
by Ocellus
(pilot-fish, et libidinis expers, of Tyre;

CANTO XCI **ab lo . . . vai** With the sweetness that comes to my heart. Modification of lines from troubadour poetry. [6]**Reina** possibly the goddess Aphrodite. [12]**Undine** Ondine, a mythical sea-creature with a seductive appeal to men. [13]**Circeo** town on the coast of Italy. [15]**Apollonius** a first-century mystic, seer, and Pythagorean sun-worshipper. [17]**Helen of Tyre** Helen of Troy. [18]**Pithagoras** Pythagoras, the Greek mathematician and philosopher of the sixth-century B.C. [19]**Ocellus** Greek philosopher, a contemporary of Pythagoras.

From *Canto XCII*

And from far
                    il tremolar della marina
chh   chh
        the pebbles turn with the wave
chh   ch'u
                        "fui chiamat'
                                        e qui refulgo"
Le Paradis n'est pas artificiel
                                        but is jagged,
For a flash,
                for an hour.
Then agony,
                    then an hour,
                                    then agony,
Hilary stumbles, but the Divine Mind is abundant
                        unceasing
                        improvisatore

[2]**il tremolar della marina** "the trembling of the sea." Dante: *Purgatorio* I, 116–117. [3–5]**chh . . . ch'u** onomatopoeia: sounds of the sea. [6–7]**fui . . . refulgo** "I was called and here I glow." Dante: *Paradiso* IX, 32. [8]**Le Paradis . . . artificiel** "Paradise is not artificial." Nealt, *Pai,* 4–1, 35. [15]**Hilary** Hilary of Poitiers. Pound was interested in the light in the Church of St. Hilary in Poitiers. [17]**improvisatore** "improviser."

Marianne Moore

[1887–1972]

With one of the freshest voices in twentieth-century American poetry, Marianne Moore brought an intellectual sense of play and an emotional sincerity to a poetry that thrives on hope, accuracy, and delight. Avoiding conventional poetic subjects, Moore wrote about animals and works of art, people and places, sports and society in eclectic and unpredictable ways. She valued in her animals and athletes their unconsciousness, their quirkiness, their elegant simplicity of action, and their surprising, sometimes astonishing behavior.

In addition to their singular subjects, Moore's poems are characterized by a wide-ranging diction and imagistic concreteness, unusual rhythms, unexpected rhymes, and stanzaic intricacy. Commenting on the diction in her familiar poem "Poetry," she states that a poet should not "discriminate against 'business documents and / school-books.' " T. S. Eliot suggests that her word choice is brilliant, precise, and at times a refinement of the speech that characterizes the American language and inspires "both the jargon of the laboratory and the slang of the comic strip." As such, Moore was as capable of describing a mussel shell

> opening and shutting itself like
>
> an
>
> injured fan

as she was capable of writing jargon such as "a liability rather than an asset," or "diminished vitality." This sense of diction, combined with her sense of a poem's possible rhythms, catches some readers off guard. Somehow it doesn't seem "poetic." We find no driving meter, no poetic rhetoric, only the cool, controlled illusion of everyday American speech. Moore's rhythms are spoken rhythms, but not the rhythms of the oral tradition. We find none of Whitman's biblical lists, no long chant-like invocations, no theatrical gestures. Her lines sound cleanly spoken, almost written, in a voice free of connectives. As Hugh Kenner remarks, her diction is "urbane without slickness and brisk without imprecision."

"I have a passion for rhythm and accent," Marianne Moore once told an interviewer, "and so I blundered into versifying." She enjoyed what she termed "inconspicuous rhymes and unpompous conspicuous rhymes" and considered the stanza, not the line, as the unit of poetry and "thus came to hazard hyphens at the end of the line." This stylistic feature is evident in one of her best poems, "The Fish," whose title is made up of its opening words. Notice the uneven line lengths within each stanza and the symmetry between stanzas. Notice, too, how the rhymes are sometimes hidden, displaced from accented syllables to less obtrusive words.

The Fish

wade
through black jade.
  Of the crow-blue mussel-shells, one keeps
  adjusting the ash-heaps;
    opening and shutting itself like

an
injured fan.
  The barnacles which encrust the side
  of the wave, cannot hide
    there for the submerged shafts of the

sun,
split like spun

glass, move themselves with spotlight swiftness
into the crevices—
in and out, illuminating

the
turquoise sea
of bodies. The water drives a wedge
of iron through the iron edge
of the cliff; whereupon the stars,

pink
rice-grains, ink-
bespattered jelly-fish, crabs like green
lilies, and submarine
toadstools, slide each on the other.

All
external
marks of abuse are present on this
defiant edifice—
all the physical features of

ac-
cident—lack
of cornice, dynamic grooves, burns, and
hatchet strokes, these things stand
out on it; the chasm-side is

dead.
Repeated
evidence has proved that it can live
on what can not revive
its youth. The sea grows old in it.

"The Fish" highlights more than Moore's stylistic virtuosity, poetic ingenuity, and linguistic extravagance. Beyond these admirable qualities, "The Fish" demonstrates an aptness of phrase and form suited to the scope of the subject, which one critic has identified as the "scars of experience." It also illustrates how in Moore's poems the number of syllables rather than a pattern of stress determines the poetic line.

Moore returns, as Bonnie Costello has noted, to premodernist assumptions about the moral value of poetry, particularly its capacity for teaching human values. And while her poems are not laced with didacticism, many do offer advice in the form of witty parables and of examples drawn from natural history. Unlike Robert Frost and Thomas Hardy, whose poetry is modernist in its philosophical premises while being cast in traditional poetic forms, Moore is modern in technique but traditional, even classical, in disposition and values. Her poetry is an original blend of classical reserve and modern candor. Her poems are "imaginary gardens with real toads in them."

Born in Missouri in 1887, Marianne Moore was educated at Bryn Mawr College in Pennsylvania, receiving her B.A. in 1909. She then taught commercial subjects at Carlisle Commercial College (1911–1915), where her pupils included the famous Native American athlete, Jim Thorpe. She began editing *The Dial,* an influential literary journal, from 1925 until it ceased publication in 1929. Her early poems appeared in the literary magazines *The Egoist, Poetry,* and *Others,* all of which published experimental modernist work. Her published writings also include a play, translations from the French and German, and the collections of critical essays *Predilections* (1955) and *Poetry and Criticism* (1965). She has received several prestigious honors, including the National Book Award (1952), the Bollingen Poetry Prize (1953), and the National Medal for Literature (1968) as well as honorary doctorates from eight universities.

In her later years she became a celebrity. In 1955 the Ford Motor Company engaged her help in the naming of Ford's then-new car, the Edsel. In 1968 at the invitation of the team's owners she opened the baseball season at Yankee Stadium. She appeared on television. Even people who had never read a poem could identify her by her flowing black cape and tricorn hat.

Moore's poetry testifies to the joy she took in life. She loved animals, slang, jargon—she loved to tango. Focusing her attention on the less exalted aspects of ordinary life, she wrote a poetry as Byzantine and explosive as the game of baseball she so admired. Gracefully muscling each line to the page, she created from these subjects, as T. S. Eliot has suggested, "part of the durable poetry written in our time."

To a Snail

If "compression is the first grace of style,"
you have it. Contractility is a virtue
as modesty is a virtue.
It is not the acquisition of any one thing
that is able to adorn,
or the incidental quality that occurs
as a concomitant of something well said,
that we value in style,
but the principle that is hid:
in the absence of feet, "a method of conclusions";
"a knowledge of principles,"
in the curious phenomenon of your occipital horn.

The Past Is the Present

If external action is effete
  and rhyme is outmoded,
    I shall revert to you,
  Habakkak, as when in a Bible class
    the teacher was speaking of unrhymed verse.
He said—and I think I repeat his exact words,
    "Hebrew poetry is prose
  with a sort of heightened consciousness." Ecstasy affords
    the occasion and expediency determines the form.

A Grave

Man looking into the sea,
taking the view from those who have as much right to it as
you have to it yourself,
it is human nature to stand in the middle of a thing,
but you cannot stand in the middle of this;
the sea has nothing to give but a well excavated grave.
The firs stand in a procession, each with an emerald turkey-foot
at the top,
reserved as their contours, saying nothing;
repression, however, is not the most obvious characteristic of
the sea;

the sea is a collector, quick to return a rapacious look.
There are others besides you who have worn that look—
whose expression is no longer a protest; the fish no longer
investigate them
for their bones have not lasted:
men lower nets, unconscious of the fact that they are
desecrating a grave,
and row quickly away—the blades of the oars
moving together like the feet of water-spiders as if there were no
such thing as death.
The wrinkles progress among themselves in a phalanx—beautiful
under networks of foam,
and fade breathlessly while the sea rustles in and out of the
seaweed;
the birds swim through the air at top speed, emitting cat-calls
as heretofore—
the tortoise-shell scourges about the feet of the cliffs, in motion
beneath them;
and the ocean, under the pulsation of lighthouses and noise of
bell-buoys,
advances as usual, looking as if it were not that ocean in which
dropped things are bound to sink—
in which if they turn and twist, it is neither with volition nor
consciousness.

Nevertheless

you've seen a strawberry
that's had a struggle; yet
was, where the fragments met,

a hedgehog or a star-
fish for the multitude
of seeds. What better food

than apple-seeds—the fruit
within the fruit—locked in
like counter-curved twin

hazel-nuts? Frost that kills
    the little rubber-plant-
    leaves of *kok-saghyz*-stalks, can't

harm the roots; they still grow
    in frozen ground. Once where
    there was a prickly-pear-

leaf clinging to barbed wire,
    a root shot down to grow
    in earth two feet below;

as carrots form mandrakes
    or a ram's-horn root some-
    times. Victory won't come

to me unless I go
    to it; a grape-tendril
    ties a knot in knots till

knotted thirty times,—so
    the bound twig that's under-
    gone and over-gone, can't stir.

The weak overcomes its
    menace, the strong over-
    comes itself. What is there

like fortitude! What sap
    went through that little thread
    to make the cherry red!

In the Days of Prismatic Color

not in the days of Adam and Eve, but when Adam
    was alone; when there was no smoke and color was
fine, not with the refinement
    of early civilization art, but because
of its originality; with nothing to modify it but the

mist that went up, obliqueness was a variation
   of the perpendicular, plain to see and
to account for: it is no
   longer that; nor did the blue-red-yellow band
of incandescence that was color keep its stripe: it also is one of

those things into which much that is peculiar can be
   read; complexity is not a crime, but carry
it to the point of murkiness
   and nothing is plain. Complexity,
moreover, that has been committed to darkness, instead of

granting itself to be the pestilence that it is, moves all a-
   bout as if to bewilder us with the dismal
fallacy that insistence
   is the measure of achievement and that all
truth must be dark. Principally throat, sophistication is as it al-

ways has been—at the antipodes from the init-
   ial great truths. "Part of it was crawling, part of it
was about to crawl, the rest
   was torpid in its lair." In the short-legged, fit-
ful advance, the gurgling and all the minutiae—we have the classic

multitude of feet. To what purpose! Truth is no Apollo
   Belvedere, no formal thing. The wave may go over it if it likes.
Know that it will be there when it says,
   "I shall be there when the wave has gone by."

A Jelly-fish

Visible, invisible,
   a fluctuating charm
an amber-tinctured amethyst
   inhabits it, your arm
approaches and it opens
   and it closes; you had meant
to catch it and it quivers;
   you abandon your intent.

His Shield

The pin-swin or spine-swine
(the edgehog miscalled hedgehog) with all his edges out,
echidna and echinoderm in distressed-
pin-cushion thorn-fur coats, the spiny pig or porcupine,
the rhino with horned snout—
everything is battle-dressed.

Pig-fur won't do, I'll wrap
myself in salamander-skin like Presbyter John.
A lizard in the midst of flames, a firebrand
that is life, asbestos-eyed asbestos-eared, with tattooed nap
and permanent pig on
the instep; he can withstand

fire and won't drown. In his
unconquerable country of unpompous gusto,
gold was so common none considered it; greed
and flattery were unknown. Though rubies large as tennis-
balls conjoined in streams so
that the mountain seemed to bleed,

the inextinguishable
salamander styled himself but presbyter. His shield
was his humility. In Carpasian
linen coat, flanked by his household lion-cubs and sable
retinue, he revealed
a formula safer than

an armorer's: the power of relinquishing
what one would keep; that is freedom. Become dinosaur-
skulled, quilled or salamander-wooled, more ironshod
and javelin-dressed than a hedgehog battalion of steel, but be
dull. Don't be envied or
armed with a measuring-rod.

The Student

"In America," began
the lecturer, "everyone must have a
degree. The French do not think that
all can have it, they don't say everyone
must go to college." We

incline to feel, here,
    that although it may be unnecessary

to know fifteen languages,
one degree is not too much. With us, a
school—like the singing tree of which
the leaves were mouths that sang in concert—
    is both a tree of knowledge
and of liberty,—
  seen in the unanimity of college

mottoes, *lux et veritas,*
Christo et ecclesiae, sapiet
felici. It may be that we
have not knowledge, just opinions, that we
    are undergraduates,
not students; we know
  we have been told with smiles, by expatriates

of whom we had asked "When will
your experiment be finished?" "Science
is never finished." Secluded
from domestic strife, Jack Bookworm led a
  college life, says Goldsmith;
and here also as
  in France or Oxford, study is beset with

dangers—with bookworms, mildews,
and complaisancies. But someone in New
England has known enough to say
that the student is patience personified,
  a variety
of hero, "patient
  of neglect and of reproach,"—who can "hold by

himself." You can't beat hens to
make them lay. Wolf's wool is the best of wool,
but it cannot be sheared, because
the wolf will not comply. With knowledge as
  with wolves' surliness,

the student studies
voluntarily, refusing to be less

than individual. He
"gives his opinion and then rests upon it";
he renders service when there is
no reward, and is too reclusive for
some things to seem to touch
him; not because he
has no feeling but because he has so much.

When I Buy Pictures

or what is closer to the truth,
when I look at that of which I may regard myself as the imaginary possessor,
I fix upon what would give me pleasure in my average moments:
the satire upon curiosity in which no more is discernible
than the intensity of the mood;
or quite the opposite—the old thing, the medieval decorated hat-box,
in which there are hounds with waists diminishing like the waist of the hour-glass,
and deer and birds and seated people;
it may be no more than a square of parquetry; the literal biography perhaps,
in letters standing well apart upon a parchment-like expanse;
an artichoke in six varieties of blue; the snipe-legged hieroglyphic in three parts;
the silver fence protecting Adam's grave, or Michael taking Adam by the wrist.
Too stern an intellectual emphasis upon this quality or that detracts from one's enjoyment.
It must not wish to disarm anything; nor may the approved triumph easily be honored—
that which is great because something else is small.
It comes to this: of whatever sort it is,
it must be "lit with piercing glances into the life of things";
it must acknowledge the spiritual forces which have made it.

To a Prize Bird

You suit me well, for you can make me laugh,
nor are you blinded by the chaff
  that every wind sends spinning from the rick.

You know to think, and what you think you speak
with much of Samson's pride and bleak
  finality, and none dare bid you stop.

Pride sits you well, so strut, colossal bird.
No barnyard makes you look absurd;
  your brazen claws are staunch against defeat.

The Monkeys

winked too much and were afraid of snakes. The zebras,
supreme in
their abnormality; the elephants with their fog-colored skin
  and strictly practical appendages
    were there, the small cats; and the parakeet—
      trivial and humdrum on examination, destroying
    bark and portions of the food it could not eat.

I recall their magnificence, now not more magnificent
than it is dim. It is difficult to recall the ornament,
  speech, and precise manner of what one might
    call the minor acquaintances twenty
      years back; but I shall not forget him—that Gilgamesh
among
    the hairy carnivora—that cat with the

wedge-shaped, slate-gray marks on its forelegs and the resolute
tail,
astringently remarking, "They have imposed on us with their pale
  half-fledged protestations, trembling about
    in inarticulate frenzy, saying
      it is not for us to understand art; finding it
    all so difficult, examining the thing

as if it were inconceivably arcanic, as symmet-
rically frigid as if it had been carved out of chrysoprase
or marble—strict with tension, malignant
in its power over us and deeper
than the sea when it proffers flattery in exchange for hemp,
rye, flax, horses, platinum, timber, and fur."

The Labors of Hercules

To popularize the mule, its neat exterior
expressing the principle of accommodation reduced to a minimum:
to persuade one of austere taste, proud in the possession of home, and a musician—
that the piano is a free field for etching; that his "charming tadpole notes"
belong to the past when one had time to play them:
to persuade those self-wrought Midases of brains
whose fourteen-carat ignorance aspires to rise in value, augurs disappointment,
that one must not borrow a long white beard and tie it on
and threaten with the scythe of time the casually curious:
to teach the bard with too elastic a selectiveness
that one detects creative power by its capacity to conquer one's detachment,
that while it may have more elasticity than logic;
it flies along in a straight line like electricity,
depopulating areas that boast of their remoteness,
to prove to the high priests of caste
that snobbishness is a stupidity,
the best side out, of age-old toadyism,
kissing the feet of the man above,
kicking the face of the man below;
to teach the patron-saints-to-atheists
that we are sick of the earth,
sick of the pig-sty, wild geese and wild men;
to convince snake-charming controversialists
that one keeps on knowing
"that the Negro is not brutal,
that the Jew is not greedy,
that the Oriental is not immoral,
that the German is not a Hun."

The Hero

Where there is personal liking we go.
  Where the ground is sour; where there are
  weeds of beanstalk height,
  snakes' hypodermic teeth, or
  the wind brings the "scarebabe voice"
  from the neglected yew set with
  the semi-precious cat's eyes of the owl—
awake, asleep, "raised ears extended to fine points," and so
on—love won't grow.

We do not like some things, and the hero
  doesn't; deviating head-stones
  and uncertainty;
  going where one does not wish
  to go; suffering and not
  saying so; standing and listening where something
  is hiding. The hero shrinks
as what it is flies out on muffled wings, with twin yellow
eyes—to and fro—

with quavering water-whistle note, low,
  high, in basso-falsetto chirps
  until the skin creeps.
  Jacob when a-dying, asked
  Joseph: Who are these? and blessed
  both sons, the younger most, vexing Joseph. And
  Joseph was vexing to some.
Cincinnatus was; Regulus; and some of our fellow
men have been, although devout,

like Pilgrim having to go slow
  to find his roll; tired but hopeful—
  hope not being hope
  until all ground for hope has
  vanished; and lenient, looking
  upon a fellow creature's error with the
  feelings of a mother—a
woman or a cat. The decorous frock-coated Negro
by the grotto

answers the fearless sightseeing hobo
  who asks the man she's with, what's this,
  what's that, where's Martha
  buried, "Gen-ral Washington
  there; his lady, here"; speaking
  as if in a play—not seeing her; with a
  sense of human dignity
and reverence for mystery, standing like the shadow
of the willow.

Moses would not be grandson to Pharaoh.
  It is not what I eat that is
  my natural meat,
  the hero says. He's not out
  seeing a sight but the rock
  crystal thing to see—the startling El Greco
  brimming with inner light—that
covets nothing that it has let go. This then you may know
as the hero.

Sojourn in the Whale

Trying to open locked doors with a sword, threading
  the points of needles, planting shade trees
  upside down; swallowed by the opaqueness of one whom
  the seas
love better than they love you, Ireland—

you have lived and lived on every kind of shortage.
  You have been compelled by hags to spin
  gold thread from straw and have heard men say:
"There is a feminine temperament in direct contrast to ours,

which makes her do these things. Circumscribed by a
  heritage of blindness and native
  incompetence, she will become wise and will be forced to
  give in.
Compelled by experience, she will turn back;

water seeks its own level":
and you have smiled. "Water in motion is far
from level." You have seen it, when obstacles happened to bar
the path, rise automatically.

Critics and Connoisseurs

There is a great amount of poetry in unconscious
fastidiousness. Certain Ming
products, imperial floor-coverings of coach-
wheel yellow, are well enough in their way but I have seen
something
that I like better—a
mere childish attempt to make an imperfectly bal-
lasted animal stand up,
similar determination to make a pup
eat his meat from the plate.

I remember a swan under the willows in Oxford,
with flamingo-colored, maple-
leaflike feet. It reconnoitered like a battle-
ship. Disbelief and conscious fastidiousness were
ingredients in its
disinclination to move. Finally its hardihood was
not proof against its
proclivity to more fully appraise such bits
of food as the stream

bore counter to it; it made away with what I gave it
to eat. I have seen this swan and
I have seen you; I have seen ambition without
understanding in a variety of forms. Happening to stand
by an ant-hill, I have
seen a fastidious ant carrying a stick north, south,
east, west, till it turned on
itself, struck out from the flower-bed into the lawn,
and returned to the point

from which it had started. Then abandoning the stick as
useless and overtaxing its
jaws with a particle of whitewash—pill-like but
heavy, it again went through the same course of procedure.
What is
there in being able
to say that one has dominated the stream in an attitude
of self-defense;
in proving that one has had the experience
of carrying a stick?

Propriety

is some such word
as the chord
Brahms had heard
from a bird,
sung down near the root of the throat;
it's the little downy woodpecker
spiraling a tree—
up up up like mercury;

a not long
sparrow-song
of hayseed
magnitude—
a tuned reticence with rigor
from strength at the source. Propriety is
Bach's Solfegietto—
harmonica and basso.

The fish-spine
on firs, on
somber trees
by the sea's
walls of wave-worn rock—have it; and
a moonbow and Bach's cheerful firmness
in a minor key.
It's an owl-and-a-pussy-

both-content
agreement.
Come, come. It's
mixed with wits;
it's not a graceful sadness. It's
resistance with bent head, like foxtail
millet's. Brahms and Bach,
no; Bach and Brahms. To thank Bach

for his song
first, is wrong.
Pardon me;
both are the
unintentional pansy-face
uncursed by self-inspection; blackened
because born that way.

England

with its baby rivers and little towns, each with its abbey or its
cathedral,
with voices—one voice perhaps, echoing through the transept—the
criterion of suitability and convenience: and Italy
with its equal shores—contriving an epicureanism
from which the grossness has been extracted:

and Greece with its goat and its gourds,
the nest of modified illusions: and France,
the "chrysalis of the nocturnal butterfly,"
in whose products mystery of construction
diverts one from what was originally one's object—
substance at the core: and the East with its snails, its emotional

shorthand and jade cockroaches, its rock crystal and its
imperturbability,
all of museum quality: and America where there
is the little old ramshackle victoria in the south,
where cigars are smoked on the street in the north;
where there are no proof-readers, no silkworms, no digressions;

the wild man's land; grassless, linksless, languageless country in
which letters are written
not in Spanish, not in Greek, not in Latin, not in shorthand,
but in plain American which cats and dogs can read!
The letter *a* in psalm and calm when
pronounced with the sound of *a* in candle, is very noticeable, but

why should continents of misapprehension
have to be accounted for by the fact?
Does it follow that because there are poisonous toadstools
which resemble mushrooms, both are dangerous?
Of mettlesomeness which may be mistaken for appetite,
of heat which may appear to be haste,
no conclusions may be drawn.

To have misapprehended the matter is to have confessed that one
has not looked far enough.
The sublimated wisdom of China, Egyptian discernment,
the cataclysmic torrent of emotion
compressed in the verbs of the Hebrew language,
the books of the man who is able to say,
"I envy nobody but him, and him only,
who catches more fish than I do"—
the flower and fruit of all that noted superiority—
if not stumbled upon in America,
must one imagine that it is not there?
It has never been confined to one locality.

In Distrust of Merits

Strengthened to live, strengthened to die for
medals and positioned victories?
They're fighting, fighting, fighting the blind
man who thinks he sees,—
who cannot see that the enslaver is
enslaved; the hater, harmed. O shining O
firm star, O tumultuous
ocean lashed till small things go

as they will, the mountainous
wave makes us who look, know

depth. Lost at sea before they fought! O
star of David, star of Bethlehem,
O black imperial lion
of the Lord—emblem
of a risen world—be joined at last, be
joined. There is hate's crown beneath which all is
death; there's love's without which none
is king; the blessed deeds bless
the halo. As contagion
of sickness makes sickness,

contagion of trust can make trust. They're
fighting in deserts and caves, one by
one, in battalions and squadrons;
they're fighting that I
may yet recover from the disease, My
Self; some have it lightly; some will die. "Man's
wolf to man" and we devour
ourselves. The enemy could not
have made a greater breach in our
defenses. One pilot-

ing a blind man can escape him, but
Job disheartened by false comfort knew
that nothing can be so defeating
as a blind man who
can see. O alive who are dead, who are
proud not to see, O small dust of the earth
that walks so arrogantly,
trust begets power and faith is
an affectionate thing. We
vow, we make this promise

to the fighting—it's a promise—"We'll
never hate black, white, red, yellow, Jew,
Gentile, Untouchable." We are
not competent to

make our vows. With set jaw they are fighting,
fighting, fighting,—some we love whom we know,
some we love but know not—that
hearts may feel and not be numb.
It cures me; or am I what
I can't believe in? Some

in snow, some on crags, some in quicksands,
little by little, much by much, they
are fighting fighting fighting that where
there was death there may
be life. "When a man is prey to anger,
he is moved by outside things; when he holds
his ground in patience patience
patience, that is action or
beauty," the soldier's defense
and hardest armor for

the fight. The world's an orphans' home. Shall
we never have peace without sorrow?
without please of the dying for
help that won't come? O
quiet form upon the dust, I cannot
look and yet I must. If these great patient
dyings—all these agonies
and wound bearings and bloodshed—
can teach us how to live, these
dyings were not wasted.

Hate-hardened heart, O heart of iron,
iron is iron till it is rust.
There never was a war that was
not inward; I must
fight till I have conquered in myself what
causes war, but I would not believe it.
I inwardly did nothing.
O Iscariot-like crime!
Beauty is everlasting
and dust is for a time.

A Face

"I am not treacherous, callous, jealous, superstitious,
supercilious, venomous, or absolutely hideous":
studying and studying its expression,
exasperated desperation
though at no real impasse,
would gladly break the mirror,

when love of order, ardor, uncircuitous simplicity
with an expression of inquiry, are all one needs to be!
Certain faces, a few, one or two—or one
face photographed by recollection—
to my mind, to my sight,
must remain a delight.

No Swan so Fine

"No water so still as the
dead fountains of Versailles." No swan,
with swart blind look askance
and gondoliering legs, so fine
as the chintz china one with fawn-
brown eyes and toothed gold
collar on to show whose bird it was.

Lodged in the Louis Fifteenth
candelabrum-tree of cockscomb-
tinted buttons, dahlias,
sea-urchins, and everlastings,
it perches on the branching foam
of polished sculptured
flowers—at ease and tall. The king is dead.

Four Quartz Crystal Clocks

There are four vibrators, the world's exactest clocks;
and these quartz time-pieces that tell
time intervals to other clocks,
these worksless clocks work well;

independently the same, kept in
the 41° Bell
Laboratory time

vault. Checked by a comparator with Arlington,
they punctualize the "radio,
cinéma," and "presse,"—a group the
Giraudoux truth-bureau
of hoped-for accuracy has termed
"instruments of truth." We know—
as Jean Giraudoux says,

certain Arabs have not heard—that Napoleon
is dead; that a quartz prism when
the temperature changes, feels
the change and that the then
electrified alternate edges
oppositely charged, threaten
careful timing; so that

this water-clear crystal as the Greeks used to say,
this "clear ice" must be kept at the
same coolness. Repetition, with
the scientist, should be
synonymous with accuracy.
The lemur-student can see
that an aye-aye is not

an angwan-tíbo, potto, or loris. The sea-
side burden should not embarrass
the bell-boy with the buoy-ball
endeavoring to pass
hotel patronesses; nor could a
practiced ear confuse the glass
eyes for taxidermists

with eye-glasses from the optometrist. And as
MEridian-7 one-two
one-two gives, each fifteenth second
in the same voice, the new
data—"The time will be" so and so—
you realize that "when you
hear the signal," you'll be

hearing Jupiter or jour pater, the day god—
the salvaged son of Father Time—
telling the cannibal Chronos
(eater of his proxime
newborn progeny) that punctuality
is not a crime.

The Steeple-Jack

Dürer would have seen a reason for living
in a town like this, with eight stranded whales
to look at; with the sweet sea air coming into your house
on a fine day, from water etched
with waves as formal as the scales
on a fish.

One by one in two's and three's, the seagulls keep
flying back and forth over the town clock,
or sailing around the lighthouse without moving their wings—
rising steadily with a slight
quiver of the body—or flock
mewing where

a sea the purple of the peacock's neck is
paled to greenish azure as Dürer changed
the pine green of the Tyrol to peacock blue and guinea
gray. You can see a twenty-five-
pound lobster; and fish nets arranged
to dry. The

whirlwind fife-and-drum of the storm bends the salt
marsh grass, disturbs stars in the sky and the
star on the steeple; it is a privilege to see so
much confusion. Disguised by what
might seem the opposite, the sea-
side flowers and

trees are favored by the fog so that you have
the tropics at first hand: the trumpet vine,
fox-glove, giant snap-dragon, a salpiglossis that has

spots and stripes; morning-glories, gourds,
or moon-vines trained on fishing-twine
at the back door;

cat-tails, flags, blueberries and spiderwort,
striped grass, lichens, sunflowers, asters, daisies—
yellow and crab-claw ragged sailors with green bracts—toad-plant,
petunias, ferns; pink lilies, blue
ones, tigers; poppies; black sweet-peas.
The climate

is not right for the banyan, frangipani, or
jack-fruit trees; or for exotic serpent
life. Ring lizard and snake-skin for the foot, if you see fit;
but here they've cats, not cobras, to
keep down the rats. The diffident
little newt

with white pin-dots on black horizontal spaced-
out bands lives here; yet there is nothing that
ambition can buy or take away. The college student
named Ambrose sits on the hillside
with his not-native books and hat
and sees boats

at sea progress white and rigid as if in
a groove. Liking an elegance of which
the source is not bravado, he knows by heart the antique
sugar-bowl shaped summer-house of
interlacing slats, and the pitch
of the church

spire, not true, from which a man in scarlet lets
down a rope as a spider spins a thread;
he might be part of a novel, but on the sidewalk a
sign says C. J. Poole, Steeple-Jack,
in black and white; and one in red
and white says

Danger. The church portico has four fluted
columns, each a single piece of stone, made

modester by white-wash. This would be a fit haven for
waifs, children, animals, prisoners,
and presidents who have repaid
sin-driven

senators by not thinking about them. The
place has a school-house, a post-office in a
store, fish-houses, hen-houses, a three-masted
schooner on
the stocks. The hero, the student,
the steeple-jack, each in his way,
is at home.

It could not be dangerous to be living
in a town like this, of simple people,
who have a steeple-jack placing danger-signs by the church
while he is gilding the solid-
pointed star, which on a steeple
stands for hope.

The Jerboa

Too Much

A Roman had an
artist, a freedman,
contrive a cone—pine-cone
or fir-cone—with holes for a fountain. Placed on
the Prison of St. Angelo, this cone
of the Pompeys which is known

now as the Popes', passed
for art. A huge cast
bronze, dwarfing the peacock
statue in the garden of the Vatican,
it looks like a work of art made to give
to a Pompey, or native

of Thebes. Others could
build, and understood
making colossi and
how to use slaves, and kept crocodiles and put

baboons on the necks of giraffes to pick
fruit, and used serpent magic.

They had their men tie
hippopotami
and bring out dappled dog-
cats to course antelopes, dikdik, and ibex;
or used small eagles. They looked on as theirs,
impalas and onigers,

the wild ostrich herd
with hard feet and bird
necks rearing back in the
dust like a serpent preparing to strike, cranes,
mongooses, storks, anoas, Nile geese;
and there were gardens for these—

combining planes, dates,
limes, and pomegranates,
in avenues—with square
pools of pink flowers, tame fish, and small frogs. Besides
yarns dyed with indigo, and red cotton,
they had a flax which they spun

into fine linen
cordage for yachtsmen.
These people liked small things;
they gave to boys little paired playthings such as
nests of eggs, ichneumon and snake, paddle
and raft, badger and camel;

and made toys for them-
selves: the royal totem;
and toilet-boxes marked
with the contents. Lords and ladies put goose-grease
paint in round bone boxes—the pivoting
lid incised with a duck-wing

or reverted duck-
head; kept in a buck
or rhinoceros horn,
the ground horn; and locust oil in stone locusts.

It was a picture with a fine distance;
of drought, and of assistance

in time, from the Nile
rising slowly, while
the pig-tailed monkey on
slab-hands, with arched-up slack-slung gait, and the brown
dandy looked at the jasmine two-leafed twig
and bud, cactus-pads, and fig.

Dwarfs here and there, lent
to an evident
poetry of frog grays,
duck-egg greens, and egg-plant blues, a fantasy
and a verisimilitude that were
right to those with, everywhere,

power over the poor.
The bees' food is your
food. Those who tended flower-
beds and stables were like the king's cane in the
form of a hand, or the folding bedroom
made for his mother of whom

he was fond. Princes
clad in queens' dresses,
calla or petunia
white, that trembled at the edge, and queens in a
king's underskirt of fine-twilled thread like silk-
worm gut, as bee-man and milk-

maid, kept divine cows
and bees; limestone brows,
and gold-foil wings. They made
basalt serpents and portraits of beetles; the
king gave his name to them and he was named
for them. He feared snakes, and tamed

Pharaoh's rat, the rust-
backed mongoose. No bust
of it was made, but there
was pleasure for the rat. Its restlessness was

its excellence; it was praised for its wit;
and the jerboa, like it,

a small desert rat,
and not famous, that
lives without water, has
happiness. Abroad seeking food, or at home
in its burrow, the Sahara field-mouse
has a shining silver house

of sand. O rest and
joy, the boundless sand,
the stupendous sand-spout,
no water, no palm-trees, no ivory bed,
tiny cactus; but one would not be he
who has nothing but plenty.

Abundance

Africanus meant
the conqueror sent
from Rome. It should mean the
untouched: the sand-brown jumping-rat—free-born; and
the blacks, that choice race with an elegance
ignored by one's ignorance.

Part terrestrial,
and part celestial,
Jacob saw, cudgel staff
in claw-hand—steps of air and air angels; his
friends were the stones. The translucent mistake
of the desert, does not make

hardship for one who
can rest and then do
the opposite—launching
as if on wings, from its match-thin hind legs, in
daytime or at night; with the tail as a weight,
undulated out by speed, straight.

Looked at by daylight,
the underside's white,

though the fur on the back
is buff-brown like the breast of the fawn-breasted
bower-bird. It hops like the fawn-breast, but has
chipmunk contours—perceived as

it turns its bird head—
the nap directed
neatly back and blending
with the ear which reiterates the slimness
of the body. The fine hairs on the tail,
repeating the other pale

markings, lengthen until
at the tip they fill
out in a tuft—black and
white; strange detail of the simplified creature,
fish-shaped and silvered to steel by the force
of the large desert moon. Course

the jerboa, or
plunder its food store,
and you will be cursed. It
honors the sand by assuming its color;
closed upper paws seeming one with the fur
in its flight from a danger.

By fifths and sevenths,
in leaps of two lengths,
like the uneven notes
of the Bedouin flute, it stops its gleaning
on little wheel castors, and makes fern-seed
foot-prints with kangaroo speed.

Its leaps should be set
to the flageolet;
pillar body erect
on a three-cornered smooth-working Chippendale
claw—propped on hind legs, and tail as third toe,
between leaps to its burrow.

Marriage

This institution,
perhaps one should say enterprise
out of respect for which
one says one need not change one's mind
about a thing one has believed in,
requiring public promises
of one's intention
to fulfil a private obligation:
I wonder what Adam and Eve
think of it by this time,
this fire-gilt steel
alive with goldenness;
how bright it shows—
"of circular traditions and impostures,
committing many spoils,"
requiring all one's criminal ingenuity
to avoid!
Psychology which explains everything
explains nothing,
and we are still in doubt.
Eve: beautiful woman—
I have seen her
when she was so handsome
she gave me a start,
able to write simultaneously
in three languages—
English, German and French—
and talk in the meantime;
equally positive in demanding a commotion
and in stipulating quiet:
"*I* should like to be alone";
to which the visitor replies,
"I should like to be alone;
why not be alone together?"
Below the incandescent stars
below the incandescent fruit,
the strange experience of beauty;
its existence is too much;
it tears one to pieces

and each fresh wave of consciousness
is poison.
"See her, see her in this common world,"
the central flaw
in that first crystal-fine experiment,
this amalgamation which can never be more
than an interesting impossibility,
describing it
as "that strange paradise
unlike flesh, stones,
gold or stately buildings,
the choicest piece of my life:
the heart rising
in its estate of peace
as a boat rises
with the rising of the water";
constrained in speaking of the serpent—
shed snakeskin in the history of politeness
not to be returned to again—
that invaluable accident
exonerating Adam.
And he has beauty also;
it's distressing—the O thou
to whom from whom,
without whom nothing—Adam;
"something feline,
something colubrine"—how true!
a crouching mythological monster
in that Persian miniature of emerald mines,
raw silk—ivory white, snow white,
oyster white and six others—
that paddock full of leopards and giraffes—
long lemon-yellow bodies
sown with trapezoids of blue.
Alive with words,
vibrating like a cymbal
touched before it has been struck,
he has prophesied correctly—
the industrious waterfall,
"the speedy stream
which violently bears all before it,

at one time silent as the air
and now as powerful as the wind."
"Treading chasms
on the uncertain footing of a spear,"
forgetting that there is in woman
a quality of mind
which as an instinctive manifestation
is unsafe,
he goes on speaking
in a formal customary strain,
of "past states, the present state,
seals, promises,
the evil one suffered,
the good one enjoys,
hell, heaven,
everything convenient
to promote one's joy."
In him a state of mind
perceives what it was not
intended that he should;
"he experiences a solemn joy
in seeing that he has become an idol."
Plagued by the nightingale
in the new leaves,
with its silence—
not its silence but its silences,
he says of it:
"It clothes me with a shirt of fire."
"He dares not clap his hands
to make it go on
lest it should fly off;
if he does nothing, it will sleep;
if he cries out, it will not understand."
Unnerved by the nightingale
and dazzled by the apple,
impelled by "the illusion of a fire
effectual to extinguish fire,"
compared with which
the shining of the earth
is but deformity—a fire
"as high as deep
as bright as broad

as long as life itself,"
he stumbles over marriage,
"a very trivial object indeed"
to have destroyed the attitude
in which he stood—
the ease of the philosopher
unfathered by a woman.
Unhelpful Hymen!
a kind of overgrown cupid
reduced to insignificance
by the mechanical advertising
parading as involuntary comment,
by that experiment of Adam's
with ways out but no way in—
the ritual of marriage,
augmenting all its lavishness;
its fiddle-head ferns,
lotus flowers, opuntias, white dromedaries,
its hippopotamus—
nose and mouth combined
in one magnificent hopper—
its snake and the potent apple.
He tells us
that "for love that will
gaze an eagle blind,
that is with Hercules
climbing the trees
in the garden of the Hesperides,
from forty-five to seventy
is the best age,"
commending it
as a fine art, as an experiment,
a duty or as merely recreation.
One must not call him ruffian
nor friction a calamity—
the fight to be affectionate:
"no truth can be fully known
until it has been tried
by the tooth of disputation."
The blue panther with black eyes,
the basalt panther with blue eyes,
entirely graceful—

one must give them the path—
the black obsidian Diana
who "darkeneth her countenance
as a bear doth,"
the spiked hand
that has an affection for one
and proves it to the bone,
impatient to assure you
that impatience is the mark of independence,
not of bondage.
"Married people often look that way"—
"seldom and cold, up and down,
mixed and malarial
with a good day and a bad."
We Occidentals are so unemotional,
self lost, the irony preserved
in "the Ahasuerus *tête-à-tête* banquet"
with its small orchids like snakes' tongues,
with its "good monster, lead the way,"
with little laughter
and munificence of humor
in that quixotic atmosphere of frankness
in which "four o'clock does not exist,
but at five o'clock
the ladies in their imperious humility
are ready to receive you";
in which experience attests
that men have power
and sometimes one is made to feel it.
He says, "What monarch would not blush
to have a wife
with hair like a shaving-brush?"
The fact of woman
is "not the sound of the flute
but very poison."
She says, "Men are monopolists
of 'stars, garters, buttons
and other shining baubles'—
unfit to be the guardians
of another person's happiness."
He says, "These mummies
must be handled carefully—
'the crumbs from a lion's meal,

a couple of shins and the bit of an ear';
turn to the letter M
and you will find
that 'a wife is a coffin,'
that severe object
with the pleasing geometry
stipulating space not people,
refusing to be buried
and uniquely disappointing,
revengefully wrought in the attitude
of an adoring child
to a distinguished parent."
She says, "This butterfly,
this waterfly, this nomad
that has 'proposed
to settle on my hand for life'—
What can one do with it?
There must have been more time
in Shakespeare's day
to sit and watch a play.
You know so many artists who are fools."
He says, "You know so many fools
who are not artists."
The fact forgot
that "some have merely rights
while some have obligations,"
he loves himself so much,
he can permit himself
no rival in that love.
She loves herself so much,
she cannot see herself enough—
a statuette of ivory on ivory,
the logical last touch
to an expansive splendor
earned as wages for work done:
one is not rich but poor
when one can always seem so right.
What can one do for them—
these savages
condemned to disaffect
all those who are not visionaries
alert to undertake the silly task
of making people noble?

This model of petrine fidelity
who "leaves her peaceful husband
only because she has seen enough of him"—
that orator reminding you,
"I am yours to command."
"Everything to do with love is mystery;
it is more than a day's work
to investigate this science."
One sees that it is rare—
that striking grasp of opposites
opposed each to the other, not to unity,
which in cycloid inclusiveness
has dwarfed the demonstration
of Columbus with the egg—
a triumph of simplicity—
that charitive Euroclydon
of frightening disinterestedness
which the world hates,
admitting:

"I am such a cow,
if I had a sorrow
I should feel it a long time;
I am not one of those
who have a great sorrow
in the morning
and a great joy at noon";

which says: "I have encountered it
among those unpretentious
protégés of wisdom,
where seeming to parade
as the debater and the Roman,
the statesmanship
of an archaic Daniel Webster
persists to their simplicity of temper
as the essence of the matter:

'Liberty and union
now and forever';

the Book on the writing-table;
the hand in the breast-pocket."

An Octopus

of ice. Deceptively reserved and flat,
it lies "in grandeur and in mass"
beneath a sea of shifting snow-dunes;
dots of cyclamen-red and maroon on its clearly defined
pseudo-podia
made of glass that will bend—a much needed invention—
comprising twenty-eight ice-fields from fifty to five hundred
feet thick,
of unimagined delicacy.
"Picking periwinkles from the cracks"
or killing prey with the concentric crushing rigor of the python,
it hovers forward "spider fashion
on its arms" misleadingly like lace;
its "ghostly pallor changing
to the green metallic tinge of an anemone-starred pool."
The fir-trees, in "the magnitude of their root systems,"
rise aloof from these maneuvers "creepy to behold,"
austere specimens of our American royal families,
"each like the shadow of the one beside it.
The rock seems frail compared with their dark energy of life,"
its vermilion and onyx and manganese-blue interior expensiveness
left at the mercy of the weather;
"stained transversely by iron where the water drips down,"
recognized by its plants and its animals.
Completing a circle,
you have been deceived into thinking that you have progressed,
under the polite needles of the larches
"hung to filter, not to intercept the sunlight"—
met by tightly wattled spruce-twigs
"conformed to an edge like clipped cypress
as if no branch could penetrate the cold beyond its company";
and dumps of gold and silver ore enclosing The Goat's Mirror—
that lady-fingerlike depression in the shape of the left human
foot,
which prejudices you in favor of itself
before you have had time to see the others;
its indigo, pea-green, blue-green, and turquoise,
from a hundred to two hundred feet deep,
"merging in irregular patches in the middle lake
where, like gusts of a storm

obliterating the shadows of the fir-trees, the wind makes lanes
of ripples."
What spot could have merits of equal importance
for bears, elk, deer, wolves, goats, and ducks?
Pre-empted by their ancestors,
this is the property of the exacting porcupine,
and of the rat "slipping along to its burrow in the swamp
or pausing on high ground to smell the heather";
of "thoughtful beavers
making drains which seem the work of careful men with shovels,"
and of the bears inspecting unexpectedly
ant-hills and berry-bushes.
Composed of calcium gems and alabaster pillars,
topaz, tourmaline crystals and amethyst quartz,
their den is somewhere else, concealed in the confusion
of "blue forests thrown together with marble and jasper and agate
as if whole quarries had been dynamited."
And farther up, in stag-at-bay position
as a scintillating fragment of these terrible stalagmites,
stands the goat,
its eye fixed on the waterfall which never seems to fall—
an endless skein swayed by the wind,
immune to force of gravity in the perspective of the peaks.
A special antelope
acclimated to "grottoes from which issue penetrating draughts
which make you wonder why you came,"
it stands its ground
on cliffs the color of the clouds, of petrified white vapor—
black feet, eyes, nose, and horns, engraved on dazzling ice-fields,
the ermine body on the crystal peak;
the sun kindling its shoulders to maximum heat like acetylene,
dyeing them white—
upon this antique pedestal,
"a mountain with those graceful lines which prove it a volcano,"
its top a complete cone like Fujiyama's
till an explosion blew it off.
Distinguished by a beauty
of which "the visitor dare never fully speak at home
for fear of being stoned as an impostor,"
Big Snow Mountain is the home of a diversity of creatures:
those who "have lived in hotels
but who now live in camps—who prefer to";

the mountain guide evolving from the trapper,
"in two pairs of trousers, the outer one older,
wearing slowly away from the feet to the knees";
"the nine-striped chipmunk
running with unmammal-like agility along a log";
the water ouzel
with "its passion for rapids and high-pressured falls,"
building under the arch of some tiny Niagara;
the white-tailed ptarmigan "in winter solid white,
feeding on heather-bells and alpine buckwheat";
and the eleven eagles of the west,
"fond of the spring fragrance and the winter colors,"
used to the unegoistic action of the glaciers
and "several hours of frost every midsummer night."
"They make a nice appearance, don't they,"
happy seeing nothing?
Perched on treacherous lava and pumice—
those unadjusted chimney-pots and cleavers
which stipulate "names and addresses of persons to notify
in case of disaster"—
they hear the roar of ice and supervise the water
winding slowly through the cliffs,
the road "climbing like the thread
which forms the groove around a snail-shell,
doubling back and forth until where snow begins, it ends."
No "deliberate wide-eyed wistfulness" is here
among the boulders sunk in ripples and white water
where "when you hear the best wild music of the forest
it is sure to be a marmot,"
the victim on some slight observatory,
of "a struggle between curiosity and caution,"
inquiring what has scared it:
a stone from the moraine descending in leaps,
another marmot, or the spotted ponies with glass eyes,
brought up on frosty grass and flowers
and rapid draughts of ice-water.
Instructed none knows how, to climb the mountain,
by business men who require for recreation
three hundred and sixty-five holidays in the year,
these conspicuously spotted little horses are peculiar;
hard to discern among the birch-trees, ferns, and lily-pads,
avalanche lilies, Indian paint-brushes,

bear's ears and kittentails,
and miniature cavalcades of chlorophylless fungi
magnified in profile on the moss-beds like moonstones in the water;
the cavalcade of calico competing
with the original American menagerie of styles
among the white flowers of the rhododendron surmounting rigid leaves
upon which moisture works its alchemy,
transmuting verdure into onyx.

"Like happy souls in Hell," enjoying mental difficulties, the Greeks
amused themselves with delicate behavior
because it was "so noble and so fair";
not practised in adapting their intelligence
to eagle-traps and snow-shoes,
to alpenstocks and other toys contrived by those
"alive to the advantage of invigorating pleasures."
Bows, arrows, oars, and paddles, for which trees provide the wood,
in new countries more eloquent than elsewhere—
augmenting the assertion that, essentially humane,
"the forest affords wood for dwellings and by its beauty
stimulates the moral vigor of its citizens."
The Greeks liked smoothness, distrusting what was back
of what could not be clearly seen,
resolving with benevolent conclusiveness,
"complexities which still will be complexities
as long as the world lasts";
ascribing what we clumsily call happiness,
to "an accident or a quality,
a spiritual substance or the soul itself,
an act, a disposition, or a habit,
or a habit infused, to which the soul has been persuaded,
or something distinct from a habit, a power"—
such power as Adam had and we are still devoid of.
"Emotionally sensitive, their hearts were hard";
their wisdom was remote
from that of these odd oracles of cool official sarcasm,
upon this game preserve
where "guns, nets, seines, traps and explosives,
hired vehicles, gambling and intoxicants are prohibited;

disobedient persons being summarily removed
and not allowed to return without permission in writing."
It is self-evident
that it is frightful to have everything afraid of one;
that one must do as one is told
and eat rice, prunes, dates, raisins, hardtack, and tomatoes
if one would "conquer the main peak of Mount Tacoma,
this fossil flower concise without a shiver,
intact when it is cut,
damned for its sacrosanct remoteness—
like Henry James "damned by the public for decorum";
not decorum, but restraint;
it is the love of doing hard things
that rebuffed and wore them out—a public out of sympathy with neatness.
Neatness of finish! Neatness of finish!
Relentless accuracy is the nature of this octopus
with its capacity for fact.
"Creeping slowly as with meditated stealth,
its arms seeming to approach from all directions,"
it receives one under winds that "tear the snow to bits
and hurl it like a sandblast
shearing off twigs and loose bark from the trees."
Is "tree" the word for these things
"flat on the ground like vines"?
some "bent in a half circle with branches on one side
suggesting dust-brushes, not trees;
some finding strength in union, forming little stunted groves
their flattened mats of branches shrunk in trying to escape"
from the hard mountain "planed by ice and polished by the wind"—
the white volcano with no weather side;
the lightning flashing at its base,
rain falling in the valleys, and snow falling on the peak—
the glassy octopus symmetrically pointed,
its claw cut by the avalanche
"with a sound like the crack of a rifle,
in a curtain of powdered snow launched like a waterfall."

T. S. Eliot

[1888–1965]

Some readers believe that T. S. Eliot was more English than American, not only since he lived in England for much of his life and converted to its state religion, Anglicanism, but also because he subscribed to its cultural values. His description of himself as a "royalist in politics, classicist in literature, and Anglo-Catholic in religion" seems to support this view. So too does Eliot's assumption of British citizenship in 1927. Yet rather than losing his American cultural identity, Eliot seems to have grafted a British one onto it. Eliot thus became a poet of two worlds rather than one.

Ezra Pound and Thomas Stearns Eliot are generally recognized as the founders of modernist poetry in English (with Walt Whitman and Emily Dickinson serving as their American precursors). Their influence has been far greater than that of any other modern American poet. What made their poetry so important for modernism? Why did it become so prominent? And what distinguished it from the work of other modern poets writing in English? Three things at least: its difficulty, its technical innovation, its thematic preoccupations.

Both Eliot and Pound are considered "difficult" poets whose major works present formidable obstacles for all but the most experienced readers. The difficulty in reading Eliot's poems is attributable primarily to three factors: its heavy use of allusion, its borrowings from foreign languages, and its use of juxtaposed images. When considering Eliot's late religious poems, especially *Four Quartets,* one must also reckon with mystical and paradoxical ideas about time, death, and spirituality. Like Pound's work, much of Eliot's poetry includes numerous references to history, philosophy, and literature—especially medieval and Renaissance drama and the classical literature of Greece and Rome. Eliot expected his readers to be familiar with Greek mythology, to recognize references to Dante, Shakespeare, and Wagner (among others), and to make sense of the allusions by considering them in the context of the poem. Even if we cannot recognize all of Eliot's literary allusions or historical references, we can, nevertheless, gain a sense of the poem's meaning, intention, and power by attending to its images, especially by establishing connections among them.

Another dragon guarding the gate of Eliot's poetry is the apparent lack of connection among sections, stanzas, lines, and sentences. Eliot's poems are often highly imagistic. In *The Waste Land,* for example, he makes the image an instrument of ironic commentary by juxtaposing details of the present with more idealized images of the past. The images may be included as part of brief dramatic scenes, as in the typist's encounter with the "young man carbuncular." They may be presented as static pictorial details, as in the many examples of dryness and sterility. Or they may be primarily allusive, as in the references to the mythological rape of Philomel.

Eliot's poems employ fragmentation as a deliberate structural principle, one consequence of which is that their coherence must be inferred by the reader. One advantage, in fact, of poems that eschew discursive explanation is increased intensity and compression. Another is that they demand readers' active participation in making sense of a fragmented structure. Still another benefit is an opportunity for the poet to create new structural patterns, new ways to organize forms. Many of Eliot's poems, for example, employ musical structures. *The Waste Land,* to cite one example, is arranged in movements much like a symphony.

An additional reason that Eliot's poems are seen as difficult derives from his belief that poetry, especially modern poetry, *should be* difficult. In *The Use of Poetry and the Use of Criticism* he discusses his reason: "The difficulty in reading some poems is caused by the author's having left something out that the reader is used to finding; so that the reader, bewildered, gropes about for what is absent." Alongside this remark we should place Eliot's notion that great poetry need not be understood in every line and detail. Eliot believed that readers could apprehend poems in languages they could neither read nor translate. Eliot also believed that poetry should reflect the complexities and ambiguities of experience. His poetic forms typify the fragmentation, disconnection, and confusion at the heart of modern history, which he once described as an "immense panorama of futility and anarchy."

Thomas Stearns Eliot's life reflects some of the tensions and divisions of his poetry. He was born in St. Louis, Missouri, in 1888. Though raised in the Southwest, his family had its roots in New England, and they vacationed at a summer home in Gloucester, Massachusetts. Solidifying this aspect of Eliot's life was his education at Harvard University (1906–1910), where he edited *The Harvard Advocate* and earned both bachelor's and master's degrees. Eliot then went abroad to attend the Sorbonne and to Merton College, Oxford, where he studied philosophy. He wrote his master's thesis there on the British philosopher F. H. Bradley and was working toward a doctorate in philosophy and an academic career when the outbreak of World War I prevented his return from England to complete his degree at Harvard.

Instead of pursuing an academic life, Eliot turned to business and to poetry. Eliot's employment ranged from teaching at the High Wycombe and Highgate schools (1915–1917) through working as a clerk for Lloyd's Bank of London (1917–1925) to serving as editor and later as director of Faber and Faber, a London publishing house (1926–1965). In addition, Eliot founded *The Criterion,* an important literary quarterly that flourished from 1922 to 1939. He received many distinctions and awards, including the Nobel Prize for Literature (1948), the New York Drama Critics Circle Award (1950), the Dante Gold Medal, Florence (1959), and the Order of Merit, Bonn (1959). He also received seventeen honorary doctorates from the most prestigious universities in six countries, including Harvard, Yale, Oxford, and Cambridge.

Eliot's most influential poem, *The Waste Land,* burst upon the literary scene in 1922. Nearly fifty years later, in 1971, a facsimile edition of this important document of literary modernism was published with transcripts of Eliot's original drafts, including extensive annotations made by Ezra Pound. Edited by Eliot's widow, this edition revealed the extent of Eliot's debt to Pound and the degree of Pound's editorial skill and judgment. Pound advised Eliot to revise the poem by excising discursive explanation and cutting seventy-two lines of rhymed couplets at the beginning of "The Fire Sermon." Pound also dissuaded Eliot from using "Gerontion" as a preface to the poem and suggested numerous small-scale alterations that resulted in a more unified poem. In gratitude Eliot dedicated *The Waste Land* to Pound, designating him *il miglior fabbro* ("the better craftsman"). *The Waste Land* is important not only as a poetic achievement but also as a remarkable influence exerted on an entire generation of poets, both those who were converted to Eliot's techniques and those who, like William Carlos Williams, resisted them.

Eliot's poetic output included a 1936 volume that collected his verse of 1906–1935 and a larger collection, *The Collected Poems 1909–1962.* This final book featured Eliot's last major poetic enterprise, *Four Quartets,* originally published in 1943. In addition to this modest poetic production, Eliot also wrote five plays and a collection of humorous verse, *Old Possum's Book of Practical Cats,* which inspired the musical *Cats.*

His literary criticism includes brief books on Dante, George Herbert, Elizabethan drama, and seventeenth-century poetry, among many essays. Eliot's criticism reflects an effort to find solutions to his own poetic problems. Like his plays, his criticism is interesting for the light it sheds on his own poetry, especially his emphasis on the poem itself rather than on the personality of the poet. His criticism is perhaps even more important for its influential reevaluation of seventeenth-century literature, especially the poetry of John Donne and Andrew Marvell, and the plays of a number of Elizabethan and Jacobean dramatists.

Eliot's most popular and best-known poem after *The Waste Land* is "The Love Song of J. Alfred Prufrock." It portrays an inhibited, timid man who is unable to declare his feelings for a woman. In a series of self-deprecating excuses, he reveals his fear of human connection, identifying himself as a diminished, ineffectual person. Considered by some readers to be a dramatic monologue, "Prufrock" lacks the steady narrative drive and consistent voice characteristic of the form as practiced by Robert Browning and Alfred, Lord Tennyson. With its ironies, its fragmentation, and its elaborate conceits, "Prufrock" displays the influence of both the seventeenth-century metaphysical poets and the French Symbolists. The poem also exhibits Eliot's lifelong concern with human relationships.

The Waste Land, however, is Eliot's modernist masterpiece. It is the single most widely read and most frequently analyzed American poem of the twentieth century. Much celebrated as a modernist document, it offers an account of the dismal state of the world following World War I. The world of *The Waste Land* lacks value and meaning. Human relationships are based on misuse and self-gratification. The poem's various voices depict a place devoid of faith, hope, and love. Read with a biographical emphasis, *The Waste Land* reflects aspects of Eliot's personal problems, particularly his unhappy first marriage. From a historical perspective, the poem offers a critique of a world without an ultimate purpose. From a mythic standpoint, it suggests how heroic virtues and traditional cultural and religious values are necessary to restore a more vital, hopeful world. To see the poem as "only the relief of a personal and insignificant grouse against life" (as Eliot once described it) or to emphasize too heavily its connections with the Grail legend and fertility rituals (directions Eliot also suggested) is to restrict our understanding and impoverish our experience of it. *The Waste Land* shares with other ambitious American poems a multiplicity of facets. It is partly a language experiment, partly an ambiguous allegory, partly a puzzle, partly a game of wit. It is, for many, the most challenging poem of the century, and certainly the most famous.

Eliot was only thirty-four when *The Waste Land* was published. It would be more than twenty years before he would publish his next major poetic work, *Four Quartets,* a series of expansive meditations on time, change, age, suffering, love, spirituality, and history. Even more explicitly than *The Waste Land,* each of the quartets assumes a musical structure. Each contains five movements varied in rhythm; each contains themes or statements followed by counterthemes, repetitions, and variations of the original statements.

The last of the quartets, "Little Gidding," presents an opportunity to see Eliot in a more hopeful, less critical mode than is characteristic of his earlier work. In "Little Gidding," as in the other quartets, Eliot offers a positive image of community and an encouraging vision of life. Although generally recognized as a major achievement, the *Quartets* have never captured the imagination of readers the way *The Waste Land* has. It was

The Waste Land that spread Eliot's fame and influence. And it was *The Waste Land,* along with the critical theory Eliot developed to support it, that largely created the taste of the age, a taste that would ultimately judge Eliot the supreme poet of his time.

The Love Song of J. Alfred Prufrock

S'io credesse che mia risposta fosse
A persona che mai tornasse al mondo,
Questa fiamma staria senza più scosse.
Ma perciocche giammai di questo fondo
Non tornò vivo alcun, s'i'odo il vero,
Senza tema d'infamia ti rispondo.

Let us go then, you and I,
When the evening is spread out against the sky
Like a patient etherized upon a table;
Let us go, through certain half-deserted streets,
The muttering retreats
Of restless nights in one-night cheap hotels
And sawdust restaurants with oyster-shells:
Streets that follow like a tedious argument
Of insidious intent
To lead you to an overwhelming question . . .
Oh, do not ask, 'What is it?'
Let us go and make our visit.

In the room the women come and go
Talking of Michelangelo.

The yellow fog that rubs its back upon the window-panes,
The yellow smoke that rubs its muzzle on the window-panes,
Licked its tongue into the corners of the evening,
Lingered upon the pools that stand in drains,
Let fall upon its back the soot that falls from chimneys,
Slipped by the terrace, made a sudden leap,

THE LOVE SONG OF J. ALFRED PRUFROCK Epigraph from Dante's Inferno, canto XXVII, 61–66. The words are spoken by Guido da Montefeltro when asked to identify himself: "If I thought my answer were given to anyone who could ever return to the world, this flame would shake no more; but since none ever did return above from this depth, if what I hear is true, without fear of infamy I answer thee."

And seeing that it was a soft October night,
Curled once about the house, and fell asleep.

And indeed there will be time
For the yellow smoke that slides along the street
Rubbing its back upon the window-panes;
There will be time, there will be time
To prepare a face to meet the faces that you meet;
There will be time to murder and create,
And time for all the works and days of hands
That lift and drop a question on your plate;
Time for you and time for me,
And time yet for a hundred indecisions,
And for a hundred visions and revisions,
Before the taking of a toast and tea.

In the room the women come and go
Talking of Michelangelo.

And indeed there will be time
To wonder, 'Do I dare?' and, 'Do I dare?'
Time to turn back and descend the stair,
With a bald spot in the middle of my hair—
(They will say: 'How his hair is growing thin!')
My morning coat, my collar mounting firmly to the chin,
My necktie rich and modest, but asserted by a simple pin—
(They will say: 'But how his arms and legs are thin!')
Do I dare
Disturb the universe?
In a minute there is time
For decisions and revisions which a minute will reverse.

For I have known them all already, known them all—
Have known the evenings, mornings, afternoons,
I have measured out my life with coffee spoons;
I know the voices dying with a dying fall

[29]**works and days:** *Works and Days* is the title of a poem by the Greek poet Hesiod (eighth century B.C.) that combines an account of an agrarian life with moral teaching. [52]**I know . . . dying fall:** echoes Shakespeare's *Twelfth Night* I, i, 1–4. "If music be the food of love, play on; / Give me excess of it, that, surfeiting / The appetite may sicken, and so die. / That strain again! it had a dying fall."

Beneath the music from a farther room.
  So how should I presume?

And I have known the eyes already, known them all—
The eyes that fix you in a formulated phrase,
And when I am formulated, sprawling on a pin,
When I am pinned and wriggling on the wall,
Then how should I begin
To spit out all the butt-ends of my days and ways?
  And how should I presume?

And I have known the arms already, known them all—
Arms that are braceleted and white and bare
(But in the lamplight, downed with light brown hair!)
Is it perfume from a dress
That makes me so digress?
Arms that lie along a table, or wrap about a shawl.
  And should I then presume?
  And how should I begin?

. . . . .

Shall I say, I have gone at dusk through narrow streets
And watched the smoke that rises from the pipes
Of lonely men in shirt-sleeves, leaning out of windows? . . .

I should have been a pair of ragged claws
Scuttling across the floors of silent seas.

. . . . .

And the afternoon, the evening, sleeps so peacefully!
Smoothed by long fingers,
Asleep . . . tired . . . or it malingers,
Stretched on the floor, here beside you and me.
Should I, after tea and cakes and ices,
Have the strength to force the moment to its crisis?
But though I have wept and fasted, wept and prayed,
Though I have seen my head (grown slightly bald) brought in
  upon a platter,
I am no prophet—and here's no greater matter;
I have seen the moment of my greatness flicker,

[82]**my head . . . upon a platter:** John the Baptist was beheaded at the order of King Herod to please his wife, Herodias, and daughter, Salome. See Matthew 14:1–11.

And I have seen the eternal Footman hold my coat, and
snicker,
And in short, I was afraid.

And would it have been worth it, after all,
After the cups, the marmalade, the tea,
Among the porcelain, among some talk of you and me,
Would it have been worth while,
To have bitten off the matter with a smile,
To have squeezed the universe into a ball
To roll it towards some overwhelming question,
To say: 'I am Lazarus, come from the dead,
Come back to tell you all, I shall tell you all'—
If one, settling a pillow by her head,
Should say: 'That is not what I meant at all.
That is not it, at all.'

And would it have been worth it, after all,
Would it have been worth while,
After the sunsets and the dooryards and the sprinkled streets,
After the novels, after the teacups, after the skirts that trail
along the floor—
And this, and so much more?—
It is impossible to say just what I mean!
But as if a magic lantern threw the nerves in patterns on a
screen:
Would it have been worth while
If one, settling a pillow or throwing off a shawl,
And turning toward the window, should say:
'That is not it at all,
That is not what I meant, at all.'

. . . . .

No! I am not Prince Hamlet, nor was meant to be;
Am an attendant lord, one that will do
To swell a progress, start a scene or two,

[91–92]**To have bitten . . . into a ball:** An allusion to Andrew Marvell's poem "To His Coy Mistress": Let us roll all our strength and all / Our sweetness up into one ball / And tear our pleasures with rough strife / Thorough the iron gates of life." Eliot also alludes to the first line of Marvell's poem, "Had we world enough and time," in line 23: "And indeed there will be time." [94]**Lazarus:** a man whom Jesus raised from the dead. See John 11:1–44. [113]**progress:** a procession or royal journey made by members of the court.

Advise the prince; no doubt, an easy tool,
Deferential, glad to be of use,
Politic, cautious, and meticulous;
Full of high sentence, but a bit obtuse;
At times, indeed, almost ridiculous—
Almost, at times, the Fool.

I grow old . . . I grow old . . .
I shall wear the bottoms of my trousers rolled.

Shall I part my hair behind? Do I dare to eat a peach?
I shall wear white flannel trousers, and walk upon the beach.
I have heard the mermaids singing, each to each.

I do not think that they will sing to me.

I have seen them riding seaward on the waves
Combing the white hair of the waves blown back
When the wind blows the water white and black.

We have lingered in the chambers of the sea
By sea-girls wreathed with seaweed red and brown
Till human voices wake us, and we drown.

Preludes

I

The winter evening settles down
With smell of steaks in passageways.
Six o'clock.
The burnt-out ends of smoky days.
And now a gusty shower wraps
The grimy scraps
Of withered leaves about your feet
And newspapers from vacant lots;
The showers beat
On broken blinds and chimney-pots,
And at the corner of the street

A lonely cab-horse steams and stamps.
And then the lighting of the lamps.

II

The morning comes to consciousness
Of faint stale smells of beer
From the sawdust-trampled street
With all its muddy feet that press
To early coffee-stands.
With the other masquerades
That time resumes,
One thinks of all the hands
That are raising dingy shades
In a thousand furnished rooms.

III

You tossed a blanket from the bed,
You lay upon your back, and waited;
You dozed, and watched the night revealing
The thousand sordid images
Of which your soul was constituted;
They flickered against the ceiling.
And when all the world came back
And the light crept up between the shutters
And you heard the sparrows in the gutters,
You had such a vision of the street
As the street hardly understands;
Sitting along the bed's edge, where
You curled the papers from your hair,
Or clasped the yellow soles of feet
In the palms of both soiled hands.

IV

His soul stretched tight across the skies
That fade behind a city block,
Or trampled by insistent feet
At four and five and six o'clock;

And short square fingers stuffing pipes,
And evening newspapers, and eyes
Assured of certain certainties,
The conscience of a blackened street
Impatient to assume the world.

I am moved by fancies that are curled
Around these images, and cling:
The notion of some infinitely gentle
Infinitely suffering thing.

Wipe your hand across your mouth, and laugh;
The worlds revolve like ancient women
Gathering fuel in vacant lots.

Gerontion

Thou hast nor youth nor age
But as it were an after dinner sleep
Dreaming of both.

Here I am, an old man in a dry month,
Being read to by a boy, waiting for rain.
I was neither at the hot gates
Nor fought in the warm rain
Nor knee deep in the salt-marsh, heaving a cutlass,
Bitten by flies, fought.
My house is a decayed house,
And the Jew squats on the window sill, the owner,
Spawned in some estaminet of Antwerp,
Blistered in Brussels, patched and peeled in London.
The goat coughs at night in the field overhead;
Rocks, moss, stonecrop, iron, merds.
The woman keeps the kitchen, makes tea,
Sneezes at evening, poking the peevish gutter.
I an old man,
A dull head among windy spaces.

GERONTION The title is coined from the Greek *geron,* "old man." The epigraph is from Shakespeare's *Measure for Measure,* III, i, 32–34. [3]**hot gates:** an allusion to Thermopylae (Greek for "hot gates"), the mountain pass where the Spartans defeated the Persians in 480 B.C.. [12]**merds:** French for "dung."

Signs are taken for wonders. 'We would see a sign!'
The word within a word, unable to speak a word,
Swaddled with darkness. In the juvescence of the year
Came Christ the tiger

In depraved May, dogwood and chestnut, flowering judas,
To be eaten, to be divided, to be drunk
Among whispers; by Mr. Silvero
With caressing hands, at Limoges
Who walked all night in the next room;

By Hakagawa, bowing among the Titians;
By Madame de Tornquist, in the dark room
Shifting the candles; Fräulein von Kulp
Who turned in the hall, one hand on the door.
Vacant shuttles
Weave the wind. I have no ghosts,
An old man in a draughty house
Under a windy knob.

After such knowledge, what forgiveness? Think now
History has many cunning passages, contrived corridors
And issues, deceives with whispering ambitions,
Guides us by vanities. Think now
She gives when our attention is distracted
And what she gives, gives with such supple confusions
That the giving famishes the craving. Gives too late
What's not believed in, or is still believed,

[17]**'We would see a sign!':** see Matthew 12:38: "Master we would see a sign from you," in which the disciples asked Jesus for an indication of his divinity. And also Luke 2:12: "And this will be a sign for you; you will find a babe wrapped in swaddling cloths and lying in a manger." [18]**The word . . . a word:** see John 1:1, 14: "In the beginning was the Word, and the Word was with God, and the Word was God. . . . And the Word became flesh and dwelt among us." Lines 17–18 also allude to a sermon by Lancelot Andrewes (1555–1626) in which Andrewes discusses the gospel and the life of Jesus as signs and wonders and refers to the infant Jesus as *"verbum infans,* the Word without a word; the eternal Word not able to speak a word." [19]**juvescence:** juvenescence, or youth. [21]**depraved May:** a reference to Henry Adams's autobiography, *The Education of Henry Adams,* Chapter 18, in which he describes the "passionate depravity that marked the Maryland May." [23–28]**Mr. Silvero . . . Fräulein von Kulp:** Eliot invented these names.

In memory only, reconsidered passion. Gives too soon
Into weak hands, what's thought can be dispensed with
Till the refusal propagates a fear. Think
Neither fear nor courage saves us. Unnatural vices
Are fathered by our heroism. Virtues
Are forced upon us by our impudent crimes.
These tears are shaken from the wrath-bearing tree.

The tiger springs in the new year. Us he devours. Think at last
We have not reached conclusion, when I
Stiffen in a rented house. Think at last
I have not made this show purposelessly
And it is not by any concitation
Of the backward devils.
I would meet you upon this honestly.
I that was near your heart was removed therefrom
To lose beauty in terror, terror in inquisition.
I have lost my passion: why should I need to keep it
Since what is kept must be adulterated?
I have lost my sight, smell, hearing, taste and touch:
How should I use them for your closer contact?

These with a thousand small deliberations
Protract the profit of their chilled delirium,
Excite the membrane, when the sense has cooled,
With pungent sauces, multiply variety
In a wilderness of mirrors. What will the spider do,
Suspend its operations, will the weevil
Delay? De Bailhache, Fresca, Mrs. Cammel, whirled
Beyond the circuit of the shuddering Bear
In fractured atoms. Gull against the wind, in the windy straits
Of Belle Isle, or running on the Horn.
White feathers in the snow, the Gulf claims,
And an old man driven by the Trades
To a sleepy corner.
                                        Tenants of the house,
Thoughts of a dry brain in a dry season.

[52]**concitation:** stirring up. [67–68]**De Bailhache . . . shuddering Bear:** unidentified, perhaps invented, persons who will be hurled around Polaris, the pole-star, the outermost star in the handle of the Little Bear.

The Waste Land

'Nam Sibyllam quidem Cumis ego ipse oculis meis vidi in ampulla pendere, et cum illi pueri dicerent: Σίβυλλα τί θέλεις; *respondebat illa:* αποθανεῖν θέλω.'

FOR EZRA POUND

il miglior fabbro.

I. The Burial of the Dead

April is the cruellest month, breeding
Lilacs out of the dead land, mixing
Memory and desire, stirring
Dull roots with spring rain.
Winter kept us warm, covering
Earth in forgetful snow, feeding
A little life with dried tubers.
Summer surprised us, coming over the Starnbergersee
With a shower of rain; we stopped in the colonnade,
And went on in sunlight, into the Hofgarten,
And drank coffee, and talked for a hour.
Bin gar keine Russin, stamm' aus Litauen, echt deutsch.
And when we were children, staying at the arch-duke's,
My cousin's, he took me out on a sled,
And I was frightened. He said, Marie,
Marie, hold on tight. And down we went.

THE WASTE LAND Eliot acknowledged that the poem's title, plan, and symbolism were influenced by Jesse L. Weston's book on the Grail legend, *From Ritual to Romance* (1920). He also recognized the importance for the poem of James G. Frazer's *The Golden Bough* (1890–1915), especially the portions that concern vegetation myths and fertility rituals. Eliot's fifty-two footnotes are incorporated among those of the editor and identified as his. The epigraph quotes Petronius's *Satyricon* (first century A.D.): "For with my own eyes I saw the Sibyl hanging in a jar at Cumae, and when the boys said to her, 'Sibyl, what do you want?' she replied, 'I want to die.' " The Sibyl, a prophetess, had been granted immortal life but not immortal youth by Apollo. Her shriveled form was kept in a jar in the temple of Hercules at Cumae. Eliot's dedication acknowledges the editorial assistance of Ezra Pound, whom he designates "the better craftsman." The Italian quotation is taken from Dante's *Purgatorio,* XXVI, 17, in which Guido Guinizelli pays tribute to the Provençal poet Arnaut Daniel as a better maker of poems. **The Burial of the Dead:** a phrase from the Anglican burial service. 8**Starnbergersee:** a resort lake near Munich. 10**Hofgarten:** a public park that had once been a royal palace garden. 12**Bin gar keine . . . echt deutsch:** German for "I'm not Russian; I come from Lithuania, a true German."

In the mountains, there you feel free.
I read, much of the night, and go south in the winter.

What are the roots that clutch, what branches grow
Out of this stony rubbish? Son of man,
You cannot say, or guess, for you know only
A heap of broken images, where the sun beats,
And the dead tree gives no shelter, the cricket no relief,
And the dry stone no sound of water. Only
There is shadow under this red rock,
(Come in under the shadow of this red rock),
And I will show you something different from either
Your shadow at morning striding behind you
Or your shadow at evening rising to meet you;
I will show you fear in a handful of dust.
Frisch weht der Wind
Der Heimat zu
Mein Irisch Kind,
Wo weilest du?
'You gave me hyacinths first a year ago;
'They called me the hyacinth girl.'
—Yet when we came back, late, from the hyacinth garden,
Your arms full, and your hair wet, I could not
Speak, and my eyes failed, I was neither
Living nor dead, and I knew nothing,
Looking into the heart of light, the silence.
Oed' und leer das Meer.

Madame Sosostris, famous clairvoyante,
Had a bad cold, nevertheless

[20]**Son of man:** Eliot's note: Cf. Ezekiel II, i: "Son of man, stand upon thy feet, and I will speak to thee." [23]**the cricket no relief:** Eliot's note: Cf. Ecclesiastes XII, v: "the grasshopper shall be a burden, and desire shall fail." [24–25]**And the dry stone . . . under this red rock:** The prophet Isaiah had foretold the coming of a Messiah who would be "a river of water in a dry place, as the shadow of a great rock in a weary land." [31–34]**Frisch weht der Wind . . . Wo weilest du?:** Eliot's note: *V.*[*ide*] [see] *Tristan and Isolde,* I, verses 5–8. The lines mean: "Fresh blows the wind to the homeland, my Irish child, where do you tarry." It is sung in Wagner's opera by a sailor who thinks about his beloved. [42]**Oed' und leer das Meer:** Eliot's note reads: "Id.[em] [the same] III, verse 24." In Wagner's *Tristan,* this line is sung by a shepherd looking out to sea for a sign of Isolde's ship, which Tristan eagerly awaits. Tristan lies wounded at his castle. The line translates: "Empty and waste is the sea."

Is known to be the wisest woman in Europe,
With a wicked pack of cards. Here, said she,
Is your card, the drowned Phoenician Sailor,
(Those are pearls that were his eyes. Look!)
Here is Belladonna, the Lady of the Rocks,
The lady of situations.
Here is the man with three staves, and here the Wheel,
And here is the one-eyed merchant and this card,
Which is blank, is something he carries on his back,
Which I am forbidden to see. I do not find
The Hanged Man. Fear death by water.
I see crowds of people, walking round in a ring.
Thank you. If you see dear Mrs. Equitone,
Tell her I bring the horoscope myself:
One must be so careful these days.

Unreal City,
Under the brown fog of a winter dawn,
A crowd flowed over London Bridge, so many
I had not thought death had undone so many.
Sighs, short and infrequent, were exhaled,
And each man fixed his eyes before his feet.

[46]**wicked pack of cards:** tarot cards have been used for fortunetelling. Eliot's note on the passage reads: "I am not familiar with the exact constitution of the Tarot pack of cards, from which I have obviously departed to suit my own convenience. The Hanged Man, a member of the traditional pack, fits my purpose in two ways: because he is associated in my mind with the Hanged God of Frazer, and because I associate him with the hooded figure in the passage of the disciples to Emmaus in Part V. The Phoenician Sailor and the Merchant appear later; also the 'crowds of people', and Death by Water is executed in Part IV. The Man with Three Staves (an authentic member of the Tarot pack) I associate, quite arbitrarily, with the Fisher King himself." [48]**Those pearls that were his eyes:** a quotation from Shakespeare's *The Tempest* I, ii, 398. Prince Ferdinand, who has been shipwrecked with his father on an island, is told falsely that his father has died. The line suggests that the supposed death involved a miraculous change into something rich and beautiful. [49]**Belladonna:** literally "beautiful lady," belladonna also refers to nightshade, a poisonous plant. [60]**Unreal City:** Eliot's note: Cf. Baudelaire: "Fourmillante cité, cité pleine de rêves / Où le spectre en plein jour raccroche le passant." The lines can be translated: "Swarming city, city full of dreams, / Where the specter in broad daylight accosts the passersby." [63]**I had not thought . . . so many:** Eliot's note: Cf. *Inferno,* III, 55–57. Eliot quotes the Italian, which can be translated: "so long a train of people, that I would never have believed death had undone so many." [64]**Sighs . . . were exhaled:** Eliot's note: Cf. *Inferno,* IV, 25–27. Eliot again refers to the Italian, which translates: "Here, to my hearing, there was no weeping, but sighs which caused the eternal air to tremble."

Flowed up the hill and down King William Street,
To where Saint Mary Woolnoth kept the hours
With a dead sound on the final stroke of nine.
There I saw one I knew, and stopped him, crying: 'Stetson!
'You who were with me in the ships at Mylae!
'That corpse you planted last year in your garden,
'Has it begun to sprout? Will it bloom this year?
'Or has the sudden frost disturbed its bed?
'O keep the Dog far hence, that's friend to men,
'Or with his nails he'll dig it up again!
'You! hypocrite lecteur!—mon semblable,—mon frère!'

II. A Game of Chess

The Chair she sat in, like a burnished throne,
Glowed on the marble, where the glass
Held up by standards wrought with fruited vines
From which a golden Cupidon peeped out
(Another hid his eyes behind his wing)
Doubled the flames of sevenbranched candelabra
Reflecting light upon the table as
The glitter of her jewels rose to meet it,
From satin cases poured in rich profusion.
In vials of ivory and coloured glass
Unstoppered, lurked her strange synthetic perfumes,
Unguent, powdered, or liquid—troubled, confused
And drowned the sense in odours; stirred by the air
That freshened from the window, these ascended
In fattening the prolonged candle-flames,

[66–68] **King William Street . . . stroke of nine:** Eliot's note: "A phenomenon which I have often noticed." The church of St. Mary Woolnoth is in London's financial district. [70] **Mylae:** site of a naval battle in the Punic War (260 B.C.). [74–75] **'O keep the Dog . . . dig it up again!':** Eliot's note: Cf. the dirge in Webster's *White Devil,* V, iv, 97–98 which reads: "But keep the wolf far thence, that's foe to man, / For with his nails he'll dig them up again." [76] **'You! . . . mon frère!':** Eliot's note: V. Baudelaire, Preface to *Fleurs du Mal.* The last line of Baudelaire's introductory poem "To the Reader" can be translated: "Hypocrite reader!—my likeness—my brother!" **A Game of Chess:** Thomas Middleton's play (1627). The title also alludes to another play in which a seduction occurring on one part of the stage parallels a game of chess on another. [77–78] **The Chair she sat in . . . Glowed on the marble:** Eliot's note: Cf. *Antony and Cleopatra,* II, ii, 190. The allusion is to Cleopatra's barge, which is described by the Roman soldier Enobarbus: "The barge she sat in, like a burnish'd throne, / Burn'd on the water."

Flung their smoke into the laquearia,
Stirring the pattern on the coffered ceiling.
Huge sea-wood fed with copper
Burned green and orange, framed by the coloured stone,
In which sad light a carvèd dolphin swam.
Above the antique mantel was displayed
As though a window gave upon the sylvan scene
The change of Philomel, by the barbarous king
So rudely forced; yet there the nightingale
Filled all the desert with inviolable voice
And still she cried, and still the world pursues,
'Jug Jug' to dirty ears.
And other withered stumps of time
Were told upon the walls; staring forms
Leaned out, leaning, hushing the room enclosed.
Footsteps shuffled on the stair.
Under the firelight, under the brush, her hair
Spread out in fiery points
Glowed into words, then would be savagely still.

'My nerves are bad to-night. Yes, bad. Stay with me.
'Speak to me. Why do you never speak. Speak.
  'What are you thinking of? What thinking? What?
'I never know what you are thinking. Think.'

I think we are in rats' alley
Where the dead men lost their bones.

'What is that noise?'
                    The wind under the door.

[91–93]**In fattening . . . the coffered ceiling:** Eliot's note: V. *Aeneid,* I, 276. The reference is to Vergil's description of the banquet given by Dido, Queen of Carthage, for her Trojan lover, Aeneas. Eliot quotes two lines, which may be translated: "blazing torches hang from the golden paneled ceiling, and the torches conquer the night with flames." [98]**As though . . . the sylvan scene:** Eliot's note: V. Milton, *Paradise Lost,* IV, 140. Milton's description is of Satan looking at Eden. [99–100]**The change of Philomel . . . there the nightingale:** Eliot's note: V. Ovid, *Metamorphoses,* VI, Philomela. King Tereus raped Philomela, his wife's sister, and cut out her tongue. Procne, his wife, found out and revenged herself on Tereus by killing his son Itys and serving him to the king as food. Philomela was transformed into a nightingale by the gods. [115]**rats' alley:** Eliot's note: Cf. Part III, line 195. [118]**The wind under the door:** Eliot's note: Cf. Webster: 'Is the wind in that door still?'

'What is that noise now? What is the wind doing?'
                                        Nothing again nothing.
                                                                        'Do
'You know nothing? Do you see nothing? Do you remember
'Nothing?'

        I remember
Those are pearls that were his eyes.
'Are you alive, or not? Is there nothing in your head?'
                                                                            But
O O O O that Shakespeherian Rag—
It's so elegant
So intelligent
'What shall I do now? What shall I do?'
'I shall rush out as I am, and walk the street
'With my hair down, so. What shall we do tomorrow?
'What shall we ever do?'
                                                The hot water at ten.
And if it rains, a closed car at four.
And we shall play a game of chess.
Pressing lidless eyes and waiting for a knock upon the door.

When Lil's husband got demobbed, I said—
I didn't mince my words, I said to her myself,
HURRY UP PLEASE ITS TIME
Now Albert's coming back, make yourself a bit smart.
He'll want to know what you done with that money he
    gave you
To get yourself some teeth. He did, I was there.
You have them all out, Lil, and get a nice set,
He said, I swear, I can't bear to look at you.
And no more can't I, I said, and think of poor Albert,
He's been in the army four years, he wants a good time,
And if you don't give it him, there's others will, I said.
Oh is there, she said. Something o' that, I said.
Then I'll know who to thank, she said, and give me a
    straight look.
HURRY UP PLEASE ITS TIME
If you don't like it you can get on with it, I said.
Others can pick and choose if you can't.

[139]**demobbed:** demobilized from the army after World War I. [141]**HURRY UP PLEASE ITS TIME:** barkeeper's call at closing time in a British pub.

But if Albert makes off, it won't be for lack of telling.
You ought to be ashamed, I said, to look so antique.
(And her only thirty-one.)
I can't help it, she said, pulling a long face,
It's them pills I took, to bring it off, she said.
(She's had five already, and nearly died of young George.)
The chemist said it would be all right, but I've never been the same.
You *are* a proper fool, I said.
Well, if Albert won't leave you alone, there it is, I said,
What you get married for if you don't want children?
HURRY UP PLEASE ITS TIME
Well, that Sunday Albert was home, they had a hot gammon,
And they asked me in to dinner, to get the beauty of it hot—
HURRY UP PLEASE ITS TIME
HURRY UP PLEASE ITS TIME
Goonight Bill. Goonight Lou. Goonight May. Goonight.
Ta ta. Goonight. Goonight.
Good night, ladies, good night, sweet ladies, good night, good night.

III. THE FIRE SERMON

The river's tent is broken; the last fingers of leaf
Clutch and sink into the wet bank. The wind
Crosses the brown land, unheard. The nymphs are departed.
Sweet Thames, run softly, till I end my song.
The river bears no empty bottles, sandwich papers,
Silk handkerchiefs, cardboard boxes, cigarette ends
Or other testimony of summer nights. The nymphs are departed.
And their friends, the loitering heirs of City directors;
Departed, have left no addresses.
By the waters of Leman I sat down and wept . . .

161**chemist:** druggist. 166**gammon:** ham. 172**Good night, ladies . . . good night:** allusions to the popular song "Good Night, Ladies" and to Shakespeare's *Hamlet* IV, v, 72, in which Ophelia sings her mad song before drowning herself. **The Fire Sermon:** an allusion to Buddha's Fire Sermon, which urges the elimination of desire, the fire of passion. 176**Sweet Thames . . . end my song:** Eliot's note: V. Spenser *Prothalamion*. The line is the refrain of Spenser's poem celebrating marriage. 182**By the waters . . . wept:** in Psalm 137, the exiled Jews lament the loss of their homeland: "By the waters of Babylon, there we sat down, yea, we wept, when we remembered Zion."

Sweet Thames, run softly till I end my song,
Sweet Thames, run softly, for I speak not loud or long.
But at my back in a cold blast I hear
The rattle of the bones, and chuckle spread from ear to ear.

A rat crept softly through the vegetation
Dragging its slimy belly on the bank
While I was fishing in the dull canal
On a winter evening round behind the gashouse
Musing upon the king my brother's wreck
And on the king my father's death before him.
White bodies naked on the low damp ground
And bones cast in a little low dry garret,
Rattled by the rat's foot only, year to year.
But at my back from time to time I hear
The sound of horns and motors, which shall bring
Sweeney to Mrs. Porter in the spring.
O the moon shone bright on Mrs. Porter
And on her daughter
They wash their feet in soda water
Et O ces voix d'enfants, chantant dans la coupole!

Twit twit twit
Jug jug jug jug jug
So rudely forc'd.
Tereu
Unreal City
Under the brown fog of a winter noon
Mr. Eugenides, the Smyrna merchant

185**But at my back . . . I hear:** an echo of Andrew Marvell (1621–1678) in "To His Coy Mistress": "But at my back I always hear / Time's winged chariot hurrying near, / And yonder all before us lie / Deserts of vast eternity." Also echoed in line 196. See below. 192**And on the king . . . before him:** Eliot's note: Cf. *The Tempest,* I, ii. 197–198**The sound of horns . . . Mrs. Porter in the spring:** Eliot's note: Cf. Day, *Parliament of Bees:* "When of the sudden, listening, you shall hear, / A noise of horns and hunting, which shall bring Actaeon to Diana in the spring, / Where all shall see her naked skin." 200–201**And on her daughter . . . soda water:** Eliot's note: "I do not know the origin of the ballad from which these lines are taken: it was reported to me from Sydney, Australia." 202**Et O ces voix . . . dans la coupole:** Eliot's note: V. Verlaine, *Parsifal.* The last line of the poem by Paul Verlaine (1844–1896) can be translated: "And O those children's voices singing in the dome." 206**Tereu:** Tereus; along with "jug" it is a way of alluding to the nightingale's song. See note on lines 99–100.

Unshaven, with a pocket full of currants
C.i.f. London: documents at sight,
Asked me in demotic French
To luncheon at the Cannon Street Hotel
Followed by a weekend at the Metropole.

At the violet hour, when the eyes and back
Turn upward from the desk, when the human engine waits
Like a taxi throbbing waiting,
I Tiresias, though blind, throbbing between two lives,
Old man with wrinkled female breasts, can see
At the violet hour, the evening hour that strives
Homeward, and brings the sailor home from sea,
The typist home at teatime, clears her breakfast, lights
Her stove, and lays out food in tins.
Out of the window perilously spread
Her drying combinations touched by the sun's last rays,
On the divan are piled (at night her bed)
Stockings, slippers, camisoles, and stays.
I Tiresias, old man with wrinkled dugs
Perceived the scene, and foretold the rest—
I too awaited the expected guest.
He, the young man carbuncular, arrives,
A small house agent's clerk, with one bold stare,
One of the low on whom assurance sits
As a silk hat on a Bradford millionaire.
The time is now propitious, as he guesses,

[211]**C.i.f. London: documents at sight:** Eliot's note: "The currants were quoted at a price 'cost insurance and freight to London'; and the Bill of Lading, etc., were to be handed to the buyer upon payment of the sight draft." [218]**Tiresias:** Eliot's note: "Tiresias, although a mere spectator and not indeed a 'character,' is yet the most important personage in the poem, uniting all the rest. Just as the one-eyed merchant, seller of currants, melts into the Phoenician Sailor, and the latter is not wholly distinct from Ferdinand, Prince of Naples, so all the women are one woman, and the two sexes meet in Tiresias. What Tiresias *sees,* in fact, is the substance of the poem. The whole passage from Ovid is of great anthropological interest. . . ." [221]**and brings the sailor home from sea:** Eliot's note: "This may not appear as exact as Sappho's lines, but I had in mind the 'longshore' or 'dory' fisherman, who returns at nightfall." Eliot echoes both the Greek poet Sappho (600 B.C.) and the Scottish writer Robert Louis Stevenson (1850–1894), who wrote in *Requiem:* "Home is the sailor, home from sea." [234]**Bradford millionaire:** the manufacturers of Bradford, an English industrial city, were reputed to have profited handsomely from war industry in World War I.

The meal is ended, she is bored and tired,
Endeavours to engage her in caresses
Which still are unreproved, if undesired.
Flushed and decided, he assaults at once;
Exploring hands encounter no defence;
His vanity requires no response,
And makes a welcome of indifference.
(And I Tiresias have foresuffered all
Enacted on this same divan or bed;
I who have sat by Thebes below the wall
And walked among the lowest of the dead.)
Bestows one final patronising kiss,
And gropes his way, finding the stairs unlit.

She turns and looks a moment in the glass,
Hardly aware of her departed lover;
Her brain allows one half-formed thought to pass:
'Well now that's done: and I'm glad it's over.'
When lovely woman stoops to folly and
Paces about her room again, alone,
She smoothes her hair with automatic hand,
And puts a record on the gramophone.

'This music crept by me upon the waters'
And along the Strand, up Queen Victoria Street.
O City city, I can sometimes hear
Beside a public bar in Lower Thames Street,
The pleasant whining of a mandoline
And a clatter and a chatter from within
Where fishmen lounge at noon: where the walls
Of Magnus Martyr hold
Inexplicable splendour of Ionian white and gold.

[253–256]**When lovely woman stoops . . . on the gramophone:** Eliot's note: V. Goldsmith, the song in *The Vicar of Wakefield.* The seduced woman's song reads: "When lovely woman stoops to folly / And finds too late that men betray / What charm can soothe her melancholy, / What art can wash her guilt away?"
[257]**'This music . . . upon the waters':** Eliot's note: V. *The Tempest,* as above.
[263–265]**where the walls / Of Magnus Martyr . . . Ionian white and gold.** Eliot's note: "The interior of St. Magnus Martyr is to my mind one of the finest among Wren's interiors."

The river sweats
Oil and tar
The barges drift
With the turning tide
Red sails
Wide
To leeward, swing on the heavy spar.
The barges wash
Drifting logs
Down Greenwich reach
Past the Isle of Dogs.
Weialala leia
Wallala leialala

Elizabeth and Leicester
Beating oars
The stern was formed
A gilded shell
Red and gold
The brisk swell
Rippled both shores
Southwest wind
Carried down stream
The peal of bells
White towers
Weialala leia
Wallala leialala

'Trams and dusty trees.
Highbury bore me. Richmond and Kew

275–276**Greenwich reach . . . Dogs:** a bend in the River Thames that forms a peninsula called the Isle of Dogs. 279**Elizabeth and Leicester:** refers to the love affair of Queen Elizabeth and the Earl of Leicester. Eliot's note quotes the historian J. A. Froude's *Elizabeth,* Vol. I, chapter 4, letter of De Quadra to Philip of Spain: "In the afternoon we were in a barge, watching the games on the river. [The queen] was alone with Lord Robert and myself on the poop, when they began to talk nonsense, and went so far that Lord Robert at last said, as I was on the spot there was no reason why they should not be married if the queen pleased."
293–294**Highbury . . . Undid me.:** Eliot's note: Cf. *Purgatorio* V. 133. Eliot quotes the Italian, which translates as: "Remember me, who am La Pia. / Siena made me, Maremma undid me." Highbury is a London neighborhood; Richmond and Kew, boating places on the Thames.

Undid me. By Richmond I raised my knees
Supine on the floor of a narrow canoe.'

'My feet are at Moorgate, and my heart
Under my feet. After the event
He wept. He promised "a new start."
I made no comment. What should I resent?'

'On Margate Sands.
I can connect
Nothing with nothing.
The broken fingernails of dirty hands.
My people humble people who expect
Nothing.'
                        la la

To Carthage then I came
Burning burning burning burning
O Lord Thou pluckest me out
O Lord Thou pluckest

burning

IV. Death by Water

Phlebas the Phoenician, a fortnight dead,
Forgot the cry of gulls, and the deep sea swell
And the profit and loss.
                                        A current under sea
Picked his bones in whispers. As he rose and fell

[292–305]**'Trams and dusty trees . . . people who expect / Nothing.'** Eliot's note: "The Song of the (three) Thames daughters begins here. From lines 292 to 305 inclusive they speak in turn. V. *Gotterdammerung,* III, i: the Rhinedaughters." In Wagner's opera, the Rhine maidens attempt to seduce the hero, Siegfried, and threaten and implore him to retrieve their stolen gold. Eliot quotes their refrain. [296]**Moorgate:** a London slum. [300]**Margate Sands:** an English seaside resort. [307]**To Carthage then I came:** Eliot's note: V. St Augustine's *Confessions:* "To Carthage then I came, where a cauldron of unholy loves sang all about mine ears." [308]**Burning burning burning:** Eliot's note to this line alludes to Buddha's Fire Sermon, without quoting any of it. [309]**O Lord Thou pluckest me out:** Eliot's note: "From St. Augustine's *Confessions* again. The collocation of these two representatives of eastern and western asceticism, as the culmination of this part of the poem is not an accident." **Death by Water:** Eliot offered no notes for Part IV.

He passed the stages of his age and youth
Entering the whirlpool.
                                        Gentile or Jew
O you who turn the wheel and look to windward,
Consider Phlebas, who was once handsome and tall as you.

V. WHAT THE THUNDER SAID

After the torchlight red on sweaty faces
After the frosty silence in the gardens
After the agony in stony places
The shouting and the crying
Prison and palace and reverberation
Of thunder of spring over distant mountains
He who was living is now dead
We who were living are now dying
With a little patience

Here is no water but only rock
Rock and no water and the sandy road
The road winding above among the mountains
Which are mountains of rock without water
If there were water we should stop and drink
Amongst the rock one cannot stop or think
Sweat is dry and feet are in the sand
If there were only water amongst the rock
Dead mountain mouth of carious teeth that cannot spit
Here one can neither stand nor lie nor sit
There is not even silence in the mountains
But dry sterile thunder without rain
There is not even solitude in the mountains
But red sullen faces sneer and snarl
From doors of mudcracked houses
                                        If there were water
    And no rock
    If there were rock
    And also water
    And water

What the Thunder Said: Eliot's note: "In the first part of V three themes are employed: the journey to Emmaus, the approach to the Chapel Perilous (see Miss Weston's book) and the present decay of Eastern Europe." 322–327 **After the torchlight . . . distant mountains:** an allusion to Christ's agony in the garden of Gethsemane, his arrest, and his crucifixion.

A spring
A pool among the rock
If there were the sound of water only
Not the cicada
And dry grass singing
But sound of water over a rock
Where the hermit-thrush sings in the pine trees
Drip drop drip drop drop drop drop
But there is no water

Who is the third who walks always beside you?
When I count, there are only you and I together
But when I look ahead up the white road
There is always another one walking beside you
Gliding wrapt in a brown mantle, hooded
I do not know whether a man or a woman
—But who is that on the other side of you?

What is that sound high in the air
Murmur of maternal lamentation
Who are those hooded hordes swarming
Over endless plains, stumbling in cracked earth
Ringed by the flat horizon only
What is the city over the mountains
Cracks and reforms and bursts in the violet air
Falling towers
Jerusalem Athens Alexandria
Vienna London
Unreal

[357]**hermit-thrush:** Eliot's note: "This is . . . the hermit-thrush which I have heard in Quebec Province. . . . Its water-dripping is justly celebrated." [360]**Who is the third . . . beside you?** Eliot's note: "The following lines were stimulated by the account of one of the Antarctic expeditions (I forget which, but think one of Shackleton's): it was related that the party of explorers, at the extremity of their strength, had the constant delusion that there was *one more member* than could actually be counted." Also relevant is Luke 24: 13–16, which describes Jesus on the way to Emmaus with two of his disciples who were unaware of who he was. [367–370]**What is that sound . . . Over endless plains:** Eliot's note quotes *A Glimpse of Chaos* by Hermann Hesse. In English translation: "Already half of Europe, already at least half of Eastern Europe is on the way to Chaos, drives drunkenly in sacred madness along the edge of the abyss, and moreover, sings, sings drunken hymns as Dmitri Karamasoff sang. The offended bourgeois laughs at these songs, the saint and seer hear them with tears."

A woman drew her long black hair out tight
And fiddled whisper music on those strings
And bats with baby faces in the violet light
Whistled, and beat their wings
And crawled head downward down a blackened wall
And upside down in air were towers
Tolling reminiscent bells, that kept the hours
And voices singing out of empty cisterns and exhausted wells.

In this decayed hole among the mountains
In the faint moonlight, the grass is singing
Over the tumbled graves, about the chapel
There is the empty chapel, only the wind's home.
It has no windows, and the door swings,
Dry bones can harm no one.
Only a cock stood on the rooftree
Co co rico co co rico
In a flash of lightning. Then a damp gust
Bringing rain

Ganga was sunken, and the limp leaves
Waited for rain, while the black clouds
Gathered far distant, over Himavant.
The jungle crouched, humped in silence.
Then spoke the thunder
DA
Datta: what have we given?
My friend, blood shaking my heart
The awful daring of a moment's surrender
Which an age of prudence can never retract
By this, and this only, we have existed
Which is not to be found in our obituaries
Or in memories draped by the beneficent spider

[396]**Ganga:** the River Ganges, sacred in India. [398]**Himavant:** a Himalayan mountain. [402–419]**Datta . . . Dayadhvam . . . Damyata:** Eliot's note: Datta, dayadhvam, damyata (Give, sympathize, control). The fable of the meaning of the thunder is found in Brihandaranyaka, *Upanishad,* V, I. The fable describes how when the Creator speaks "Da," gods, men, and demons hear and respond to different commands. [408]**Or in memories . . . beneficent spider:** Eliot's note: Cf. Webster, *The White Devil,* V, vi: "they'll remarry / Ere the worm pierce your winding-sheet, ere the spider / Make a thin curtain for your epitaphs."

Or under seals broken by the lean solicitor
In our empty rooms
DA
Dayadhvam: I have heard the key
Turn in the door once and turn once only
We think of the key, each in his prison
Thinking of the key, each confirms a prison
Only at nightfall, aethereal rumours
Revive for a moment a broken Coriolanus
DA
Damyata: The boat responded
Gaily, to the hand expert with sail and oar
The sea was calm, your heart would have responded
Gaily, when invited, beating obedient
To controlling hands

I sat upon the shore
Fishing, with the arid plain behind me
Shall I at least set my lands in order?
London Bridge is falling down falling down falling down
Poi s'ascose nel foco che gli affina
Quando fiam uti chelidon—O swallow swallow

412**I have heard the key:** Eliot refers to Dante's *Inferno,* XXXIII, 46, which describes Ugolino and his children, who were locked in a tower to starve to death. Eliot quotes the Italian, which translates: "And I heard below the door of the horrible tower being locked up." Eliot also quotes the philosopher F. H. Bradley's *Appearance and Reality:* "My external sensations are no less private to myself than are my thoughts or my feelings. In either case my experience falls within my own circle, a circle closed on the outside, and, with all its elements alike, every sphere is opaque to the others which surround it. . . . In brief, regarded as an existence which appears in a soul, the whole world for each is peculiar and private to that soul." 417**Coriolanus:** the tragic hero of Shakespeare's *Coriolanus,* a Roman general who, exiled from Rome, led the enemy against his former city. 424–425**sat upon the shore / Fishing:** Eliot's note: "V. Weston. *From Ritual to Romance,* chapter on the Fisher King." 426**Shall I at least set my lands in order?:** Cf. Isaiah: 38, 1: "Thus saith the Lord. Set thine house in order: for thou shalt die, and not live." 428**Poi s'ascose . . . gli affina:** Eliot's note: V. [for "Vide"] *Purgatorio* XXVI, 148. In the note, he quotes four lines that translate: "Now I pray you by that virtue / that guides you to the top of the stair / be mindful in time of my suffering / Then he hid himself in the fire that refines them." In the poem, Eliot quotes only the last line of the four. The lines are spoken by the Provençal poet Arnaut Daniel, who was an important influence on Dante. 429**Quando fiam uti chelidon:** Eliot's note: V. *Pervigilium Veneris.* Cf. Philomela in Parts II and III. See note on lines 99–100. The line translates: "She sings when will my spring come."

Le Prince d'Aquitaine à la tour abolie
These fragments I have shored against my ruins
Why then Ile fit you. Hieronymo's mad againe.
Datta. Dayadhvam. Damyata.
Shantih shantih shantih

Little Gidding

I

Midwinter spring is its own season
Sempiternal though sodden towards sundown,
Suspended in time, between pole and tropic.
When the short day is brightest, with frost and fire,
The brief sun flames the ice, on pond and ditches,
In windless cold that is the heart's heat,
Reflecting in a watery mirror
A glare that is blindness in the early afternoon.
And glow more intense than blaze of branch, or brazier,
Stirs the dumb spirit: no wind, but pentecostal fire
In the dark time of the year. Between melting and freezing
The soul's sap quivers. There is no earth smell
Or smell of living thing. This is the spring time
But not in time's covenant. Now the hedgerow
Is blanched for an hour with transitory blossom
Of snow, a bloom more sudden

THE WASTE LAND [430]**Le Prince d'Aquitaine à la tour abolie:** Eliot's note: V. Gerard de Nerval, sonnet *El Desdichado.* The title means "The Disinherited"; the line, "The Prince of Aquitaine at the ruined tower." [432]**Hieronymo:** Eliot's note: V. Kyd's (1558–1594) *Spanish Tragedy* with the subtitle *Hieronymo's Mad Againe.* In the play, Hieronymo avenges the murder of his son. [434]**Shantih shantih shantih:** Eliot's note: "Shantih. Repeated as here a formal ending to an Upanishad. 'The Peace which passeth understanding' is our equivalent to this word."
LITTLE GIDDING "Little Gidding" is the last of Eliot's *Four Quartets.* Little Gidding was the name of an Anglican religious community founded in 1625 by Nicholas Ferrar. It lasted twenty-five years, until it was destroyed by the Puritans under Oliver Cromwell. [10]**pentecostal fire:** on the feast of Pentecost (the seventh Sunday after Easter) Christ's disciples were assembled when "suddenly there came a sound from heaven, as of a rushing mighty wind, and it filled all the house where they were sitting. And there appeared unto them cloven tongues, like as of fire. . . . And they were all filled with the Holy Ghost, and began to speak with other tongues, as the Spirit gave them utterance." (Acts II:2–4).

Than that of summer, neither budding nor fading,
Not in the scheme of generation.
Where is the summer, the unimaginable
Zero summer?

If you came this way,
Taking the route you would be likely to take
From the place you would be likely to come from,
If you came this way in may time, you would find the hedges
White again, in May, with voluptuary sweetness.
It would be the same at the end of the journey,
If you came at night like a broken king,
If you came by day not knowing what you came for,
It would be the same, when you leave the rough road
And turn behind the pig-sty to the dull façade
And the tombstone. And what you thought you came for
Is only a shell, a husk of meaning
From which the purpose breaks only when it is fulfilled
If at all. Either you had no purpose
Or the purpose is beyond the end you figured
And is altered in fulfilment. There are other places
Which also are the world's end, some at the sea jaws,
Or over a dark lake, in a desert or a city—
But this is the nearest, in place and time,
Now and in England.

If you came this way,
Taking any route, starting from anywhere,
At any time or at any season,
It would always be the same: you would have to put off
Sense and notion. You are not here to verify,
Instruct yourself, or inform curiosity
Or carry report. You are here to kneel
Where prayer has been valid. And prayer is more
Than an order of words, the conscious occupation
Of the praying mind, or the sound of the voice praying.
And what the dead had no speech for, when living,
They can tell you, being dead: the communication

[27] **a broken king:** King Charles I, who visited Little Gidding after a defeat in the English Civil War.

Of the dead is tongued with fire beyond the language of
  the living.
Here, the intersection of the timeless moment
Is England and nowhere. Never and always.

II

Ash on an old man's sleeve
Is all the ash the burnt roses leave.
Dust in the air suspended
Marks the place where a story ended.
Dust inbreathed was a house—
The wall, the wainscot and the mouse.
The death of hope and despair,
    This is the death of air.

There are flood and drouth
Over the eyes and in the mouth,
Dead water and dead sand
Contending for the upper hand.
The parched eviscerate soil
Gapes at the vanity of toil,
Laughs without mirth.
    This is the death of earth.

Water and fire succeed
The town, the pasture and the weed.
Water and fire deride
The sacrifice that we denied.
Water and fire shall rot
The marred foundations we forgot,
Of sanctuary and choir.
    This is the death of water and fire.

In the uncertain hour before the morning
  Near the ending of interminable night
  At the recurrent end of the unending

80–151 Eliot imitates and varies Dante's terza rima in this section of the poem, which, he wrote, "cost me far more time and trouble and vexation than any passage of the same length I have ever written."

After the dark dove with the flickering tongue
  Had passed below the horizon of his homing
  While the dead leaves still rattled on like tin
Over the asphalt where no other sound was
  Between three districts whence the smoke arose
  I met one walking, loitering and hurried
As if blown towards me like the metal leaves
  Before the urban dawn wind unresisting.
  And as I fixed upon the down-turned face
That pointed scrutiny with which we challenge
  The first-met stranger in the waning dusk
  I caught the sudden look of some dead master
Whom I had known, forgotten, half recalled
  Both one and many; in the brown baked features
  The eyes of a familiar compound ghost
Both intimate and unidentifiable.
  So I assumed a double part, and cried
  And heard another's voice cry: 'What! are *you* here?'
Although we were not. I was still the same,
  Knowing myself yet being someone other—
  And he a face still forming; yet the words sufficed
To compel the recognition they preceded.
  And so, compliant to the common wind,
  Too strange to each other for misunderstanding,
In concord at this intersection time
  Of meeting nowhere, no before and after,
  We trod the pavement in a dead patrol.
I said: 'The wonder that I feel is easy,
  Yet ease is cause of wonder. Therefore speak:
  I may not comprehend, may not remember.'
And he: 'I am not eager to rehearse
  My thoughts and theory which you have forgotten.
  These things have served their purpose: let them be.
So with your own, and pray they be forgiven
  By others, as I pray you to forgive
  Both bad and good. Last season's fruit is eaten
And the fullfed beast shall kick the empty pail.
  For last year's words belong to last year's language
  And next year's words await another voice.
But, as the passage now presents no hindrance
  To the spirit unappeased and peregrine
  Between two worlds become much like each other,

So I find words I never thought to speak
  In streets I never thought I should revisit
  When I left my body on a distant shore.
Since our concern was speech, and speech impelled us
  To purify the dialect of the tribe
  And urge the mind to aftersight and foresight,
Let me disclose the gifts reserved for age
  To set a crown upon your lifetime's effort.
  First, the cold friction of expiring sense
Without enchantment, offering no promise
  But bitter tastelessness of shadow fruit
  As body and soul begin to fall asunder.
Second, the conscious impotence of rage
  At human folly, and the laceration
  Of laughter at what ceases to amuse.
And last, the rending pain of re-enactment
  Of all that you have done, and been; the shame
  Of motives late revealed, and the awareness
Of things ill done and done to others' harm
  Which once you took for exercise of virtue.
  Then fools' approval stings, and honour stains.
From wrong to wrong the exasperated spirit
  Proceeds, unless restored by that refining fire
  Where you must move in measure, like a dancer.'
The day was breaking. In the disfigured street
  He left me, with a kind of valediction,
  And faded on the blowing of the horn.

III

There are three conditions which often look alike
Yet differ completely, flourish in the same hedgerow:
Attachment to self and to things and to persons, detachment
From self and from things and from persons; and, growing
  between them, indifference
Which resembles the others as death resembles life,
Being between two lives—unflowering, between
The live and the dead nettle. This is the use of memory:

[129]**To purify the dialect of the tribe:** this line translates Stéphane Mallarmé's "Le Tombeau d'Edgar Poe."

For liberation—not less of love but expanding
Of love beyond desire, and so liberation
From the future as well as the past. Thus, love of a country
Begins as attachment to our own field of action
And comes to find that action of little importance
Though never indifferent. History may be servitude,
History may be freedom. See, now they vanish,
The faces and places, with the self which, as it could,
  loved them,
To become renewed, transfigured, in another pattern.

Sin is Behovely, but
All shall be well, and
All manner of thing shall be well.
If I think, again, of this place,
And of people, not wholly commendable,
Of no immediate kin or kindness,
But some of peculiar genius,
All touched by a common genius,
United in the strife which divided them;
If I think of a king at nightfall,
Of three men, and more, on the scaffold
And a few who died forgotten
In other places, here and abroad,
And of one who died blind and quiet,
Why should we celebrate
These dead men more than the dying?
It is not to ring the bell backward
Nor is it an incantation
To summon the spectre of a Rose.
We cannot revive old factions
We cannot restore old policies
Or follow an antique drum.
These men, and those who opposed them

[168–180] **Sin is Behovely . . . here and abroad:** Eliot took these lines from Dame Julian of Norwich, a fourteenth-century English mystic. [177–178] **a king at nightfall . . . on the scaffold:** Charles I was beheaded, as were some of his followers. [181] **one who died blind and quiet:** a reference to John Milton, a supporter of Cromwell. [186] **spectre of a Rose:** suggestive of both historical and symbolic considerations, the Tudor rose represented the English monarchy before the accession of the Stuart kings, of which Charles I was one.

And those whom they opposed
Accept the constitution of silence
And are folded in a single party.
Whatever we inherit from the fortunate
We have taken from the defeated
What they had to leave us—a symbol:
A symbol perfected in death.
And all shall be well and
All manner of thing shall be well
By the purification of the motive
In the ground of our beseeching.

IV

The dove descending breaks the air
With flame of incandescent terror
Of which the tongues declare
The one discharge from sin and error.
The only hope, or else despair
  Lies in the choice of pyre or pyre—
  To be redeemed from fire by fire.

Who then devised the torment? Love.
Love is the unfamiliar Name
Behind the hands that wove
The intolerable shirt of flame
Which human power cannot remove.
  We only live, only suspire
  Consumed by either fire or fire.

V

What we call the beginning is often the end
And to make an end is to make a beginning.
The end is where we start from. And every phrase
And sentence that is right (where every word is at home,

[201]**In the ground of our beseeching:** Julian of Norwich held that "the ground of our beseeching is love." [212]**The intolerable shirt of flame:** a reference to the shirt of Nessus, which Heracles's wife had him put on in the false hope she would win back her husband's love. The shirt burst into flames, adhered to his flesh, and caused such agonizing pain that he immolated himself.

Taking its place to support the others,
The word neither diffident nor ostentatious,
An easy commerce of the old and the new,
The common word exact without vulgarity,
The formal word precise but not pedantic,
The complete consort dancing together)
Every phrase and every sentence is an end and a beginning,
Every poem an epitaph. And any action
Is a step to the block, to the fire, down the sea's throat
Or to an illegible stone: and that is where we start.
We die with the dying:
See, they depart, and we go with them.
We are born with the dead:
See, they return, and bring us with them.
The moment of the rose and the moment of the yew-tree
Are of equal duration. A people without history
Is not redeemed from time, for history is a pattern
Of timeless moments. So, while the light fails
On a winter's afternoon, in a secluded chapel
History is now and England.

With the drawing of this Love and the voice of this Calling

We shall not cease from exploration
And the end of all our exploring
Will be to arrive where we started
And know the place for the first time.
Through the unknown, remembering gate
When the last of earth left to discover
Is that which was the beginning;
At the source of the longest river
The voice of the hidden waterfall
And the children in the apple-tree
Not known, because not looked for
But heard, half-heard, in the stillness
Between two waves of the sea.
Quick now, here, now, always—
A condition of complete simplicity

240**With the drawing . . . of this Calling:** from *The Cloud of Unknowing,* a fourteenth-century religious work.

(Costing not less than everything)
And all shall be well and
All manner of thing shall be well
When the tongues of flame are in-folded
Into the crowned knot of fire
And the fire and the rose are one.

[261]**And the fire and the rose are one:** a reference to Dante's *Paradiso* XXXIII, which, for Eliot, is "the highest point that poetry has ever reached or ever can reach."

Hart Crane

[1899–1932]

Among modern American poets, Hart Crane is the one whose work has inspired the strongest and most pervasive critical disagreement. Some readers see Crane as an ambitious but failed poet whose reach far exceeded his grasp and whose poems are frustratingly obscure. Others, while acknowledging Crane's difficulty, nonetheless see him as a powerful visionary with deep roots in the tradition of Emersonian Romanticism. These readers admire Crane's rhetorical brilliance, his intense lyricism, and his metaphorical ingenuity.

As Alan Williamson points out in *Voices and Visions,* Crane is a poet of intense feeling, one for whom everyday life and ordinary language are inadequate. In both, Crane struggled to find ways to reach an intense level of experience. One of the ways he chose was as a Romantic artist who, though regarded with scorn and incomprehension, is inspired to heights of visionary insight. As a poet, he seeks to extol his vision in exalted language, inscribe it in vivid images, and embody it in an enduring voice.

The Romantic element in Crane's work is partly a legacy from Whitman, whose optimism and affirmative spirit he echoes. Like Whitman, Crane accepted America's developing technology and envisioned a glorious future. Also like Whitman, Crane celebrated America's people and places. In addition, Crane strove, in the manner of Whitman, to create a strong tie between himself and his readers, to abolish distinctions of time and place, and to establish connections between past and present, high culture and popular experience.

But the differences between Crane and Whitman are as important as their similarities. Where Whitman was intensely political, Crane studiously avoided political and social issues. He was far more concerned with his theory of poetry and with matters of technique than with philosophical and political perspectives. His poetry, as a result, lacks the philosophical depth and social breadth of Whitman's work. More important, it differs sharply from Whitman's verse in its style, especially in its disavowal of speech. Missing from Crane's poems are the direct addresses to the reader so prominent in Whitman. Missing, too, is the oratorical splendor of Whitman's grand manner—though Crane's rich language possesses an eloquence of the imagistic gesture. Crane's poems are usually comprised of a dense texture of image, allusion, and personal reference that soars, at times, into a remarkable lyricism. The following passage—the last four stanzas of "To Brooklyn Bridge"—illustrates these tendencies.

O harp and altar, of the fury fused,
(How could mere toil align thy choiring strings!)
Terrific threshold of the prophet's pledge,
Prayer of pariah, and the lover's cry,—

Again the traffic lights that skim thy swift
Unfractioned idiom, immaculate sigh of stars,
Beading thy path—condense eternity:
And we have seen night lifted in thine arms.

Under thy shadow by the piers I waited;
Only in darkness is thy shadow clear.
The City's fiery parcels all undone,
Already snow submerges an iron year . . .

O Sleepless as the river under thee,
Vaulting the sea, the prairies' dreaming sod,
Unto us lowliest sometime sweep, descend
And of the curveship lend a myth to God.

Crane's poetry blends Emersonian attitudes and Whitmanesque ideals with complex amalgams of images characteristic of the verse of T. S. Eliot and Ezra Pound. Like Eliot and Pound, Crane was fond of alluding to classical myth and Renaissance literature. From Eliot, Crane learned the power of the nondiscursive, the power of the image to evoke feeling and to stimulate desire. Crane's images, however, are less sharply delineated than the precise images of Pound and Eliot. They are multi-faceted, kaleidoscopic in their shifting contours. Furthermore, Crane strove to adapt Eliot's use of fragmented images and nonlogical poetic structures in an effort to counter what he saw as a pessimistic overemphasis on despair and hopelessness in Eliot's poetry. Crane wrote his ambitious Romantic epic, *The Bridge,* in fact, as a rebuttal to *The Waste Land,* thus taking Eliot's poem as both a model to imitate and a manifesto to undermine.

Offering a positive image of the modern metropolis, *The Bridge* is Crane's longest and most complex work and the one that has sparked the sharpest critical debate. The poem is organized as a series of separate lyrics in different voices. It moves backward through time from 1930, when it was written, to the nineteenth century, invoking Whitman and Poe, and then still further back to Columbus's discovery of America. It also spans the country's ample geography, moving westward from New York to California and then back. The bridge itself, gloriously celebrated in the opening Proem, stands as a symbol of American unity and achievement. Crane described the Proem and the Brooklyn Bridge, which inspired it, as "symbol[s] of our constructive future, our unique identity, in which is included also our scientific hopes and achievement of the future." Of the poem in its entirety he wrote to a friend that it contained a "mystical synthesis of America."

Crane was born in Ohio in 1899. He spent his childhood and youth there, largely in Cleveland and Akron. His life was splintered by the constant quarreling of his parents, who eventually divorced. It was further upset by Crane's refusal to go into his father's candy business and by his unsuccessful attempts at a series of varied, briefly held jobs—reporter, clerk, printer, stevedore, and advertising copywriter. He was also bisexual. Together, these complications of Crane's personal life spurred his identification with agonized figures like the French poet Arthur Rimbaud, with whom Crane shared a romantic temperament and an impulse toward excess. Crane eventually killed himself by leaping from the stern of a ship that was returning to America from Mexico. Before he died, however, he had begun to fulfill his poetic promise, publishing two volumes, *White Buildings* (1926) and *The Bridge* (1930).

For some readers, Crane's life was more interesting than his poems. For others, his life became a reason to dismiss his poetry. We return inevitably to the competing assessments of his work. On the one hand, it is seen as excessively hyperbolic and overburdened with inaccessible symbols; it is held to strain after intensities it cannot sustain; it is said to lack coherence, consistency, and cultural perspective. On the other hand, Crane's intuitive vision is praised, and his sensuous and suggestive images, especially their power to stimulate memory and to evoke feeling, are admired. This counter view sees his poetry as idealistic in the best sense—as a search for the ideal and as an attempt to achieve communion between poet and reader. And further, this admiring view relishes the strange and surrealistic beauty of his best work.

Whatever our final judgment of the value and success of Crane's poetry, to assess it with reasonable fairness we need to approach it with an understanding of what Crane attempted and with a recognition of its special difficulties. First, Crane's poetry is more highly compressed, more densely textured than that of many of his contemporaries. Second, the connotations of his language vastly outweigh its denotations. Refusing to be bound by a word's dictionary meaning, Crane exploited its suggestive resonances and emotional reverberations. He attempted to break free of both grammatical and logical constraints. In "At Melville's Tomb," for example, as Alan Williamson has noted, we find unusual combinations of subjects and verbs: stars bleed infinity; dice bequeath an embassy. By themselves, such phrases don't make sense. Even in the context of the poem the sense we make of them is tenuous, arrived at with difficulty, and more important, not strictly logical. But such nonlogical meaning is precisely what Crane strove for. He sought what he called a "logic of metaphor" that was not bound by the structure of rational thought. Its center was, instead, the poet's intense, vivid, and extravagant feelings, evoked by the associations of words, especially by compressed, mutually illuminating constellations of metaphors. The consequence of this poetic method is that in reading Crane we may require explanations of the poet's feelings, thoughts, and intentions—in short, his meaning—if we are not to be left puzzling over what amounts to a private symbolism. Alan Williamson has described the situation exactly. It is as if, he suggests, "Crane allows us to glimpse the objective world only through a screen of subjective associations or emotional responses. . . . He wishes the reader to have the *same* consciousness as the poet, for the duration of the poem." When we share the poet's consciousness successfully, we share the experience of intensely felt perceptions, and we are carried on a surge of energized eloquence, notable for its power and its beauty and utterly distinctive among the poetry of our time.

My Grandmother's Love Letters

There are no stars to-night
But those of memory.
Yet how much room for memory there is
In the loose girdle of soft rain.

There is even room enough
For the letters of my mother's mother,
Elizabeth,
That have been pressed so long
Into a corner of the roof
That they are brown and soft,
And liable to melt as snow.

Over the greatness of such space
Steps must be gentle.
It is all hung by an invisible white hair.
It trembles as birch limbs webbing the air.

And I ask myself:

"Are your fingers long enough to play
Old keys that are but echoes:
Is the silence strong enough
To carry back the music to its source
And back to you again
As though to her?"

Yet I would lead my grandmother by the hand
Through much of what she would not understand;
And so I stumble. And the rain continues on the roof
With such a sound of gently pitying laughter.

Chaplinesque

We make our meek adjustments,
Contented with such random consolations
As the wind deposits
In slithered and too ample pockets.

For we can still love the world, who find
A famished kitten on the step, and know
Recesses for it from the fury of the street
Or warm torn elbow coverts.

We will sidestep, and to the final smirk
Dally the doom of that inevitable thumb
That slowly chafes its puckered index toward us,
Facing the dull squint with what innocence
And what surprise!

And yet these fine collapses are not lies
More than the pirouettes of any pliant cane;
Our obsequies are, in a way, no enterprise.
We can evade you, and all else but the heart:
What blame to us if the heart live on.

Chaplinesque: about this poem, Crane wrote the following in letters to friends: "I am moved to put Chaplin with the poets [of today]; hence the 'we'. In other words, he, especially in *The Kid,* made me feel myself, as a poet, as being 'in the same boat' with him. Poetry, the human feelings, 'the kitten,' is so crowded out of the humdrum, rushing, mechanical scramble of today that the man who would preserve them must duck and camouflage for dear life to keep them or keep himself from annihilation. I have since learned that I am by no means alone in seeing these things in the buffooneries of the tragedian, Chaplin . . . and in the poem I have tried to express these 'social sympathies' in words corresponding somewhat to the antics of the actor. . . . Chaplin may be a sentimentalist, after all, but he carries the theme with such power . . . that sentimentality is made to transcend itself into a new kind of tragedy, eccentric, homely and yet brilliant. It is because I feel that I have captured the arrested climaxes and evasive victories of his gestures in words, somehow, that I like the poem as much as anything I have done." (*Letters* 68, 69).

The game enforces smirks; but we have seen
The moon in lonely alleys make
A grail of laughter of an empty ash can,
And through all sound of gaiety and quest
Have heard a kitten in the wilderness.

Praise for an Urn

IN MEMORIAM: ERNEST NELSON

It was a kind and northern face
That mingled in such exile guise
The everlasting eyes of Pierrot
And, of Gargantua, the laughter.

His thoughts, delivered to me
From the white coverlet and pillow,
I see now, were inheritances—
Delicate riders of the storm.

The slant moon on the slanting hill
Once moved us toward presentiments
Of what the dead keep, living still,
And such assessments of the soul

As, perched in the crematory lobby,
The insistent clock commented on,
Touching as well upon our praise
Of glories proper to the time.

PRAISE FOR AN URN **Ernest Nelson:** "Nelson," Crane wrote in a letter of 1922, "was a Norwegian who rebelled against the religious restrictions of home and came to America when a mere kid. Went to art school in Washington and won some kind of distinguished medal there. As soon as he was through school, an aunt of his in America who had been paying his tuition abruptly withdrew all her help and forced him into the prostitution of all his ideals and a cheap lithographic work that he was never able to pull out of afterward. He wrote several good poems . . . got married, and I finally met him here in Cleveland where he had been living in seclusion for a number of years. One of the best-read people I ever met, wonderful kindliness and tolerance and a true Nietzschean. He was one of many broken against the stupidity of American life in such places as here. I think he has had a lasting influence on me." [3]**Pierrot:** in French pantomime, a pathetic clown. [4]**Gargantua:** a character from François Rabelais (c 1494–1553) who possessed a robust enjoyment of life.

Still, having in mind gold hair,
I cannot see that broken brow
And miss the dry sound of bees
Stretching across a lucid space.

Scatter these well-meant idioms
Into the smoky spring that fills
The suburbs, where they will be lost.
They are no trophies of the sun.

Repose of Rivers

The willows carried a slow sound,
A sarabande the wind mowed on the mead.
I could never remember
That seething, steady leveling of the marshes
Till age had brought me to the sea.

Flags, weeds. And remembrance of steep alcoves
Where cypresses shared the noon's
Tyranny; they drew me into hades almost.
And mammoth turtles climbing sulphur dreams
Yielded, while sun-silt rippled them
Asunder . . .

How much I would have bartered! the black gorge
And all the singular nestings in the hills
Where beavers learn stitch and tooth.
The pond I entered once and quickly fled—
I remember now its singing willow rim.

And finally, in that memory all things nurse;
After the city that I finally passed
With scalding unguents spread and smoking darts
The monsoon cut across the delta
At gulf gates . . . There, beyond the dykes

I heard wind flaking sapphire, like this summer,
And willows could not hold more steady sound.

Passage

Where the cedar leaf divides the sky
I heard the sea.
In sapphire arenas of the hills
I was promised an improved infancy.

Sulking, sanctioning the sun,
My memory I left in a ravine,—
Casual louse that tissues the buckwheat,
Aprons rocks, congregates pears
In moonlit bushels
And wakens alleys with a hidden cough.

Dangerously the summer burned
(I had joined the entrainments of the wind).
The shadows of boulders lengthened my back:
In the bronze gongs of my cheeks
The rain dried without odour.

"It is not long, it is not long;
See where the red and black
Vine-stanchioned valleys—"; but the wind
Died speaking through the ages that you know
And hug, chimney-sooted heart of man!
So was I turned about and back, much as your smoke
Compiles a too well-known biography.

The evening was a spear in the ravine
That throve through very oak. And had I walked
The dozen particular decimals of time?
Touching an opening laurel, I found
A thief beneath, my stolen book in hand.

"Why are you back here—smiling an iron coffin?"
"To argue with the laurel," I replied:
"Am justified in transience, fleeing
Under the constant wonder of your eyes—."

[29]**laurel:** the laurel wreath is a traditional symbol of poetic achievement.

He closed the book. And from the Ptolemies
Sand troughed us in a glittering abyss.
A serpent swam a vertex to the sun
—On unpaced beaches leaned its tongue and drummed.
What fountains did I hear? what icy speeches?
Memory, committed to the page, had broke.

Legend

As silent as a mirror is believed
Realities plunge in silence by . . .

I am not ready for repentance;
Nor to match regrets. For the moth
Bends no more than the still
Imploring flame. And tremorous
In the white falling flakes
Kisses are,—
The only worth all granting.

It is to be learned—
This cleaving and this burning,
But only by the one who
Spends out himself again.

Twice and twice
(Again the smoking souvenir,
Bleeding eidolon!) and yet again.
Until the bright logic is won
Unwhispering as a mirror
Is believed.

Then, drop by caustic drop, a perfect cry
Shall string some constant harmony,—
Relentless caper for all those who step
The legend of their youth into the noon.

[32]**Ptolemies:** rulers of ancient Egypt.

Legende

The tossing loneliness of many nights
Rounds off my memory of her.
Like a shell surrendered to evening sands,
Yet called adrift again at every dawn,
She has become a pathos,—
Waif of the tides.

The sand and sea have had their way,
And moons of spring and autumn,—
All, save I.
And even my vision will be erased
As a cameo the waves claim again.

The Wine Menagerie

Invariably when wine redeems the sight,
Narrowing the mustard scansions of the eyes,
A leopard ranging always in the brow
Asserts a vision in the slumbering gaze.

Then glozening decanters that reflect the street
Wear me in crescents on their bellies. Slow
Applause flows into liquid cynosures:
—I am conscripted to their shadows' glow.

Against the imitation onyx wainscoting
(Painted emulsion of snow, eggs, yarn, coal, manure)
Regard the forceps of the smile that takes her.
Percussive sweat is spreading to his hair. Mallets,
Her eyes, unmake an instant of the world . . .

What is it in this heap the serpent pries—
Whose skin, facsimile of time, unskeins
Octagon, sapphire transepts round the eyes;
—From whom some whispered carillon assures
Speed to the arrow into feathered skies?

Sharp to the windowpane guile drags a face,
And as the alcove of her jealousy recedes
An urchin who has left the snow
Nudges a cannister across the bar
While August meadows somewhere clasp his brow.

Each chamber, transept, coins some squint,
Remorseless line, minting their separate wills—
Poor streaked bodies wreathing up and out,
Unwitting the stigma that each turn repeals:
Between black tusks the roses shine!

New thresholds, new anatomies! Wine talons
Build freedom up about me and distill
This competence—to travel in a tear
Sparkling alone, within another's will.

Until my blood dreams a receptive smile
Wherein new purities are snared; where chimes
Before some flame of gaunt repose a shell
Tolled once, perhaps, by every tongue in hell.
—Anguished, the wit that cries out of me:

"Alas,—these frozen billows of your skill!
Invent new dominoes of love and bile . . .
Ruddy, the tooth implicit of the world
Has followed you. Though in the end you know
And count some dim inheritance of sand,
How much yet meets the treason of the snow.

"Rise from the dates and crumbs. And walk away,
Stepping over Holofernes' shins—
Beyond the wall, whose severed head floats by
With Baptist John's. Their whispering begins.

"—And fold your exile on your back again;
Petrushka's valentine pivots on its pin."

At Melville's Tomb

Often beneath the wave, wide from this ledge
The dice of drowned men's bones he saw bequeath
An embassy. Their numbers as he watched,
Beat on the dusty shore and were obscured.

And wrecks passed without sound of bells,
The calyx of death's bounty giving back
A scattered chapter, livid hieroglyph,
The portent wound in corridors of shells.

Then in the circuit calm of one vast coil,
Its lashings charmed and malice reconciled,
Frosted eyes there were that lifted altars;
And silent answers crept across the stars.

Compass, quadrant and sextant contrive
No farther tides . . . High in the azure steeps
Monody shall not wake the mariner.
This fabulous shadow only the sea keeps.

2–3**The dice . . . bequeath / An embassy:** Crane's note: "Dice bequeath an embassy, in the first place, by being ground (in this connection only, of course) in little cubes from the bones of drowned men by the action of the sea, and are finally thrown up on the sand, having 'numbers' but no identification. These being the bones of dead who never completed their voyage, it seems legitimate to refer to them as the only surviving evidence of certain messages undelivered, mute evidence. . . . Dice as a symbol of chance and circumstances is also implied." 6–8**The calyx . . . in corridors of shells:** Crane's note: "This calyx refers in a double ironic sense both to a cornucopia and the vortex made by a sinking vessel. As soon as the water has closed over a ship this whirlpool sends up broken spars, wreckage, etc., which can be alluded to as livid *hieroglyphs,* making a *scattered chapter* so far as any complete record of the recent ship and crew is concerned. In fact, about as much definite knowledge might come from all this as anyone might gain from the roar of his own veins, which is easily heard (haven't you ever done it?) by holding a shell close to one's ear." A calyx is the outermost group of sepals on a flower. 11**Frosted eyes . . . lifted altars:** Crane's note: "Refers simply to a conviction that a man, not knowing perhaps a definite god yet being endowed with a reverence for deity—such a man naturally postulates a deity somehow, and the altar of that deity by the very *action* of the eyes *lifted* in searching." 13–14**Compass, quadrant . . . No farther tides:** Crane's note: "Hasn't it often occurred that instruments originally invented for record and computation have inadvertently so extended the concepts of the entity they were invented to measure (concepts of space, etc.) in the mind and imagination that employed them, that they may metaphorically be said to have extended the original boundaries of the entity measured? This little bit of relativity ought not to be discredited in poetry now that scientists are proceeding to measure the universe on principles of pure *ratio,* quite as metaphorical, so far as previous standards of scientific methods extended, as some of the axioms in Job."

For the Marriage of Faustus and Helen

"And so we may arrive by Talmud skill
And profane Greek to raise the building up
Of Helen's house against the Ismaelite,
King of Thogarma, and his habergeons
Brimstony, blue and fiery; and the force
Of King Abaddon, and the beast of Cittim;
Which Rabbi David Kimchi, Onkelos,
And Aben Ezra do interpret Rome."
—THE ALCHEMIST

I

The mind has shown itself at times
Too much the baked and labeled dough
Divided by accepted multitudes.
Across the stacked partitions of the day—
Across the memoranda, baseball scores,
The stenographic smiles and stock quotations
Smutty wings flash out equivocations.

The mind is brushed by sparrow wings;
Numbers, rebuffed by asphalt, crowd
The margins of the day, accent the curbs,
Convoying divers dawns on every corner
To druggist, barber and tobacconist,
Until the graduate opacities of evening
Take them away as suddenly to somewhere
Virginal perhaps, less fragmentary, cool.

In 1923, Crane wrote the following to Waldo Frank about this poem: "A few planks of the scaffolding may interest you, so I'll roughly indicate a few of my intentions. Part I starts out from the quotidian, rises to evocation, ecstasy, and statement. The whole poem is a kind of fusion of our own time with the past. Almost every symbol of current significance is matched by a correlative, suggested or actually stated, 'of ancient days.' Helen, the symbol of this abstract 'sense of beauty,' Faustus the symbol of myself, the poetic or imaginative man of all times. The street car device is the most concrete symbol I could find for the transition of the imagination from quotidian details to the universal consideration of beauty—the body still 'centered in traffic,' the imagination eluding its daily nets and self-consciousness. Symbolically, also, and in relation to Homer, this first part has significance of the rape of Helen by Paris. In one word, however, Part I stands simply for the EVOCATION of beauty" (*Letters*, 120–121). Dr. Faustus is a figure in Christopher Marlowe's play of the same name. He sells his soul to the devil and has a vision of Helen of Troy. The epigraph is taken from Ben Johnson's play *The Alchemist,* a satiric comedy about human gullibility centered on the false science of alchemy.

There is the world dimensional for
Those untwisted by the love of things
irreconcilable . . .

And yet, suppose some evening I forgot
The fare and transfer, yet got by that way
Without recall,—lost yet poised in traffic.
Then I might find your eyes across an aisle,
Still flickering with those prefigurations—
Prodigal, yet uncontested now,
Half-riant before the jerky window frame.

There is some way, I think, to touch
Those hands of yours that count the nights
Stippled with pink and green advertisements.
And now, before its arteries turn dark
I would have you meet this bartered blood.
Imminent in his dream, none better knows
The white wafer cheek of love, or offers words
Lightly as moonlight on the eaves meets snow.

Reflective conversion of all things
At your deep blush, when ecstasies thread
The limbs and belly, when rainbows spread
Impinging on the throat and sides . . .
Inevitable, the body of the world
Weeps in inventive dust for the hiatus
That winks above it, bluet in your breasts.

The earth may glide diaphanous to death;
But if I lift my arms it is to bend
To you who turned away once, Helen, knowing
The press of troubled hands, too alternate
With steel and soil to hold you endlessly.
I meet you, therefore, in that eventual flame
You found in final chains, no captive then—
Beyond their million brittle, bloodshot eyes;
White, through white cities passed on to assume
That world which comes to each of us alone.
Accept a lone eye riveted to your plane,

25**Half-riant:** half-laughing.

Bent axle of devotion along companion ways
That beat, continuous, to hourless days—
One inconspicuous, glowing orb of praise.

II

Brazen hypnotics glitter here;
Glee shifts from foot to foot,
Magnetic to their tremolo.
This crashing opéra bouffe,
Blest excursion! this ricochet
From roof to roof—
Know, Olympians, we are breathless
While nigger cupids scour the stars!

A thousand light shrugs balance us
Through snarling hails of melody.
White shadows slip across the floor
Splayed like cards from a loose hand;
Rhythmic ellipses lead into canters
Until somewhere a rooster banters.

Greet naïvely—yet intrepidly
New soothings, new amazements
That cornets introduce at every turn—
And you may fall downstairs with me
With perfect grace and equanimity.
Or, plaintively scud past shores
Where, by strange harmonic laws
All relatives, serene and cool,
Sit rocked in patent armchairs.

O, I have known metallic paradises
Where cuckoos clucked to finches
Above the deft catastrophes of drums.
While titters hailed the groans of death
Beneath gyrating awnings I have seen
The incunabula of the divine grotesque.
This music has a reassuring way.

61 **Olympians:** the Greek gods who inhabit Mount Olympus.

The siren of the springs of guilty song—
Let us take her on the incandescent wax
Striated with nuances, nervosities
That we are heir to: she is still so young,
We cannot frown upon her as she smiles,
Dipping here in this cultivated storm
Among slim skaters of the gardened skies.

III

Capped arbiter of beauty in this street
That narrows darkly into motor dawn,—
You, here beside me, delicate ambassador
Of intricate slain numbers that arise
In whispers, naked of steel;
religious gunman!
Who faithfully, yourself, will fall too soon,
And in other ways than as the wind settles
On the sixteen thrifty bridges of the city:
Let us unbind our throats of fear and pity.

We even,
Who drove speediest destruction
In corymbulous formations of mechanics,—
Who hurried the hill breezes, spouting malice
Plangent over meadows, and looked down
On rifts of torn and empty houses
Like old women with teeth unjubilant
That waited faintly, briefly and in vain:

We know, eternal gunman, our flesh remembers
The tensile boughs, the nimble blue plateaus,
The mounted, yielding cities of the air!

That saddled sky that shook down vertical
Repeated play of fire—no hypogeum
Of wave or rock was good against one hour.
We did not ask for that, but have survived,
And will persist to speak again before
All stubble streets that have not curved
To memory, or known the ominous lifted arm

That lowers down the arc of Helen's brow
To saturate with blessing and dismay.
A goose, tobacco and cologne—
Three-winged and gold-shod prophecies of heaven,
The lavish heart shall always have to leaven
And spread with bells and voices, and atone
The abating shadows of our conscript dust.

Anchises' navel, dripping of the sea,—
The hands Erasmus dipped in gleaming tides,
Gathered the voltage of blown blood and vine;
Delve upward for the new and scattered wine,
O brother-thief of time, that we recall.
Laugh out the meager penance of their days
Who dare not share with us the breath released,
The substance drilled and spent beyond repair
For golden, or the shadow of gold hair.

Distinctly praise the years, whose volatile
Blamed bleeding hands extend and thresh the height
The imagination spans beyond despair,
Outpacing bargain, vocable and prayer.

Voyages

I

Above the fresh ruffles of the surf
Bright striped urchins flay each other with sand.
They have contrived a conquest for shell shucks,
And their fingers crumble fragments of baked weed
Gaily digging and scattering.

And in answer to their treble interjections
The sun beats lightning on the waves,
The waves fold thunder on the sand;
And could they hear me I would tell them:

FOR THE MARRIAGE OF FAUSTUS AND HELEN [126]**Anchises:** father of Aeneas, founder of Rome. [127]**Erasmus:** medieval humanist philosopher.

O brilliant kids, frisk with your dog,
Fondle your shells and sticks, bleached
By time and the elements; but there is a line
You must not cross nor ever trust beyond it
Spry cordage of your bodies to caresses
Too lichen-faithful from too wide a breast.
The bottom of the sea is cruel.

II

—And yet this great wink of eternity,
Of rimless floods, unfettered leewardings,
Samite sheeted and processioned where
Her undinal vast belly moonward bends,
Laughing the wrapt inflections of our love;

Take this Sea, whose diapason knells
On scrolls of silver snowy sentences,
The sceptred terror of whose sessions rends
As her demeanors motion well or ill,
All but the pieties of lovers' hands.

And onward, as bells off San Salvador
Salute the crocus lustres of the stars,
In these poinsettia meadows of her tides,—
Adagios of islands, O my Prodigal,
Complete the dark confessions her veins spell.

Mark how her turning shoulders wind the hours,
And hasten while her penniless rich palms
Pass superscription of bent foam and wave,—
Hasten, while they are true,—sleep, death, desire,
Close round one instant in one floating flower.

[22]**this Sea:** the Caribbean. [30]**Adagios of islands:** In his essay "General Aims and Theories," Crane wrote: "When . . . I speak of 'adagios of islands,' the reference is to the motion of a boat through islands clustered thickly, the rhythm of the motion, etc. And it seems a much more direct and creative statement than any more logical employment of words, such as 'coasting slowly through the islands,' besides ushering in a whole world of music." *Adagio* is a musical term denoting a slow tempo.

Bind us in time, O Seasons clear, and awe.
O minstrel galleons of Carib fire,
Bequeath us to no earthly shore until
Is answered in the vortex of our grave
The seal's wide spindrift gaze toward paradise.

O Carib Isle!

The tarantula rattling at the lily's foot
Across the feet of the dead, laid in white sand
Near the coral beach—nor zigzag fiddle crabs
Side-stilting from the path (that shift, subvert
And anagrammatize your name)—No, nothing here
Below the palsy that one eucalyptus lifts
In wrinkled shadows—mourns.

And yet suppose
I count these nacreous frames of tropic death,
Brutal necklaces of shells around each grave
Squared off so carefully. Then

To the white sand I may speak a name, fertile
Albeit in a stranger tongue. Tree names, flower names
Deliberate, gainsay death's brittle crypt. Meanwhile
The wind that knots itself in one great death—
Coils and withdraws. So syllables want breath.

But where is the Captain of this doubloon isle
Without a turnstile? Who but catchword crabs
Patrols the dry groins of the underbrush?
What man, or What
Is Commissioner of mildew throughout the ambushed senses?
His Carib mathematics web the eyes' baked lenses!

Under the poinciana, of a noon or afternoon
Let fiery blossoms clot the light, render my ghost
Sieved upward, white and black along the air
Until it meets the blue's comedian host.

Let not the pilgrim see himself again
For slow evisceration bound like those huge terrapin
Each daybreak on the wharf, their brine-caked eyes;

—Spiked, overturned; such thunder in their strain!
And clenched beaks coughing for the surge again!

Slagged of the hurricane—I, cast within its flow,
Congeal by afternoons here, satin and vacant.
You have given me the shell, Satan,—carbonic amulet
Sere of the sun exploded in the sea.

To Emily Dickinson

You who desired so much—in vain to ask—
Yet fed your hunger like an endless task,
Dared dignify the labor, bless the quest—
Achieved that stillness ultimately best,

Being, of all, least sought for: Emily, hear!
O sweet, dead Silencer, most suddenly clear
When singing that Eternity possessed
And plundered momently in every breast;

—Truly no flower yet withers in your hand,
The harvest you described and understand
Needs more than wit to gather, love to bind.
Some reconcilement of remotest mind—

Leaves Ormus rubyless, and Ophir chill.
Else tears heap all within one clay-cold hill.

The Broken Tower

The bell-rope that gathers God at dawn
Dispatches me as though I dropped down the knell
Of a spent day—to wander the cathedral lawn
From pit to crucifix, feet chill on steps from hell.

Have you not heard, have you not seen that corps
Of shadows in the tower, whose shoulders sway

TO EMILY DICKINSON [13]**Ormus, Ophir:** Ormus (Ormuz) was an ancient city on the Persian Gulf. Ophir was an ancient country noted for its precious stones and metals.

Antiphonal carillons launched before
The stars are caught and hived in the sun's ray?

The bells, I say, the bells break down their tower;
And swing I know not where. Their tongues engrave
Membrane through marrow, my long-scattered score
Of broken intervals . . . And I, their sexton slave!

Oval encyclicals in canyons heaping
The impasse high with choir. Banked voices slain!
Pagodas, campaniles with reveilles outleaping—
O terraced echoes prostrate on the plain! . . .

And so it was I entered the broken world
To trace the visionary company of love, its voice
An instant in the wind (I know not whither hurled)
But not for long to hold each desperate choice.

My word I poured. But was it cognate, scored
Of that tribunal monarch of the air
Whose thigh embronzes earth, strikes crystal Word
In wounds pledged once to hope—cleft to despair?

The steep encroachments of my blood left me
No answer (could blood hold such a lofty tower
As flings the question true?)—or is it she
Whose sweet mortality stirs latent power?—

And through whose pulse I hear, counting the strokes
My veins recall and add, revived and sure
The angelus of wars my chest evokes:
What I hold healed, original now, and pure . . .

And builds, within, a tower that is not stone
(Not stone can jacket heaven)—but slip
Of pebbles,—visible wings of silence sown
In azure circles, widening as they dip

The matrix of the heart, lift down the eye
That shrines the quiet lake and swells a tower . . .
The commodious, tall decorum of that sky
Unseals her earth, and lifts love in its shower.

From *The Bridge*

From going to and fro in the earth,
and from walking up and down in it.
—THE BOOK OF JOB

PROEM: TO BROOKLYN BRIDGE

How many dawns, chill from his rippling rest
The seagull's wings shall dip and pivot him,
Shedding white rings of tumult, building high
Over the chained bay waters Liberty—

Then, with inviolate curve, forsake our eyes
As apparitional as sails that cross
Some page of figures to be filed away;
—Till elevators drop us from our day . . .

I think of cinemas, panoramic sleights
With multitudes bent toward some flashing scene
Never disclosed, but hastened to again,
Foretold to other eyes on the same screen;

And Thee, across the harbor, silver-paced
As though the sun took step of thee, yet left
Some motion ever unspent in thy stride,—
Implicitly thy freedom staying thee!

Out of some subway scuttle, cell or loft
A bedlamite speeds to thy parapets,
Tilting there momently, shrill shirt ballooning,
A jest falls from the speechless caravan.

Down Wall, from girder into street noon leaks,
A rip-tooth of the sky's acetylene;

In his letters, Crane said of *The Bridge:* "Very roughly, it concerns a mystical synthesis of 'America.' History and fact, location, etc., all have to be transfigured into abstract form that would almost function independently of its subject matter. The initial impulses of 'our people' will have to be gathered up toward the climax of the bridge, symbol of our constructive future, our unique identity, in which is included also our scientific hopes and achievements of the future. . . . The actual statement of the thing . . . will take me months, at best; and I may have to give it up entirely before that; it may be too impossible an ambition. But if I do succeed, such a waving of banners, such ascent of towers, such dancing, etc., will never before have been put down on paper!" [18]**bedlamite:** an inmate of a mental hospital.

All afternoon the cloud-flown derricks turn . . .
Thy cables breathe the North Atlantic still.

And obscure as that heaven of the Jews,
Thy guerdon . . . Accolade thou dost bestow
Of anonymity time cannot raise:
Vibrant reprieve and pardon thou dost show.

O harp and altar, of the fury fused,
(How could mere toil align thy choiring strings!)
Terrific threshold of the prophet's pledge,
Prayer of pariah, and the lover's cry,—

Again the traffic lights that skim thy swift
Unfractioned idiom, immaculate sigh of stars,
Beading thy path—condense eternity:
And we have seen night lifted in thine arms.

Under thy shadow by the piers I waited;
Only in darkness is thy shadow clear.
The City's fiery parcels all undone,
Already snow submerges an iron year . . .

O Sleepless as the river under thee,
Vaulting the sea, the prairies' dreaming sod,
Unto us lowliest sometime sweep, descend
And of the curveship lend a myth to God.

I. AVE MARIA

Venient annis, saecula seris,
Quibus Oceanus vincula rerum
Laxet et ingens pateat tellus
Tiphysque novos detegat orbes
Nec sit terris ultima Thule.

—SENECA

Ave Maria: Hail Mary—the traditional way of invoking the mother of God in prayer. The epigraph to Part I is from *Medea,* a tragedy by the Roman dramatist Seneca. It can be translated: "A time will come in distant years when Ocean will loosen the bonds of things and the whole earth's surface will be open to view, and Tiphys [the pilot of Jason's ship] will discover new worlds; and Thule will no longer be the outer edge of the world."

Columbus, alone, gazing toward Spain, invokes the presence of two faithful partisans of his quest . . .

Be with me, Luis de San Angel, now—
Witness before the tides can wrest away
The word I bring, O you who reined my suit
Into the Queen's great heart that doubtful day;
For I have seen now what no perjured breath
Of clown nor sage can riddle or gainsay:—
To you, too, Juan Perez, whose counsel fear
And greed adjourned,—I bring you back Cathay!

Here waves climb into dusk on gleaming mail;
Invisible valves of the sea,—locks, tendons
Crested and creeping, troughing corridors
That fall back yawning to another plunge.
Slowly the sun's red caravel drops light
Once more behind us. . . . It is morning there—
O where our Indian emperies lie revealed,
Yet lost, all, let this keel one instant yield!

I thought of Genoa; and this truth, now proved,
That made me exile in her streets, stood me
More absolute than ever—biding the moon
Till dawn should clear that dim frontier, first seen
—The Chan's great continent. . . . Then faith, not fear
Nigh surged me witless. . . . Hearing the surf near—
I, wonder-breathing, kept the watch,—saw
The first palm chevron the first lighted hill.

And lowered. And they came out to us crying,
"The Great White Birds!" (O Madre María, still
One ship of these thou grantest safe returning;
Assure us through thy mantle's ageless blue!)
And record of more, floating in a casque,
Was tumbled from us under bare poles scudding;
And later hurricanes may claim more pawn. . . .
For her between two worlds, another, harsh,

[45]**Luis de San Angel:** a collector of church revenues in Spain and an advocate of Christopher Columbus at the court of Queen Isabella. [61]**Genoa:** city in Italy, birthplace of Columbus. [65]**Chan:** Khan, the Chinese emperor.

This third, of water, tests the word; lo, here
Bewilderment and mutiny heap whelming
Laughter, and shadow cuts sleep from the heart
Almost as though the Moor's flung scimitar
Found more than flesh to fathom in its fall.
Yet under tempest-lash and surfeitings
Some inmost sob, half-heard, dissuades the abyss,
Merges the wind in measure to the waves,

Series on series, infinite,—till eyes
Starved wide on blackened tides,
accrete—enclose
This turning rondure whole, this crescent ring
Sun-cusped and zoned with modulated fire
Like pearls that whisper through the Doge's hands
—Yet no delirium of jewels! O Fernando,
Take of that eastern shore, this western sea,
Yet yield thy God's, thy Virgin's charity!

—Rush down the plenitude, and you shall see
Isaiah counting famine on this lee!

. . .

An herb, a stray branch among salty teeth,
The jellied weeds that drag the shore,—perhaps
Tomorrow's moon will grant us Saltes Bar—
Palos again,—a land cleared of long war.
Some Angelus environs the cordage tree,
Dark waters onward shake the dark prow free.

. . .

O Thou who sleepest on Thyself, apart
Like ocean athwart lanes of death and birth,
And all the eddying breath between dost search

[89]**Doge:** ruler of Venice. [90]**Fernando:** King Ferdinand V of Spain. [94]**Isaiah . . . on this lee:** Isaiah, the Biblical prophet, warns: "Rejoice not thou, O Philistia. . . . I will kill thy root with famine." (Isaiah 14:29–30). [98]**Palos:** Spanish port. [99]**Angelus:** the bells calling people to prayer.

Cruelly with love thy parable of man,—
Inquisitor! incognizable Word
Of Eden and the enchained Sepulchre,
Into thy steep savannahs, burning blue,
Utter to loneliness the sail is true.

Who grindest oar, and arguing the mast
Subscribest holocaust of ships, O Thou
Within whose primal scan consummately
The glistening seignories of Ganges swim;—
Who sendest greeting by the corposant,
And Teneriffe's garnet—flamed it in a cloud,
Urging through night our passage to the Chan;—
Te Deum laudamus, for thy teeming span!

Of all that amplitude that time explores,
A needle in the sight, suspended north,—
Yielding by inference and discard, faith
And true appointment from the hidden shoal:
This disposition that thy night relates
From Moon to Saturn in one sapphire wheel:
The orbic wake of thy once whirling feet,
Elohim, still I hear thy sounding heel!

White toil of heaven's cordons, mustering
In holy rings all sails charged to the far
Hushed gleaming fields and pendant
   seething wheat
Of knowledge,—round thy brows unhooded now
—The kindled Crown! acceded of the poles
And biassed by full sails, meridians reel
Thy purpose—still one shore beyond desire!
The sea's green crying towers a-sway, Beyond
And kingdoms
                    naked in the
                                        trembling heart—
      Te Deum laudamus
                                        O Thou Hand of Fire

[113–115]**Who sendest greeting . . . our passage to the Chan:** Columbus reported in his journal that he saw a glowing ball of fire, which he took to be a sign from God. [116]**Te Deum laudamus:** Latin for "O Lord we praise Thee."

II. POWHATAN'S DAUGHTER

"—Pocahuntus, a well-featured but wanton yong girle . . . of the age of eleven or twelve years, get the boyes forth with her into the market place, and make them wheele, falling on their hands, turning their heels upwards, whom she would followe, and wheele so herself, naked as she was, all the fort over."

The Harbor Dawn

400 years and more . . . or is it from the soundless shore of sleep that time

Insistently through the sleep—a tide of voices—
They meet you listening midway in your dream,
The long, tired sounds, fog-insulated noises:
Gongs in white surplices, beshrouded wails,
Far strum of fog horns . . . signals dispersed in veils.

And then a truck will lumber past the wharves
As winch engines begin throbbing on some deck;
Or a drunken stevedore's howl and thud below
Comes echoing alley-upward through dim snow.

And if they take your sleep away sometimes
They give it back again. Soft sleeves of sound
Attend the darkling harbor, the pillowed bay;
Somewhere out there in blankness steam

Spills into steam, and wanders, washed away
—Flurried by keen fifings, eddied
Among distant chiming buoys—adrift. The sky,
Cool feathery fold, suspends, distills
This wavering slumber. . . . Slowly—
Immemorially the window, the half-covered chair
Ask nothing but this sheath of pallid air.

recalls you to your love, there in a waking dream to merge your seed

And you beside me, blessed now while sirens
Sing to us, stealthily weave us into day—
Serenely now, before day claims our eyes
Your cool arms murmurously about me lay.

Powhatan's Daughter: Pocahontas. The epigraph is taken from William Strachey's *History of Travaile into Virginia Britannica.*

While myriad snowy hands are clustering at
 the panes—

your hands within my hands are deeds;
my tongue upon your throat—singing
arms close; eyes wide, undoubtful
 dark
 drink the dawn—
a forest shudders in your hair!

—with whom?

The window goes blond slowly. Frostily clears.
From Cyclopean towers across Manhattan waters
—Two—three bright window-eyes aglitter, disk
The sun, released—aloft with cold gulls hither.

Who is the woman with us in the dawn? . . . whose is the flesh our feet have moved upon?

The fog leans one last moment on the sill.
Under the mistletoe of dreams, a star—
As though to join us at some distant hill—
Turns in the waking west and goes to sleep.

Van Winkle

Streets spread past store and factory—sped by sunlight and her smile . . .

Macadam, gun-grey as the tunny's belt,
Leaps from Far Rockaway to Golden Gate:
Listen! the miles a hurdy-gurdy grinds—
Down gold arpeggios mile on mile unwinds.

Times earlier, when you hurried off to school,
—It is the same hour though a later day—
You walked with Pizarro in a copybook,
And Cortes rode up, reining tautly in—
Firmly as coffee grips the taste,—and away!

[168]**Cyclopean:** the Cyclops was the one-eyed giant Odysseus blinded in Homer's *Odyssey.* **Van Winkle:** In Washington Irving's tale from *The Sketch Book,* Rip Van Winkle falls asleep for twenty years to wake to an America he doesn't recognize. Crane uses him as a guide on a journey through the past to encounters with Spanish conquistadors Francisco Pizarro (c. 1470–1541) and Hernando Cortés (1485–1547), Priscilla Alden, who was courted by the hero of Henry Wadsworth Longfellow's poem *The Courtship of Miles Standish,* and Captain John Smith (1580–1631), the Virginia colonial leader whose life was supposed to have been saved by Pocahontas (1595–1617). [175]**tunny:** tuna. [176]**Far Rockaway to Golden Gate:** Far Rockaway is on Long Island, New York; the Golden Gate Bridge spans the entrance to San Francisco Bay.

There was Priscilla's cheek close in the wind,
And Captain Smith, all beard and certainty,
And Rip Van Winkle bowing by the way,—
"Is this Sleepy Hollow, friend—?" And he—

Like Memory, she is time's truant, shall take you by the hand . . .

And Rip forgot the office hours,
and he forgot the pay;
Van Winkle sweeps a tenement
way down on Avenue A,—

The grind-organ says . . . Remember, remember
The cinder pile at the end of the backyard
Where we stoned the family of young
Garter snakes under . . . And the monoplanes
We launched—with paper wings and twisted
Rubber bands . . . Recall—recall
the rapid tongues
That flittered from under the ash heap day
After day whenever your stick discovered
Some sunning inch of unsuspecting fibre—
It flashed back at your thrust, as clean as fire.

And Rip was slowly made aware
that he, Van Winkle, was not here
nor there. He woke and swore he'd seen Broadway
a Catskill daisy chain in May—

So memory, that strikes a rhyme out of a box,
Or splits a random smell of flowers through glass—
Is it the whip stripped from the lilac tree
One day in spring my father took to me,
Or is it the Sabbatical, unconscious smile
My mother almost brought me once from church
And once only, as I recall—?

[187]**Sleepy Hollow:** home of the Dutch settlers in Washington Irving's *The Legend of Sleepy Hollow.*

It flickered through the snow screen, blindly
It forsook her at the doorway, it was gone
Before I had left the window. It
Did not return with the kiss in the hall.

Macadam, gun-grey as the tunny's belt,
Leaps from Far Rockaway to Golden Gate. . . .
Keep hold of that nickel for car-change, Rip,—
Have you got your *"Times"—?*
And hurry along, Van Winkle—it's getting late!

The River

. . . and past the din and slogans of the year—

Stick your patent name on a signboard
brother—all over—going west—young man
Tintex—Japalac—Certain-teed Overalls ads
and land sakes! under the new playbill ripped
in the guaranteed corner—see Bert Williams what?
Minstrels when you steal a chicken just
save me the wing for if it isn't
Erie it ain't for miles around a
Mazda—and the telegraphic night coming
on Thomas

a Ediford—and whistling down the tracks
a headlight rushing with the sound—can you
imagine—while an EXPRESS makes time like

The River: Crane's note: "I'm trying in this part of the poem to chart the pioneer experience of our forefathers—and to tell the story backwards . . . on the 'backs' of hoboes. These hoboes are simply 'psychological ponies' to carry the reader across the country and back to the Mississippi, which you will notice is described as a great River of Time. I also unlatch the door to the pure Indian world which opens out in 'The Dance' section, so the reader is gradually led back in time to the pure savage world, while existing at the same time in the present." He also wrote: "The subway is simply a figurative, psychological 'vehicle' for transporting the reader to the Middle West. He lands on the railroad tracks in the company of several tramps in the twilight. The extravagance of the first twenty-three lines of this section is an intentional burlesque on the conglomeration of noises analogous to the strident impression of a fast express rushing by." [226]**Bert Williams:** a popular entertainer of the black minstrel shows. [231]**Ediford:** a playful conflation of the names of Thomas A. Edison (1847–1931), the trade name of whose electric light bulb was Mazda, and Henry Ford (1863–1947), the automobile manufacturer.

SCIENCE—COMMERCE and the HOLYGHOST
RADIO ROARS IN EVERY HOME WE HAVE THE
NORTHPOLE
WALLSTREET AND VIRGINBIRTH WITHOUT STONES OR
WIRES OR EVEN RUNNING brooks connecting ears
and no more sermons windows flashing roar
breathtaking—as you like it . . . eh?

So the 20th Century—so
whizzed the Limited—roared by and left
three men, still hungry on the tracks, ploddingly
watching the tail lights wizen and converge, slip-
ping gimleted and nearly out of sight.

. . . .

to those whose addresses are never near

The last bear, shot drinking in the Dakotas
Loped under wires that span the mountain stream.
Keen instruments, strung to a vast precision
Bind town to town and dream to ticking dream.
But some men take their liquor slow—and count
—Though they'll confess no rosary nor clue—
The river's minute by the far brook's year.
Under a world of whistles, wires and steam
Caboose-like they go ruminating through
Ohio, Indiana—blind baggage—
To Cheyenne tagging . . . Maybe Kalamazoo.

Time's rendings, time's blendings they construe
As final reckonings of fire and snow;
Strange bird-wit, like the elemental gist
Of unwalled winds they offer, singing low
My Old Kentucky Home and *Casey Jones,*
Some Sunny Day. I heard a road-gang chanting so.
And afterwards, who had a colt's eyes—one said,
"Jesus! Oh I remember watermelon days!"
And sped
High in a cloud of merriment, recalled
"—And when my Aunt Sally Simpson smiled,"
he drawled—

"It was almost Louisiana, long ago."
"There's no place like Booneville though, Buddy,"
One said, excising a last burr from his vest,
"—For early trouting." Then peering in the can,
"—But I kept on the tracks." Possessed, resigned,
He trod the fire down pensively and grinned,
Spreading dry shingles of a beard. . . .

Behind
My father's cannery works I used to see
Rail-squatters ranged in nomad raillery,
The ancient men—wifeless or runaway
Hobo-trekkers that forever search
An empire wilderness of freight and rails.
Each seemed a child, like me, on a loose perch,
Holding to childhood like some termless play.
John, Jake or Charley, hopping the slow freight
—Memphis to Tallahassee—riding the rods,
Blind fists of nothing, humpty-dumpty clods.

but who have touched her, knowing her without name

Yet they touch something like a key perhaps.
From pole to pole across the hills, the states
—They know a body under the wide rain;
Youngsters with eyes like fjords, old reprobates
With racetrack jargon,—dotting immensity
They lurk across her, knowing her yonder breast
Snow-silvered, sumac-stained or smoky blue—
Is past the valley-sleepers, south or west.
—As I have trod the rumorous midnights, too,

And past the circuit of the lamp's thin flame
(O Nights that brought me to her body bare!)
Have dreamed beyond the print that bound
her name.
Trains sounding the long blizzards out—I heard
Wail into distances I knew were hers.
Papooses crying on the wind's long mane
Screamed redskin dynasties that fled the brain,
—Dead echoes! But I knew her body there,
Time like a serpent down her shoulder, dark
And space, an eaglet's wing, laid on her hair.

Under the Ozarks, domed by Iron Mountain,
The old gods of the rain lie wrapped in pools
Where eyeless fish curvet a sunken fountain
And re-descend with corn from querulous crows.
Such pilferings make up their timeless eatage,
Propitiate them for their timber torn
By iron, iron—always the iron dealt cleavage!
They doze now, below axe and powder horn.
And Pullman breakfasters glide glistening steel
From tunnel into field—iron strides the dew—
Straddles the hill, a dance of wheel on wheel.
You have a half-hour's wait at Siskiyou,
Or stay the night and take the next train through.
Southward, near Cairo passing, you can see
The Ohio merging,—borne down Tennessee;
And if it's summer and the sun's in dusk
Maybe the breeze will lift the River's musk
—As though the waters breathed that you might know
Memphis Johnny, Steamboat Bill, Missouri Joe.
Oh, lean from the window, if the train slows down,
As though you touched hands with some ancient clown,
—A little while gaze absently below
And hum Deep River with them while they go.

nor the myths of her fathers . . .

Yes, turn again and sniff once more—look see,
O Sheriff, Brakeman and Authority—
Hitch up your pants and crunch another quid,
For you, too, feed the River timelessly.
And few evade full measure of their fate;
Always they smile out eerily what they seem.
I could believe he joked at heaven's gate—
Dan Midland—jolted from the cold brake-beam.

Down, down—born pioneers in time's despite,
Grimed tributaries to an ancient flow—

[327]**quid:** chewing tobacco. [332]**Dan Midland:** a hobo who fell to his death from a train.

They win no frontier by their wayward plight,
But drift in stillness, as from Jordan's brow.

You will not hear it as the sea; even stone
Is not more hushed by gravity . . . But slow,
As loath to take more tribute—sliding prone
Like one whose eyes were buried long ago
The River, spreading, flows—and spends
  your dream.
What are you, lost within this tideless spell?
You are your father's father, and the stream—
A liquid theme that floating niggers swell.

Damp tonnage and alluvial march of days—
Nights turbid, vascular with silted shale
And roots surrendered down of moraine clays:
The Mississippi drinks the farthest dale.

O quarrying passion, undertowed sunlight!
The basalt surface drags a jungle grace
Ochreous and lynx-barred in lengthening might;
Patience! and you shall reach the biding place!

Over De Soto's bones the freighted floors
Throb past the City storied of three thrones
Down two more turns the Mississippi pours
(Anon tall ironsides up from salt lagoons)

And flows within itself, heaps itself free.
All fades but one thin skyline 'round . . . Ahead
No embrace opens but the stinging sea;
The River lifts itself from its long bed,

Poised wholly on its dream, a mustard glow
Tortured with history, its one will—flow!
—The Passion spreads in wide tongues, choked
  and slow,
Meeting the Gulf, hosannas silently below.

[353]**De Soto:** Fernando De Soto (1496–1542) discovered the Mississippi in 1541.
[354]**the City storied of three thrones:** New Orleans, which was held at various times by the English, French, and Spanish.

VII. THE TUNNEL

To Find the Western path
Right thro' the Gates of Wrath.
—BLAKE

Performances, assortments, résumés—
Up Times Square to Columbus Circle lights
Channel the congresses, nightly sessions,
Refractions of the thousand theatres, faces—
Mysterious kitchens. . . . You shall search them
all.
Someday by heart you'll learn each famous sight
And watch the curtain lift in hell's despite;
You'll find the garden in the third act dead,
Finger your knees—and wish yourself in bed
With tabloid crime-sheets perched in easy sight.

Then let you reach your hat
and go.
As usual, let you—also
walking down—exclaim
to twelve upward leaving
a subscription praise
for what time slays.

Or can't you quite make up your mind to ride;
A walk is better underneath the L a brisk
Ten blocks or so before? But you find yourself
Preparing penguin flexions of the arms,—
As usual you will meet the scuttle yawn:
The subway yawns the quickest promise home.

Be minimum, then, to swim the hiving swarms
Out of the Square, the Circle burning bright—
Avoid the glass doors gyring at your right,
Where boxed alone a second, eyes take fright
—Quite unprepared rush naked back to light:
And down beside the turnstile press the coin
Into the slot. The gongs already rattle.

The epigraph to Part VII is from "Morning," a visionary poem by William Blake (1757–1827). **383L:** abbreviation for "elevated railway."

And so
of cities you bespeak
subways, rivered under streets
and rivers. . . . In the car
the overtone of motion
underground, the monotone
of motion is the sound
of other faces, also underground—

"Let's have a pencil Jimmy—living now
at Floral Park
Flatbush—on the fourth of July—
like a pigeon's muddy dream—potatoes
to dig in the field—travlin the town—too—
night after night—the Culver line—the
girls all shaping up—it used to be—"

Our tongues recant like beaten weather vanes.
This answer lives like verdigris, like hair
Beyond extinction, surcease of the bone;
And repetition freezes—"What

"what do you want? getting weak on the links?
fandaddle daddy don't ask for change—IS THIS
FOURTEENTH? it's half past six she said—if
you don't like my gate why did you
swing on it, why didja
swing on it
anyhow—"

And somehow anyhow swing—

The phonographs of hades in the brain
Are tunnels that re-wind themselves, and love
A burnt match skating in a urinal—
Somewhere above Fourteenth TAKE THE EXPRESS
To brush some new presentiment of pain—

"But I want service in this office SERVICE
I said—after
the show she cried a little afterwards but—"

Whose head is swinging from the swollen strap?
Whose body smokes along the bitten rails,
Bursts from a smoldering bundle far behind
In back forks of the chasms of the brain,—
Puffs from a riven stump far out behind
In interborough fissures of the mind . . . ?

And why do I often meet your visage here,
Your eyes like agate lanterns—on and on
Below the toothpaste and the dandruff ads?
—And did their riding eyes right through your side,
And did their eyes like unwashed platters ride?
And Death, aloft,—gigantically down
Probing through you—toward me, O evermore!
And when they dragged your retching flesh,
Your trembling hands that night through Baltimore—
That last night on the ballot rounds, did you
Shaking, did you deny the ticket, Poe?

For Gravesend Manor change at Chambers Street.
The platform hurries along to a dead stop.

The intent escalator lifts a serenade
Stilly
Of shoes, umbrellas, each eye attending its shoe, then
Bolting outright somewhere above where streets
Burst suddenly in rain. . . . The gongs recur:
Elbows and levers, guard and hissing door.
Thunder is galvothermic here below. . . . The car
Wheels off. The train rounds, bending to a scream,
Taking the final level for the dive
Under the river—
And somewhat emptier than before,
Demented, for a hitching second, humps; then
Lets go. . . . Toward corners of the floor
Newspapers wing, revolve and wing.
Blank windows gargle signals through the roar.

And does the Daemon take you home, also,
Wop washerwoman, with the bandaged hair?

[442]**Probing through you . . . evermore!:** Echoes of Edgar Allan Poe's poems "The City in the Sea" and "The Raven." [455]**galvothermic:** producing heat by electricity.

After the corridors are swept, the cuspidors—
The gaunt sky-barracks cleanly now, and bare,
O Genoese, do you bring mother eyes and hands
Back home to children and to golden hair?

Daemon, demurring and eventful yawn!
Whose hideous laughter is a bellows mirth
—Or the muffled slaughter of a day in birth—
O cruelly to inoculate the brinking dawn
With antennae toward worlds that glow and sink;—
To spoon us out more liquid than the dim
Locution of the eldest star, and pack
The conscience navelled in the plunging wind,
Umbilical to call—and straightway die!

O caught like pennies beneath soot and steam,
Kiss of our agony thou gatherest;
Condensed, thou takest all—shrill ganglia
Impassioned with some song we fail to keep.
And yet, like Lazarus, to feel the slope,
The sod and billow breaking,—lifting ground,
—A sound of waters bending astride the sky
Unceasing with some Word that will not die . . . !

. . . .

A tugboat, wheezing wreaths of steam,
Lunged past, with one galvanic blare stove up the
        River.
I counted the echoes assembling, one after one,
Searching, thumbing the midnight on the piers.
Lights, coasting, left the oily tympanum of waters;
The blackness somewhere gouged glass on a sky.

And this thy harbor, O my City, I have driven under,
Tossed from the coil of ticking towers. . . .
        Tomorrow,
And to be. . . . Here by the River that is East—
Here at the waters' edge the hands drop memory;
Shadowless in that abyss they unaccounting lie.

[483]**Lazarus:** man brought back from the dead by Jesus. See John 11:43–44.

How far away the star has pooled the sea—
Or shall the hands be drawn away, to die?

Kiss of our agony Thou gatherest,
O Hand of Fire
gatherest—

VIII. ATLANTIS

Music is then the knowledge of that which relates to love in harmony and system.

PLATO

Through the bound cable strands, the arching path
Upward, veering with light, the flight of strings,—
Taut miles of shuttling moonlight syncopate
The whispered rush, telepathy of wires.
Up the index of night, granite and steel—
Transparent meshes—fleckless the gleaming staves—
Sibylline voices flicker, waveringly stream
As though a god were issue of the strings. . . .

And through that cordage, threading with its call
One arc synoptic of all tides below—
Their labyrinthine mouths of history
Pouring reply as though all ships at sea
Complighted in one vibrant breath made cry,—
"Make thy love sure—to weave whose song we ply!"
—From black embankments, moveless soundings hailed,
So seven oceans answer from their dream.

And on, obliquely up bright carrier bars
New octaves trestle the twin monoliths
Beyond whose frosted capes the moon bequeaths
Two worlds of sleep (O arching strands of song!)—
Onward and up the crystal-flooded aisle
White tempest nets file upward, upward ring
With silver terraces the humming spars,
The loft of vision, palladium helm of stars.
Sheerly the eyes, like seagulls stung with rime—
Slit and propelled by glistening fins of light—

The epigraph to Part VIII is from *The Republic.* [511]**Sibylline:** Oracular, enigmatic; referring to the ancient oracle, the Sibyl of Cumae.

Pick biting way up towering looms that press
Sidelong with flight of blade on tendon blade
—Tomorrows into yesteryear—and link
What cipher-script of time no traveller reads
But who, through smoking pyres of love and death,
Searches the timeless laugh of mythic spears.
Like hails, farewells—up planet-sequined heights
Some trillion whispering hammers glimmer Tyre:
Serenely, sharply up the long anvil cry
Of inchling aeons silence rivets Troy.
And you, aloft there—Jason! hesting Shout!
Still wrapping harness to the swarming air!
Silvery the rushing wake, surpassing call,
Beams yelling Aeolus! splintered in the straits!

From gulfs unfolding, terrible of drums,
Tall Vision-of-the-Voyage, tensely spare—
Bridge, lifting night to cycloramic crest
Of deepest day—O Choir, translating time
Into what multitudinous Verb the suns
And synergy of waters ever fuse, recast
In myriad syllables,—Psalm of Cathay!
O Love, thy white, pervasive Paradigm . . . !

We left the haven hanging in the night—
Sheened harbor lanterns backward fled the keel.
Pacific here at time's end, bearing corn,—
Eyes stammer through the pangs of dust and steel.
And still the circular, indubitable frieze
Of heaven's meditation, yoking wave
To kneeling wave, one song devoutly binds—
The vernal strophe chimes from deathless strings!

O Thou steeled Cognizance whose leap commits
The agile precincts of the lark's return;
Within whose lariat sweep encinctured sing
In single chrysalis the many twain,—
Of stars Thou art the stitch and stallion glow
And like an organ, Thou, with sound of doom—

[538]**Tyre:** ancient Phoenician seaport. [541]**Jason:** leader of the Greek sailors who sought the Golden Fleece. [544]**Aeolus:** the Greek god of the winds.

Sight, sound and flesh Thou leadest from time's realm
As love strikes clear direction for the helm.

Swift peal of secular light, intrinsic Myth
Whose fell unshadow is death's utter wound,—
O River-throated—iridescently upborne
Through the bright drench and fabric of our veins;
With white escarpments swinging into light,
Sustained in tears the cities are endowed
And justified conclamant with ripe fields
Revolving through their harvests in sweet torment.

Forever Deity's glittering Pledge, O Thou
Whose canticle fresh chemistry assigns
To wrapt inception and beatitude,—
Always through blinding cables, to our joy,
Of thy white seizure springs the prophecy:
Always through spiring cordage, pyramids
Of silver sequel, Deity's young name
Kinetic of white choiring wings . . . ascends.

Migrations that must needs void memory,
Inventions that cobblestone the heart,—
Unspeakable Thou Bridge to Thee, O Love.
Thy pardon for this history, whitest Flower,
O Answerer of all,—Anemone,—
Now while thy petals spend the suns about us, hold—
(O Thou whose radiance doth inherit me)
Atlantis,—hold thy floating singer late!

So to thine Everpresence, beyond time,
Like spears ensanguined of one tolling star
That bleeds infinity—the orphic strings,
Sidereal phalanxes, leap and converge:
—One Song, one Bridge of Fire! Is it Cathay,
Now pity steeps the grass and rainbows ring
The serpent with the eagle in the leaves . . . ?
Whispers antiphonal in azure swing.

595**orphic:** reference to Orpheus, whose musical powers could charm the animals and the dead.

Langston Hughes

[1902–1967]

"Poetry," Langston Hughes once remarked, "should be direct, comprehensible, and the epitome of simplicity." His poems illustrate these guidelines with remarkable consistency. Avoiding the obscure and the difficult, Hughes wrote poems that could be understood by readers and listeners who had little prior experience with poetry. He sought to write poems that were immediately understandable, poems that express concretely the concerns of daily black life.

Hughes's poetry offers a transcription of urban life through a portrayal of the speech, habits, attitudes, and feelings of an oppressed people. The poems do more, however, than reveal the pain of poverty. They also illustrate racial pride and dignity. Hughes's poems cling, moreover, to the spoken language. They derive from an oral tradition in which folk poetry is recited and performed, rather than published in written form. In the oral tradition poems are passed down from one generation to the next through performance and recitation. As a result Hughes's poems, more than most, need to be read aloud to be fully appreciated. Hughes himself became famous for his public readings, which were sometimes accompanied by a glee club or jazz combo.

Music, in fact, is a central feature of Hughes's poetry. And the kind of music most evident in his work is the blues, an important influence in the work of many modern black writers, especially those associated with the Harlem Renaissance, a flowering of artistic activity among black artists and writers of Harlem in the 1920s. Hughes once described the blues as "sad funny songs—too sad to be funny and too funny to be sad," songs that contain "laughter and pain, hunger and heartache." The bittersweet tone and view of life reflected in Hughes's perspective on the blues is consistently mirrored in his poems, which sometimes adapt the stanza form of the typical blues song. This stanza includes two nearly identical lines followed by a third that contrasts with the first two. "Same in Blues" exhibits this characteristic with only slight modifications. In this and other poems, Hughes succeeds in grafting the inflections of the urban black dialect onto the rhythms of the blues.

But the blues is not the only musical influence on Hughes's poetry; his work also makes use of jazz as both subject and style, though Hughes's jazz poems are freer and looser in form than his blues poems. This difference reflects the improvisatory nature of jazz as well as its energy and vitality, which contrast with the more controlled idiom of the blues. The aggressive exuberance of jazz, its relaxed but vigorous informality is evident in poems like "Mulatto" and "Trumpet Player."

Hughes was a prolific writer whose published books span forty years (1926–1967). His output includes sixteen volumes of poems; two novels; three collections of short stories; four documentary works; three historical works; twenty dramatic pieces, including plays, musicals, and operettas; two volumes of autobiography; eight children's books; and twelve radio and television scripts. In addition, Hughes edited seven books—mostly collections of poems by black writers—and translated four others, including the poems of the renowned modern Spanish poet Federico García Lorca. Such versatility established Hughes as an important man of letters, contributing to his stature as a leading figure in the arts, especially the theater, whose audience Hughes was instrumental in enlarging.

The writers who influenced Hughes included Paul Dunbar, whose poems re-created the black vernacular, and W. E. B. DuBois, whose collection of essays on Afro-American life, *The Souls of Black Folk,* exerted a lasting influence on many writers, including novelists Richard Wright and James Baldwin. Hughes was also strongly influenced by the democratic idealism of Walt Whitman and the populism of Carl Sandburg, whom Hughes designated his "guiding star." From Sandburg, Hughes learned to write free verse. From Dunbar, he learned a method of incorporating local dialect into poems. And from DuBois, he derived what later came to be called black pride. These influences were combined and amalgamated in myriad ways, resulting in poems that provided insight into urban life.

Hughes's life was as varied as his writing. Born in Joplin, Missouri, in 1902, Hughes lived in Kansas and Ohio before studying at Columbia University in New York and later and more fully at Lincoln University in Nebraska. He worked as a seaman and as a newspaper correspondent and columnist for the *Chicago Defender,* the *Baltimore Afro-American,* and the New York *Post.* He also worked briefly as a cook at a fashionable restaurant in France and as a busboy in a Washington, D.C., hotel. It was there that Hughes left three of his poems beside the plate of a hotel dinner guest, the poet Vachel Lindsay, who recognized their merit and helped Hughes to secure their publication.

Hughes also founded theaters on both coasts—the Harlem Suitcase Theatre (New York, 1938) and the New Negro Theatre (Los Angeles, 1939)—and, in the Midwest, the Skyloft Players (Chicago, 1941). He traveled extensively, visiting and at various times living in Africa and Europe, especially Italy and France, as well as in Cuba, Haiti, Russia, Korea, and Japan. His life and travels are richly and engagingly chronicled in his two volumes of autobiography, *The Big Sea* (1940) and *I Wonder As I Wander* (1956).

As a writer who believed it was his vocation to "explain and illuminate the Negro condition in America," Hughes captured the experience as "the hurt of their lives, the monotony of their jobs, and the veiled weariness of their songs." He accomplished this in poems remarkable not only for their directness and simplicity but for their economy, lucidity, and wit. Whether he was writing poems of racial protest like "Dream Deferred" and "Ballad of the Landlord" or poems of racial affirmation like "Mother to Son" and "The Negro Speaks of Rivers," Hughes was able to find language and forms to express not only the pain of urban life but also its splendid vitality.

The Negro Speaks of Rivers

I've known rivers:
I've known rivers ancient as the world and older than the flow
  of human blood in human veins.
My soul has grown deep like the rivers.

I bathed in the Euphrates when dawns were young.
I built my hut near the Congo and it lulled me to sleep.
I looked upon the Nile and raised the pyramids above it.
I heard the singing of the Mississippi when Abe Lincoln
went down to New Orleans, and I've seen its muddy
bosom turn all golden in the sunset.

I've known rivers:
Ancient, dusky rivers.

My soul has grown deep like the rivers.

Mother to Son

Well, son, I'll tell you:
Life for me ain't been no crystal stair.
It's had tacks in it,
And splinters,
And boards torn up,
And places with no carpet on the floor—
Bare.
But all the time
I'se been a-climbin' on,
And reachin' landin's,
And turnin' corners,
And sometimes goin' in the dark
Where there ain't been no light.
So boy, don't you turn back.
Don't you set down on the steps
'Cause you finds it's kinder hard.
Don't you fall now—
For I'se still goin', honey,
I'se still climbin',
And life for me ain't been no crystal stair.

Dream Variations

To fling my arms wide
In some place of the sun,
To whirl and to dance
Till the white day is done.

Then rest at cool evening
Beneath a tall tree
While night comes on gently.
      Dark like me—
That is my dream!

To fling my arms wide
In the face of the sun,
Dance! Whirl! Whirl!
Till the quick day is done.
Rest at pale evening . . .
A tall, slim tree . . .
Night coming tenderly
      Black like me.

Mulatto

I am your son, white man!

Georgia dusk
And the turpentine woods.
One of the pillars of the temple fell.

      You are my son!
      Like hell!

The moon over the turpentine woods.
The Southern night
Full of stars
Great big yellow stars.
   What's a body but a toy?
      Juicy bodies
      Of nigger wenches
      Blue black
      Against black fences.
      O, you little bastard boy,
      What's a body but a toy?
The scent of pine wood stings the soft night air.
      What's the body of your mother?
Silver moonlight everywhere.

What's the body of your mother?
Sharp pine scent in the evening air.
A nigger night,
A nigger joy,
A little yellow
Bastard boy.

Naw, you ain't my brother.
Niggers ain't my brother.

Not ever.
Niggers ain't my brother.

The Southern night is full of stars,
Great big yellow stars.
O, sweet as earth,
Dusk dark bodies
Give sweet birth
To little yellow bastard boys.

Git on back there in the night,
You ain't white.

The bright stars scatter everywhere.
Pine wood scent in the evening air.
A nigger night,
A nigger joy.

I am your son, white man!

A little yellow
Bastard boy.

I, Too

I, too, sing America.

I am the darker brother.
They send me to eat in the kitchen
When company comes,
But I laugh,

And eat well,
And grow strong.

Tomorrow,
I'll be at the table
When company comes.
Nobody'll dare
Say to me,
"Eat in the kitchen,"
Then.

Besides,
They'll see how beautiful I am
And be ashamed—

I, too, am America.

My People

The night is beautiful,
So the faces of my people.

The stars are beautiful,
So the eyes of my people.

Beautiful, also, is the sun.
Beautiful, also, are the souls of my people.

The Weary Blues

Droning a drowsy syncopated tune,
Rocking back and forth to a mellow croon,
        I heard a Negro play.
Down on Lenox Avenue the other night
By the pale dull pallor of an old gas light
        He did a lazy sway. . . .
        He did a lazy sway. . . .
To the tune o' those Weary Blues.
With his ebony hands on each ivory key
He made that poor piano moan with melody.
        O Blues!

Swaying to and fro on his rickety stool
He played that sad raggy tune like a musical fool.
    Sweet Blues!
Coming from a black man's soul.
    O Blues!
In a deep song voice with a melancholy tone
I heard that Negro sing, that old piano moan—
    "Ain't got nobody in all this world,
    Ain't got nobody but ma self.
    I's gwine to quit ma frownin'
    And put ma troubles on the shelf."
Thump, thump, thump, went his foot on the floor.
He played a few chords then he sang some more—
    "I got the Weary Blues
    And I can't be satisfied.
    Got the Weary Blues
    And can't be satisfied—
    I ain't happy no mo'
    And I wish that I had died."
And far into the night he crooned that tune.
The stars went out and so did the moon.
The singer stopped playing and went to bed
While the Weary Blues echoed through his head.
He slept like a rock or a man that's dead.

Song for a Dark Girl

Way Down South in Dixie
    (Break the heart of me)
They hung my black young lover
    To a cross roads tree.
Way Down South in Dixie
    (Bruised body high in air)
I asked the white Lord Jesus
    What was the use of prayer.

Way Down South in Dixie
    (Break the heart of me)
Love is a naked shadow
    On a gnarled and naked tree.

Young Gal's Blues

I'm gonna walk to the graveyard
'Hind ma friend Miss Cora Lee.
Gonna walk to the graveyard
'Hind ma dear friend Cora Lee
Cause when I'm dead some
Body'll have to walk behind me.

I'm goin' to the po' house
To see ma old Aunt Clew.
Goin' to the po' house
To see ma old Aunt Clew.
When I'm old an' ugly
I'll want to see somebody, too.

The po' house is lonely
An' the grave is cold.
O, the po' house is lonely,
The graveyard grave is cold.
But I'd rather be dead than
To be ugly an' old.

When love is gone what
Can a young gal do?
When love is gone, O,
What can a young gal do?
Keep on a-lovin' me, daddy,
Cause I don't want to be blue.

Morning After

I was so sick last night I
Didn't hardly know my mind.
So sick last night I
Didn't know my mind.
I drunk some bad licker that
Almost made me blind.

Had a dream last night I
Thought I was in hell.
I drempt last night I
Thought I was in hell.
Woke up and looked around me—
Babe, your mouth was open like a well.
I said, Baby! Baby!
Please don't snore so loud.
Baby! Please!
Please don't snore so loud.
You jest a little bit o' woman but you
Sound like a great big crowd.

Trumpet Player

The Negro
With the trumpet at his lips
Has dark moons of weariness
Beneath his eyes
Where the smoldering memory
Of slave ships
Blazed to the crack of whips
About his thighs.

The Negro
With the trumpet at his lips
Has a head of vibrant hair
Tamed down,
Patent-leathered now
Until it gleams
Like jet—
Were jet a crown.

The music
From the trumpet at his lips
Is honey
Mixed with liquid fire.
The rhythm
From the trumpet at his lips
Is ecstasy
Distilled from old desire—

Desire
That is longing for the moon
Where the moonlight's but a spotlight
In his eyes,
Desire
That is longing for the sea
Where the sea's a bar-glass
Sucker size.

The Negro
With the trumpet at his lips
Whose jacket
Has a *fine* one-button roll,
Does not know
Upon what riff the music slips
Its hypodermic needle
To his soul—

But softly
As the tune comes from his throat
Trouble
Mellows to a golden note.

When Sue Wears Red

When Susanna Jones wears red
Her face is like an ancient cameo
Turned brown by the ages.

Come with a blast of trumpets,
    Jesus!

When Susanna Jones wears red
A queen from some time-dead Egyptian night
Walks once again.

Blow trumpets, Jesus!

And the beauty of Susanna Jones in red
Burns in my heart a love-fire sharp like pain.

Sweet silver trumpets,
Jesus!

Same in Blues

I said to my baby,
Baby, take it slow.
I can't, she said, I can't!
I got to go!

There's a certain
amount of traveling
in a dream deferred.

Lulu said to Leonard,
I want a diamond ring.
Leonard said to Lulu,
You won't get a goddamn thing!

A certain
amount of nothing
in a dream deferred.

Daddy, daddy, daddy,
All I want is you.
You can have me, baby—
but my lovin' days is through.

A certain
amount of impotence
in a dream deferred.

Three parties
On my party line—
But that third party,
Lord, ain't mine!

There's liable
to be confusion
in a dream deferred.

From river to river,
Uptown and down,
There's liable to be confusion
when a dream gets kicked around.

Dream Boogie

Good morning, daddy!
Ain't you heard
The boogie-woogie rumble
Of a dream deferred?

Listen closely:
You'll hear their feet
Beating out and beating out a—

You think
It's a happy beat?

Listen to it closely:
Ain't you heard
something underneath
like a—

What did I say?

Sure,
I'm happy!
Take it away!

Hey, pop!
Re-bop!
Mop!

Y-e-a-h!

What don't bug
them white kids
sure bugs me:
We knows everybody
ain't free!

Some of these young ones is cert'ly bad—
One batted a hard ball right through my window
and my gold fish et the glass.

What's written down
for white folks
ain't for us a-tall:
"Liberty And Justice—
Huh—For All."

Oop-pop-a-da!
Skee! Daddle-de-do!
Be-bop!

Salt'peanuts!

De-dop!

Madam and the Rent Man

The rent man knocked.
He said, Howdy-do?
I said, What
Can I do for you?
He said, You know
Your rent is due.

I said, Listen,
Before I'd pay
I'd go to Hades
And rot away!

The sink is broke,
The water don't run,
And you ain't done a thing
You promised to've done.

Back window's cracked,
Kitchen floor squeaks,
There's rats in the cellar,
And the attic leaks.

He said, Madam,
It's not up to me.
I'm just the agent,
Don't you see?

I said, Naturally,
You pass the buck.
If it's money you want
You're out of luck.

He said, Madam,
I ain't pleased!
I said, Neither am I.

So we agrees!

Theme for English B

The instructor said,

Go home and write
a page tonight.
And let that page come out of you—
Then, it will be true.

I wonder if it's that simple?

I am twenty-two, colored, born in Winston-Salem.
I went to school there, then Durham, then here
to this college on the hill above Harlem.
I am the only colored student in my class.
The steps from the hill lead down into Harlem,
through a park, then I cross St. Nicholas,
Eighth Avenue, Seventh, and I come to the Y,
the Harlem Branch Y, where I take the elevator
up to my room, sit down, and write this page:

It's not easy to know what is true for you or me
at twenty-two, my age. But I guess I'm what
I feel and see and hear. Harlem, I hear you:
hear you, hear me—we two—you, me, talk on this page.
(I hear New York, too.) Me—who?

Well, I like to eat, sleep, drink, and be in love.
I like to work, read, learn, and understand life.
I like a pipe for a Christmas present,
or records—Bessie, bop, or Bach.
I guess being colored doesn't make me *not* like
the same things other folks like who are other races.

So will my page be colored that I write?
Being me, it will not be white.
But it will be
a part of you, instructor.
You are white—
yet a part of me, as I am a part of you.
That's American.
Sometimes perhaps you don't want to be a part of me.
Nor do I often want to be a part of you.
But we are, that's true!
As I learn from you,
I guess you learn from me—
although you're older—and white—
and somewhat more free.

This is my page for English B.

Aunt Sue's Stories

Aunt Sue has a head full of stories.
Aunt Sue has a whole heart full of stories.
Summer nights on the front porch
Aunt Sue cuddles a brown-faced child to her bosom
And tells him stories.

Black slaves
Working in the hot sun,
And black slaves

Walking in the dewy night,
And black slaves
Singing sorrow songs on the banks of a mighty river
Mingle themselves softly
In the flow of old Aunt Sue's voice,
Mingle themselves softly
In the dark shadows that cross and recross
Aunt Sue's stories.

And the dark-faced child, listening,
Knows that Aunt Sue's stories are real stories.
He knows that Aunt Sue never got her stories
Out of any book at all,
But that they came
Right out of her own life.

The dark-faced child is quiet
Of a summer night
Listening to Aunt Sue's stories.

Feet o' Jesus

At the feet o' Jesus,
Sorrow like a sea.
Lordy, let yo' mercy
Come driftin' down on me.

At the feet o' Jesus
At yo' feet I stand.
O, ma little Jesus,
Please reach out yo' hand.

Genius Child

This is a song for the genius child.
Sing it softly, for the song is wild.
Sing it softly as ever you can—
Lest the song get out of hand.

Nobody loves a genius child.

Can you love an eagle,
Tame or wild?

Wild or tame,
Can you love a monster
Of frightening name?

Nobody loves a genius child.

Kill him—and let his soul run wild!

Listen Here Blues

Sweet girls, sweet girls,
Listen here to me.
All you sweet girls,
Listen here to me:
Gin an' whiskey
Kin make you lose yo' 'ginity.

I used to be a good chile,
Lawd, in Sunday School.
Used to be a good chile,—
In de Sunday School,
Till these licker-headed rounders
Made me everbody's fool.

Good girls, good girls,
Listen here to me.
Oh, you good girls,
Better listen to me:
Don't you fool wid no men 'cause
They'll bring you misery.

Consider Me

Consider me,
A colored boy,
Once sixteen,
Once five, once three,
Once nobody,
Now me.

Let America Be America Again

Let America be America again.
Let it be the dream it used to be.
Let it be the pioneer on the plain
Seeking the home where he himself is free.

(America never was America to me.)

Let America be the dream the dreamers dreamed—
Let it be that great strong land of love
Where never kings connive nor tyrants scheme
That any man be crushed by one above.

(It never was America to me.)

Madrid—1937

Damaged by shells, many of the clocks on the public buildings in Madrid have stopped. At night, the streets are pitch dark.

—*News Item*

Put out the lights and stop the clocks.
Let time stand still,
Again man mocks himself
And all his human will to build and grow.
    Madrid!
The fact and symbol of man's woe.
    Madrid!
Time's end and throw-back,
Birth of darkness,
Years of light reduced:
The ever minus of the brute,
The nothingness of barren land
And stone and metal,
Emptiness of gold,
The dullness of a bill of sale:
BOUGHT AND PAID FOR! SOLD!
Stupidity of hours that do not move
Because all clocks are stopped.
Blackness of nights that do not see
Because all lights are out.
    Madrid!

Beneath the bullets!
        Madrid!
Beneath the bombing planes!
        Madrid!
In the fearful dark!

Oh, mind of man!
So long to make a light
Of fire,
        of oil,
                of gas,
And now electric rays.
So long to make a clock
Of sun-dial,
        sand-dial,
                figures,
And now two hands that mark the hours.
Oh, mind of man!
So long to struggle upward out of darkness
To a measurement of time—
And now:
These guns,
These brainless killers in the Guadarrama hills
Trained on Madrid
To stop the clocks in the towers
And shatter all their faces
Into a million bits of nothingness
In the city
That will not bow its head
To darkness and to greed again:
That dares to dream a cleaner dream!
Oh, mind of man
Moulded into a metal shell—
Left-overs of the past
That rain dull hell and misery
On the world again—
Have your way
And stop the clocks!
Bomb out the lights!
And mock yourself!
Mock all the rights of those
Who live like decent folk.
Let guns alone salute

The wisdom of our age
With dusty powder marks
On yet another page of history.
Let there be no sense of time,
Nor measurement of light and dark,
In fact, no light at all!
Let mankind fall
Into the deepest pit that ignorance can dig
For us all!
Descent is quick.
To rise again is slow.
In the darkness of her broken clocks
Madrid cries NO!
In the timeless midnight of the Fasicst guns,
Madrid cries NO!
To all the killers of man's dreams,
Madrid cries NO!

To break that NO apart
Will be to break the human heart.

Madrid, September 24, 1937.

Negro Ghetto

I looked at their black faces
And this is what I saw:
The wind imprisoned in the flesh,
The sun bound down by law.
I watched them moving, moving,
Like water down the street,
And this is what moved in my heart:
Their far-too-humble feet.

Note on Commercial Theatre

You've taken my blues and gone—
You sing 'em on Broadway
And sing 'em in Hollywood Bowl,

MADRID Unpublished poem. Inscribed: "To Arthur Spingarn, Sincerely, Langston." The Arthur B. Spingarn Papers, Moorland-Spingarn Collection, Howard University Library.

And you mixed 'em up with symphonies
And you fixed 'em
So they don't sound like me.
Yep, you done taken my blues and gone.
You also took my spirituals and gone.
You put me in *Macbeth* and *Carmen Jones*
And all kinds of *Swing Mikados*
And in everything but what's about me—
But someday somebody'll
Stand up and talk about me,
And write about me—
Black and beautiful—
And sing about me,
And put on plays about me!
I reckon it'll be
Me myself!

Yes, it'll be me.

I'm Still Here

I've been scarred and battered.
My hopes the wind done scattered.
Snow has friz me, sun has baked me.
Looks like between 'em
They done tried to make me
Stop laughin', stop lovin', stop livin'—
But I don't care!
I'm still here!

Elizabeth Bishop

[1911–1979]

Elizabeth Bishop's poems, rooted in a stunning precision of observation, are grounded in clarity and attentiveness. Bishop is noted for the purity and exactness of her language as well as for its range and unpredictability. Avoiding the learned allusions to history and literature that characterize the poems of her contemporaries T. S. Eliot and Ezra Pound, Bishop also eschews the confessional, self-revelatory mode of Sylvia Plath. Her poems hold the private self in reserve, their emotion controlled and restrained. Though her poems offer a close inspection of experience, Bishop leaves much unsaid. She is a master of silence and suggestion.

Bishop's life was relatively quiet and undisturbed by the literary revolution that was occurring among her contemporaries. She was born in Massachusetts in 1911 and grew up in New England and Nova Scotia. Her father died before she reached her first birthday, and her mother was taken to a sanitarium when she was five. Bishop never saw her again. Educated at Vassar College, she later lived in Key West, Florida, and then for nearly seventeen years in Brazil. She served as poetry consultant to the Library of Congress, and she taught briefly at New York University, the University of Washington, the Massachusetts Institute of Technology, and at Harvard. She received numerous awards, including a Pulitzer Prize (1956) and a National Book Award (1970). In addition to her poetry, she wrote short fiction and she also translated Brazilian poetry.

Bishop's poetic subjects are conveniently reflected in the titles of her books, especially *North and South* (1946), *Questions of Travel* (1965), and *Geography III* (1976). Her poems, however, are not merely about the literal places that inspired them; they are more than pictures of those places. Characteristically speculative in tone, Bishop's poems raise questions about foreign landscapes and experiences, conveying a sense of their strangeness. In "Questions of Travel," for example, she asks whether it is right "to be watching strangers in a play / in this strangest of theatres?"—a foreign country. She also wonders whether it is a "lack of imagination that makes us come / to imagined places."

Bishop's poems exhibit a tendency to combine the factual with the fanciful, the imaginary with the real. Her poems are both realistic and surrealistic, a combination evident in the following lines from "The Monument":

> What is that?"
>   It is the monument.
> "It's piled-up boxes
> outlined with shoddy fret-work, half-fallen off,
> cracked and unpainted. It looks old."
> —The strong sunlight, the wind from the sea,
> all the conditions of its existence,
> may have flaked off the paint, if ever it was painted,
> and made it homelier than it was.
> "Why did you bring me here to see it?
> A temple of crates in cramped and created scenery,
> what can it prove?
> I am tired of breathing this eroded air,
> this dryness in which the monument is cracking."
> It is an artifact
> of wood. Wood holds together better
> than sea or cloud or sand could by itself,
> much better than real sea or sand or cloud.
> It chose that way to grow and not to move.
> The monument's an object, yet those decorations,
> carelessly nailed, looking like nothing at all,
> give it away as having life, and wishing;
> wanting to be a monument, to cherish something.

The crudest scroll-work says "commemorate,"
while once each day the light goes around it
like a prowling animal,
or the rain falls on it, or the wind blows into it.
It may be solid, may be hollow.
The bones of the artist-prince may be inside
or far away on even drier soil.
But roughly but adequately it can shelter
what is within (which after all
cannot have been intended to be seen).
It is the beginning of a painting,
a piece of sculpture, or poem, or monument,
and all of wood. Watch it closely.

These lines invite the reader to watch closely—not just the monument but any object of perception—since the mind can transform reality, embroidering fact with fanciful imaginings. In the poem, Bishop's speaker demonstrates the process, commemorating both the unlikely monument itself and the act of imaginative perception whereby it is observed and transfigured. The acts of mind involved share something with the work of the naturalist observer who is part scientist and part visionary poet; for Bishop, Charles Darwin represents such a luminous conjunction of reality and imaginative vision. But Bishop's acts of seeing were more important than even this blending of reality and imagination would suggest. For Bishop, as Helen McNeil has pointed out, "to look was to act, an action that for her carried moral weight." The pleasures of perception thus extend beyond precision of seeing through dreamlike imagining and into moral imperative.

The qualities that distinguish Bishop's poetry include more, however, than her keen observations and imaginings. They extend, as Joseph Summers has noted, to an impeccable ear for language, a purity of diction, and a delicacy of tone that echo the work of the seventeenth-century metaphysical poet George Herbert. Like Herbert, though not as extensively, Bishop wrote poems in a wide variety of forms—among them prose poems, blank verse, song, quatrain, sonnet, sestina, and villanelle. The following poem reveals both Bishop's attention to external detail and her precision of language. It also illustrates her striking ability to offer a fresh perspective—in this case, the point of view of a bird running along an ocean beach.

Sandpiper

The roaring alongside he takes for granted,
and that every so often the world is bound to shake.
He runs, he runs to the south, finical, awkward,
in a state of controlled panic, a student of Blake.

The beach hisses like fat. On his left, a sheet
of interrupting water comes and goes
and glazes over his dark and brittle feet.
He runs, he runs straight through it, watching his toes.

—Watching, rather, the spaces of sand between them,
where (no detail too small) the Atlantic drains
rapidly backwards and downwards. As he runs,
he stares at the dragging grains.

The world is a mist. And then the world is
minute and vast and clear. The tide
is higher or lower. He couldn't tell you which.
His beak is focussed; he is preoccupied,

looking for something, something, something.
Poor bird, he is obsessed!
The millions of grains are black, white, tan, and gray,
mixed with quartz grains, rose and amethyst.

Bishop suggests the bird's acceptance of the way its "world is bound to shake" as the surf hits the beach. That the bird runs is not surprising and is easy enough to imagine. What is surprising is Bishop's description of that running as a "state of controlled panic" and as something "finical," an archaic word meaning finicky, or overdetailed. Equally original is the humorous allusion to William Blake, who wrote, in "Auguries of Innocence," that it is possible to see "a world in a grain of sand." Whereas for Blake such an act of imaginative perception was a sign of human wonder in the face of the splendor of nature, Bishop's ironic wit readapts Blake's perspective to illustrate the sandpiper's obsessive failure of imagination. The sandpiper is unable to see large things like the relative height of the tide because it is obsessed with minutiae like the grains of sand. Without Bishop's stating it directly, the poem describes the limitations of perception that result from a relentless preoccupation with detail, a focused narrowness that blocks the meditative imagination.

The details of stanza 2 are just as fresh: the beach hissing "like fat"; the "sheet" of sea water "interrupting" the sandpiper's watchful searching; the water glazing the bird's toes. Bishop's descriptive precision extends to the bird's direction: he runs south with the ocean on his left. And it accurately reflects the direction of the ocean's draining: "rapidly backwards and downwards"—from the bird's point of view. The linguistic precision includes the aptly chosen "dragging" to describe the grains of sand, and the repetition of "something, something, something" to mimic the sandpiper's obsessive looking. In noticing such attention to detail, we begin to appreciate Bishop's poetic accomplishment. Perhaps even more remarkable is the way Bishop surrenders herself to the object, an ability she shares with the great English Romantic poet John Keats, for whom this empathic capability was the essential poetic act. This imaginative empathy is among Bishop's most astonishing poetic qualities.

The Man-Moth

Here, above,
cracks in the buildings are filled with battered moonlight.
The whole shadow of Man is only as big as his hat.
It lies at his feet like a circle for a doll to stand on,
and he makes an inverted pin, the point magnetized to the moon.
He does not see the moon; he observes only her vast properties,
feeling the queer light on his hands, neither warm nor cold,
of a temperature impossible to record in thermometers.

But when the Man-Moth
pays his rare, although occasional, visits to the surface,
the moon looks rather different to him. He emerges
from an opening under the edge of one of the sidewalks
and nervously begins to scale the faces of the buildings.

Man-Moth: *Newspaper misprint for "mammoth."*

He thinks the moon is a small hole at the top of the sky,
proving the sky quite useless for protection.
He trembles, but must investigate as high as he can climb.

Up the façades,
his shadow dragging like a photographer's cloth behind him,
he climbs fearfully, thinking that this time he will manage
to push his small head through that round clean opening
and be forced through, as from a tube, in black scrolls on the light.
(Man, standing below him, has no such illusions.)
But what the Man-Moth fears most he must do, although
he fails, of course, and falls back scared but quite unhurt.

Then he returns
to the pale subways of cement he calls his home. He flits,
he flutters, and cannot get aboard the silent trains
fast enough to suit him. The doors close swiftly.
The Man-Moth always seats himself facing the wrong way
and the train starts at once at its full, terrible speed,
without a shift in gears or a gradation of any sort.
He cannot tell the rate at which he travels backwards.

Each night he must
be carried through artificial tunnels and dream recurrent dreams.
Just as the ties recur beneath his train, these underlie
his rushing brain. He does not dare look out the window,
for the third rail, the unbroken draught of poison,
runs there beside him. He regards it as a disease
he has inherited the susceptibility to. He has to keep
his hands in his pockets, as others must wear mufflers.

If you catch him,
hold up a flashlight to his eye. It's all dark pupil,
an entire night itself, whose haired horizon tightens
as he stares back, and closes up the eye. Then from the lids
one tear, his only possession, like the bee's sting, slips.
Slyly he palms it, and if you're not paying attention
he'll swallow it. However, if you watch, he'll hand it over,
cool as from underground springs and pure enough to drink.

Elizabeth Bishop

The Shampoo

The still explosions on the rocks,
the lichens, grow
by spreading, gray, concentric shocks.
They have arranged
to meet the rings around the moon, although
within our memories they have not changed.

And since the heavens will attend
as long on us,
you've been, dear friend,
precipitate and pragmatical;
and look what happens. For Time is
nothing if not amenable.

The shooting stars in your black hair
in bright formation
are flocking where,
so straight, so soon?
—Come, let me wash it in this big tin basin,
battered and shiny like the moon.

Seascape

This celestial seascape, with white herons got up as angels,
flying as high as they want and as far as they want sidewise
in tiers and tiers of immaculate reflections;
the whole region, from the highest heron
down to the weightless mangrove island
with bright green leaves edged neatly with bird-droppings
like illumination in silver,
and down to the suggestively Gothic arches of the mangrove
   roots
and the beautiful pea-green back-pasture
where occasionally a fish jumps, like a wild-flower
in an ornamental spray of spray;
this cartoon by Raphael for a tapestry for a Pope:
it does look like heaven.
But a skeletal lighthouse standing there
in black and white clerical dress,

on his nerves, thinks he knows better.
, that hell rages below his iron feet,
is why the shallow water is so warm,
knows that heaven is not like this.
is not like flying or swimming,
Bu s something to do with blackness and a strong glare
and when it gets dark he will remember something
strongly worded to say on the subject.

The Map

Land lies in water; it is shadowed green.
Shadows, or are they shallows, at its edges
showing the line of long sea-weeded ledges
where weeds hang to the simple blue from green.
Or does the land lean down to lift the sea from under,
drawing it unperturbed around itself?
Along the fine tan sandy shelf
is the land tugging at the sea from under?

The shadow of Newfoundland lies flat and still.
Labrador's yellow, where the moony Eskimo
has oiled it. We can stroke these lovely bays,
under a glass as if they were expected to blossom,
or as if to provide a clean cage for invisible fish.
The names of seashore towns run out to sea,
the names of cities cross the neighboring mountains
—the printer here experiencing the same excitement
as when emotion too far exceeds its cause.
These peninsulas take the water between thumb and finger
like women feeling for the smoothness of yard-goods.

Mapped waters are more quiet than the land is,
lending the land their waves' own conformation:
and Norway's hare runs south in agitation,
profiles investigate the sea, where land is.
Are they assigned, or can the countries pick their colors?
—What suits the character or the native waters best.
Topography displays no favorites; North's as near as West.
More delicate than the historians' are the map-makers' colors.

The Monument

Now can you see the monument? It is of wood
built somewhat like a box. No. Built
like several boxes in descending sizes
one above the other.
Each is turned half-way round so that
its corners point toward the sides
of the one below and the angles alternate.
Then on the topmost cube is set
a sort of fleur-de-lys of weathered wood,
long petals of board, pierced with odd holes,
four-sided, stiff, ecclesiastical.
From it four thin, warped poles spring out,
(slanted like fishing-poles or flag-poles)
and from them jig-saw work hangs down,
four lines of vaguely whittled ornament
over the edges of the boxes
to the ground.
The monument is one-third set against
a sea; two-thirds against a sky.
The view is geared
(that is, the view's perspective)
so low there is no "far away,"
and we are far away within the view.
A sea of narrow, horizontal boards
lies out behind our lonely monument,
its long grains alternating right and left
like floor-boards—spotted, swarming-still,
and motionless. A sky runs parallel,
and it is palings, coarser than the sea's:
splintery sunlight and long-fibred clouds.
"Why does that strange sea make no sound?
Is it because we're far away?
Where are we? Are we in Asia Minor,
or in Mongolia?"
                An ancient promontory,
an ancient principality whose artist-prince
might have wanted to build a monument
to mark a tomb or boundary, or make
a melancholy or romantic scene of it . . .

"But that queer sea looks made of wood,
half-shining, like a driftwood sea.
And the sky looks wooden, grained with cloud.
It's like a stage-set; it is all so flat!
Those clouds are full of glistening splinters!
What is that?"
It is the monument.
"It's piled-up boxes,
outlined with shoddy fret-work, half-fallen off,
cracked and unpainted. It looks old."
—The strong sunlight, the wind from the sea,
all the conditions of its existence,
may have flaked off the paint, if ever it was painted,
and made it homelier than it was.
"Why did you bring me here to see it?
A temple of crates in cramped and crated scenery,
what can it prove?
I am tired of breathing this eroded air,
this dryness in which the monument is cracking."
It is an artifact
of wood. Wood holds together better
than sea or cloud or sand could by itself,
much better than real sea or sand or cloud.
It chose that way to grow and not to move.
The monument's an object, yet those decorations,
carelessly nailed, looking like nothing at all,
give it away as having life, and wishing;
wanting to be a monument, to cherish something.
The crudest scroll-work says "commemorate,"
while once each day the light goes around it
like a prowling animal,
or the rain falls on it, or the wind blows into it.
It may be solid, may be hollow.
The bones of the artist-prince may be inside
or far away on even drier soil.
But roughly but adequately it can shelter
what is within (which after all
cannot have been intended to be seen).
It is the beginning of a painting,
a piece of sculpture, or poem, or monument,
and all of wood. Watch it closely.

The Unbeliever

He sleeps on the top of a mast.
—BUNYAN

He sleeps on the top of a mast
with his eyes fast closed.
The sails fall away below him
like the sheets of his bed,
leaving out in the air of the night the sleeper's head.

Asleep he was transported there,
asleep he curled
in a gilded ball on the mast's top,
or climbed inside
a gilded bird, or blindly seated himself astride.

"I am founded on marble pillars,"
said a cloud. "I never move.
See the pillars there in the sea?"
Secure in introspection
he peers at the watery pillars of his reflection.

A gull had wings under his
and remarked that the air
was "like marble." He said: "Up here
I tower through the sky
for the marble wings on my tower-top fly."

But he sleeps on the top of his mast
with his eyes closed tight.
The gull inquired into his dream,
which was, "I must not fall.
The spangled sea below wants me to fall.
It is hard as diamonds; it wants to destroy us all."

The Fish

I caught a tremendous fish
and held him beside the boat
half out of water, with my hook
fast in a corner of his mouth.
He didn't fight.

He hadn't fought at all.
He hung a grunting weight,
battered and venerable
and homely. Here and there
his brown skin hung in strips
like ancient wallpaper,
and its pattern of darker brown
was like wallpaper:
shapes like full-blown roses
stained and lost through age.
He was speckled with barnacles,
fine rosettes of lime,
and infested
with tiny white sea-lice,
and underneath two or three
rags of green weed hung down.
While his gills were breathing in
the terrible oxygen
—the frightening gills,
fresh and crisp with blood,
that can cut so badly—
I thought of the coarse white flesh
packed in like feathers,
the big bones and the little bones,
the dramatic reds and blacks
of his shiny entrails,
and the pink swim-bladder
like a big peony.
I looked into his eyes
which were far larger than mine
but shallower, and yellowed,
the irises backed and packed
with tarnished tinfoil
seen through the lenses
of old scratched isinglass.
They shifted a little, but not
to return my stare.
—It was more like the tipping
of an object toward the light.
I admired his sullen face,
the mechanism of his jaw,
and then I saw

that from his lower lip
—if you could call it a lip—
grim, wet, and weaponlike,
hung five old pieces of fish-line,
or four and a wire leader
with the swivel still attached,
with all their five big hooks
grown firmly in his mouth.
A green line, frayed at the end
where he broke it, two heavier lines,
and a fine black thread
still crimped from the strain and snap
when it broke and he got away.
Like medals with their ribbons
frayed and wavering,
a five-haired beard of wisdom
trailing from his aching jaw.
I stared and stared
and victory filled up
the little rented boat,
from the pool of bilge
where oil had spread a rainbow
around the rusted engine
to the bailer rusted orange,
the sun-cracked thwarts,
the oarlocks on their strings,
the gunnels—until everything
was rainbow, rainbow, rainbow!
And I let the fish go.

At the Fishhouses

Although it is a cold evening,
down by one of the fishhouses
an old man sits netting,
his net, in the gloaming almost invisible
a dark purple-brown
and his shuttle worn and polished.
The air smells so strong of codfish
it makes one's nose run and one's eyes water.
The five fishhouses have steeply peaked roofs

and narrow, cleated gangplanks slant up
to storerooms in the gables
for the wheelbarrows to be pushed up and down on.
All is silver: the heavy surface of the sea,
swelling slowly as if considering spilling over,
is opaque, but the silver of the benches,
the lobster pots, and masts, scattered
among the wild jagged rocks,
is of an apparent translucence
like the small old buildings with an emerald moss
growing on their shoreward walls.
The big fish tubs are completely lined
with layers of beautiful herring scales
and the wheelbarrows are similarly plastered
with creamy iridescent coats of mail,
with small iridescent flies crawling on them.
Up on the little slope behind the houses,
set in the sparse bright sprinkle of grass,
is an ancient wooden capstan,
cracked, with two long bleached handles
and some melancholy stains, like dried blood,
where the ironwork has rusted.
The old man accepts a Lucky Strike.
He was a friend of my grandfather.
We talk of the decline in the population
and of codfish and herring
while he waits for a herring boat to come in.
There are sequins on his vest and on his thumb.
He has scraped the scales, the principal beauty,
from unnumbered fish with that black old knife,
the blade of which is almost worn away.

Down at the water's edge, at the place
where they haul up the boats, up the long ramp
descending into the water, thin silver
tree trunks are laid horizontally
across the gray stones, down and down
at intervals of four or five feet.

Cold dark deep and absolutely clear,
element bearable to no mortal,
to fish and to seals . . . One seal particularly
I have seen here evening after evening.

He was curious about me. He was interested in music;
like me a believer in total immersion,
so I used to sing him Baptist hymns.
I also sang "A Mighty Fortress Is Our God."
He stood up in the water and regarded me
steadily, moving his head a little.
Then he would disappear, then suddenly emerge
almost in the same spot, with a sort of shrug
as if it were against his better judgment.
Cold dark deep and absolutely clear,
the clear gray icy water . . . Back, behind us,
the dignified tall firs begin.
Bluish, associating with their shadows,
a million Christmas trees stand
waiting for Christmas. The water seems suspended
above the rounded gray and blue-gray stones.
I have seen it over and over, the same sea, the same,
slightly, indifferently swinging above the stones,
icily free above the stones,
above the stones and then the world.
If you should dip your hand in,
your wrist would ache immediately,
your bones would begin to ache and your hand would burn
as if the water were a transmutation of fire
that feeds on stones and burns with a dark gray flame.
If you tasted it, it would first taste bitter,
then briny, then surely burn your tongue.
It is like what we imagine knowledge to be:
dark, salt, clear, moving, utterly free,
drawn from the cold hard mouth
of the world, derived from the rocky breasts
forever, flowing and drawn, and since
our knowledge is historical, flowing, and flown.

The Moose

FOR GRACE BULMER BOWERS

From narrow provinces
of fish and bread and tea,
home of the long tides
where the bay leaves the sea

twice a day and takes
the herrings long rides,

where if the river
enters or retreats
in a wall of brown foam
depends on if it meets
the bay coming in,
the bay not at home;

where, silted red,
sometimes the sun sets
facing a red sea,
and others, veins the flats'
lavender, rich mud
in burning rivulets;

on red, gravelly roads,
down rows of sugar maples,
past clapboard farmhouses
and neat, clapboard churches,
bleached, ridged as clamshells,
past twin silver birches,

through late afternoon
a bus journeys west,
the windshield flashing pink,
pink glancing off of metal,
brushing the dented flank
of blue, beat-up enamel;

down hollows, up rises,
and waits, patient, while
a lone traveller gives
kisses and embraces
to seven relatives
and a collie supervises.

Goodbye to the elms,
to the farm, to the dog.
The bus starts. The light
grows richer; the fog,
shifting, salty, thin,
comes closing in.

Its cold, round crystals
form and slide and settle
in the white hens' feathers,
in gray glazed cabbages,
on the cabbage roses
and lupins like apostles;

the sweet peas cling
to their wet white string
on the whitewashed fences;
bumblebees creep
inside the foxgloves,
and evening commences.

One stop at Bass River.
Then the Economies—
Lower, Middle, Upper;
Five Islands, Five Houses,
where a woman shakes a tablecloth
out after supper.

A pale flickering. Gone.
The Tantramar marshes
and the smell of salt hay.
An iron bridge trembles
and a loose plank rattles
but doesn't give way.

On the left, a red light
swims through the dark:
a ship's port lantern.
Two rubber boots show,
illuminated, solemn.
A dog gives one bark.

A woman climbs in
with two market bags,
brisk, freckled, elderly.
"A grand night. Yes, sir,
all the way to Boston."
She regards us amicably.

Moonlight as we enter
the New Brunswick woods,
hairy, scratchy, splintery;
moonlight and mist
caught in them like lamb's wool
on bushes in a pasture.

The passengers lie back.
Snores. Some long sighs.
A dreamy divagation
begins in the night,
a gentle, auditory,
slow hallucination. . . .

In the creakings and noises,
an old conversation
—not concerning us,
but recognizable, somewhere,
back in the bus:
Grandparents' voices

uninterruptedly
talking, in Eternity:
names being mentioned,
things cleared up finally;
what he said, what she said,
who got pensioned;

deaths, deaths and sicknesses;
the year he remarried;
the year (something) happened.
She died in childbirth.
That was the son lost
when the schooner foundered.

He took to drink. Yes.
She went to the bad.
When Amos began to pray
even in the store and
finally the family had
to put him away.

"Yes . . ." that peculiar
affirmative. "Yes . . ."
A sharp, indrawn breath,
half groan, half acceptance,
that means "Life's like that.
We know *it* (also death)."

Talking the way they talked
in the old featherbed,
peacefully, on and on,
dim lamplight in the hall,
down in the kitchen, the dog
tucked in her shawl.

Now, it's all right now
even to fall asleep
just as on all those nights
—Suddenly the bus driver
stops with a jolt,
turns off his lights.

A moose has come out of
the impenetrable wood
and stands there, looms, rather,
in the middle of the road.
It approaches; it sniffs at
the bus's hot hood.

Towering, antlerless,
high as a church,
homely as a house
(or, safe as houses).
A man's voice assures us
"Perfectly harmless. . . ."

Some of the passengers
exclaim in whispers,
childishly, softly,
"Sure are big creatures."
"It's awful plain."
"Look! It's a she!"

Taking her time,
she looks the bus over,
grand, otherworldly.
Why, why do we feel
(we all feel) this sweet
sensation of joy?

"Curious creatures,"
says our quiet driver,
rolling his *r*'s.
"Look at that, would you."
Then he shifts gears.
For a moment longer,

by craning backward,
the moose can be seen
on the moonlit macadam;
then there's a dim
smell of moose, an acrid
smell of gasoline.

Questions of Travel

There are too many waterfalls here; the crowded streams
hurry too rapidly down to the sea,
and the pressure of so many clouds on the mountaintops
makes them spill over the sides in soft slow-motion,
turning to waterfalls under our very eyes.
—For if those streaks, those mile-long, shiny, tearstains,
aren't waterfalls yet,
in a quick age or so, as ages go here,
they probably will be.
But if the streams and clouds keep travelling, travelling,
the mountains look like the hulls of capsized ships,
slime-hung and barnacled.

Think of the long trip home.
Should we have stayed at home and thought of here?
Where should we be today?
Is it right to be watching strangers in a play
in this strangest of theatres?
What childishness is it that while there's a breath of life

in our bodies, we are determined to rush
to see the sun the other way around?
The tiniest green hummingbird in the world?
To stare at some inexplicable old stonework,
inexplicable and impenetrable,
at any view,
instantly seen and always, always delightful?
Oh, must we dream our dreams
and have them, too?
And have we room
for one more folded sunset, still quite warm?

But surely it would have been a pity
not to have seen the trees along this road,
really exaggerated in their beauty,
not to have seen them gesturing
like noble pantomimists, robed in pink.
—Not to have had to stop for gas and heard
the sad, two-noted, wooden tune
of disparate wooden clogs
carelessly clacking over
a grease-stained filling-station floor.
(In another country the clogs would all be tested.
Each pair there would have identical pitch.)
—A pity not to have heard
the other, less primitive music of the fat brown bird
who sings above the broken gasoline pump
in a bamboo church of Jesuit baroque:
three towers, five silver crosses.
—Yes, a pity not to have pondered,
blurr'dly and inconclusively,
on what connection can exist for centuries
between the crudest wooden footwear
and, careful and finicky,
the whittled fantasies of wooden cages.
—Never to have studied history in
the weak calligraphy of songbirds' cages.
—And never to have had to listen to rain
so much like politicians' speeches:
two hours of unrelenting oratory
and then a sudden golden silence
in which the traveller takes a notebook, writes:

"Is it lack of imagination that makes us come
to imagined places, not just stay at home?
Or could Pascal have been not entirely right
about just sitting quietly in one's room?

Continent, city, country, society:
the choice is never wide and never free.
And here, or there . . . No. Should we have stayed at home,
wherever that may be?"

The Armadillo

FOR ROBERT LOWELL

This is the time of year
when almost every night
the frail, illegal fire balloons appear.
Climbing the mountain height,

rising toward a saint
still honored in these parts,
the paper chambers flush and fill with light
that comes and goes, like hearts.

Once up against the sky it's hard
to tell them from the stars—
planets, that is—the tinted ones:
Venus going down, or Mars,

or the pale green one. With a wind,
they flare and falter, wobble and toss;
but if it's still they steer between
the kite sticks of the Southern Cross,

receding, dwindling, solemnly
and steadily forsaking us,
or, in the downdraft from a peak,
suddenly turning dangerous.

Last night another big one fell.
It splattered like an egg of fire
against the cliff behind the house.
The flame ran down. We saw the pair

of owls who nest there flying up
and up, their whirling black-and-white
stained bright pink underneath, until
they shrieked up out of sight.

The ancient owls' nest must have burned.
Hastily, all alone,
a glistening armadillo left the scene,
rose-flecked, head down, tail down,

and then a baby rabbit jumped out,
short-eared, to our surprise.
So soft!—a handful of intangible ash
with fixed, ignited eyes.

Too pretty, dreamlike mimicry!
O falling fire and piercing cry
and panic, and a weak mailed fist
clenched ignorant against the sky!

Argument

Days that cannot bring you near
or will not,
Distance trying to appear
something more than obstinate,
argue argue argue with me
endlessly
neither proving you less wanted nor less dear.

Distance: Remember all that land
beneath the plane;
that coastline
of dim beaches deep in sand
stretching indistinguishably
all the way,
all the way to where my reasons end?

Days: And think
of all those cluttered instruments,
one to a fact,
canceling each other's experience;
how they were

like some hideous calendar
"Compliments of Never & Forever, Inc."

The intimidating sound
of these voices
we must separately find
can and shall be vanquished:
Days and Distance disarrayed again
and gone
both for good and from the gentle battleground.

Sestina

September rain falls on the house.
In the failing light, the old grandmother
sits in the kitchen with the child
beside the Little Marvel Stove,
reading the jokes from the almanac,
laughing and talking to hide her tears.

She thinks that her equinoctial tears
and the rain that beats on the roof of the house
were both foretold by the almanac,
but only known to a grandmother.
The iron kettle sings on the stove.
She cuts some bread and says to the child,

It's time for tea now; but the child
is watching the teakettle's small hard tears
dance like mad on the hot black stove,
the way the rain must dance on the house.
Tidying up, the old grandmother
hangs up the clever almanac

on its string. Birdlike, the almanac
hovers half open above the child,
hovers above the old grandmother
and her teacup full of dark brown tears.
She shivers and says she thinks the house
feels chilly and puts more wood on the stove.

It was to be, says the Marvel Stove.
I know what I know, says the almanac.
With crayons the child draws a rigid house
and a winding pathway. Then the child
puts in a man with buttons like tears
and shows it proudly to the grandmother.

But secretly, while the grandmother
busies herself about the stove,
the little moons fall down like tears
from between the pages of the almanac
into the flower bed the child
has carefully placed in the front of the house.

Time to plant tears, says the almanac.
The grandmother sings to the marvellous stove
and the child draws another inscrutable house.

The Prodigal

The brown enormous odor he lived by
was too close, with its breathing and thick hair,
for him to judge. The floor was rotten; the sty
was plastered halfway up with glass-smooth dung.
Light-lashed, self-righteous, above moving snouts,
the pigs' eyes followed him, a cheerful stare—
even to the sow that always ate her young—
till, sickening, he leaned to scratch her head.
But sometimes mornings after drinking bouts
(he hid the pints behind a two-by-four),
the sunrise glazed the barnyard mud with red;
the burning puddles seemed to reassure.
And then he thought he almost might endure
his exile yet another year or more.

But evenings the first star came to warn.
The farmer whom he worked for came at dark
to shut the cows and horses in the barn
beneath their overhanging clouds of hay,
with pitchforks, faint forked lightnings, catching light,
safe and companionable as in the Ark.

The pigs stuck out their little feet and snored.
The lantern—like the sun, going away—
laid on the mud a pacing aureole.
Carrying a bucket along a slimy board,
he felt the bats' uncertain staggering flight,
his shuddering insights, beyond his control,
touching him. But it took him a long time
finally to make his mind up to go home.

In the Waiting Room

In Worcester, Massachusetts,
I went with Aunt Consuelo
to keep her dentist's appointment
and sat and waited for her
in the dentist's waiting room.

It was winter. It got dark
early. The waiting room
was full of grown-up people,
arctics and overcoats,
lamps and magazines.
My aunt was inside
what seemed like a long time
and while I waited I read
the *National Geographic*
(I could read) and carefully
studied the photographs:
the inside of a volcano,
black, and full of ashes;
then it was spilling over
in rivulets of fire.
Osa and Martin Johnson
dressed in riding breeches,
laced boots, and pith helmets.
A dead man slung on a pole
—"Long Pig," the caption said.
Babies with pointed heads
wound round and round with string;
black, naked women with necks
wound round and round with wire

like the necks of light bulbs.
Their breasts were horrifying.
I read it right straight through.
I was too shy to stop.
And then I looked at the cover:
the yellow margins, the date.

Suddenly, from inside,
came an *oh!* of pain
—Aunt Consuelo's voice—
not very loud or long.
I wasn't at all surprised;
even then I knew she was
a foolish, timid woman.
I might have been embarrassed,
but wasn't. What took me
completely by surprise
was that it was *me:*
my voice, in my mouth.
Without thinking at all
I was my foolish aunt,
I—we—were falling, falling,
our eyes glued to the cover
of the *National Geographic,*
February, 1918.

I said to myself: three days
and you'll be seven years old.
I was saying it to stop
the sensation of falling off
the round, turning world
into cold, blue-black space.
But I felt: you are an *I,*
you are an *Elizabeth,*
you are one of *them.*
Why should you be one, too?
I scarcely dared to look
to see what it was I was.
I gave a sidelong glance
—I couldn't look any higher—
at shadowy gray knees,
trousers and skirts and boots

and different pairs of hands
lying under the lamps.
I knew that nothing stranger
had ever happened, that nothing
stranger could ever happen.
Why should I be my aunt,
or me, or anyone?
What similarities—
boots, hands, the family voice
I felt in my throat, or even
the *National Geographic*
and those awful hanging breasts—
held us all together
or made us all just one?
How—I didn't know any
word for it—how "unlikely" . . .
How had I come to be here,
like them, and overhear
a cry of pain that could have
got loud and worse but hadn't?
The waiting room was bright
and too hot. It was sliding
beneath a big black wave,
another, and another.

Then I was back in it.
The War was on. Outside,
in Worcester, Massachusetts,
were night and slush and cold,
and it was still the fifth
of February, 1918.

Santarém

Of course I may be remembering it all wrong
after, after—how many years?

That golden evening I really wanted to go no farther;
more than anything else I wanted to stay awhile
in that conflux of two great rivers, Tapajós, Amazon,
grandly, silently flowing, flowing east.

Suddenly there'd been houses, people, and lots of mongrel
riverboats skittering back and forth
under a sky of gorgeous, under-lit clouds,
with everything gilded, burnished along one side,
and everything bright, cheerful, casual—or so it looked.
I liked the place; I liked the idea of the place.
Two rivers. Hadn't two rivers sprung
from the Garden of Eden? No, that was four
and they'd diverged. Here only two
and coming together. Even if one were tempted
to literary interpretations
such as: life/death, right/wrong, male/female
—such notions would have resolved, dissolved, straight off
in that watery, dazzling dialectic.

In front of the church, the Cathedral, rather,
there was a modest promenade and a belvedere
about to fall into the river,
stubby palms, flamboyants like pans of embers,
buildings one story high, stucco, blue or yellow,
and one house faced with *azulejos,* buttercup yellow.
The street was deep in dark-gold river sand
damp from the ritual afternoon rain,
and teams of zebus plodded, gentle, proud,
and *blue,* with down-curved horns and hanging ears,
pulling carts with solid wheels.
The zebus' hooves, the people's feet
waded in golden sand,
dampered by golden sand,
so that almost the only sounds
were creaks and *shush, shush, shush.*

Two rivers full of crazy shipping—people
all apparently changing their minds, embarking,
disembarking, rowing clumsy dories.
(After the Civil War some Southern families
came here; here they could still own slaves.
They left occasional blue eyes, English names,
and *oars.* No other place, no one
on all the Amazon's four thousand miles
does anything but paddle.)
A dozen or so young nuns, white-habited,

waved gaily from an old stern-wheeler
getting up steam, already hung with hammocks
—off to their mission, days and days away
up God knows what lost tributary.
Side-wheelers, countless wobbling dugouts . . .
A cow stood up in one, quite calm,
chewing her cud while being ferried,
tipping, wobbling, somewhere, to be married.
A river schooner with raked masts
and violet-colored sails tacked in so close
her bowsprit seemed to touch the church

(Cathedral, rather!). A week or so before
there'd been a thunderstorm and the Cathedral'd
been struck by lightning. One tower had
a widening zigzag crack all the way down.
It was a miracle. The priest's house right next door
had been struck, too, and his brass bed
(the only one in town) galvanized black.
Graças a deus—he'd been in Belém.

In the blue pharmacy the pharmacist
had hung an empty wasps' nest from a shelf:
small, exquisite, clean matte white,
and hard as stucco. I admired it
so much he gave it to me.

Then—my ship's whistle blew. I couldn't stay.
Back on board, a fellow-passenger, Mr. Swan,
Dutch, the retiring head of Philips Electric,
really a very nice old man,
who wanted to see the Amazon before he died,
asked, "What's that ugly thing?"

Pink Dog

[Rio de Janeiro]

The sun is blazing and the sky is blue.
Umbrellas clothe the beach in every hue.
Naked, you trot across the avenue.

Oh, never have I seen a dog so bare!
Naked and pink, without a single hair . . .
Startled, the passersby draw back and stare.

Of course they're mortally afraid of rabies.
You are not mad; you have a case of scabies
but look intelligent. Where are your babies?

(A nursing mother, by those hanging teats.)
In what slum have you hidden them, poor bitch,
while you go begging, living by your wits?

Didn't you know? It's been in all the papers,
to solve this problem, how they deal with beggars?
They take and throw them in the tidal rivers.

Yes, idiots, paralytics, parasites
go bobbing in the ebbing sewage, nights
out in the suburbs, where there are no lights.

If they do this to anyone who begs,
drugged, drunk, or sober, with or without legs,
what would they do to sick, four-leggèd dogs?

In the cafés and on the sidewalk corners
the joke is going round that all the beggars
who can afford them now wear life preservers.

In your condition you would not be able
even to float, much less to dog-paddle.
Now look, the practical, the sensible

solution is to wear a *fantasía*.
Tonight you simply can't afford to be a-
n eyesore. But no one will ever see a

dog in *máscara* this time of year.
Ash Wednesday'll come but Carnival is here.
What sambas can you dance? What will you wear?

[28]**fantasía:** Carnival costume.

They say that Carnival's degenerating
—radios, Americans, or something,
have ruined it completely. They're just talking.

Carnival is always wonderful!
A depilated dog would not look well.
Dress up! Dress up and dance at Carnival!

Crusoe in England

A new volcano has erupted,
the papers say, and last week I was reading
where some ship saw an island being born:
at first a breath of steam, ten miles away;
and then a black fleck—basalt, probably—
rose in the mate's binoculars
and caught on the horizon like a fly.
They named it. But my poor old island's still
un-rediscovered, un-renamable.
None of the books has ever got it right.

Well, I had fifty-two
miserable, small volcanoes I could climb
with a few slithery strides—
volcanoes dead as ash heaps.
I used to sit on the edge of the highest one
and count the others standing up,
naked and leaden, with their heads blown off.
I'd think that if they were the size
I thought volcanoes should be, then I had
become a giant;
and if I had become a giant,
I couldn't bear to think what size
the goats and turtles were,
or the gulls, or the overlapping rollers
—a glittering hexagon of rollers
closing and closing in, but never quite,
glittering and glittering, though the sky
was mostly overcast.

My island seemed to be
a sort of cloud-dump. All the hemisphere's

left-over clouds arrived and hung
above the craters—their parched throats
were hot to touch.
Was that why it rained so much?
And why sometimes the whole place hissed?
The turtles lumbered by, high-domed,
hissing like teakettles.
(And I'd have given years, or taken a few,
for any sort of kettle, of course.)
The folds of lava, running out to sea,
would hiss. I'd turn. And then they'd prove
to be more turtles.
The beaches were all lava, variegated,
black, red, and white, and gray;
the marbled colors made a fine display.
And I had waterspouts. Oh,
half a dozen at a time, far out,
they'd come and go, advancing and retreating,
their heads in cloud, their feet in moving patches
of scuffed-up white.
Glass chimneys, flexible, attenuated,
sacerdotal beings of glass . . . I watched
the water spiral up in them like smoke.
Beautiful, yes, but not much company.

I often gave way to self-pity.
"Do I deserve this? I suppose I must.
I wouldn't be here otherwise. Was there
a moment when I actually chose this?
I don't remember, but there could have been."
What's wrong about self-pity, anyway?
With my legs dangling down familiarly
over a crater's edge, I told myself
"Pity should begin at home." So the more
pity I felt, the more I felt at home.

The sun set in the sea; the same odd sun
rose from the sea,
and there was one of it and one of me.
The island had one kind of everything:
one tree snail, a bright violet-blue
with a thin shell, crept over everything,
over the one variety of tree,

a sooty, scrub affair.
Snail shells lay under these in drifts
and, at a distance,
you'd swear that they were beds of irises.
There was one kind of berry, a dark red.
I tried it, one by one, and hours apart.
Sub-acid, and not bad, no ill effects;
and so I made home-brew. I'd drink
the awful, fizzy, stinging stuff
that went straight to my head
and play my home-made flute
(I think it had the weirdest scale on earth)
and, dizzy, whoop and dance among the goats.
Home-made, home-made! But aren't we all?
I felt a deep affection for
the smallest of my island industries.
No, not exactly, since the smallest was
a miserable philosophy.

Because I didn't know enough.
Why didn't I know enough of something?
Greek drama or astronomy? The books
I'd read were full of blanks;
the poems—well, I tried
reciting to my iris-beds,
"They flash upon that inward eye,
which is the bliss . . ." The bliss of what?
One of the first things that I did
when I got back was look it up.

The island smelled of goat and guano.
The goats were white, so were the gulls,
and both too tame, or else they thought
I was a goat, too, or a gull.
Baa, baa, baa and *shriek, shriek, shriek,*
baa . . . shriek . . . baa . . . I still can't shake
them from my ears; they're hurting now.
The questioning shrieks, the equivocal replies
over a ground of hissing rain
and hissing, ambulating turtles
got on my nerves.

When all the gulls flew up at once, they sounded
like a big tree in a strong wind, its leaves.
I'd shut my eyes and think about a tree,
an oak, say, with real shade, somewhere.
I'd heard of cattle getting island-sick.
I thought the goats were.
One billy-goat would stand on the volcano
I'd christened *Mont d'Espoir* or *Mount Despair*
(I'd time enough to play with names),
and bleat and bleat, and sniff the air.
I'd grab his beard and look at him.
His pupils, horizontal, narrowed up
and expressed nothing, or a little malice.
I got so tired of the very colors!
One day I dyed a baby goat bright red
with my red berries, just to see
something a little different.
And then his mother wouldn't recognize him.

Dreams were the worst. Of course I dreamed of food
and love, but they were pleasant rather
than otherwise. But then I'd dream of things
like slitting a baby's throat, mistaking it
for a baby goat. I'd have
nightmares of other islands
stretching away from mine, infinities
of islands, islands spawning islands,
like frogs' eggs turning into polliwogs
of islands, knowing that I had to live
on each and every one, eventually,
for ages, registering their flora,
their fauna, their geography.

Just when I thought I couldn't stand it
another minute longer, Friday came.
(Accounts of that have everything all wrong.)
Friday was nice.
Friday was nice, and we were friends.
If only he had been a woman!
I wanted to propagate my kind,
and so did he, I think, poor boy.
He'd pet the baby goats sometimes,

and race with them, or carry one around.
—Pretty to watch; he had a pretty body.

And then one day they came and took us off.

Now I live here, another island,
that doesn't seem like one, but who decides?
My blood was full of them; my brain
bred islands. But that archipelago
has petered out. I'm old.
I'm bored, too, drinking my real tea,
surrounded by uninteresting lumber.
The knife there on the shelf—
it reeked of meaning, like a crucifix.
It lived. How many years did I
beg it, implore it, not to break?
I knew each nick and scratch by heart,
the bluish blade, the broken tip,
the lines of wood-grain on the handle . . .
Now it won't look at me at all.
The living soul has dribbled away.
My eyes rest on it and pass on.

The local museum's asked me to
leave everything to them:
the flute, the knife, the shrivelled shoes,
my shedding goatskin trousers
(moths have got in the fur),
the parasol that took me such a time
remembering the way the ribs should go.
It still will work but, folded up,
looks like a plucked and skinny fowl.
How can anyone want such things?
—And Friday, my dear Friday, died of measles
seventeen years ago come March.

Robert Lowell

[1917–1977]

Robert Lowell is a poet for whom writing was as important as living. Lowell's personal experience, particularly his family history, was the animating impulse of his art. He was born into a prominent patrician Boston family that included his great-great-uncle, the nineteenth-century poet James Russell Lowell, a figure of dignified conservatism. The family also included the modern American poet and editor Amy Lowell, a distant cousin of Robert's. While his own work resembles neither the Imagist poems of Amy nor the Victorian pieties of James Russell, the curious disparity in the work of these two relatives (experimentalist versus traditionalist) is encompassed in Robert's own artistic direction. Spanning a poetic career of more than thirty years, Lowell combines in his poems conventional formalism and rebellious innovation, which at their best fuse in taut and emotionally charged verse.

True to his patrician background, Lowell enrolled at Harvard University, but after a brief unhappy stint there he transferred to Kenyon College, in Ohio, where he studied with the influential poet and critic John Crowe Ransom. After graduation, he studied at Louisiana State University, where he came under the influence of the prominent critics Cleanth Brooks and Robert Penn Warren. Lowell's early work shows the influence of all three in its tight formal structure, its imagistic cohesiveness, its religious disposition, and its richly metaphorical rhetoric—poetic strategies he would modify and reconstitute in his later work.

Lowell later worked briefly as an editorial assistant for the Catholic publishing house of Sheed and Ward (1941–1942) and served as poetry consultant for the Library of Congress (1947–1948). He taught at a number of universities including the University of Iowa, Boston University, Harvard University, and the University of Essex, in England. He was awarded a number of prizes, including a Pulitzer Prize in 1947 for *Lord Weary's Castle,* a National Book Award in 1960 for *Life Studies,* and in 1962 a Bollingen Poetry Prize for *Imitations.*

Lowell is also noteworthy for his political activity. During World War II he refused to register for the draft on grounds of conscientious objection. Sentenced to a year in prison, Lowell served five months. In the mid-1960s he declined an invitation from President Lyndon Johnson to attend the White House Festival of the Arts; Lowell instead took the opportunity to protest the Vietnam War. During the same period, he campaigned for Senator Eugene McCarthy, a presidential candidate whose antiwar views he shared. Lowell was also one of a group of writers, which included Norman Mailer, who led a small army of peaceful protesters to the Pentagon in 1967.

Lowell was married three times, first to the fiction writer Jean Stafford, later to the critic Elizabeth Hardwick, and finally to Lady Caroline Blackwood. He treated his marriages and divorces as subjects for his poems, especially in the three volumes published together in 1973—*For Lizzie and Harriet, History,* and *The Dolphin.* Domestic turmoil forms one of four central concerns of Lowell's life and work; the others are alcoholism, mental illness, for which he was twice hospitalized, and the impoverished quality of contemporary life. After an illustrious and influential career as a commanding presence in American poetry, Lowell died of a heart attack in 1977.

Lowell's poetry can be divided into three phases, represented respectively by *Lord Weary's Castle, Life Studies,* and *History* and *The Dolphin.* The poetry of the early stage is formally tight, with heavy doses of Christian and classical allusion and a high voltage of angry rhetoric, as "The Quaker Graveyard in Nantucket" reveals. In his middle stage, Lowell's subjects are more personal and his style looser. These poems are more restrained in tone and are occasionally almost proselike in their familiar diction and syntax; see, for example, "My Last Afternoon with Uncle Devereux Winslow" (p. 590). In his final phase, Lowell returns to the dense poetic textures of the early period, but his work is more compressed and he has firmer control over his linguistic resources, especially tone. "Epilogue" is a memorable example. Though not without their anguish and pain, the later poems are generally more elegiac than those that preceded them, with the possible exception of some of the work from *Life Studies*.

Lowell's poetry is generally energized by struggle and galvanized by guilt. His poems reflect his rebellion against his patrician upbringing and his eminent New England lineage. Even so, however, they retain a significant aspect of that legacy: the complex soul searching, the agonized quest to know the self and connect with a personal history. A central theme of his work from beginning to end is the diminishment of the present as measured against the grandeur of the past. Lowell's poems, especially the early ones, protest fiercely against the reigning secularism and corrupting materialism of his time. And although his poems are not didactic, there is something in them of the passionate intensity of the New England Puritan divine and the Biblical prophet. Relating his own troubles, marital and emotional, to the problems of the age, Lowell often makes public occasions out of his private experience, as Charles Molesworth has noted in *The Fierce Embrace,* thereby both complicating those experiences and clarifying them. Rooted in personal history and the subjectivity of memory, Lowell's poems represent, as M. L. Rosenthal has observed, an objective, artistic fashioning of private experience. Exhibiting a delicate balance between subjective experience and its objectification in language, Lowell's poetry blends the personal with the historical, the private with the public, the traditional with the modern. These combinations, moreover, are reflected in Lowell's blending of his classical background, reflected in the use of allusion and myth, combined with a democratic impulse. These aspects relate Lowell's poetry to the classical aesthetics of Eliot and Pound and to the American Romanticism of Williams and Whitman.

One additional feature of Lowell's poetic work should be mentioned: his impulse to revise. He rewrote his poems frequently, seeing published versions as no more than revisable drafts. He rewrote, for example, some of the poems originally published in *Notebook* (1967), a work whose title suggests its provisional nature, republishing them in *History* (1973). He also rewrote his life in his poems, recording his family history in *Life*

Studies (1959) and his emotional biography in that book and in later work. As David Kalstone has noted in *Five Temperaments,* "No poet since Whitman has made such continuous public revisions of his life."

In addition to his poetry and his political activism, Lowell was active in theatrical enterprises. He translated a number of plays, including Aeschylus's *Prometheus Bound* and Racine's *Phaedra*—both works with strong political and psychological implications. He adapted for the stage Herman Melville's short novel *Benito Cereno* and Nathaniel Hawthorne's stories "Endicott and the Red Cross," "The Maypole of Merry Mount," and "My Kinsman Major Molineux." He also translated and adapted a number of classical and modern poems from Greek, Latin, French, and Russian, published as *Imitations* (1961).

Lowell's life and art were one. Reading his poetry requires an acknowledgment of this central fact. It also requires a willingness to confront images of disgust, to come to terms with cruelty, and with what Helen Vendler has termed "an edge of malice." As with other modern American poets, especially Eliot and Pound, Lowell requires us to know something of Christian theology and classical myth, though he does not use these as extensively as Eliot and Pound do. Finally, in reading Lowell, we need to remain alert for the way he rapidly shifts among details, introduces different voices unexpectedly, or changes tune and tone without warning. Such difficulties, however, are no more insurmountable than they are in the work of other poets.

Lowell himself best summed up his poetic intentions—while simultaneously offering a perspective on the poetic life he lived. In his late poem "Epilogue," he touches on central facets of his work: its restless exploration of formal and technical problems; its autobiographical impulse; its struggle against the recalcitrant and only partly yielding material of life.

Epilogue

Those blessèd structures, plot and rhyme—
why are they no help to me now
I want to make
something imagined, not recalled?
I hear the noise of my own voice:
The painter's vision is not a lens,

it trembles to caress the light.
But sometimes everything I write
with the threadbare art of my eye
seems a snapshot,
lurid, rapid, garish, grouped,
heightened from life,
yet paralyzed by fact.
All's misalliance.
Yet why not say what happened?
Pray for the grace of accuracy
Vermeer gave to the sun's illumination
stealing like the tide across a map
to his girl solid with yearning.
We are poor passing facts,
warned by that to give
each figure in the photograph
his living name.

"Epilogue" is Lowell's eloquent yet humble testament to his poetic ambitions. It epitomizes the intense feeling of his work and the unremitting honesty of its vision.

The Quaker Graveyard in Nantucket

[FOR WARREN WINSLOW, DEAD AT SEA]

Let man have dominion over the fishes of the sea and the fowls of the air and the beasts of the whole earth, and every creeping creature that moveth upon the earth.

I

A brackish reach of shoal off Madaket—
The sea was still breaking violently and night
Had steamed into our North Atlantic Fleet,
When the drowned sailor clutched the drag-net. Light
Flashed from his matted head and marble feet,
He grappled at the net
With the coiled, hurdling muscles of his thighs:
The corpse was bloodless, a botch of reds and whites,

THE QUAKER GRAVEYARD **Warren Winslow:** Lowell's cousin, who died on a sinking naval vessel during World War II. The epigraph paraphrases Genesis 1:26. [1]**Madaket:** on Nantucket Island.

Its open, staring eyes
Were lustreless dead-lights
Or cabin-windows on a stranded hulk
Heavy with sand. We weight the body, close
Its eyes and heave it seaward whence it came
Where the heel-headed dogfish barks its nose
On Ahab's void and forehead; and the name
Is blocked in yellow chalk.
Sailors, who pitch this portent at the sea
Where dreadnaughts shall confess
Its hell-bent deity,
When you are powerless
To sand-bag this Atlantic bulwark, faced
By the earth-shaker, green, unwearied, chaste
In his steel scales: ask for no Orphean lute
To pluck life back. The guns of the steeled fleet
Recoil and then repeat
The hoarse salute.

II

Whenever winds are moving and their breath
Heaves at the roped-in bulwarks of this pier,
The terns and sea-gulls tremble at your death
In these home waters. Sailor, can you hear
The Pequod's sea wings, beating landward, fall
Headlong and break on our Atlantic wall
Off 'Sconset, where the yawing S-boats splash
The bellbuoy, with ballooning spinnakers,
As the entangled, screeching mainsheet clears
The blocks: off Madaket, where lubbers lash
The heavy surf and throw their long lead squids
For blue-fish? Sea-gulls blink their heavy lids
Seaward. The winds' wings beat upon the stones,
Cousin, and scream for you and the claws rush
At the sea's throat and wring it in the slush

[10]**dead-lights:** porthole covers to keep out water during a storm. Cf. Henry David Thoreau (1817–1862), *Cape Cod* chapter one. [15]**Ahab:** the monomaniacal captain of the *Pequod,* the whaling ship destroyed by Moby Dick in Herman Melville's novel of that name. [23–24]**no Orphean lute / To pluck life back:** Through his music, Orpheus brought his wife, Eurydice, up from the Underworld. [33]**S-boats:** racing sailboats.

Of this old Quaker graveyard where the bones
Cry out in the long night for the hurt beast
Bobbing by Ahab's whaleboats in the East.

III

All you recovered from Poseidon died
With you, my cousin, and the harrowed brine
Is fruitless on the blue beard of the god,
Stretching beyond us to the castles in Spain,
Nantucket's westward haven. To Cape Cod
Guns, cradled on the tide,
Blast the eelgrass about a waterclock
Of bilge and backwash, roil the salt and sand
Lashing earth's scaffold, rock
Our warships in the hand
Of the great God, where time's contrition blues
Whatever it was these Quaker sailors lost
In the mad scramble of their lives. They died
When time was open-eyed,
Wooden and childish; only bones abide
There, in the nowhere, where their boats were tossed
Sky-high, where mariners had fabled news
Of IS, the whited monster. What it cost
Them is their secret. In the sperm-whale's slick
I see the Quakers drown and hear their cry:
"If God himself had not been on our side,
If God himself had not been on our side,
When the Atlantic rose against us, why,
Then it had swallowed us up quick."

IV

This is the end of the whaleroad and the whale
Who spewed Nantucket bones on the thrashed swell
And stirred the troubled waters to whirlpools
To send the Pequod packing off to hell:
This is the end of them, three-quarters fools,
Snatching at straws to sail
Seaward and seaward on the turntail whale,

[45]**Poseidon:** Greek god of the sea. [62]**IS:** a reference to Exodus 3:14 in which God identifies himself as "I Am That I Am."

Spouting out blood and water as it rolls,
Sick as a dog to these Atlantic shoals:
Clamavimus, O depth. Let the sea-gulls wail

For water, for the deep where the high tide
Mutters to its hurt self, mutters and ebbs.
Waves wallow in their wash, go out and out,
Leave only the death-rattle of the crabs,
The beach increasing, its enormous snout
Sucking the ocean's side.
This is the end of running on the waves;
We are poured out like water. Who will dance
The mast-lashed master of Leviathans
Up from this field of Quakers in their unstoned graves?

V

When the whale's viscera go and the roll
Of its corruption overruns this world
Beyond tree-swept Nantucket and Woods Hole
And Martha's Vineyard, Sailor, will your sword
Whistle and fall and sink into the fat?
In the great ash-pit of Jehoshaphat
The bones cry for the blood of the white whale,
The fat flukes arch and whack about its ears,
The death-lance churns into the sanctuary, tears
The gun-blue swingle, heaving like a flail,
And hacks the coiling life out: it works and drags
And rips the sperm-whale's midriff into rags,
Gobbets of blubber spill to wind and weather,
Sailor, and gulls go round the stoven timbers
Where the morning stars sing out together
And thunder shakes the white surf and dismembers
The red flag hammered in the mast-head. Hide,
Our steel, Jonas Messias, in Thy side.

[78]**Clamavimus:** Latin: "We have called." [87]**Leviathans:** Biblical sea monsters. [94]**Jehoshaphat:** Lowell's note: "The day of judgment. The world, according to some prophets, will end in fire." [98]**Swingle:** knifelike wooden instrument. [105]**The red flag hammered in the mast-head:** At the end of *Moby Dick,* as the *Pequod* sinks, Tashtego, one of the harpooners, nails Ahab's flag to the sinking mast. [106]**Our steel . . . in Thy side:** conflated references to Jonah, an Old Testament prophet who was swallowed by a whale, and to Jesus, pierced by the lance of a Roman soldier.

VI. OUR LADY OF WALSINGHAM

There once the penitents took off their shoes
And then walked barefoot the remaining mile;
And the small trees, a stream and hedgerows file
Slowly along the munching English lane,
Like cows to the old shrine, until you lose
Track of your dragging pain.
The stream flows down under the druid tree,
Shiloah's whirlpools gurgle and make glad
The castle of God. Sailor, you were glad
And whistled Sion by that stream. But see:

Our Lady, too small for her canopy,
Sits near the altar. There's no comeliness
At all or charm in that expressionless
Face with its heavy eyelids. As before,
This face, for centuries a memory,
Non est species, neque decor,
Expressionless, expresses God: it goes
Past castled Sion. She knows what God knows,
Not Calvary's Cross nor crib at Bethlehem
Now, and the world shall come to Walsingham.

VII

The empty winds are creaking and the oak
Splatters and splatters on the cenotaph,
The boughs are trembling and a gaff
Bobs on the untimely stroke
Of the greased wash exploding on a shoal-bell
In the old mouth of the Atlantic. It's well;
Atlantic, you are fouled with the blue sailors,
Sea-monsters, upward angel, downward fish:
Unmarried and corroding, spare of flesh
Mart once of supercilious, wing'd clippers,
Atlantic, where your bell-trap guts its spoil
You could cut the brackish winds with a knife
Here in Nantucket, and cast up the time

Our Lady of Walsingham: a reference to the medieval shrine of the Virgin Mary at Walsingham, England. [122]**Non est species, neque decor:** Latin for "There is no ostentation or elegance."

When the Lord God formed man from the sea's slime
And breathed into his face the breath of life,
And blue-lung'd combers lumbered to the kill.
The Lord survives the rainbow of His will.

Mr. Edwards and the Spider

I saw the spiders marching through the air,
Swimming from tree to tree that mildewed day
In latter August when the hay
Came creaking to the barn. But where
The wind is westerly,
Where gnarled November makes the spiders fly
Into the apparitions of the sky,
They purpose nothing but their ease and die
Urgently beating east to sunrise and the sea;

What are we in the hands of the great God?
It was in vain you set up thorn and briar
In battle array against the fire
And treason crackling in your blood;
For the wild thorns grow tame
And will do nothing to oppose the flame;
Your lacerations tell the losing game
You play against a sickness past your cure.
How will the hands be strong? How will the heart endure?

A very little thing, a little worm,
Or hourglass-blazoned spider, it is said,
Can kill a tiger. Will the dead
Hold up his mirror and affirm
To the four winds the smell
And flash of his authority? It's well
If God who holds you to the pit of hell,

THE QUAKER GRAVEYARD [143]**The Lord . . . of His will:** an allusion to Genesis 9:11, in which God makes an agreement with Noah never again to destroy mankind by flood, a promise symbolized by the rainbow.

MR. EDWARDS AND THE SPIDER **Mr. Edwards:** Jonathan Edwards, Puritan theologian and preacher (1703–1758). Stanza 2 alludes to Edwards's sermon "Sinners in the Hands of an Angry God." [20]**hourglass-blazoned spider:** the black widow spider exhibits this marking.

Much as one holds a spider, will destroy,
Baffle and dissipate your soul. As a small boy

On Windsor Marsh, I saw the spider die
When thrown into the bowels of fierce fire:
There's no long struggle, no desire
To get up on its feet and fly—
It stretches out its feet
And dies. This is the sinner's last retreat;
Yes, and no strength exerted on the heat
Then sinews the abolished will, when sick
And full of burning, it will whistle on a brick.

But who can plumb the sinking of that soul?
Josiah Hawley, picture yourself cast
Into a brick-kiln where the blast
Fans your quick vitals to a coal—
If measured by a glass,
How long would it seem burning! Let there pass
A minute, ten, ten trillion; but the blaze
Is infinite, eternal: this is death,
To die and know it. This is the Black Widow, death.

After the Surprising Conversions

September twenty-second, Sir: today
I answer. In the latter part of May,
Hard on our Lord's Ascension, it began
To be more sensible. A gentleman
Of more than common understanding, strict
In morals, pious in behavior, kicked
Against our goad. A man of some renown,
An useful, honored person in the town,
He came of melancholy parents; prone
To secret spells, for years they kept alone—
His uncle, I believe, was killed of it:
Good people, but of too much or little wit.
I preached one Sabbath on a text from Kings;

MR. EDWARDS [28]**Windsor Marsh:** in Connecticut, where Edwards lived as a child. [38]**Josiah Hawley:** Edwards's uncle.

"After the Surprising Conversions" was based on letters and journals of the Puritan divine Jonathan Edwards, who described the revival of Christian faith in Massachusetts. [3]**our Lord's Ascension:** Christ ascended into heaven forty days after Easter.

He showed concernment for his soul. Some things
In his experience were hopeful. He
Would sit and watch the wind knocking a tree
And praise this countryside our Lord has made.
Once when a poor man's heifer died, he laid
A shilling on the doorsill; though a thirst
For loving shook him like a snake, he durst
Not entertain much hope of his estate
In heaven. Once we saw him sitting late
Behind his attic window by a light
That guttered on his Bible; through that night
He meditated terror, and he seemed
Beyond advice or reason, for he dreamed
That he was called to trumpet Judgment Day
To Concord. In the latter part of May
He cut his throat. And though the coroner
Judged him delirious, soon a noisome stir
Palsied our village. At Jehovah's nod
Satan seemed more let loose amongst us: God
Abandoned us to Satan, and he pressed
Us hard, until we thought we could not rest
Till we had done with life. Content was gone.
All the good work was quashed. We were undone.
The breath of God had carried out a planned
And sensible withdrawal from this land;
The multitude, once unconcerned with doubt,
Once neither callous, curious nor devout,
Jumped at broad noon, as though some peddler groaned
At it in its familiar twang: "My friend,
Cut your own throat. Cut your own throat. Now! Now!"
September twenty-second, Sir, the bough
Cracks with the unpicked apples, and at dawn
The small-mouth bass breaks water, gorged with spawn.

My Last Afternoon with Uncle Devereux Winslow

1922: THE STONE PORCH OF MY GRANDFATHER'S SUMMER HOUSE

I

"I won't go with you. I want to stay with Grandpa!"
That's how I threw cold water
on my Mother and Father's

watery martini pipe dreams at Sunday dinner.
. . . Fontainebleau, Mattapoisett, Puget Sound. . . .
Nowhere was anywhere after a summer
at my Grandfather's farm.
Diamond-pointed, athirst and Norman,
its alley of poplars
paraded from Grandmother's rose garden
to a scary stand of virgin pine,
scrub, and paths forever pioneering.

One afternoon in 1922,
I sat on the stone porch, looking through
screens as black-grained as drifting coal.
Tockytock, tockytock
clumped our Alpine, Edwardian cuckoo clock,
slung with strangled, wooden game.
Our farmer was cementing a root-house under the hill.
One of my hands was cool on a pile
of black earth, the other warm
on a pile of lime. All about me
were the works of my Grandfather's hands:
snapshots of his *Liberty Bell* silver mine;
his high school at *Stuttgart am Neckar;*
stogie-brown beams; fools'-gold nuggets;
octagonal red tiles,
sweaty with a secret dank, crummy with ant-stale;
a Rocky Mountain chaise longue,
its legs, shellacked saplings.
A pastel-pale Huckleberry Finn
fished with a broom straw in a basin
hollowed out of a millstone.
Like my Grandfather, the décor
was manly, comfortable,
overbearing, disproportioned.

What were those sunflowers? Pumpkins floating
   shoulder-high?
It was sunset, Sadie and Nellie
bearing pitchers of ice-tea,
oranges, lemons, mint, and peppermints,
and the jug of shandygaff,
which Grandpa made by blending half and half

yeasty, wheezing homemade sarsaparilla with beer.
The farm, entitled *Char-de-sa*
in the Social Register,
was named for my Grandfather's children:
Charlotte, Devereux, and Sarah.
No one had died there in my lifetime . . .
Only Cinder, our Scottie puppy
paralyzed from gobbling toads.
I sat mixing black earth and lime.

2

I was five and a half.
My formal pearl gray shorts
had been worn for three minutes.
My perfection was the Olympian
poise of my models in the imperishable autumn
display windows
of Rogers Peet's boys' store below the State House
in Boston. Distorting drops of water
pinpricked my face in the basin's mirror.
I was a stuffed toucan
with a bibulous, multicolored beak.

3

Up in the air
by the lakeview window in the billiards-room,
lurid in the doldrums of the sunset hour,
my Great Aunt Sarah
was learning *Samson and Delilah*.
She thundered on the keyboard of her dummy piano,
with gauze curtains like a boudoir table,
accordionlike yet soundless.
It had been bought to spare the nerves
of my Grandmother,
tone-deaf, quick as a cricket,
now needing a fourth for "Auction,"
and casting a thirsty eye

67–68 **Samson and Delilah . . . her dummy piano:** an opera by Camille Saint-Saens (1835–1921), in a version for piano.

on Aunt Sarah, risen like the phoenix
from her bed of troublesome snacks and Tauchnitz classics.
Forty years earlier,
twenty, auburn headed,
grasshopper notes of genius!
Family gossip says Aunt Sarah
tilted her archaic Athenian nose
and jilted an Astor.
Each morning she practiced
on the grand piano at Symphony Hall,
deathlike in the off-season summer—
its naked Greek statues draped with purple
like the saints in Holy Week. . . .
On the recital day, she failed to appear.

4

I picked with a clean finger nail at the blue anchor
on my sailor blouse washed white as a spinnaker.
What in the world was I wishing?
. . . A sail-colored horse browsing in the bullrushes . . .
A fluff of the west wind puffing
my blouse, kiting me over our seven chimneys,
troubling the waters. . . .
As small as sapphires were the ponds: *Quittacus, Snippituit,*
and *Assawompset,* halved by "the Island,"
where my Uncle's duck blind
floated in a barrage of smoke-clouds.
Double-barreled shotguns
stuck out like bundles of baby crow-bars.
A single sculler in a camouflaged kayak
was quacking to the decoys. . . .

At the cabin between the waters,
the nearest windows were already boarded.
Uncle Devereux was closing camp for the winter.
As if posed for "the engagement photograph,"
he was wearing his severe
war-uniform of a volunteer Canadian officer.
Daylight from the doorway riddled his student posters,

77 **Tauchnitz classics:** German paperbound books, including classic British and American works.

tacked helter-skelter on walls as raw as a boardwalk.
Mr. Punch, a water melon in hockey tights,
was tossing off a decanter of Scotch.
La Belle France in a red, white and blue toga
was accepting the arm of her "protector,"
the ingenu and porcine Edward VII.
The pre-war music hall belles
had goose necks, glorious signatures, beauty-moles,
and coils of hair like rooster tails.
The finest poster was two or three young men in khaki kilts
being bushwhacked on the veldt—
They were almost life-size. . . .

My Uncle was dying at twenty-nine.
"You are behaving like children,"
said my Grandfather,
when my Uncle and Aunt left their three baby daughters,
and sailed for Europe on a last honeymoon . . .
I cowered in terror.
I wasn't a child at all—
unseen and all-seeing, I was Agrippina
in the Golden House of Nero. . . .
Near me was the white measuring-door
my Grandfather had penciled with my Uncle's heights.
In 1911, he had stopped growing at just six feet.
While I sat on the tiles,
and dug at the anchor on my sailor blouse,
Uncle Devereux stood behind me.
He was as brushed as Bayard, our riding horse.
His face was putty.
His blue coat and white trousers
grew sharper and straighter.
His coat was a blue jay's tail,
his trousers were solid cream from the top of the bottle.
He was animated, hierarchical,
like a ginger snap man in a clothes-press.
He was dying of the incurable Hodgkin's disease. . . .

113**Mr. Punch:** a cartoon figure representing the British humor magazine *Punch*. 115–117**La Belle France . . . Edward VII:** an allusion to a poster representing the political alliance between France and Britain. 131**Agrippina:** Nero's mother, murdered on his orders.

My hands were warm, then cool, on the piles
of earth and lime,
a black pile and a white pile. . . .
Come winter,
Uncle Devereux would blend to the one color.

Florence

[FOR MARY MCCARTHY]

I long for the black ink,
cuttlefish, April, Communists
and brothels of Florence—
everything, even the British
fairies who haunted the hills,
even the chills and fever
that came once a month
and forced me to think.
The apple was more human there than here,
but it took a long time for the blinding
golden rind to mellow.

How vulnerable the horseshoe crabs
dredging the bottom like flat-irons
in their antique armor,
with their swordgrass blackbone tails,
made for a child to grab
and throw strangling ashore!

Oh Florence, Florence, patroness
of the lovely tyrannicides!
Where the tower of the Old Palace
pierces the sky
like a hypodermic needle,
Perseus, David and Judith,
lords and ladies of the Blood,
Greek demi-gods of the Cross,
rise sword in hand
above the unshaven,
formless decapitation
of the monsters, tubs of guts,
mortifying chunks for the pack.

Pity the monsters!
Pity the monsters!
Perhaps, one always took the wrong side—
Ah, to have known, to have loved
too many Davids and Judiths!
My heart bleeds black blood for the monster.
I have seen the Gorgon.
The erotic terror
of her helpless, big bosomed body
lay like slop.
Wall-eyed, staring the despot to stone,
her severed head swung
like a lantern in the victor's hand.

Beyond the Alps

(On the train from Rome to Paris. 1950, the year Pius XII defined the dogma of Mary's bodily assumption.)

Reading how even the Swiss had thrown the sponge
in once again and Everest was still
unscaled, I watched our Paris Pullman lunge
mooning across the fallow Alpine snow.
O bella Roma! I saw our stewards go
forward on tiptoe banging on their gongs.
Life changed to landscape. Much against my will
I left the City of God where it belongs.
There the skirt-mad Mussolini unfurled
the eagle of Caesar. He was one of us
only, pure prose. I envy the conspicuous
waste of our grandparents on their grand tours—
long-haired Victorian sages bought the universe,
while breezing on their trust funds through the world.

When the Vatican made Mary's Assumption dogma,
the crowds at San Pietro screamed *Papá.*
The Holy Father dropped his shaving glass,
and listened. His electric razor purred,
his pet canary chirped on his left hand.
The lights of science couldn't hold a candle
to Mary risen—at one miraculous stroke,

angel-wing'd, gorgeous as a jungle bird!
But who believed this? Who could understand?
Pilgrims still kissed Saint Peter's brazen sandal.
The Duce's lynched, bare, booted skull still spoke.
God herded his people to the *coup de grâce*—
the costumed Switzers sloped their pikes to push,
O Pius, through the monstrous human crush. . . .

Our mountain-climbing train had come to earth.
Tired of the querulous hush-hush of the wheels,
the blear-eyed ego kicking in my berth
lay still, and saw Apollo plant his heels
on terra firma through the morning's thigh . . .
each backward, wasted Alp, a Parthenon,
fire-branded socket of the Cyclops' eye.
There were no tickets for that altitude
once held by Hellas, when the Goddess stood,
prince, pope, philosopher and golden bough,
pure mind and murder at the scything prow—
Minerva, the miscarriage of the brain.

Now Paris, our black classic, breaking up
like killer kings on an Etruscan cup.

Memories of West Street and Lepke

Only teaching on Tuesdays, book-worming
in pajamas fresh from the washer each morning,
I hog a whole house on Boston's
"hardly passionate Marlborough Street,"
where even the man
scavenging filth in the back alley trash cans,
has two children, a beach wagon, a helpmate,
and is a "young Republican."
I have a nine months' daughter,
young enough to be my granddaughter.
Like the sun she rises in her flame-flamingo infants' wear.

These are the tranquillized *Fifties,*
and I am forty. Ought I to regret my seedtime?

I was a fire-breathing Catholic C.O.,
and made my manic statement,
telling off the state and president, and then
sat waiting sentence in the bull pen
beside a Negro boy with curlicues
of marijuana in his hair.

Given a year,
I walked on the roof of the West Street Jail, a short
enclosure like my school soccer court,
and saw the Hudson River once a day
through sooty clothesline entanglements
and bleaching khaki tenements.
Strolling, I yammered metaphysics with Abramowitz,
a jaundice-yellow ("it's really tan")
and fly-weight pacifist,
so vegetarian,
he wore rope shoes and preferred fallen fruit.
He tried to convert Bioff and Brown,
the Hollywood pimps, to his diet.
Hairy, muscular, suburban,
wearing chocolate double-breasted suits,
they blew their tops and beat him black and blue.

I was so out of things, I'd never heard
of the Jehovah's Witnesses.
"Are you a C.O.?" I asked a fellow jailbird.
"No," he answered, "I'm a J.W."
He taught me the "hospital tuck,"
and pointed out the T-shirted back
of *Murder Incorporated's* Czar Lepke,
there piling towels on a rack,
or dawdling off to his little segregated cell full
of things forbidden the common man:
a portable radio, a dresser, two toy American
flags tied together with a ribbon of Easter palm.
Flabby, bald, lobotomized,
he drifted in a sheepish calm,
where no agonizing reappraisal
jarred his concentration on the electric chair—
hanging like an oasis in his air
of lost connections. . . .

Man and Wife

Tamed by *Miltown,* we lie on Mother's bed;
the rising sun in war paint dyes us red;
in broad daylight her gilded bed-posts shine,
abandoned, almost Dionysian.
At last the trees are green on Marlborough Street,
blossoms on our magnolia ignite
the morning with their murderous five days' white.
All night I've held your hand,
as if you had
a fourth time faced the kingdom of the mad—
its hackneyed speech, its homicidal eye—
and dragged me home alive. . . . Oh my *Petite,*
clearest of all God's creatures, still air and nerve:
you were in your twenties, and I,
once hand on glass
and heart in mouth,
outdrank the Rahvs in the heat
of Greenwich Village, fainting at your feet—
too boiled and shy
and poker-faced to make a pass,
while the shrill verve
of your invective scorched the traditional South.

Now twelve years later, you turn your back.
Sleepless, you hold
your pillow to your hollows like a child;
your old-fashioned tirade—
loving, rapid, merciless—
breaks like the Atlantic Ocean on my head.

Sailing Home from Rapallo

[FEBRUARY 1954]

Your nurse could only speak Italian,
but after twenty minutes I could imagine your final week,
and tears ran down my cheeks. . . .

MAN AND WIFE [1]**Miltown:** a tranquilizer. [4]**Dionysian:** reference to the Greek god Dionysus, associated with wine, revelry, and frenzy. [5]**Marlborough Street:** in Boston.

When I embarked from Italy with my Mother's body,
the whole shoreline of the *Golfo di Genova*
was breaking into fiery flower.
The crazy yellow and azure sea-sleds
blasting like jack-hammers across
the *spumante*-bubbling wake of our liner,
recalled the clashing colors of my Ford.
Mother traveled first-class in the hold;
her *Risorgimento* black and gold casket
was like Napoleon's at the *Invalides*. . . .

While the passengers were tanning
on the Mediterranean in deck-chairs,
our family cemetery in Dunbarton
lay under the White Mountains
in the sub-zero weather.
The graveyard's soil was changing to stone—
so many of its deaths had been midwinter.
Dour and dark against the blinding snowdrifts,
its black brook and fir trunks were as smooth as masts.
A fence of iron spear-hafts
black-bordered its mostly Colonial grave-slates.
The only "unhistoric" soul to come here
was Father, now buried beneath his recent
unweathered pink-veined slice of marble.
Even the Latin of his Lowell motto:
Occasionem cognosce,
seemed too businesslike and pushing here,
where the burning cold illuminated
the hewn inscriptions of Mother's relatives:
twenty or thirty Winslows and Starks.
Frost had given their names a diamond edge. . . .

In the grandiloquent lettering on Mother's coffin,
Lowell had been misspelled LOVEL.
The corpse
was wrapped like *panettone* in Italian tinfoil.

[12]**Risorgimento:** Italy's great mid-nineteenth-century national revival. [13]**Invalides:** Paris building that houses Napoleon's casket. [29]**Occasionem cognosce:** Latin for "Recognize the occasion." [38]**panettone:** a sweet Italian cake.

Skunk Hour

[FOR ELIZABETH BISHOP]

Nautilus Island's hermit
heiress still lives through winter in her Spartan cottage;
her sheep still graze above the sea.
Her son's a bishop. Her farmer
is first selectman in our village;
she's in her dotage.

Thirsting for
the hierarchic privacy
of Queen Victoria's century,
she buys up all
the eyesores facing her shore,
and lets them fall.

The season's ill—
we've lost our summer millionaire,
who seemed to leap from an L. L. Bean
catalogue. His nine-knot yawl
was auctioned off to lobstermen.
A red fox stain covers Blue Hill.

And now our fairy
decorator brightens his shop for fall;
his fishnet's filled with orange cork,
orange, his cobbler's bench and awl;
there is no money in his work,
he'd rather marry.

One dark night,
my Tudor Ford climbed the hill's skull;
I watched for love-cars. Lights turned down,
they lay together, hull to hull,

The poem responds to and is modeled on Bishop's "The Armadillo," pages 564–565. Lowell's note: "The dedication is to Elizabeth Bishop, because rereading her suggested a way of breaking through the shell of my old manner." [1]**Nautilus Island:** in Maine, where Lowell had a summer house. [15]**L. L. Bean:** a mail-order company in Maine, specializing in outdoor clothes and sporting equipment.

where the graveyard shelves on the town. . . .
My mind's not right.

A car radio bleats,
"Love, O careless Love. . . ." I hear
my ill-spirit sob in each blood cell,
as if my hand were at its throat. . . .
I myself am hell;
nobody's here—

only skunks, that search
in the moonlight for a bite to eat.
They march on their soles up Main Street:
white stripes, moonstruck eyes' red fire
under the chalk-dry and spar spire
of the Trinitarian Church.

I stand on top
of our back steps and breathe the rich air—
a mother skunk with her column of kittens swills the garbage
pail.
She jabs her wedge-head in a cup
of sour cream, drops her ostrich tail,
and will not scare.

For the Union Dead

"Relinquunt Omnia Servare Rem Publicam."

The old South Boston Aquarium stands
in a Sahara of snow now. Its broken windows are boarded.
The bronze weathervane cod has lost half its scales.
The airy tanks are dry.

SKUNK HOUR [35]**I myself am hell:** Cf. Milton's *Paradise Lost* IV. 75, in which Satan says, "Which way I fly is Hell, myself am Hell."

"For the Union Dead," originally entitled "Colonel Shaw and the Massachusetts 54," refers to a bronze relief by Augustus Saint-Gaudens (1848–1907), that depicts the commander of the first black regiment, Robert Gould Shaw (1837–1863), killed in a Civil War battle. The monument stands on Boston Common, opposite the Massachusetts State House. The epigraph is a Latin inscription on the monument, which translates: "He leaves all behind to serve the Republic."

Once my nose crawled like a snail on the glass;
my hand tingled
to burst the bubbles
drifting from the noses of the cowed, compliant fish.

My hand draws back. I often sigh still
for the dark downward and vegetating kingdom
of the fish and reptile. One morning last March,
I pressed against the new barbed and galvanized

fence on the Boston Common. Behind their cage,
yellow dinosaur steamshovels were grunting
as they cropped up tons of mush and grass
to gouge their underworld garage.

Parking spaces luxuriate like civic
sandpiles in the heart of Boston.
A girdle of orange, Puritan-pumpkin colored girders
braces the tingling Statehouse,

shaking over the excavations, as it faces Colonel Shaw
and his bell-cheeked Negro infantry
on St. Gaudens' shaking Civil War relief,
propped by a plank splint against the garage's earthquake.

Two months after marching through Boston,
half the regiment was dead;
at the dedication,
William James could almost hear the bronze Negroes breathe.

Their monument sticks like a fishbone
in the city's throat.
Its Colonel is as lean
as a compass-needle.

He has an angry wrenlike vigilance,
a greyhound's gentle tautness;

[28]**William James:** American philosopher and psychologist (1842–1912) who taught at Harvard.

he seems to wince at pleasure,
and suffocate for privacy.

He is out of bounds now. He rejoices in man's lovely,
peculiar power to choose life and die—
when he leads his black soldiers to death,
he cannot bend his back.

On a thousand small town New England greens,
the old white churches hold their air
of sparse, sincere rebellion; frayed flags
quilt the graveyards of the Grand Army of the Republic.

The stone statues of the abstract Union Soldier
grow slimmer and younger each year—
wasp-waisted, they doze over muskets
and muse through their sideburns . . .

Shaw's father wanted no monument
except the ditch,
where his son's body was thrown
and lost with his "niggers."

The ditch is nearer.
There are no statues for the last war here;
on Boylston Street, a commercial photograph
shows Hiroshima boiling

over a Mosler Safe, the "Rock of Ages"
that survived the blast. Space is nearer.
When I crouch to my television set,
the drained faces of Negro school-children rise like balloons.

Colonel Shaw
is riding on his bubble,
he waits
for the blessed break.

The Aquarium is gone. Everywhere,
giant finned cars nose forward like fish;
a savage servility
slides by on grease.

[55]**Boylston Street:** in Boston.

Robert Kennedy: 1925–1968

R.F.K.

Here in my workroom, in its listlessness
of Vacancy, some old Victorian house,
airtight and sheeted for old summers,
far from the hornet yatter of the bond—
is loneliness, a thin smoke thread of vital
air. What can I catch from you now?
Doom was woven in your nerves, your shirt,
woven in the great clan; they too were loyal,
and you too more than loyal to them, to death.
For them like a prince, you daily left your tower
to walk through dirt in your best cloth. Untouched,
alone in my Plutarchan bubble, I miss
you, you out of Plutarch, made by hand—
forever approaching our maturity.

Two Walls

[1968, MARTIN LUTHER KING'S MURDER]

Somewhere a white wall faces a white wall,
one wakes the other, the other wakes the first,
each burning with the other's borrowed splendor—
the walls, awake, are forced to go on talking,
their color looks much alike, two shadings of white,
each living in the shadow of the other.
How fine our distinctions when we cannot choose!
Don Giovanni can't stick his sword through stone,
two contracting, white stone walls—their pursuit
of happiness and his, coincident. . . .
At this point of civilization, this point of the world,
the only satisfactory companion we
can imagine is death—this morning, skin lumping in my throat
I lie here, heavily breathing, the soul of New York.

May

THE PACIFICATION OF COLUMBIA

A patch of tan, a blood-warm roof-tile, then tan
patch, then sky patch, as the jigsaw flung some mosque of Omar
to vaultless consummation and blue consumption,

exhalation of the sands of the desert to fire.
I got the message, one the puzzle never sent. . . .
No destructive element emaciates
Columbia this Mayday afternoon;
the thickened buildings look like buildings out
of Raphael, colossal classic, dungeon feudal;
horses, higher artistic types than their grooms,
forage Broadway's median trees, as if
nature were liberated . . . the police
lean on the burnished, nervous hides, show they,
at least, have learned to meet and reason together.

Robert Frost

Robert Frost at midnight, the audience gone
to vapor, the great act laid on the shelf in mothballs,
his voice is musical and raw—he writes in the flyleaf:
For Robert from Robert, his friend in the art.
"Sometimes I feel too full of myself," I say.
And he, misunderstanding, "When I am low,
I stray away. My son wasn't your kind. The night
we told him Merrill Moore would come to treat him,
he said, 'I'll kill him first.' One of my daughters thought
things,
thought every male she met was out to make her;
the way she dressed, she couldn't make a whorehouse."
And I, "Sometimes I'm so happy I can't stand myself."
And he, "When I am too full of joy, I think
how little good my health did anyone near me."

Reading Myself

Like thousands, I took just pride and more than just,
struck matches that brought my blood to a boil;
I memorized the tricks to set the river on fire—
somehow never wrote something to go back to.
Can I suppose I am finished with wax flowers
and have earned my grass on the minor slopes of Parnassus. . . .
No honeycomb is built without a bee
adding circle to circle, cell to cell,

READING MYSELF [6]**Parnassus:** a traditional symbol of poetic achievement, from Greek mythology.

the wax and honey of a mausoleum—
this round dome proves its maker is alive;
the corpse of the insect lives embalmed in honey,
prays that its perishable work live long
enough for the sweet-tooth bear to desecrate—
this open book . . . my open coffin.

The Mouth of the Hudson

[FOR ESTHER BROOKS]

A single man stands like a bird-watcher,
and scuffles the pepper and salt snow
from a discarded, gray
Westinghouse Electric cable drum.
He cannot discover America by counting
the chains of condemned freight-trains
from thirty states. They jolt and jar
and junk in the siding below him.
He has trouble with his balance.
His eyes drop,
and he drifts with the wild ice
ticking seaward down the Hudson,
like the blank sides of a jig-saw puzzle.

The ice ticks seaward like a clock.
A Negro toasts
wheat-seeds over the coke-fumes
of a punctured barrel.
Chemical air
sweeps in from New Jersey,
and smells of coffee.

Across the river,
ledges of suburban factories tan
in the sulphur-yellow sun
of the unforgivable landscape.

Fall 1961

Back and forth, back and forth
goes the tock, tock, tock
of the orange, bland, ambassadorial

face of the moon
on the grandfather clock.

All autumn, the chafe and jar
of nuclear war;
we have talked our extinction to death.
I swim like a minnow
behind my studio window.

Our end drifts nearer,
the moon lifts,
radiant with terror.
The state
is a diver under a glass bell.

A father's no shield
for his child.
We are like a lot of wild
spiders crying together,
but without tears.

Nature holds up a mirror.
One swallow makes a summer.
It's easy to tick
off the minutes,
but the clockhands stick.

Back and forth!
Back and forth, back and forth—
my one point of rest
is the orange and black
oriole's swinging nest!

Waking Early Sunday Morning

O to break loose, like the chinook
salmon jumping and falling back,
nosing up to the impossible
stone and bone-crushing waterfall—
raw-jawed, weak-fleshed there, stopped by ten
steps of the roaring ladder, and then

to clear the top on the last try,
alive enough to spawn and die.

Stop, back off. The salmon breaks
water, and now my body wakes
to feel the unpolluted joy
and criminal leisure of a boy—
no rainbow smashing a dry fly
in the white run is free as I,
here squatting like a dragon on
time's hoard before the day's begun!

Fierce, fireless mind, running downhill.
Look up and see the harbor fill:
business as usual in eclipse
goes down to the sea in ships—
wake of refuse, dacron rope,
bound for Bermuda or Good Hope,
all bright before the morning watch
the wine-dark hulls of yawl and ketch.

I watch a glass of water wet
with a fine fuzz of icy sweat,
silvery colors touched with sky,
serene in their neutrality—
yet if I shift, or change my mood,
I see some object made of wood,
background behind it of brown grain,
to darken it, but not to stain.

O that the spirit could remain
tinged but untarnished by its strain!
Better dressed and stacking birch,
or lost with the Faithful at Church—
anywhere, but somewhere else!
And now the new electric bells,
clearly chiming, "Faith of our fathers,"
and now the congregation gathers.

O Bible chopped and crucified
in hymns we hear but do not read,
none of the milder subtleties

of grace or art will sweeten these
stiff quatrains shoveled out four-square—
they sing of peace, and preach despair;
yet they gave darkness some control,
and left a loophole for the soul.

When will we see Him face to face?
Each day, He shines through darker glass.
In this small town where everything
is known, I see His vanishing
emblems, His white spire and flag-
pole sticking out above the fog,
like old white china doorknobs, sad,
slight, useless things to calm the mad.

Hammering military splendor,
top-heavy Goliath in full armor—
little redemption in the mass
liquidations of their brass,
elephant and phalanx moving
with the times and still improving,
when that kingdom hit the crash:
a million foreskins stacked like trash . . .

Sing softer! But what if a new
diminuendo brings no true
tenderness, only restlessness,
excess, the hunger for success,
sanity of self-deception
fixed and kicked by reckless caution,
while we listen to the bells—
anywhere, but somewhere else!

O to break loose. All life's grandeur
is something with a girl in summer . . .
elated as the President
girdled by his establishment
this Sunday morning, free to chaff
his own thoughts with his bear-cuffed staff,
swimming nude, unbuttoned, sick
of his ghost-written rhetoric!

No weekends for the gods now. Wars
flicker, earth licks its open sores,

fresh breakage, fresh promotions, chance
assassinations, no advance.
Only man thinning out his kind
sounds through the Sabbath noon, the blind
swipe of the pruner and his knife
busy about the tree of life . . .

Pity the planet, all joy gone
from this sweet volcanic cone;
peace to our children when they fall
in small war on the heels of small
war—until the end of time
to police the earth, a ghost
orbiting forever lost
in our monotonous sublime.

The Old Flame

My old flame, my wife!
Remember our lists of birds?
One morning last summer, I drove
by our house in Maine. It was still
on top of its hill—

Now a red ear of Indian maize
was splashed on the door.
Old Glory with thirteen stars
hung on a pole. The clapboard
was old-red schoolhouse red.

Inside, a new landlord,
a new wife, a new broom!
Atlantic seaboard antique shop
pewter and plunder
shone in each room.

A new frontier!
No running next door
now to phone the sheriff
for his taxi to Bath
and the State Liquor Store!

No one saw your ghostly
imaginary lover
stare through the window,
and tighten
the scarf at his throat.

Health to the new people,
health to their flag, to their old
restored house on the hill!
Everything had been swept bare,
furnished, garnished, and aired.

Everything's changed for the best—
how quivering and fierce we were,
there snowbound together,
simmering like wasps
in our tent of books!

Poor ghost, old love, speak
with your old voice
of flaming insight
that kept us awake all night.
In one bed and apart,

we heard the plow
groaning up hill—
a red light, then a blue,
as it tossed off the snow
to the side of the road.

Home After Three Months Away

Gone now the baby's nurse,
a lioness who ruled the roost
and made the Mother cry.
She used to tie
gobbets of porkrind in bowknots of gauze—
three months they hung like soggy toast
on our eight foot magnolia tree,
and helped the English sparrows
weather a Boston winter.

Three months, three months!
Is Richard now himself again?
Dimpled with exaltation,
my daughter holds her levee in the tub.
Our noses rub,
each of us pats a stringy lock of hair—
they tell me nothing's gone.
Though I am forty-one,
not forty now, the time I put away
was child's play. After thirteen weeks
my child still dabs her cheeks
to start me shaving. When
we dress her in her sky-blue corduroy,
she changes to a boy,
and floats my shaving brush
and washcloth in the flush . . .
Dearest, I cannot loiter here
in lather like a polar bear.
Recuperating, I neither spin nor toil.
Three stories down below,
a choreman tends our coffin's length of soil,
and seven horizontal tulips blow.
Just twelve months ago,
these flowers were pedigreed
imported Dutchmen, now no one need
distinguish them from weed.
Bushed by the late spring snow,
they cannot meet
another year's snowballing enervation.

I keep no rank nor station.
Cured, I am frizzled, stale and small.

Waking in the Blue

The night attendant, a B.U. sophomore,
rouses from the mare's-nest of his drowsy head
propped on *The Meaning of Meaning.*
He catwalks down our corridor.
Azure day
makes my agonized blue window bleaker.

Crows maunder on the petrified fairway.
Absence! My heart grows tense
as though a harpoon were sparring for the kill.
(This is the house for the "mentally ill.")

What use is my sense of humor?
I grin at Stanley, now sunk in his sixties,
once a Harvard all-American fullback
(if such were possible!),
still hoarding the build of a boy in his twenties,
as he soaks, a ramrod
with the muscle of a seal
in his long tub,
vaguely urinous from the Victorian plumbing.
A kingly granite profile in a crimson golf cap,
worn all day, all night,
he thinks only of his figure,
of slimming on sherbet and ginger ale—
more cut off from words than a seal.

This is the way day breaks in Bowditch Hall at McLean's;
the hooded night lights bring out "Bobbie,"
Porcellian '29,
a replica of Louis XVI
without the wig—
redolent and roly-poly as a sperm whale,
as he swashbuckles about in his birthday suit
and horses at chairs.
These victorious figures of bravado ossified young.

In between the limits of day,
hours and hours go by under the crew haircuts
and slightly too little nonsensical bachelor twinkle
of the Roman Catholic attendants.
(There are no Mayflower
screwballs in the Catholic Church.)

After a hearty New England breakfast,
I weigh two hundred pounds
this morning. Cock of the walk,
I strut in my turtle-necked French sailor's jersey
before the metal shaving mirrors,

and see the shaky future grow familiar
in the pinched, indigenous faces
of these thoroughbred mental cases,
twice my age and half my weight.
We are all old-timers,
each of us holds a locked razor.

Turtle

I pray for memory—
an old turtle,
absentminded, inelastic,
kept afloat by losing touch . . .
no longer able to hiss or lift
a useless shield against the killer.

Turtles age, but wade out amorously,
half-frozen fossils, yet knight-errant
in a foolsdream of armor.
The smaller ones climb rocks to broil in comfort.
Snapping turtles only submerge.
They have survived . . . not by man's philanthropy.

I hunted them in school vacations.
I trampled an acre of driftstraw
floating off the muskrats' loose nests.
Here and there, a solitary turtle
craned its brown Franciscan cowl
from one of twenty waterholes.
In that brew, I stepped
on a turtle's smooth, invisible back.
It was like escaping quicksand.
I drew it in my arms by what I thought was tail—
a tail? I held a foreleg.
I could have lost a finger.

This morning when
the double-brightness of the winter sun
wakes me from the film of dreaming,
my bedroom is unfamiliar. I see

three snapping turtles squatted on my drifting clothes—
two rough black logs . . . the third is a nuzzler
dressed in see-through yellow tortoiseshell,
a puppy squeaking and tweaking
my empty shirt for milk.

They are stale and panting;
what is dead in me wakes their appetite.
When they breathe, they seem to crack apart,
crouched motionless on tiptoe
with crooked smiles
and high-school nicknames on their tongues,
as if they wished to relive
the rawness that let us meet as animals.
Nothing has passed between us but time.

"You've wondered where we were these years?
Here are we."

They lie like luggage—
my old friend the turtle . . . Too many pictures
have screamed from the reel . . . in the rerun,
the snapper holds on till sunset—
in the awful instantness of retrospect,
its beak
works me underwater drowning by my neck,
as it claws away pieces of my flesh
to make me small enough to swallow.

Returning Turtle

Weeks hitting the road, one fasting in the bathtub,
raw hamburger mossing in the watery stoppage,
the room drenched with musk like kerosene—
no one shaved, and only the turtle washed.
He was so beautiful when we flipped him over:
greens, reds, yellows, fringe of the faded savage,
the last Sioux, old and worn, saying with weariness,
'Why doesn't the Great White Father put his red
children on wheels, and move us as he will?'
We drove to the Orland River, and watched the turtle

rush for water like rushing into marriage,
swimming in uncontaminated joy,
lovely the flies that fed that sleazy surface,
a turtle looking back at us, and blinking.

Dolphin

My Dolphin, you only guide me by surprise,
a captive as Racine, the man of craft,
drawn through his maze of iron composition
by the incomparable wandering voice of Phèdre.
When I was troubled in mind, you made for my body
caught in its hangman's-knot of sinking lines,
the glassy bowing and scraping of my will. . . .
I have sat and listened to too many
words of the collaborating muse,
and plotted perhaps too freely with my life,
not avoiding injury to others,
not avoiding injury to myself—
to ask compassion . . . this book, half fiction,
an eelnet made by man for the eel fighting—

my eyes have seen what my hand did.

Sylvia Plath

[1932–1963]

Sylvia Plath emerges out of a tradition older than Euripides, one that includes Baudelaire, Poe, Dostoyevsky, and Kafka, among others. Exploring the innermost reaches of the mind, Sylvia Plath wrote a lyric poetry of the psyche's often painful journey toward self-actualization. Notable for its combination of powerful imagery and intense vision, her poetry is fueled by extravagance, irony, and wonder.

Plath's poems describe the truth of horror. The "boot in the face" we encounter in "Daddy" is reminiscent of Orwell's "boot stamping on a human face—forever" transposed from political to human relationships. Her speaker lives the "truth" of her terrifying struggle as an awakening self out of the psychological prison of her father's demands: "Daddy, I've had to kill you." Through Plath's poem, the reader can experience the powerful and sometimes terrible forces at play in the human mind.

But Plath did more than just paint the truth of horror; she also painted the horror of truth. For Plath, the truth sometimes meant a world in which people are pressed with humiliating questions about rubber breasts and crotches, as in "The Applicant," and where a suicidal patient glows "Bright as a Nazi lampshade" before the professional indifference of her doctors, as in "Lady Lazarus." It is a world in which we sometimes rage, delirious, as in "Fever 103°," a world that chokes "the aged and the meek."

And yet Plath was too honest and perceptive a poet to limit herself to a world of dread and aversion. Her poetry also acknowledges that "Miracles occur," as she stated in "Black Rook in Rainy Weather." And there are moments of wonder, as in "Crossing the Water" where "Stars open among the lilies" in the "silence of astounded souls."

For Sylvia Plath the truth and difficulty of self-realization also entailed the arduous and frustrating process of finding herself as a woman. Helen McNeil suggests that we accept Plath's validity on the subject of women's struggle because of the intensity and honesty with which she depicted the plight of women caught remorselessly between the expectations associated with traditional roles of wife and mother and the driving force of her own poetic vocation. In this regard, Plath's commanding voice is assertive and authoritative. As the mother of two children and the wife of an accomplished poet, she expressed the irony, resentment, and anguish of women attempting to live their own lives while struggling with predetermined roles. Plath dealt with these competing roles, moreover, not only in her poetry but also in her novel, *The Bell Jar.* In that work, the protagonist, Esther Greenwood, a thinly disguised version of Plath herself, remembers once being told that when she had children she would no longer want to write poems.

Born in Boston in 1932, Sylvia Plath has been the subject of intensive biographical scholarship. What we have come to know of her background as a child offers only a few subtle clues to her tragic later life. Her father, Otto Plath, was of German descent and worked as a professor of biology and German at Boston University. He published a scholarly treatise on bees (a subject the poet went on to pursue later in life) and seems to have been a quiet, academically ambitious man. Colleagues remember how vehemently Professor Plath hated his Calvinistic schooling in the Midwest and how he detested the Nazis in Germany. Nevertheless, he was considered an "authoritarian head of the house." Plath went out of her way at an early age to earn his approval and became a "model child," and he is cited as the "panzer man" in her poem "Daddy." He died in November 1940, when his daughter was eight. Plath's mother, Aurelia Schober, who was of Austrian descent, met her husband while she was his student working on a master's degree in English and German. Upon their marriage, Aurelia Plath seemed content to play the role of academic wife and homemaker. She is remembered by her neighbors as an urbane, congenial, hardworking woman.

Sifting through these images of normalcy, many biographical and psychological critics have attempted to find associations between Plath's poems and her subsequent life. But surely biographical data only hint at future events. While still in high school, Plath wrote in a letter, "I have erected in my mind an image of myself—idealistic and beautiful. Is not that image, free from blemish, the true self—the true perfection? Am I wrong when this image insinuates itself between me and the merciless mirror?" Three years later she attempted suicide.

In 1955 Sylvia Plath graduated from Smith College, where she had written an honors thesis on Dostoyevsky, and then went to England as a Fulbright scholar. In June 1956 she married the English poet Ted Hughes, with whom she had two children. However, their marriage began to disintegrate, and in October 1962, Plath wrote home to her mother, "I am fighting now, against hard odds and alone." On the morning of February 11, 1963, Sylvia Plath attempted suicide again and this time succeeded.

Because we know a considerable amount about her troubled life, and because Plath, like so many other poets, drew from her own experiences, some critics treat her poetry, especially her later poems, as "confessional," emphasizing their biographical revelations rather than considering them as works of art. Such a restricted reading robs her poetry of its uniqueness. Her early poetry, which reveals the influence of W. H. Auden and W. B. Yeats, is complex, formal, and often brilliantly orchestrated. Her later poetry is more direct and intense. Like the paintings of Hieronymus Bosch, her distortions and exaggerations seem much like the startling images of nightmares. We approach her poems with the expectation that we will find in them not the logical order of rational thought, but an urgently insistent retelling of the necessities of our often terrifying lives.

Black Rook in Rainy Weather

On the stiff twig up there
Hunches a wet black rook
Arranging and rearranging its feathers in the rain.
I do not expect miracle
Or an accident

To set the sight on fire
In my eye, nor seek
Any more in the desultory weather some design,
But let spotted leaves fall as they fall,
Without ceremony, or portent

Although, I admit, I desire,
Occasionally, some backtalk
From the mute sky, I can't honestly complain:
A certain minor light may still
Leap incandescent

Out of kitchen table or chair
As if a celestial burning took
Possession of the most obtuse objects now and then—
Thus hallowing an interval
Otherwise inconsequent

By bestowing largesse, honor,
One might say love. At any rate, I now walk
Wary (for it could happen
Even in this dull, ruinous landscape); skeptical,
Yet politic; ignorant

Of whatever angel may choose to flare
Suddenly at my elbow. I only know that a rook
Ordering its black feathers can so shine
As to seize my senses, haul
My eyelids up, and grant

A brief respite from fear
Of total neutrality. With luck,
Trekking stubborn through this season
Of fatigue, I shall
Patch together a content

Of sorts. Miracles occur,
if you care to call those spasmodic
Tricks of radiance miracles. The wait's begun again,
The long wait for the angel,
For that rare, random descent.

The Colossus

I shall never get you put together entirely,
Pieced, glued, and properly jointed.
Mule-bray, pig-grunt and bawdy cackles
Proceed from your great lips.
It's worse than a barnyard.

Perhaps you consider yourself an oracle,
Mouthpiece of the dead, or of some god or other.
Thirty years now I have labored
To dredge the silt from your throat.
I am none the wiser.

Scaling little ladders with gluepots and pails of Lysol
I crawl like an ant in mourning
Over the weedy acres of your brow
To mend the immense skull-plates and clear
The bald, white tumuli of your eyes.

A blue sky out of the Oresteia
Arches above us. O father, all by yourself
You are pithy and historical as the Roman Forum.
I open my lunch on a hill of black cypress.
Your fluted bones and acanthine hair are littered

In their old anarchy to the horizon-line.
It would take more than a lightning-stroke
To create such a ruin.
Nights, I squat in the cornucopia
Of your left ear, out of the wind,

Counting the red stars and those of plum-color.
The sun rises under the pillar of your tongue.
My hours are married to shadow.
No longer do I listen for the scrape of a keel
On the blank stones of the landing.

[16]**Oresteia:** a dramatic trilogy by the Greek tragic playwright Aeschylus (525–456 B.C.). Clytemnestra, wife of King Agamemnon, murders him for sacrificing their daughter Iphigenia. Electra and Orestes, their other children, in turn murder Clytemnestra to avenge the death of their father.

Morning Song

Love set you going like a fat gold watch.
The midwife slapped your footsoles, and your bald cry
Took its place among the elements.

Our voices echo, magnifying your arrival. New statue.
In a drafty museum, your nakedness
Shadows our safety. We stand round blankly as walls.

I'm no more your mother
Than the cloud that distills a mirror to reflect its own slow
Effacement at the wind's hand.

All night your moth-breath
Flickers among the flat pink roses. I wake to listen:
A far sea moves in my ear.

One cry, and I stumble from bed, cow-heavy and floral
In my Victorian nightgown.
Your mouth opens clean as a cat's. The window square

Whitens and swallows its dull stars. And now you try
Your handful of notes;
The clear vowels rise like balloons.

The Applicant

First, are you our sort of a person?
Do you wear
A glass eye, false teeth or a crutch,
A brace or a hook,
Rubber breasts or a rubber crotch,

Stitches to show something's missing? No, no? Then
How can we give you a thing?
Stop crying.
Open your hand.
Empty? Empty. Here is a hand

To fill it and willing
To bring teacups and roll away headaches

And do whatever you tell it.
Will you marry it?
It is guaranteed

To thumb shut your eyes at the end
And dissolve of sorrow.
We make new stock from the salt.
I notice you are stark naked.
How about this suit—

Black and stiff, but not a bad fit.
Will you marry it?
It is waterproof, shatterproof, proof
Against fire and bombs through the roof.
Believe me, they'll bury you in it.

Now your head, excuse me, is empty.
I have the ticket for that.
Come here, sweetie, out of the closet.
Well, what do you think of *that?*
Naked as paper to start

But in twenty-five years she'll be silver,
In fifty, gold.
A living doll, everywhere you look.
It can sew, it can cook,
It can talk, talk, talk.

It works, there is nothing wrong with it.
You have a hole, it's a poultice.
You have an eye, it's an image.
My boy, it's your last resort.
Will you marry it, marry it, marry it.

Lady Lazarus

I have done it again.
One year in every ten
I manage it—

LADY LAZARUS Lazarus was raised from the dead by Jesus (See John 11:1–45).

A sort of walking miracle, my skin
Bright as a Nazi lampshade,
My right foot

A paperweight,
My face a featureless, fine
Jew linen.

Peel off the napkin
O my enemy.
Do I terrify?—

The nose, the eye pits, the full set of teeth?
The sour breath
Will vanish in a day.

Soon, soon the flesh
The grave cave ate will be
At home on me

And I a smiling woman.
I am only thirty.
And like the cat I have nine times to die.

This is Number Three.
What a trash
To annihilate each decade.

What a million filaments.
The peanut-crunching crowd
Shoves in to see

Them unwrap me hand and foot—
The big strip tease.
Gentlemen, ladies,

These are my hands,
My knees.
I may be skin and bone,

[5]**Nazi lampshade:** the skin of some Jewish victims of the Holocaust was made into lampshades.

Nevertheless, I am the same, identical woman.
The first time it happened I was ten.
It was an accident.

The second time I meant
To last it out and not come back at all.
I rocked shut

As a seashell.
They had to call and call
And pick the worms off me like sticky pearls.

Dying
Is an art, like everything else.
I do it exceptionally well.

I do it so it feels like hell.
I do it so it feels real.
I guess you could say I've a call.

It's easy enough to do it in a cell.
It's easy enough to do it and stay put.
It's the theatrical

Comeback in broad day
To the same place, the same face, the same brute
Amused shout:

"A miracle!"
That knocks me out.
There is a charge

For the eyeing of my scars, there is a charge
For the hearing of my heart—
It really goes.

And there is a charge, a very large charge,
For a word or a touch
Or a bit of blood

Or a piece of my hair or my clothes.
So, so, Herr Doktor.
So, Herr Enemy.

I am your opus,
I am your valuable,
The pure gold baby

That melts to a shriek.
I turn and burn.
Do not think I underestimate your great concern.

Ash, ash—
You poke and stir.
Flesh, bone, there is nothing there—

A cake of soap,
A wedding ring,
A gold filling.

Herr God, Herr Lucifer,
Beware
Beware.

Out of the ash
I rise with my red hair
And I eat men like air.

Death & Co.

Two, of course there are two.
It seems perfectly natural now—
The one who never looks up, whose eyes are lidded
And balled, like Blake's,
Who exhibits

The birthmarks that are his trademark—
The scald scar of water,

LADY LAZARUS 65**Herr:** German for "mister."
DEATH & CO. 4**Blake:** William Blake (1757–1827), English poet.

The nude
Verdigris of the condor.
I am red meat. His beak

Claps sidewise: I am not his yet.
He tells me how badly I photograph.
He tells me how sweet
The babies look in their hospital
Icebox, a simple

Frill at the neck,
Then the flutings of their Ionian
Death-gowns,
Then two little feet.
He does not smile or smoke.

The other does that,
His hair long and plausive.
Bastard
Masturbating a glitter,
He wants to be loved.

I do not stir.
The frost makes a flower,
The dew makes a star,
The dead bell,
The dead bell.

Somebody's done for.

The Beekeeper's Daughter

A garden of mouthings. Purple, scarlet-speckled, black
The great corollas dilate, peeling back their silks.
Their musk encroaches, circle after circle,
A well of scents almost too dense to breathe in.
Hieratical in your frock coat, maestro of the bees,
You move among the many-breasted hives,

My heart under your foot, sister of a stone.

Trumpet-throats open to the beaks of birds.
The Golden Rain Tree drips its powders down.
In these little boudoirs streaked with orange and red
The anthers nod their heads, potent as kings
To father dynasties. The air is rich.
Here is a queenship no mother can contest—

A fruit that's death to taste: dark flesh, dark parings.

In burrows narrow as a finger, solitary bees
Keep house among the grasses. Kneeling down
I set my eye to a hole-mouth and meet an eye
Round, green, disconsolate as a tear.
Father, bridegroom, in this Easter egg
Under the coronal of sugar roses

The queen bee marries the winter of your year.

The Disquieting Muses

Mother, mother, what illbred aunt
Or what disfigured and unsightly
Cousin did you so unwisely keep
Unasked to my christening, that she
Sent these ladies in her stead
With heads like darning-eggs to nod
And nod and nod at foot and head
And at the left side of my crib?

Mother, who made to order stories
Of Mixie Blackshort the heroic bear,
Mother, whose witches always, always
Got baked into gingerbread, I wonder
Whether you saw them, whether you said
Words to rid me of those three ladies
Nodding by night around my bed,
Mouthless, eyeless, with stitched bald head.

In the hurricane, when father's twelve
Study windows bellied in
Like bubbles about to break, you fed

My brother and me cookies and Ovaltine
And helped the two of us to choir:
'Thor is angry: boom boom boom!
Thor is angry: we don't care!'
But those ladies broke the panes.

When on tiptoe the schoolgirls danced,
Blinking flashlights like fireflies
And singing the glowworm song, I could
Not lift a foot in the twinkle-dress
But, heavy-footed, stood aside
In the shadow cast by my dismal-headed
Godmothers, and you cried and cried:
And the shadow stretched, the lights went out.

Mother, you sent me to piano lessons
And praised my arabesques and trills
Although each teacher found my touch
Oddly wooden in spite of scales
And the hours of practicing, my ear
Tone-deaf and yes, unteachable.
I learned, I learned, I learned elsewhere,
From muses unhired by you, dear mother.

I woke one day to see you, mother,
Floating above me in bluest air
On a green balloon bright with a million
Flowers and bluebirds that never were
Never, never, found anywhere.
But the little planet bobbed away
Like a soap-bubble as you called: Come here!
And I faced my traveling companions.

Day now, night now, at head, side, feet,
They stand their vigil in gowns of stone,
Faces blank as the day I was born,
Their shadows long in the setting sun
That never brightens or goes down.
And this is the kingdom you bore me to,
Mother, mother. But no frown of mine
Will betray the company I keep.

Ariel

Stasis in darkness.
Then the substanceless blue
Pour of tor and distances.

God's lioness,
How one we grow,
Pivot of heels and knees!—The furrow

Splits and passes, sister to
The brown arc
Of the neck I cannot catch,

Nigger-eye
Berries cast dark
Hooks—

Black sweet blood mouthfuls,
Shadows.
Something else

Hauls me through air—
Thighs, hair;
Flakes from my heels.

White
Godiva, I unpeel—
Dead hands, dead stringencies.

And now I
Foam to wheat, a glitter of seas.
The child's cry

Melts in the wall.
And I
Am the arrow,

Ariel: an airy sprite in Shakespeare's play *The Tempest;* also the name of a horse Plath rode. [3]**tor:** a rocky peak.

The dew that flies
Suicidal, at one with the drive
Into the red

Eye, the cauldron of morning.

Daddy

You do not do, you do not do
Any more, black shoe
In which I have lived like a foot
For thirty years, poor and white,
Barely daring to breathe or Achoo.

Daddy, I have had to kill you.
You died before I had time—
Marble-heavy, a bag full of God,
Ghastly statue with one grey toe
Big as a Frisco seal

And a head in the freakish Atlantic
Where it pours bean green over blue
In the waters off beautiful Nauset.
I used to pray to recover you.
Ach, du.

In the German tongue, in the Polish town
Scraped flat by the roller
Of wars, wars, wars.
But the name of the town is common.
My Polack friend

Says there are a dozen or two.
So I never could tell where you
Put your foot, your root,
I never could talk to you.
The tongue stuck in my jaw.

DADDY [13]**Nauset:** a beach north of Boston. [15]**Ach, du:** German for "ah, you," a reference to Plath's father.

It stuck in a barb wire snare.
Ich, ich, ich, ich,
I could hardly speak.
I thought every German was you.
And the language obscene

An engine, an engine
Chuffing me off like a Jew.
A Jew to Dachau, Auschwitz, Belsen.
I began to talk like a Jew.
I think I may well be a Jew.

The snows of the Tyrol, the clear beer of Vienna
Are not very pure or true.
With my gypsy ancestress and my weird luck
And my Taroc pack and my Taroc pack
I may be a bit of a Jew.

I have always been scared of *you,*
With your Luftwaffe, your gobbledygoo.
And your neat moustache
And your Aryan eye, bright blue.
Panzer-man, panzer-man, O You—

Not God but a swastika
So black no sky could squeak through.
Every woman adores a Fascist,
The boot in the face, the brute
Brute heart of a brute like you.

You stand at the blackboard, daddy,
In the picture I have of you,
A cleft in your chin instead of your foot
But no less a devil for that, no not
Any less the black man who

[27]**Ich:** German for "I." [33]**Dachau, Auschwitz, Belsen:** German concentration camps where millions of Jews were murdered during World War II. [36]**Tyrol:** in the Austrian Alps. [39]**Taroc:** tarot cards, used in fortunetelling. [42]**Luftwaffe:** German air force in World War II. [45]**Panzer:** German for "armor." "Panzer-man" is a reference to Hitler.

Bit my pretty red heart in two.
I was ten when they buried you.
At twenty I tried to die
And get back, back, back to you.
I thought even the bones would do.

But they pulled me out of the sack,
And they stuck me together with glue.
And then I knew what to do.
I made a model of you,
A man in black with a Meinkampf look

And a love of the rack and the screw.
And I said I do, I do.
So daddy, I'm finally through.
The black telephone's off at the root,
The voices just can't worm through.

If I've killed one man, I've killed two—
The vampire who said he was you
And drank my blood for a year,
Seven years, if you want to know.
Daddy, you can lie back now.

There's a stake in your fat black heart
And the villagers never liked you.
They are dancing and stamping on you.
They always *knew* it was you.
Daddy, daddy, you bastard, I'm through.

Fever 103°

Pure? What does it mean?
The tongues of hell
Are dull, dull as the triple

Tongues of dull, fat Cerberus
Who wheezes at the gate. Incapable
Of licking clean

FEVER [4]**Cerberus:** in Greek mythology, the three-headed dog that guarded the gate to the Underworld. He also guards the gate of hell in Dante's *Inferno*.

The aguey tendon, the sin, the sin.
The tinder cries.
The indelible smell

Of a snuffed candle!
Love, love, the low smokes roll
From me like Isadora's scarves, I'm in a fright

One scarf will catch and anchor in the wheel.
Such yellow sullen smokes
Make their own element. They will not rise,

But trundle round the globe
Choking the aged and the meek,
The weak

Hothouse baby in its crib,
The ghastly orchid
Hanging its hanging garden in the air,

Devilish leopard!
Radiation turned it white
And killed it in an hour.

Greasing the bodies of adulterers
Like Hiroshima ash and eating in.
The sin. The sin.

Darling, all night
I have been flickering, off, on, off, on.
The sheets grow heavy as a lecher's kiss.

Three days. Three nights.
Lemon water, chicken
Water, water make me retch.

I am too pure for you or anyone.
Your body
Hurts me as the world hurts God. I am a lantern—

[12–13]**like Isadora's scarves . . . in the wheel:** Isadora Duncan (1878–1927), ballet dancer who was strangled when her long scarf caught in the wheel of her car.

My head a moon
Of Japanese paper, my gold beaten skin
Infinitely delicate and infinitely expensive.

Does not my heat astound you. And my light.
All by myself I am a huge camellia
Glowing and coming and going, flush on flush.

I think I am going up,
I think I may rise—
The beads of hot metal fly, and I, love, I

Am a pure acetylene
Virgin
Attended by roses,

By kisses, by cherubim,
By whatever these pink things mean.
Not you, nor him

Not him, nor him
(My selves dissolving, old whore petticoats)—
To Paradise.

Edge

The woman is perfected.
Her dead

Body wears the smile of accomplishment,
The illusion of a Greek necessity

Flows in the scrolls of her toga,
Her bare

Feet seem to be saying:
We have come so far, it is over.

Each dead child coiled, a white serpent,
One at each little

Pitcher of milk, now empty.
She has folded

Them back into her body as petals
Of a rose close when the garden

Stiffens and odors bleed
From the sweet, deep throats of the night flower.

The moon has nothing to be sad about,
Staring from her hood of bone.

She is used to this sort of thing.
Her blacks crackle and drag.

Words

Axes
After whose stroke the wood rings,
And the echoes!
Echoes travelling
Off from the center like horses.

The sap
Wells like tears, like the
Water striving
To re-establish its mirror
Over the rock

That drops and turns,
A white skull,
Eaten by weedy greens.
Years later I
Encounter them on the road—

Words dry and riderless,
The indefatigable hoof-taps.
While
From the bottom of the pool, fixed stars
Govern a life.

Mirror

I am silver and exact. I have no preconceptions.
Whatever I see I swallow immediately
Just as it is, unmisted by love or dislike.
I am not cruel, only truthful—
The eye of a little god, four-cornered.
Most of the time I meditate on the opposite wall.
It is pink, with speckles. I have looked at it so long
I think it is a part of my heart. But it flickers.
Faces and darkness separate us over and over.

Now I am a lake. A woman bends over me,
Searching my reaches for what she really is.
Then she turns to those liars, the candles or the moon.
I see her back, and reflect it faithfully.
She rewards me with tears and an agitation of hands.
I am important to her. She comes and goes.
Each morning it is her face that replaces the darkness.
In me she has drowned a young girl, and in me an old woman
Rises toward her day after day, like a terrible fish.

Heavy Women

Irrefutable, beautifully smug
As Venus, pedestalled on a half-shell
Shawled in blond hair and the salt
Scrim of a sea breeze, the women
Settle in their belling dresses.
Over each weighty stomach a face
Floats calm as a moon or a cloud.

Smiling to themselves, they meditate
Devoutly as the Dutch bulb
Forming its twenty petals.
The dark still nurses its secret.
On the green hill, under the thorn trees,
They listen for the millennium,
The knock of the small, new heart.

Pink-buttocked infants attend them.
Looping wool, doing nothing in particular,

They step among the archetypes.
Dusk hoods them in Mary-blue
While far off, the axle of winter
Grinds round, bearing down with the straw,
The star, the wise grey men.

The Moon and the Yew Tree

This is the light of the mind, cold and planetary.
The trees of the mind are black. The light is blue.
The grasses unload their griefs on my feet as if I were God,
Prickling my ankles and murmuring of their humility.
Fumy, spiritous mists inhabit this place
Separated from my house by a row of headstones.
I simply cannot see where there is to get to.

The moon is no door. It is a face in its own right,
White as a knuckle and terribly upset.
It drags the sea after it like a dark crime; it is quiet
With the O-gape of complete despair. I live here.
Twice on Sunday, the bells startle the sky—
Eight great tongues affirming the Resurrection.
At the end, they soberly bong out their names.

The yew tree points up. It has a Gothic shape.
The eyes lift after it and find the moon.
The moon is my mother. She is not sweet like Mary.
Her blue garments unloose small bats and owls.
How I would like to believe in tenderness—
The face of the effigy, gentled by candles,
Bending, on me in particular, its mild eyes.

I have fallen a long way. Clouds are flowering
Blue and mystical over the face of the stars.
Inside the church, the saints will be all blue,
Floating on their delicate feet over the cold pews,
Their hands and faces stiff with holiness.
The moon sees nothing of this. She is bald and wild.
And the message of the yew tree is blackness—blackness and silence.

Tulips

The tulips are too excitable, it is winter here.
Look how white everything is, how quiet, how snowed-in.
I am learning peacefulness, lying by myself quietly
As the light lies on these white walls, this bed, these hands.
I am nobody; I have nothing to do with explosions.
I have given my name and my day-clothes up to the nurses
And my history to the anaesthetist and my body to surgeons.

They have propped my head between the pillow and the sheet-cuff
Like an eye between two white lids that will not shut.
Stupid pupil, it has to take everything in.
The nurses pass and pass, they are no trouble,
They pass the way gulls pass inland in their white caps,
Doing things with their hands, one just the same as another,
So it is impossible to tell how many there are.

My body is a pebble to them, they tend it as water
Tends to the pebbles it must run over, smoothing them gently.
They bring me numbness in their bright needles, they bring me sleep.
Now I have lost myself I am sick of baggage—
My patent leather overnight case like a black pillbox,
My husband and child smiling out of the family photo;
Their smiles catch onto my skin, little smiling hooks.

I have let things slip, a thirty-year-old cargo boat
Stubbornly hanging on to my name and address.
They have swabbed me clear of my loving associations.
Scared and bare on the green plastic-pillowed trolley
I watched my tea-set, my bureaus of linen, my books
Sink out of sight, and the water went over my head.
I am a nun now, I have never been so pure.

I didn't want any flowers, I only wanted
To lie with my hands turned up and be utterly empty.
How free it is, you have no idea how free—
The peacefulness is so big it dazes you,
And it asks nothing, a name tag, a few trinkets.
It is what the dead close on, finally; I imagine them
Shutting their mouths on it, like a Communion tablet.

The tulips are too red in the first place, they hurt me.
Even through the gift paper I could hear them breathe
Lightly, through their white swaddlings, like an awful baby.
Their redness talks to my wound, it corresponds.
They are subtle: they seem to float, though they weigh me down,
Upsetting me with their sudden tongues and their color,
A dozen red lead sinkers round my neck.

Nobody watched me before, now I am watched.
The tulips turn to me, and the window behind me
Where once a day the light slowly widens and slowly thins,
And I see myself, flat, ridiculous, a cut-paper shadow
Between the eye of the sun and the eyes of the tulips,
And I have no face, I have wanted to efface myself.
The vivid tulips eat my oxygen.

Before they came the air was calm enough,
Coming and going, breath by breath, without any fuss.
Then the tulips filled it up like a loud noise.
Now the air snags and eddies round them the way a river
Snags and eddies round a sunken rust-red engine.
They concentrate my attention, that was happy
Playing and resting without committing itself.

They are opening like the mouth of some great African cat,
And I am aware of my heart: it opens and closes
Its bowl of red blooms out of sheer love of me.
The water I taste is warm and salt, like the sea,
And comes from a country far away as health.

Elm

FOR RUTH FAINLIGHT

I know the bottom, she says. I know it with my great tap root:
It is what you fear.
I do not fear it: I have been there.

Is it the sea you hear in me,
Its dissatisfactions?
Or the voice of nothing, that was your madness?

Love is a shadow.
How you lie and cry after it.
Listen: these are its hooves: it has gone off, like a horse.

All night I shall gallop thus, impetuously,
Till your head is a stone, your pillow a little turf,
Echoing, echoing.

Or shall I bring you the sound of poisons?
This is rain now, this big hush.
And this is the fruit of it: tin-white, like arsenic.

I have suffered the atrocity of sunsets.
Scorched to the root
My red filaments burn and stand, a hand of wires.

Now I break up in pieces that fly about like clubs.
A wind of such violence
Will tolerate no bystanding: I must shriek.

The moon, also, is merciless: she would drag me
Cruelly, being barren.
Her radiance scathes me. Or perhaps I have caught her.

I let her go. I let her go
Diminished and flat, as after radical surgery.
How your bad dreams possess and endow me.

I am inhabited by a cry.
Nightly it flaps out
Looking, with its hooks, for something to love.

I am terrified by this dark thing
That sleeps in me;
All day I feel its soft, feathery turnings, its malignity.

Clouds pass and disperse.
Are those the faces of love, those pale irretrievables?
Is it for such I agitate my heart?

I am incapable of more knowledge.
What is this, this face
So murderous in its strangle of branches?—

Its snaky acids kiss.
It petrifies the will. These are the isolate, slow faults
That kill, that kill, that kill.

Cut

FOR SUSAN O'NEILL ROE

What a thrill—
My thumb instead of an onion.
The top quite gone
Except for a sort of a hinge

Of skin,
A flap like a hat,
Dead white.
Then that red plush.

Little pilgrim,
The Indian's axed your scalp.
Your turkey wattle
Carpet rolls

Straight from the heart.
I step on it,
Clutching my bottle
Of pink fizz.

A celebration, this is.
Out of a gap
A million soldiers run,
Redcoats, every one.

Whose side are they on?
O my

Homunculus, I am ill.
I have taken a pill to kill

The thin
Papery feeling.
Saboteur,
Kamikaze man—

The stain on your
Gauze Ku Klux Klan
Babushka
Darkens and tarnishes and when

The balled
Pulp of your heart
Confronts its small
Mill of silence

How you jump—
Trepanned veteran,
Dirty girl,
Thumb stump.

Nick and the Candlestick

I am a miner. The light burns blue.
Waxy stalactites
Drip and thicken, tears

The earthen womb
Exudes from its dead boredom.
Black bat airs

Wrap me, raggy shawls,
Cold homicides.
They weld to me like plums.

Old cave of calcium
Icicles, old echoer.
Even the newts are white,

Those holy Joes.
And the fish, the fish—
Christ! They are panes of ice,

A vice of knives,
A piranha
Religion, drinking

Its first communion out of my live toes.
The candle
Gulps and recovers its small altitude,

Its yellows hearten.
O love, how did you get here?
O embryo

Remembering, even in sleep,
Your crossed position.
The blood blooms clean

In you, ruby.
The pain
You wake to is not yours.

Love, love,
I have hung our cave with roses.
With soft rugs—

The last of Victoriana.
Let the stars
Plummet to their dark address,

Let the mercuric
Atoms that cripple drip
Into the terrible well,

You are the one
Solid the spaces lean on, envious.
You are the baby in the barn.

Crossing the Water

Black lake, black boat, two black, cut-paper people.
Where do the black trees go that drink here?
Their shadows must cover Canada.

A little light is filtering from the water flowers.
Their leaves do not wish us to hurry:
They are round and flat and full of dark advice.

Cold worlds shake from the oar.
The spirit of blackness is in us, it is in the fishes.
A snag is lifting a valedictory, pale hand;

Stars open among the lilies.
Are you not blinded by such expressionless sirens?
This is the silence of astounded souls.

Blackberrying

Nobody in the lane, and nothing, nothing but blackberries,
Blackberries on either side, though on the right mainly,
A blackberry alley, going down in hooks, and a sea
Somewhere at the end of it, heaving. Blackberries
Big as the ball of my thumb, and dumb as eyes
Ebon in the hedges, fat
With blue-red juices. These they squander on my fingers.
I had not asked for such a blood sisterhood; they must love
me.
They accommodate themselves to my milkbottle, flattening
their sides.

Overhead go the choughs in black, cacophonous flocks—
Bits of burnt paper wheeling in a blown sky.
Theirs is the only voice, protesting, protesting.
I do not think the sea will appear at all.
The high, green meadows are glowing, as if lit from within.
I come to one bush of berries so ripe it is a bush of flies,
Hanging their blue-green bellies and their wing panes in a
Chinese screen.

The honey-feast of the berries has stunned them; they believe
  in heaven.
One more hook, and the berries and bushes end.

The only thing to come now is the sea.
From between two hills a sudden wind funnels at me,
Slapping its phantom laundry in my face.
These hills are too green and sweet to have tasted salt.
I follow the sheep path between them. A last hook brings me
To the hills' northern face, and the face is orange rock
That looks out on nothing, nothing but a great space
Of white and pewter lights, and a din like silversmiths
Beating and beating at an intractable metal.

PART THREE

Other Voices and Visions: Modern and Contemporary Poets

EDWIN ARLINGTON ROBINSON

[1869–1935]

Edwin Arlington Robinson was born and raised in Maine. After working there as a freelance writer and studying for two years at Harvard University, he moved to New York in 1896. Robinson settled in Greenwich Village and, through the patronage of Theodore Roosevelt, was appointed a clerk in the New York Customs House. After the financial struggles of his early years and the initial difficulty of getting his poems published, Robinson acquired both fame and financial stability. He was awarded three Pulitzer prizes and various medals, distinctions, and honorary degrees. He spent the last twenty-four summers of his life at the MacDowell colony for artists in New Hampshire. His poetry—traditional in rhythm, language, and structure—is notable for its compassionate yet ironically realistic portraits of characters whose pervasive experience is one of sadness and loss.

Richard Cory

Whenever Richard Cory went down town,
We people on the pavement looked at him:
He was a gentleman from sole to crown,
Clean favored, and imperially slim.

And he was always quietly arrayed,
And he was always human when he talked;
But still he fluttered pulses when he said,
"Good-morning," and he glittered when he walked.

And he was rich—yes, richer than a king—
And admirably schooled in every grace:
In fine, we thought that he was everything
To make us wish that we were in his place.

So on we worked, and waited for the light,
And went without the meat, and cursed the bread;
And Richard Cory, one calm summer night,
Went home and put a bullet through his head.

Mr. Flood's Party

Old Eben Flood, climbing alone one night
Over the hill between the town below
And the forsaken upland hermitage
That held as much as he should ever know
On earth again of home, paused warily.
The road was his with not a native near;
And Eben, having leisure, said aloud,
For no man else in Tilbury Town to hear:

"Well, Mr. Flood, we have the harvest moon
Again, and we may not have many more;
The bird is on the wing, the poet says,
And you and I have said it here before.
Drink to the bird." He raised up to the light
The jug that he had gone so far to fill,
And answered huskily: "Well, Mr. Flood,
Since you propose it, I believe I will."

Alone, as if enduring to the end
A valiant armor of scarred hopes outworn,
He stood there in the middle of the road
Like Roland's ghost winding a silent horn.
Below him, in the town among the trees,
Where friends of other days had honored him,
A phantom salutation of the dead
Rang thinly till old Eben's eyes were dim.

Then, as a mother lays her sleeping child
Down tenderly, fearing it may awake,
He set the jug down slowly at his feet

MR. FLOYD'S PARTY [11]**the poet:** Omar Khayyam, whose *Rubaiyat* was translated into English by Edward Fitzgerald. [20]**Roland's ghost winding a silent horn:** in the *Song of Roland,* a medieval French epic, the courageous and proud Roland refuses to sound his horn to call for aid.

With trembling care, knowing that most things break;
And only when assured that on firm earth
It stood, as the uncertain lives of men
Assuredly did not, he paced away,
And with his hand extended paused again:

"Well, Mr. Flood, we have not met like this
In a long time; and many a change has come
To both of us, I fear, since last it was
We had a drop together. Welcome home!"
Convivially returning with himself,
Again he raised the jug up to the light;
And with an acquiescent quaver said:
"Well, Mr. Flood, if you insist, I might.

"Only a very little, Mr. Flood—
For auld lang syne. No more, sir; that will do."
So, for the time, apparently it did,
And Eben evidently thought so too;
For soon amid the silver loneliness
Of night he lifted up his voice and sang,
Secure, with only two moons listening,
Until the whole harmonious landscape rang—

"For auld lang syne." The weary throat gave out,
The last word wavered; and the song was done.
He raised again the jug regretfully
And shook his head, and was again alone.
There was not much that was ahead of him,
And there was nothing in the town below—
Where strangers would have shut the many doors
That many friends had opened long ago.

HD (HILDA DOOLITTLE)

[1886–1961]

Hilda Doolittle was born in Pennsylvania. She was educated at private schools in Philadelphia and then attended Bryn Mawr College. In college, she resumed a friendship she had established earlier with Ezra Pound, who introduced her to William Carlos Williams—then a student, as was Pound, at the University of Pennsylvania. Doolittle settled in Europe, first in England, where she met and married the English poet and classical scholar Richard Aldington, and later in Switzerland after her divorce. Her published work includes fiction, plays, translations, and a tribute to Sigmund Freud, with whom she underwent psychoanalysis. She is best known for her spare and compelling Imagist poems, characterized by short lines, free rhythmic cadences, and vivid images.

Sea Rose

Rose, harsh rose,
marred and with stint of petals,
meagre flower, thin,
sparse of leaf,

more precious
than a wet rose,
single on a stem—
you are caught in the drift.

Stunted, with small leaf,
you are flung on the sand,
you are lifted
in the crisp sand
that drives in the wind.

Can the spice-rose
drip such acrid fragrance
hardened in a leaf?

Evening

The light passes
from ridge to ridge,
from flower to flower—
the hypaticas, wide-spread
under the light
grow faint—
the petals reach inward,
the blue tips bend
toward the bluer heart

and the flowers are lost.
The cornel-buds are still white,
but shadows dart
from the cornel-roots—
black creeps from root to root,
each leaf
cuts another leaf on the grass,
shadow seeks shadow,
then both leaf
and leaf-shadow are lost.

JOHN CROWE RANSOM

[1888–1974]

John Crowe Ransom was born in Tennessee and was educated there at Vanderbilt University. After studying as a Rhodes scholar at Oxford (1910–1913), Ransom returned to Vanderbilt, where he taught from 1914 until 1937, with time out to serve in the army and to take a year's leave as a Guggenheim fellow. Ransom taught at a number of other colleges and universities, the most important of which was Kenyon College, in Ohio, where he worked from 1937 until 1974. There, he established the influential literary journal *The Kenyon Review,* which was published in 1937–1959. Ransom's poetry illustrates a set of poetic values that also inform his literary criticism: wit, irony, traditional structures, and density of implication.

Bells for John Whiteside's Daughter

There was such speed in her little body,
And such lightness in her footfall,
It is no wonder her brown study
Astonishes us all.

Her wars were bruited in our high window.
We looked among orchard trees and beyond
Where she took arms against her shadow,
Or harried unto the pond

The lazy geese, like a snow cloud
Dripping their snow on the green grass,

Tricking and stopping, sleepy and proud,
Who cried in goose, Alas,

For the tireless heart within the little
Lady with rod that made them rise
From their noon apple-dreams and scuttle
Goose-fashion under the skies!

But now go the bells, and we are ready,
In one house we are sternly stopped
To say we are vexed at her brown study,
Lying so primly propped.

Blue Girls

Twirling your blue skirts, travelling the sward
Under the towers of your seminary,
Go listen to your teachers old and contrary
Without believing a word.

Tie the white fillets then about your hair
And think no more of what will come to pass
Than bluebirds that go walking on the grass
And chattering on the air.

Practise your beauty, blue girls, before it fail;
And I will cry with my loud lips and publish
Beauty which all our power shall never establish,
It is so frail.

For I could tell you a story which is true;
I know a woman with a terrible tongue,
Blear eyes fallen from blue,
All her perfections tarnished—yet it is not long
Since she was lovelier than any of you.

Janet Waking

Beautifully Janet slept
Till it was deeply morning. She woke then
And thought about her dainty-feathered hen,
To see how it had kept.

One kiss she gave her mother.
Only a small one gave she to her daddy
Who would have kissed each curl of his shining baby;
No kiss at all for her brother.

"Old Chucky, old Chucky!" she cried,
Running across the world upon the grass
To Chucky's house, and listening. But alas,
Her Chucky had died.

It was a transmogrifying bee
Came droning down on Chucky's old bald head
And sat and put the poison. It scarcely bled,
But how exceedingly

And purply did the knot
Swell with the venom and communicate
Its rigor! Now the poor comb stood up straight
But Chucky did not.

So there was Janet
Kneeling on the wet grass, crying her brown hen
(Translated far beyond the daughters of men)
To rise and walk upon it.

And weeping fast as she had breath
Janet implored us, "Wake her from her sleep!"
And would not be instructed in how deep
Was the forgetful kingdom of death.

E. E. CUMMINGS

[1894–1962]

Edward Estlin Cummings was born in Massachusetts. He was educated at Cambridge High and Latin School and at Harvard University. During World War I, he served as a member of the Norton Harjes Ambulance Corps. Due to an administrative error, cummings and a companion spent three months in a French detention camp, an experience he later described in his novel *The Enormous Room*. He lived at times in Paris and New York, working in both cities at his painting and his poetry. His poems are noted for their experimental structure and language, especially their unconventional punctuation and grammatical inventiveness. He is adept at satire and charming in the lyrical mode, especially in love poetry.

anyone lived in a pretty how town

anyone lived in a pretty how town
(with up so floating many bells down)
spring summer autumn winter
he sang his didn't he danced his did.

Women and men(both little and small)
cared for anyone not at all
they sowed their isn't they reaped their same
sun moon stars rain

children guessed(but only a few
and down they forgot as up they grew
autumn winter spring summer)
that noone loved him more by more

when by now and tree by leaf
she laughed his joy she cried his grief
bird by snow and stir by still
anyone's any was all to her

someones married their everyones
laughed their cryings and did their dance
(sleep wake hope and then) they
said their nevers they slept their dream

stars rain sun moon
(and only the snow can begin to explain
how children are apt to forget to remember
with up so floating many bells down)

one day anyone died i guess
(and noone stooped to kiss his face)
busy folk buried them side by side
little by little and was by was

all by all and deep by deep
and more by more they dream their sleep

noone and anyone earth by april
wish by spirit and if by yes.

Women and men(both dong and ding)
summer autumn winter spring
reaped their sowing and went their came
sun moon stars rain

i like my body when it is with your

i like my body when it is with your
body. It is so quite new a thing.
Muscles better and nerves more.
i like your body.— i like what it does,
i like its hows.— i like to feel the spine
of your body and its bones, and the trembling
-firm-smooth ness and which i will
again and again and again
kiss,— i like kissing this and that of you,
i like, slowing stroking the, shocking fuzz
of your electric fur, and what-is-it comes
over parting flesh . . . . And eyes big love-crumbs,

and possibly i like the thrill

of under me you so quite new

may i feel said he

may i feel said he
(i'll squeal said she
just once said he)
it's fun said she

(may i touch said he
how much said she
a lot said he)
why not said she

(let's go said he
not too far said she

what's too far said he
where you are said she)

may i stay said he
(which way said she
like this said he
if you kiss said she

may i move said he
is it love said she)
if you're willing said he
(but you're killing said she

but it's life said he
but your wife said she
now said he)
ow said she

(tiptop said he
don't stop said she
oh no said he)
go slow said she

(cccome?said he
ummm said she)
you're divine!said he
(you are Mine said she)

my father moved through dooms of love

my father moved through dooms of love
through sames of am through haves of give,
singing each morning out of each night
my father moved through depths of height

this motionless forgetful where
turned at his glance to shining here;
that if(so timid air is firm)
under his eyes would stir and squirm

newly as from unburied which
floats the first who,his april touch

drove sleeping selves to swarm their fates
woke dreamers to their ghostly roots

and should some why completely weep
my father's fingers brought her sleep:
vainly no smallest voice might cry
for he could feel the mountains grow.

Lifting the valleys of the sea
my father moved through griefs of joy;
praising a forehead called the moon
singing desire into begin

joy was his song and joy so pure
a heart of star by him could steer
and pure so now and now so yes
the wrists of twilight would rejoice

keen as midsummer's keen beyond
conceiving mind of sun will stand,
so strictly(over utmost him
so hugely)stood my father's dream

his flesh was flesh his blood was blood:
no hungry man but wished him food;
no cripple wouldn't creep one mile
uphill to only see him smile.

Scorning the pomp of must and shall
my father moved through dooms of feel;
his anger was as right as rain
his pity was as green as grain

septembering arms of year extend
less humbly wealth to foe and friend
than he to foolish and to wise
offered immeasurable is

proudly and(by octobering flame
beckoned)as earth will downward climb,
so naked for immortal work
his shoulders marched against the dark

his sorrow was as true as bread:
no liar looked him in the head;
if every friend became his foe
he'd laugh and build a world with snow.

My father moved through theys of we,
singing each new leaf out of each tree
(and every child was sure that spring
danced when she heard my father sing)

then let men kill which cannot share,
let blood and flesh be mud and mire,
scheming imagine,passion willed,
freedom a drug that's bought and sold

giving to steal and cruel kind,
a heart to fear,to doubt a mind,
to differ a disease of same,
conform the pinnacle of am

though dull were all we taste as bright,
bitter all utterly things sweet,
maggoty minus and dumb death
all we inherit,all bequeath

and nothing quite so least as truth
—i say though hate were why men breathe—
because my father lived his soul
love is the whole and more than all

LOUISE BOGAN

[1897–1970]

Louise Bogan was born in Maine and educated at Boston University. She taught at a number of universities, including Chicago and Brandeis. For nearly forty years, she was poetry editor of *The New Yorker* magazine. Her awards and prizes include a Bollingen Poetry Prize and two Guggenheim fellowships. She published criticism and letters, as well as verse. Her poems are noted for their spareness of detail and their finely distilled thought.

Men Loved Wholly Beyond Wisdom

Men loved wholly beyond wisdom
Have the staff without the banner.
Like a fire in a dry thicket
Rising within women's eyes
Is the love men must return.
Heart, so subtle now, and trembling,
What a marvel to be wise,
To love never in this manner!
To be quiet in the fern
Like a thing gone dead and still,
Listening to the prisoned cricket
Shake its terrible, dissembling
Music in the granite hill.

Women

Women have no wilderness in them,
They are provident instead,
Content in the tight hot cell of their hearts
To eat dusty bread.

They do not see cattle cropping red winter grass,
They do not hear
Snow water going down under culverts
Shallow and clear.

They wait, when they should turn to journeys,
They stiffen, when they should bend.
They use against themselves that benevolence
To which no man is friend.

They cannot think of so many crops to a field
Or of clean wood cleft by an axe.
Their love is an eager meaninglessness
Too tense, or too lax.

They hear in every whisper that speaks to them
A shout and a cry.
As like as not, when they take life over their door-sills
They should let it go by.

RICHARD EBERHART

[b. 1904]

Richard Eberhart was born in Minnesota and educated at the University of Minnesota, Dartmouth College, St. John's College, Cambridge University, and Harvard University. During World War II he was an aerial gunnery officer in the navy, an experience reflected in his poem "The Fury of Aerial Bombardment." He has had a distinguished and varied teaching career; he once served as tutor to the son of the king of Siam. He taught at many American universities and at St. Mark's School in Massachusetts, where Robert Lowell was among his pupils. He has received numerous distinctions and awards, including a Bollingen Prize, a Pulitzer Prize, and a National Book Award. His poems are characterized by a transforming vision that transcends fact into a spiritual and imaginative realm.

The Groundhog

In June, amid the golden fields,
I saw a groundhog lying dead.
Dead lay he; my senses shook,
And mind outshot our naked frailty.
There lowly in the vigorous summer
His form began its senseless change,
And made my senses waver dim
Seeing nature ferocious in him.
Inspecting close his maggots' might
And seething cauldron of his being,
Half with loathing, half with a strange love,
I poked him with an angry stick.
The fever arose, became a flame
And Vigour circumscribed the skies,
Immense energy in the sun,
And through my frame a sunless trembling.
My stick had done nor good nor harm.
Then stood I silent in the day
Watching the object, as before;
And kept my reverence for knowledge
Trying for control, to be still,
To quell the passion of the blood;

Until I had bent down on my knees
Praying for joy in the sight of decay.
And so I left; and I returned
In Autumn strict of eye, to see
The sap gone out of the groundhog,
But the bony sodden hulk remained.
But the year had lost its meaning,
And in intellectual chains
I lost both love and loathing,
Mured up in the wall of wisdom.
Another summer took the fields again
Massive and burning, full of life,
But when I chanced upon the spot
There was only a little hair left,
And bones bleaching in the sunlight
Beautiful as architecture;
I watched them like a geometer,
And cut a walking stick from a birch.
It has been three years, now.
There is no sign of the groundhog.
I stood there in the whirling summer,
My hand capped a withered heart,
And thought of China and of Greece,
Of Alexander in his tent;
Of Montaigne in his tower,
Of Saint Theresa in her wild lament.

ROBERT PENN WARREN

[1905–1989]

Robert Penn Warren, born in Kentucky, is generally considered to be one of America's most distinguished writers. He has excelled at both fiction and poetry, winning the Pulitzer Prize in 1946 for his novel *All the King's Men* and again in 1958 for his volume of poems *Promises*. He spent the first twenty years of his life in the South, attending Vanderbilt University, in Tennessee, where he studied with John Crowe Ransom. Warren continued his studies at the University of California, at Oxford, where he was a Rhodes scholar, and finally at Yale, where he taught for many years. With Cleanth Brooks, he wrote the influential textbook *Understanding Poetry,* which taught more than one generation of students how to read poems. His own poems reflect a strong interest in the ambiguity and complexity of experience. They are cast in a variety of forms and voices, from the ironic wit of the brief metaphysical lyric to speculative sequential narratives in free verse.

The Corner of the Eye

The poem is just beyond the corner of the eye.
You cannot see it—not yet—but sense the faint gleam,

Or stir. It may be like a poor little shivering fieldmouse,
One tiny paw lifted from snow while, far off, the owl

Utters. Or like breakers, far off, almost as soundless as dream.
Or the rhythmic rasp of your father's last breath, harsh

As the grind of a great file the blacksmith sets to hoof.
Or the whispering slither the torn morning newspaper makes,

Blown down an empty slum street in New York, at midnight,
Past dog shit and garbage cans, while the full moon,

Phthisic and wan, above the East River, presides
Over that last fragment of history which is

Our lives. Or the foggy glint of old eyes of
The sleepless patient who no longer wonders

If he will once more see in that window the dun-
Bleached dawn that promises what. Or the street corner

Where always, for years, in passing you felt, unexplained, a pang
Of despair, like nausea, till one night, late, late on that spot

You were struck stock-still and again remembered—felt
Her head thrust to your shoulder, she clinging, while you

Mechanically pat the fur coat, hear sobs, and stare up
Where tall buildings, frailer than reed-stalks, reel among stars.

Yes, something there at eye-edge lurks, hears ball creak in
socket,
Knows, before you do, tension of muscle, change

Of blood pressure, heart-heave of sadness, foot's falter, for
It has stalked you all day, or years, breath rarely heard, fangs
dripping.

And now, any moment, great hindquarters may hunch,
ready—
Or is it merely a poem, after all?

W. H. AUDEN

[1907–1973]

Wystan Hugh Auden, son of a physician, was born in York, England. He attended private schools throughout England and studied at Oxford University. After teaching school for a few years, Auden traveled extensively in the 1930s through Europe, Iceland, and China. During the Spanish Civil War he served as an ambulance driver for the anti-Franco forces. He became a naturalized American citizen in 1946, living mostly in New York City and summering in Austria. He has received many distinguished honors, including Pulitzer and Bollingen prizes and a National Book Award. His poems are noted for their wit, their incisive intelligence, their social and moral impulses, and their careful craftsmanship.

The Unknown Citizen

(TO JS/07/M/378
THIS MARBLE MONUMENT IS ERECTED BY THE STATE)

He was found by the Bureau of Statistics to be
One against whom there was no official complaint,
And all the reports on his conduct agree
That, in the modern sense of an old-fashioned word, he was a
saint,
For in everything he did he served the Greater Community.
Except for the War till the day he retired
He worked in a factory and never got fired
But satisfied his employers, Fudge Motors Inc.

Yet he wasn't a scab or odd in his views,
For his Union reports that he paid his dues,
(Our report on his Union shows it was sound)
And our Social Psychology workers found
That he was popular with his mates and liked a drink.
The Press are convinced that he bought a paper every day
And that his reactions to advertisements were normal in every way.
Policies taken out in his name prove that he was fully insured,
And his Health-card shows he was once in hospital but left it cured.
Both Producers Research and High-Grade Living declare
He was fully sensible to the advantages of the Installment Plan
And had everything necessary to the Modern Man,
A phonograph, a radio, a car and a frigidaire.
Our researchers into Public Opinion are content
That he held the proper opinions for the time of year;
When there was peace, he was for peace; when there was war, he went.
He was married and added five children to the population,
Which our Eugenist says was the right number for a parent of his generation.
And our teachers report that he never interfered with their education.

Was he free? Was he happy? The question is absurd:
Had anything been wrong, we should certainly have heard.

In Memory of W. B. Yeats

[D. JANUARY 1939]

I

He disappeared in the dead of winter:
The brooks were frozen, the air-ports almost deserted,
And snow disfigured the public statues;
The mercury sank in the mouth of the dying day.
O all the instruments agree
The day of his death was a dark cold day.

Far from his illness
The wolves ran on through the evergreen forests,
The peasant river was untempted by the fashionable quays;

By mourning tongues
The death of the poet was kept from his poems.
But for him it was his last afternoon as himself,
An afternoon of nurses and rumours;
The provinces of his body revolted,
The squares of his mind were empty,
Silence invaded the suburbs,
The current of his feeling failed: he became his admirers.

Now he is scattered among a hundred cities
And wholly given over to unfamiliar affections;
To find his happiness in another kind of wood
And be punished under a foreign code of conscience.
The words of a dead man
Are modified in the guts of the living.

But in the importance and noise of to-morrow
When the brokers are roaring like beasts on the floor of the
  Bourse,
And the poor have the sufferings to which they are fairly
  accustomed,
And each in the cell of himself is almost convinced of his
  freedom;
A few thousand will think of this day
As one thinks of a day when one did something slightly
  unusual.

O all the instruments agree
The day of his death was a dark cold day.

2

You were silly like us: your gift survived it all;
The parish of rich women, physical decay,
Yourself; mad Ireland hurt you into poetry.
Now Ireland has her madness and her weather still,
For poetry makes nothing happen: it survives
In the valley of its saying where executives
Would never want to tamper; it flows south
From ranches of isolation and the busy griefs,
Raw towns that we believe and die in; it survives,
A way of happening, a mouth.

3

Earth, receive an honoured guest;
William Yeats is laid to rest:
Let the Irish vessel lie
Emptied of its poetry.

Time that is intolerant
Of the brave and innocent,
And indifferent in a week
To a beautiful physique,

Worships language and forgives
Everyone by whom it lives;
Pardons cowardice, conceit,
Lays its honours at their feet.

Time that with this strange excuse
Pardoned Kipling and his views,
And will pardon Paul Claudel,
Pardons him for writing well.

In the nightmare of the dark
All the dogs of Europe bark,
And the living nations wait,
Each sequestered in its hate;

Intellectual disgrace
Stares from every human face,
And the seas of pity lie
Locked and frozen in each eye.

Follow, poet, follow right
To the bottom of the night,
With your unconstraining Voice
Still persuade us to rejoice;

With the farming of a verse
Make a vineyard of the curse,

55**Kipling:** Rudyard Kipling (1865–1936), British writer with imperialist views. 56**Paul Claudel:** French Catholic writer (1868–1955) who was extremely conservative politically. 58–61**In the nightmare . . . in its hate:** World War II broke out only a few months after Auden wrote this poem.

Sing of human unsuccess
In a rapture of distress;

In the deserts of the heart
Let the healing fountain start,
In the prison of his days
Teach the free man how to praise.

THEODORE ROETHKE

[1908–1963]

Theodore Roethke was born in 1908 in Saginaw, Michigan, where his family owned and operated a large greenhouse nursery. Roethke earned both his B.A. and M.A. degrees at the University of Michigan. He taught at Lafayette, Penn State, Bennington, and the University of Washington, serving as varsity tennis coach at the first two schools and remaining at the last for seventeen years until his death in 1963. Roethke won many prizes and awards, including two Guggenheim fellowships (1945, 1950), two Ford Foundation grants (1952, 1959), the Bollingen Poetry Prize (1959), the Pulitzer Prize (1954), and a pair of National Book awards (1959, 1965). His success as a poet was paralleled by his fame as a teacher, a number of notable American poets having studied with him, including David Wagoner, Richard Hugo, and James Wright. His own poetry displays a Romanticist's passionate interest in the natural world and an autobiographer's concern with fashioning a self from fragments of the past.

The Premonition

Walking this field I remember
Days of another summer.
Oh that was long ago! I kept
Close to the heels of my father,
Matching his stride with half-steps
Until we came to a river.
He dipped his hand in the shallow:
Water ran over and under
Hair on a narrow wrist bone;
His image kept following after,—
Flashed with the sun in the ripple.
But when he stood up, that face
Was lost in a maze of water.

Child on Top of a Greenhouse

The wind billowing out the seat of my britches,
My feet crackling splinters of glass and dried putty,
The half-grown chrysanthemums staring up like accusers,
Up through the streaked glass, flashing with sunlight,
A few white clouds all rushing eastward,
A line of elms plunging and tossing like horses,
And everyone, everyone pointing up and shouting!

I Knew a Woman

I knew a woman, lovely in her bones,
When small birds sighed, she would sigh back at them;
Ah, when she moved, she moved more ways than one:
The shapes a bright container can contain!
Of her choice virtues only gods should speak,
Or English poets who grew up on Greek
(I'd have them sing in chorus, cheek to cheek).

How well her wishes went! She stroked my chin,
She taught me Turn, and Counter-turn, and Stand;
She taught me Touch, that undulant white skin;
I nibbled meekly from her proffered hand;
She was the sickle; I, poor I, the rake,
Coming behind her for her pretty sake
(But what prodigious mowing we did make).

Love likes a gander, and adores a goose:
Her full lips pursed, the errant note to seize;
She played it quick, she played it light and loose;
My eyes, they dazzled at her flowing knees;
Her several parts could keep a pure repose,
Or one hip quiver with a mobile nose
(She moved in circles, and those circles moved).

Let seed be grass, and grass turn into hay:
I'm martyr to a motion not my own;
What's freedom for? To know eternity.
I swear she cast a shadow white as stone.
But who would count eternity in days?
These old bones live to learn her wanton ways:
(I measure time by how a body sways).

The Far Field

1

I dream of journeys repeatedly:
Of flying like a bat deep into a narrowing tunnel,
Of driving alone, without luggage, out a long peninsula,
The road lined with snow-laden second growth,
A fine dry snow ticking the windshield,
Alternate snow and sleet, no on-coming traffic,
And no lights behind, in the blurred side-mirror,
The road changing from glazed tarface to a rubble of stone,
Ending at last in a hopeless sand-rut,
Where the car stalls,
Churning in a snowdrift
Until the headlights darken.

2

At the field's end, in the corner missed by the mower,
Where the turf drops off into a grass-hidden culvert,
Haunt of the cat-bird, nesting-place of the field-mouse,
Not too far away from the ever-changing flower-dump,
Among the tin cans, tires, rusted pipes, broken machinery,—
One learned of the eternal;
And in the shrunken face of a dead rat, eaten by rain and
ground-beetles
(I found it lying among the rubble of an old coal bin)
And the tom-cat, caught near the pheasant-run,
Its entrails strewn over the half-grown flowers,
Blasted to death by the night watchman.

I suffered for birds, for young rabbits caught in the mower,
My grief was not excessive.
For to come upon warblers in early May
Was to forget time and death:
How they filled the oriole's elm, a twittering restless cloud, all
one morning,
And I watched and watched till my eyes blurred from the bird
shapes,—
Cape May, Blackburnian, Cerulean,—
Moving, elusive as fish, fearless,
Hanging, bunched like young fruit, bending the end branches,
Still for a moment,

Then pitching away in half-flight,
Lighter than finches,
While the wrens bickered and sang in the half-green
  hedgerows,
And the flicker drummed from his dead tree in the
  chicken-yard.

—Or to lie naked in sand,
In the silted shallows of a slow river,
Fingering a shell,
Thinking:
Once I was something like this, mindless,
Or perhaps with another mind, less peculiar;
Or to sink down to the hips in a mossy quagmire;
Or, with skinny knees, to sit astride a wet log,
Believing:
I'll return again,
As a snake or a raucous bird,
Or, with luck, as a lion.

I learned not to fear infinity,
The far field, the windy cliffs of forever,
The dying of time in the white light of tomorrow,
The wheel turning away from itself,
The sprawl of the wave,
The on-coming water.

3

The river turns on itself,
The tree retreats into its own shadow.
I feel a weightless change, a moving forward
As of water quickening before a narrowing channel
When banks converge, and the wide river whitens;
Or when two rivers combine, the blue glacial torrent
And the yellowish-green from the mountainy upland,—
At first a swift rippling between rocks,
Then a long running over flat stones
Before descending to the alluvial plain,
To the clay banks, and the wild grapes hanging from the
  elmtrees.
The slightly trembling water

Dropping a fine yellow silt where the sun stays;
And the crabs bask near the edge,
The weedy edge, alive with small snakes and bloodsuckers,—
I have come to a still, but not a deep center,
A point outside the glittering current;
My eyes stare at the bottom of a river,
At the irregular stones, iridescent sandgrains,
My mind moves in more than one place,
In a country half-land, half-water.

I am renewed by death, thought of my death,
The dry scent of a dying garden in September,
The wind fanning the ash of a low fire.
What I love is near at hand,
Always, in earth and air.

4

The lost self changes,
Turning toward the sea,
A sea-shape turning around,—
An old man with his feet before the fire,
In robes of green, in garments of adieu.

A man faced with his own immensity
Wakes all the waves, all their loose wandering fire.
The murmur of the absolute, the why
Of being born fails on his naked ears.
His spirit moves like monumental wind
That gentles on a sunny blue plateau.
He is the end of things, the final man.

All finite things reveal infinitude:
The mountain with its singular bright shade
Like the blue shine on freshly frozen snow,
The after-light upon ice-burdened pines;
Odor of basswood on a mountain-slope,
A scent beloved of bees;
Silence of water above a sunken tree:
The pure serene of memory in one man,—
A ripple widening from a single stone
Winding around the waters of the world.

CHARLES OLSON

[1910–1970]

Charles Olson was born in Massachusetts and educated in New England at Wesleyan, Yale, and Harvard. He taught at a number of universities, including Harvard, Connecticut, and the State University of New York at Buffalo. More important, however, was Olson's connection with Black Mountain College, in North Carolina, where he was professor and rector in 1948–1956. In Black Mountain's experimental environment, Olson worked with avant-garde artists such as composer John Cage, choreographer Merce Cunningham, and painter Robert Rauschenberg. At Black Mountain, Olson was also at the center of a group of experimental poets who included Robert Duncan, Denise Levertov, and Robert Creeley. Olson's poems reflect the theoretical assumptions he was developing during the 1950s. They attempt to project the poet's energy and perceptions directly to the reader by means of freely placed lines and phrases over the open field of the page, distributed according to rhythms corresponding to the poet's breath, rather than to conventional metrical patterns.

Maximus, to Gloucester, Sunday, July 19

and they stopped before that bad sculpture of a fisherman

—"as if one were to talk to a man's house,
knowing not what gods or heroes are"—

not knowing what a fisherman is
instead of going straight to the Bridge
and doing no more than—saying no more than—
in the Charybdises of the
Cut waters the flowers tear off

the wreaths

the flowers
turn

Gloucester: fishing town in Massachusetts, where Olson grew up. On July 19 the town holds a memorial service for fishermen lost at sea. [7]**Charybdises:** a whirlpool that Odysseus, in Homer's *Odyssey,* must sail around.

the character of the sea The sea jumps
the fate of the flower The drowned men are undrowned
in the eddies
                    of the eyes
                    of the flowers
                    opening
                    the sea's eyes
The disaster
is undone
What was received as alien
—the flower
on the water, that a man drowns
that he dies in water as he dies on earth, the impossible
      that this gross fact can return to us
            in this upset
on a summer day
of a particular tide

that the sensation is true,
that the transformations of fire are, first of all, sea—
      "as gold for wares wares for gold"

      Let them be told who stopped first
      by a bronze idol

      A fisherman is not a successful man
      he is not a famous man he is not a man
      of power, these are the damned by God

II

whose surface bubbles
with these gimlets
which screw-in like

potholes, caustic
caked earth in painted
pools, Yellowstone

Park of holes
is death the diseased
presence on us, the spilling lesion

of the brilliance
it is to be alive: to walk onto it,
as Jim Bridger the first into it,

it is more true a scabious
field than it is a pretty
meadow

When a man's coffin is the sea
the whole of creation shall come to his funeral,

it turns out; the globe
is below, all lapis

and its blue surface golded
by what happened

this afternoon: there are eyes
in this water

the flowers
from the shore,

awakened
the sea

Men are so sure they know very many things,
they don't even know night and day are one

A fisherman works without reference to
that difference. It is possible he also

by lying there when he does lie, jowl
to the sea, has another advantage: it is said,

"You rectify what can be rectified," and when a man's heart
cannot see this, the door of his divine intelligence is shut

let you who paraded to the Cut today
to hold memorial services to all fishermen

48 **Jim Bridger:** fur trader and Indian scout (1804–1881).

who have been lost at sea in a year
when for the first time not one life was lost

radar sonar radio telephone good engines
bed-check seaplanes goodness over and
under us

no difference
when men come back

ROBERT HAYDEN

[1913–1980]

Robert Hayden was born in Michigan and educated at Wayne State University and the University of Michigan. For most of his academic life, he taught at Fisk University, in Tennessee, but he also served on the faculties of the universities of Michigan, Louisville, and Washington and on that of the Breadloaf Writers' Conference. His awards include a Ford Foundation grant, an American Academy of Poets fellowship, and a poetry consultantship at the Library of Congress. His poems are characterized by a directness of language in rendering character and action, a descriptive vividness of detail, and a strong moral tone.

O Daedalus, Fly Away Home

(FOR MAIA AND JULIE)

Drifting night in the Georgia pines,
coonskin drum and jubilee banjo.
Pretty Malinda, dance with me.

Night is juba, night is conjo.
Pretty Malinda, dance with me.

Night is an African juju man
weaving a wish and a weariness together
to make two wings.

O fly away home fly away

Do you remember Africa?

O cleave the air fly away home

My gran, he flew back to Africa,
just spread his arms and
flew away home.

Drifting night in the windy pines;
night is a laughing, night is a longing.
Pretty Malinda, come to me.

Night is a mourning juju man
weaving a wish and a weariness together
to make two wings.

O fly away home fly away

The Whipping

The old woman across the way
is whipping the boy again
and shouting to the neighborhood
her goodness and his wrongs.

Wildly he crashes through elephant ears,
pleads in dusty zinnias,
while she in spite of crippling fat
pursues and corners him.

She strikes and strikes the shrilly circling
boy till the stick breaks
in her hand. His tears are rainy weather
to woundlike memories:

My head gripped in bony vise
of knees, the writhing struggle
to wrench free, the blows, the fear
worse than blows that hateful

Words could bring, the face that I
no longer knew or loved . . . .
Well, it is over now, it is over,
and the boy sobs in his room,

And the woman leans muttering against
a tree, exhausted, purged—
avenged in part for lifelong hidings
she has had to bear.

JOHN BERRYMAN

[1914–1972]

John Berryman was born in Oklahoma as John Smith, the son of a banker. He took the name Berryman from his stepfather, whom his mother married after his father committed suicide when the boy was twelve. Berryman was educated at Columbia University and at Clare College, Cambridge. He taught at Wayne State, Princeton, and Harvard universities before beginning his long association with the University of Minnesota, which lasted from 1954 until 1972, when he committed suicide. Berryman's major poetic effort was a series of 385 "Dream Songs" that comprise a loose narrative about the life of a semiautobiographical character, Henry, whom Berryman described as "a white American in early middle age . . . who has suffered an irreversible loss and talks to himself." Each "Dream Song" is eighteen lines, written in iambic stanzas of six lines each, two in trimeter and four in pentameter.

From *Dream Songs*

1

Huffy Henry hid the day,
unappeasable Henry sulked.
I see his point,—a trying to put things over.
It was the thought that they thought
they could *do* it made Henry wicked & away.
But he should have come out and talked.

All the world like a woolen lover
once did seem on Henry's side.

Then came a departure.
Thereafter nothing fell out as it might or ought.
I don't see how Henry, pried
open for all the world to see, survived.

What he has now to say is a long
wonder the world can bear & be.
Once in a sycamore I was glad
all at the top, and I sang.
Hard on the land wears the strong sea
and empty grows every bed.

14

Life, friends, is boring. We must not say so.
After all, the sky flashes, the great sea yearns,
we ourselves flash and yearn,
and moreover my mother told me as a boy
(repeatingly) 'Ever to confess you're bored
means you have no

Inner Resources.' I conclude now I have no
inner resources, because I am heavy bored.
Peoples bore me,
literature bores me, especially great literature,
Henry bores me, with his plights & gripes
as bad as achilles,

who loves people and valiant art, which bores me.
And the tranquil hills, & gin, look like a drag
and somehow a dog
has taken itself & its tail considerably away
into mountains or sea or sky, leaving
behind: me, wag.

29

There sat down, once, a thing on Henry's heart
so heavy, if he had a hundred years
& more, & weeping, sleepless, in all them time
Henry could not make good.
Starts again always in Henry's ears
the little cough somewhere, an odour, a chime.

And there is another thing he has in mind
like a grave Sienese face a thousand years
would fail to blur the still profiled reproach of. Ghastly,
with open eyes, he attends, blind.
All the bells say: too late. This is not for tears;
thinking.

But never did Henry, as he thought he did,
end anyone and hacks her body up
and hide the pieces, where they may be found.
He knows: he went over everyone, & nobody's missing.
Often he reckons, in the dawn, them up.
Nobody is ever missing.

40

I'm scared a lonely. Never see my son,
easy be not to see anyone,
combers out to sea
know they're goin somewhere but not me.
Got a little poison, got a little gun,
I'm scared a lonely.

I'm scared a only one thing, which is me,
from othering I don't take nothin, see,
for any hound dog's sake.
But this is where I livin, where I rake
my leaves and cop my promise, this' where we
cry oursel's awake.

Wishin was dyin but I gotta make
it all this way to that bed on these feet
where peoples said to meet.
Maybe but even if I see my son
forever never, get back on the take,
free, black & forty-one.

45

He stared at ruin. Ruin stared straight back.
He thought they was old friends. He felt on the stair
where her papa found them bare

they became familiar. When the papers were lost
rich with pals' secrets, he thought he had the knack
of ruin. Their paths crossed

and once they crossed in jail; they crossed in bed;
and over an unsigned letter their eyes met,
and in an Asian city
directionless & lurchy at two & three,
or trembling to a telephone's fresh threat,
and when some wired his head

to reach a wrong opinion, 'Epileptic'.
But he noted now that: they were not old friends.
He did not know this one.
This one was a stranger, come to make amends
for all the imposters, and to make it stick.
Henry nodded, un-.

GWENDOLYN BROOKS

[b. 1917]

Gwendolyn Brooks was born in Kansas but has spent most of her life in Chicago, where she attended Wilson Junior College. She has taught at a number of universities in the Chicago area, as well as at the University of Wisconsin and the City University of New York. She has won many honors and awards, including a Pulitzer Prize. Since 1968 she has been poet laureate of Illinois, an honor formerly held by Carl Sandburg. Her poetry blends the language and concerns of urban blacks, particularly their street talk, with the poetic diction and forms characteristic of traditional English poetry. Her poetic voice is authoritative and occasionally satirical, without being either militant or didactic.

A Song in the Front Yard

I've stayed in the front yard all my life.
I want a peek at the back
Where it's rough and untended and hungry weed grows.
A girl gets sick of a rose.

I want to go in the back yard now
And maybe down the alley,
To where the charity children play.
I want a good time today.

They do some wonderful things.
They have some wonderful fun.
My mother sneers, but I say it's fine
How they don't have to go in at quarter to nine.
My mother, she tells me that Johnnie Mae
Will grow up to be a bad woman.
That George'll be taken to Jail soon or late
(On account of last winter he sold our back gate.)

But I say it's fine. Honest, I do.
And I'd like to be a bad woman, too,
And wear the brave stockings of night-black lace
And strut down the streets with paint on my face.

ROBERT DUNCAN

[1919–1988]

Robert Duncan, a native of California, was educated at the University of California, Berkeley. He has taught at San Francisco State, Black Mountain College, and the University of British Columbia, and has won prestigious poetry awards including the Harriet Monroe Memorial Prize, the National Poetry Award, a Guggenheim Fellowship, and grants from the National Endowment for the Arts. His poems are richly imaginative and deeply spiritual.

Often I Am Permitted to Return to a Meadow

as if it were a scene made-up by the mind,
that is not mine, but is a made place,

that is mine, it is so near to the heart,
an eternal pasture folded in all thought
so that there is a hall therein

that is a made place, created by light
wherefrom the shadows that are forms fall.

Wherefrom fall all architectures I am
I say are likenesses of the First Beloved
whose flowers are flames lit to the Lady.

She it is Queen Under The Hill
whose hosts are a disturbance of words within words
that is a field folded.

It is only a dream of the grass blowing
east against the source of the sun
in an hour before the sun's going down

whose secret we see in a children's game
of ring a round of roses told.

Often I am permitted to return to a meadow
as if it were a given property of the mind
that certain bounds hold against chaos,

that is a place of first permission,
everlasting omen of what is.

MAY SWENSON

[b. 1919]

May Swenson was born in Utah and educated at Utah State University. She has worked as a reporter for a Salt Lake City newspaper and as an editor for New Directions, a New York publishing house. Her university affiliations include Purdue, Bryn Mawr, and North Carolina at Greensboro. Her published work includes poems, stories, drama, translations from Swedish poetry, and books for children. Her poems are characteristically playful and witty, sometimes visually so.

How Everything Happens

(BASED ON A STUDY OF THE WAVE)

happen.
to
up
stacking
is
something
When nothing is happening

When it happens
something
pulls
back
not
to
happen.

When has happened.
pulling back stacking up
happens

has happened stacks up.
When it something nothing
pulls back while

Then nothing is happening.

happens.
and
forward
pushes
up
stacks
something
Then

Women

Women   Or they
should be   should be
pedestals   little horses
moving   those wooden
pedestals   sweet
moving   oldfashioned
to the   painted
motions   rocking
of men   horses

the gladdest things in the toyroom.

the   feelingly
pegs   and then
of their   unfeelingly
ears   To be
so familiar   joyfully
and dear   ridden
to the trusting   rockingly
fists   ridden until
To be chafed   the restored

egos dismount and the legs stride away

Immobile   willing
sweetlipped   to be set
sturdy   into motion
and smiling   Women
women   should be
should always   pedestals
be waiting   to men

The Centaur

The summer that I was ten—
Can it be there was only one
summer that I was ten? It must

have been a long one then—
each day I'd go out to choose
a fresh horse from my stable

which was a willow grove
down by the old canal.
I'd go on my two bare feet.

But when, with my brother's jack-knife,
I had cut me a long limber horse
with a good thick knob for a head,

and peeled him slick and clean
except a few leaves for the tail,
and cinched my brother's belt

around his head for a rein,
I'd straddle and canter him fast
up the grass bank to the path,

trot along in the lovely dust
that talcumed over his hoofs,
hiding my toes, and turning

his feet to swift half-moons.
The willow knob with the strap
jouncing between my thighs

was the pommel and yet the poll
of my nickering pony's head.
My head and my neck were mine,

yet they were shaped like a horse.
My hair flopped to the side
like the mane of a horse in the wind.

My forelock swung in my eyes,
my neck arched and I snorted.
I shied and skittered and reared,

stopped and raised my knees,
pawed at the ground and quivered.
My teeth bared as we wheeled

and swished through the dust again.
I was the horse and the rider,
and the leather I slapped to his rump

spanked my own behind.
Doubled, my two hoofs beat
a gallop along the bank,

the wind twanged in my mane,
my mouth squared to the bit.
And yet I sat on my steed

quiet, negligent riding,
my toes standing the stirrups,
my thighs hugging his ribs.

At a walk we drew up to the porch.
I tethered him to a paling.
Dismounting, I smoothed my skirt

and entered the dusky hall.
My feet on the clean linoleum
left ghostly toes in the hall.

Where have you been? said my mother.
Been riding. I said from the sink,
and filled me a glass of water.

What's that in your pocket? she said.
Just my knife. It weighted my pocket
and stretched my dress awry.

Go tie back your hair, said my mother,
and *Why is your mouth all green?*
*Rob Roy, he pulled some clover
as we crossed the field,* I told her.

RICHARD WILBUR

[b. 1921]

Richard Wilbur was born in New York and educated in New England at Amherst College and Harvard University. During World War II, he served as an infantryman in Italy and France. He has taught at Harvard, Wellesley, Wesleyan, and Smith, where he currently teaches. His numerous awards and prizes include Guggenheim and Ford Foundation fellowships, a Pulitzer Prize, a National Book Award, and a Bollingen Poetry Prize for translation. His translations of Molière's comedies are judged by many to be the supreme English renderings of these works. His own poems are cast in traditional stanzaic forms, and they exhibit a striking command of versification and rhyme. They demonstrate an unswerving recognition of the need for strict adherence to form, which Wilbur believes is essential for poetic achievement. "The strength of the genie," he has remarked, "comes from his being confined in a bottle."

Mind

Mind in the purest play is like some bat
That beats about in caverns all alone,
Contriving by a kind of senseless wit
Not to conclude against a wall of stone.

It has no need to falter or explore;
Darkly it knows what obstacles are there,
And so may weave and flitter, dip and soar
In perfect courses through the blackest air.

And has this simile a like perfection?
The mind is like a bat. Precisely. Save
That in the very happiest intellection
A graceful error may correct the cave.

Juggler

A ball will bounce, but less and less. It's not
A light-hearted thing, resents its own resilience.
Falling is what it loves, and the earth falls

So in our hearts from brilliance,
Settles and is forgot.
It takes a skyblue juggler with five red balls

To shake our gravity up. Whee, in the air
The balls roll round, wheel on his wheeling hands,
Learning the ways of lightness, alter to spheres
Grazing his finger ends,
Cling to their courses there,
Swinging a small heaven about his ears.

But a heaven is easier made of nothing at all
Than the earth regained, and still and sole within
The spin of worlds, with a gesture sure and noble
He reels that heaven in,
Landing it ball by ball,
And trades it all for a broom, a plate, a table.

Oh, on his toe the table is turning, the broom's
Balancing up on his nose, and the plate whirls
On the tip of the broom! Damn, what a show, we cry:
The boys stamp, and the girls
Shriek, and the drum booms
And all comes down, and he bows and says good-bye.

If the juggler is tired now, if the broom stands
In the dust again, if the table starts to drop
Through the daily dark again, and though the plate
Lies flat on the table top,
For him we batter our hands
Who has won for once over the world's weight.

LOUIS SIMPSON

[b. 1923]

Louis Simpson was born in Jamaica, West Indies. He was educated there at Munro College and in New York at Columbia University, where he received his master's and doctorate. He served in the United States Army during World War II, earning both a Purple Heart and a Bronze Star. He has taught at Columbia and at the University of California at Berkeley and is currently professor of English at the State University of New York at Stony Brook. His numerous distinctions include a Guggenheim fellowship, a Pulitzer Prize, and an award from the American Academy of Arts and Letters. His poetry intricately blends the familiar and the strange in both ordinary and surrealistic evocations. He also exhibits a concern for American history, traditions, and cultural values, especially those inspired by the American dream.

The Heroes

I dreamed of war-heroes, of wounded war-heroes
With just enough of their charms shot away
To make them more handsome. The women moved nearer
To touch their brave wounds and their hair steaked with gray.

I saw them in long ranks ascending the gang-planks;
The girls with the doughnuts were cheerful and gay.
They minded their manners and muttered their thanks;
The Chaplain advised them to watch and to pray.

They shipped these rapscallions, these sea-sick battalions
To a patriotic and picturesque spot;
They gave them new bibles and marksmen's medallions,
Compasses, maps, and committed the lot.

A fine dust has settled on all that scrap metal.
The heroes were packaged and sent home in parts
To pluck at a poppy and sew on a petal
And count the long night by the stroke of their hearts.

American Poetry

Whatever it is, it must have
A stomach that can digest
Rubber, coal, uranium, moons, poems.

Like the shark, it contains a shoe.
It must swim for miles through the desert
Uttering cries that are almost human.

Walt Whitman at Bear Mountain

. . . life which does not give the preference to any other life, of any previous period, which therefore prefers its own existence . . .

ORTEGA Y GASSET

Neither on horseback nor seated,
But like himself, squarely on two feet,
The poet of death and lilacs
Loafs by the footpath. Even the bronze looks alive
Where it is folded like cloth. And he seems friendly.

"Where is the Mississippi panorama
And the girl who played the piano?
What are you, Walt?
The Open Road goes to the used-car lot.

"Where is the nation you promised?
These houses built of wood sustain
Colossal snows,
And the light above the street is sick to death.

"As for the people—see how they neglect you!
Only a poet pauses to read the inscription."

"I am here," he answered.
"It seems you have found me out.
Yet, did I not warn you that it was Myself
I advertised? Were my words not sufficiently plain?

"I gave no prescriptions,
And those who have taken my moods for prophecies
Mistake the matter."
Then, vastly amused—"Why do you reproach me?
I freely confess I am wholly disreputable.
Yet I am happy, because you have found me out."

A crocodile in wrinkled metal loafing . . .

Then all the realtors,
Pickpockets, salesmen, and the actors performing
Official scenarios,

Turned a deaf ear, for they had contracted
American dreams.

But the man who keeps a store on a lonely road,
And the housewife who knows she's dumb,
And the earth, are relieved.

All that grave weight of America
Cancelled! Like Greece and Rome.
The future in ruins!
The castles, the prisons, the cathedrals
Unbuilding, and roses
Blossoming from the stones that are not there . . .

The clouds are lifting from the high Sierras.
The Bay mists clearing;
And the angel in the gate, the flowering plum,
Dances like Italy, imagining red.

KENNETH KOCH

[b. 1925]

Kenneth Koch was born in Ohio and educated at Harvard, where he became friends with John Ashbery and Frank O'Hara, and at Columbia. He spent three years abroad in Italy and France soaking up the influence of French surrealistic verse, especially that of Jacques Prévert. Koch has taught at several universities but mostly at Columbia, where he is currently established. Besides his own poetry, Koch has edited a series of anthologies designed to teach children to read and write poetry. His poems exhibit a debt to Whitman as well as French Surrealism. They are characterized by open forms, incongruous images, and zany humor.

To You

I love you as a sheriff searches for a walnut
That will solve a murder case unsolved for years
Because the murderer left it in the snow beside a window

Through which he saw her head, connecting with
Her shoulders by a neck, and laid a red
Roof in her heart. For this we live a thousand years;
For this we love, and we live because we love, we are not
Inside a bottle, thank goodness! I love you as a
Kid searches for a goat; I am crazier than shirttails
In the wind, when you're near, a wind that blows from
The big blue sea, so shiny so deep and so unlike us;
I think I am bicycling across an Africa of green and white fields
Always, to be near you, even in my heart
When I'm awake, which swims, and also I believe that you
Are trustworthy as the sidewalk which leads me to
The place where I again think of you, a new
Harmony of thoughts! I love you as the sunlight leads the prow
Of a ship which sails
From Hartford to Miami, and I love you
Best at dawn, when even before I am awake the sun
Receives me in the questions which you always pose.

You Were Wearing

You were wearing your Edgar Allan Poe printed cotton blouse.
In each divided up square of the blouse was a picture of Edgar Allan Poe.
Your hair was blonde and you were cute. You asked me, "Do most boys think that most girls are bad?"
I smelled the mold of your seaside resort hotel bedroom on your hair held in place by a John Greenleaf Whittier clip.
"No," I said, "it's girls who think that boys are bad." Then we read *Snowbound* together
And ran around in an attic, so that a little of the blue enamel was scraped off my George Washington, Father of His Country, shoes.

Mother was walking in the living room, her Strauss Waltzes comb in her hair.
We waited for a time and then joined her, only to be served tea in cups painted with pictures of Herman Melville

As well as with illustrations from his book *Moby Dick* and from
his novella, *Benito Cereno.*
Father came in wearing his Dick Tracy necktie: "How about a
drink, everyone?"
I said, "Let's go outside a while." Then we went onto the
porch and sat on the Abraham Lincoln swing.
You sat on the eyes, mouth, and beard part, and I sat on the
knees.
In the yard across the street we saw a snowman holding a
garbage can lid smashed into a likeness of the mad English
king, George the Third.

A. R. AMMONS

[b. 1926]

Archibald Randolph Ammons was born and raised on a farm in North Carolina. He was educated at Wake Forest College, where he studied science, and at the University of California at Berkeley. He has worked as the principal of an elementary school and as an executive vice-president of a company that manufactured biological glassware. Since 1964 he has taught at Cornell University. Ammons has received a number of honors including a Bollingen Poetry Prize and a National Book Award for his *Collected Poems*. In its meditative cast, his poetry shows the influence of Wallace Stevens. In its metrical innovation and experiments with the poetic line, it has affinities with William Carlos Williams.

Reflective

I found a
weed
that had a

mirror in it
and that
mirror

looked in at
a mirror
in

me that
had a
weed in it.

The City Limits

When you consider the radiance, that it does not withhold
itself but pours its abundance without selection into every
nook and cranny not overhung or hidden; when you consider

that birds' bones make no awful noise against the light but
lie low in the light as in a high testimony; when you consider
the radiance, that it will look into the guiltiest

swervings of the weaving heart and bear itself upon them,
not flinching into disguise or darkening; when you consider
the abundance of such resource as illuminates the glow-blue

bodies and gold-skeined wings of flies swarming the dumped
guts of a natural slaughter or the coil of shit and in no
way winces from its storms of generosity; when you consider

that air or vacuum, snow or shale, squid or wolf, rose or
lichen,
each is accepted into as much light as it will take, then
the heart moves roomier, the man stands and looks about, the

leaf does not increase itself above the grass, and the dark
work of the deepest cells is of a tune with May bushes
and fear lit by the breadth of such calmly turns to praise.

Extrication

I tangled with
the world to
let it go
but couldn't free

it: so I made
words
to wrestle in my
stead and went

off silent to
the quick flow
of brooks, the
slow flow of stone

ROBERT CREELEY

[b. 1926]

Robert Creeley was born in Massachusetts and educated at Harvard University, Black Mountain College, and the University of New Mexico. He has worked with the American Field Service in India and Burma, and has lived on a farm in New Hampshire. He has also traveled in France and Majorca, where he started the Divers Press. He has taught on a coffee plantation in Guatemala, at the University of New Mexico, and, since 1966, at the State University of New York at Buffalo. His poems reveal the influence of William Carlos Williams in their minimalism, intimacy, and openness to language and experience. They are usually short, plain, direct, casual, and personal in their attempt to offer transitory glimpses of feelings and relationships.

I Know a Man

As I sd to my
friend, because I am
always talking,—John, I

sd, which was not his
name, the darkness sur-
rounds us, what

can we do against
it, or else, shall we &
why not, buy a goddamn big car,

drive, he sd, for
christ's sake, look
out where yr going.

The Language

Locate *I*
love you some-
where in

teeth and
eyes, bite
it but

take care not
to hurt, you
want so

much so
little. Words
say everything,

I
love you
again,

then what
is emptiness
for. To

fill, fill.
I heard words
and words full

of holes
aching. Speech
is a mouth.

ALLEN GINSBERG

[b. 1926]

Allen Ginsberg was born in New Jersey and educated at Columbia University. His formal academic education was, however, less important to him than the literary education he received from William Burroughs, author of the experimental novel *Naked Lunch.* For a while, Ginsberg lived in San

Francisco and became associated with the "Beat" generation of writers that included Burroughs, Jack Kerouac, Gary Snyder, and Lawrence Ferlinghetti. In the 1960s he traveled extensively through the Far East, where he studied Buddhism and Hinduism. His poetry, which reveals the influence of Walt Whitman, William Blake, and William Carlos Williams, is largely motivated by a prophetic impulse to set society straight. It is characterized by a confessional tendency and is generally recognizable by its long lines cast in incantatory repetitive patterns.

A Supermarket in California

What thoughts I have of you tonight, Walt Whitman, for I walked down the sidestreets under the trees with a headache self-conscious looking at the full moon.

In my hungry fatigue, and shopping for images, I went into the neon fruit supermarket, dreaming of your enumerations!

What peaches and what penumbras! Whole families shopping at night! Aisles full of husbands! Wives in the avocados, babies in the tomatoes!—and you, Garcia Lorca, what were you doing down by the watermelons?

I saw you, Walt Whitman, childless, lonely old grubber, poking among the meats in the refrigerator and eyeing the grocery boys.

I heard you asking questions of each: Who killed the pork chops? What price bananas? Are you my Angel?

I wandered in and out of the brilliant stacks of cans following you, and followed in my imagination by the store detective.

We strode down the open corridors together in our solitary fancy tasting artichokes, possessing every frozen delicacy, and never passing the cashier.

Where are we going, Walt Whitman? The doors close in an hour. Which way does your beard point tonight?

(I touch your book and dream of our odyssey in the supermarket and feel absurd.)

Will we walk all night through solitary streets? The trees add shade to shade, lights out in the houses, we'll both be lonely.

Will we stroll dreaming of the lost America of love past

blue automobiles in driveways, home to our silent cottage?

Ah, dear father, graybeard, lonely old courage-teacher, what America did you have when Charon quit poling his ferry and you got out on a smoking bank and stood watching the boat disappear on the black waters of Lethe?

Howl

FOR CARL SOLOMON

I

I saw the best minds of my generation destroyed by madness,
 starving hysterical naked,
dragging themselves through the negro streets at dawn looking
 for an angry fix,
angelheaded hipsters burning for the ancient heavenly
 connection to the starry dynamo in the machinery of night,
who poverty and tatters and hollow-eyed and high sat up
 smoking in the supernatural darkness of cold-water flats
 floating across the tops of cities contemplating jazz,
who bared their brains to Heaven under the El and saw
 Mohammedan angels staggering on tenement roofs
 illuminated,
who passed through universities with radiant cool eyes
 hallucinating Arkansas and Blake-light tragedy among the
 scholars of war,
who were expelled from the academies for crazy & publishing
 obscene odes on the windows of the skull,
who cowered in unshaven rooms in underwear, burning their
 money in wastebaskets and listening to the Terror through
 the wall,
who got busted in their pubic beards returning through Laredo
 with a belt of marijuana for New York,
who ate fire in paint hotels or drank turpentine in Paradise
 Alley, death, or purgatoried their torsos night after night
with dreams, with drugs, with waking nightmares, alcohol and
 cock and endless balls,
incomparable blind streets of shuddering cloud and lightning
 in the mind leaping toward poles of Canada & Paterson,
 illuminating all the motionless world of Time between,
Peyote solidities of halls, backyard green tree cemetery dawns,

wine drunkenness over the rooftops, storefront boroughs of
teahead joyride neon blinking traffic light, sun and moon
and tree vibrations in the roaring winter dusks of Brooklyn,
ashcan rantings and kind king light of mind,
who chained themselves to subways for the endless ride from
Battery to holy Bronx on benzedrine until the noise of
wheels and children brought them down shuddering
mouth-wracked and battered bleak of brain all drained of
brilliance in the drear light of Zoo,
who sank all night in submarine light of Bickford's floated out
and sat through the stale beer afternoon in desolate
Fugazzi's, listening to the crack of doom on the hydrogen
jukebox,
who talked continuously seventy hours from park to pad to
bar to Bellevue to museum to the Brooklyn Bridge,
a lost battalion of platonic conversationalists jumping down the
stoops off fire escapes off windowsills off Empire State out
of the moon,
yacketayakking screaming vomiting whispering facts and
memories and anecdotes and eyeball kicks and shocks of
hospitals and jails and wars,
whole intellects disgorged in total recall for seven days and
nights with brilliant eyes, meat for the Synagogue cast on
the pavement,
who vanished into nowhere Zen New Jersey leaving a trail of
ambiguous picture postcards of Atlantic City Hall,
suffering Eastern sweats and Tangerian bone-grindings and
migraines of China under junk-withdrawal in Newark's
bleak furnished room,
who wandered around and around at midnight in the railroad
yard wondering where to go, and went, leaving no broken
hearts,
who lit cigarettes in boxcars boxcars boxcars racketing through
snow toward lonesome farms in grandfather night,
who studied Plotinus Poe St. John of the Cross telepathy and
bop kaballa because the cosmos instinctively vibrated at their
feet in Kansas,
who loned it through the streets of Idaho seeking visionary
indian angels who were visionary indian angels,
who thought they were only mad when Baltimore gleamed in
supernatural ecstasy,
who jumped in limousines with the Chinaman of Oklahoma

on the impulse of winter midnight streetlight smalltown rain,
who lounged hungry and lonesome through Houston seeking jazz or sex or soup, and followed the brilliant Spaniard to converse about America and Eternity, a hopeless task, and so took ship to Africa,
who disappeared into the volcanoes of Mexico leaving behind nothing but the shadow of dungarees and the lava and ash of poetry scattered in fireplace Chicago,
who reappeared on the West Coast investigating the F.B.I. in beards and shorts with big pacifist eyes sexy in their dark skin passing out incomprehensible leaflets,
who burned cigarette holes in their arms protesting the narcotic tobacco haze of Capitalism,
who distributed Supercommunist pamphlets in Union Square weeping and undressing while the sirens of Los Alamos wailed them down, and wailed down Wall, and the Staten Island ferry also wailed,
who broke down crying in white gymnasiums naked and trembling before the machinery of other skeletons,
who bit detectives in the neck and shrieked with delight in policecars for committing no crime but their own wild cooking pederasty and intoxication,
who howled on their knees in the subway and were dragged off the roof waving genitals and manuscripts,
who let themselves be fucked in the ass by saintly motorcyclists, and screamed with joy,
who blew and were blown by those human seraphim, the sailors, caresses of Atlantic and Caribbean love,
who balled in the morning in the evenings in rosegardens and the grass of public parks and cemeteries scattering their semen freely to whomever come who may,
who hiccupped endlessly trying to giggle but wound up with a sob behind a partition in a Turkish Bath when the blonde & naked angel came to pierce them with a sword,
who lost their loveboys to the three old shrews of fate the one eyed shrew of the heterosexual dollar the one eyed shrew that winks out of the womb and the one eyed shrew that does nothing but sit on her ass and snip the intellectual golden threads of the craftsman's loom,
who copulated ecstatic and insatiate with a bottle of beer a sweetheart a package of cigarettes a candle and fell off the

bed, and continued along the floor and down the hall and
ended fainting on the wall with a vision of ultimate cunt
and come eluding the last gyzym of consciousness,
who sweetened the snatches of a million girls trembling in the
sunset, and were red eyed in the morning but prepared to
sweeten the snatch of the sunrise, flashing buttocks under
barns and naked in the lake,
who went out whoring through Colorado in myriad stolen
night-cars, N.C., secret hero of these poems, cocksman and
Adonis of Denver—joy to the memory of his innumerable
lays of girls in empty lots & diner backyards, moviehouses'
rickety rows, on mountaintops in caves or with gaunt
waitresses in familiar roadside lonely petticoat upliftings &
especially secret gas-station solipsisms of johns, &
hometown alleys too,
who faded out in vast sordid movies, were shifted in dreams,
woke on a sudden Manhattan, and picked themselves up
out of basements hungover with heartless Tokay and
horrors of Third Avenue iron dreams & stumbled to
unemployment offices,
who walked all night with their shoes full of blood on the
snowbank docks waiting for a door in the East River to
open to a room full of steamheat and opium,
who created great suicidal dramas on the apartment cliff-banks
of the Hudson under the wartime blue floodlight of the
moon & their heads shall be crowned with laurel in
oblivion,
who ate the lamb stew of the imagination or digested the crab
at the muddy bottom of the rivers of Bowery,
who wept at the romance of the streets with their pushcarts
full of onions and bad music,
who sat in boxes breathing in the darkness under the bridge,
and rose up to build harpsichords in their lofts,
who coughed on the sixth floor of Harlem crowned with
flame under the tubercular sky surrounded by orange crates
of theology,
who scribbled all night rocking and rolling over lofty
incantations which in the yellow morning were stanzas of
gibberish,
who cooked rotten animals lung heart feet tail borsht &
tortillas dreaming of the pure vegetable kingdom,
who plunged themselves under meat trucks looking for an egg,

who threw their watches off the roof to cast their ballot for
Eternity outside of Time, & alarm clocks fell on their heads
every day for the next decade,
who cut their wrists three times successively unsuccessfully,
gave up and were forced to open antique stores where they
thought they were growing old and cried,
who were burned alive in their innocent flannel suits on
Madison Avenue amid blasts of leaden verse & the
tanked-up clatter of the iron regiments of fashion & the
nitroglycerine shrieks of the fairies of advertising & the
mustard gas of sinister intelligent editors, or were run down
by the drunken taxicabs of Absolute Reality,
who jumped off the Brooklyn Bridge this actually happened
and walked away unknown and forgotten into the ghostly
daze of Chinatown soup alleyways & firetrucks, not even
one free beer,
who sang out of their windows in despair, fell out of the
subway window, jumped in the filthy Passaic, leaped on
negroes, cried all over the street, danced on broken
wineglasses barefoot smashed phonograph records of
nostalgic European 1930's German jazz finished the whiskey
and threw up groaning into the bloody toilet, moans in
their ears and the blast of colossal steamwhistles,
who barreled down the highways of the past journeying to
each other's hotrod-Golgotha jail-solitude watch or
Birmingham jazz incarnation,
who drove crosscountry seventytwo hours to find out if I had
a vision or you had a vision or he had a vision to find out
Eternity,
who journeyed to Denver, who died in Denver, who came
back to Denver & waited in vain, who watched over
Denver & brooded & loned in Denver and finally went
away to find out the Time, & now Denver is lonesome for
her heroes,
who fell on their knees in hopeless cathedrals praying for each
other's salvation and light and breasts, until the soul
illuminated its hair for a second,
who crashed through their minds in jail waiting for impossible
criminals with golden heads and the charm of reality in their
hearts who sang sweet blues to Alcatraz,
who retired to Mexico to cultivate a habit, or Rocky Mount

to tender Buddha or Tangiers to boys or Southern Pacific to
the black locomotive or Harvard to Narcissus to Woodlawn
to the daisychain or grave,
who demanded sanity trials accusing the radio of hypnotism &
were left with their insanity & their hands & a hung jury,
who threw potato salad at CCNY lecturers on Dadaism and
subsequently presented themselves on the granite steps of
the madhouse with shaven heads and harlequin speech of
suicide, demanding instantaneous lobotomy,
and who were given instead the concrete void of insulin
metrasol electricity hydrotherapy psychotherapy
occupational therapy pingpong & amnesia,
who in humorless protest overturned only one symbolic
pingpong table, resting briefly in catatonia,
returning years later truly bald except for a wig of blood, and
tears and fingers, to the visible madman doom of the wards
of the madtowns of the East,
Pilgrim State's Rockland's and Greystone's foetid halls,
bickering with the echoes of the soul, rocking and rolling in
the midnight solitude-bench dolmen-realms of love, dream
of life a nightmare, bodies turned to stone as heavy as the
moon,
with mother finally ******, and the last fantastic book flung
out of the tenement window, and the last door closed at 4
AM and the last telephone slammed at the wall in reply and
the last furnished room emptied down to the last piece of
mental furniture, a yellow paper rose twisted on a wire
hanger in the closet, and even that imaginary, nothing but a
hopeful little bit of hallucination—
ah, Carl, while you are not safe I am not safe, and now you're
really in the total animal soup of time—
and who therefore ran through the icy streets obsessed with a
sudden flash of the alchemy of the use of the ellipse the
catalog the meter & the vibrating plane,
who dreamt and made incarnate gaps in Time & Space
through images juxtaposed, and trapped the archangel of the
soul between 2 visual images and joined the elemental verbs
and set the noun and dash of consciousness together
jumping with sensation of Pater Omnipotens Aeterna Deus
to recreate the syntax and measure of poor human prose and
stand before you speechless and intelligent and shaking with

shame, rejected yet confessing out the soul to conform to
the rhythm of thought in his naked and endless head,
the madman bum and angel beat in Time, unknown, yet
putting down here what might be left to say in time come
after death,
and rose reincarnate in the ghostly clothes of jazz in the
goldhorn shadow of the band and blew the suffering of
America's naked mind for love into an eli eli lamma lamma
sabacthani saxophone cry that shivered the cities down to
the last radio
with the absolute heart of the poem of life butchered out of
their own bodies good to eat a thousand years.

II

What sphinx of cement and aluminum bashed open their
skulls and ate up their brains and imagination?
Moloch! Solitude! Filth! Ugliness! Ashcans and unobtainable
dollars! Children screaming under the stairways! Boys
sobbing in armies! Old men weeping in the parks!
Moloch! Moloch! Nightmare of Moloch! Moloch the loveless!
Mental Moloch! Moloch the heavy judger of men!
Moloch the incomprehensible prison! Moloch the crossbone
soulless jailhouse and Congress of sorrows! Moloch whose
buildings are judgement! Moloch the vast stone of war!
Moloch the stunned governments!
Moloch whose mind is pure machinery! Moloch whose blood
is running money! Moloch whose fingers are ten armies!
Moloch whose breast is a cannibal dynamo! Moloch whose
ear is a smoking tomb!
Moloch whose eyes are a thousand blind windows! Moloch
whose skyscrapers stand in the long streets like endless
Jehovahs! Moloch whose factories dream and croak in the
fog! Moloch whose smokestacks and antennae crown the
cities!
Moloch whose love is endless oil and stone! Moloch whose
soul is electricity and banks! Moloch whose poverty is the
specter of genius! Moloch whose fate is a cloud of sexless
hydrogen! Moloch whose name is the Mind!
Moloch in whom I sit lonely! Moloch in whom I dream
Angels! Crazy in Moloch! Cocksucker in Moloch! Lacklove
and manless in Moloch!

Moloch who entered my soul early! Moloch in whom I am a consciousness without a body! Moloch who frightened me out of my natural ecstasy! Moloch whom I abandon! Wake up in Moloch! Light streaming out of the sky!
Moloch! Moloch! Robot apartments! invisible suburbs! skeleton treasuries! blind capitals! demonic industries! spectral nations! invincible madhouses! granite cocks! monstrous bombs!
They broke their backs lifting Moloch to Heaven! Pavements, trees, radios, tons! lifting the city to Heaven which exists and is everywhere about us!
Visions! omens! hallucinations! miracles! ecstasies! gone down the American river!
Dreams! adorations! illuminations! religions! the whole boatload of sensitive bullshit!
Breakthroughs! over the river! flips and crucifixions! gone down the flood! Highs! Epiphanies! Despairs! Ten years' animal screams and suicides! Minds! New loves! Mad generation! down on the rocks of Time!
Real holy laughter in the river! They saw it all! the wild eyes! the holy yells! They bade farewell! They jumped off the roof! to solitude! waving! carrying flowers! Down to the river! into the street!

III

Carl Solomon! I'm with you in Rockland
   where you're madder than I am
I'm with you in Rockland
   where you must feel very strange
I'm with you in Rockland
   where you imitate the shade of my mother
I'm with you in Rockland
   where you've murdered your twelve secretaries
I'm with you in Rockland
   where you laugh at this invisible humor
I'm with you in Rockland
   where we are great writers on the same dreadful typewriter
I'm with you in Rockland
   where your condition has become serious and is reported on the radio

I'm with you Rockland
where the faculties of the skull no longer admit the worms of the senses
I'm with you in Rockland
where you drink the tea of the breasts of the spinsters of Utica
I'm with you in Rockland
where you pun on the bodies of your nurses the harpies of the Bronx
I'm with you in Rockland
where you scream in a straightjacket that you're losing the game of the actual pingpong of the abyss
I'm with you in Rockland
where you bang on the catatonic piano the soul is innocent and immortal it should never die ungodly in an armed madhouse
I'm with you in Rockland
where fifty more shocks will never return your soul to its body again from its pilgrimage to a cross in the void
I'm with you in Rockland
where you accuse your doctors of insanity and plot the Hebrew socialist revolution against the fascist national Golgotha
I'm with you in Rockland
where you will split the heavens of Long Island and resurrect your living human Jesus from the superhuman tomb
I'm with you in Rockland
where there are twentyfive-thousand mad comrades all together singing the final stanzas of the Internationale
I'm with you in Rockland
where we hug and kiss the United States under our bedsheets the United States that coughs all night and won't let us sleep
I'm with you in Rockland
where we wake up electrified out of the coma by our own souls' airplanes roaring over the roof they've come to drop angelic bombs the hospital illuminates itself imaginary walls collapse O skinny legions run outside O starry spangled shock of mercy the eternal war is here O victory forget your underwear we're free

I'm with you in Rockland
  in my dreams you walk dripping from a sea-journey on the
  highway across America in tears to the door of my cottage
  in the Western night

FRANK O'HARA

[1926–1966]

Frank O'Hara was born in Maryland and grew up in Massachusetts. He was educated at Harvard University, the University of Michigan, and the New England Conservatory of Music. During World War II he served in the navy. Later he worked as a curator at the Museum of Modern Art in New York, where he met important artists and helped organize exhibitions to introduce modern American art to the world. He belonged to a group of poets loosely identified as the New York School, which included John Ashbery and Kenneth Koch. O'Hara was influenced as much by modern art as by modern poetry, and he expressed a liking for the poems of Walt Whitman, Hart Crane, and William Carlos Williams. His own poetry attempts to be spontaneous, natural, direct, and unassuming.

Autobiographia Literaria

When I was a child
I played by myself in a
corner of the schoolyard
all alone.

I hated dolls and I
hated games, animals were
not friendly and birds
flew away.

If anyone was looking
for me I hid behind a
tree and cried out "I am
an orphan."

And here I am, the
center of all beauty!
writing these poems!
Imagine!

Ave Maria

Mothers of America
let your kids go to the movies!
get them out of the house so they won't know what you're up to
it's true that fresh air is good for the body
but what about the soul
that grows in darkness, embossed by silvery images
and when you grow old as grow old you must
they won't hate you
they won't criticize you they won't know
they'll be in some glamorous country
they first saw on a Saturday afternoon or playing hookey
they may even be grateful to you
for their first sexual experience
which only cost you a quarter
and didn't upset the peaceful home
they will know where candy bars come from
and gratuitous bags of popcorn
as gratuitous as leaving the movie before it's over
with a pleasant stranger whose apartment is in the Heaven on Earth Bldg
near the Williamsburg Bridge
oh mothers you will have made the little tykes
so happy because if nobody does pick them up in the movies
they won't know the difference
and if somebody does it'll be sheer gravy
and they'll have been truly entertained either way
instead of hanging around the yard
or up in their room
hating you
prematurely since you won't have done anything horribly mean yet
except keeping them from the darker joys
it's unforgivable the latter

so don't blame me if you won't take this advice
    and the family breaks up
and your children grow old and blind in front of a TV set
    seeing
movies you wouldn't let them see when they were young

JOHN ASHBERY

[b. 1927]

John Ashbery was born in New York and educated at Harvard, Columbia, and New York universities. For ten years he lived in France and worked as a critic for the *New York Herald Tribune* and *Art International*. Later he was an executive editor of *ARTnews* in New York. With Kenneth Koch and Frank O'Hara he is considered one of the New York School of poets, a group that has found inspiration in painting and in contemporary French Surrealism. A professor at Brooklyn College of the City University of New York, Ashbery has written plays and fiction as well as poetry. He has received many awards, including a Pulitzer Prize and a National Book Award for his *Self Portrait in a Convex Mirror*. His poems are intellectually challenging with their abrupt changes of intention and direction, their circular structures, and their enigmatic self-reference.

Some Trees

These are amazing: each
Joining a neighbor, as though speech
Were a still performance.
Arranging by chance

To meet as far this morning
From the world as agreeing
With it, you and I
Are suddenly what the trees try

To tell us we are:
That their merely being there
Means something; that soon
We may touch, love, explain.

And glad not to have invented
Such comeliness, we are surrounded:
A silence already filled with noises,
A canvas on which emerges

A chorus of smiles, a winter morning.
Placed in a puzzling light, and moving,
Our days put on such reticence
These accents seem their own defense.

GALWAY KINNELL

[b. 1927]

Galway Kinnell was born and raised in Rhode Island. His education at Princeton (B.A., 1948) and the University of Rochester (M.A., 1949) was interrupted by a year of service in the U.S. Navy. Kinnell has traveled widely in Europe and the Middle East and has taught in Iran and France, as well as at a number of prominent American universities. He is currently professor of English at New York University. His honors and prizes include awards from the National Institute of Arts and Letters and a Pulitzer Prize in 1982 for his *Selected Poems*. He has also written criticism and fiction and has translated the poetry of François Villon. Kinnell's poems reveal the influence of the American Romantics, especially Whitman, Crane, and Williams, the modern German poet Rainer Maria Rilke, and the modern Chilean poet Pablo Neruda. Kinnell's poetry is at once personal and mythic, sometimes blending primal and personal experience in a tone of prayerful affirmation.

To Christ Our Lord

The legs of the elk punctured the snow's crust
And wolves floated lightfooted on the land
Hunting Christmas elk living and frozen;
Inside snow melted in a basin, and a woman basted
A bird spread over coals by its wings and head.

Snow had sealed the windows; candles lit
The Christmas meal. The Christmas grace chilled

The cooked bird, being long-winded and the room cold.
During the words a boy thought, is it fitting
To eat this creature killed on the wing?

He had killed it himself, climbing out
Alone on snowshoes in the Christmas dawn,
The fallen snow swirling and the snowfall gone,
Heard its throat scream as the gunshot scattered,
Watched it drop, and fished from the snow the dead.

He had not wanted to shoot. The sound
Of wings beating into the hushed air
Had stirred his love, and his fingers
Froze in his gloves, and he wondered,
Famishing, could he fire? Then he fired.

Now the grace praised his wicked act. At its end
The bird on the plate
Stared at his stricken appetite.
There had been nothing to do but surrender,
To kill and to eat; he ate as he had killed, with wonder.

At night on snowshoes on the drifting field
He wondered again, for whom had love stirred?
The stars glittered on the snow and nothing answered.
Then the Swan spread her wings, cross of the cold north,
The pattern and mirror of the acts of earth.

The Bear

1

In late winter
I sometimes glimpse bits of steam
coming up from
some fault in the old snow
and bend close and see it is lung-colored
and put down my nose
and know
the chilly, enduring odor of bear.

2

I take a wolf's rib and whittle
it sharp at both ends
and coil it up
and freeze it in blubber and place it out
on the fairway of the bears.

And when it has vanished
I move out on the bear tracks,
roaming in circles
until I come to the first, tentative, dark
splash on the earth.

And I set out
running, following the splashes
of blood wandering over the world.
At the cut, gashed resting places
I stop and rest,
at the crawl-marks
where he lay out on his belly
to overpass some stretch of bauchy ice
I lie out
dragging myself forward with bear-knives in my fists.

3

On the third day I begin to starve,
at nightfall I bend down as I knew I would
at a turd sopped in blood,
and hesitate, and pick it up,
and thrust it in my mouth, and gnash it down,
and rise
and go on running.

4

On the seventh day,
living by now on bear blood alone,
I can see his upturned carcass far out ahead, a scraggled,
steamy hulk,
the heavy fur riffling in the wind.

I come up to him
and stare at the narrow-spaced, petty eyes,
the dismayed
face laid back on the shoulder, the nostrils
flared, catching
perhaps the first taint of me as he
died.

I hack
a ravine in his thigh, and eat and drink,
and tear him down his whole length
and open him and climb in
and close him up after me, against the wind,
and sleep.

5

And dream
of lumbering flatfooted
over the tundra,
stabbed twice from within,
splattering a trail behind me,
splattering it out no matter which way I lurch,
no matter which parabola of bear-transcendence,
which dance of solitude I attempt,
which gravity-clutched leap,
which trudge, which groan.

6

Until one day I totter and fall—
fall on this
stomach that has tried so hard to keep up,
to digest the blood as it leaked in,
to break up
and digest the bone itself: and now the breeze
blows over me, blows off
the hideous belches of ill-digested bear blood
and rotted stomach
and the ordinary, wretched odor of bear,

blows across
my sore, lolled tongue a song
or screech, until I think I must rise up
and dance. And I lie still.

7

I awaken I think. Marshlights
reappear, geese
come trailing again up the flyway.
In her ravine under old snow the dam-bear
lies, licking
lumps of smeared fur
and drizzly eyes into shapes
with her tongue. And one
hairy-soled trudge stuck out before me,
the next groaned out,
the next,
the next,
the rest of my days I spend
wandering: wondering
what, anyway,
was that sticky infusion, that rank flavor of blood, that poetry,
  by which I lived?

Saint Francis and the Sow

The bud
stands for all things,
even for those things that don't flower,
for everything flowers, from within, of self-blessing;
though sometimes it is necessary
to reteach a thing its loveliness,
to put a hand on its brow
of the flower
and retell it in words and in touch
it is lovely
until it flowers again from within, of self-blessing;
as Saint Francis
put his hand on the creased forehead
of the sow, and told her in words and in touch
blessings of earth on the sow, and the sow

began remembering all down her thick length,
from the earthen snout all the way
through the fodder and slops to the spiritual curl of the tail,
from the hard spininess spiked out from the spine
down through the great broken heart
to the sheer blue milken dreaminess spurting and shuddering
from the fourteen teats into the fourteen mouths sucking and
  blowing beneath them:
the long, perfect loveliness of sow.

Blackberry Eating

I love to go out in late September
among the fat, overripe, icy, black blackberries
to eat blackberries for breakfast,
the stalks very prickly, a penalty
they earn for knowing the black art
of blackberry-making; and as I stand among them
lifting the stalks to my mouth, the ripest berries
fall almost unbidden to my tongue,
as words sometimes do, certain peculiar words
like *strengths* or *squinched,*
many-lettered, one-syllabled lumps,
which I squeeze, squinch open, and splurge well
in the silent, startled, icy, black language
of blackberry-eating in late September.

W. S. MERWIN

[b. 1927]

William Stanley Merwin was born in New York and grew up in New Jersey and Pennsylvania. He received a B.A. from Princeton, where he studied foreign languages and literatures. He has lived in England, Mexico, France, and Hawaii. In addition to writing his own poetry, he has translated numerous works from French, Spanish, Latin, Greek, Russian, Portuguese, Chinese, and Japanese. Among his translations are two medieval epics, the French *Song of Roland* and the Spanish *Poem of the Cid.* His own poems are notable for their brevity and austerity, their avoidance of traditional meters and forms, and their reliance on the spoken voice.

When You Go Away

When you go away the wind clicks around to the north
The painters work all day but at sundown the paint falls
Showing the black walls
The clock goes back to striking the same hour
That has no place in the years

And at night wrapped in the bed of ashes
In one breath I wake
It is the time when the beards of the dead get their growth
I remember that I am falling
That I am the reason
And that my words are the garment of what I shall never be
Like the tucked sleeve of a one-armed boy

Separation

Your absence has gone through me
Like thread through a needle.
Everything I do is stitched with its color.

Elegy

Who would I show it to

JAMES WRIGHT

[1927–1980]

James Wright was born in Ohio and educated at Kenyon College, where he studied with John Crowe Ransom, and at the University of Washington, where he was instructed by Theodore Roethke. Wright taught at the University of Minnesota and at Hunter College of the City University of New York. With Robert Bly, he translated poems of George Trakl from German and the poems of Pablo Neruda and Cesar Vallejo from Spanish. His own poems reflect the influence of Robert Frost and Edwin Arlington Robinson in their depiction of isolated, troubled outcasts and in their recognition of both the bleakness and beauty of nature.

Lying in a Hammock at William Duffy's Farm in Pine Island, Minnesota

Over my head, I see the bronze butterfly,
Asleep on the black trunk,
Blowing like a leaf in green shadow.
Down the ravine behind the empty house,
The cowbells follow one another
Into the distances of the afternoon.
To my right,
In a field of sunlight between two pines,
The droppings of last year's horses
Blaze up into golden stones.
I lean back, as the evening darkens and comes on.
A chicken hawk floats over, looking for home.
I have wasted my life.

A Blessing

Just off the highway to Rochester, Minnesota,
Twilight bounds softly forth on the grass.
And the eyes of those two Indian ponies
Darken with kindness.
They have come gladly out of the willows
To welcome my friend and me.
We step over the barbed wire into the pasture
Where they have been grazing all day, alone.
They ripple tensely, they can hardly contain their happiness
That we have come.
They bow shyly as wet swans. They love each other.
There is no loneliness like theirs.
At home once more,
They begin munching the young tufts of spring in the darkness.
I would like to hold the slenderer one in my arms,
For she has walked over to me
And nuzzled my left hand.
She is black and white,
Her mane falls wild on her forehead,
And the light breeze moves me to caress her long ear

That is delicate as the skin over a girl's wrist.
Suddenly I realize
That if I stepped out of my body I would break
Into blossom.

ANNE SEXTON

[1928–1974]

Anne Sexton was born in Newton, Massachusetts, in 1928. She worked briefly as a librarian and a fashion model, married, and had two daughters. She taught English at a number of colleges and universities, including Tufts, Colgate, Fairfield, and Boston University. She was also the recipient of numerous awards: a Bread Loaf Fellowship (1959), a fellowship from the American Academy of Arts and Sciences (1963), a Ford Foundation grant (1964), a Pulitzer Prize, and a Guggenheim fellowship (1969). She committed suicide in 1974 after a series of mental breakdowns. Her poetry, which takes as its subject her experience as a woman, wife, and mother, attempts to appeal directly and immediately to the emotions, from which it derives its primary impulse.

Her Kind

I have gone out, a possessed witch,
haunting the black air, braver at night;
dreaming evil, I have done my hitch
over the plain houses, light by light:
lonely thing, twelve-fingered, out of mind.
A woman like that is not a woman, quite.
I have been her kind.

I have found the warm caves in the woods,
filled them with skillets, carvings, shelves,
closets, silks, innumerable goods;
fixed the suppers for the worms and the elves:
whining, rearranging the disaligned.
A woman like that is misunderstood.
I have been her kind.

I have ridden in your cart, driver,
waved my nude arms at villages going by,
learning the last bright routes, survivor
where your flames still bite my thigh
and my ribs crack where your wheels wind.
A woman like that is not ashamed to die.
I have been her kind.

Us

I was wrapped in black
fur and white fur and
you undid me and then
you placed me in gold light
and then you crowned me,
while snow fell outside
the door in diagonal darts.
While a ten-inch snow
came down like stars
in small calcium fragments,
we were in our own bodies
(that room that will bury us)
and you were in my body
(that room that will outlive us)
and at first I rubbed your
feet dry with a towel
because I was your slave
and then you called me princess.
Princess!

Oh then
I stood up in my gold skin
and I beat down the psalms
and I beat down the clothes
and you undid the bridle
and you undid the reins
and I undid the buttons,
the bones, the confusion,
the New England postcards,
the January ten o'clock night,

and we rose up like wheat,
acre after acre of gold,
and we harvested,
we harvested.

DONALD HALL

[b. 1928]

Donald Hall was born in Connecticut and studied at Harvard, Stanford, and Oxford universities. He taught for ten years at the University of Michigan before moving to a New Hampshire farm that had belonged to his great-grandfather. There, Hall has continued writing prolifically in a variety of forms—poetry, essay, reportage, criticism, autobiography, verse play—and editing textbooks on the teaching of writing and literature. His own poems combine the discipline of traditional forms with the spontaneity and naturalness of open forms in free verse.

My Son, My Executioner

My son, my executioner,
  I take you in my arms,
Quiet and small and just astir,
  And whom my body warms.

Sweet death, small son, our instrument
  Of immortality,
Your cries and hungers document
  Our bodily decay.

We twenty-five and twenty-two,
  Who seemed to live forever,
Observe enduring life in you
  And start to die together.

Kicking the Leaves

1

Kicking the leaves, October, as we walk home together
from the game, in Ann Arbor,
on a day the color of soot, rain in the air;

I kick at the leaves of maples,
reds of seventy different shades, yellow
like old paper; and poplar leaves, fragile and pale;
and elm leaves, flags of a doomed race.
I kick at the leaves, making a sound I remember
as the leaves swirl upward from my boot,
and flutter; and I remember
Octobers walking to school in Connecticut,
wearing corduroy knickers that swished
with a sound like leaves; and a Sunday buying
a cup of cider at a roadside stand
on a dirt road in New Hampshire; and kicking the leaves,
autumn 1955 in Massachusetts, knowing
my father would die when the leaves were gone.

2

Each fall in New Hampshire, on the farm
where my mother grew up, a girl in the country,
my grandfather and grandmother
finished the autumn work, taking the last vegetables in
from the cold fields, canning, storing roots and apples
in the cellar under the kitchen. Then my grandfather
raked leaves against the house
as the final chore of autumn.
One November I drove up from college to see them.
We pulled big rakes, as we did when we hayed in summer,
pulling the leaves against the granite foundations
around the house, on every side of the house,
and then, to keep them in place, we cut spruce boughs
and laid them across the leaves,
green on red, until the house
was tucked up, ready for snow
that would freeze the leaves in tight, like a stiff skirt.
Then we puffed through the shed door,
taking off boots and overcoats, slapping our hands,
and sat in the kitchen, rocking, and drank
black coffee my grandmother made,
three of us sitting together, silent, in gray November.

3

One Saturday when I was little, before the war,
my father came home at noon from his half day at the office
and wore his Bates sweater, black on red,
with the crossed hockey sticks on it, and raked beside me
in the back yard, and tumbled in the leaves with me,
laughing, and carried me, laughing, my hair full of leaves,
to the kitchen window
where my mother could see us, and smile, and motion
to set me down, afraid I would fall and be hurt.

4

Kicking the leaves today, as we walk home together
from the game, among crowds of people
with their bright pennants, as many and bright as leaves,
my daughter's hair is the red-yellow color
of birch leaves, and she is tall like a birch,
growing up, fifteen, growing older; and my son
flamboyant as maple, twenty,
visits from college, and walks ahead of us, his step
springing, impatient to travel
the woods of the earth. Now I watch them
from a pile of leaves beside this clapboard house
in Ann Arbor, across from the school
where they learned to read,
as their shapes grow small with distance, waving,
and I know that I
diminish, not them, as I go first
into the leaves, taking
the step they will follow, Octobers and years from now.

5

This year the poems came back, when the leaves fell.
Kicking the leaves, I heard the leaves tell stories,
remembering, and therefore looking ahead, and building
the house of dying. I looked up into the maples
and found them, the vowels of bright desire.
I thought they had gone forever
while the bird sang *I love you, I love you*
and shook its black head

from side to side, and its red eye with no lid,
through years of winter, cold
as the taste of chicken wire, the music of cinder block.

6

Kicking the leaves, I uncover the lids of graves.
My grandfather died at seventy-seven, in March
when the sap was running; and I remember my father
twenty years ago,
coughing himself to death at fifty-two in the house
in the suburbs. Oh, how we flung
leaves in the air! How they tumbled and fluttered around us,
like slowly cascading water, when we walked together
in Hamden, before the war, when Johnson's Pond
had not surrendered to houses, the two of us
hand in hand, and in the wet air the smell of leaves
burning;
and in six years I will be fifty-two.

7

Now I fall, now I leap and fall
to feel the leaves crush under my body, to feel my body
buoyant in the ocean of leaves, the night of them,
night heaving with death and leaves, rocking like the ocean.
Oh, this delicious falling into the arms of leaves,
into the soft laps of leaves!
Face down, I swim into the leaves, feathery,
breathing the acrid odor of maple, swooping
in long glides to the bottom of October—
where the farm lies curled against winter, and soup steams
its breath of onion and carrot
onto damp curtains and windows; and past the windows
I see the tall bare maple trunks and branches, the oak
with its few brown weathery remnant leaves,
and the spruce trees, holding their green.
Now I leap and fall, exultant, recovering
from death, on account of death, in accord with the dead,
the smell and taste of leaves again,
and the pleasure, the only long pleasure, of taking a place
in the story of leaves.

JOHN HOLLANDER

[b. 1929]

John Hollander was born in New York City and was educated there at Columbia University (B.A., 1950, M.A., 1952). He received a doctorate from Indiana University in 1959. Hollander has taught at Harvard and Yale universities and at Hunter and Connecticut colleges. His poetry is typically witty, allusive, and verbally intricate.

Adam's Task

"And Adam gave names to all cattle, and to the fowl of the air, and to every beast of the field . . ."

GEN. 2:20

Thou, paw-paw-paw; thou, glurd; thou, spotted
Glurd; thou, whitesap, lurching through
The high-grown brush; thou, pliant-footed,
Implex; thou, awagabu.

Every burrower, each flier
Came for the name he had to give:
Gay, first work, ever to be prior,
Not yet sunk to primitive.

Thou, verdle; thou, McFleery's pomma;
Thou; thou; thou—three types of grawl;
Thou, flisket; thou, kabasch; thou, comma-
Eared mashawk; thou, all; thou, all.

Were, in a fire of becoming,
Laboring to be burned away,
Then work, half-measuring, half-humming,
Would be as serious as play.

Thou, pambler; thou, rivarn; thou, greater
Wherret, and thou, lesser one;
Thou, sproal; thou, zant; thou, lily-eater.
Naming's over. Day is done.

Swan and Shadow

Dusk
Above the
water hang the
loud
flies
Here
O so
gray
then
What A pale signal will appear
When Soon before its shadow fades
Where Here in this pool of opened eye
In us No Upon us As at the very edges
of where we take shape in the dark air
this object bares its image awakening
ripples of recognition that will
brush darkness up into light
even after this bird this hour both drift by atop the perfect sad instant now
already passing out of sight
toward yet-untroubled reflection
this image bears its object darkening
into memorial shades Scattered bits of
light No of water Or something across
water Breaking up No Being regathered
soon Yet by then a swan will have
gone Yes out of mind into what
vast
pale
hush
of a
place
past
sudden dark as
if a swan
sang

X. J. KENNEDY

[b. 1929]

Joseph Kennedy was born in Dover, New Jersey, and educated at Seton Hall University and the University of Michigan. He taught for many years at Tufts University before retiring and devoting himself to an array of writing projects. Besides his own poetry, Kennedy has written children's books and has edited a number of college text books. His poems display an engaging sense of humor and an eye for the apt detail.

First Confession

Blood thudded in my ears. I scuffed,
Steps stubborn, to the telltale booth
Beyond whose curtained portal coughed
The robed repositor of truth.

The slat shot back. The universe
Bowed down his cratered dome to hear
Enumerated my each curse,
The sip snitched from my old man's beer,

My sloth pride envy lechery,
The dime held back from Peter's Pence
With which I'd bribed my girl to pee
That I might spy her instruments.

Hovering scale-pans when I'd done
Settled their balance slow as silt
While in the restless dark I burned
Bright as a brimstone in my guilt

Until as one feeds birds he doled
Seven Our Fathers and a Hail
Which I to double-scrub my soul
Intoned twice at the altar rail

Where Sunday in seraphic light
I knelt, as full of grace as most,
And stuck my tongue out at the priest:
A fresh roost for the Holy Ghost.

In a Prominent Bar in Secaucus One Day

(To the tune of 'The Old Orange Flute' or the tune of 'Sweet Betsy from Pike')

In a prominent bar in Secaucus one day
Rose a lady in skunk with a topheavy sway,

Raised a knobby red finger—all turned from their beer—
While with eyes bright as snowcrust she sang high and clear:

'Now who of you'd think from an eyeload of me
That I once was a lady as proud as could be?
Oh I'd never sit down by a tumbledown drunk
If it wasn't, my dears, for the high cost of junk.

'All the gents used to swear that the white of my calf
Beat the down of the swan by a length and a half.
In the kerchief of linen I caught to my nose
Ah, there never fell snot, but a little gold rose.

'I had seven gold teeth and a toothpick of gold,
My Virginia cheroot was a leaf of it rolled
And I'd light it each time with a thousand in cash—
Why the bums used to fight if I flicked them an ash.

'Once the toast of the Biltmore, the belle of the Taft,
I would drink bottle beer at the Drake, never draft,
And dine at the Astor on Salisbury steak
With a clean tablecloth for each bite I did take.

'In a car like the Roxy I'd roll to the track,
A steel-guitar trio, a bar in the back,
And the wheels made no noise, they turned over so fast,
Still it took you ten minutes to see me go past.

'When the horses bowed down to me that I might choose,
I bet on them all, for I hated to lose.
Now I'm saddled each night for my butter and eggs
And the broken threads race down the backs of my legs.

'Let you hold in mind, girls, that your beauty must pass
Like a lovely white clover that rusts with its grass.
Keep your bottoms off barstools and marry you young
Or be left—an old barrel with many a bung.

'For when time takes you out for a spin in his car
You'll be hard-pressed to stop him from going too far
And be left by the roadside, for all your good deeds,
Two toadstools for tits and a face full of weeds.'

All the house raised a cheer, but the man at the bar
Made a phonecall and up pulled a red patrol car
And she blew us a kiss as they copped her away
From that prominent bar in Secaucus, N.J.

ADRIENNE RICH

[b. 1929]

Adrienne Rich was born in Maryland and educated at Radcliffe College (B.A., 1951). She has taught at a number of colleges and universities, including Bryn Mawr, Brandeis, Rutgers, and Columbia. Among her honors is a 1974 National Book Award for *Diving into the Wreck.* In addition to her poetry, Rich has published two volumes of prose on feminist subjects and has translated Dutch poetry. Her own poetry exhibits the strengths of her formalist precursors, particularly W. H. Auden, yet it breaks free of them into a more open style and a more contemporary voice and vision.

Storm Warnings

The glass has been falling all the afternoon,
And knowing better than the instrument
What winds are walking overhead, what zone
Of gray unrest is moving across the land,
I leave the book upon a pillowed chair
And walk from window to closed window, watching
Boughs strain against the sky

And think again, as often when the air
Moves inward toward a silent core of waiting,
How with a single purpose time has traveled
By secret currents of the undiscerned
Into this polar realm. Weather abroad
And weather in the heart alike come on
Regardless of prediction.

Between foreseeing and averting change
Lies all the mastery of elements
Which clocks and weatherglasses cannot alter.
Time in the hand is not control of time,
Nor shattered fragments of an instrument

A proof against the wind; the wind will rise
We can only close the shutters.

I draw the curtains as the sky goes black
And set a match to candles sheathed in glass
Against the keyhole draught, the insistent whine
Of weather through the unsealed aperture.
This is our sole defense against the season;
These are the things that we have learned to do
Who live in troubled regions.

Aunt Jennifer's Tigers

Aunt Jennifer's tigers prance across a screen,
Bright topaz denizens of a world of green.
They do not fear the men beneath the tree;
They pace in sleek chivalric certainty.

Aunt Jennifer's fingers fluttering through her wool
Find even the ivory needle hard to pull.
The massive weight of Uncle's wedding band
Sits heavily upon Aunt Jennifer's hand.

When Aunt is dead, her terrified hands will lie
Still ringed with ordeals she was mastered by.
The tigers in the panel that she made
Will go on prancing, proud and unafraid.

The Knight

A knight rides into the noon,
and his helmet points to the sun,
and a thousand splintered suns
are the gaiety of his mail.
The soles of his feet glitter
and his palms flash in reply,
and under his crackling banner
he rides like a ship in sail.

A knight rides into the noon,
and only his eye is living,
a lump of bitter jelly

set in a metal mask,
betraying rags and tatters
that cling to the flesh beneath
and wear his nerves to ribbons
under the radiant casque.

Who will unhorse this rider
and free him from between
the walls of iron, the emblems
crushing his chest with their weight?
Will they defeat him gently,
or leave him hurled on the green,
his rags and wounds still hidden
under the great breastplate?

Diving into the Wreck

First having read the book of myths,
and loaded the camera,
and checked the edge of the knife-blade,
I put on
the body-armor of black rubber
the absurd flippers
the grave and awkward mask.
I am having to do this
not like Cousteau with his
assiduous team
aboard the sun-flooded schooner
but here alone.

There is a ladder.
The ladder is always there
hanging innocently
close to the side of the schooner.
We know what it is for,
we who have used it.
Otherwise
it's a piece of maritime floss
some sundry equipment.

I go down.
Rung after rung and still
the oxygen immerses me

the blue light
the clear atoms
of our human air.
I go down.
My flippers cripple me,
I crawl like an insect down the ladder
and there is no one
to tell me when the ocean
will begin.

First the air is blue and then
it is bluer and then green and then
black I am blacking out and yet
my mask is powerful
it pumps my blood with power
the sea is another story
the sea is not a question of power
I have to learn alone
to turn my body without force
in the deep element.

And now: it is easy to forget
what I came for
among so many who have always
lived here
swaying their crenellated fans
between the reefs
and besides
you breathe differently down here.

I came to explore the wreck.
The words are purposes.
The words are maps.
I came to see the damage that was done
and the treasures that prevail.
I stroke the beam of my lamp
slowly along the flank
of something more permanent
than fish or weed

the thing I came for:
the wreck and not the story of the wreck
the thing itself and not the myth

the drowned face always staring
toward the sun
the evidence of damage
worn by salt and sway into this threadbare beauty
the ribs of the disaster
curving their assertion
among the tentative haunters.

This is the place.
And I am here, the mermaid whose dark hair
streams black, the merman in his armored body
We circle silently
about the wreck
we dive into the hold.
I am she: I am he

whose drowned face sleeps with open eyes
whose breasts still bear the stress
whose silver, copper, vermeil cargo lies
obscurely inside barrels
half-wedged and left to rot
we are the half-destroyed instruments
that once held to a course
the water-eaten log
the fouled compass

We are, I am, you are
by cowardice or courage
the one who find our way
back to this scene
carrying a knife, a camera
a book of myths
in which
our names do not appear.

From *An Atlas of the Difficult World*

II

Here is a map of our country:
here is the Sea of Indifference, glazed with salt
This is the haunted river flowing from brow to groin

we dare not taste its water
This is the desert where missiles are planted like corms
This is the breadbasket of foreclosed farms
This is the birthplace of the rockabilly boy
This is the cemetery of the poor
who died for democracy   This is a battlefield
from a nineteenth-century war   the shrine is famous
This is the sea-town of myth and story   when the fishing fleets
went bankrupt   here is where the jobs were   on the pier
processing frozen fishsticks   hourly wages and no shares
These are other battlefields   Centralia   Detroit
here are the forests primeval   the copper   the silver lodes
These are the suburbs of acquiescence   silence rising fumelike
  from the streets
This is the capital of money and dolor whose spires
flare up through air inversions whose bridges are crumbling
whose children are drifting blind alleys pent
between coiled rolls of razor wire
I promised to show you a map you say but this is a mural
then yes let it be   these are small distinctions
where do we see it from is the question

XIII (DEDICATIONS)

I know you are reading this poem
late, before leaving your office
of the one intense yellow lamp-spot and the darkening
  window
in the lassitude of a building faded to quiet
long after rush-hour.   I know you are reading this poem
standing up in a bookstore far from the ocean
on a grey day of early spring, faint flakes driven
across the plains' enormous spaces around you.
I know you are reading this poem
in a room where too much has happened for you to bear
where the bedclothes lie in stagnant coils on the bed
and the open valise speaks of flight
but you cannot leave yet.   I know you are reading this poem
as the underground train loses momentum and before running
  up the stairs
toward a new kind of love

your life has never allowed.
I know you are reading this poem by the light
of the television screen where soundless images jerk and slide
while you wait for the newscast from the *intifada*.
I know you are reading this poem in a waiting-room
of eyes met and unmeeting, of identity with strangers.
I know you are reading this poem by fluorescent light
in the boredom and fatigue of the young who are counted
out,
count themselves out, at too early an age. I know
you are reading this poem through your failing sight, the thick
lens enlarging these letters beyond all meaning yet you read on
because even the alphabet is precious.
I know you are reading this poem as you pace beside the stove
warming milk, a crying child on your shoulder, a book in your
hand
because life is short and you too are thirsty.
I know you are reading this poem which is not in your
language
guessing at some words while others keep you reading
and I want to know which words they are.
I know you are reading this poem listening for something,
torn between bitterness and hope
turning back once again to the task you cannot refuse.
I know you are reading this poem because there is nothing else
left to read
there where you have landed, stripped as you are.

GARY SNYDER

[b. 1930]

Gary Snyder was born in California and raised on a farm outside Seattle, Washington. He was educated at Reed College (B.A., 1951), at Indiana University, and at the University of California at Berkeley, where he specialized in Oriental languages and cultures. Snyder also studied Zen Buddhism in Kyoto, Japan. His awards have included a Bollingen grant for Buddhist studies and a 1975 Pulitzer Prize for *Turtle Island*. His poetry reflects a strong commitment to the primitive, the mythic, and the natural, along with a deep respect for non-Western ideals.

Riprap

Lay down these words
Before your mind like rocks.
placed solid, by hands
In choice of place, set
Before the body of the mind
in space and time:
Solidity of bark, leaf, or wall
riprap of things:
Cobble of milky way,
straying planets,
These poems, people,
lost ponies with
Dragging saddles—
and rocky sure-foot trails.
The worlds like an endless
four-dimensional
Game of *Go*.
ants and pebbles
In the thin loam, each rock a word
a creek-washed stone
Granite: ingrained
with torment of fire and weight
Crystal and sediment linked hot
all change, in thoughts,
As well as things.

Prayer for the Great Family

Gratitude to Mother Earth, sailing through night and day—
and to her soil: rich, rare, and sweet
in our minds so be it.

Gratitude to Plants, the sun-facing light-changing leaf
and fine root-hairs; standing still through wind
and rain; their dance is in the flowing spiral grain
in our minds so be it.

Gratitude to Air, bearing the soaring Swift and the silent
Owl at dawn. Breath of our song
clear spirit breeze
in our minds so be it.

Gratitude to Wild Beings, our brothers, teaching secrets,
freedoms, and ways; who share with us their milk;
self-complete, brave, and aware
in our minds so be it.

Gratitude to Water: clouds, lakes, rivers, glaciers;
holding or releasing; streaming through all
our bodies salty seas
in our minds so be it.

Gratitude to the Sun: blinding pulsing light through
trunks of trees, through mists, warming caves where
bears and snakes sleep—he who wakes us—
in our minds so be it.

Gratitude to the Great Sky
who holds billions of stars—and goes yet beyond that—
beyond all powers, and thoughts
and yet is within us—

Grandfather Space.
the Mind is his Wife.

so be it.

after a Mohawk prayer

SANDRA SCHOR

[1932–1990]

Sandra Schor was a novelists, poet, and professor of English. She taught at Queens College, CUNY, from 1970 until her death in 1990. Her poems and short stories have appeared in such journals as the *South Carolina Quarterly, Northwest Review*, and *Carleton Miscellany*. Her critically acclaimed novel, *The Great Letter*, was published by North Point Press in 1990.

At Point Hope on the Chukchi Sea

Senator Buckley admired the clear roles of men and women there. "Better than receiving welfare," he stated.

Eskimo girls
play hopscotch
on the ice,
the lines and squares
etched near
the edge of it
in sight of men
harpooning creatures
never hunted by
a woman.

Deep in the ice
the men lock the whale
hooked and butchered into
steaks, skin, blubber
enough to feed
a village for a year.
The women clean the blades
and far into the night,
over the fires they tend,
bend the iron rods.

Atop the ice
a sentry of birds in fur
takes the morning off
and happy men go down in sleds;
they trade oil and furs,
and toast a distant fair
in wirephotos.

But at the edge
the ice has voices.
The shoreline shifts
and campsites of women
keep on working,
for a footing if nothing else,
toes curled from infancies of hopscotch
against premonitions
of a slide.

ETHERIDGE KNIGHT

[b. 1933]

Etheridge Knight was born in Mississippi. He attended high school for two years before a two-year stint in the U.S. Army and the Korean War. He has worked as a factory hand and has been imprisoned for robbery. His own words best describe the power and purpose of his poetry:

> I died in Korea from a shrapnel wound and narcotics resurrected me. I died in 1960 from a prison sentence and poetry brought me back to life.

As a black writer, Knight sees his role as having to conceptualize "the collective aspiration, the collective vision of black people." Through his art he attempts to "give back to the people the truth he has gotten from them."

Hard Rock Returns to Prison from the Hospital for the Criminal Insane

Hard Rock was "known not to take no shit
From nobody," and he had the scars to prove it:
Split purple lips, lumped ears, welts above
His yellow eyes, and one long scar that cut
Across his temple and plowed through a thick
Canopy of kinky hair.

The WORD was that Hard Rock wasn't a mean nigger
Anymore, that the doctors had bored a hole in his head,
Cut out part of his brain, and shot electricity
Through the rest. When they brought Hard Rock back,
Handcuffed and chained, he was turned loose,
Like a freshly gelded stallion, to try his new status.
And we all waited and watched, like indians at a corral,
To see if the WORD was true.

As we waited we wrapped ourselves in the cloak
Of his exploits: "Man, the last time, it took eight
Screws to put him in the Hole." "Yeah, remember when he
Smacked the captain with his dinner tray?" "He set
The record for time in the Hole—67 straight days!"
"Ol Hard Rock! man, that's one crazy nigger."

And then the jewel of a myth that Hard Rock had once bit
A screw on the thumb and poisoned him with syphilitic spit.

The testing came, to see if Hard Rock was really tame.
A hillbilly called him a black son of a bitch
And didn't lose his teeth, a screw who knew Hard Rock
From before shook him down and barked in his face.
And Hard Rock did *nothing*. Just grinned and looked silly,
His eyes empty like knot holes in a fence.

And even after we discovered that it took Hard Rock
Exactly 3 minutes to tell you his first name,
We told ourselves that he had just wised up,
Was being cool; but we could not fool ourselves for long,
And we turned away, our eyes on the ground. Crushed.
He had been our Destroyer, the doer of things
We dreamed of doing but could not bring ourselves to do,
The fears of years, like a biting whip,
Had cut grooves too deeply across our backs.

Haiku

1

Eastern guard tower
glints in sunset; convicts rest
like lizards on rocks.

2

The piano man
is sting at 3 am
his songs drop like plum.

3

Morning sun slants cell.
Drunks stagger like cripple flies
On Jailhouse floor.

4

To write a blues song
is to regiment riots
and pluck gems from graves.

5

A bare pecan tree
slips a pencil shadow down
a moonlit snow slope.

6

The falling snow flakes
Can not blunt the hard aches nor
Match the steel stillness.

7

Under moon shadows
A tall boy flashes knife and
Slices star bright ice.

8

In the August grass
Struck by the last rays of sun
The cracked teacup screams.

9

Making jazz swing in
Seventeen syllables AIN'T
No square poet's job.

IMAMU AMIRI BARAKA (LEROI JONES)

[b. 1934]

LeRoi Jones was born in New Jersey and educated at Howard University and at Columbia, where he was awarded an M.A. in German literature. He served in the U.S. Air Force as a weatherman and gunner. In an effort to identify more completely with his racial heritage, Jones assumed the Muslim name of Imamu Amiri Baraka. His poems and plays exhibit a fierce pride in his racial consciousness, and their strident militancy and rhetoric urge political and social action.

An Agony. As now.

I am inside someone
who hates me. I look
out from his eyes. Smell
what fouled tunes come in
to his breath. Love his
wretched women.

Slits in the metal, for sun. Where
my eyes sit turning, at the cool air
the glance of light, or hard flesh
rubbed against me, a woman, a man,
without shadow, or voice, or meaning.

This is the enclosure (flesh,
where innocence is a weapon. An
abstraction. Touch. (Not mine.
Or yours, if you are the soul I had
and abandoned when I was blind and had
my enemies carry me as a dead man
(if he is beautiful, or pitied.

It can be pain. (As now, as all his
flesh hurts me.) It can be that. Or
pain. As when she ran from me into
that forest.
                                        Or pain, the mind
silver spiraled whirled against the
sun, higher than even old men thought
God would be. Or pain. And the other. The
yes. (Inside his books, his fingers. They
are withered yellow flowers and were never
beautiful.) The yes. You will, lost soul, say
'beauty.' Beauty, practiced, as the tree. The
slow river. A white sun in its wet sentences.
Or, the cold men in their gale. Ecstasy. Flesh
or souls. The yes. (Their robes blown. Their bowls
empty. They chant at my heels, not at yours.) Flesh
or soul, as corrupt. Where the answer moves too quickly.
Where the God is a self, after all.)

Cold air blown through narrow blind eyes. Flesh,
white hot metal. Glows as the day with its sun.
It is a human love, I live inside. A bony skeleton
you recognize as words or simple feeling.

But it has no feeling. As the metal, is hot, it is not,
given to love.

It burns the thing
inside it. And that thing
screams.

Ka 'Ba

A closed window looks down
on a dirty courtyard, and black people
call across or scream across or walk across
defying physics in the stream of their will

Our world is full of sound
Our world is more lovely than anyone's
tho we suffer, and kill each other
and sometimes fail to walk the air

We are beautiful people
with african imaginations
full of masks and dances and swelling chants
with african eyes, and noses, and arms,
though we sprawl in grey chains in a place
full of winters, when what we want is sun.

We have been captured,
brothers. And we labor
to make our getaway, into
the ancient image, into a new
correspondence with ourselves
and our black family. We need magic
now we need the spells, to raise up
return, destroy, and create. What will be

the sacred words?

AUDRE LORDE

[1934–1992]

Audre Lorde was born in Harlem. She received a B.A. from Hunter College in 1961, and a Master's in Library Science from Columbia University. She has worked as a librarian and has taught school, spending a year as poet-in-residence at Tougaloo College in Mississippi. She has also taught at other colleges in New York, and since 1961 has been Professor of English at Hunter College, City University of New York. She has written more than a dozen books, including ten volumes of poems and prose accounts of her lesbianism and her bout with breast cancer. Her poetry is intensely passionate and powerful in its directness.

Now That I Am Forever with Child

How the days went
while you were blooming within me
I remember each upon each—
the swelling changed planes of my body
and how you first fluttered, then jumped
and I thought it was my heart.

How the days wound down
and the turning of winter
I recall, with you growing heavy
against the wind. I thought
now her hands
are formed, and her hair
has started to curl
now her teeth are done
now she sneezes.
Then the seed opened
I bore you one morning just before spring
My head rang like a fiery piston
my legs were towers between which
A new world was passing.

Since then
I can only distinguish
one thread within running hours
You, flowing through selves
toward You.

MARY OLIVER

[b. 1934]

Mary Oliver was born in Cleveland and educated at Ohio State University and Vassar College. She has taught at Case Western Reserve University, where she has been poet-in-residence. Among her many awards are a Guggenheim fellowship, a creative writing fellowship from the National Endowment for the Arts, and a Pulitzer Prize for her volume of poems, *American Primitive.* Her poetry has been compared with that of Theodore Roethke and James Wright in its sharp observation of the natural world and its strong physical impact.

Poem for My Father's Ghost

Now is my father
A traveler, like all the bold men
He talked of, endlessly
And with boundless admiration,
Over the supper table,
Or gazing up from his white pillow—
Book on his lap always, until
Even that grew too heavy to hold.
Now is my father free of all binding fevers.
Now is my father
Traveling where there is no road.

Finally, he could not lift a hand
To cover his eyes.
Now he climbs to the eye of the river,
He strides through the Dakotas,
He disappears into the mountains. And though he looks
Cold and hungry as any man
At the end of a questing season,

He is one of *them* now:
He cannot be stopped.
Now is my father
Walking the wind,
Sniffing the deep Pacific
That begins at the end of the world.

Vanished from us utterly,
Now is my father circling the deepest forest—
Then turning in to the last red campfire burning
In the final hills,

Where chieftains, warriors and heroes
Rise and make him welcome,
Recognizing, under the shambles of his body,
A brother who has walked his thousand miles.

MARK STRAND

[b. 1934]

Mark Strand was born to American parents on Prince Edward Island, Canada. He was educated at Antioch College (B.A.), Yale University (B.F.A.), and the University of Iowa (M.A.). He has taught at various universities, including Princeton, Virginia, and Utah, whose program in creative writing he currently directs. His published work includes translations, fiction, and children's books as well as poetry. His verse is characterized by an effacement of the poet's personality, a directness of language tinged with irony, and a factuality leavened with dreamlike images.

Elegy for My Father

(ROBERT STRAND, 1908–1968)

1. THE EMPTY BODY

The hands were yours, the arms were yours,
But you were not there.
The eyes were yours, but they were closed and would not
open.
The distant sun was there.
The moon poised on the hill's white shoulder was there.
The wind on Bedford Basin was there.
The pale green light of winter was there.
Your mouth was there,
But you were not there.
When somebody spoke, there was no answer.
Clouds came down
And buried the buildings along the water,
And the water was silent.

The gulls stared.
The years, the hours, that would not find you
Turned in the wrists of others.
There was no pain. It had gone.
There were no secrets. There was nothing to say.
The shade scattered its ashes.
The body was yours, but you were not there.
The air shivered against its skin.
The dark leaned into its eyes.
But you were not there.

2. ANSWERS

Why did you travel?
Because the house was cold.
Why did you travel?
Because it is what I have always done between sunset and sunrise.
What did you wear?
I wore a blue suit, a white shirt, yellow tie, and yellow socks.
What did you wear?
I wore nothing. A scarf of pain kept me warm.
Who did you sleep with?
I slept with a different woman each night.
Who did you sleep with?
I slept alone. I have always slept alone.
Why did you lie to me?
I always thought I told the truth.
Why did you lie to me?
Because the truth lies like nothing else and I love the truth.
Why are you going?
Because nothing means much to me anymore.
Why are you going?
I don't know. I have never known.
How long shall I wait for you?
Do not wait for me. I am tired and I want to lie down.
Are you tired and do you want to lie down?
Yes, I am tired and I want to lie down.

3. YOUR DYING

Nothing could stop you.
Not the best day. Not the quiet. Not the ocean rocking.
You went on with your dying.

Not the trees
Under which you walked, not the trees that shaded you.
Not the doctor
Who warned you, the white-haired young doctor who saved you once.
You went on with your dying.
Nothing could stop you. Not your son. Not your daughter
Who fed you and made you into a child again.
Not your son who thought you would live forever.
Not the wind that shook your lapels.
Not the stillness that offered itself to your motion.
Not your shoes that grew heavier.
Not your eyes that refused to look ahead.
Nothing could stop you.
You sat in your room and stared at the city
And went on with your dying.
You went to work and let the cold enter your clothes.
You let blood seep into your socks.
Your face turned white.
Your voice cracked in two.
You leaned on your cane.
But nothing could stop you.
Not your friends who gave you advice.
Not your son. Not your daughter who watched you grow small.
Not fatigue that lived in your sighs.
Not your lungs that would fill with water.
Not your sleeves that carried the pain of your arms.
Nothing could stop you.
You went on with your dying.
When you played with children you went on with your dying.
When you sat down to eat,
When you woke up at night, wet with tears, your body sobbing,
You went on with your dying.
Nothing could stop you.
Not the past.
Not the future with its good weather.
Not the view from your window, the view of the graveyard.
Not the city. Not the terrible city with its wooden buildings.
Not defeat. Not success.
You did nothing but go on with your dying.

You put your watch to your ear.
You felt yourself slipping.
You lay on the bed.
You folded your arms over your chest and you dreamed of the world without you,
Of the space under the trees,
Of the space in your room,
Of the spaces that would now be empty of you,
And you went on with your dying.
Nothing could stop you.
Not your breathing. Not your life.
Not the life you wanted.
Not the life you had.
Nothing could stop you.

4. YOUR SHADOW

You have your shadow.
The places where you were have given it back.
The hallways and bare lawns of the orphanage have given it back.
The Newsboys Home has given it back.
The streets of New York have given it back and so have the streets of Montreal.
The rooms in Belém where lizards would snap at mosquitos have given it back.
The dark streets of Manaus and the damp streets of Rio have given it back.
Mexico City where you wanted to leave it has given it back.
And Halifax where the harbor would wash its hands of you has given it back.
You have your shadow.
When you traveled the white wake of your going sent your shadow below, but when you arrived it was there to greet you. You had your shadow.
The doorways you entered lifted your shadow from you and when you went out, gave it back. You had your shadow.
Even when you forgot your shadow, you found it again; it had been with you.
Once in the country the shade of a tree covered your shadow and you were not known.
Once in the country you thought your shadow had been cast by somebody else. Your shadow said nothing.

Your clothes carried your shadow inside; when you took
them off, it spread like the dark of your past.
And your words that float like leaves in an air that is lost, in a
place no one knows, gave you back your shadow.
Your friends gave you back your shadow.
Your enemies gave you back your shadow. They said it was
heavy and would cover your grave.
When you died your shadow slept at the mouth of the
furnace and ate ashes for bread.
It rejoiced among ruins.
It watched while others slept.
It shone like crystal among the tombs.
It composed itself like air.
It wanted to be like snow on water.
It wanted to be nothing, but that was not possible.
It came to my house.
It sat on my shoulders.
Your shadow is yours. I told it so. I said it was yours.
I have carried it with me too long. I give it back.

5. MOURNING

They mourn for you.
When you rise at midnight,
And the dew glitters on the stone of your cheeks,
They mourn for you.
They lead you back into the empty house.
They carry the chairs and tables inside.
They sit you down and teach you to breathe.
And your breath burns,
It burns the pine box and the ashes fall like sunlight.
They give you a book and tell you to read.
They listen and their eyes fill with tears.
The women stroke your fingers.
They comb the yellow back into your hair.
They shave the frost from your beard.
They knead your thighs.
They dress you in fine clothes.
They rub your hands to keep them warm.
They feed you. They offer you money.
They get on their knees and beg you not to die.
When you rise at midnight they mourn for you.
They close their eyes and whisper you name over and over.

But they cannot drag the buried light from your veins.
They cannot reach your dreams.
Old man, there is no way.
Rise and keep rising, it does no good.
They mourn for you the way they can.

6. THE NEW YEAR

It is winter and the new year.
Nobody knows you.
Away from the stars, from the rain of light,
You lie under the weather of stones.
There is no thread to lead you back.
Your friends doze in the dark
Of pleasure and cannot remember.
Nobody knows you. You are the neighbor of nothing.
You do not see the rain falling and the man walking away,
The soiled wind blowing its ashes across the city.
You do not see the sun dragging the moon like an echo.
You do not see the bruised heart go up in flames,
The skulls of the innocent turn into smoke.
You do not see the scars of plenty, the eyes without light.
It is over. It is winter and the new year.
The meek are hauling their skins into heaven.
The hopeless are suffering the cold with those who have
  nothing to hide.
It is over and nobody knows you.
There is starlight drifting on the black water.
There are stones in the sea no one has seen.
There is a shore and people are waiting.
And nothing comes back.
Because it is over.
Because there is silence instead of a name.
Because it is winter and the new year.

LUCILLE CLIFTON

[b. 1936]

Lucille Clifton was born in Depew, New York, and educated at the State University of New York at Fredonia and Howard University. She has taught at a number of universities, including Fisk, George Washington, and the University of Cincinnati. In addition to half a dozen volumes of poems, the most recent of which is *Quilting* (1991) Clifton has also written a memoir, *Generations of Americans*. Her poems, written in a distinctive idiomatic voice, express powerfully a comfortable sense of physical being and a jaunty and spirited individualism.

Homage to My Hips

these hips are big hips.
they need space to
move around in.
they don't fit into little
pretty places. these hips
are free hips.
they don't like to be held back.
these hips have never been enslaved,
they go where they want to go
they do what they want to do.
these hips are mighty hips.
these hips are magic hips.
i have known them
to put a spell on a man and
spin him like a top!

The Lost Baby Poem

the time i dropped your almost body down
down to meet the waters under the city
and run one with the sewage to the sea
what did i know about waters rushing back
what did i know about drowning
or being drowned

you would have been born into winter
in the year of the disconnected gas
and no car   we would have made the thin
walk over Genesee hill into the Canada wind
to watch you slip like ice into strangers' hands
you would have fallen naked as snow into winter
if you were here i could tell you these
and some other things

if i am ever less than a mountain
for your definite brothers and sisters
let the rivers pour over my head
let the sea take me for a spiller
of seas let black men call me stranger
always for your never named sake

MICHAEL HARPER

[b. 1938]

Michael Harper was born and raised in New York. Educated at California State College and the University of Iowa, he has taught at Reed College and Brown University, where he directs the creative writing program. His poems, like those of Langston Hughes, exhibit the influence of jazz and the blues. Though rooted in personal history, they also reveal a strong concern for racial, musical, and literary history.

American History

Those four black girls blown up
in that Alabama church
remind me of five hundred
middle passage blacks,
in a net, under water
in Charleston harbor
so *redcoats* wouldn't find them.
Can't find what you can't see
can you?

Martin's Blues

He came apart in the open,
the slow motion cameras
falling quickly
neither alive nor kicking;
stone blind dead
on the balcony

MARTIN'S BLUES **Martin:** Martin Luther King, Jr. (1929–1968), black civil rights leader assassinated.

that old melody
etched his black lips
in a pruned echo:
We shall overcome
some day—
Yes we did!
Yes we did!

Nightmare Begins Responsibility

I placed these numbed wrists to the pane
watching white uniforms whisk over
him in the tube-kept
prison
fear what they will do in experiment
watch my gloved stickshifting gasolined hands
breathe *boxcar-information-please* infirmary tubes
distrusting white-pink mending paperthin
silkened end hairs, distrusting tubes
shrunk in his *trunk-skincapped*
shaven head, in thighs
distrusting-white-hands-picking-baboon-light
on this son who will not make his second night
of this wardstrewn intensive airpocket
where his father's asthmatic
hymns of *night-train,* train done gone
his mother can only know that he has flown
up into essential calm unseen corridor
going boxscarred home, *mamaborn, sweetsonchild*
gonedowntown into *researchtestingwarehousebatteryacid*
mama-son-done-gone/me telling her 'nother
train tonight, no music, no breathstroked
heartbeat in my infinite distrust of them:

and of my distrusting self
white-doctor-who-breathed-for-him-all-night
say it for two sons gone,
say nightmare, say it loud
panebreaking heartmadness:
nightmare begins responsibility.

CHARLES SIMIC

[b. 1938]

Charles Simic was born in Belgrade, Yugoslavia, and raised in Paris, Chicago, and New York, where he received a B.A. from New York University. He has taught at a number of colleges and universities, including the University of New Hampshire, and he has won fellowships and awards including those from the National Endowment for the Arts and a Pulitzer Prize for poetry. His poems tend toward the minimal and the surreal, with Simic compressing intense feeling into descriptions of common things within a brief compass.

Stone

Go inside a stone
That would be my way.
Let somebody else become a dove
Or gnash with a tiger's tooth.
I am happy to be a stone.

From the outside the stone is a riddle:
No one knows how to answer it.
Yet within, it must be cool and quiet
Even though a cow steps on it full weight,
Even though a child throws it in a river;
The stone sinks, slow, unperturbed
To the river bottom
Where the fishes come to knock on it
And listen.

I have seen sparks fly out
When two stones are rubbed,
So perhaps it is not dark inside after all;
Perhaps there is a moon shining
From somewhere, as though behind a hill—
Just enough light to make out
The strange writings, the star-charts
On the inner walls.

BARBARA HOLDER

(b. 1939)

Barbara Holder was born in Brooklyn, New York. She studied and taught ballet for many years, and received her B.A., M.A., and M. Phil. from Columbia University. She teaches at Pace University and Westchester Community College, and runs writing and journaling workshops. Her poems have appeared in numerous magazines.

First Death

I will wait for the dawn to come
before I remember her, before I recall the earth
thumping against her coffin and the guttural
lyrics of the rabbi's words.

Only when sun shines, can I think of the dead—
my grandmother's worn face and stone-black eyes
confused by her body's failing. Only when sun comes,
can I see her swollen belly, the flat pies
of her breasts.

I didn't believe in death, the dirt scattered by my
mother and uncles blinding her eyes, packing
her nose, sealing her mouth. Only then she was gone.

She gave me sweets. Her keen fingers lifted and spread
dough to a thin, milky tent to stuff with apples,
the pungence of strudel filling our rooms.

But her silence was ponderous, black Russia
in her eyes, the snow of the tundra flaked over
her hands, her kiss stiffly whiskered like a beaver's—
hidden woman of few joys, Annetta, Annetta.

ROBERT PINSKY

[b. 1940]

Robert Pinsky was born in New Jersey and educated at Rutgers University, where he received his B.A. and at Stanford, from which he received a Ph.D. in English. After teaching at Wellesley and the University of California at Berkeley, he assumed a position at Boston University. In addition to a number of volumes of poems, Pinsky has also published an important critical book on contemporary American poetry, *The Situation of Poetry,* as well as an interactive computer novel, *Mindwheel.*

Dying

Nothing to be said about it, and everything—
The change of changes, closer or further away:
The Golden Retriever next door, Gussie, is dead,

Like Sandy, the Cocker Spaniel from three doors down
Who died when I was small; and every day
Things that were in my memory fade and die.

Phrases die out: first, everyone forgets
What doornails are; then after certain decades
As a dead metaphor, *"dead as a doornail"* flickers

And fades away. But someone I know is dying—
And though one might say glibly, "everyone is,"
The different pace makes the difference absolute.

The tiny invisible spores in the air we breathe,
That settle harmlessly on our drinking water
And on our skin, happen to come together

With certain conditions on the forest floor,
Or even a shady corner of the lawn—
And overnight the fleshy, pale stalks gather,

The colorless growth without a leaf or flower;
And around the stalks, the summer grass keeps growing
With steady pressure, like the insistent whiskers

That grow between shaves on a face, the nails
Growing and dying from the toes and fingers
At their own humble pace, oblivious

As the nerveless moths, that live their night or two—
Though like a moth a bright soul keeps on beating,
Bored and impatient in the monster's mouth.

ROBERT HASS

[b. 1941]

Robert Hass was born in San Francisco and raised in San Rafael, California. He received a B.A. from St. Mary's College and a Ph.D. from Stanford. Since 1989 he has taught at the University of California at Berkeley. Among his numerous awards is a MacArthur Fellowship. In addition to three volumes of poems, Hass has also published a collection of essays on poetry, *Twentieth-Century Pleasures*. He has also translated the poetry of Czeslaw Milosz. His own poems frequently reveal an intensely passionate engagement with the physical world in language that expresses its sensuous pleasures.

Meditation at Lagunitas

All the new thinking is about loss.
In this it resembles all the old thinking.
The idea, for example, that each particular erases
the luminous clarity of a general idea. That the clown-
faced woodpecker probing the dead sculpted trunk
of that black birch is, by his presence,
some tragic falling off from a first world
of undivided light. Or the other notion that,
because there is in this world no one thing
to which the bramble of *blackberry* corresponds,
a word is elegy to what it signifies.
We talked about it late last night and in the voice

of my friend, there was a thin wire of grief, a tone
almost querulous. After a while I understood that,
talking this way, everything dissolves: *justice,*
pine, hair, woman, you and *I.* There was a woman
I made love to and I remembered how, holding
her small shoulders in my hands sometimes,
I felt a violent wonder at her presence
like a thirst for salt, for my childhood river
with its island willows, silly music from the pleasure boat,
muddy places where we caught the little orange-silver fish
called *pumpkinseed.* It hardly had to do with her.
Longing, we say, because desire is full
of endless distances. I must have been the same to her.
But I remember so much, the way her hands dismantled bread,
the thing her father said that hurt her, what
she dreamed. There are moments when the body is as
  numinous
as words, days that are the good flesh continuing.
Such tenderness, those afternoons and evenings,
saying *blackberry, blackberry, blackberry.*

MARILYN HACKER

[b. 1942]

Marilyn Hacker was born in New York City and educated there at the Bronx High of Science, New York University, and the Art Students League. She has worked as an antiquarian bookseller and as a teacher, as well as performing editorial work for books and magazines. Among her awards is a National Book Award in 1975 for her volume, *Presentation Piece.* Her poems are often playful and witty, taking and revealing the pleasures of verbal suggestion through sound and form.

Canzone

Consider the three functions of the tongue:
taste, speech, the telegraphy of pleasure,
are not confused in any human tongue:
yet, sinewy and singular, the tongue
accomplishes what, perhaps, no other organ

can. Were I to speak of giving tongue,
you'd think two things at least; and a cooked tongue,
sliced, on a plate, with caper sauce, which I give
my guest for lunch, is one more, to which she'd give
the careful concentration of her tongue
twice over, to appreciate the taste
and to express—it would be in good taste—

a gastronomic memory the taste
called to mind, and mind brought back to tongue.
There is a paucity of words for taste:
sweet, sour, bitter, salty. Any taste,
however multiplicitous its pleasure,
complex its execution (I might taste
that sauce ten times in cooking, change its taste
with herbal subtleties, chromatic organ
tones of clove and basil, good with organ
meats) must be described with those few taste-
words, or with metaphors, to give
my version of sensations it would give

a neophyte, deciding whether to give
it a try. She might develop a taste.
(you try things once; I think you have to give
two chances, though, to know your mind, or give
up on novelties.) Your mother tongue
nurtures, has the subtleties which give
flavor to words, and words to flavor, give
the by no means subsidiary pleasure
of being able to describe a pleasure
and recreate it. Making words, we give
the private contemplations of each organ
to the others, and to others, organ-

ize sensations into thoughts. Sentient organ-
isms, we symbolize feeling, give
the spectrum (that's a symbol) each sense organ
perceives, by analogy, to others. Disorgan-
ization of the senses is an acquired taste
we all acquire; as speaking beasts, it's organ-
ic to our discourse. The first organ
of acknowledged communion is the tongue

(tripartite diplomat, which after tongu-
ing a less voluble expressive organ
to wordless efflorescences of pleasure
offers up words to reaffirm the pleasure).

That's a primary difficulty: pleasure
means something, and something different, for each organ;
each person, too. I may take exquisite pleasure
in boiled eel, or blancmange—or not. One pleasure
of language is making known what not to give.
And think of a bar of lavender soap, a pleasure
to see and, moistened, rub on your skin, a pleasure
especially to smell, but if you taste
it (though smell is most akin to taste)
what you experience will not be pleasure;
you almost retch, grimace, stick out your tongue,
slosh rinses of ice water over your tongue.
But I would rather think about your tongue
experiencing and transmitting pleasure
to one or another multi-sensual organ
—like memory. Whoever wants to give
only one meaning to that, has untutored taste.

LOUISE GLÜCK

[b. 1943]

Louise Glück was born in New York City and studied at Sarah Lawrence College and Columbia University. She has taught at Goddard, Warren Wilson, and Williams colleges and has received awards from the National Endowment for the Arts and from the Rockefeller Foundation. Her poems are evocative and stirring in their blend of sensuousness and austerity.

The School Children

The children go forward with their little satchels.
And all morning the mothers have labored
to gather the late apples, red and gold,
like words of another language.

And on the other shore
are those who wait behind great desks
to receive these offerings.

How orderly they are—the nails
on which the children hang
their overcoats of blue or yellow wool.

And the teachers shall instruct them in silence
and the mothers shall scour the orchards for a way out,
drawing to themselves the gray limbs of the fruit trees
bearing so little ammunition.

The Garden

1. THE FEAR OF BIRTH

One sound. Then the hiss and whir
of houses gliding into their places.
And the wind
leafs through the bodies of animals—

But my body that could not content itself
with health—why should it be sprung back
into the chord of sunlight?

It will be the same again.
This fear, this inwardness,
until I am forced into a field
without immunity
even to the least shrub that walks
stiffly out of the dirt, trailing
the twisted signature of its root,
even to a tulip, a red claw.

And then the losses,
one after another,
all supportable.

2. GARDEN

The garden admires you.
For your sake it smears itself with green pigment,

the ecstatic reds of the roses,
so that you will come to it with your lovers.

And the willows—
see how it has shaped these green
tents of silence. Yet
there is still something you need,
your body so soft, so alive, among the stone animals.

Admit that it is terrible to be like them,
beyond harm.

3. THE FEAR OF LOVE

That body lying beside me like obedient stone—
once its eyes seemed to be opening,
we could have spoken.

At that time it was winter already.
By day the sun rose in its helmet of fire
and at night also, mirrored in the moon.
Its light passed over us freely,
as though we had lain down
in order to leave no shadows,
only these two shallow dents in the snow.
And the past, as always, stretched before us,
still, complex, impenetrable.

How long did we lie there
as, arm in arm in their cloaks of feathers,
the gods walked down
from the mountain we built for them?

4. ORIGINS

As though a voice were saying
You should be asleep by now—
But there was no one. Nor
had the air darkened,
though the moon was there,
already filled in with marble.

As though, in a garden crowded with flowers,
a voice had said
How dull they are, these golds,
so sonorous, so repetitious
until you closed your eyes,
lying among them, all
stammering flame:

And yet you could not sleep,
poor body, the earth
still clinging to you—

5. THE FEAR OF BURIAL

In the empty field, in the morning,
the body waits to be claimed.
The spirit sits beside it, on a small rock—
nothing comes to give it form again.

Think of the body's loneliness.
At night pacing the sheared field,
its shadow buckled tightly around.
Such a long journey.
And already the remote, trembling lights of the village
not pausing for it as they scan the rows.
How far away they seem,
the wooden doors, the bread and milk
laid like weights on the table.

JAMES TATE

[b. 1943]

James Tate was born in Missouri and educated at Kansas State College, the University of Missouri, and later at the University of Iowa, from which he received a Master of Fine Arts degree. He has taught at Berkeley, Columbia, and the University of Massachusetts. His honors include a Guggenheim fellowship and an award from the National Institute for Arts and Letters. His poems contain surprising details and unpredictable turns of thought; their tone is a blend of matter-of-factness with bemused astonishment.

The Lost Pilot

FOR MY FATHER, 1922–1944

Your face did not rot
like the others—the co-pilot,
for example, I saw him

yesterday. His face is corn-
mush: his wife and daughter,
the poor ignorant people, stare

as if he will compose soon.
He was more wronged than Job.
But your face did not rot

like the others—it grew dark,
and hard like ebony;
the features progressed in their

distinction. If I could cajole
you to come back for an evening,
down from your compulsive

orbiting, I would touch you,
read your face as Dallas,
your hoodlum gunner, now,

with the blistered eyes, reads
his braille editions. I would
touch your face as a disinterested

scholar touches an original page.
However frightening, I would
discover you, and I would not

turn you in; I would not make
you face your wife, or Dallas,
or the co-pilot, Jim. You

could return to your crazy
orbiting, and I would not try
to fully understand what

it means to you. All I know
is this: when I see you,
as I have seen you at least

once every year of my life,
spin across the wilds of the sky
like a tiny, African god,

I feel dead. I feel as if I were
the residue of a stranger's life,
that I should pursue you.

My head cocked toward the sky,
I cannot get off the ground,
and, you, passing over again,

fast, perfect, and unwilling
to tell me that you are doing
well, or that it was mistake

that placed you in that world,
and me in this; or that misfortune
placed these worlds in us.

JERRY W. WARD, JR.

[b. 1943]

Jerry W. Ward, Jr., was born in Washington, D.C., and raised in Mississippi. He received his B.S. from Tougaloo College and his Ph.D. from the University of Virgina. The Lawrence Durgin Professor of Literature at Tougaloo College, Ward is a critic and poet as well as a teacher. His work has appeared in such publications as *New Orleans Review, The Southern Quarterly,* and *Black American Literature Forum.* With A. LaVonne Brown Ruoff he has coedited *Redefining American Literary History* (1980), and with John Oliver Killens he has edited *Black Southern Voices* (1993).

Jazz to Jackson to John

FOR JOHN REESE

movement one: genesis

it must have been something like
sheets of sound wrinkled

with riffs and scats,
the aftermath of a fierce night
breezing through the grits and gravy;
or something like a blind leviathan
squeezing through solid rock,
marking chaos in the water
when his lady of graveyard love went
turning tricks on the ocean's bottom;
or something like a vision
so blazing basic, so gutbucket, so blessed
the lowdown blues flew out: jazz

jazz to jackson and
dust to dawn and
words for John

it must have been something like
Farish Street in the bebop forties,
a ragtag holy ghost baptizing Mississippi
on an unexpected Sunday, a brilliant revelation
for Billie telling you about these foolish things
back in your own backyard, angel eyes in the rose room,
Monk's changing piano into horn because it was zero in the sun,
and around midnight there was nobody but you
to walk Parker and his jazz to Jackson;
yeah, brother, it must have been something
striking you like an eargasm,
a baritone ax laid into soprano wood,

like loving madly in hurting silence,
waiting to fingerpop this heathen air
with innovations of classical black
at decibels to wake the deaf, the dumb, and the dead;
because around midnight there was nobody but you
who dug whether race records were
lamentations or lynchings: jazz
jazz to jackson and
sunset to dawn and
words for John

movement two: blues people in the corn

steal away, steal away, steal away
the heart blow/horn blow/drum drop
to bass/five-four time beat
making a one o'clock comeback creep
behind all that jazz
beat—beepbeep—beat
steal way back to beginning
beginning
is the water
is the soul
is the source
is the foundation with my brothers
is Pharaoh jamming in the pyramid,
sketches of Spain for a night in Tunisia;
is MJQ, Tatum, Turrentine, Tyner,
the Jazz Messengers, messiahs, crusading
headhunters tracking down the mind

cause, Lord yes, all God's people got sold
and who'da thought
owning rhythm was a crime like stealing a nickel
and snitching a dime, when we had coffers packed
with golden music and time, golden music and time

sliding from the flesh, the bone, honeysweet music;
them lollipopcicle people
and they sardine ships
(and no music to speak of)
they stole it all and sold it all
for wooden nickels, for frozen dimes: jazz

behind all that jazz
blues people in the corn, in the vale of cotton tears,
blues people in the corn,
waiting, waiting, waiting,
wrapped in esoteric patience,
waiting to steal away,
steal away, steal away
soon as Miles runs down the voodoo avenue

with some jazz to Jackson
and pipes a private number
to call a tune for John

movement three: and this, John, is our new day

and this, John, is our new day.
never say goodbye to the blues that saw you through,
nor put down the spirituals and the salty sermonnettes
the drugs, the junkies, the jukebox juice, the sweat
and the pain of shelling hot peanuts, hot peanuts: jazz

and the jazz you gave to us
we give to you as jazz to Jackson and
because we really want to thank you
words for John

CHRISTOPHER JANE CORKERY

[b. 1946]

Christopher Jane Corkery is the author of *Blessing* (Princeton Series of Contemporary Poets). Recent work of hers has appeared in *The Atlantic* and in *Partisan Review*. She lives in Dorchester, Massachussetts, and teaches each summer at Harvard University.

As in the Days of the Prophets

Love took the words right out of my mouth.
Not the making of love, the clinging and plunge,
The tongue's deep spiral, but the acts of days,
The sun up and down, the dish and the pot,
The light on the head of first one, then another,
The stairs unswept, the bed cold, the light out,
The papers brought in, the bed made, the money
Paid out, the bulbs dug, the children reverent
At what came next, the rise and the fall
Of coral and ocher, the folding and sorting,
The endless numbering of things, the walking
With babies in slings, in backpacks, in strollers,
Then hand in hand, then the hand dropped

And one of them up to my shoulder, eyeing,
Before I do, the hawk or the waxwing,
The junco, the hermit thrush in the depths
Of our gun-shot city, and just to the south
The great hill we climb, by season, together,
Alone, in pairs, in trios, the slapping
Of mud from our shoes on the back steps again,
The chastening memory of the otter plunging
In the icy water of his adequate tank
At the base of that hill, and love made the otter,
Love made the mud, the ice-slicked bark.
The meals, the shining heads, and the sleep,
The risings, the children, the hawk's spiral.
Love took the words right out of my mouth.

NEAL BOWERS

[b. 1948]

Neal Bowers, who was born in Tennessee, earned his Ph.D. at the University of Florida, and is currently professor of English at Iowa State University. His publications include two volumes of poems, *Lost in the Heartland* and *The Golf Ball Driver,* and two critical books, *James Dickey: The Poet as Pitchman* and *Theodore Roethke: The Journey from I to Otherwise.* His poetry and scholarly work have appeared in such periodicals as *The New Yorker, Poetry, Harper's,* and *The Sewanee Review.* His awards include the *Yankee* Poetry Prize, *Poetry* magazine's Frederick Bock Prize, and a National Endowment for the Arts Fellowship.

Divining Love

FOR NANCY

After a while, the drought dried up
all talk of itself,
grew beyond notice
the way a steady noise
slips out of hearing
but still envelops everything.
All day the sky was parchment;
each night the sheets were powder,
and the cracked moon chalked the floor.

Drinking from the same cup
or sharing bathwater,
we spoke of love
for the first time in years,
drew closer in our intimate austerity,
felt how the heart
may blossom under stress.

Thriving on less and less,
we let the houseplants shrivel
in their pots, stopped
lugging buckets to the lilac
and the stunted redbud,
watched the land go
dry as kindling,
ourselves already smoldering.

Enthralled by an exquisite thirst,
we pared down with the trees, withdrew
into our roots, our deepest veins,
driving deep for the molten core,
the hidden river of fire
that could ignite our limbs, our souls,
and quench the grasses of the world.

BARON WORMSER

[b. 1948]

Baron Wormser is the author of *The White Words,* and *Good Trembling* (Houghton Mifflin, 1983, 1985) and of *Atoms, Soul Music and Other Poems* (Paris Review Editions, 1989). He lives in Mercer, Maine, and works as a librarian.

Friday Night

Dinner winds down, and the bottom
Of the accompanying bottle appears
With the abruptness of a smile
Or a plainclothesman's badge. The people

Are friends. The moments are idle as jewels.
It is not written into any constitution or
Call to arms but this takes place all over the world.
Praise to conviviality!
Praise to the flesh of the broiled fish!
Praise to the ardor that dissipates
In words and cigarettes!
These evenings are accomplishments—
That is why they disappear.
The hostess hunches over the table,
Shakes her head, speaks rapidly.
The host flips an apple into the air.
Everyone has lived through another work week,
Everyone has a story to tell:
Tanks, jokes, sickness, boots.
Myths are not dead. This is the table
Of life—one and many, human.
It is worth the journey.

JORIE GRAHAM

[b. 1951]

Jorie Graham was brought up in Italy, attended a French lycee in Rome, and became fluent in French, Italian, and English. After attending the Sorbonne, she pursued a program in cinema studies at New York University before taking an M.F.A. at the University of Iowa, where she has been professor of English. Her poems, which reveal a fascination with the visual in both landscape and painting, are richly philosophical, pursuing questions of creativity and consciousness.

Mind

The slow overture of rain,
each drop breaking
without breaking into
the next, describes
the unrelenting, syncopated
mind. Not unlike
the hummingbirds

imagining their wings
to be their heart, and swallows
believing the horizon
to be a line they lift
and drop. What is it
they cast for? The poplars,
advancing or retreating,
lose their stature
equally, and yet stand firm,
making arrangements
in order to become
imaginary. The city
draws the mind in streets,
and streets compel it
from their intersections
where a little
belongs to no one. It is
what is driven through
all stationary portions
of the world, gravity's
stake in things, the leaves,
pressed against the dank
window of November
soil, remain unwelcome
till transformed, parts
of a puzzle unsolvable
till the edges give a bit
and soften. See how
then the picture becomes clear,
the mind entering the ground
more easily in pieces,
and all the richer for it.

JIMMY SANTIAGO BACA

[b. 1952]

Jimmy Santiago Baca was born in Santa Fe, New Mexico, and has lived in Norch Carolina, California, and Arizona. He dropped out of school in the seventh grade and did not return until he was thirty-two. After receiving his B.A. from the University of New Mexico in 1987, Baca conducted writing workshops and programs for children, prison inmates at the Santa Fe prison, and adults in treatment for alcohol and drug abuse. He has also taught creative writing at the University of New Mexico.

From *Meditations on the South Valley*

XVII

I love the wind
when it blows through my barrio.
It hisses its snake love
down calles de polvo,
and cracks egg-shell skins
of abandoned homes.
Stray dogs find shelter
along the river,
where great cottonwoods rattle
like old covered wagons,
stuck in stagnant waterholes.
Days when the wind blows
full of sand and grit,
men and women make decisions
that change their whole lives.
Windy days in the barrio
give birth to divorce papers
and squalling separation. The wind tells us
what others refuse to tell us,
informing men and women of a secret,
that they move away to hide from.

RITA DOVE

[b. 1952]

Rita Dove was born and raised in Akron, Ohio. Her degrees include a B.A. from Miami University, and an M.F.A. from the University of Iowa, following the study of modern European literature at the University of Tübingen, Germany, on a Fulbright fellowship. She has taught at the University of Virginia and the University of Arizona. In 1987 she won the Pulitzer Prize for *Tohmas and Beulah,* which includes poems on the black experience in America, with particular emphasis on family history. She was named U.S. Poet Laureate for 1993.

Canary

FOR MICHAEL S. HARPER

Billie Holiday's burned voice
had as many shadows as lights,
a mournful candelabra against a sleek piano,
the gardenia her signature under that ruined face.

(Now you're cooking, drummer to bass,
magic spoon, magic needle.
Take all day if you have to
with your mirror and your bracelet of song.)

Fact is, the invention of women under siege
has been to sharpen love in the service of myth.

If you can't be free, be a mystery.

ALICE FULTON

[b. 1952]

Alice Fulton was born in Troy, New York, where she lived for twenty-five years. Her first book of poems, *Dance Script with Electric Ballerina,* won the 1982 Associated Writing Programs Award in poetry and was followed by her 1986 collection, *Palladium.* She has published in *The New Yorker, The Yale Review, Poetry,* and *Parnassus,* among other magazines. Her honors include the 1980 Emily Dickinson Award and the 1984 Consuelo Ford Award from the Poetry Society of America. A Professor of English at the University of Michigan, Ann Arbor, Alice Fulton has won numerous awards, among them fellowships from the John Simon Guggenheim Memorial Foundation and the MacArthur Foundation.

My Second Marriage to My First Husband

We married for acceptance: to stall the nagging
married friends who wanted us
to do it there and then—

with them. In the downy wedlocked bed
we ask "Is there life after
one-day honeymoons to Kissamee Springs?
Was I all right?" The answers, woefully,
are no and no. And yes,

we lollygagged down the aisle, vowed
to forsake dallying, shilly-shallying, and cleave
only onto one another, to forever romp
in the swampy rumpus
room of our eccentricities: that sanctum
sanctorum where I sport
bedsocks and never rise
till noon. What did we know?
Did you know my love for animals
has always been acute? Perhaps in time
I will become a shepherdess, a jockey.

At the reception every table was adorned
with toilet tissue cy-
cloned into swans. When I unraveled one
to find the charm, the management
was shocked. Dismembering swans!
No bride had ever . . . And the prize, a little gizzard
of a ring, was disappointing. Oh Person,
was it worth it? Of course,
we fit at dinner parties. But as one part warbles
to be normal, another puts a spin on things.
I see you striving to frolic
in your steel-mesh tweeds as I model
chiffon voluptuaries the color of exhaust.

In the wedding album we end or commence
our revels. There we are! doing the cha-cha-cha
to the boom-chick-chick band
in our dyed-to-match togs.
We're getting fat
on the eats, foaming
white crumbs, "Honey" and "Dear"
cumbersome as live doves
on our tongues.

Bring squeezeboxes, gardenias,
a hybrid of the two. Congratulate us,
chums. Smile and freeze: our dimples stiffen
to resolute framed stares. How adult
we look! Our eyes burn
stoplights in the Instamatic squares.

ALBERTO RIOS

[b. 1952]

Alberto Rios was born in Jogales, Arizona, a town on the Mexican border. His mother is Mexican and his father English, which as Rios has noted, enriches his linguistic and cultural heritage. He has published a volume of stories, *The Iguana Killer,* which won the 1984 Western States Book Award, and two collections of poems, *Whispering to Fool the Wind* (1982) and *Five Indiscretions* (1985). His poems often move deftly between the imaginary and the real.

A Dream of Husbands

Though we thought it, Doña Carolina did not die.
She was too old for that nonsense, and too set.
That morning she walked off just a little farther
into her favorite dream, favorite but not nice
so much, not nice and not bad, so it was not death.
She dreamed the dream of husbands
and over there she found him after all the years.
Cabrón, she called him, *animal,* very loud
so we could hear it, for us it was a loud truck
passing, or thunder, or too many cats, very loud
for having left her for so long and so far. Days now
her voice is the squeak of the rocking chair
as she complains, we hear it, it will not go
not with oils or sanding or shouts back at her.
But it becomes too the sound a spoon makes, her old
very large wooden spoon as it stirs a pot of soup.
Dinnertimes, we think of her, the good parts, of her
cooking, we like her best then, even the smell of her.
But then, *cabrones* she calls us, *animales,* irritated,

from over there, from the dream, they come, her words
they are the worst sounds of the street in the night
so that we will not get so comfortable about her,
so comfortable with her having left us
we thinking that her husband and her long dream
are so perfect, because no, they are not, not so much,
she is not so happy this way, not in this dream,
this is not heaven, don't think it. She tells us this,
sadness too is hers, a half measure, sadness at having
no time for the old things, for rice, for chairs.

SHERYL NOETHE

[b. 1954]

Sheryl Noethe was born in Minneapolis, Minnesota, of Norwegian and German ancestry. She has taught at various public and private schools in the west, especially in Idaho and Montana. A member of Teachers and Writers Collaborative, Noethe has been Resident Poet at the New York School for the Deaf.

Slow Dancing with Billy

Last night I dreamt that you and I
were slow dancing in a wet field in
South Dakota, and that your hair
smelled like wheat and is somehow
still long and yellow enough for me
to breathe in a dream. When I woke
up I wanted to call South Dakota,
tell the operator that when I was
14 years old I thought you looked
just like Apollo, describe how you
look walking out of seven-foot high
Sunflowers with 13 inch heads so heavy
it is all they can do to follow the sun
in a day. Tell her how the dog crept
off to the chicken farm to play tag,
how the outhouse blew away in a winter
storm and when we went to get another

the old man came to the door and called
me your boy. How you ran your fingers
through my short hair and across my
round, willful forehead, and said
yes, my beautiful boy.
All day long I kept thinking about
that 20 mile drive into Aberdeen for a glass of
whiskey. It was 14 years now since I
sat next to you on the tractor waiting
for dark. Last night when we slow-danced
in my dream it was all just the same.
Why didn't I marry you?
Why did I take that hostess job in Minneapolis?
We drove out of town and the collected reflections
of cities hit the northern ice caps and a shimmering
curtain of light illuminated the sky over the
winter prairie. Another winter passed and you met
another mean girl in some downtown bar.
I started going out with the motorcyclist and
then a musician and at your wedding your grandma
shouted IT WON'T LAST and winked at me.
At the reception the weeping bride drove me
out the back door with her champagne glass
and after that I never saw you again.
When I was eleven I met you and married you in my heart.
It's been 25 years and I spent so far this whole day
remembering some dancing we never even did.

CATHY SONG

[b. 1955]

Cathy Song is the product of two cultures, the older Asian culture of her Korean grandmother and the more modern Hawaiian culture of her upbringing. Following her early schooling in Hawaii, Song attended Wellesley College and Boston University, where she earned her graduate and undergraduate degrees, respectively. Her poems frequently depict a movement between the worlds of her Asian heritage and contemporary American life.

Lost Sister

1

In China,
even the peasants
named their first daughters
Jade—
the stone that in the far fields
could moisten the dry season,
could make men move mountains
for the healing green of the inner hills
glistening like slices of winter melon.

And the daughters were grateful:
They never left home.
To move freely was a luxury
stolen from them at birth.
Instead, they gathered patience,
learning to walk in shoes
the size of teacups,
without breaking—
the arc of their movements
as dormant as the rooted willow,
as redundant as the farmyard hens.
But they traveled far
in surviving,
learning to stretch the family rice,
to quiet the demons,
the noisy stomachs.

2

There is a sister
across the ocean,
who relinquished her name,
diluting jade green
with the blue of the Pacific.
Rising with a tide of locusts,
she swarmed with others
to inundate another shore.
In America,
there are many roads
and women can stride along with men.

But in another wilderness,
the possibilities,
the loneliness,
can strangulate like jungle vines.
The meager provisions and sentiments
of once belonging—
fermented roots, Mah-Jong tiles and firecrackers—set but
a flimsy household
in a forest of nightless cities.
A giant snake rattles above,
spewing black clouds into your kitchen.
Dough-faced landlords
slip in and out of your keyholes,
making claims you don't understand,
tapping into your communication systems
of laundry lines and restaurant chains.

You find you need China:
your one fragile identification,
a jade link
handcuffed to your wrist.
You remember your mother
who walked for centuries,
footless—
and like her,
you have left no footprints,
but only because
there is an ocean in between,
the unremitting space of your rebellion.

JULIA ALVAREZ

[b. 1960]

Julia Alvarez was raised in the Dominican Republic and emigrated to the United States in 1960. She has earned undergraduate and graduate degrees in literature and writing, and is Professor of English at Middlebury College. A fiction writer as well as a poet, Alvarez has received grants from the National Endowment for the Arts and the Ingram Merrill Foundation.

Bookmaking

Words, let water from an unseen infinite Ocean
Come into this place as energy for the dying
and even the dead.

Rumi

At the Pierpont Morgan I go up and down
the glass cases of the East Room,
studying bindings, toolings, papercutting,
as if by learning your craft,
I will know you in the books exposed before me,
the thick seams clasping
the packets together the way your hand will
fold around my forearm,
your urgent fingers whitening my skin
as if to bind us in a certain moment
of knowing; the pearled vellum lucent
as lovemaking, the leather covers
pockmarked in a scarred masculine pattern
as if we undressed hastily
and your jacket's rough tweed pressed
against my leg as you bore down,
parting me, the way I've seen you take
a book in both hands, parting
its thick wedge of pages to the exact passage
you want me to read.
I go slowly over each display, accustoming myself
to this new way of looking
at books: gold leaf, embossed crescents, Dove's bindings,
Zaehendorf's aquamarine fancies:
I read each legend card carefully
as if to know you better
without the distraction of your body
beside my body,
the vocabulary of your craft still odd on my tongue
like the taste of you at first,
an uncertain pleasure, the self posed between
its celibate single-mindedness
and its being cracked open with the creaking give
of a new binding in a book you've made.
I study them now—books I've known, abstractly,
books we've both loved with a passion

almost of the body: *Leaves of Grass, The Marriage*
of Heaven and Hell, To the Lighthouse,
changed utterly as I pass by, taking each one in,
marveling. Now they have become objects:
physical shapes: the filigreed leaves closed
into solid gold, the leather tooled
into splendid, intricate beds of flowers,
the embossed medallion like the spiral
swirl of an ear the finger pleasures
to follow. Now they have become
texts, tomes, volumes—books I would touch
were they not encased in their carefully
monitored boxes for the generations to come.
Now the words become flesh,
your body, my body, side by side in my small twin bed.
I lean over, closer, clouding the glass
with my frank breath, wanting you,
the idea of you no longer enough
to hold me until the next time we meet,
the body keen to the hunger you have awakened.
I lean forward for the righting touch
of the physical world: the dark warm
wood of the case gleaming with polish.
Now, I am knowing my body,
late into its fourth decade in the passionate way
you have known it: the great seam
of the spine centered in the jacket of the shoulders,
the ligaments tooled on the plates
of the clavicles, the legible bones of the wrists
and the ankles. And my breath comes
quickly for time seems suddenly short
for all the knowing of the body
of the world, the touching all the body of the world,
and the handing down to the generations to come
the world's body loved by our passionate arts.

Glossary

Allegory A symbolic narrative whose surface details imply a secondary meaning, often both generalized and moral.

Alliteration The repetition of consonant sounds, especially at the beginning of words.

Allusion A reference to a person, event, or literary work outside the poem.

Anapest Two unaccented syllables followed by an accented one as in com̆-prĕ-hénd or iñ-tĕr-véne.

Archetype An image, character, or event recurrent in literature and suggestive of mythological patterns of experience.

Assonance The repetition of similar vowel sounds in a sentence or a line of poetry, as in "I r*o*se and t*o*ld him of my w*o*e."

Aubade A love lyric in which the speaker rues the arrival of the dawn, when he must part from his lover.

Ballad A narrative poem written in four-line stanzas, characterized by swift action and told in a direct style.

Blank verse A line of poetry or prose in unrhymed iambic pentameter.

Caesura A strong pause within a line of verse.

Closed form A type of poetic form or structure characterized by regularity and consistency in such elements as rhyme, line length, and metrical pattern.

Connotation The personal and emotional associations called up by a word.

Convention A customary feature of a type of literary work, such as the use of iambic pentameter in the sonnet.

Couplet A pair of rhymed lines that may or may not constitute a separate stanza in a poem.

Dactyl A stressed syllable followed by two unstressed ones as in flút-tĕr-iňg or blúe-bĕr-rў.

Denotation The dictionary meaning of a word.

Diction The selection of words in a literary work.

Dramatic monologue A type of poem in which a speaker addresses a silent listener.

Elegy A lyric poem that laments or remembers the dead.

Elision The omission of an unstressed vowel or syllable to preserve the meter of a line of poetry.

Enjambment A run-on line of poetry in which logical and grammatical sense carries over from one line into the next. An enjambed line differs from an *end-stopped line,* in which the grammatical and logical sense is completed within the line.

Epic A long narrative poem that records the adventures of a hero. Epics typically chronicle the origins of a civilization and embody its central values.

Epigram A brief, witty poem, often satirical.

Falling meter Poetic meters, such as trochaic and dactylic, that move or fall from a stressed to an unstressed syllable.

Figurative language Language in which writers and speakers intend something other than the literal meaning of their words. See *allegory, hyperbole, metaphor, metonymy, simile, synecdoche,* and *understatement.*

Foot A metrical unit composed of stressed and unstressed syllables. For example, an *iamb* or *iambic foot* is represented by ˘ˊ—that is, by an unaccented syllable followed by an accented one. See the table on page 68.

Free verse Poetry without a regular pattern of meter or rhyme.

Hyperbole A figure of speech involving exaggeration.

Iamb An unstressed syllable followed by a stressed one, as in tŏ-dáy.

Image A concrete representation of a sense impression, a feeling, or an idea. Imagery refers to the pattern of related details in a work.

Irony A contrast or discrepancy between what is said and what is meant, or between what happens and what is expected to happen. In verbal irony characters say the opposite of what they mean. In irony of circumstance or situation the opposite of what is expected happens. In dramatic irony a character speaks in ignorance of a situation or event known to the audience or to other characters.

Literal language A form of language in which writers and speakers mean exactly what their words denote.

Lyric poem A type of poem characterized by brevity, compression, and the expression of feeling.

Metaphor A comparison between essentially unlike things without a word such as *like* or *as* to designate the comparison. An example: "My love is a red, red rose."

Meter The measured pattern of rhythmic accents in poems.

Metonymy A figure of speech in which a term is substituted for a closely related object or idea. An example: "We have always remained loyal to the crown."

Narrative poem A poem that tells a story.

Narrator The voice and implied speaker (often called a *speaker*) of a literary work, to be distinguished from the actual living author.

Octave An eight-line unit that may constitute a stanza or a section of a poem, as in the octave of a sonnet.

Ode A long, stately poem in stanzas of varied length, meter, and form. Usually a serious poem on an exalted subject.

Onomatopoeia The use of words to imitate the sounds they describe. *Buzz* and *crack* are onomatopoetic.

Open form A type of literary structure or form in poetry characterized by freedom from regularity and consistency in such elements as rhyme, line length, and metrical pattern.

Parody A humorous, mocking imitation of a literary work.

Personification The endowment of inanimate objects or abstract concepts with animate or living qualities. An example: "The yellow leaves flaunted their color gaily in the wind."

Quatrain A four-line stanza in a poem.

Rhyme The matching of final vowel or consonant sounds in two or more words. Masculine rhymes end with a stressed syllable, feminine rhymes with an unstressed one. Approximate or imperfect rhymes are called "slant" or "near" rhymes.

Rhythm The recurrence of accent or stress in lines of verse.

Rising meter Poetic meters, such as iambic and anapestic, that move or ascend from an unstressed to a stressed syllable.

Satire A literary work that criticizes human misconduct and ridicules vice, stupidity, and folly.

Sestet A six-line unit of verse constituting a stanza or section of a poem; the last six lines of an Italian sonnet.

Sestina A poem of thirty-nine lines written in iambic pentameter. Its six-line stanzas repeat, in an intricate and prescribed order, the six last words of each line in the opening stanza. After the sixth stanza there is a three-line *envoi,* which uses the six repeating words, two to a line.

Simile A figure of speech involving a comparison between unlike things using *like, as,* or *as though.* An example: "My love is like a red, red rose."

Sonnet A fourteen-line poem in iambic pentameter. The *Shakespearean,* or *English, sonnet* is arranged as three quatrains and a couplet, rhyming *abab cdcd efef gg.* The *Petrarchan,* or *Italian, sonnet* divides into two parts: an eight-line octave and a six-line sestet, rhyming *abbaabba cde cde* or *cd cd cd.*

Spondee A metrical foot represented by two stressed syllables such as knínck-knáck.

Stanza A division or unit of a poem that is repeated in the same form—with similar or identical patterns of rhyme and meter.

Structure The design or form of a literary work.

Style The way an author chooses words, arranges them in sentences or lines, and develops actions, ideas, and forms.

Symbol An object or action in a literary work that stands for something beyond itself.

Synecdoche A figure of speech in which a part is substituted for the whole. An example: "Lend me a hand."

Synesthesia An attempt to fuse different senses by describing one in terms of another.

Syntax The grammatical order of words in a sentence or line of verse or dialogue.

Tercet A three-line stanza.

Terza rima Interlocking tercets rhyming *aba bcb cdc,* and so on.

Theme The idea of a literary work abstracted from its details of language, character, and action and cast in the form of a generalization.

Tone The implied attitude of a poet toward the subject and materials of a poem.

Understatement A figure of speech in which a writer or speaker says less than what he or she means; the converse of exaggeration or *hyperbole.*

Villanelle A nineteen-line lyric poem that relies heavily on repetition. The first and third lines alternate throughout the poem, which is structured in six stanzas—five tercets and a final quatrain.

Copyrights and Acknowledgments

Alvarez, Julia. "Bookmaking," by Julia Alvarez, first published in *The Best American Poetry, 1991,* Charles Scribner's Sons. Copyright © by Julia Alvarez 1991. Reprinted by permission of Susan Bergholz Literary Services, New York.

Ammons, A. R. "Poetics," "Reflective," "The City Limits" from *Collected Poems, 1951–1971,* by A. R. Ammons. Copyright © 1972 by A. R. Ammons. Reprinted by permission of W. W. Norton & Co., Inc. "Extrication" is reprinted from *Worldly Hopes: Poems by A. R. Ammons,* by permission of W. W. Norton & Company, Inc., Copyright © 1982 by A. R. Ammons.

Ashbery, John. "Some Trees," from *Some Trees* by John Ashbery. Reprinted by permission of Georges Borchardt, Inc., and the author. Copyright © 1956 by John Ashbery.

Auden, W. H. "Musée des Beaux Arts," "The Unknown Citizen," and "In Memory of W. B. Yeats" from *W. H. Auden: Collected Poems* by W. H. Auden, edited by Edward Mendelson. Copyright 1940, renewed 1968, by W. H. Auden. Reprinted by permission of Random House, Inc.

Baca, Jimmy Santiago. "XVII" from *Meditations on the South Valley* by Jimmy Santiago Baca. Copyright © 1987 by Jimmy Santiago Baca. Reprinted by permission of New Directions Publishing Corp.

Baraka, Imamu Amiri. "Ka 'Ba" and "An Agony As Now" by Imamu Amiri Baraka from *Black Magic Poetry,* published by Bobbs Merrill Co., 1969. Copyright © 1969 by Amiri Baraka. Reprinted by permission of Sterling Lord Literistic, Inc.

Berryman, John. "Winter Landscape" from *Collected Poems, 1937–1971* by John Berryman. Copyright © 1989 by Kate Donahue Berryman. Reprinted by permission of Farrar, Straus & Giroux, Inc.
Poems 1, 14, 29, 40, 45 from *The Dream Songs* by John Berryman. Copyright © 1969 by John Berryman. Reprinted by permission of Farrar, Straus & Giroux, Inc.

Bishop, Elizabeth. "Filling Station," "First Death in Nova Scotia," "One Art," "Sandpiper," "The Man-Moth," "The Shampoo," "Seascape," "The Map," "The Monument," "The Unbeliever," "At the Fishhouses," "The Moose," "Questions of

Travel," "The Armadillo," "Argument," "Sestina," "The Prodigal," "In the Waiting Room," "Santarem," "Pink Dog," "Crusoe in England," and "The Fish" from *The Complete Poems, 1927–1979,* by Elizabeth Bishop. Copyright © 1979, 1983 by Alice Helen Methfessel. Reprinted by permission of Farrar, Straus & Giroux, Inc.

Bogen, Louise. "Women" and "Men Loved Wholly Beyond Wisdom" from *The Blue Estuaries* by Louise Bogan. Copyright © 1968 by Louise Bogan. Reprinted by permission of Farrar, Straus & Giroux, Inc.

Bowers, Neal. "Divining Love" by Neal Bowers, from *Poetry,* vol. 160, no. 4 (July 1992), pp. 197. Copyright © 1992. Reprinted by permission of the author.

Brooks, Gwendolyn. "The Mother," and "A Song in the Front Yard," copyright © 1991 from *Blacks* by Gwendolyn Brooks, published by Third World Press.

Chasin, Helen. "The Word *Plum*" by Helen Chasin, from *Coming Close and Other Poems* published by Yale University Press. Copyright © 1968. Reprinted by permission.

Clifton, Lucille. "Homage to My Hips" by Lucille Clifton from *Two-Headed Woman* published by University of Massachusetts Press, 1980. Copyright © 1980 by Lucille Clifton. Reprinted by permission of Curtis Brown, Ltd.

"The Lost Baby Poem," copyright © 1987 by Lucille Clifton. Reprinted from *Good Woman: Poems and a Memoir, 1969–1980* with the permission of BOA Editions, Ltd., Park Ave., Brockport, NY 14420.

Corkery, Christopher Jane. "As in the Days of the Prophets" by Christopher Jane Corkery. Originally published in the June 1992 issue of *The Atlantic Monthly.* Copyright © 1992. Used by permission of the author.

Crane, Hart. "Royal Palm," "My Grandmother's Love Letters," "Chaplinesque," "Praise for an Urn," "Repose of Rivers," "Passage," "Legend," "The Wine Menagerie," "At Melville's Tomb," "For the Marriage of Faustus and Helen," "Voyages," "O Carib Isle," "To Emily Dickinson," "Legende," "The Broken Tower" and, from *The Bridge* "Proem: To Brooklyn Bridge," "I. Ave Maria," "II. Powhatan's Daughter," "VII. The Tunnel," "VIII. Atlantis," and the last four stanzas of "To Brooklyn Bridge" from *The Complete Poems and Selected Letters and Prose of Hart Crane,* edited by Brom Weber. Copyright © 1933, © 1958, 1966 by Liveright Publishing Corporation. Reprinted by permission of Liveright Publishing Corporation.

Creeley, Robert. "I Know a Man" and "The Language" by Robert Creeley from *Collected Poems of Robert Creeley, 1945–1975.* Copyright © 1983 The Regents of the University of California. Used by permission of the Regents of the University of California and the University of California Press.

cummings, e. e. "may i feel said he" from *No Thanks* by e. e. cummings, edited by George James Firmage. Copyright 1935 by e. e. cummings. Copyright © 1968 by Marion Morehouse Cummings. © 1973, 1978 by The Trustees for the E. E. Cummings Trust. Copyright © 1973, 1978 by George James Firmage. Reprinted by permission of Liveright Publishing Corporation.

"[Buffalo Bill's]," and "i like my body when it is with your" from *Tulips & Chimneys* by e. e. cummings, edited by George James Firmage. Copyright 1923, 1925, renewed 1951, 1953 by e. e. cummings. Copyright © 1973, 1976 by the Trustees for the E. E. Cummings Estate. Copyright © 1973, 1976 by George James Firmage. Reprinted by permission of Liveright Publishing Corp.

Dickinson, Emily. Poem 1072 from *Life and Letters of Emily Dickinson,* edited by Martha Dickinson Bianchi. Copyright 1924 by Martha Dickinson Bianchi, © renewed 1952 by Alfred Leete Hampson. Reprinted by permission of Houghton Mifflin Co. All rights reserved.

Poems 108, 306, 321, 326, 341, 448, 480, 569, 599, 657, 668, 709, 754, 1100, 1142, 1705 from *The Complete Poems of Emily Dickinson,* edited by Thomas H. Johnson. Copyright 1929, 1935 by Martha Dickinson Bianchi: Copyright © renewed 1957, 1963 by Mary L. Hampson. By permission of Little, Brown and Company.

"Because I could not stop for Death," "Safe in Their Alabaster Chambers" (1859 and 1861 versions), and poems 67, 185, 199, 241, 249, 252, 258, 280, 303, 324, 328, 365, 435, 449, 465, 501, 508, 512, 536, 547, 632, 640, 650, 744, 959, 986, 1078, 1129, 1138, 1770, 1732. Reprinted by permission of the publishers and the Trustees of Amherst College from *The Poems of Emily Dickinson,* Thomas H. Johnson, ed., Cambridge, Mass.: The Belknap Press of Harvard University Press. Copyright © 1951, 1955, 1983 by the President and Fellows of Harvard College.

Poems 480, 569, 599, 657, 1100, reprinted by permission of the publishers and the Trustees of Amherst College from *The Poems of Emily Dickinson,* Thomas H. Johnson, ed., Cambridge, Mass.: The Belknap Press of Harvard University Press. Copyright © 1951, 1955, 1983 by the President and Fellows of Harvard College.

Dove, Rita. "Canary" from *Grace Notes* by Rita Dove. Copyright © 1989 by Rita Dove. Reprinted by permission of W. W. Norton & Co., Inc.

Duncan, Robert. "Often I Am Permitted to Return to a Meadow" from *The Opening of the Field* by Robert Duncan. Copyright © 1960 by Robert Duncan. Reprinted by permission of New Directions Publishing Corp.

Eberhart, Richard. "The Groundhog" from *Collected Poems, 1930–1986* by Richard Eberhart. Copyright © 1988 by Richard Eberhart. Reprinted by permission of Oxford University Press, Inc.

Eliot, T.S. "Journey of the Magi," "The Love Song of J. Alfred Prufrock," "Preludes," "Gerontion," and "The Waste Land." From *Collected Poems: 1909–1962* by T. S. Eliot, copyright 1936 by Harcourt Brace Jovanovich, Inc.; copyright © 1963 by T. S. Eliot; renewed 1971 by Esme Valerie Eliot. Reprinted by permission of the publisher and Faber and Faber, Ltd., London.

"Little Gidding." From *Four Quartets* by T. S. Eliot, copyright 1943 by T. S. Eliot; renewed 1971 by Esme Valerie Eliot. Reprinted by permission of Harcourt Brace Jovanovich, Inc., and Faber and Faber Ltd., London.

Frost, Robert "The Silken Tent," "Stopping by Woods on a Snowy Evening," "The Span of Life," "Design," "Fire and Ice," "Nothing Gold Can Stay," "The Need of Being Versed in Country Things," "Tree at My Window," "On Looking Up by Chance at the Constellations," "West-Running Brook," "Once by the Pacific," "Acquainted with the Night," "Desert Places," "Departmental," "Provide, Provide," "Never Again Would Birds' Song Be the Same," "The Gift Outright," "The Most of It," "Two Look at Two," from *The Poetry of Robert Frost* edited by Edward Frost. Copyright 1936, 1942, 1951 © 1956 by Robert Frost. Copyright © 1964, 1970 by Lesley Frost Ballantine. Copyright 1923, 1928, © 1968, 1969 by Henry Holt and Company, Inc. Reprinted by permission of Henry Holt and Company, Inc.

"In White" from *The Dimensions of Robert Frost* by Reginald L. Cook. Copyright © 1958 by Reginald L. Cook. Reprinted by permission of Henry Holt and Company, Inc.

Fulton, Alice. "My Second Marriage to My First Husband" from *Palladium* (University of Illinois Press). Copyright © 1982, 1984, 1986 by Alice Fulton. Reprinted by permission of the author and the University of Illinois Press.

Ginsberg, Alan. "A Supermarket in California," "Howl" from *The Collected Poems of Allen Ginsberg, 1947–1980.* Copyright © 1984 by Allen Ginsberg. Reprinted by permission of HarperCollins Publishers, Inc.

Glück, Louise. "The Garden" © 1976, 1977, 1978, 1979, 1980 by Louise Glück. From *Descending Figure* by Louise Glück, published by The Ecco Press. Reprinted by permission.

"The School Children" © 1971, 1972, 1973, 1974, 1975 by Louise Glück. From *The House on Marshland* by Louise Glück, published by The Ecco Press. Reprinted by permission.

Graham, Jorie. "Mind" from *Erosion.* Copyright © 1983 by Princeton University Press. Reprinted by permission of Princeton University Press.

HD (Doolittle, Hilda). "Sea Rose," "Evening," and "Heat" from *Collected Poems, 1912–1944* by H.D. Copyright © 1982 by The Estate of Hilda Doolittle. Reprinted by permission of New Directions Publishing Corp.

Hacker, Marilyn. "Canzone" by Marilyn Hacker, from *Taking Notice,* published by Alfred A. Knopf, Inc, 1980. Copyright © 1980 by Marilyn Hacker. Reprinted by permission of the author

Hall, Donald. "Kicking the Leaves" from *Old and New Poems* by Donald Hall. Copyright © 1990 by Donald Hall. Reprinted by permission of Ticknor & Fields/Houghton Mifflin Co. All rights reserved.

Harper, Michael. "American History," "Martin's Blues," and "Nightmare Begins Responsibility" from *Images of Kin,* University of Illinois Press, © 1977. Reprinted by permission of the University of Illinois Press and the author.

Hass, Robert. "Meditation at Lagunitas" © 1974, 1975, 1976, 1977, 1978, 1979 by Robert Hass. From *Praise* by Robert Hass, published by The Ecco Press. Reprinted by permission.

Hayden, Robert. "O Daedalus, Fly Away Home," "The Whipping," and "Those Winter Sundays" from *Angle of Ascent: New and Selected Poems* by Robert Hayden. Copyright © 1975, 1972, 1970, 1966 by Robert Hayden. Reprinted by permission of Liveright Publishing Corporation.

Hollander, John. "Adam's Task," and "Swan and Shadow" by John Hollander from *The Night Mirror.* Copyright © 1969, 1991 by John Hollander. Used by permission.

Holder, Barbara. "First Death," © 1993 Barbara Holder. Reprinted by permission of the author.

Hughes, Langston. "The Negro Speaks of Rivers," "Mother to Son," "Dream Variations," "Mulatto," "I, Too," "My People," "The Weary Blues," "Song for a Dark Girl," "Madam and the Rent Man," "Morning After," "Trumpet Player," "When Sue Wears Red," "Aunt Sue's Stories," "Feet o' Jesus," "Consider Me," "Note on Commercial Theater" from *Selected Poems of Langston Hughes,* by Langston Hughes. Copyright © 1959 by Langston Hughes. Reprinted by permission of Alfred A. Knopf, Inc.

"Ballad of the Landlord," "Theme for English B," "Same in Blue," "Dream Boogie" by Langston Hughes from *Montage of a Dream Deferred,* published by Henry Holt & Co., 1951. Copyright 1951 by Langston Hughes. Copyright renewed 1979 by George Houston Bass. Reprinted by permission of Harold Ober Associates Incorporated.

"Madrid—1937" from *Good Morning Revolution,* Citadel Press, Carol Publishing Group. 600 Madison Ave., New York, NY. Copyright © 1973, 1992 by Faith Berry. Reprinted by special arrangement of executors and trustees of the Estate of Langston Hughes.

Kennedy, X. J. "First Confession" and "In a Prominent Bar in Secaucus One Day" by X. J. Kennedy from *Cross Ties: Selected Poems.* © 1985 by X. J. Kennedy. Published by The University of Georgia Press. All rights reserved.

Kinnell, Galway. "The Bear" from *Body Rags* by Galway Kinnell. Copyright © 1965, 1966, 1967 by Galway Kinnell. Reprinted by permission of Houghton Mifflin Co. All rights reserved.

"Saint Francis and the Sow," and "Blackberry Eating" from *Mortal Acts, Mortal Words* by Galway Kinnell. Copyright © 1980 by Galway Kinnell. Reprinted by permission of Houghton Mifflin Co. All rights reserved.

"To Christ Our Lord" from *What a Kingdom It Was* by Galway Kinnell. Copyright © 1960, © renewed 1988 by Galway Kinnell. Reprinted by permission of Houghton Mifflin Co. All rights reserved.

Knight, Etheridge. "Hard Rock Returns to Prison from the Hospital for the Criminally Insane" and "Haiku" by Etheridge Knight from *Poems from Prison.* Copyright © 1968 by Etheridge Knight. Used by permission of Broadside Press.

Koch, Kenneth. "Variations on a Theme by William Carlos Williams," "To You," and "You Were Wearing" from *Selected Poems* by Kenneth Koch. Copyright © 1985 by Kenneth Koch. Reprinted by permission of the author.

Lorde, Audre. "Now That I Am Forever with Child" from *Chosen Poems, Old and New* by Audre Lord. Copyright © 1982, 1976, 1974, 1973, 1970, 1968 by Audre Lorde. Reprinted by permission of W. W. Norton & Co., Inc., and by permission of Audre Lorde.

Lowell, Robert. "R.F.K.," "Two Walls," and "Pacification of Columbia" from *Notebook, 1967–1968* by Robert Lowell. Copyright © 1969 by Robert Lowell. Reprinted by permission of Farrar, Straus & Giroux, Inc.
"The Quaker Graveyard at Nantucket," "Mr. Edwards and the Spider," and "After the Surprising Conversations" from *Lord Weary's Castle* by Robert Lowell. Copyright © 1946, renewed 1974, by Robert Lowell. Reprinted by permission of Harcourt Brace & Company.
"Epilogue" and "Turtle" from *Day by Day* by Robert Lowell. Copyright © 1977 by Robert Lowell. Reprinted by permission of Farrar, Straus & Giroux, Inc.
"The Drinker," "My Last Afternoon with Uncle Devereux Winslow," "Beyond the Alps," "Memories of West Street and Lepke," "Man and Wife," "Sailing Home from Rapallo," "Skunk Hour," "For the Union Dead," "Robert Frost," "Reading Myself," "The Mouth of the Hudson," "Fall 1961," "Waking Early Sunday Morning," "The Old Flame," "Home after Three Months Away," "Waking in the Blue," "Returning Turtle," and "Dolphin" from *Selected Poems* by Robert Lowell. Copyright © 1976 by Robert Lowell. Reprinted by permission of Farrar, Straus & Giroux, Inc.
"Florence" from *Selected Poems* by Robert Lowell. Copyright © 1976 by Robert Lowell. Reprinted by permission of Farrar, Straus & Giroux, Inc.

Meinke, Peter. "Advice to My Son" by Peter Meinke from *Trying to Surprise God,* University of Pittsburgh Press, 1981. Copyright © Peter Meinke. Used by permission.

Merwin, W. S. "Elegy" from *The Carrier of Ladders* by W. S. Merwin. Copyright © by W. S. Merwin. Reprinted by permission of Georges Borchardt, Inc.
"When You Go Away" from *The Lice* by W. S. Merwin. Copyright © 1967 by W. S. Merwin. Reprinted by permission of Georges Borchardt, Inc.
"Separation" from *The Moving Target* by W. S. Merwin. Copyright © 1963 by W. S. Merwin. Reprinted by permission of Georges Borchardt, Inc.

Millay, Edna St. Vincent. "Sonnets XLII, XLIX, and LXXV" from *The Collected Poems of Edna St. Vincent Millay,* edited by Norma Millay. Copyright 1923, 1931, 1956 by Norma Millay Ellis. Reprinted by permission of HarperCollins Publishers, Inc.

Moore, Marianne. "A Face," "His Shield," and "Propriety" by Marianne Moore. Reprinted with permission of Macmillan Publishing Company from *Collected Poems of Marianne Moore.* Copyright 1951 by Marianne Moore, renewed 1979 by Lawrence E. Brinn and Louise Crane.
"The Mind Is an Enchanting Thing," "Nevertheless," and "In Distrust of Merits" by Marianne Moore. Reprinted with permission of Macmillan Publishing Company from *Collected Poems of Marianne Moore.* Copyright 1944, and renewed 1972, by Marianne Moore.
"Four Quartz Crystal Clocks" by Marianne Moore. Reprinted with permission of Macmillan Publishing Company from *Collected Poems of Marianne Moore.* Copyright 1941, and renewed 1969, by Marianne Moore.
"To a Prize Bird" by Marianne Moore from *Observations,* published by Dial.
"A Jelly-Fish," copyright © 1959 by Marianne Moore, © renewed 1987 by Lawrence E. Brinn and Louise Crane, Executors of the Estate of Marianne Moore, from *The Complete Poems of Marianne Moore* by Marianne Moore. Used by permission of Viking Penguin, a division of Penguin Books USA, Inc.
"The Steeple-Jack," copyright 1951, © 1970 by Marianne Moore, © renewed 1979 by

Lawrence E. Brinn and Louise Crane, Executors of the Estate of Marianne Moore, from *The Complete Poems of Marianne Moore* by Marianne Moore. Used by permission of Viking Penguin, a division of Penguin Books USA, Inc.

"The Student" by Marianne Moore. Reprinted with permission of Macmillan Publishing Company from *What Are Years* by Marianne Moore. Copyright 1941, and renewed 1969, by Marianne Moore.

"No Swan So Fine," "The Jerboa," "Marriage," "An Octopus," "Poetry" (1924 version), "The Fish," "To a Snail," "The Past Is the Present," "A Grave," "In the Days of Prismatic Colour," "When I Buy Pictures," "The Monkeys," "The Labours of Hercules," "The Hero," "Sojourn in the Whale," "Critics and Connoisseurs," and "England" by Marianne Moore. Reprinted with permission of Macmillan Publishing Company from *Collected Poems of Marianne Moore.* Copyright 1935 by Marianne Moore, renewed 1963 by Marianne Moore and T. S. Eliot.

"Poetry" (1921 version) from *Observations* by Marianne Moore (The Dial Press, Inc., 1924). Copyright © by the Estate of Marianne Moore. Used by permission of Marianne Craig Moore, Literary Executor for the Estate of Marianne Moore.

Noethe, Sheryl. "Slow Dancing with Billy" by Sheryl Noethe. © 1992 Sheryl Noethe. Used by permission.

O'Hara, Frank. "Autobiographia Literaria" from *Collected Poems* by Frank O'Hara. Copyright © 1967 by Maureen Granville-Smith, Administratrix of the Estate of Frank O'Hara. Reprinted by permission of Alfred A. Knopf, Inc.

"Ave Maria" from *Lunch Poems* by Frank O'Hara. Copyright © 1964 by Frank O'Hara. Reprinted by permission of City Lights Books.

Oliver, Mary. "Poem for My Father's Ghost" from *Twelve Moons* by Mary Oliver. Copyright © 1976 by Mary Oliver. By permission of Little, Brown and Company.

Olson, Charles. "Maximus, to Gloucester, Sunday, July 19" by Charles Olson from *Maximus Poems,* trans./ed. by George Butterick. Copyright © 1983, The Regents of the University of California. Reprinted by permission of the Regents of the University of California and the University of California Press.

Pinsky, Robert. "Dying" © 1984 by Robert Pinsky. From *History of My Heart* by Robert Pinsky, published by The Ecco Press. Reprinted by permission.

Plath, Sylvia. "Metaphors," "Black Rook in Rainy Weather" (1960), "Morning Song" (1961), "Heavy Woman," "Crossing the Water" (1962), "The Applicant," "Lady Lazarus," "Death & Co.," "Ariel," "Fever 103," "Edge," "Elm," "Cut" (1963), and "Words" from *The Collected Poems of Sylvia Plath* by Sylvia Plath. Copyright © 1981 by the Estate of Sylvia Plath. Reprinted by permission of HarperCollins Publishers, Inc.

"Mirror" (1963), "The Moon and the Yew Tree" (1963), and "Blackberrying" (1962) from *The Collected Poems of Sylvia Plath.* First published in *The New Yorker.* Copyright © 1981 by The Estate of Sylvia Plath. Reprinted by permission of HarperCollins Publishers, Inc.

"Nick and the Candlestick" from *The Collected Poems of Sylvia Plath.* Copyright © 1981 by The Estate of Sylvia Plath. Reprinted by permission of HarperCollins Publishers, Inc.

"Daddy" by Sylvia Plath from *The Collected Poems of Sylvia Plath,* edited by Ted Hughes. Copyright © 1963 by Ted Hughes. Reprinted by permission of HarperCollins Publishers, Inc.

"Tulips" by Sylvia Plath from *The Collected Poems of Sylvia Plath,* edited by Ted Hughes. Copyright © 1962 by Ted Hughes. Reprinted by permission of HarperCollins Publishers, Inc.

"The Colossus," and "The Beekeeper's Daughter" from *The Colossus and Other Poems* by Sylvia Plath. Copyright © 1961 by Sylvia Plath. Reprinted by permission of Alfred A. Knopf, Inc.

"The Disquieting Muses" from *The Colossus and Other Poems* by Sylvia Plath. Copyright © 1962 by Sylvia Plath. Reprinted by permission of Alfred A. Knopf, Inc.

Simpson, Louis. "The Heroes" by Louis Simpson from *People Live Here: Selected Poems."* Copyright © 1983. Reprinted by permission of Louis Simpson.
"American Poetry," and "Walt Whitman at Bear Mountain" from *At the End of the Open Road,* copyright 1963 by Louis Simpson, Wesleyan University Press. By permission of University Press of New England.

Snyder, Gary. "Riprap" from *Riprap and Cold Mountain Poems* by Gary Snyder. Copyright © 1958, 1959, 1965 by Gary Snyder. Reprinted by permission of North Point Press, a division of Farrar, Straus & Giroux, Inc.
"Prayer for the Great Family" from *Turtle Island* by Gary Snyder. Copyright © 1974 by Gary Snyder. Reprinted by permission of New Directions Publishing Corp.

Song, Cathy. "Lost Sister" by Cathy Song, from *Picture Bride* published by Yale University Press. Copyright © 1983. Reprinted by permission.

Stevens, Wallace. "No Possum, No Sop, No Taters," "No Man Made Out of Words," "Chaos in Motion and Not in Motion," and "The House Was Quiet and the World Was Calm" from *Collected Poems* by Wallace Stevens. Copyright 1947 by Wallace Stevens. Reprinted by permission of Alfred A. Knopf, Inc.
"Peter Quince at the Clavier," "Sunday Morning," "Anecdote of the Jar," "The Emperor of Ice-Cream," "Disillusionment of Ten O'Clock," "The Snow Man," "A High-Toned Old Christian Woman," "O Florida, Venereal Soil," "To the One of Fictive Music," "Thirteen Ways of Looking at a Blackbird," and "To the Roaring Wind" from *Collected Poems* by Wallace Stevens. Copyright 1923 and renewed 1951 by Wallace Stevens. Reprinted by permission of Alfred A. Knopf, Inc.
"The Poems of Our Climate," "The Sense of the Sleight-of-Hand Man," "Study of Two Pears," "The Glass of Water," "Of Modern Poetry," and "Notes Toward a Supreme Fiction" from *Collected Poems* by Wallace Stevens. Copyright 1942 and renewed 1970 by Wallace Stevens. Reprinted by permission of Alfred A. Knopf, Inc.
"The Idea of Order at Key West," "The Man with the Blue Guitar," "A Postcard from the Volcano" from *Collected Poems* by Wallace Stevens. Copyright 1936 by Wallace Stevens and renewed 1964 by Holly Stevens. Reprinted by permission of Alfred A. Knopf, Inc.
"Angel Surrounded by Paysans," from *Collected Poems* by Wallace Stevens. Copyright 1950 by Wallace Stevens. Reprinted by permission of Alfred A. Knopf, Inc.
"The Plain Sense of Things" from *Collected Poems* by Wallace Stevens. Copyright 1952 by Wallace Stevens. Reprinted by permission of Alfred A. Knopf, Inc.
"The Planet on the Table," "The River of Rivers in Connecticut," "Not Ideas about the Thing but the Thing Itself," and "The Rock" from *Collected Poems* by Wallace Stevens. Copyright 1954 by Wallace Stevens. Reprinted by permission of Alfred A. Knopf, Inc.
"The Course of a Particular" from *Collected Poems* by Wallace Stevens. Copyright 1957 by Elsie Stevens and Holly Stevens. Reprinted by permission of Alfred A. Knopf, Inc.
"Final Soliloquy of the Interior Paramour" from *Collected Poems* by Wallace Stevens. Copyright 1951 by Wallace Stevens. Reprinted by permission of Alfred A. Knopf, Inc.
"The Auroras of Autumn" from *Collected Poems* by Wallace Stevens. Copyright 1948 by Wallace Stevens. Reprinted by permission of Alfred A. Knopf, Inc.

Strand, Mark. "Elegy for My Father" from *Selected Poems* by Mark Strand. Copyright © 1979, 1980 by Mark Strand. Reprinted by permission of Alfred A. Knopf, Inc.

Swenson, May. "The Universe" by May Swenson, © 1963, © renewed 1991. "How Everything Happens" by May Swenson, © 1969. Both poems used with permission of the Literary Estate of May Swenson.

Tate, James. "The Lost Pilot," © 1978 by James Tate. From *The Lost Pilot* by James Tate, first published by The Ecco Press in 1982. Reprinted by permission.

Wallace, Robert. "The Double-Play" by Robert Wallace from *Views of a Ferris Wheel.* Copyright © 1965 by Robert Wallace. Reprinted by permission.

Index of Authors, Titles, and First Lines